Warfare in Medieval Europe c.400–c.1453

Warfare in Medieval Europe, now in its second edition, offers considerably more attention to the transition from the later Roman Empire to the early Middle Ages, the composition of the armies of the opponents of the West, and the experience of commanders and individual combatants on the battlefield.

This second revised and expanded edition provides a more in-depth thematic discussion of the nature and conduct of war, with an emphasis on its overall impact on society, from the late Roman Empire to the end of the Hundred Years' War. The authors explore the origins of the institutions, physical infrastructure, and intellectual underpinnings of warfare, with chapters on military topography, military technology, logistics, combat, and strategy. Bernard and David S. Bachrach have also added a new chapter, which provides two detailed campaign narratives that highlight the themes treated throughout the text. The geographical scope of the volume encompasses Latin Europe, the Slavic world, Scandinavia, and the eastern Mediterranean, with a particular focus on the conflict between Western Christianity and the Islamic Near East.

Written in an accessible and engaging way, *Warfare in Medieval Europe* is the ideal resource for all students of the history of medieval warfare.

Bernard S. Bachrach, a fellow of the Medieval Academy, is a professor emeritus of medieval history at the University of Minnesota. His research focuses on the military history of pre-crusade Europe. He is the author of more than 160 scholarly articles and twenty-five books, including *Early Carolingian Warfare: Prelude to Empire* (2002); *Charlemagne's Early Campaigns (768–777): A Diplomatic and Military Analysis* (2013); and *Writing the Military History of Pre-Crusade Europe: Studies in Sources and Source Criticism* (2020), with David S. Bachrach.

David S. Bachrach is a professor of medieval history at the University of New Hampshire. His research focuses on the military and administrative history of Carolingian East Francia/Ottonian Germany in the ninth–eleventh centuries, and the kingdom of England in the thirteenth and early fourteenth centuries. He is the author of more than sixty scholarly articles and a dozen books, including *Religion and the Conduct of War c. 300–c.1215* (2003); *Warfare in Tenth-Century Germany* (2012); and *Administration and Organization of War in Thirteenth-Century England* (2020).

Praise for the previous edition:

This book is a masterpiece, bringing together the collected scholarship of the past several decades and more in a brilliant synthesis that illuminates not only medieval military matters, but the whole 'medieval millennium' as well.

Paul F. Crawford, California University of Pennsylvania, USA

The perfect introduction to medieval warfare for students of history and strategic or security studies. Firmly rooted in source evidence, this remains faithful to contemporary terminology yet helps us interpret it in the light of today's military-strategic vocabulary.

Beatrice Heuser, University of Reading, UK

Warfare in Medieval Europe c.400–c.1453

Second Edition

**Bernard S. Bachrach and
David S. Bachrach**

Routledge
Taylor & Francis Group

LONDON AND NEW YORK

Second edition published 2022
by Routledge
2 Park Square, Milton Park, Abingdon, Oxon, OX14 4RN

and by Routledge
605 Third Avenue, New York, NY 10158

Routledge is an imprint of the Taylor & Francis Group, an informa business

© 2022 Bernard S. Bachrach and David S. Bachrach

The right of Bernard S. Bachrach and David S. Bachrach to be identified as authors of this work has been asserted by them in accordance with sections 77 and 78 of the Copyright, Designs and Patents Act 1988.

First edition published by Routledge 2017

British Library Cataloguing-in-Publication Data
A catalogue record for this book is available from the British Library

Library of Congress Cataloging-in-Publication Data
Names: Bachrach, Bernard S., 1939– author. | Bachrach, David S., 1971– author.
Title: Warfare in Medieval Europe c.400–c.1453 / Bernard S. Bachrach, and David S. Bachrach.
Description: Second edition. | Abingdon, Oxon ; New York : Routledge, 2022. | Includes bibliographical references and index. | Contents: Sources: The writing of medieval military history—Military topography—Military organization of medieval Europe—Military logistics—Military technology—Medieval combat—Strategy—Two Campaigns in Focus.
Identifiers: LCCN 2021010058
Subjects: LCSH: Military art and science—History—Medieval, 500–1500. | Europe—History, Military—476–1492
Classification: LCC U37 .B332 2022 | DDC 355.02094/0902—dc23
LC record available at https://lccn.loc.gov/2021010058

ISBN: 978-0-367-47018-0 (hbk)
ISBN: 978-0-367-47019-7 (pbk)
ISBN: 978-1-003-03287-8 (ebk)

DOI: 10.4324/9781003032878

Typeset in Galliard
by Apex CoVantage, LLC

We dedicate this text to all of our students, past, present, and future.

Contents

List of figures   viii
List of maps   x
Preface to the second edition   xii
Acknowledgements   xiii

Introduction   1

1   Sources: the writing of medieval military history   6

2   Military topography   32

3   Military organization of medieval Europe   95

4   Military logistics   164

5   Military technology   222

6   Medieval combat   274

7   Strategy   329

8   Two campaigns in focus   375

    Conclusion   395

    Index   397

Figures

1.1	An illustrated page from the Gutenberg Bible	13
1.2	Facsimile of Widukind of Corvey's Res Gestae Saxonicae	16
1.3	Supplies for Charlemagne's army	22
1.4	Frankish spatha, eighth century	26
1.5	Above-ground remains of a fortification in the Lake District, UK	26
1.6	Excavated foundations of a fortification in Northumberland, UK	27
2.1	An example of a Roman milestone	39
2.2	An example of Roman walls in Spain	54
2.3	Crac des Chevaliers, Syria	78
2.4	Conwy Castle in Wales	81
2.5	The fortified village of Fort Bourtange, The Netherlands	86
2.6	Offa's Dyke in Shropshire, UK	90
3.1	Magister Militum per Orientem 2	98
3.2	Large numbers of Roman soldiers from the Arch of Constantine	99
3.3	Danish Army arriving East Anglia in 866	104
3.4	Crusader army from a contemporary illustration	144
3.5	Two massed opposing armies from the Hundred Years' War period	152
4.1	Eleventh-century Anglo-Saxon manuscript depiction of mounted soldiers	168
4.2a	Example of a Roman road surface	172
4.2b	Cobble stone at the end of the Appian Way	172
4.3	A Medieval ship from excavation	174
4.4	Anglo-Saxon view of a Viking dragon ship, tenth century	174
4.5	Amphorae	177
4.6	Col du Tourmalet mountain pass in the Pyrenees	199
4.7	An example of a medieval bridge in France	208
5.1	Norman armour from the Bayeux Tapestry	224
5.2	An example of late Roman mail	225
5.3	Flügellanz	229
5.4	Slingers	236
5.5	Man loading a crossbow	240
5.6	Reconstruction of a motte-and-bailey castle	249
5.7	Château Gaillard in Les Andelys, France	261
6.1	Battle of Roosebeke, 1382, French against Flemish militiamen	279
6.2	Illustration of the Battle of Stirling Bridge	282
6.3	Reconstruction of a miniature depicting the Battle of Formigny	287

7.1   Francia on the Peutinger Map   337
7.2   King and court   338
7.3   Medieval woodcut from the story of Melusine   356

Maps

2.1	The Roman Empire in AD 395	33
2.2	Empire of Justinian	37
2.3	Barbarian kingdoms, c.534	45
2.4	France and its principalities, c.1000	50
2.5	Byzantium and the expansion of Islam in the Mediterranean area, seventh–ninth centuries	51
2.6	Magyars	52
2.7	Frederick I Barbarossa and the Lombard League	55
2.8	Map of fortresses of Henry I on the Eastern Frontier	66
2.9	England, c.1000	71
2.10	Angevins and Capetians in the late twelfth century	73
2.11	The Spanish and Portuguese reconquest to c.1140	74
2.12	The Crusader states	76
2.13	Wales: the Principality and the Marches	80
2.14	The Mercian supremacy	89
3.1	The Empire of Charlemagne, 768–814	113
3.2	The division of the Carolingian Empire, 843	120
3.3	The Ottonian Empire, 962	122
3.4	The East European states, c.1000	127
3.5	The larger towns of Europe	131
3.6	Where did the Crusaders come from?	133
3.7	Expansion of French royal control, 1180–1226	135
3.8	England under William I	138
3.9	The Hohenstaufen Empire, c.1150–1250	142
3.10	The Templar network	146
3.11	The Hundred Years' War	151
3.12	The growth of the Burgundian state	155
3.13	The German Hanse	157
4.1	Carolingian residential villas	183
4.2	The Scottish wars of independence	192
4.3	The Alpine passes	200
4.4	The routes of the First Crusade	203
4.5	The Empire of the Comneni, 1081–1185	205
4.6	The Second and Third Crusades	207
4.7	The Fourth Crusade	209
4.8	The crusades of Emperor Frederick II and St. Louis	210

8.1	Muslim Spain	378
8.2	Map of 929 campaign objectives	386
8.3	Brandenburg defence in depth	388
8.4	Fortifications constructed by Henry I in context of the 929 campaign	390

Preface to the second edition

We have been fortunate to receive considerable feedback and constructive criticism about the first edition of the text from anonymous readers, our colleagues, and – above all – our students. Based on this feedback, we have made numerous additions and some changes to the text. Readers will note that we have added an eighth chapter in which we discuss in detail two early medieval campaigns that permit us to highlight many of the topics treated throughout the volume, including questions of logistics, diplomacy, intelligence gathering, and the great importance of the Roman inheritance of military topography. Throughout the first seven chapters, we have added material to address lacunae noted by readers. These include a closer focus on developments in Late Antiquity from the fifth through seventh centuries; additional attention to the Near East, both in terms of the crusader states and their Arab and Turkish opponents; and also to developments in the later Middle Ages. We also have had the opportunity to develop further ideas that we only touched upon in the first edition. These include new sections on military discipline, chivalry, plague, and demography; the participation of military commanders in combat; and the relationship between taxation and military service. In order to facilitate the use of the text, we have changed the format somewhat so that the maps appear throughout the book rather than grouped together in the beginning. We have also added about a dozen new maps to help our readers gain a better appreciation of the geographical contexts that we discuss. We also have modified the bibliographic sections for each chapter to include a new section we call 'Conflicting perspectives'. These additional sections provide readers with a selection of books and articles whose authors have taken very different positions regarding topics of central importance to the study of medieval warfare. Finally, we would like to offer a brief note regarding the new cover image for the second edition. This manuscript illustration, from the fourteenth century, depicts the siege of Jerusalem during the First Crusade. Attentive readers will note that the siege engine deployed by the crusaders is a trebuchet – that is, a counter-weight traction engine. Engines of this type did not exist in the late eleventh century, and probably were not developed by Muslim engineers for another 60–90 years. Trebuchets were not introduced into the West until the early thirteenth century. The anachronistic depiction of a trebuchet by the artist, who designed this illustration, highlights one of the challenges faced by military historians in trying to use images to draw conclusions about the types of technology that were available in a particular time or place.

Acknowledgements

A synthesis, such as the present volume, is necessarily a collaborative project that owes a tremendous debt to the work of hundreds of scholars whose articles and books we have read over the course of our careers. In addition, we both have benefitted from advice and criticism offered in conferences and in private conversations over the years with numerous colleagues, and this includes advice that we have sought with respect to writing this current book. We would like to offer our particular thanks to Richard Abels, the late Chuck Bowlus, Anne Curry, Kelly DeVries, John France, John Gillingham, John Haldon, John Hosler, Stephen Morillo, Lief Petersen, Michael Prestwich, John Pryor, Cliff Rogers, and Manuel Rojas. Naturally, all errors of commission and omission in the text are our own.

The publishers would like to thank PLSclear, as well as the map creators from David Ditchburn, Simon MacLean and Angus Mackay (eds.), *Atlas of Medieval Europe, Second Edition* (Routledge, 2007) for granting the permission to use the maps in this volume. Copyright information and acknowledgement are included in the list of maps.

Introduction

War, the preparation for war, and war's aftermath consumed the greater part of the surplus economic resources of society throughout the long millennium of the European Middle Ages. Massive sums of money, material resources, and labour were expended on the training and payment of soldiers; the production and procurement of arms and supplies; the construction and repair of roads, ports, and ships; and perhaps most significantly, the construction and maintenance of a vast number of fortifications that were built throughout Europe and in the crusading states of the Near East. To these expenses can be added the costs for repairing damage done in war, in lost crops, burned homes, destroyed villages, and the incalculable toll in the loss of human life. Warfare at one time or another likely affected the lives of almost every man, woman, and child in medieval Europe either directly as participants in or as victims of military operations, or indirectly through the imposition of military-related obligations, taxes, and labour duties.

Medieval Europeans also were exposed to war through the practices of their religion, including the very sacraments of their faith, especially the celebration of mass and confession, as well as through technological innovations, new foods, architectural techniques, languages, and communication networks that were transmitted and established through the vectors of armies on campaign, and soldiers returning from war. The production of food, the practices of commerce and trade – indeed, the economic systems of medieval Europe as a whole – developed, in large part, to meet the military needs of polities large and small. In sum, it is correct to say that during the entirety of the Middle Ages, European societies were organized for war. For all of these reasons, warfare deserves to be at the centre of the discussion of the history of medieval Europe if this society is to be understood in its own context.

This volume is intended as a synthesis of scholarship dealing with medieval warfare that will serve as an introduction to the subject for general readers with an interest in the history of the Middle Ages and for use in the classroom, in both medieval history and military history courses. We also believe that this synthesis will be of use to those who already work in one or another field of medieval studies and are seeking an entrée into the field of military history to understand its central and critical place in the history of the Middle Ages. As this work is a synthesis and not a monograph, we have provided very few notes, limiting these to direct quotations from scholarly works. Unless otherwise noted, all of the translations in this volume are our own.

At the end of each chapter, we have provided a selection of further readings for those interested in pursuing their interest in either the Middle Ages or military history in general. We have listed most of the studies only once in these selected readings, although in many cases, a single work is relevant to a number of the themes that we treat in the seven chapters of the text. The additional readings are all in English, although we have included

DOI: 10.4324/9781003032878-1

translations of some seminal works that originally were written in languages other than English. Because, as previously mentioned, this work is intended as a synthesis rather than as a monograph, it was not our intention to provide a comprehensive or exhaustive list of pertinent scholarly works, even in English. However, in making our selections, we chose to call readers' attention to articles and books that would provide both general readers and students with access to the much broader corpus of scholarship on medieval warfare. Finally, in this second edition of our text, we have added a section to each chapter bibliography entitled 'Conflicting perspectives' where we bring to our readers' attention to scholarly works that present divergent views among historians regarding a particular topic or topic that has been addressed in that chapter.

We have striven to provide a synthesis of scholarly views, as well as to give attention to a range of historical models, some of which we do not, ourselves, accept as valid, but about which the reader should be informed. Nevertheless, when we set out to write this work, we intended it to be thesis-driven and ultimately to reflect our own views regarding the nature and conduct of medieval warfare. As indicated previously, we see warfare as intertwined with almost every significant aspect of medieval society. Consequently, we have attempted to show the impact of warfare *inter alia* on Christian doctrine and practice, the social organization of medieval societies, the development and diffusion of new technologies, and the adoption of new agricultural and administrative practices, as well as the role played by warfare in stimulating the development of representative institutions whose members demanded a voice in how their taxes were spent by the ruler. In short, our major point is to illustrate the numerous ways in which warfare was embedded within the medieval world.

The second important and somewhat controversial thesis that we pursue in this volume is the importance of the Roman inheritance on the nature and conduct of warfare in medieval Europe. We do not hold doctrinaire positions, arguing that military practices, technology, organization, and the conduct of war itself were marked by stasis, or that medieval warfare was simply a slavish copy of Roman warfare at a later date. Rather, we, in a manner similar to historians of medieval Christianity, start from the proposition that early medieval European kingdoms inherited a wide range of practices, institutions, physical topography, and ways of thinking from the late imperial government in the West.

We have argued consistently over our careers that the elements of governmental and societal organization inherited from Rome were marked by gradual change and development over time, rather than by any kind of abrupt disjuncture or revolution. Our views in this regard are consistent with a large and growing body of scholarship over the past three decades that demonstrates considerable economic, administrative, religious, and social continuities across the period AD 400–700, and in many cases even later, which have led to the new periodization of the post-Roman world as Late Antiquity. With respect to warfare, continuities in both the military topography of Western Europe – consisting of Roman roads, ports, and fortifications, and also aspects of military organization – are especially relevant to understanding warfare not only during Late Antiquity, but also throughout the medieval period as a whole.

Our third and final thesis in this work is that warfare in the Middle Ages was marked both by its complexity and its considerable – and, on occasion, massive – scale. A main reason why warfare affected so many people and so many institutions in medieval Europe was that very large numbers of combatants, requiring vast quantities of arms and supplies, were needed, in general, to conduct important military operations. For the most part, such military efforts were directed toward the capture or defence of fortifications, many of Roman origin, which dominated both the urban and rural topography of medieval Europe. The large scale of military operations required, in turn, the maintenance and further development of advanced techniques in administration, logistics, transportation, and architecture. The complexity of military operations also brought with it the necessity for the extensive education of future and current military commanders in a manner again consistent with what both they and we know to have been late Roman practice.

This volume differs from its numerous predecessors in its examination of military history across both a much broader geographical stage, and over a much longer temporal plane. These rather expansive chronological and geographical perspectives include a major emphasis on the Roman inheritance of medieval Europe and the importation of western traditions of warfare east of the Rhine River, including not only *into* the German world but also in the Slavic world, into the eastern Mediterranean, and throughout the North Sea world. These factors give us the opportunity to explain the conduct and nature of medieval warfare in a more nuanced manner than has heretofore been possible in a synthetic format. In contrast to earlier syntheses, we account for the origins of institutions, physical infrastructure, and intellectual underpinnings of medieval warfare, and trace the diffusion of western practices beyond those regions such as France and England that have been the traditional focus of scholars in the English-language tradition. This volume is also equipped with an extensive series of maps and images that are intended to help our readers in assimilating the information provided in the text, itself.

The second edition of this volume is organized in eight chapters, the first seven of which each focuses on a specific theme regarding the conduct of war during the Middle Ages. Each of these chapters is further sub-divided into sections that provide focused attention to particular issues, regions, or periods. Within this thematic format, Chapters 2–7 are each organized in a roughly chronological manner. The text as a whole is made easier to follow through a detailed 'timeline' that is part of the digital accompaniment of the volume, as well as numerous maps.

The two exceptions to this pattern are Chapter 1 and Chapter 8. In Chapter 1, we discuss both the broad range of sources that are available for the writing of medieval military history, and the successful approaches that scholars have used in order to understand the reality of warfare during the Middle Ages. These approaches include developing an understanding of the strengths and weaknesses of various types of written works, and the assimilation of material sources of information that have been produced through the efforts of paleographers, numismatists, specialists in onomastics, codicologists, art historians, literary theorists, and especially archaeologists. Finally, we introduce the reader to the wide range of disciplines, such as animal husbandry, physics, and physiology that can be deployed to provide crucial insights regarding the context in which war was conducted during the Middle Ages.

Chapter 2, which focuses on the military topography of medieval Europe, begins with the Roman inheritance of fortress cities, lesser fortifications, roads, bridges, and ports, and then examines further developments in the construction and maintenance of fortifications and transportation infrastructure over the course of the medieval period. An important element of this chapter is the discussion of the ways in which western-style military infrastructure was brought into or adopted within regions that once were outside of or largely peripheral to the Roman Empire. Another central question addressed in this chapter is the relationship between the enormous investment of human and material resources in this military topography, and the development or increasing sophistication of medieval governments, particularly with regard to administrative matters.

In Chapter 3, we discuss the military organization of medieval Europe, again beginning with the institutions inherited from Rome, and then examining how these developed and were altered over time in response to contemporary developments. In this chapter, we treat both land-based and naval forces. Throughout the chapter, moreover, we focus on the central questions of who served in war and under what circumstances, as well as the relationship between military service and economic and social status. We also address the hotly contested issues of the rise of the so-called 'warrior aristocracy', including the thorny questions of the nature of knighthood, the roles of women in combat, and chivalry. In addition, we treat the relationship between military service and the development of representative government.

The focus in Chapter 4 is on logistics, which is the fundamental issue of supplying an army with food, arms, and equipment. Logistics lies at the nexus of economic, administrative, fiscal, and military history. As a result, we discuss the ways in which the conduct of war played a role in the development of market economies and the so-called administrative state. In this context, we consider the establishment of systems of magazines and commissaries, taxation of the broader population, and the management of royal, ecclesiastical, and princely estates. The discussion of logistics necessarily also bears on the history of transportation technology, and so we consider developments in the technology of both land-based and water-based transportation resources. Everyone knows the cliché that an army travels on its stomach, but few medievalists venture to investigate this key aspect of warfare, or its implications for the impact of war on society.

In Chapter 5, we analyze the wide range of military equipment utilized by combatants from the late Roman period up through the end of the medieval millennium. We consider personal arms and armour, as well as large-scale weapons systems, including artillery and naval assets, and finally fortifications. Our discussion of these subjects is accompanied by medieval illustrations and sculpted reliefs that will help the reader visualize the equipment that is being discussed. We devote considerable attention to developments in these various weapons and weapons systems, and how these developments affected the conduct of both offensive and defensive military operations. The investigation of military technology also illuminates the matter of cultural transmission both across time and space during the course of the medieval millennium.

In Chapter 6, we turn our attention to combat, with a focus on tactics, training, and morale. As is the case in the earlier chapters, we begin our discussion with an analysis of late Roman traditions, which were well-known to military leaders during the Middle Ages. We then consider how developments in technology and military organization during the course of the Middle Ages impacted the ways in which military commanders oversaw the training and deployment of their troops in the field, including for sieges, as well as on the sea. We also consider the ways in which the Christianization of the Roman Empire affected the conduct of military operations, and how the needs of war impacted Christian doctrine and religious practice. Looking at religion in both directions, i.e. cause and effect, illuminates the importance of treating warfare as central to the human experience during the Middle Ages.

Chapter 7 considers strategy with a focus on the interplay between warfare and geopolitical relations. We give considerable attention to the distinctions between 'grand strategy', or long-term strategy, and campaign strategy. We devote attention as well to important elements in the development of both long-term and campaign strategy such as planning, intelligence gathering, diplomacy, and the use of calculated destruction or restraint, with the concomitant issue of 'collateral damage'. We conclude this chapter with a discussion of military education, once more providing an overview of late Roman practice and then continue with a focus on continuities as well as new developments during the Middle Ages. The intellectual part of warfare is a subject that is neglected at the reader's peril.

Chapter 8, a final chapter which is a new addition to this second edition of our text, focuses on two military campaigns from the early medieval period, which we chose in order to highlight several of the major themes discussed in the previous chapters. The first of these campaigns is Charlemagne's 'invasion' of Muslim-ruled Spain in the spring of 778, which provides considerable scope for an examination of the role of diplomacy in warfare, as well as the crucial importance of the Roman legacy of roads and fortresses for early medieval military planners. The second campaign is King Henry I of Germany's conquest of the lands of the Hevelli and Sorbs in the winter of 928–929, which substantially expanded the territory under his rule, and pushed the frontiers of the nascent German kingdom beyond those ever achieved by his Carolingian predecessors. The relative dearth of written sources about Henry I's major military effort offers an opportunity to explore the methodological approaches to examining the conduct of war through material sources of information developed through archaeological excavations.

1   Sources

The writing of medieval military history

Introduction

On the eve of the Second World War, the great British historian Sir Charles Oman wrote:

> both the medieval monastic chroniclers and the modern liberal historiographers had often no closer notion of the meaning of war than that it involves various horrors and is attended by a lamentable loss of life. Both classes strove to disguise their personal ignorance or dislike of military matters by deprecating their importance and significance in history.[1]

This distaste for the writing about, and thereby teaching about, war did not lead to the end of warfare, as the events of 1939–1945 and since have demonstrated so starkly. Rather, with the honourable exception of Oman and a small handful of other scholars, the writing of medieval military history up through the late 1950s was left to retired military officers, who focused most of their attention on battles. These were viewed and evaluated on the basis of the conformity of medieval commanders to the military doctrines of the modern world, chief among them Clausewitz's argument, based on his observations of the success of Napoleon Bonaparte, that the main task of a general was to seek out the enemy army and destroy it in the field. Because most successful military commanders assiduously avoided battle throughout most of the Middle Ages, they were deemed deficient by their modern successors, who asserted that military science overall was at a nadir in the millennium following the fall of the Western Roman Empire.

Medieval military history was rescued from the margins of scholarly discourse in the decades after the end of the Second World War as a new generation of academics, many of whom had seen military service but not made a career of it, devoted their intellectual energies to evaluating medieval warfare on its own terms. Among their important insights were that battle-seeking strategies generally were not relevant to medieval warfare, which was dominated by sieges, and the control of territory through the construction and garrisoning of fortifications. In addition, scholars began to turn away from a focus on battles to investigate the relationship of military affairs to other aspects of society, particularly social status. During the 1980s, medieval military history was further revitalized through the development of the 'war and society' school of inquiry that sought to understand the impact of warfare on society at large. Historians began systemically to investigate topics such as logistics

---

1 Charles Oman, *On the Writing of History* (New York, 1939), 159–160.

DOI: 10.4324/9781003032878-2

and the impact of warfare on the economy and culture, and also to develop a more nuanced understanding of medieval military technology.

The increasing sophistication over the past two generations of the study of medieval warfare has been accompanied and also driven, in part, by the growth of available source materials. In many cases, sources of information such as administrative documents and charters had been edited and published by the late nineteenth century, but were not used by historians, trained in older methodologies, who focused their attention on easily accessible narrative texts. By contrast, the veritable explosion of archaeological studies in the period since the Second World War has opened up vast quantities of information about the Middle Ages that simply was not available to earlier generations of scholars. Ironically, the great destruction wrought by this war, particularly in urban settings, opened up large areas for archaeological investigation that previously had been inaccessible. This is especially the case in the field that is now known as 'landscape archaeology', a term used to describe the efforts of scholars from across a wide range of disciplines to read human intention into the natural and man-made topography and the relationship between the two.

From a methodological perspective, the historian working today to investigate warfare during the Middle Ages is responsible for understanding and using a wide array of sources, some of which have a long pedigree, and others that only recently have been applied to the study of medieval history. Perhaps even more importantly, the traditional model of picking one or two of the supposed 'best' narrative texts and refining them to create a narrative is no longer viable. Indeed, such a method, although common, never was viable for the development of an accurate depiction of the past, as is revealed in the critiques levelled against their colleagues by scholars such as John E. Morris, who pioneered the use of administrative documents in writing about the campaigns in Wales that were conducted by King Edward I of England (1272–1307).

The present chapter is intended to provide an overview of the great variety of sources of information that are available for the study of medieval warfare, and to give guidance about how to use them effectively to write military history. Somewhat arbitrarily, we have divided our discussion between written and non-written sources, although it is the case that some illustrations in manuscripts, stone carvings, and above all coins, often contain written information, as well. In addition, we have divided our discussion of written sources between those whose authors were motivated explicitly to provide an account of past events, and other types of documents that were produced in large part for prescriptive, didactic, administrative, personal, or entertainment purposes.

Historiographical texts

Historiographical texts – that is, written sources that purport to offer information about the past – generally have been favoured by modern medieval military historians because they tend to offer the greatest detail in a collective sense regarding both the overall conduct of military operations and the actions, including the supposed thoughts, of individual participants, and especially of the leadership. By contrast, many dozens of administrative documents often need to be accessed to get a similar range of information. In addition, it is rare that administrative documents are published in large quantities and even rarer to have translations of such texts. In comparison, a great many narrative sources have been translated during the past two centuries into numerous modern languages, albeit with varying degrees of quality, completeness, and accuracy.

It is certainly true that the many genres of historiographical texts (more on this in what follows) are essential for the writing of military history, or perhaps it is better to say, for answering specific questions that relate to the military history of medieval Europe. However, before the historian can draw effectively upon information in these texts to develop an accurate understanding of past events, it is necessary to understand not only the strengths but also the limitations of each type of historiographical source, and also of each individual exemplar within a genre. Taking a selection of quotations from a particular text, for example, either to prove its value or to reject its usefulness is methodologically unsound. Rather, the entire text must be evaluated as a whole. In this context, it also must be kept in mind that the authors of many historiographical texts drew upon more than one literary tradition when writing so that differentiating between genres must be done in a nuanced rather than dogmatic or rigid manner. In short, historiographical works must be understood both as works of literature and as sources.

As we begin this discussion of both the strengths and limitations of various types of historiographical sources of information, it is also important to draw attention to at least some of the most important current scholarly arguments regarding the epistemology of historical knowledge. This is the question of how we can obtain accurate information about past human action. The two authors of this volume espouse what might be termed an optimistic epistemology, meaning that we believe that it is possible to come to an accurate understanding of what happened in the past by using historiographical texts in conjunction with a wide range of additional types of sources, especially archaeological materials, which will be discussed in later sections.

This optimistic epistemology can be contrasted with a pessimistic approach to historiographical texts that has been illuminated recently in the works of the prominent German medieval historian Johannes Fried. In a series of books and articles, which draw upon older scholarship, Fried has argued that a true understanding of what actually happened in medieval Europe, particularly early medieval Europe, is impossible because written texts, by their very nature, cannot convey reality of the type necessary to write political history, and consequently military history as well. This pessimistic view of the value of historiographical sources for ascertaining aspects of what actually happened in the past depends on two basic premises. The first of these is that it was impossible for the putatively 'oral society' of medieval Europe, and particularly early medieval Europe, to provide an accurate record of past events. This is because humans not only forget most of the things that they have experienced; it is also the case that they remember past events inaccurately in order to suit their present needs. The second fundamental reason offered for rejecting the information provided by historiographical texts is that the authors were not concerned with providing an account of events as they happened in the past, but rather sought to use accounts of the past to shape the present in pursuit of a political, or even more commonly, an ideological agenda. In short, the distortion of the past by writers during the Middle Ages was purposeful.

The premises espoused by scholars such as Professor Fried depends on a *reductio ad absurdum* with respect to realities inherent in the human condition, on the one hand, and the nature of historical writing in the pre-modern period, on the other hand. It is certainly the case that human beings in the present, as well as in the past, forget much of what they have experienced, and engage, sometimes intentionally, in 'misremembering' for a wide range of purposes. And yet, it is also the case that all of us rely upon our memories to navigate effectively among all of our daily activities, relationships, and tasks. In short, we rely on our memories every day, and they are sufficiently reliable to enable to us to succeed far more often than not. As a corollary to this point, the written word played a much larger part in all aspects of medieval life than is granted by scholars such as Professor Fried, and this was certainly true with regard to the conduct of military affairs. In effect, the use of memory was strengthened by the equally effective use of documents.

Fried and others also are correct to point out that medieval authors generally did not write in order to provide information about 'how things really were'. Indeed, we endorse the proposition made by scholars such as the early medieval historian Walter Goffart that medieval writers did not naïvely transmit fact, but rather were engaged in complex dialogues with their contemporaries about the proper organization of human society, at both theological and political levels. From the perspective of military history, one of the most important of these biases is the emphasis on aristocrats and their participation in warfare at the expense of all other members of society. However, the blanket rejection of all of the information provided by a historiographical text because it is clear that the author added, left out, or misrepresented some information relating to the narrative arc of the work is methodologically unsound, or to put it colloquially, is tantamount to throwing out the baby with the bathwater.

In this context, it bears emphasis that in order to create a view of the past, the authors of historiographical texts deployed facts – that is, accurate information concerning events that actually happened – to make their case. Such facts, many of which are verifiable through a wide variety of means, are of considerable importance for the writing of history by modern scholars. As a consequence, unless it can be shown that a particular medieval writer made things up – that is, produced phony information all the time in all cases – and made no use in any way of contemporary speech, dress, culture, or thought in his text, it is the task of the historian to identify what is accurate and what is not.

As a corollary to these questions with regard to the value of historiographical texts in providing accurate information about the past, we also wish to draw the readers' attention to one further aspect of epistemological pessimism. This is the idea that historiographical sources, particularly from the early Middle Ages, are so laconic with regard to military matters that they offer very little scope for anything other than a bare bones recitation of the names of conquerors and lists of battles or sieges. This approach to historiographical sources, in our view, is a manifestation of the old-style positivistic approach to history, in which the historian's task was to collect data points provided by the text and then develop a coherent image from them. What is missing is the use of historical imagination, which makes it possible to pose a series of questions that are raised if the information provided by a source is, in fact, accurate.

For example, the observation made by Bishop Gregory of Tours (died c.594) in his *Histories* that in 531 the Thuringian king Hermanfrid prepared the battlefield along the Unstrut River with ditches to thwart a potential Frankish cavalry attack opens up a number of fruitful avenues for questions. It is clear that Hermanfrid had to obtain information regarding both Frankish military organization and tactics. He had to have specific information considerably prior to the Frankish attack in order to prepare the field of battle. Consequently, the modern historian must ask, how did Hermanfrid obtain information about the approach of the Franks, how did the Thuringians know about Frankish tactics, and how did the Thuringians know that preparing a field with ditches was the proper response to the typical Frankish style of attack? These questions open the way to investigating matters such as military training and intelligence that are discussed in Chapters 6–7.

Interrogating historiographical sources

Rather than making wholesale judgements about historiographical texts, whether positive or negative, each individual medieval work that is considered by the modern historian must be evaluated according to a wide range of criteria. The interrogation of a particular text should begin by ascertaining the potential access of an author to reliable or accurate information, the ability or inability of an author to understand the information that he had obtained, and the variety of influences – such as bias, audience, and purpose – that impinged upon the decisions by the author about what information to include, exclude, misrepresent, or even falsify. With these criteria in mind, it also important to understand that if a text is of little or no value in answering one particular question about the past, this does not mean it lacks usefulness for answering a different question about the past.

An important starting point for an interrogation of a text is understanding that most authors of medieval historiographical works were familiar, either directly or indirectly, with the *Etymologies*, written by Bishop Isidore of Seville (died 636). In this work, which was a standard textbook for students throughout the medieval millennium, Isidore defined *historia* as the presentation of events that actually happened in the past. Isidore contrasted history with the writing of fables, which were events that did not take place. Isidore's definition of *historia* was quoted or paraphrased in many hundreds of historiographical texts throughout the Middle Ages. Neither Isidore's definition nor its repetition by medieval authors requires a modern reader to accept any particular claim in a text as representing factual accuracy, in the sense that an event took place precisely how an author explained it, or even that the event took place at all. However, the ubiquitous repetition of and commentary on Isidore's definition is very important, because it illuminates a broad understanding among both authors and their audiences that historical works did not deal with fantasy – that is, fables – but rather with reality – that is, events that actually took place in the past. In short, the principle itself was not at issue, only its execution.

Once we understand that historical works brought with them an expectation of presenting information about events that had happened in the past, an analysis of the intended audience for a historiographical text provides a powerful tool to the historian for examining the ways in which an author was constrained to discuss reality as he understood it. The Roman politician, lawyer, and writer Cicero (died 43 BC) composed a manual *On Rhetoric* that was widely copied, read, and discussed in medieval Europe, most frequently because of its common use as a school text. Among Cicero's main points in this text was that a successful writer, or speaker, made his case or offered his historical account in a manner that was plausible to the audience. From a practical perspective, this meant that an author of a history had to avoid alienating his audience by writing something that they would recognize as obviously false, incorrect, or foolish. When writing for an audience of men experienced in war, for example, an author who purported to write history had to 'get it right' with respect to military matters if he expected the audience to accept the other claims made in the work. The audience, when it is known, therefore provides the modern historian with a control, although not a total control, on the text that is being analyzed.

A corollary to a proper understanding of the 'rhetoric of plausibility' in evaluating a historiographical text is ascertaining the narrative arc – that is, the main story line of a work. It is here that an author's intentions for the text become manifest as he offers praise, condemnation, and exculpation, shades what he knows to be true, adds information that he knows to be false, and excludes information that is likely to undermine his case. By contrast, information provided by an author that is not part of the narrative arc is very likely to be accurate, insofar as the author has accurate information available to him. This is the case because the author, working within the context of the rhetoric of plausibility, has an interest in maintaining the confidence of his audience with respect to his own reliability, particularly when providing accurate information does not impinge upon the overall point or points that he is making in the text. Such information might be considered 'local colour'.

One of the medieval authors who has received considerable scholarly attention with regard to the narrative arc of his text is William of Poitiers (died c.1090), whose *Deeds of Duke William II of the Normans* has been the subject of dozens of historical and literary commentaries. The popularity of this work for scholarly studies is due to the author's previous career as a soldier, his close relationship to William the Conqueror, and his access to first-hand accounts of the Norman duke's reign and information regarding the victory at Hastings in 1066, that either came from the duke or from others who participated in the battle. William of Poitiers' work variously has been accepted in its entirety, rejected completely, and identified as offering accurate information about one or another aspect of Duke William's career, the conquest of England, and contemporary military affairs. This last interpretation is the one to which we subscribe, and is based on the idea that in framing his political claims about William the Conqueror, William of Poitiers accurately described contemporary mores, practices, and institutions, including those relating to the conduct of war.

However, one point that often is made by scholars who try to discredit the accuracy of the information provided by William of Poitiers, aside from his obvious and exceptionally strong bias in favour of the Conqueror, is the author's considerable debt to classical Roman texts. Many historians have argued that William was less interested in describing the reality of contemporary affairs than he was in demonstrating his own erudition. As a consequence, they conclude that William of Poitiers' quotation – or better said, adaptation – of the works of Roman authors in describing the military organization of the Norman duchy or Duke William's conduct of military campaigns actually provides no information about these or other topics.

This argument is based on the premise that William of Poitiers, and the many hundreds of other medieval writers who demonstrated their familiarity with Roman texts, must have been interested *either* in 'showing off' *or* in providing accurate information about contemporary affairs. In our view, this either/or approach not only discounts the complexity of human behaviour, but also ignores the issue of the rhetoric of plausibility. Authors such as William of Poitiers almost certainly had the capacity to embrace multiple goals at the same time, so long as these goals were not mutually contradictory. For example, the choice to describe William the Conqueror undertaking a reconnaissance mission in a manner consistent with Julius Caesar's account of just such as mission in his *Gallic Wars* reasonably can be understood both as an attempt to demonstrate knowledge of Caesar's text and also as an effort to describe what William the Conqueror really did. In fact, it may be suggested that Duke William undertook a reconnaissance because he had learned that such an effort was important through conversing with military advisors who had studied Roman history. Indeed, scholars now agree that Duke William himself received a thorough education and may also have read Roman histories, which helped inform his understanding of military affairs. As we shall discuss in more detail in Chapter 7, it simply is not tenable that Duke William somehow simply knew how to fight a war without being taught how to do so.

In addition to understanding the importance of both the rhetoric of plausibility and the narrative arc as internal controls on the text, an important external control is provided by what the great German military historian Hans Delbrück denoted as *Sachkritik*, which can be translated into English as the study of material reality. When the authors of texts make claims about the size of armies, their rate of march, or other quantifiable matters, these can be tested against the known realities of human physiology, physical topography, and technological capacity at a given time and place. For example, the techniques of *Sachkritik* were employed effectively by classical military historians more than a century ago to show that Herodotos' account of the size of the Persian army that was mobilized to invade Greece in 480 BC was not physically possible. If the numbers provided by Herodotos were accepted at face value, the Persian rear guard would still have been crossing the Hellespont, the narrow strip of water separating Europe from Asia, while the vanguard was already in Greece.

One area of considerable debate among military historians, and medievalists more generally, which is particularly amenable to analysis through the principles of *Sachkritik*, concerns the number of fighting men who served in an army. Many scholars argue that medieval writers were simply hopeless in providing accurate figures for the size of military forces. To support this contention, they draw attention to the occasional use by medieval writers of terminology such as an army numbered more than the stars in sky, or to claims that an army numbered in the hundreds of thousands. As a consequence, it is sometimes claimed by scholars that it is impossible to use any numbers offered by any medieval author to develop an accurate assessment of the scale of an army. Other modern scholars, who start with the assumption that medieval armies must have been small, readily accept claims by medieval authors that one side had just a few thousand or even a few hundred men, but reject out of hand statements by these very same authors that armies numbered in the many thousands or even tens of thousands. This inconsistency in the approach to the numbers provided in medieval sources led the renowned scholar of early medieval Europe Karl Ferdinand Werner to rebuke his fellow historians, insisting that: 'the effective scholar does not gain distinction simply because he estimates the smallest possible number but because his methods bring him closer to the truth and, in addition, he can prove his point'.[2]

The proper approach, as Werner made clear, was to assess each text on its own terms, and to consider the specific context in which the army was functioning. The application of the principles of *Sachkritik* is particularly apropos in this process, because a knowledge of human and animal dietary requirements, including both food and liquid, allows the historian, for example, to determine the minimum quantity of calories that were required to sustain a fighting force over any length of time. Information about caloric needs and diet of both men and animals can be obtained by the historian through the work of paleobotanists, specialists in pre-modern animal husbandry, and physical anthropologists. An understanding of contemporary medieval transportation technology permits the historian to understand what quantity and types of animals, vehicles, or ships were necessary to transport these supplies to an army.

At a more complex level, an understanding of medieval military technology, which has been made available through the work of archaeologists, sometimes in conjunction with

---

2 Karl Ferdinand Werner, 'Heeresorganization und Kriegsführung im deutschen Königreich des 10. und 11. Jahrhunderts' in *Settimane di Studio de Centro Italiano sull'alto Medioevo* 15 (Spoleto, 1968), 791–843, here 813–814 for the quotation.

specialists in physics and ballistics, provides the historian with information about the number of men who were required to defend a fortification of a known size, and how many men were required to assault it. Information about the size of fortifications also is made available to historians through the work of archaeologists. In short, *Sachkritik* relies upon a synthesis of many strands of knowledge, much as the study of history, as a whole, stands at the nexus of a vast array of disciplines.

Historiographical genres

Histories and chronicles

Throughout the medieval millennium, men and some women stood at their writing desks and composed self-consciously historical works, in which they focused on providing an account of past events. Texts in one genre, which often are denoted by scholars as histories or chronicles, were composed, in general, by a single author with a set theme or themes in mind. However, with a few notable exceptions, most histories and chronicles written in the period before the First Crusade, in the late eleventh century, presented contemporary affairs as an 'addendum' to a lengthy pre-history, often dating back to the creation of the universe. This was the case even when contemporary affairs were the primary focus of the author's text. It was important in rhetorical terms for Christian writers to put contemporary affairs in a universal context, in order to show the unfolding of God's plan in historical time.

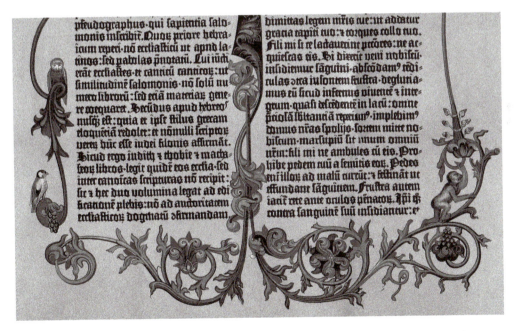

Figure 1.1 This illustrated page from the Gutenberg Bible, produced around 1453–1456

Source: © Ivy Close Images/Alamy Stock Photo CFMJ3N

One important model for this historical approach in the Christian tradition was Eusebius' *Ecclesiastical History*, written during the late third and early fourth century, which was popularized in the West through St. Jerome's Latin translation of the later fourth or early fifth century. Eusebius' account begins with the life of Jesus, and one of the implicit lessons of his text was that the victory of Christianity under Constantine the Great (306–337) revealed God's hand in the direction of human affairs. A second important model of history writing was Gregory of Tours' *Historiae*, written during the late sixth century, which begins with the creation of the universe, and ends with observations on events during the author's own lifetime.

Although not constructed as a universal history in the same manner as Eusebius' text, Gregory's history nevertheless provides a biblical setting for current affairs as a vehicle for Christian instruction to make clear God's hand in earthly matters. He also sought to emphasize to his contemporaries that if they did not live up to Christian ideals, they would suffer the same punishments as evil-doers in the past. For the numerous medieval writers whose education included deep reading in Roman authors, works such as Livy's *From the Foundation of the City* (*Ab Urbe Condita*) also illustrated the importance of placing current affairs within a much longer historical context.

Of course, other Roman authors such as Caesar provided alternative models, such as his *Gallic Wars*, in which the focus was entirely on contemporary matters. Some medieval authors in the pre-crusade period also followed this model. However, they usually felt compelled to justify this decision. For example, Charlemagne's grandson Nithard (died 843), a layman and experienced military commander who wrote a detailed account of the events from the 820s up to his present day in 843, recorded that he had done so at the command of his cousin, the West Frankish King Charles the Bald (840–877). In the early eleventh century, the cleric Alpert of Metz went even further, offering a lengthy defence of having written about contemporary affairs in his dedicatory letter to Bishop Burchard of Worms (1000–1025).

The tendency to imbed a discussion of the recent past or contemporary affairs within a broader history of the world began to recede rapidly by the early twelfth century. It is likely that the impetus here was the vast outpouring of narratives about the First Crusade (1096–1099). Many of the surviving Latin narrative texts from the decades immediately following the capture of Jerusalem by the crusaders in 1099 focused almost exclusively on contemporary events. From the twelfth century onward, the authors of histories and chronicles tended to focus largely on contemporary affairs, although some continued to place these events into a context that fit their *parti pris*. A good example of this is provided by William the Breton (died 1225), who included a history of the origin of the French, whom he traced to the Trojans, in his account of the reign of King Philip II Augustus of France (1180–1223).

The tendency of the authors of medieval histories and chronicles to draw upon earlier historical works provides yet another means for modern scholars to assess how a particular text can be used to answer specific questions regarding medieval warfare. Of particular importance is analyzing the ways in which a later author manipulates or adapts earlier historical texts or information from previous eras to fit his current narrative. For example, when writing about a battle that took place in 882, the eleventh-century author Hermann of Reichenau changed the text of his source, the ninth-century *Annals of Fulda*, in order to make it understandable to his present audience. The *Annals of Fulda* recorded that eighteen royal *satellites* of the king (in this case, the Carolingian ruler Louis the Younger), along with their military units, were killed in this battle against the Vikings. The term *satellites* did not have the meaning of military officer or commander in the eleventh century as it did in the ninth. So Hermann altered his source to read eighteen royal *milites*, along with their men were killed, because the term *milites* conformed to the contemporary terminology with respect to denoting military commanders. It is clear that Hermann, as a scholar and historian, knew the meaning of the ninth-century text, but he was uncertain as to whether his readers or listeners would be as well informed.

Annales and *gestae*

In addition to histories, the two most common genres of explicitly historical works are *annales* and *gestae*. The first of these genres, the *annales*, were characterized by their format of presenting events in chronological sequence in year-by-year instalments, rather than creating synthetic histories that focused on chosen sets of topics. In most cases, especially in pre-crusade Europe, the authors of the *annales* are not known, and many of these texts appear to have been composite works that were begun and then continued at intervals determined by the internal needs of the monastery or bishopric in which they were produced. Consequently, the information provided by any single work must be evaluated quite carefully to determine the nature of the *parti pris* of the man who was the author of that portion of the text, what sources of information he had available, and what expectations his audience might have had. On the positive side of the ledger, because the texts of the *annales* were presented in a year-by-year fashion, it is often possible to pinpoint the dates of specific events, particularly those that were of local significance, or were regarded as important by the author. In addition, when a large number of written works survive from a particular monastic scriptorium, it is often possible to identify the specific handwriting of the author of one or more parts of the annals produced at that monastery. An analysis of these other works produced at the monastery by this same hand sometimes permits a close dating of the portion of the historical text he wrote.

However, recent studies of *annales* indicate that the appearance of a year-by-year record is sometimes deceiving to the modern reader because some medieval authors wrote a series of entries at a single point in time, sometimes long after the events that they described, and consequently did not add to their texts on an annual basis. The implication of this latter practice is that an author refined his text to fit a particular agenda that was pertinent in his own day, but which might not have been very important in earlier years. In order to proceed on a sound methodological basis, the modern scholar must treat each segment of these texts as part of the whole, but also individually. In addition, as Rosamond McKitterick has shown in a number of studies, it is very important to analyze the surviving manuscripts of *annales* to determine the identity of the authors, through an analysis of their handwriting, and also to see which passages were erased or crossed out and then replaced. The earliest editors of these texts in the nineteenth and early twentieth centuries often were not sufficiently attuned to these nuances, and produced editions that obscured the complexities of these texts.

The *gestae*, literally deeds, of bishops and abbots follow a rather different format than the *annales* in that they present information regarding the abbatiate or episcopate of each of the leaders of their particular institution. Nevertheless, like the *annales*, the *gestae* tend to have multiple authors, and to have been written over the course of many decades. Consequently, many of the source problems posed by the *annales* are also present in the *gestae*. However, one very important characteristic of the *gestae* is that many of the abbots and bishops whose deeds they record played significant roles not only in the history of the local areas in which

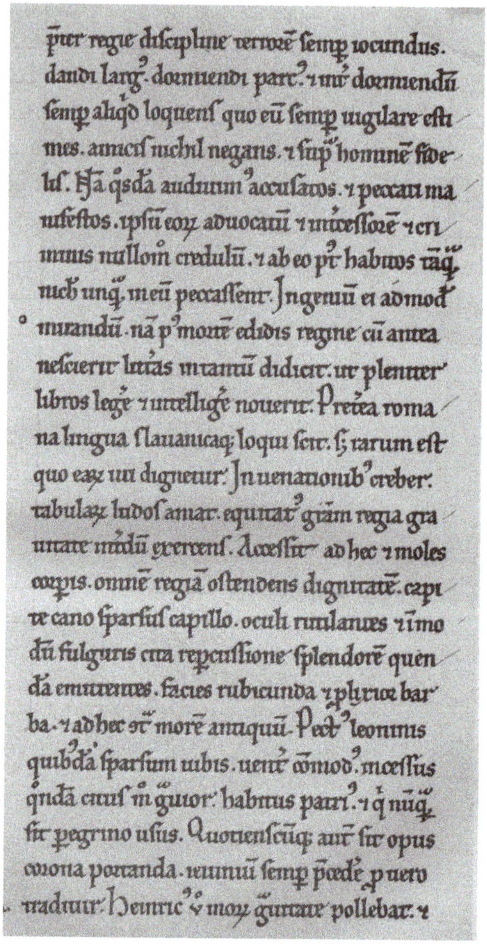

Figure 1.2 Facsimile of Widukind of Corvey's Res Gestae Saxonicae
Source: © FALKENSTEINFOTO/Alamy Stock Photo HKK0GH

they functioned, but also on a regional, kingdom-wide, or even international stage. As a result, the *gestae* are particularly valuable in shedding light on the activities of a king, prince, or great magnate from a local or regional perspective.

In addition, the authors of *gestae* typically recorded administrative records, charters, wills, letters, and even treaties in their texts in an effort to demonstrate the veracity of the claims that they were making about the past. These recorded documents sometimes are preserved only in *gestae*, with the originals having been lost over time. As a consequence, in addition to providing a narrative from the point of view of the author regarding past events, the *gestae* can also shed light on the activities of numerous local, regional, and even princely or royal actors. These magnates often made donations to religious institutions in order to win support during a military campaign. In other cases, the documents preserved in *gestae* can be compared with other surviving exemplars, including sometimes the original document. This is especially the case in regard to lands claimed by a particular monastery or bishopric.

When this happens, the modern historian can learn whether the author of a *gesta* accurately copied the original text, or rather manipulated the document in order to support his particular agenda or that of his patrons.

Vitae

Yet another type of historical source is the *vita* – that is, the biography of a holy man or woman. These texts generally were not self-consciously historical in the sense that the authors set out to provide a narrative of the past, even if the author described earlier events. Instead, the primary purpose of a *vita* was to establish the bona fides of a particular individual as a saintly person. Most *vitae* in medieval Europe owe their form and construction to the model established by Sulpicius Severus (died 425) in his exceptionally influential early fifth-century *vita* of St. Martin of Tours (died 397). Despite the very large number of surviving *vitae*, it was common until the 1950s for many medieval historians to reject these texts as having any useful information to provide concerning 'properly' historical matters, including medieval warfare. In large part, the refusal by scholars to consider *vitae* as providing insights into contemporary reality was due to the inclusion of numerous miracles in these texts that were intended to serve as proof of the hero's saintliness. The argument was that because the miracle stories must have been invented, the text as a whole should be treated as fiction, good only for gaining a glimpse of the contemporary understanding of saintliness.

However, detailed studies of *vitae* over the past half century have made clear that the authors of these texts actually were constrained by the rhetoric of plausibility in a manner similar, when dealing with non-supernatural matters, to the authors of explicitly historical works. When making the case about the sanctity of the hero of the *vita*, including the miracles carried out by this saintly figure, it was very important to maintain the trust of the audience about the author's truthfulness. This was done by providing an accurate 'frame' in which to tell the story of the saint, with the consequence that matters that were not part of the author's narrative arc often can be understood as reflecting contemporary reality at the time the *vita* was written, such as the depredations of Vikings and the responses of monks in the ninth and tenth centuries. The efforts of authors of *vitae* to provide an accurate frame for their accounts can be seen quite clearly when *vitae* were revised over time. It is usually the case that the specific details about the saint's life and career, as well as the miracles that the author depicted the holy person performing, remain the same. However, the context in which this life took place was altered by the author to fit the realities of the later time in which the text was revised.

A counterpart to the *vita* as a sacred biography is the biographical account of a ruler or important ecclesiastical magnate, which has the intent of preserving the supposed greatness of this individual in the written record, but without the additional claim that this individual was saintly. The archetype of this type of secularized *vita* is Einhard's *Life of Charlemagne*, written in the 820s. Einhard (died 840) himself borrowed much of the form of his text, if not the content, from the Roman author Suetonius' *Lives of the Caesars*, written early in the second century. In many cases, however, authors denoted these secular biographies as *gestae*, drawing on the name, although not the form, of the historical works written in monasteries and cathedrals. These secular biographies – and, in some cases, autobiographies – that appear in greater numbers during the later Middle Ages, must be evaluated by the historian using the same tools that are applied to histories and chronicles, as described earlier.

Prosimetric and poetic histories

A new genre of historiographical writing developed in the course of the eleventh century that is denoted by scholars as prosimetric history. Works of this type, such as Dudo of St. Quentin's *History of the Customs and Deeds of the First Dukes of Normandy* (*De moribus et actis primorum normaniae ducum*), written in the early eleventh century, and Ralph of Caen's *Deeds of Tancred* (*Gesta Tancredi*), written in the early twelfth, combine a prose narrative with lengthy passages in verse. Dudo, Ralph, and other authors who wrote texts in this genre made clear to their audiences that they intended to provide an accurate account of what had happened in the past, often by making a statement to this effect in the preface of the work. However, there is a striking difference between the types of accounts that are provided in the prose and poetic sections of the texts. While writing in prose, the authors focus on making a plausible case regarding the course of the events. By contrast, when writing in poetry, they offer highly exaggerated vignettes of their heroes' accomplishments, accounts of dreams, and descriptions of fantastic or even miraculous events. Ralph of Caen was quite explicit about this point, making clear that when he wrote poetry, the reader should treat this in the same manner that he understood an epic poem. The bifurcated approach to the narration indicates that the authors of prosimetric texts felt constrained by factors such as the rhetoric of plausibility when writing in prose, but considered themselves free to indulge in fables or fantasy when writing in poetry. In fact, authors of historiographical works in the eleventh century, such as William of Poitiers, commented that verse histories were really just pseudo-histories because the poet could write anything he pleased without being constrained by fact.

The use of poetry by authors of prosimetric works stands in stark contrast to self-consciously historiographical works that are presented in verse from the twelfth century onward. It was once argued by scholars that histories written in verse suffered from the same liabilities as epic poetry that was written largely for entertainment purposes, such as *The Song of Roland* or the early medieval *Beowulf*. However, detailed analysis of the sources and presentation of information in verse histories such as the late twelfth century *Roman de Rou* by the Norman writer Wace, or the early thirteenth century *Philippide* by William the Breton, make clear that these texts should be read and interpreted in the same manner as prose histories and chronicles. The number of verse histories proliferated during the later Middle Ages, both in Latin and in the vernacular. Many of the latter were produced in urban settings, particularly in Germany, which indicates a burgeoning interest in the past among the increasingly wealthy and literate urban elites.

Literary works

In contrast to historiographical texts, the authors of literary works including epic poetry such as *Beowulf, Song of Roland,* and the *Arthurian Cycle*, were not bound by the conventions of the rhetoric of plausibility, or the Isidorean definition of history as describing events that actually took place in the past. Consequently, historians must tread very carefully when attempting to discern what kinds of questions a particular literary work might help to answer. For example, many works of entertainment literature, in addition to depicting monsters and magic, also present combatants regularly cleaving through the armour and bodies of their opponents, as well as the horses of their adversaries. Such feats of human strength and skill are impossible and did not happen on medieval battlefields. In a similar vein, the authors of medieval romances and epic literature tended to focus much of their attention on describing, in loving detail, every sword or lance stroke in a duel between champions. Such duels, while they did take place on occasion, were also quite rare and usually had very little to do with the conduct of warfare generally, or with the course of any particular battle.

Sometimes, the details provided in these literary accounts are accurate, such as the description of the proper method to butcher a deer that is recounted in *Tristan and Isolde*. However, all too many historians and specialists in literary studies have been enthralled by the great detail offered in romances and epic poems, and treat entertainment literature as having the same claims to the depiction of reality as historiographical texts. Indeed, much of the basis for the development of chivalry as an element in medieval warfare by modern scholars is based on the uncritical acceptance of the stories recounted in works such as *Sir Gawain and the Green Knight*, first set down in writing in the fourteenth century. This can be contrasted with the study of chivalry by scholars such as John Gillingham and Matthew Strickland, who focus their attention on historiographical texts.

In addition to simply telling tales, the authors of literary works also used satire to entertain, and perhaps also to educate their audiences. In some cases, the individuals whom modern scholars have identified as heroes were, in fact, presented as fools by contemporary authors. In the context of medieval warfare, some of these supposed heroes, such as Roland in the Norman version of the *Song of Roland*, are shown as acting in ways that were completely contrary to contemporary military practice and doctrine, leading to their deaths and the deaths of their men. By contrast, Oliver in this work is used as something of a foil to demonstrate Roland's failure to adhere to established military doctrine.

Nevertheless, despite the danger of accepting the stories in entertainment literature at face value, it is not necessary or desirable simply to discard these numerous texts when attempting to answer questions about the nature of medieval warfare. Rather, they can be understood as reflecting important aspects of contemporary mores, beliefs, and also equipment and technology, which can be compared with material remains and contemporary images. In order to be effective, stories must be comprehensible to their audiences. This requirement for comprehensibility often entailed that the authors of entertainment literature were constrained, in a manner quite similar to the authors of *vitae*, to present their stories within a frame that was familiar to their audiences. Even when undertaking extraordinary actions, heroes still had to bear arms and travel in ways that an audience recognized. In a similar vein, when authors presented the 'good guys' in their narrative, these characters had to conform to contemporary modes of propriety. Even in cases when authors sought to subvert conventional norms, they had to do so in a manner that was comprehensible to their audiences. Because of these constraints on the authors of entertainment literature, it is often possible to pick out certain elements of the text that can be used, but with great care, to help answer questions about military affairs.

Letters

Letters written in Latin present an important literary genre in the Latin West dating back to Late Antiquity, and indeed to the Roman Empire and Republic. Both secular and ecclesiastical figures used letters as an important form of communication throughout the medieval era, and these documents provide crucial insights into an exceptionally broad array of social, economic, political, religious, and military events. However, the survival of letters, particularly during the pre-crusade period, is exceptionally variable. Although, for example, thousands of letters have survived as individual documents or in collections from the Carolingian period, the tenth century and early part of the eleventh century present a veritable desert in surviving examples of the epistolary art, particularly east of the Rhine. From the twelfth century onwards, the number of surviving letters increases dramatically, so that we can point to collections numbering in the many hundreds or even thousands for kings and princes during the later Middle Ages.

Letters are a valuable source of information about military matters, not only because of their practical content, but also as a clear expression of the views, hopes, and intentions of their authors. In addition, many letters provide glimpses of the correspondent, whose letters have not survived, by responding to specific points or questions that were raised in now-lost texts. It is true that many letters survive in collections, which had a practical or ideological purpose, so that the original intention of the author in a particular letter might be subsumed within a broader programme. However, in a great many cases, letters survive fortuitously as originals, or because they were copied into large works such as *gestae*, as previously mentioned. In these circumstances, letters permit the modern scholar to get into the mind of the author in much more personal and direct ways than is possible even in autobiographies, which are in effect memoirs that are written long after the event and illuminate an individual's reflections rather than his 'real-time' thinking. One additional benefit of letters is that they cast light on diplomacy and planning that often took place before military operations were undertaken.

Charters

Both governments and quasi-governmental institutions such as monasteries and bishoprics produced a wide range of documents throughout the medieval millennium. Up through the late twelfth century, the most commonly surviving types of documents are those denoted by scholars broadly as charters. The great majority of these texts, whether produced by governments, ecclesiastical institutions, or private individuals, relate to the transfer of property from one individual or institution to another. These texts provide a considerable body of information about a broad range of matters that can illuminate questions relating to military history, such as the identities of men receiving land to perform military service, the identities of individuals who were present at a particular location on a specific date, and an idea of the overall expendable wealth belonging to a particular ruler. In addition, such documents provide information regarding the building of fortifications, the destruction of property, and the funds raised for military projects, as well as the identities of particular individuals who were killed in war.

In contrast to either fundamentally historiographical or literary texts, these documents tend to be less subject to bias as they describe real-time actions that are validated by government officials or witnesses. Indeed, one aspect of charters that has received considerable attention from scholars recently is the tendency for rulers and lesser officials to have charters read out in public at court, so that the content of the documents could be vetted and validated by a large number of people. Partly as a result of the public nature of the ratification of charters, these documents often include a narrative section that sets out the background for the action that they are codifying. Consequently, these documents often provide time-conditioned historical information that has been vetted by witnesses, in addition to the information that pertains directly to the action being undertaken in the charter. In addition, some scholars have argued that the physical appearance of the document also was significant in that a splendid charter, written in gold ink on a dyed purple surface, lent additional authority to its content and is thought to impress the audience greatly.

However, because charters generally deal with the transfer of property, they often were forged, particularly by ecclesiastical institutions, in order to claim lands that they had lost, or to justify their possession of lands for which they lacked legitimate documentation. In some cases, these forgeries were based upon once existing texts that had been lost. In other cases, however, forgeries were simply inventions that had no basis in reality. Another difficulty that scholars face in using charters is that original documents often were recopied in a collection, called a cartulary, by monasteries. In such cases, much of the original information in the charters was stripped out, including witness lists and dating clauses. Fortunately for scholars interested in using charters for the study of history, very large numbers of these texts have been subject to detailed analysis by specialists in fields such as diplomatics, paleography, and codicology. As a consequence, many of the issues relating to the reliability of charters already have been resolved, particularly for the early and high Middle Ages.

Administrative documents

Following on late Roman practice, governments throughout the Latin West during the entirety of the medieval millennium made considerable use of the written word to carry out their administrative functions. However, due to a number of factors, the vast majority, comprising over 99 per cent of all administrative documents produced in the period before c.1100, have been lost. To put this into perspective, there are more extant royal administrative documents from England during the reign of Edward I (1272–1307) than there are total administrative documents from secular and ecclesiastical sources, including those of the papacy, combined for all of Europe in the period 500–1100. The survival of these later medieval English documents is due to the fortuitous fact that they were kept for storage in repositories that were not subject to destruction in medieval or early modern wars, and also escaped damage from bombing during the Second World War.

The comparative dearth of administrative documents, particularly in pre-crusade Europe, has led many scholars, who believe that the early Middle Ages experienced a 'dark age', to conclude that these types of texts never were produced, or had any role in the conduct of warfare. We disagree with this assessment on a number of grounds. First, even though they survive in only small numbers, extant administrative documents make clear to the attentive reader that they are a mere fragment of a much larger corpus of texts that was used to carry out administrative tasks. In many cases, these documents refer to other now-lost documents. In other cases, we have a small handful or just one exemplar of an entire class of documents, such as mobilization orders, receipts for supplies, or commands to undertake the maintenance of the physical infrastructure of roads, bridges, ports, and fortifications. In yet other cases, particularly for the early Middle Ages, we have compendia of model administrative documents, known as formularies. These documents were produced in royal chanceries, and in the writing offices of lesser rulers, to provide a guide to scribes for documents that were produced on a regular basis. The model documents in these formularies often have been stripped of specific information, such as the date on which they were issued and the identity of the recipients. However, as a group, they provide valuable information about the types of administrative documents produced by the governments of various rulers.

The information provided in historiographical sources and other types of documents regarding the conduct of war implies – and, on occasion, provides – direct information not only regarding the need for documents to carry out administrative functions, but also specific information that such efforts were executed. Finally, the increasing survival of administrative documents from the twelfth century onwards makes clear the need for governments

Figure 1.3 Supplies for Charlemagne's army
Source: © Biblioteca Nazionale Marciana, Venice, Italy/Bridgeman Images

to use the written word in order to organize large-scale military operations, and to construct fortifications. These later medieval documents provide information about every aspect of the conduct of war, from the selection and mobilization of fighting men to the acquisition and transportation of supplies to the production of arms and equipment. As a consequence, it stretches credulity to conclude that early medieval governments, such as those of the Carolingian kings and emperors, were able to carry out military operations on a scale similar to or even greater than those of the later Middle Ages without making similar use of the practical technology of storing information in writing.

Prescriptive texts

Letters, charters, and administrative documents all have in common that they purport to describe actual human activity. By contrast, there are a wide range of extant texts from the entire medieval period that describe how people ought to behave. These documents – which include royal and ecclesiastical law codes, ordinances issued by a wide variety of governments and institutions, including cities and towns, treaties, handbooks, and even individual edicts by a ruler – are often denoted by scholars as prescriptive texts. It is clear that such documents must be treated with some care when attempting to use them to answer questions about particular aspects of medieval warfare. As is the case with regard to historiographical sources, there is a range of scholarly views concerning how closely prescriptive texts touch on contemporary reality. Some historians, who are epistemologically pessimistic, conclude that law codes, and particularly those from early medieval Europe, should be understood merely as wish lists. Similarly, handbooks such as the late Roman author Vegetius' *Epitoma rei militaris*, are depicted as appealing only to the antiquarian interests of medieval monks rather than having real-world applications.[3] Other historians take what is perhaps an overly optimistic approach by assuming that if a ruler issued a law, or if a copy of a military handbook was possessed by a ruler, then it follows that this law was followed in all cases, or the handbook provided a 'blueprint' for the conduct of military operations.

In our view, it is appropriate to treat all types of prescriptive documents carefully, but also to evaluate each one on its own merits, and in conjunction with the wide range of other sources that shed light on matters relating to the conduct of war. For example, we agree with the concern raised by the early medieval historian Karl Brunner that: 'With official regulations such as the famous *Capitulare de villis* of Charlemagne the problem is to what extent these were descriptions of the ideal state, never, or at least never fully, implemented in reality'.[4] However, the matter cannot be left there. Specifically with respect to the set of commands issued by Charlemagne in *Capitulare de villis*, noted by Brunner, a wide range of surviving administrative documents make clear that the rules for estate management set out by the great Frankish king were enforced by his agents throughout his empire with such vigour that we have records of complaints about their actions.

Images

There is a wide range of images from the Middle Ages, such as the one on the cover of this book, that depict various aspects of medieval warfare. These images include illustrations in manuscripts, as well as full-scale paintings such as murals on church walls. In addition to these two-dimensional forms, military historians have available very large numbers of three-dimensional images such as the carved stone figures around the gateways of churches and on sarcophagi. On a smaller scale, military imagery and even entire battles are depicted on numerous artefacts such as portable altars and small chests. These latter include the famous Franks Casket, produced c.700, which depicts an Anglo-Saxon army formed up in an infantry phalanx as well as a *testudo* (a group of soldiers holding their shields over their heads), and the Courtrai Chest, which depicts the then contemporary Battle of Courtrai, fought in 1302.

When properly dated, images of weapons, armour, and even military formations can be quite helpful in augmenting information that is provided by textual and material sources (more on this in what follows). However, there are also considerable challenges in using images to help answer questions about medieval warfare. First, artists working with paint, wood, ivory, bone, metal, and stone did not necessarily have first-hand experience with the weapons, armour, or combat that they were attempting to depict. As a consequence, they often made basic errors in their compositions that have the potential to mislead unwary

---

3 For the conflicting perspectives on this issue, see the studies by Bernard S. Bachrach, and by Stephen Morillo and Richard Abels.

4 Karl Brunner, 'Continuity and Discontinuity of Roman Agricultural Knowledge in the Early Middle Ages' in *Agriculture in the Middle Ages: Technology, Practice, and Representation*, ed. Del Sweeney (Philadelphia, 1995), 21–40, here 23.

observers. For example, it is clear that the horse transports that are depicted in the Bayeux Tapestry are the result of the imagination of the artist, who had no knowledge of how war horses were transported or how they were off-loaded from ships.

Second, even if they did have first-hand experience with the objects or events that they sought to present, they did not necessarily have the skill to depict them accurately. For example, the knowledge of how to show perspective in painting did not develop until the later Middle Ages. Third, even in those cases when artists had both the experience and skill that was required to depict an object or event accurately, they often chose not to do so because the genre of their work required a different sort of presentation. Typical in this regard is the conservatism of artists who drew upon the models of older works for their compositions, even when the arms or armour they depicted were more predominant in an earlier age. For example, Carolingian and Byzantine manuscript illustrators tended to avoid depicting stirrups until the ninth century, even though this equestrian equipment had already been introduced in the West a century earlier.

In other cases, however, artists made a point of demonstrating up-to-date knowledge regarding military technology. Consequently, drawing conclusions about the accuracy of a particular artist in a doctrinaire manner on the basis of the general tendency toward conservatism in their approach also can lead modern scholars astray. For example, the bodyguards of the West Frankish ruler Charles the Bald (840–877) are depicted in manuscript illustrations produced in the late ninth century in a type of armour that appears very similar to the armour that is worn by the bodyguards of Roman emperors in images that were produced at earlier dates. The possibility exists that Charles dressed up his bodyguards in this type of armour specifically because of its Roman connections, which he, like we, discovered from examining late Roman images. In fact, he likely had access to actual pieces of surviving armour of this type, such as still survive today and can be seen in modern museums.

Material sources

In contrast to images and written descriptions, information developed by archaeologists has the potential to provide direct access to the material reality of warfare in medieval Europe. However, caution is also warranted with regard to material sources to avoid the mistake of assuming that artefacts are 'unbiased'. The danger inherent in this assumption was highlighted by the numismatist Phillip Grierson, who observed trenchantly: 'it is said that the spade cannot lie, but it owes this merit in part to the fact that it cannot speak'.[5] As Grierson's comment makes clear, it is the archaeologist, historian, or other specialist who interprets a material source, and decides what value that it has to answer questions about the past. Obviously, modern scholars, however well-trained and however well-meaning, often cannot keep their biases from creeping into their interpretations.

In fact, determining what kinds of questions to ask about material sources can have considerable impact on their utility for historical inquiry. This process is illuminated, for example, by the treatment by historians of the defensive works known as Offa's Dyke, which ran along the frontier between the Anglo-Saxon kingdom of Mercia and the Welsh kingdom of Powys, and the Danevirke, located between the southern frontier of Denmark and the Saxon region (more about this in Chapter 2). Both of these linear defences, which

---

5 Phillip Grierson, 'Commerce in the Dark Ages: A Critique of the Evidence' in *Transactions of the Royal Historical Society*, 5th ser., 9 (1958), 123–140, here 129.

were constructed during the eighth century, were dismissed by scholars in the nineteenth century and much of the twentieth century as examples of primitive technology that did not meet the high standards once set by the Roman Empire. By contrast, during the past three decades, more thorough excavations combined with a new analytic framework have transformed scholarly opinion regarding both the defensive systems of Offa's Dyke and the Danevirke, and the interpretation of the polities that constructed them. It is now understood that both defensive complexes provided highly effective protection against land-based raids across the frontier, and that these linear defences were combined with a network of fortifications and – in the case of Denmark – fleets. In addition, analyses of the labour inputs for both the Danevirke and Offa's Dyke illuminate the vast resources that were required to construct them, and the concomitant administrative sophistication of both Mercia and the Danish kingdom during the eighth century.

Of particular interest to specialists in military history has been the discovery of arms, armour, and other military equipment, such as stirrups and horseshoes, through excavations. From the late Roman period up through the early eighth century, the burial of weapons remained a common practice in the regions that once had been part of the Western Empire. Over the course of the eighth century, however, Christian burial practices were revised throughout much of the Latin West, as well as in Anglo-Saxon England, to discourage the placement of goods, including military equipment, in graves. By contrast, weapons burials remained quite common among the pagan Slavs and Scandinavians well into the tenth century, and in some places, into the eleventh. Graves provide considerable scope for the close dating of weapons because they often included other elements, such as pottery, wooden material, or even coins.

The gradual end of the practice of burying weapons and equipment has meant that fewer exemplars of equipment survive from the high Middle Ages than from the earlier period, despite both the greater numbers of weapons in circulation in the later period and also its closer proximity temporally to the present. Most of the weapons that survive within Latin Europe from the later eighth century onwards were accidental losses, often buried in the mud of river bottoms or in bogs, where the anaerobic environment protected the iron from corrosion. However, these latter finds are difficult to date closely because of the lack of stratigraphic context. In place of this analytical framework, it is necessary to use stylistic analogies regarding its decoration and also to compare its metallurgical characteristics with other swords.

Equally – if not more – important, for the understanding of medieval warfare is the excavation of fortifications, including defensive systems such as Offa's Dyke, and individual strongholds. However, until very recently, scholars have tended not to devote significant attention to the vast quantity of data developed by archaeologists with respect to fortifications, or to integrate these data into their understanding of the conduct of war, including both the economic and strategic implications of the construction of these strongholds. This has been the case for a number of reasons, despite the general recognition among specialists in medieval military history that warfare during the Middle Ages was dominated by sieges – that is, the capture and defence of fortifications. In particular, many modern historians have remained wedded to the use of historiographical works, and to a lesser extent, documentary texts, as their primary source materials.

Such a focus on narrative works, however, is highly problematic in the context of understanding the role played by fortifications in medieval warfare. This is true because the overwhelming majority of the fortifications constructed during the medieval millennium are not mentioned in any written source. For example, of the 250 fortifications that have been

Figure 1.4 Frankish spatha, eighth century
Source: © INTERFOTO/Alamy Stock Photo T4TH48

Figure 1.5 Above-ground remains of a fortification, Galava Roman Fort in Ambleside in the
        Lake District, UK
Source: © Roger Coulam/Alamy Stock Photo C3Y7YA

Figure 1.6 Excavated foundations of a fortification at Vindolanda Roman Fort in Northumberland, UK
Source: © Clearview/Alamy Stock Photo C6654C

identified by archaeologists as being constructed during the period c.700–c.1000 in the northern part of the *Bundesland* of Bavaria in modern Germany, just thirty are mentioned in the surviving written sources. Obviously relying on written sources alone would lead a historian to underestimate by a full 80 per cent the number of strongholds and the concomitant resources and organization that were required for their construction, supply, and defence. In addition, even when fortifications appear in written sources, it is usually not until at least fifty or a hundred years after they initially were built. For example, the stronghold of Rosstal in Bavaria, which is first mentioned in a written source c.960, already was a formidable stone fortress by the turn of the ninth century. Even in the later Middle Ages, when the vastly increased quantity of surviving administrative documents provides considerable insight into governmental efforts to construct fortresses, a great many of these strongholds are only known through the work of archaeologists.

History at the nexus of interdisciplinary scholarly investigation

All of the types of sources, both written and material, discussed in the previous sections have the potential to illuminate aspects of medieval warfare on the basis of the information that they provide about specific people, equipment, and infrastructure at a particular place and time. This information, however, can be contextualized even further by bringing to bear insights provided by a large number of disciplines that treat what the philosopher John Searle has described as 'brute fact'. Searle uses this term to denote realities that are unchanged whether or not they are ever considered by human beings at all. One typical example of brute fact offered by Searle is the atomic composition of a hydrogen atom, which had this composition long before there were any humans, and will have this atomic composition long after the last trace of mankind has disappeared from the universe.

Understanding that there are today, and were in the Middle Ages, unalterable physical realities provides historians with a basis for establishing a solid foundation on which to ask and answer questions about the conduct of medieval warfare. At the simplest level, the mass of 1 cubic metre of granite, oak, or water has not changed in any noteworthy manner over the past millennia, although there are different grades of stone and different species of oak. Arrows in medieval Europe fell from the sky at 32 feet per second squared, just as they do today. Similarly, the impact of a stone of a given weight and given velocity against a stone wall had the same force in the Middle Ages as it does today. The brute fact of the tensile strength of wood, bone, iron, and steel of various types and grades also means that it is possible for modern specialists in experimental archaeology and physics to calculate accurately the potential energy that was stored in the stave of a bow or crossbow, and the thrust of a stone-throwing engine. The buoyancy inherent in wood of various types, and the interplay of geometry and physics, likewise permits calculations for the carrying capacity of medieval vessels that have been unearthed through the work of archaeologists on both land and in the sea.

At a more complex level, the concept of brute fact can be broadened for use in historical inquiry by providing an understanding of the physical limits within which humans, animals, and even mechanical devices operate. Human physiology, for example, has remained largely unchanged for the past 75,000–100,000 years, as is well understood by specialists in physical anthropology. As a consequence, it is possible for the historian to develop models, based on the findings of physiologists, regarding the minimum number of calories that were required of a man of a given age, height, and weight undertaking a given type of labour over a given temporal span. These calculations are indispensable in understanding the logistics of medieval armies. In a similar vein, the physiology of domesticated animals such as horses, donkeys, mules, and oxen, although affected to a considerable degree by human intervention, is well understood by specialists in pre-modern animal science. As a consequence, it is also possible to develop models about the caloric and water requirements of these animals within a specific context of labour and time, and consequently what resources were required to support a specific number of these animals on campaign or during a siege.

The process that is applied to understanding human and animal physiological constraints with regard to caloric and water intake also can be applied to help us to understand physical limitations on their labour. For example, on average, stall-bred horses do not today and did not in the medieval period have the capacity to walk or run for more than five or six days without rest for two consecutive days. In fact, numerous tests of the stamina of stall-bred horses have made clear that most of these animals do not have the capacity to travel more than 30 miles in a given day before they begin to break down physically and become useless for further work. These physical limitations provide a means of testing the claims in written sources to determine whether the account provided by an author is possible within the constraints of animal physiology.

By contrast with horses, human beings have a demonstrated capacity, if provided with sufficient water, to undertake forced marches for periods extending for more than a week without suffering from debilitating physical breakdown. This capacity has been tested, for example, by numerous armies, as well as by experimental archaeologists over the course of the past two hundred years. Similar large-scale tests of human labour capacity under a variety of conditions have been made with regard to the digging of ditches, which obviously had considerable importance for the conduct of both modern and medieval warfare. Similar experimental and real-world data are available for activities such as cutting trees, laying bricks, quarrying stone, and myriad of other tasks that have relevance to the conduct of medieval warfare. These data, in turn, provide historians with a framework within which to evaluate the overall costs involved in activities such as constructing fortifications, building roads, or setting up field works, particularly in terms of labour.

Another important aspect of archaeology for military history is the study of skeletons. Such investigations provide important information about the general health and nutrition of a population. In a more specifically military context, skeletons can provide information about wounds that damaged bones, and the types of weapons that inflicted them. In addition, because human skeletons can repair themselves to a certain extent, some skeletal studies illuminate the survival of wounds suffered in battle.

Conclusion

Because history touches on all aspects of human activity in the past, it is often said that the discipline of history is the muddy lake into which flows the crystal clear streams of all of the other disciplines of human investigation. This reality is perhaps even more true of military history than most other fields of historical inquiry, because preparation for war, the conduct of war, and war's aftermath touched virtually every person and every facet of life from the late Roman Empire up through the end of the medieval period. Medieval military history has been transformed over the past century from a narrow focus on battle that relied almost exclusively on the reports found in a limited, often opportunistic selection of narrative texts, to broad-ranging explorations of dozens of facets of warfare that depend upon a vast range of sources. As medieval military historians have expanded the scope and range of their studies, so too have they developed increasingly sophisticated techniques for evaluating the ways in which both written and material sources can be deployed to come to an accurate understanding of the reality of warfare in the Middle Ages. In the following seven chapters, we will return repeatedly to the issue of historical epistemology, and consider how it is that the available sources can tell us about the past.

Bibliography

For an overview of the approaches to medieval military history over the past long century, see

Charles Oman, *The Art of War in the Middle Ages, 378–1515* (London, 1924);

John Beeler, *Warfare in Feudal Europe, 730–1200* (Ithaca, 1971);

Hans Delbrück, *History of the Art of War within the Framework of Political History III: The Middle Ages*, trans. Walter J. Renfroe, Jr. (London, 1982), originally published as *Geschichte der Kriegskunst in Rahmen der politischen Geschichte 3* (Berlin, 1907);

Philippe Contamine, *War in the Middle Ages*, trans. Michael Jones (Oxford, 1993), originally published as *La guerre au moyen âge* (Paris, 1980);

J. F. Verbruggen, *The Art of Warfare in Western Europe during the Middle Ages: From the Eighth Century to 1340*, trans. S. Willard and R. W. Southern, second English edition (Woodbridge, 1997), originally published as *De Krijgskunst in West-Europa in de Middeleeuwen IXe tot begin XIVe eeuw* (Brussels, 1954);

John France, *Western Warfare in the Age of the Crusades, 1000–1300* (Ithaca, New York, 1999);

Guy Halsall, *Warfare and Society in the Barbarian West* (London, 2003);

Helen J. Nicholson, *Medieval Warfare: Theory and Practice of War in Europe, 300–1500* (New York, 2004);

Clifford J. Rogers, *Soldiers' Lives through History* (Westport, 2007);

The collection of essays in *War and Warfare in Late Antiquity*, ed. Alexander Sarantis and Neil Christie, 2 vols (Leiden, 2013).

With respect to source criticism and the use of narrative works for the writing of medieval military history, see

John France, 'Anna Comnena, the Alexiad and the First Crusade' in *Reading Medieval Studies* 10 (1984), 20–38;

Matthew Bennett, 'Wace and Warfare' in *Anglo-Norman Studies 11* (1989), 37–57;

John France, 'The Use of the Anonymous *Gesta Francorum* in the Early Twelfth-Century Sources for the First Crusade' in *From Clermont to Jerusalem: The Crusades and Crusader Societies, 1095–1500*, ed. Alan V. Murray (Turnhout, 1998), 29–42;

Steven C. Fanning, 'Tacitus, Beowulf and the Comitatus' in *The Haskins Society Journal 9* (2001), 17–38;

Bachrach, Bernard S., 'Gregory of Tours as a Military Historian' in *The World of Gregory of Tours*, ed. Kathleen Mitchell and Ian Wood (Leiden, 2002), 351–363;

Bernard S. Bachrach, 'Dudo of St. Quentin as an Historian of Military Organization' in *The Haskins Society Journal 12* (2003), 165–185;

John France, 'War and Sanctity: Saints' Lives as Sources for Early Medieval Warfare' in *Journal of Medieval Military History 3* (2005), 14–22;

Bernard S. Bachrach, '"A Lying Legacy" Revisited: The Abels-Morillo Defense of Discontinuity' in *Journal of Medieval Military History 5* (2007), 153–193;

David S. Bachrach, 'Memory, Epistemology, and the Writing of Early Medieval Military History: The Example of Bishop Thietmar of Merseburg (1009–1018)' in *Viator 38* (2007), 63–90;

Rosamond McKitterick, *Charlemagne: The Formation of a European Identity* (Cambridge, 2008);

Justin C. Lake, 'Truth, Plausibility, and the Virtues of Narrative at the Millennium' in *Journal of Medieval History 35* (2009), 221–238;

Bernard S. Bachrach, 'Writing Latin History for a Lay Audience c. 1000: Dudo of Saint Quentin at the Norman Court' in *Haskins Society Journal 20* (2009);

Jay Rubenstein, 'William of Poitiers Talks about War' in *The Middle Ages in Texts and Texture: Reflections on Medieval Sources*, ed. Jason Glenn (Toronto, 2011), 129–140;

David S. Bachrach, 'Feudalism, Romanticism, and Source Criticism: Writing the Military History of Salian Germany' in *Journal of Medieval Military History 15* (2015), 1–25.

Also see Walter Goffart, *The Narrators of Barbarian History: Jordanes, Gregory of Tours, Bede, and Paul the Deacon* (Princeton, 1988), which is crucial for its methodological insights.

Regarding the use of images for understanding medieval warfare, see

Jennie Kiff, 'Images of War: Illustrations of Warfare in Early Eleventh-Century England' in *Anglo-Norman Studies 7* (1984), 177–194;

Bernard S. Bachrach, 'A Picture of Avar-Frankish Warfare from a Carolingian Psalter of the Early Ninth Century in Light of the *Strategicon*' in *Archivum Eurasiae Medii Aevi 4* (1984), 5–27, reprinted with the same pagination in Bernard S. Bachrach, *Armies and Politics in the Early Medieval West* (London, 1993);

Jonathan Alexander, 'Ideological Representation of Military Combat in Anglo-Norman Art' in *Anglo-Norman Studies 15* (1993), 1–24;

Pamela Porter, 'The Ways of War in Medieval Manuscript Illumination: Tracing and Assessing the Evidence' in *Armies, Chivalry and Warfare in Medieval Britain and France*, ed. Paul Watkins (Stamford, 1998), 100–114;

Graeme Cruickshank, 'The Battle of Dunnichen and the Aberlemno Battle-Scene' in *Alba: Celtic Scotland in the Middle Ages*, ed. Edward J. Cowan and R. Andrew McDonald (Tuckwell, 2000), 69–87;

Christopher T. Allmand, *The De Re Militari of Vegetius: The Reception, Transmission and Legacy of a Roman Text in the Middle Ages* (Cambridge, 2011);

Richard Abels, 'Cultural Representations of Warfare in the High Middle Ages: The Morgan Picture Bible' in *Crusading and Warfare in the Middle Ages: Realities and Representations: Essays in Honour of John France*, ed. Simon John and Nicholas Morton (Aldershot, 2014), 13–35.

With respect to the opportunities and challenges posed by using entertainment literature to discuss the conduct of medieval warfare, see

Jill Mann, 'Knightly Combat in Malory's *Morte d'Arthur*' in *New Pelican Guide to English Literature*, ed. Boris Ford (Harmondsworth, 1982), 331–339;

Ronald Murphy, 'From Germanic Warrior to Christian Knight: The *Heliand* Transformation' in *Arthurian Literature and Christianity: Notes from the Twentieth Century*, ed. Peter Meister (New York, 1999), 11–28;

Catherine Hanley, *War and Combat, 1150–1270: The Evidence from Old French Literature* (Rochester, 2003);

Françoise H. M. Le Saux, 'War and Knighthood in Christine de Pizan's *Livre des faits d'armes et de chevallerie*' in *Writing War: Medieval Literary Responses to Warfare*, ed. Corinne Saunders, Françoise le Saux, and Neil Thomas (Cambridge, 2004), 93–105;

Matthieu Chan Tsin, 'Medieval Romances and Military History: Marching Orders in Jean de Bueil's *Le Jouvencel introduit aux armes*' in *Journal of Medieval Military History 7* (2009), 127–134;

Francisco Garcia Fitz, 'War in the *Lay of the Cid*' in *Journal of Medieval Military History 10* (2012), 61–87;

David Wallace, 'Chaucer, Langland and the Hundred Years' War' in *The Medieval Python: The Purposive and Provocative Work of Terry Jones*, ed. R. F. Yeager and Toshiyuki Takamiya (New York, 2012), 195–205.

For an introduction to reading the natural and man-made topography to gain an understanding of military operations and decision making, see

Charles R. Bowlus, *The Battle of the Lechfeld and Its Aftermath, August 955: The End of the Age of Migrations in the Latin West* (Aldershot, 2006);

David S. Bachrach, 'Henry I of Germany's 929 Military Campaign in Archaeological Perspective' in *Early Medieval Europe 21* (2013), 307–337;

Bernard S. Bachrach and David S. Bachrach, 'Landscapes of Defense: At the Nexus of Archaeology and History in the Early Middle Ages' in *Francia 42*, (2015) 231–252;

The collection of essays in *Landscapes of Defence in Early Medieval Europe*, ed. John Baker, Stuart Brooke, and Andrew Reynolds (Turnhout, 2013).

Conflicting perspectives

The use of military manuals by medieval military commanders

Stephen Morillo and Richard Abels, 'Lying Legacy? A Preliminary Discussion of Images of Antiquity and Altered Reality in Medieval Military History' in *Journal of Medieval Military History 3* (2005), 1–13.

Bernard S. Bachrach, 'sA Lying Legacy Revisited: The Abels-Morillo Defense of Discontinuity' in *Journal of Medieval Military History 5* (2007), 153–193.

2 Military topography

Introduction

Throughout the medieval period, warfare – and particularly warfare directed at conquest and long-term territorial control – focused on the capture and defence of fortifications. In order to illuminate the physical realities that shaped the conduct of medieval warfare, this chapter traces out the military topography of fortifications, along with their associated infrastructure of roads, ports, and bridges, inherited by medieval Europe from the Roman Empire, and then discusses the multifaceted ways in which medieval polities sought to maintain, expand upon, renew, and ultimately transform this physical infrastructure to suit their needs. It was not, however, only physical structures that the medieval world inherited from Rome, but also legal and administrative practices, practical engineering handbooks, and even patterns of military thinking. Consequently, we draw attention to the ongoing influence of Roman law and institutions, as well as technological expertise on the organization by medieval governments of the human, material, and financial resources that were necessary to construct and sustain their own military topographies.

In geographical terms, this chapter considers not only those regions that once were part of the Western Roman Empire but also territories that were brought into the orbit of the Latin West through both conquest and cultural exchange. These include the Slavic lands east of the Elbe and Saale river systems, and the eastern shores of the Mediterranean during the crusades. One additional important focus in this chapter is on the ways in which historians can use insights from other disciplines, and particularly archaeology, to expand our understanding of military topographies beyond what can be gleaned from textual sources. In this context, the newly emerging concept of 'landscapes of defence' permits new insights into the administrative capacities, strategic thinking, and ultimately the material resources of governments throughout the Middle Ages.

The Roman inheritance of medieval Europe

From the late third through the early fifth century, the Roman imperial government undertook a vast programme of military construction throughout large parts of its western provinces. This program was even larger than the well-known and massive fortification efforts undertaken by imperial government based in Constantinople during the later fifth and throughout much of the sixth century under Emperors Anastasius I (491–518), Justin I (518–527), and Justinian I (527–565). Many hundreds of previously inadequately defended cities in the western provinces, as well as smaller population centres, were converted into fortresses and lesser strongholds, respectively. This pattern of governmentally

DOI: 10.4324/9781003032878-3

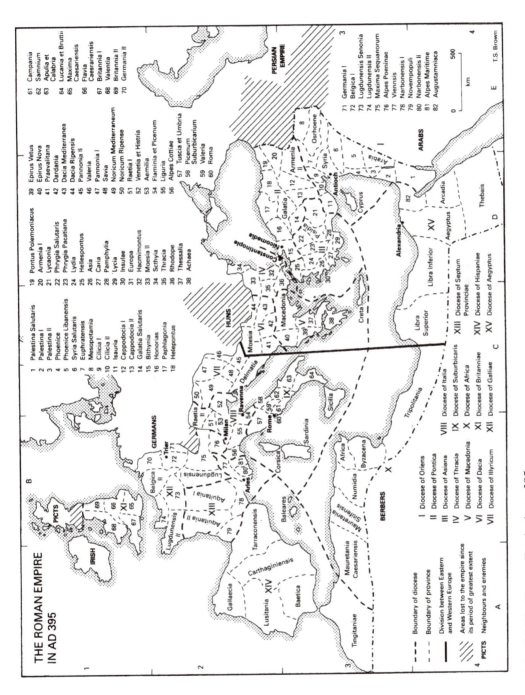

Map 2.1 The Roman Empire in AD 395

Source: *Atlas of Medieval Europe* © T.S. Brown

initiated military construction was mirrored, though on a much smaller scale, by the private efforts of the landed senatorial aristocracy to secure their estates with defensive works, and even full-scale fortifications. Rome itself benefitted from an extensive refurbishment of the city defences in 401–403, which not only included substantial efforts to make the walls higher, but also provided the city with new layers of protection by establishing firing platforms for deploying artillery.

Along the empire's Rhine and Danube frontiers, the imperial government devoted enormous resources to the refurbishment and expansion of the circuits of walls of most of the urban centres. During the later Roman Empire, these cities were the centres of political, cultural, and economic life of the provinces in which they were situated, as well as the largest concentrations of population. Following the official toleration of Christianity by Emperor Constantine the Great in 313, cities also became centres of Christian ecclesiastical administration, and would continue to play that important role during the early medieval period and beyond. These fortress cities, such as Regensburg, Augsburg, Worms, Mainz, Metz, Trier, Strasbourg, and Cologne, dominated the eastern frontier of Gaul.

As was true of Rome itself, these cities were equipped with new platforms along their walls and in their towers to accommodate artillery, including both spear-casters and various types of stone-throwing engines. These platforms have been identified through excavations and detailed investigations of the old Roman walls by archaeologists, who provide information that is not available from written sources. In addition, the stone-throwing engines, often denoted as *onageri*, literally wild asses, due to their great kick, are discussed in some detail by the contemporary author Publius Flavius Vegetius Renatus in his *Epitoma rei militaris* as being particularly useful when mounted on city walls to repel attackers.

In the provinces of Gaul, which ultimately became the most thoroughly fortified region in the western half of the empire, the construction of fortifications began in the early third century along the North Sea coast to deal with the localized problem of piracy. On the continent, a linear deployment of fortifications, as contrasted to a defence in depth (this concept is treated in detail at the end of this chapter), was established from Boulogne in the west to Brittenburg, located near the modern city of Leiden, in the east. On the northern shores of the English Channel in Britain, the Romans constructed fortifications all along the southeast coast as far east as Dover. As the threat of both entrepreneurial piracy and concerted 'barbarian' naval actions increased during the course of the third and early fourth centuries, the Romans extended this system of fortifications even further along both sides of the Channel. In Britain, the fortifications were developed westwards up to Bitterne, which is today located within the port city of Southampton. On the continent, the fortification system was expanded steadily westward and included Lillebonne, Rouen, Bayeux, Avranches, Aleth, St. Brieuc, Coz-Yaudet, Morlaix, and finally to Brest on the northwestern tip of the Breton peninsula. This North Sea/Channel defensive system, later known administratively as the 'Saxon Shore', also saw fortifications extended to the Atlantic coast of Gaul from Vannes to Nantes, Saintes, Bordeaux, and Bayonne, which was built in the early fifth century to control the mouth of the Ardour River. This system likely extended even farther into Rome's Spanish provinces, but further archaeological investigation is needed to confirm this pattern on the Iberian Peninsula.

The construction of a series of fortifications along almost the entirety of the empire's northern, and a substantial part of its western, seaboard represents an enormous expenditure of economic resources and human labour that was orchestrated by a bureaucracy of considerable size and complexity. This investment in physical defences was the consequence of conscious decisions by a series of emperors and their advisors to take an essentially defensive rather than an offensive approach to combatting large-scale piracy and raiding by various Germanic peoples from beyond the frontiers. This defensive strategy resulted from the fact that in the West, as contrasted to the piracy problem in the Mediterranean during the Republican period, the late imperial Roman government did not control territory close by the landward operation bases of the pirates and raiders. They lived a long distance to the east of the Roman frontier along the Rhine and the Danube, which made them, if not immune to, at least relatively safe from imperial reprisals.

Certainly, the Roman government had the capacity to project naval forces, for example, into the North Sea and the region of the lower Elbe or even the mouth of the Oder River, where many Saxons and other peoples dwelled. However, the Roman government had no intention of reconquering the region between the Rhine and the Elbe, which had been lost in AD 9 as a result of the victory by the Germanic tribes led by Arminius in the Teutoburg forest, in order to stop these sea-borne threats. Expeditions to deter piratical activities would have to be repeated on a regular basis because the 'barbarian' material infrastructure was primitive and could be rebuilt with relative ease after a Roman raid, regardless of how devastating it might be. Moreover, Roman naval expeditions that were intended to hunt down and destroy relatively small groups of opponents were very expensive as they required not only the construction and maintenance of fleets but also the deployment of troops, who could operate inland against enemy assets. Finally, the prospects for large quantities of booty, with the occasional acquisition of prisoners to be sold as slaves to pay for these efforts, were not great as the homelands of these pirates were developed only at a subsistence level.

In contrast to coastal defences, which most scholars agree were directed against pirates, there is a general agreement among Roman historians that the fortification of urban centres in the interior of Gaul during the third and fourth centuries was due to the fear of land-based barbarian invasions across the Rhine and the Danube. In our view, however, this explanation is not satisfactory. As the historian of the later Roman Empire Hugh Elton has demonstrated in several important studies, a thorough assessment of both the written sources and archaeological evidence for the later third and fourth centuries indicates that the small number of barbarian incursions that actually took place west of the Rhine ended in the rapid defeat, and often the annihilation of the raiding bands at the hands of imperial military units of the field army (*comitatenses*). These Roman field forces could be mobilized rapidly and enjoyed interior lines of communication for deployment, which allowed them to intercept bands of raiders with relative ease. Even if they eluded the defensive forces on the way into the empire, the barbarians were easily caught when they sought to return beyond the Rhine or Danube with whatever booty they had acquired. This was the case because the barbarian raiders had to move slowly due to the fact that the carts or wagons in which they were carrying their plunder were confined to the roads and their movements were predictable.

The explanation for the fortification of the interior of the Gallic provinces lies in another direction. The protection of the empire's northern coasts with fortifications and associated fleets proved quite effective in protecting populations and assets located in their immediate vicinity. However, the interior of Rome's Gallic provinces, and particularly the densely settled regions along the major river systems such as the Loire, Garonne, Seine, Somme, Meuse, Moselle, and the Rhine, remained highly vulnerable to river-borne raiders. The same danger would became manifest with regard to Viking raids in these same regions during the ninth century. In the late Roman period, it was not possible for the government to gain full control over the mouth of one or another river due to the fact that many were broad and made the area to be patrolled exceptionally manpower intensive. In addition, the bad weather conditions that predominated along river estuaries in the North Sea and English Channel often diminished visibility and hampered the use of signals, especially those based on fire, smoke, and mirrors. This problem was significantly worse during the later Roman period because of the general cooling of the climate and far worse weather conditions that prevailed then as contrasted with those of today.

As a consequence, the imperial government provided the interior of the Gallic provinces with a system of fortresses along major rivers that would serve the same function as those located along the Saxon Shore. For example, in the valley of the Seine and its tributaries, the imperial government ordered and oversaw the construction of walls around major urban centres including Évreux, Paris, Melun, Sens, Troyes, and as far south as Dijon. Senlis, Soissons, and Meaux, located along tributaries of the Seine, also received circuits of walls. In the west, a series of urban centres along the lower Loire were fortified, including Nantes, Angers, Tours, and Orléans. In the south, the ports of Arles and Marseilles were fortified as were cities along the Rhône valley, including Avignon, Orange, Valence, and Lyon at the confluence of the Rhône and Saône. Grenoble and Die, located on tributaries of the Rhône, also were fortified. Many of these fortress cities served the same function for the people of these regions centuries later when Viking raiders followed a strategy not very different from that of the pirates of the fifth century.

By contrast with cities that were in danger from water-borne raids because of their location along the river systems of Gaul, those cities which were not easily accessible along rivers that flowed to the coast were not fortified during this period. For example, in the province of Aquitania Prima, in the southwest of modern France, the cities of Albi, Cahors, Rodez, Javols, and St. Paulien did not receive circuits of walls during the late third or early fourth centuries. Similarly, in the province of Novempopulana, located in the angle between the Atlantic Ocean and the Pyrenees mountains, several urban centres in the interior were not fortified, including Lescar, Aire, Tarbes, Bazas, Oloron, and Eauze. By contrast, the cities in the same province that were located on the rivers Gers and Garonne, which reached the Bay of Biscay at Bordeaux, all were fortified.

The essentially defensive nature of the fortifications in the provinces of Gaul, as well as along the Rhine, can be compared with the development of new systems of fortifications in the Balkan provinces, as well as on the eastern frontiers in the fifth and sixth centuries. As Alexander Sarantis has shown in several recent publications, the generally pessimistic model of the decline of Roman power in the Balkans is at odds with recent archaeological work that demonstrates the deployment of enormous material resources there by the imperial government, beginning under Anastasius I and continuing through the reign of Justinian I. These included several layers of defences beginning along the lower Danube frontier. These frontier fortifications were complemented by fortifications to the south of the frontier in Illyricum, which protected the fertile plains of Thrace and Macedonia. East of the gorge on the Danube known as the Iron Gates, the imperial government established fortifications along the rivers and major roads in the provinces of Dacia Ripensis, Lower Moesia, and Scythia Minor. The Black Sea ports such as Odesus, Istria, and Tomis also had major fortifications. These numerous fortified cities, lesser fortifications, and fortified villages, as well as hill-top refuges, provided an opportunity for defence in depth (discussed in greater detail in what follows) for the populations of the Balkans against Slavic and Hunnic raiders. In addition, however, during Justinian's reign, the frontier fortifications served as important bases of operation for campaigns beyond the frontiers of the empire.

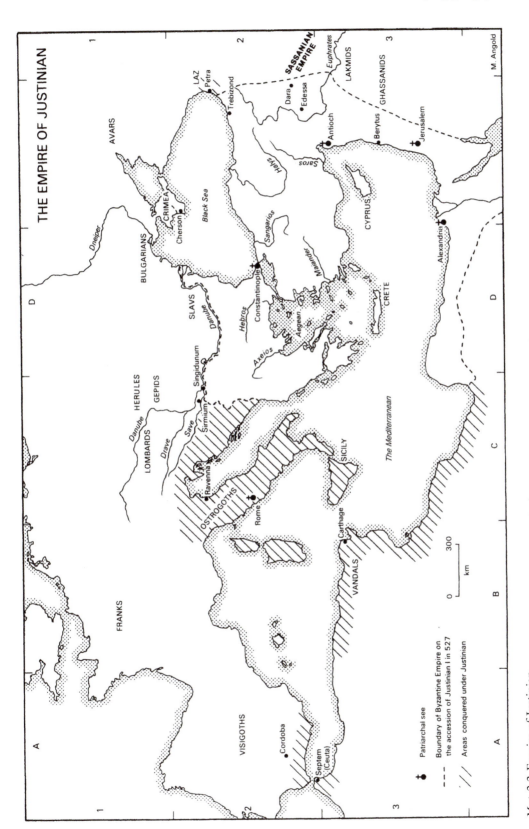

Map 2.2 Empire of Justinian

Source: *Atlas of Medieval Europe* © M. Angold

Coterminous with the development of the system of defences in the Balkans, Emperor Anastasius also undertook a massive programme of fortress building along the frontier with the Sassanian Empire, with its heartland in modern Iran and Iraq. These Roman fortifications extended from the Black Sea in the north to the Arabian desert in the south. The most powerful of these fortresses was the one constructed at Dara, located just 5 kilometres from the Persian frontier. This fortification was such a clear threat that the Persians lodged a formal diplomatic complaint with the Romans demanding that its walls be torn down. The system of fortifications on the eastern frontier was continued by Justin I and Justinian I. The latter used the forward bases that had been established to provide permanent quarters for the army to undertake a major war of conquest against the Persians in 528. All of these construction projects illuminate not only the wealth but also the long-term strategy of the empire.

Transportation infrastructure

Over the course of more than seven centuries of continuous military and military-related activity, the Roman Republic, Principate, and Empire constructed tens of thousands of miles of first-class military highways that connected the farthest reaches of the *imperium Romanum* to the city of Rome itself. These stone-paved roads, which were equipped with efficient drainage systems, permitted the movement of men, goods, and information in all seasons of the year. Every urban centre (*urbs*) in the empire was connected to this system of military highways, and even the Alpine routes were cleared of snow when necessary. Among the especially impressive elements of these roads are the thousands of bridges, constructed in both wood and stone, which spanned the vast numbers of river systems in the empire. In addition, ferry landings were established and thousands of fords were paved to facilitate their use. Many tens of thousands of miles of additional secondary and tertiary roads connected the urban centres in each district (*civitas*) to their rural hinterlands, which along with extensive river transportation resources, permitted the efficient flow of goods into the cities to feed the large urban populations.

The original construction of highways for military purposes, as well as the draining of swamps and the construction of bridges, was often carried out by the Roman government directly through the use of the army, which was well supplied with engineers as well as other technical specialists. However, a substantial body of legal evidence makes clear that the responsibility for maintaining these roads, once they had been constructed, lay with the municipal governments through whose districts (*civitates*) the highways ran. In addition, municipal governments were entirely responsible for the construction and maintenance of secondary and lesser road systems, which are labelled in legal texts as *viae vicinales*.

During the Republican period, the Roman government began placing 'mile stones' along all public roads. This practice continued through the end of imperial rule in the West during the fifth century. The word mile is a derivation of the term *milia passuum*, literally meaning 1,000 paces. This Roman mile was the equivalent of 4,841 feet or 1,480 metres, slightly shorter than the modern mile of 5,280 feet used in the United States. The stone columns that were used as milestones usually were just over 2 metres in height, one-third of which was buried below ground to guarantee their stability both in terms of erosion and attempted theft. As cut stone, these mile markers were potentially quite valuable to unscrupulous builders. Each milestone included an inscription noting the number of miles to the nearest city. At each city where a road began, there was an inscribed stone column that indicated the distance in miles to the other cities connected directly by road to this starting point.

The top third of the mile markers along the highways included an inscription indicating the distance to the forum in the city of Rome, and this helped to enforce the idea, which had considerable propaganda value that is still understood today, that 'all roads lead to Rome'.

The tens of thousands of milestones made a significant and practical impression on Roman travellers, and Roman writers frequently referred to them in their texts, often noting exactly where an event took place by reference to the nearest milestone. The widely available and detailed knowledge regarding distances between the cities in the Roman Empire, made possible in large part by the milestones, permitted travellers of all types to plan their journeys with considerable precision. To this end, Roman officials, army commanders, merchants, and even tourists were able to obtain documents known as *itineraria*, which provided a list of cities and towns along a particular highway, the distances between them, the available amenities such as inns, and the average travel time over specific distances. Much more complex illustrated maps were sometimes developed as well. Perhaps the most famous example of an illustrated map of this type is the so-called Peutinger Table, which includes more than 550 cities and more than 3,500 other locations throughout the Roman Empire. This map was long believed by scholars to have been produced in the fifth century, utilizing a large number of *itineraria* for its composition. However, the most recent scholarship indicates that the Peutinger Table likely was produced at the Carolingian court during the reign of Charlemagne in the late eighth or early ninth century, and was based on large numbers of Roman-era *itineraria* that are known to have survived into the Carolingian period, either in original or early medieval copies. The Peutinger Table itself now survives only in a thirteenth-century copy.

Although the primary road system was developed and continued to be used for the movement of armies, other types of travellers also made use of the *viae publicae*, which required

Figure 2.1 A Roman milestone from 83 CE
Source: © PhotoStock-Israel/Alamy Stock Photo A2WANF

government documents to access. Prominent among these were officials on government business, who required resting places in between urban centres. To facilitate travel by these officials, the government established a system of way stations, denoted as *mansiones*, which generally were located at intervals of about 30 kilometres, although distances between these way stations were often much shorter in areas with difficult terrain such as the Alpine passes. Thirty kilometres is about the distance that a horse can be ridden day after day for six days and recover quickly without breaking down. Although horses were used in relays to carry government orders, these animals often had to be ready for the next exchange on the following day.

In many regions of the post-Roman West, these *mansiones* continued to operate under the auspices of royal governments to maintain the *tractoria*, which was the early medieval heir of the Roman mail service (*cursus publicus*). For example, charters issued by various Merovingian kings during the sixth and seventh centuries, by Carolingian rulers in the eighth and ninth centuries, and by German kings such as Otto I (936–973) in the tenth century, indicate that the public system of way stations was still functioning centuries after the collapse of imperial rule in the West. In both the Roman and early medieval periods, a relay of messengers using this system could cover approximately 300 kilometres in a 24-hour period if the way stations were properly manned, provided with sufficient number of horses, and if weather conditions were good.

The vast network of roads in the empire was complemented by an equally intensive use of water routes as each city located along a river had well-developed docks and equipment, including the ancestor of the modern crane, for loading and unloading cargo ships. Just as was true until the steam age, water transport for the movement of goods was far less expensive than transport by land. This was due, in part, to the fact that river travel often could be maintained on a 24-hour basis, particularly during the summer, while horse-drawn carts and wagons required stops during the day for eating, drinking, and bedding down for the night. Moreover, horses could only work a six-day week and required a full day of rest on the seventh to be kept in sound condition. In addition, of course, riverboats could carry loads that were several times larger than the loads that wagons, carts, or pack animals could haul.

Throughout the Roman period, it was less expensive to transport a load of olive oil or wine across the entire Mediterranean Sea than it was to move this same cargo just 50 miles inland by pack animal or cart, even while making use of high-quality public highways. Transportation by riverboat or barge similarly provided a significant – albeit somewhat smaller – saving over transportation on land because river craft were generally quite a lot smaller than ships that operated on blue water. As a consequence of the considerable economic value of water-borne transportation, the Roman government both directly, and through mandates to municipalities, undertook enormous efforts to ensure the viability of both river- and sea-ports, and the navigability of rivers. In addition, the Romans devoted considerable resources to expanding water routes through the construction of canals, such as the Fossa Drusiana that connected the Roman army base at Fectio (modern Vechten in the Netherlands) through the Vecht River to the Ijsselmeer.

Perhaps the most important aspect of maintaining the viability of both ports and rivers was keeping them from becoming blocked with silt. Many sea-going harbours were located at the mouths of rivers that carried enormous volumes of earth to the sea. To combat this process, municipal authorities were required to undertake sustained dredging operations, which often were combined with elaborate systems of pilings to redirect silt-laden water. Perhaps the most famous and long-standing example of this type of ongoing dredging operation took place at Venice, where the modern city sits atop a foundation of wood and stone dating back more than 1,500 years. Rivers also required constant maintenance to preserve shipping channels. The Rhine, which has demonstrated a considerable propensity to switch its channels over the past 2,000 years, bears considerable evidence of Roman efforts to remove sandbars, straighten channels, and dredge silted up port facilities.

The Vecht canal, mentioned previously, was constructed by the Roman general Drusus in 12 BC to exploit the shores of Frisia along the Ijselmeer. The canal allowed the Romans to move ships along the Vecht River and canal rather than along the longer and more hazardous route from the mouth of the Rhine into the North Sea to the valleys of the Ems, Weser, and Elbe rivers. The canal stretched some 30 kilometres from the old course of the Rhine River to the Ijselmeer, with water channelled into the canal from the Waal River to keep an open water way. This canal also was used to move troops from the Roman military base at Fectio through the Ijselmeer to the mouth of the Elbe. From there, the riverboats were able to travel as far south as the area of modern Prague on the Bohemian plateau. Charlemagne used this same route, which was discussed by various Roman writers whose works were copied in the eighth and early ninth centuries, for military operations against various Slavic polities located along the lower and middle courses of the Elbe River. Similarly, King Henry I of Germany (919–936) followed this same course in a campaign during the winter of 928–929, that ended in the surrender of the city of Prague. This campaign is discussed in detail in Chapter 8. The Vecht canal was kept in working order throughout the early Middle Ages. It was used by, among others, the ill-fated missionary Boniface during his final preaching mission to the Frisians in 754 when he was martyred for this faith. His remains were returned by boat along the Vecht canal to the former Roman fortress city of Utrecht, from where his body then was transported to the monastery of Fulda for burial.

Roman military infrastructure in medieval contexts

The vast investment of human and material resources by the Roman central and municipal governments over a period of nearly 800 years, as well as the institutional and legal systems that were developed to maintain this military infrastructure, had an enduring impact on both the imagination and the practical realities of medieval Europe. Medieval writers routinely mentioned the majesty of imperial Rome, which traditionally was described as the Eternal City, as represented by its magnificent roads and walls, aqueducts, bath complexes, and even the vast numbers of governmental buildings that filled the centres of fortress cities. In fact, it became the norm for writers and especially poets during the early Middle Ages to glorify the great Roman cities that continued to flourish in their home territories. Bishop Gregory of Tours, for example, who wrote in the early 590s, described the erstwhile Roman fortress city of Dijon as being girded by a great stone wall that rose to a height of 30 Roman feet. He emphasized the massive size of the stone blocks from which the wall was constructed in the bottom 20 feet, and observed that the upper 10 feet were comprised of smaller, uniformly cut stone blocks. He went on to describe the city's thirty-five mural towers, and the impressive moat that was filled with water that had been redirected from neighbouring rivers. These walls can still be seen today and demonstrate the accuracy of Gregory's description, which was provided for the purposes of local colour, a phenomenon discussed in Chapter 1.

Alcuin (died 804), who gained great fame as one of Charlemagne's most important advisors, dedicated a poem to the glory of his home of York in Britain, which also had been a Roman fortress city. Alcuin stressed the high walls and lofty towers of the city, which he emphasized had first been constructed by the Romans. He described these walls as giving

York great security, and the city as a whole as an 'ornament' of the empire. He also described York as a 'dreaded defence' against its enemies and as a haven for ocean-going ships, which used the port facilities first constructed by the Romans. Alcuin's contemporary, the anonymous poet of Verona, similarly wrote about the Roman glories of his home city. He called attention to the status of Verona as a great and renowned fortress city, with strong stone walls that were studded with forty-eight towers.

The early eleventh-century Bishop Thietmar of Merseburg, whose *Chronicon* is one of the most important histories of the German kingdom in this period, similarly sought to emphasize the Roman origins of his city. What was particularly striking is that Thietmar sought to do so despite the lack of any such Roman connection. Thietmar claimed, for example, that it was Julius Caesar who first had given Merseburg its circuit of stone walls. Caesar, of course, never ventured as far east as the Saale River basin, although a number of Roman generals did so over the course the century following Caesar's death in 44 BC. During the reign of Augustus (died AD 14), the Elbe River, even farther east than the Saale, served as the frontier of the empire. Rather than a Roman origin, the walls of Merseburg are likely to be dated to the reign of Charlemagne in the late eighth or early ninth century when Thietmar's see was part of the Sorbian March, which will be discussed later in this chapter. Thietmar also claimed that the ruin of a fortress located near the early eleventh-century fortification of Lebusa, on the Elbe River, was a Roman-era structure. The ruined fortress was so massive, according to Thietmar, that no one other than the Romans could have constructed it. In fact, this fortress was a Bronze Age Celtic site, but there was no way for Thietmar to know this.

Physical continuity of Roman military infrastructure in medieval Europe

The efforts of early medieval writers such as Gregory of Tours, Alcuin, and Thietmar to connect the material reality of their own times to a Roman past, whether real or imagined, represents a very realistic understanding of the role that the Roman military infrastructure, discussed in the previous section, played in the conduct of war throughout the medieval millennium. Medieval writers, in general, were well aware that warfare was dominated by sieges. This was particularly true with regard to military operations that were concerned with either the defence or the conquest of territory. Efforts to maintain control over territory that had been conquered rested with the control of both large and small fortifications that were sited to play a key role in military affairs, whether in the realm of long-term strategy, campaign strategy, or campaign tactics.

Concomitantly, rulers in medieval Europe devoted enormous resources to the development of systems of fortifications to defend their lands against would-be conquerors. In light of the great expense that was involved in the construction of new fortifications, especially large strongholds built of stone, medieval rulers worked diligently to maximize their use of the enormous infrastructure of fortress cities and lesser strongholds, which originally had been constructed during the later Roman Empire, or even earlier, by Rome's Celtic predecessors. In many cases, the decision to reuse older Roman sites was based not only on an effort to economize on costs, but also on a realization that the Romans had been very adroit in siting their fortifications with respect to the natural topography and landscape, including rivers and mountain passes.

This process of reuse, often with expansion on the original Roman core resulting from population growth, can be seen throughout those regions that had been part of the Western

Empire, and continued in a significant manner throughout the entirety of the medieval period. In many cases, Roman fortress cities remained important administrative, political, ecclesiastical, and economic centres, and consequently were the focus of campaigns directed towards territorial expansion. In fact, it is exceptionally difficult to find so-called new cities that were not based on Roman foundations in various parts of the Roman Empire, even into modern times.

More subtly, the original Roman road system, which tied together the hundreds of urban centres in the Western Empire, conditioned to a major extent the movement of both the large armies that were required to undertake significant siege operations, and the movement of supplies that were needed to sustain troops involved in major military operations, especially sieges, that lasted for a significant period of time. Similarly, the systems of river- and sea-ports that were developed by the Romans, including, in some cases, long traditions of dredging operations, as identified for example at the port of Marseilles in southern Gaul, continued to provide important means of moving both men and supplies on campaign.

Rome's successor states in Late Antiquity

Some scholars, who rely heavily on the apocalyptic warnings of Christian polemicists such as St. Jerome (died 420), have argued that the cities in the western provinces of the empire were transformed into 'ghost towns' during the course of the fifth century as putative barbarian hordes supposedly sacked these urban centres and turned them into literal funeral pyres. Jerome asserted, for example, that scores of cities were burned to the ground and their populations massacred during the barbarian invasion of Gaul in AD 406. By contrast, historians who understand that these apocalyptic rants cannot be treated as transparent commentaries on current events prefer the hard evidence of documents, such as the *Notitia dignitatum* (which is discussed in greater detail in Chapter 3) that indicate that in excess of 100,000 Roman soldiers were serving in Gaul in 406 to oppose barbarian incursions, and historical narratives such as that of the Roman general Ammianus Marcellinus, writing a few years earlier, who makes clear that the barbarians were utterly inept in siege warfare.[1]

Archaeologists and historians who draw on information developed through excavations of late Roman and early medieval cities understand that there was no such collapse of urban life during Late Antiquity in the former provinces of Gaul, Italy, and Spain. There is no significant corpus of archaeological evidence, such as unambiguous layers of black earth, as evidence for widespread destruction through burning in any city in the late Roman west, much less burning by barbarians. For example, the claims by the priest Salvian, who wrote in the first half of the fifth century that the city of Trier had been 'destroyed' on at least three occasions during the period between c.410 and c.425 find no archaeological support. This lack of supporting evidence compounds Salvian's own self-contradictory reports about Trier and other matters, as well. On the positive side of the ledger, excavations in cities such as Cologne, Metz, Paris, and Marseilles demonstrate not only continued habitation, but even robust building efforts during the fifth century and beyond. In this context, the observations by Caesarius of Arles (died 542) that his city was bursting at the seams, and that new settlements had to be established beyond the walls, provide a written coda to the findings of archaeologists.

---

1 A useful comparison can be made here, for example, between the approaches of Guy Halsall, on the one hand, and Bernard S. Bachrach and Hugh Elton on the other. A selection of whose works are included in the bibliography under the 'Conflicting perspectives' heading.

The continued vitality and, indeed, centrality of cities in economic, legal, religious, and political affairs is also well attested in a wide range of written sources, including self-consciously historical works, as well as saints' lives (sacred biographies of holy men and women), legal texts, and letters. It is in this context that the rulers of the kingdoms that developed in Rome's western provinces chose to use cities as their centres of local government. This is also an important reason why cities were the primary objective of military campaigns directed towards territorial conquest. From the ecclesiastical perspective, the construction of scores of cathedrals and hundreds of urban churches, evidenced both in the written and archaeological sources, makes clear that the newly tolerated Christian population was both numerous and wealthy. The transfer of the moveable and landed resources of pagan temples to Christian churches at the local level by a series of emperors during the fourth century reinforced the trend of using the Church to help maintain important elements of public life. In many cities, bishops took a leading role in public affairs, including legal and military matters, and some bishops recruited from aristocratic families also came to govern cities directly.

In the Frankish kingdom that developed under the rule of the Merovingian dynasty throughout most of the Roman provinces of Gaul, the two provinces of Belgica, and the provinces of Germania, warfare was informed by a type of 'mercantilist' mentality. The focus of the first Merovingian king, Clovis (died 511), and most of his successors, was to gain control over one or more *civitates*, which remained the fundamental unit of political, military, economic, and religious organization following the end of Roman imperial rule in Gaul. Because the intent of Merovingian kings was to gain economic, and hence both political and military advantage, from the capture of fortress cities (*urbes*), they worked diligently to minimize the damage that they inflicted during their campaigns.

Gregory of Tours presents the informed thinking on this issue with a speech that he sets in the mouth of the Gallo-Roman magnate Aridius, who held high office in the Burgundian kingdom during the late fifth century. While the Frankish king Clovis was besieging the fortress city of Avignon, Aridius, as reported by Bishop Gregory, says:

> My king, if your highness, in all of your glory, would be willing to hear my suggestion, humbly given, even though you have little need for such counsel, I will give you my advice with complete honesty. Moreover, my counsel will be useful to you throughout the lands that you intend to traverse. Why do you keep your forces in the field when your enemy is ensconced in such a formidable fortress. You devastate the fields, you consume the produce of the meadows, you tear down the vines, and cut down the olive trees. You destroy all of the produce of the region. However, even so, you do not defeat your enemy. Instead of acting in this manner, send a messenger to him, and demand a yearly tribute in return for not devastating this region. You will then be the lord of this region and you will always receive your tribute.[2]

This advice supposedly given by Aridius encapsulates rather clearly the differences between supposedly 'barbarian' warfare of destruction and the teachings of ancient military science. The former is thought by some scholars to have seen an emphasis on taking booty, spreading terror, and wreaking destruction on both the human and material resources of the enemy. By comparison, the goals of late imperial strategy required the preservation of both

---

2 Gregory of Tours, *History of the Franks*, book 2, ch.2.

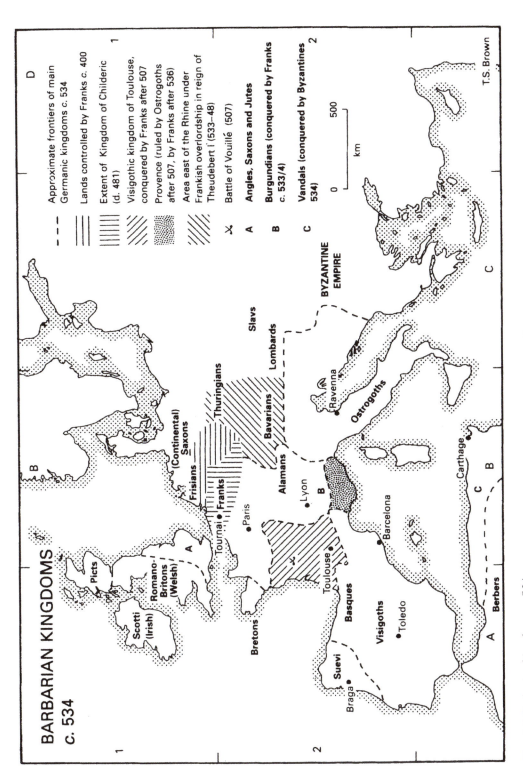

Map 2.3 Barbarian kingdoms, c.534
Source: *Atlas of Medieval Europe* © T.S. Brown

human and material resources, whenever possible, in order to obtain tribute or taxes from one's adversaries on a regular basis. Clovis made clear through his actions that he accepted this latter mode of warfare. When he invaded Aquitaine in 507, for example, Clovis issued orders to his men that his troops should not steal or wreck anything, and following Roman law were limited to taking only grass and water without offering payment to the inhabitants of the lands through which they were marching. When some of Clovis' soldiers violated this order, he had them executed.

In a manner very similar to their contemporaries in the provinces of Gaul and Germany, the Visigothic kings in what had been the Roman provinces of Hispania governed their realm from the fortress cities that they inherited from their imperial predecessors, including the Visigothic capital at Toledo, which was also the chief episcopal see of the Visigothic kingdom. These fortress cities, therefore, were the initial focus of the Muslim armies that crossed the Strait of Gibraltar in 711 under the command of Tariq ibn Ziyad. Both Christian and Muslim accounts of the rapid and successful campaign by Tariq to overthrow Visigothic rule and install largely Berber garrisons in the cities of Spain point to the pivotal military role played by Jewish communities living in these fortified urban centres.

For more than a century, the Visigothic kings had followed an inconsistent policy towards the Jews. As kings and would-be kings fought to control the royal throne, those who were supported by the Jews favoured them, and those who were opposed by the Jews persecuted them, including initiating efforts to confiscate their property, and convert them to Christianity by force. This anti-Jewish policy was in force at the time of the Muslim conquest in 711. As a result, the Jews, who were armed residents of the various fortress cities, as they also were in key cities east of the Pyrenees such as Arles and Narbonne, sided with the invaders. The Jews are depicted in the Arabic language sources as useful to the Muslim conquest and were regarded by later Christian writers, who also were opposed to the Jews in Spain, as the key element in making possible the Muslim conquest by giving them control over the fortress cities that served as the bases to establish control over almost the entire Visigothic kingdom.

In the period after the Muslim conquest, the only part of the Iberian Peninsula that remained under Christian rule was in the northwest in a region that came to be known as Asturias. Here, a Visigothic nobleman named Pelagius (685–737) established a new dynasty, and defeated repeated Muslim attempts to conquer the last vestiges of Christian rule with a major victory at the Battle of Covadonga in 719. Pelagius' successors ruled first as the kings of Asturias during the eighth and ninth centuries, and subsequently of León in the tenth century, as they moved south to reconquer parts of the Iberian Peninsula. The Christians defended their growing realm by utilizing a network of Roman-era fortified towns and lesser sites, which also had been used by the Visigoths. These fortifications provided the small Christian opposition to the Muslims with the opportunity to establish a system of defence in depth against Muslim raids, and bases for launching offensive operations against Islamic held areas. As might be expected, the pattern of continuity regarding fortress cities and lesser fortifications was just as strong within Italy as it was in the erstwhile provinces of the western half of the Empire. When Theodoric the Ostrogoth, who held office as *magister millitum* in the eastern Empire and was named consul in 484 by Emperor Zeno (474–491), seized control in Italy from another erstwhile Roman general, Odovacer, in 493, he placed garrisons of his troops in fortified cities to maintain his rule (493–526). During Justinian I's efforts to reconquer Italy in the so-called Gothic War (535–554), the main focus of both the Roman and Gothic armies was on the defence and capture of fortress cities and lesser fortifications. Similarly, when the Lombards invaded Italy in 568, they too based their rule on urban centres, each of which was governed by a Lombard duke.

The Carolingian world

The generally peaceful conditions within the *Regnum Francorum* from the mid-eighth to the third decade of the ninth century meant that the military infrastructure inherited from Rome was used largely for transporting armies to the frontiers. In the south and the west, where the Roman transportation infrastructure endured, military operations in both Italy and on the Iberian Peninsula were focused on the capture of Roman fortress cities. The Carolingian mayor of the palace and later King Pippin III/I (died 768), the father of Charlemagne, besieged and captured the Lombard capital at Pavia twice, in 755 and 756. He also undertook a successful siege of the fortress city of Bourges in 763. In 773–774, Charlemagne undertook sieges of numerous cities of Roman origin in the Lombard kingdom, including Pavia, the Lombard capital, which he captured in June 774. Charlemagne subsequently incorporated the entire Lombard kingdom into his empire. Charlemagne's military successes in the period 773–776 obviated the need for much further siege warfare in northern and central Italy for several decades to come.

In the southwest of the *Regnum Francorum*, military conflict between Muslims and Franks along the frontier between former Roman provinces of Spain and Gaul also was shaped by Roman military topography (as will be discussed in greater detail in Chapter 8). After the conquest of almost the entire Visigothic kingdom between 711 and 718 by Tariq ibn Ziyad and his military commander Musa ibn Nusayr, the new Muslim rulers of Hispania turned their attention to the Christian-ruled lands on the north side of the Pyrenees. In 721, Al-Samh ibn Malik al-Khawlani, the recently appointed governor of Spain, which was now a province of the Umayyad Caliphate, crossed the Pyrenees and captured the fortress city of Narbonne. This siege of the old Roman capital of the province of Gallia Narbonensis likely was aided by an Arab fleet that blockaded the city and prevented supplies and reinforcements from being brought in by water. Al-Samh also lay siege to a series of other former Roman cities in the region known as Septimania, including Béziers, Agde, Lodève, Montpellier, and Nîmes. However, when Al-Samh sought to capture Toulouse, which was the capital of Duke Odo of Aquitaine, he was defeated in battle and killed.

Eleven years later, in 732, Al-Samh's former lieutenant, Abd el-Rahman al Ghafiqi, undertook another major invasion across the Pyrenees, this time leading his army towards yet another fortress city of Roman origin, namely Poitiers, with the aim of deploying even farther north with a focus on the fortress city of Tours, where the famed shrine of St. Martin was located. Duke Odo, who was unable to defeat or deter Abd el-Rahman's very large army with his own more limited resources, sought support from the Frankish mayor of the palace, Charles Martel, the grandfather of Charlemagne. In response to Duke Odo's plea for aid, Charles Martel mobilized a large army, marched south and manoeuvred his forces to block the Roman road from Poitiers to Tours in order to prevent any further Muslim advance. The Carolingian mayor of the palace established his phalanx of foot soldiers in such a manner that Abd el-Rahman either had to drive the Frankish forces from the field or withdraw. The Muslim commander chose battle, and was defeated decisively about 10 kilometres north of Poitiers. This contest is therefore sometimes denoted as the Battle of Poitiers but also the Battle of Tours, which was the most important city in the region. In the ensuing rout of the Muslim army, Abd al-Rahman himself was killed.

The border regions between the Carolingian and Muslim spheres of influence on both sides of the Pyrenean mountain range remained hotly contested for the remainder of the eighth century. Following Charlemagne's failed invasion of 778 (considered in detail in Chapter 8), he began a process of reinforcing the frontier. No later than 780, Charlemagne began to establish Spanish Christians, who had escaped Muslim rule, as military colonists along the frontier (a topic discussed in Chapter 3). By c.801, Charlemagne undertook a more aggressive strategy aimed at moving the frontier well into Muslim-held territory and thereby making it very difficult for the Muslims to launch raids across the Pyrenees into the region that is now southwestern France. Charlemagne ordered his son, Louis the Pious, whom he had established as king in Aquitaine, to undertake a series of campaigns that resulted in the creation of a new frontier region, known as a march, on the formerly Muslim-held side of the Pyrenees. The first phase of this multi-year series of campaigns was directed towards the capture of the erstwhile Roman fortress city of Barcelona.

Barcelona, the early ninth-century political and commercial hub on the western coast of the Mediterranean, had received as a massive circuit wall, studded with approximately eighty towers, during the third century. Louis the Pious required an almost year-long siege operation, in which three armies and a fleet were mobilized, to capture this prize. Over the subsequent decade, Carolingian armies under Louis' command captured a series of other erstwhile Roman strongholds in the region, including Gerona, Ausona, and Huesca, as well as the major fortress cities of Tarragona (809), Tortosa (809), and Pamplona (811). Following the collapse of Carolingian rule in the West during the later ninth century, this region developed as an independent polity as the county of Barcelona, and ultimately as Catalonia. In 1137, Catalonia was integrated into the kingdom of Aragon.

Parallel with the development in the west of a frontier march with the Muslims in Spain, the Carolingians developed similar systems of fortifications in the east, some of which were based on earlier Roman networks, and others that were created *de novo*. As early as the first half of the sixth century, the Frankish kingdom under the Merovingians established the region of Bavaria as a frontier march. This region provided both a base of operations against Byzantine-ruled, and then Lombard-ruled, Italy to the south, and a defensive bulwark against the Avars to the east and southeast. The Avars were originally a nomadic people from the Eurasian steppe who filled the vacuum left by the collapse of the Hunnic Empire in the later fifth century. The Bavarian March was constructed on the basis of old Roman fortifications, as well as the imperial highway system. During the period of Merovingian weakness in the seventh century, Bavaria became an essentially independent state under its own dukes. However, Charlemagne conquered in the region in 787, and subsequently used the erstwhile fortress cities and other strongholds there as bases of operation for his conquest of the Avar realm, located in modern Hungary, which was completed in 804.

Farther north and east, Charles Martel established a series of fortifications to defend against first the Thuringians, and subsequently the Saxons, in what came to be known as the Germar March. This system, which was built in territories that were never part of the Roman Empire, ran for about 65 kilometres, and was focused on controlling crossings over the Werra and Unstrut rivers. The system included the construction of substantial fortresses at Mühlhausen, Tutinsode, Schlotheim, Eschwegen, and Frieda. The Saxons, for their part, constructed a series of fortifications on their side of the frontier in the second half of the eighth century, which similarly were intended to block Frankish attacks and expansion into their lands.

Following the conquest of Saxony by Charlemagne, which was completed in the early years of the ninth century, the Germar March lost its initial purpose. However, Charlemagne vastly expanded the system along the river valleys of the Unstrut and the Saale in order to protect the newly conquered regions from attacks by the Slavs. Information about the nineteen fortifications that comprised this new system of defence has been identified through both archaeological excavations and the so-called *Hersfeld Tithe-Register*, a document dating to the year 780, which lists hundreds of properties organized around fortified sites. The tithes – that is, taxes owed to the Church – were granted by Charlemagne to the important imperial monastery of Hersfeld, located in Thuringia. This system of fortresses eventually came to be known as the Sorbian March, because the Slavic peoples on the other side of the frontier were known to the Franks and their Ottonian successors as the Sorbs.

Even farther to the north and east, Charlemagne's conquests of various Slavic peoples brought the frontier all the way to the Elbe River. Along the middle Elbe, Charlemagne established a series of fortifications that were built on sites first developed by the government of the emperor Augustus in the brief period before AD 9, when all of the lands between the Rhine and the Elbe were included within the Roman Empire. The most prominent of these, the stronghold at Magdeburg, developed over the next 150 years into the leading royal centre of the Ottonian kingdom under Otto I, which will be discussed below.

Europe in the high and late Middle Ages

The collapse of the Carolingian rule in the West Frankish kingdom during the late ninth century did not diminish the central importance of the Roman military infrastructure for the conduct of military campaigns, although the scale of military operations in many regions was diminished greatly because kingdoms and principalities of the later ninth century and beyond had much smaller populations than those which had been available for military mobilization when the empire had been united. The fortress city of Tours, for example, was a primary objective of the counts of Anjou throughout the late tenth and the first half of the eleventh century. However, Fulk Nerra (died 1040), despite his significant military success in conquering and fortifying large swathes of land at the expense of his neighbours in Normandy, Maine, Poitou, Brittany, Aquitaine, Chartres, and Blois, was not able to gain permanent control over Tours. It was only in the reign of his son Geoffrey Martel (died 1060) that the Angevins succeeded in seizing Tours, after defeating and capturing the count of Blois, Odo II, at the Battle of Nouey in 1044.

In much of the West Frankish kingdom from the latter ninth up through the early eleventh centuries, the wealthy governmental and administrative complexes, as well as the centres of ecclesiastical administration under their bishops, were based in erstwhile Roman fortress cities. These cities, or more exactly their hinterlands, also were the objective of numerous attacks by Scandinavian raiders in the north. The focus on the hinterlands was made necessary by the fact that the Vikings, like the German-speaking "barbarians" of the fourth and fifth centuries, were ill-prepared to capture fortress cities and even lesser strongholds. Their lack of success with respect to these fortifications was due, in large part, to the lack of sufficient logistical systems and overall ignorance of siege warfare, particularly knowledge regarding sophisticated siege weapons, until relatively late in the ninth century.

However, over the course of the ninth century, the Vikings did learn the basics of western warfare, including the technological expertise necessary to construct siege engines, and also the ability to supply armies during major siege operations. The largest single campaign undertaken by Viking forces culminated in the almost year-long siege of Paris from November 885 to October 886. An exceptionally large Viking fleet sailed up the Seine and blockaded this former Roman fortress city and capital of Count Odo, whose descendants

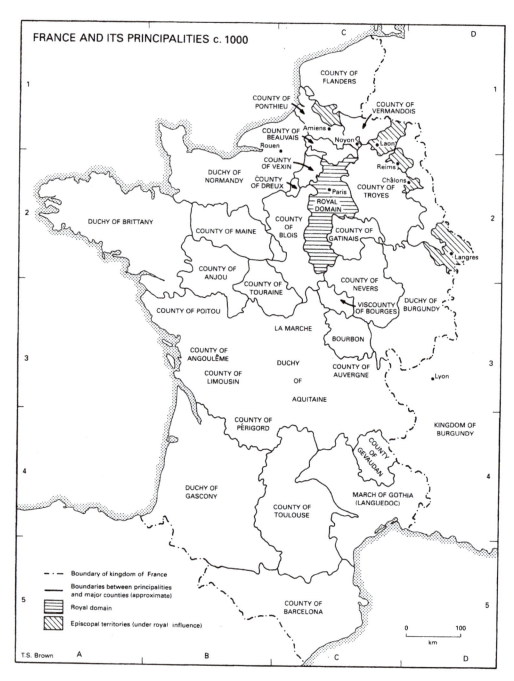

Map 2.4 France and its principalities, c.1000
Source: *Atlas of Medieval Europe* © T.S. Brown

would become the Capetian kings of France beginning in 987 under Hugh Capet. With an army numbering well over 10,000 men, the Vikings used a broad array of siege techniques to try to capture the city, including assaulting the walls with various types of stone-throwing artillery, battering the gates with rams, and launching furious assaults against the walls with troops equipped with storming ladders. The Vikings had acquired this knowledge of siege warfare through almost a century of campaigning in both England and on the continent. In the end, all of these assaults on Paris failed, in no small part due to the effective resistance of the defenders, led by Count Odo of Paris, who made very good use, in his own right, of artillery situated on the walls of the city. A bit over two years after his successful defence of Paris against the Vikings, Odo became king of West Francia following the deaths in rapid succession of the west Carolingian kings Louis III and Carloman II, and the deposition of the east Carolingian ruler Charles III by his illegitimate nephew Arnulf in 887.

In southern Europe, Muslim armies operating from North Africa and Spain continued their expansionist efforts throughout the ninth and tenth centuries. As was true of military operations that were directed towards territorial conquest within the lands of the erstwhile Carolingian Empire, the Muslims also focused their attention on the capture of fortified cities. In the west, the Muslims obtained their most significant successes against the Byzantines, who ruled Sicily and southern Italy during this period. In 831, Muslim troops from Spain besieged and captured Palermo in Sicily. Over the next seventy years, the Muslim commanders in Sicily gradually expanded their control eastwards across Sicily and conquered the entire island from the Byzantines, directing most of their major operations to the capture of its wealthy fortress cities, where the greatest concentrations of population were to be found, the centres of commerce were located, and the Church based its administration.

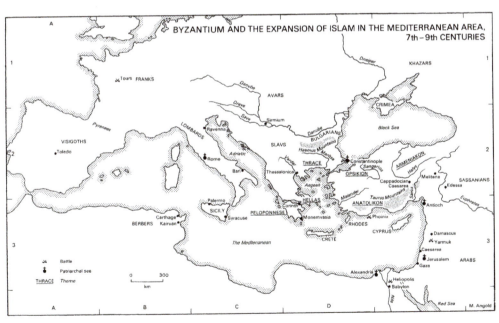

Map 2.5 Byzantium and the expansion of Islam in the Mediterranean area, seventh–ninth centuries

Source: *Atlas of Medieval Europe* © M. Angold

Even before the final conquest of Sicily, however, Muslim forces operating from bases on the island launched attacks on the Italian mainland, including a daring assault on Rome itself. In 846, Muslim raiders succeeded in sacking some of Rome's unwalled suburbs, but were kept from reaching the Eternal City by an active defence of the walls that had been refurbished during the early fifth century and had been kept in good repair ever since. In response to this dangerous Muslim raid, Pope Leo IV (847–855), with substantial support from the Carolingian Emperor Lothair I (840–855), the grandson of Charlemagne, extended the original Roman wall to the right bank of the Tiber. Lothair imposed a broad-based property tax throughout his kingdom to pay for the new walls. In the process, Pope Leo created a new fortified district that became known as the Leonine city.

In the east, the lands of the Carolingian Empire experienced a threat from the newly arrived Magyars, who settled in the region previously dominated by the Avars in the area that is today Hungary. This central Asiatic nomadic people had proved troublesome to the Byzantine Empire during the ninth century, but they did not enter Latin Europe until the 890s, when they were driven west by the Khazars, whose leadership at about this time had converted to Judaism. The Hungarians quickly established themselves as a very dangerous foe of the East Frankish and subsequent German kingdom. They launched large-scale raids throughout much of the East Frankish kingdom during the first half of the tenth century, and ranged as far west and south as the Lombard plain in Italy, and as far north and west as the lower Rhineland in the modern Netherlands. However, during two generations of raids, the Hungarians, who like the various "barbarians" discussed previously, were widely ignorant of siege methods, never succeeded in breaching the walls of any substantial fortresses, whether of Roman origin or more recent vintage. Ultimately, the Ottonian kings of

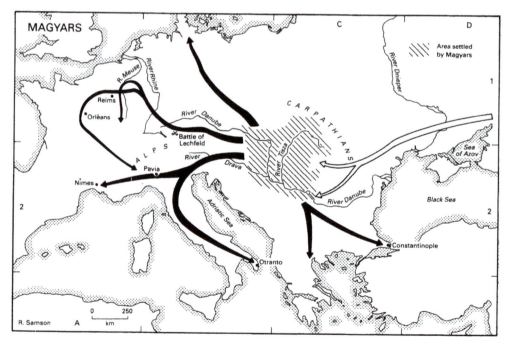

Map 2.6 Magyars

Source: *Atlas of Medieval Europe* © R. Samson

Germany, and regional magnates, developed a system of fortifications, including enhancing many of Roman origin, and established an effective system of defence in depth that stymied the Hungarians' effort to collect large numbers of slaves and wagon loads of plunder.

In response, the Hungarians developed a new strategy of attempting to establish a major territorial base within the German kingdom. In fact, the Hungarian ruler, Khan Bulksu, went to Constantinople, where he was converted to Christianity and was instructed in the development of a strategy to establish a base inside the German kingdom. The Byzantines may even have assigned advisors to Bulksu for the purpose of providing instruction regarding the construction of siege weapons and the development of siege techniques. The East Roman intervention on behalf of the Hungarians is explained by the fact that the imperial government in Constantinople was infuriated and felt threatened by the decision of Otto I to intervene in the Byzantine sphere of influence in central and southern Italy in 953.

With this Byzantine technical assistance, a very substantial Hungarian army, which included foot soldiers, their traditional mounted troops, and also a substantial siege train, marched into the German kingdom in late July 955. In August, Khan Bulksu began to besiege the fortress city of Augsburg, which had served as the capital of the Roman province of Raetia, and occupied an important economic as well as military role on the frontier between the duchies of Bavaria and Swabia. In addition, and perhaps even more important from a strategic perspective, Augsburg sat astride and controlled the main road from Germany across the lower Alps through the Brenner Pass to the fortress city of Verona in northern Italy. The Byzantines were eager to keep the German King Otto I from utilizing this strategic pass, and again intervening in a region that the Byzantines viewed as their sphere of influence.

The city of Augsburg withstood this siege under the effective leadership of Bishop Ulrich (923–973). Ultimately, the city was relieved by a large army commanded by King Otto I himself. In the battle of the Lechfeld, which was fought within sight of Augsburg's walls, Otto's relief army, which was dominated by foot soldiers fighting in phalanx formation, defeated the lightly armed Hungarian mounted archers much in the same way that Charles Martel had defeated the Muslims at Poitiers in 732. The withdrawing Hungarian forces were virtually annihilated over the next several days as they attempted to escape from the German kingdom along roads that were controlled at key choke points by garrisoned fortifications. The battle on the Lechfeld and its immediate aftermath marked a turning point in German relations with the Hungarians, who subsequently were converted as a people to Christianity and never again posed a significant military threat beyond the lands along their immediate frontier in the former Roman province of Pannonia.

The victory by Otto I at the Lechfeld and the subsequent success of Ottonian forces in the aftermath of the battle illuminate the important defensive role that Roman fortress cities, such as Augsburg, played in the conduct of war. Unlike their contemporaries in the West, however, the German kings, who were the effective rulers of a large, populous, and wealthy kingdom, were able to mobilize massive military resources for offensive campaigns, as well. As a consequence, from the tenth to the thirteenth centuries, German rulers of the Ottonian, Salian, and Staufen dynasties regularly focused their military operations on the capture of erstwhile Roman fortress cities both north and south of the Alps. In 946, for example, Otto the Great's campaign in the West Frankish kingdom was directed towards the capture of Rheims, Laon, Paris, Rouen, and Senlis, all of which possessed well-maintained Roman walls which were well defended by both urban levies and the military households of local magnates. In addition, the line of march of the Ottonian army westwards from Worms,

Figure 2.2 The Roman walls around Lugo in Spain
Source: © Peter Horree/Alamy Stock Photo C3W8MH

itself a Roman city, followed the old Roman military highways. Similarly, during the civil war of 953–954 within the German kingdom that pitted Otto I against his son Liudolf and son-in-law Conrad the Red, the major objective of all of the participants was the capture of enemy-held fortifications. The most prominent among these were fortress cities of Roman origin, including Regensburg and Mainz, both of which sustained lengthy sieges.

When German kings took their armies south of the Alps, their primary objectives also included control over the fortress cities of northern, central, and even southern Italy. Otto I and Henry II (1002–1024), following in the tradition of Charlemagne, undertook sieges of the Lombard 'capital' at Pavia in 952, 961, and 1004. Many German kings also found it necessary to besiege the highly fortified city of Rome in order to assert their political control in central Italy. Otto III (987–1002) besieged and captured Rome in 1001; Henry IV of Germany (1056–1106) besieged the city in both 1081 and 1084. The substantial military efforts of these kings, however, are dwarfed by the decades-long effort by Emperor Frederick Barbarossa, from the 1150s to the 1170s, to subjugate northern and central Italy to his direct rule, largely through sustained siege operations against dozens of fortress cities of Roman origin. The most important of these, from an economic, political, and military perspective, was the city of Milan, which Barbarossa besieged for lengthy periods on two occasions in 1158 and 1162, respectively.

By contrast with the continent, scholars generally have presented the military topography of England as experiencing a substantial break with the Roman past. However, it is clear that the Roman military highways, and other transportation infrastructure, continued to condition the movement of armies throughout the medieval millennium just as they had during the Roman period, in large part due to the obligations imposed on the population through

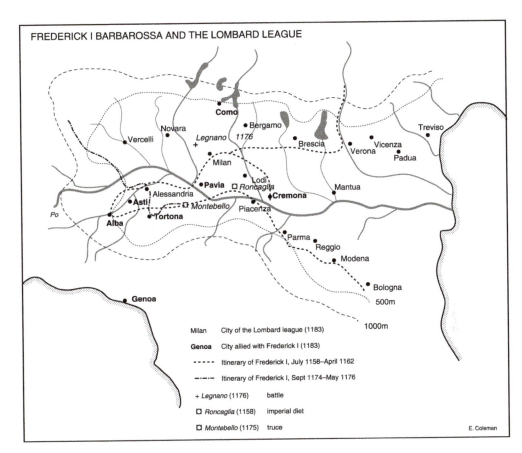

Map 2.7 Frederick I Barbarossa and the Lombard League
Source: *Atlas of Medieval Europe* © E. Coleman

the *trinoda necessitas*. This 'threefold obligation' required all landowners and dependents in England, including ecclesiastical institutions, to maintain roads and bridges, to maintain fortifications, and to provide fighting men for the king's army. Anglo-Saxon armies routinely marched along Roman roads and made good use of bridges of Roman origin, which were kept in repair. In addition, Roman ports continued to provide bases of operation for Anglo-Saxon fleets. Perhaps the most famous of these is Pevensey (Roman Anderita), which not only served as the administrative centre for the late Anglo-Saxon fleet deployed by King Harold Godwinson (1065–1066) in the summer of 1066, but also was the disembarkation site for William the Conqueror's army in September of that year. William also left his horse transports in the defensible anchorage at Pevensey when he marched along the coast with his army to ultimate victory at Hastings.

Roman fortifications within England also continued to play an important role in the conduct of war up through the eleventh century. The Roman fortress city of Winchester was a major fortification within the system of defence in depth established by the kings of Wessex during the ninth century, discussed in more detail later in this chapter, against the large Viking armies operating in England during this period. Winchester also was an important objective of William the Conqueror after his victory at Hastings in October 1066. The same was true in regard to the fortified port at Dover, which surrendered to William without a siege. Farther north, the Roman fortress city of York also remained a focus of military operations in the immediate aftermath of William's conquest. Edgar the Aetheling (1051–1126), the last Anglo-Saxon claimant to the English crown, raised a revolt against William at York in 1069. William, who at this time was operating against his Angevin enemies in Maine on the continent, crossed the channel and marched to York, where he captured the city, defeated Edgar's supporters, and wrought immense destruction within the walls and in its environs, as an element of the 'harrowing of the North'.

Medieval developments in the Roman military infrastructure

Over time, the Roman military infrastructure became incorporated into different patterns of defence to meet contemporary needs. In many cases, it became necessary to expand the walls of the original Roman fortress cities as populations grew, or as the need developed to enclose important suburbs that had grown up outside the existing circuit of walls. As mentioned earlier, Pope Leo IV expanded the walls of Rome to encompass districts on the right bank of the Tiber. In Germany, the substantial population growth of the tenth century led to the concomitant expansion of walls in many erstwhile Roman fortress cities, including Regensburg at the confluence of the Regen and Danube rivers in the south of the kingdom, to Mainz and Worms along the Rhine River in the north.

These efforts are suggestive of the effect of substantial population growth, as well as considerable surplus wealth and labour, which led in many places to a doubling of the extent of the circuit of the city wall, and consequently a quadrupling of the defended area. In other regions, the shifting of river systems or the silting up of harbours made some parts of Roman-era urban centres obsolete, and required the transfer of substantial portions of the population to new sites, which were then extensively developed. This was the case, for example, in parts of the port of Marseille. In other regions, the expansion of the Latin Christian culture and governmental structures meant that traditional Roman road networks and water-borne transportation systems, such as ports with supporting populations, had to be expanded into regions that were never part of the Roman Empire. This was the case especially east of the Rhine, in Scandinavia, and on the coasts of the North Sea and the Baltic Sea.

Despite these expansions, however, the underlying Roman infrastructure of military topography continued to play a significant and often primary role in shaping military strategy and tactics up through the late medieval period. In considering the numerous sieges that dominated the conflicts usually denoted collectively by scholars as the Hundred Years' War (1337–1453), it is clear that most were focused on the capture and defence of strongholds and fortress cities of Roman origin. For example, a major turning point in the later stages of the conflict between France and England took place during the siege of Orléans (1428–1429), where John of Lancaster (died 1435), the younger brother of King Henry V of England (1413–1422), sought to solidify the English hold on the French kingdom. His defeat at the hands of Joan of Arc (died 1431), known as the maid of Orléans, turned the tide of the war in favour of the French. Orléans, of course, was a Roman city named after Emperor Aurelian (270–275), who provided it with a circuit of Roman walls, part of which still stand today. It first gained fame from a military perspective as the site where the advance of Attila the Hun was halted in 451 when his forces were unable to capture the city, which held out until the army of the Roman general Aëtius came to relieve the siege and subsequently defeated the retreating army of the Huns at the battle of the Catalaunian Fields.

Intellectual and legal continuity of Rome's military infrastructure in medieval Europe

Many scholars, especially those specializing in ecclesiastical and religious history, have emphasized the enormous influence that late Roman authors and Church legislation, often denoted as synodal statutes, had on the organization and theology of the Church in Late Antique and medieval Europe. The books of the 'fathers of the church' such as St. Jerome (died 420) and Augustine of Hippo (died 430), and the statutes of the great ecumenical councils such as those at Nicaea (325), Constantinople (381), and Chalcedon (451) circulated widely throughout the Latin West, and were cited, analyzed, copied, and used by Church leaders as they formulated their own approaches to pastoral care, doctrinal disputes, and the organization of their churches. Similarly, historians of education have emphasized the important role played by the works of Roman and Late Antique authors such as Boethius, Cassiodorus, Isidore of Seville, Martianus Capella, Donatus, and Victorinus of Aquitaine in the curriculum for the training future monks and priests.

By contrast, there is often a great hesitance among scholars to recognize, much less to emphasize, the ongoing influence of Roman and Late Antique handbooks and training manuals in regard to the learning and pursuit of practical matters in the secular world. Such works included a substantial corpus of information regarding the construction of buildings, fortifications, roads, canals, and machines of various types; the latter included those built for military purposes. This reticence among scholars is due, in no small part, to the ongoing influence of the 'dark age' model, which takes for granted the collapse of all aspects of Roman culture, with the limited though extensively studied exception of the Church, during the centuries after the dissolution of the empire in the West.

The supposedly ignorant and illiterate 'Germanic' rulers of Rome's successor states, many scholars assume, were personally incapable of drawing on classical learning, and, in the bargain, lacked advisors who could use the significant corpus of mathematical and engineering knowledge in Latin that was required to maintain – much less, build from scratch – Roman-style roads, fortifications, and machines. Texts that treated technical matters were copied in large numbers throughout the early Middle Ages as it became increasingly necessary to replace worn papyrus manuscripts with far more durable parchment ones. Nevertheless, some scholars insist that the costly efforts in time and material were intended merely for antiquarian purposes – that is, to show off their connection to a supposedly long-dead Latin culture. This emphasis on 'antiquarianism' is intended to belittle the cultural vitality of the early medieval period, and permit the conclusion that the very large collection of technical treatises that were copied and produced, often with extensive commentary, not only had no practical impact, but were not intended to have a practical impact. The conclusion demanded by scholars enamoured of this 'dark age' model is that, while some churchmen were capable of learning from the past to plan for the future, many of these same men, who advised various governmental leaders, were incapable of thinking in this same manner with regard to practical secular matters.

This seriously biased 'dark age' model can be contrasted with the optimistic image presented by specialists in late medieval and renaissance history who focus on the wide range of Roman knowledge that is supposed to have been 'rediscovered' during the fourteenth and fifteenth centuries, including building techniques for the construction of both civilian religious and secular projects, as well as military endeavours. It is often remarked, for example, that the great renaissance architect and humanist Leon Battista Alberti (1404–1472) drew significant inspiration from the work of the Roman engineer and author Vitruvius (died c.15 BC), whose *De architectura*, which was frequently copied during the early Middle Ages, provided both illustrations and discussions of the construction of machines and complex buildings, including aqueducts. In this context, it is intriguing that some scholars associate the development of the *trace italienne*, a very late medieval style of fortification that was designed to blunt the advantages that accrued to the use of gunpowder artillery by besiegers, to Alberti's masterwork *De re aedificatoria* (*On Construction*).

However, the notion of Renaissance Italy 'rediscovering' Roman technology is a shibboleth that cannot withstand careful scrutiny. Far from being lost between the fall of the Roman Empire and the supposed 'rebirth' of classical learning during the fifteenth century, Roman engineering and mathematical knowledge remained important throughout the centuries following the dissolution of imperial rule in the West. Large numbers of Roman engineering and architectural handbooks, including those of specific concern to military builders, were copied, edited, annotated, and even updated by both government officials and others from the sixth through the eleventh centuries. These activities had a significant and ongoing impact on medieval efforts to preserve the Roman military topography, including mural defences, roads, and bridges, as well as the building of new fortifications and military infrastructure.

Among the works that proved useful were the *Institutiones*, compiled by the Roman senator Cassiodorus (died 585), who had been a very important advisor of the Ostrogothic king Theodoric the Great and a major official of his government. The *Institutiones* included Boethius' partial translation of Euclid's work on geometry into Latin, and Vitruvius' *De architectura*, mentioned earlier. Many scholars, especially specialists in the history of science, whose works often are neglected by medieval historians apparently because of their highly technical nature, believe that Einhard, the early ninth-century biographer of Charlemagne, who also undertook significant building projects during his tenure as lay abbot of the monastery of Seligenstadt in western Germany, possessed a copy of *De architectura*. It also seems very likely that the 'applied mathematician' who constructed Charlemagne's octagonal chapel at Aachen also made use of advanced engineering handbooks of Roman origin.

In addition to Vitruvius' handbook, which provided a considerable body of theoretical information, illustrated formularies also circulated throughout the Carolingian Empire and its successor kingdoms. These pamphlet-sized texts provided models for the construction of specific elements of buildings such as stone columns and towers. Similar works dealing with the techniques for constructing buildings of wood also circulated widely. Some of these texts, which included new medieval compositions, also were illustrated to facilitate their use by craftsmen and builders.

The mathematical sophistication that was required to use these texts is very well demonstrated by Alcuin's collection of problems that were used for the education of students in schools. Alcuin's *Problems for Sharpening the Youth* (*Propositiones ad acuendos juevenes*) includes puzzles that today would be solved by the use of calculus. Indeed, another shibboleth affecting modern treatments of the medieval world is that the use of Roman rather than Arabic numerals seriously hindered even simple arithmetic and – even more so – significant mathematical thought. However, this again is errant nonsense. Large numbers of people had easy access to rapid arithmetic calculations through the use of the 'finger calculus'. This system operated much in the same manner as an abacus, with which addition, subtraction, division, and multiplication of large numbers could be accomplished rapidly and for which the treatment of fractions was not problematic. In addition to such basic aspects of arithmetic, both Roman and medieval thinkers were able to solve advanced mathematical problems, such as those set out by Alcuin.

In addition to architectural handbooks, another exceptionally important collection of practical manuals that circulated throughout medieval Europe in the pre-crusade period consists of the wide range of texts that were grouped under the name *corpus agrimensorum*. These were practical manuals for surveying, which were crucial for the construction of new buildings, as well as the laying out of roads, and the designing of canals. These texts also provided models for various mathematical calculations and insights that were required for mapping. Even in early Anglo-Saxon England, where Roman learning is thought by many scholars to have 'died out', the Roman foot (*passus*) was used for measurements in military building projects. In fact, the Roman heritage was so pervasive among early medieval builders that it was even adopted by Viking raiders, who in the tenth century laid out their fortresses using the *passus* as their basic unit of measurement.

The copying of practical handbooks at great expense, not least because of the high cost of the materials such as parchment, is indicative of their perceived value. The fact that they were often copied, annotated, and updated throughout the Middle Ages indicates that many builders and their aristocratic patrons in the pre-crusade period believed that these texts were useful in practical terms, and not mere antiquarian artefacts to be used for showing off one's cultural accomplishments. Most telling, however, is the fact that highly sophisticated construction projects, utilizing technology and techniques from the Roman period, continued to be undertaken throughout Europe during the entirety of the millennium following the dissolution of imperial power in the West. Indeed, in many cases, Roman-era building techniques were surpassed, as is evidenced by the massive Gothic cathedrals that were erected throughout Europe that were taller and more magnificent than any building constructed during the period of the Roman Empire. The so-called Gothic architecture replaced the style described by modern scholars as Romanesque, which used Roman building technology, and especially the rounded Roman arch, knowledge of which obviously had not been lost during the so-called barbarian invasions.

One particularly noteworthy technical project was Charlemagne's effort to provide a direct water route from the North Sea along the Rhine and Danube rivers to the Black Sea via a canal that connected the Rhine and Danube. Many scholars during the nineteenth and first half of the twentieth century pointed towards Charlemagne's massive investment of human and material resources in this project in 793 as the ultimate act of hubris by a supposed Germanic warlord with delusions of grandeur. The great Charles was mocked by many scholars for doing little more than digging a muddy trench. This view of the Fossa Carolina, as it was called in contemporary texts, was significantly revised in the late 1960s when the German scholar Hans Hubert Hoffmann undertook a detailed study of the labour involved in digging the canal and illuminated the sophisticated administrative system that was required to provide the men and material to undertake this project. Subsequent excavations of the course of the canal and associated water-management systems made clear the enormous hydrological expertise that was possessed by the engineers who directed the canal project. Technical expertise of this sort certainly was not acquired in the primeval Germanic forests!

Indeed, it is clear from both topographical and archaeological analysis that Charlemagne's engineers chose the absolute best possible course for the canal between the Rezat, a Rhine tributary, and the Altmühl, a tributary river of the Danube. Charlemagne's engineers correctly understood the need to alter the courses of several nearby rivers in order to assure a steady flow of water through the new canal. To this end, they constructed a major dam, which was not unearthed until excavations undertaken in 1998. In sum, both topographical and archaeological excavations, supported by detailed hydrographical analysis, demonstrated that the project was much larger and more complex, and required a much greater degree of sophisticated engineering knowledge, than had been appreciated by scholars who had consulted only written accounts, or concerned themselves only with the main line of the canal. The construction of the canal was, of course, in the Roman tradition that was well-known to the Carolingians from the numerous Roman canals, such as the Fossa Drusiana, discussed earlier, that were kept in use throughout the Carolingian Empire.

Roman law and medieval practice regarding military infrastructure

As was true of Roman handbooks and practical engineering knowledge, both Roman law and administrative practices continued to exercise considerable influence throughout Late Antiquity and the Middle Ages. It was once the commonly held view of medieval historians that Roman law, with the exception of several unprepossessing epitomes of the Theodosian Code, ceased to have significance in medieval Europe until the 'rediscovery' in Italy of the law code of Emperor Justinian (527–565) during the eleventh century. This view was consistent with the early twentieth–century model of a twelfth-century renaissance postulated by the great American medieval historian Charles Homer Haskins (died 1937).

However, beginning in the early 1970s, scholars began devoting considerable attention to the structure and Roman content of so-called 'barbarian' law codes, as well as to other types of legal documents, including formularies, which are books of model letters and documents (boilerplate, to use the modern jargon) discussed in Chapter 1. In addition, scholars have identified a Roman legal substratum among other types of documents such as *polyptyques*, which are a type of administrative tax or rent record, and royal edicts, including the voluminous capitularies issued by Carolingian kings and emperors, as well as charters that treated matters such as property rights, and the obligations of property owners to the government. As scholars investigated these texts more closely, it became increasingly clear that they were infused with Roman law, including elements from both the Theodosian Code (issued in 438), not merely epitomes, and Justinian's legal compendium. When Charlemagne or his grandson Charles the Bald, for example, referred to *antiquae consuetudines* in their capitularies, they were not drawing attention to ancient Germanic customs, but rather to legal principles enunciated in Roman statutes and rescripts as embodied in the Theodosian Code. This connection between Roman law and medieval governmental practice was particularly strong with regard to matters pertaining to taxation and the conduct of war. Many of the chapters in the seventh and eighth books of the Theodosian Code that deal largely with the late Roman army, for example, are reiterated in a wide variety of texts during the Carolingian era.

In the context of this chapter, there are three matters that were stressed by the late imperial government that continued to have great importance for medieval military topographies on the continent. These were:

1   the governmental monopoly on the licensing of the construction of fortifications;
2   the obligation of those in possession of fortifications to hand them over to authorized government officials, an obligation denoted by scholars as rendition, and finally;

3   the broad-based obligation on the population to maintain the military infrastructure within their local region. This included work on roads, bridges, and fortifications. Anglo-Saxon rulers, as discussed earlier in the chapter, adopted these Roman traditions from their Carolingian continental neighbours and maintained these up through the Norman Conquest, when they were adopted by their Anglo-Norman and Angevin successors.

In considering these broad categories of legal requirements, it should be noted that the obligation of rendition applied both to governmentally constructed fortifications that were in the hands of officials appointed by the ruler and to those strongholds that had been constructed by wealthy aristocrats to protect their lands and dependents. By contrast, the governmentally imposed obligation to provide labour to maintain fortifications generally applied only to those constructed and garrisoned by the king or prince.

Licensing and rendition

The obligation to obtain a governmental license to construct any type of fortification, and the concomitant obligation to render control over all types of fortifications – from great fortress cities to the smallest stronghold – to the legally constituted authorities of the central government was constant throughout the medieval millennium. In 584, for example, the Merovingian ruler King Chilperic I (561–584) received intelligence that his kingdom was to be invaded by his nephew King Childebert II (575–595). In order to prepare for this invasion, Chilperic sent messengers to the counts, who held command in each of his fortress cities, to admit the forces of his military commanders (*duces*) so that they could take up positions within the walls. As Chilperic expected, following the imperial principle of rendition, the counts obeyed his commands and the dukes obeyed his orders despite the fact that this was regarded as being potentially costly to their own properties in local areas that might be a theatre of military operations.

In the Carolingian period, exclusive governmental control over fortifications was stated unequivocally by Charles the Bald in the Edict of Pîtres, issued in 864, whereby he commanded that any stronghold that was constructed without his license was to be destroyed. As royal power declined in West Francia during the tenth century, the late Carolingian kings nevertheless insisted on their *de iure* right to license fortifications, even if they no longer were in a position to enforce this right everywhere within their realm. Even as late as 975, the Carolingian ruler Lothair IV (954–986), working with the Angevin comital family, appointed the Angevin scion Guy as bishop and count of Le Puy, in no small part, to restore governmental control over fortifications within the *civitas*.

Even after the collapse of royal power in West Francia, regional rulers who had made themselves *de facto* rulers and who claimed to hold power on the basis of the delegation of authority to them by the monarch, maintained strong control over the possession of fortifications. In Anjou, Flanders, and Normandy, the rulers insisted on their sole right to authorize the construction of strongholds, although in periods of weak rule, this authority could slip away.

For example, when Duke William II of Normandy (1066–1087) reached his majority in 1044, he found that control over much of his duchy had been usurped by local magnates, many of whom had constructed 'adulterine' – that is, unlicensed – fortifications in order to defend their positions in the lands that they had seized from governmental control. However, William moved swiftly to reassert ducal control over these strongholds. The legal and military steps undertaken by the duke to ensure that only properly licensed fortifications remained standing are illuminated in considerable detail by the regulations (*consuetudines*) issued in 1091 by William's eldest son and successor, Robert Curthose. These *consuetudines* reflect the legal practices of Duke William's reign, but also draw upon much earlier precedents. Among the points raised in the *consuetudines* are the rules that no one was permitted to construct an earthwork higher than 1.5 metres without explicit ducal approval, no one was permitted to construct a palisade on an earthwork without a governmental license, no one was permitted to construct an earthwork on an island or on a hill, and no one was permitted to construct a stronghold (*castellum*) without first obtaining permission from the duke. Moreover, if the duke did grant permission to construct any of these types of fortifications, the holder had to turn them over to the duke or the duke's representative immediately upon demand.

In the east, the late Carolingian kings, as well as their Ottonian and Salian successors, maintained both *de iure* and *de facto* control over the military institutions of their realm, and the right to construct a fortification remained a royal monopoly. Charters issued by both late Carolingian and Ottonian rulers emphasize the necessity of obtaining a royal license before constructing a fortification, often stating explicitly that without the ruler's permission, it would be illegal to undertake such a building project. Moreover, this general recognition of the sole right of the ruler to license fortifications is seen not only in the German realm, but also in Italy.

The governmental monopoly on the ultimate disposition of fortifications also played an important role in the military policy of King Henry IV of Germany. Henry's reign witnessed a brutal and lengthy civil war that pitted, in large part, the Saxon duchy, as well as important magnates in southern Germany, against the king. The centrality of the war to all manner of contemporary affairs, and especially King Henry's conflict with Pope Gregory VII (1073–1085), elicited a broad range of written commentary by partisans on both sides of the conflict. One of Henry IV's most ardent critics, a cleric named Bruno of Merseburg, impugned the king's character in every possible manner. However, despite his hostility to Henry, Bruno acknowledged that he had the legal authority, as king, both to demand rendition of strongholds into the hands of governmentally appointed officials, and to order the destruction of fortifications that he deemed detrimental to the public good. However, as part of his rhetorical strategy of damning Henry IV whenever the opportunity presented itself, Bruno stressed that the king ordered the destruction of numerous strongholds that never had served as bases for thieves or other disturbers of the peace, thereby defending the value of these fortifications for the public good and highlighting the king's putatively irrational and partisan actions.

In the twelfth century, the period of civil war in England between Mathilda (died 1167), the daughter of King Henry I of England (1100–1135), and King Stephen of England (1135–1154), Henry I's nephew, led to the construction of numerous unauthorized fortifications. This caused great consternation among contemporary chroniclers, such as Robert of Torigni (died 1186), who claimed, undoubtedly with considerable exaggeration, that more than 1,000 of these unlicensed strongholds were built by partisans of the two sides. Upon his accession to the English throne in 1154, King Henry II announced his intention to destroy all of these adulterine fortifications for the purpose of restoring governmental authority and removing bases of operation for thieves and other promoters of civil discord. Scholars generally agree that Henry II was very successful in his efforts to restore governmental control over this crucial aspect of military policy.

Governmental control over the licensing of fortifications survived not only throughout the medieval period, but even into the early modern era. However, as fortifications evolved both in structure and function, the process of royal licensing evolved, as well. The leading specialist on the topic of royal licensing for medieval fortifications, Charles Coulson, observed that battlements on large structures eventually developed as architectural elements that demonstrated the social superiority of the inhabitants, so that by the early modern period, estate owners sought licenses for the 'crenellation' of their homes. In practice, this meant constructing faux battlements along their roof lines that gave the appearance of a medieval fortress. This might be considered a vestige of chivalric play acting.

Labour obligations and military infrastructure

The obligation to provide labour to support the military infrastructure was a central element of the system of taxation in the later Roman Empire, which was maintained throughout the medieval period. In the later Roman period, these labour obligations were called *munera publica*, and weighed most heavily on free citizens, denoted as *coloni*, who leased or rented land from great landlords. Evidence for the continuity of these obligations can be seen in early medieval law codes. For example, the sixth-century *Lex Baiuuariorum* records that free *coloni* living on the lands of the Church were required to perform duties on behalf of the government, including collecting wood, producing lime, and – of particular importance in a military context – providing horses (*parafredus*) and transport service. Notably, the transportation service with a cart (*cum carro*) is denoted in Bavarian law as an *angaria*, a standard late Roman term for a public obligation. Yet another example of the survival of late Roman imposts on free tenants – namely, the support of the *tractoria* system, which provided accommodations and horses for imperial messengers and privileged individuals – is preserved in the obligations on *coloni* in the Frankish realm under Merovingian rule.

In the Carolingian period, the famous edict issued at the royal palace of Pîtres in 864 (mentioned previously) states that those individuals who did not have sufficient wealth to go on campaign were to be identified for duty 'according to long standing practice which was also exercised among foreign peoples, for work on new fortifications (*civitates novae*), bridges, and roads through swampy regions, and were also to serve in the garrisons of fortifications and along the frontier'.[3] The governmentally imposed labour obligations on both free landowners and tenants to build and maintain the public military infrastructure, also are recorded in numerous *polyptychs* – that is, monastic inventories of properties and dues – that were produced during the ninth century. We have evidence that the Carolingians had demanded the production of these types of inventories by monasteries as early as the mid-eighth century. One of these obligations, which was very important for military logistics, was the provision of transportation resources and labour for the movement of grain, wine, and other supplies. When not required by the royal government, these obligations for *angaria*, *scara*, and *parafredus* were at the disposal of the great landowners, principally the churches. However, in times of war, or when the royal court was passing through the region, the king was able to demand that the tenants of the great landowners provide this service to the government.

We see the same kinds of obligations in the German kingdom, which developed in the eastern regions of the Carolingian Empire. Numerous charters issued by the Ottonian kings during the tenth century illustrate the duty of every able-bodied man to serve in defence

---

3 A. Boretius and V. Krause (ed.), *The Edict of Pîtres: Capitularia Regum Francorum* (Hanover, 1897) in *MGH Capitularia II*, n. 273, ch. 27.

of the kingdom, both in war and in the preparation for war. In 940, for example, Otto I assigned to Abbot Folkmar of Corvey the responsibility to mobilize the monastery's dependents within the districts (Latin *pagi*) of Auga, Netga, and Huetgo to undertake *corvée* labour to maintain royal fortifications. The abbot was also assigned the responsibility to mobilize the monastery's dependents to defend these fortifications in case of attack. Up until this point, it had been the responsibility of the royally appointed counts in these three districts to mobilize the monastery's dependents to undertake these duties. Soon after his accession, the next king in the dynasty, Otto II (973–983), made a similar grant to the bishopric of Merseburg. The royal grant delegated the responsibility to the bishops of Merseburg to mobilize all of the free men (*liberi homines*) living within the boundaries of the fortress district to perform labour in maintaining the fortress at a stronghold called Zwenkau, located near the modern city of Leipzig in Germany.

Bruno of Merseburg, mentioned earlier, also readily accepted the proposition that the king, and even supposedly evil rulers such as Henry IV, had the legal authority to construct fortresses, at the cost of his subjects, so long as the stronghold served the public good (*utilitas rei publice*). In Bruno's account of Henry IV's decision to construct the fortress at Harzburg, as well as strongholds in other locations in Saxony during the 1060s, the chronicler exclaims that had the king chosen to build these fortifications in appropriate locations, they would have been both a source of strength and an 'adornment' to the kingdom. Bruno even claims that the populations living nearby the fortifications willingly provided both financial assistance and labour in the service of the royal government as if the fortresses 'foreshadowed the king's intention to undertake military action against foreign nations'.

The government's ability to summon the population to provide labour, and also supplies and even money, to construct fortifications was transported from the medieval West across the Mediterranean in the crusader states. The Latin polities on the eastern shore of the Mediterranean were established by conquest, and the indigenous populations – Christians, Jews, and Muslims alike – were subjected to the full range of taxes and labour dues that were levied in contemporary Europe from their common origin in late Roman imperial law. In addition, newcomers to the East were generally subject to similar types of obligations, particularly in matters pertaining to the common defence. This broad-based obligation is illustrated in the construction of the fortress of *Blanche Garde* in the late 1130s or early 1140s by King Fulk of Jerusalem (1131–1143). The great historian of the Kingdom of Jerusalem, William of Tyre (died 1186), observed that when the king decided that he needed to construct a fortification on the road from Jerusalem to the coastal fortress of Ascalon, which was still held at that time by the Muslims, he summoned not only skilled builders but also the entire population because of the pressing need to finish construction of the stronghold quickly. Here, Fulk, who previously had been count of Anjou, was following customs that had been employed in his native land by ancestors such as Geoffrey Greymantle (died 987) and Fulk Nerra (died 1040), who themselves were following Carolingian practice.

Medieval topographies of defence

As we have seen, the physical, intellectual, and legal inheritance of the Roman Empire shaped and conditioned the military topography of Europe throughout the medieval millennium. But the constantly shifting political, military, and technological realities of the period between c.500 and c.1500 meant that this Roman foundation was modified, reshaped, and significantly augmented, both within the lands that once were part of the empire and in regions where Rome never had exercised direct authority. The extensive military topographies created by medieval governments offer important insights into their strategic thinking, administrative and technological capacities, and also the human and economic resources that they had available.

The Carolingian and Ottonian eastern frontiers

Charlemagne's successors in the east maintained the basic policy regarding fortifications that had been established in the late eighth century, as discussed previously. This policy entailed the protection of the frontier with the Slavic people known as the Sorbs through a system of defence in depth, combined with punitive expeditions against the Sorbs when they either raided Frankish lands or failed to pay tribute. However, the emergence of the Hungarians as a new power along the southeast frontier of the East Frankish/German kingdom changed the political calculus throughout the region. In 907, Hungarian forces inflicted a devastating defeat on the Bavarian regional levy at Pressburg (Bratislava). In 910, the Hungarians again won a decisive victory, this time against the East Carolingian ruler Louis the Child (899–911). As a result of their military success, the Hungarians had the opportunity to develop diplomatic relationships with the Slavic peoples to their north, and consequently to construct an anti-Frankish coalition along the eastern frontier of the kingdom. With material support from Slavic peoples, such as the Bohemians, with their highly fortified 'capital' at Prague on the Vltava river, and the Sorbs, who were positioned to provide considerable logistic support, the Hungarians undertook significant raids in regions to their north, including in Thuringia and Saxony in the East Frankish/German kingdom.

This increase in Hungarian military activity corresponded with a period of political uncertainty in the East Frankish/German kingdom. The last of the East Carolingian kings, Louis the Child, died in 911. He was succeeded as king not by a western Carolingian but rather one of great East Frankish magnates Conrad I (911–918), who had been duke of the region of Franconia. Conrad's accession inaugurated a decade of internecine conflicts that only came to an end when the leading magnate in Saxony, Henry I (ruled as king 919–936), seized control of the entire East Frankish realm, including Lotharingia, in a series of campaigns between 919 and 925. However, even during the reign of Conrad I, Henry, who had succeeded his father as the dominant figure in Saxony in 912, recognized the strategic problem posed by the Hungarians, and sought to inhibit their ability to undertake large-scale military operations in Saxony and Thuringia.

In order to thwart these Hungarian military enterprises, Henry made the strategic decision that the Sorbian March was no longer sufficient to provide for the protection of Saxony, and subsequently the German kingdom. Henry, therefore, undertook a multi-stage effort to obtain direct control over the Slavic polities established east of the Saale River through military conquest, and to construct systems of fortifications that expanded eastwards from the Sorbian March along the river systems of the White Elster, Mulde, and Elbe. Henry I's eastward expansion was gradual during the second and much of the third decade of the tenth century. However, in the winter of 928–929, King Henry led a major army eastwards with which he besieged and captured dozens of Slavic strongholds, including the centre of Hevelli princely power at Brandenburg, and the main seat of the Sorbian Daleminzi at the fortress of Gana. Henry also obtained the submission of the Bohemian Duke Wenceslaus I (921–935) at Prague. In the aftermath of this campaign, Henry constructed several dozen new fortresses during the early 930s, solidifying his new defensive system, and also his control over the newly conquered region between the Saale and Elbe rivers. This campaign is discussed in detail in Chapter 8.

The ultimate result of several decades of military campaigns and fortress construction was a dense constellation of approximately fifty fortifications that protected the series of river valleys extending from the Saale eastward to the Elbe. On average, these strongholds were located just 7.5 kilometres, or about an hour's march distance, from each other. The close proximity of these numerous fortifications provided considerable scope for mutual support, and also for disrupting Hungarian efforts to move either men or supplies along the Elbe River valley. These tactical and strategic matters will be discussed in Chapters 4 and 7.

The construction, refitting, and maintenance of the fifty or so fortifications along the Elbe, Mulde, White Elster, and Saale rivers represent a massive investment of human and material resources by Henry I. These capital investments were matched by an equally impressive deployment of military forces to garrison these strongholds. If a conservative estimate of just 150 men for each garrison is used, Henry required approximately 7,500 fighting men to provide the minimum possible force that was required for an adequate defence of his fifty strongholds along the Elbe, Mulde, and White Elster rivers on a permanent basis. During the early stages of Henry I's establishment of the new frontier on the Elbe, the men in these garrisons necessarily were professional soldiers because there was not yet a critical mass of trustworthy colonists in the region. By the 970s, however, the process of colonization of the region with Christian, German-speaking settlers meant that the burden of defending these strongholds could be shifted, in part, to local militia forces. This new population emerges into the historical record in a series of royal charters issued during the first years of the reign of King Otto II (973–983).

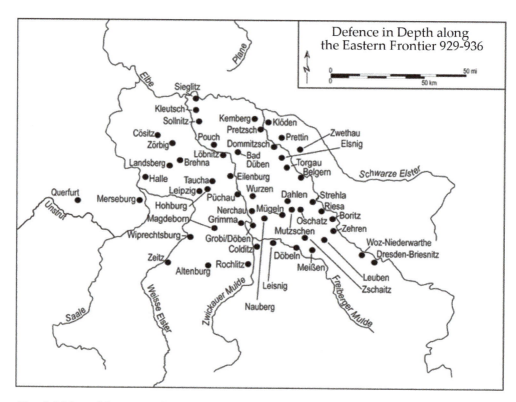

Map 2.8 Map of fortresses of Henry I on the Eastern frontier

As will be discussed in greater detail in the next chapter, King Henry I and his successors used a variety of methods to raise garrison troops. Writing retrospectively from the early eleventh century, Bishop Thietmar of Merseburg (died 1018) recorded that after constructing the fortification at Meissen, Henry provided this fortification with a garrison, 'as is common today'. As Thietmar makes clear throughout his text, one common practice of his day was for secular and ecclesiastical magnates to provide garrisons, at their own expense, in royal fortifications on a rotating basis in a manner similar, for example, to 'castle guard' in Anglo-Norman England and in Anjou.

Information from charters issued by Henry's successor Otto I makes clear that the second Saxon king also granted frontier fortifications to his faithful supporters as benefices with the requirement that these magnates would then provide garrisons of professional soldiers on a permanent basis, which could be supplemented by local militia forces. These garrisons included both the household troops of the magnates, and also colonists, who were recruited from the more densely populated western regions of the kingdom to settle on the new frontier. Finally, in addition to making demands upon their magnates for professional soldiers to serve in garrisons, Henry I and his successors, when they regarded the situation as appropriate, also deployed elements of their own military household for extended service as garrison troops.

The Slavic response

The Slavic peoples living to the east of the *Regnum Francorum* were not passive bystanders and victims of the expansionist strategies of their Carolingian and subsequently Ottonian neighbours. Rather, they also devoted enormous human and material resources to the development of their military infrastructure. This was done both to resist raids and invasions from the West, and also as bases of operation for their own offensive military efforts. The extensive military infrastructure of the various Slavic polities testifies to the development of advanced administrative systems, which likely were copied from the Carolingians and later the Ottonians. The investments that the Slavic rulers made in their strongholds also points to substantial population growth and flourishing economies that enabled them to invest considerable surplus labour and material for the construction of fortifications. The growing wealth throughout Europe, despite frequent warfare, likely was impelled in part by the climate warming trend that increased the length of the growing season and permitted greater agricultural production.

The efforts by Slavic rulers to construct systems of strongholds led the Carolingian emperor Louis the Pious (died 840) to order the compilation of a detailed intelligence survey of the number and location of the fortifications that had been constructed by Louis' adversaries, and potential adversaries, in the Slavic lands between the North Sea and the Danube. This report, entitled the *Description of the Fortresses and Regions along the Northern Banks of the Danube*, includes a region by region survey of the number of fortresses possessed by individual Slavic rulers and peoples. For example, the Obodrites in the far north of this region are listed as having fifty-three *civitates*, the Wilzi to their south ninety-five, the Hevelli eight, the Sorbs fifty, the Daleminzi fourteen, the Bohemians fifteen, and the Moravians eleven.

Although the written evidence for Slavic strongholds is limited in the period before the eleventh century, extensive archaeological work over the past fifty years has led to the close dating of large numbers of these fortifications. The results show that the construction and improvement of fortifications by the rulers of the various Slavic peoples match precisely the periods in which the Carolingian and Ottonian kings undertook sustained efforts to impose either their hegemony or direct rule through large-scale military operations. For example, we can see significant response to the efforts of Otto the Illustrious, the leading magnate in Saxony in the decades around the turn of the tenth century and his son, the future King Henry I, to extend their control eastwards. The Slavic rulers in the regions along the Havel River and in Lausatia, located between the Elbe and Kwisa rivers, rapidly constructed large numbers of fortifications to oppose the German advance. The well-fortified princely seat of the Hevelli at Brandenburg, for example, is dated to the first decade of the tenth century. Similarly, dendrochronological dating of the wooden ramparts of Slavic fortifications in the northern Lausatian region has demonstrated that at least nine substantial fortresses were built around 900. A further seven were completed by 916. It is also noteworthy that the designs of the fortifications, and the technology used to construct them, show significant western influence from the Carolingians.

Farther east along the course of the lower Oder River, the Slavic people known to the Ottonians as the Ukrani established a very strong network of fortifications to deter the expansion of the Ottonian kingdom into their lands. The entire region, known to later German writers as the Uckermark, was strongly defended by at least seventeen mutually reinforcing Slavic fortifications, each of which was supported by a large number of settlements whose inhabitants could take refuge within the walls of the large fortifications and help in the defence of the walls. One of these regional fortifications, at Drense, located 34 kilometres west of the Oder River, has benefitted from extensive excavations. These have demonstrated that over the course of the tenth century, the fortifications were continually improved, so that the walls grew from a width of 6.4 metres to 14.2 metres over a period of several decades. These earth and timber walls were protected by substantial stone facings to safeguard them from fire, as well as deep ditches, so that attackers had to surmount walls that rose in excess of 8 metres above the base of the defensive trenches.

To the east of the Oder, a new Slavic polity began coalescing in the first half of the tenth century around the aristocratic family that eventually became known as the Piasts. By 960, Miesco I (960–992), a self-proclaimed prince, had gained widespread authority throughout the watershed of the lower Oder region. No later than 965, Miesco formally converted to Christianity and married the daughter of the already converted Duke Boleslav I of Bohemia, thereby tying his realm into the broader system of Slavic Christian nations in Central Europe. During the latter half of this decade, Miesco also developed a *modus vivendi* with Otto I, whereby the Oder was established as the *de facto* eastern border of the German kingdom.

It was once thought that the Piast dynasty very gradually gained power in the regions east of the Oder beginning perhaps in the late ninth century and extending up through the accession of Miesco, and even into the reign of his son Boleslav Chrobry (992–1025). However, recent excavations of numerous fortresses in this region, including Gniezno and Ostrów Lednicki, have made clear that they were all built within a very brief time span from the late 950s to the early 960s. This not only indicates the rapid assertion of significant princely power for military purposes, but also a developing administrative system. The technical writing skills to support this administration may have been provided by the priests who served the Polish rulers in the efforts to Christianize the largely pagan population of their newly formed state, and brought with them the knowledge of the use of the written word in Latin. It is noteworthy that Miesco's son, Boleslav Chrobry, oversaw in the year 1000 the foundation of the first Polish dioceses at Gniezno and at Wroclaw, where cathedral schools for advanced study also were established.

The stimulus for the Piast seizure of control over the large Slavic population in the region east of the Oder, and their ability to exercise such enormous power, almost certainly came from the West with the advance of the Ottonian kingdom into the region between the Elbe and Oder. This expansion followed Otto I's victory at the battle at the Recknitz river (16 October 955), where he defeated and killed the Obodrite rulers Nako and Stoinef. Not incidentally, the victory at Recknitz followed shortly after Otto's victory at the Lechfeld and is a further indication of the military strength of the German kingdom. Following this victory over the Slavs, Otto I issued orders to establish a series of military districts, complete with fortresses, along the Havel and Spree river systems, including one at Spandau, the site of the infamous prison during the twentieth century. Otto also launched several campaigns against Miesco along the lower course of the Oder in the years immediately following his victory at Recknitz.

The Piast response to the German eastward advance was to establish a highly centralized military system, with a large princely military household, as well as dozens of fortresses with garrisons. These fortresses were surrounded by networks of villages that were required to supply the soldiers with food and other goods, and also to provide labour to build and maintain the strongholds. One is reminded here of the techniques used by governments throughout Western Europe. This system, which is discussed by the Judeo-Spanish traveller Abraham ben Jacob during the late tenth century, is very similar to both the Carolingian and Ottonian models for constructing and supporting systems of fortification along their eastern frontiers.

The kingdom of Wessex

During the first half of the ninth century, the kingdoms of Anglo-Saxon England suffered catastrophic losses at the hands of both large and small Viking armies, bent on substantial raids aimed at taking both moveable property and slaves. In the second half of the ninth century, the military situation for the Anglo-Saxons grew even more dire, as a very large Viking military force, denoted by the *Anglo-Saxon Chronicle* as the 'Great Heathen Army' (*mycel heathen here*) undertook sustained military operations against the kingdoms of Northumbria, Mercia, East Anglia, and Wessex. This 'great army' overwhelmed Northumbria in 867, East Anglia in 869, and most of Mercia between 874 and 877. Only the kingdom of Wessex survived, largely through long-term strategic planning of its kings Egbert (802–839), his son Aethelwulf (839–858), and Aethelwulf's four sons who served successively as king of Wessex: Aethelbald (858–860), Aethelberht (860–865), Aethelred (865–871), and Alfred the Great (871–899). In the evocative phrase of the renowned historian of Anglo-Saxon England, Nicholas Brooks, it was out of this 'crucible of defeat'[4] that the royal house of Wessex, principally under Aethelred, Alfred, and Alfred's son Edward the Elder (899–924), created a military system that finally stemmed the Viking tide.

Much as was true of the Piast rulers in Poland during the 950s, the military and political crisis posed by the 'Great Heathen Army' during the 860s permitted the kings of Wessex to impose extraordinary demands on their subjects for both active military service and labour in the construction of a new topography of defence. This dramatic militarization of the population of Wessex included the establishment of a mobile field army of 5,000 men, a permanent fleet of warships, and the vast expenditure of human and material resources on a system of

---

4 Nicholas Brooks, 'England in the Ninth Century: The Crucible of Defeat' in *Transactions of the Royal Historical Society* 5th ser., 29 (1979), 1–20.

fortifications, which collectively were garrisoned by some 27,000 men of the local militia, each of whom was supported by the surplus income produced by agricultural land associated with the stronghold where he was required to serve. All of this was accomplished on the basis of a population in Wessex that included fewer than half a million men, women, and children. By comparison, the fiscal lands of the German kingdom – that is, the lands directly under the control of the king – had a population of about the same size in the mid-tenth century.

Scholars became aware of the enormous extent and cost in men and material of the system of strongholds in Wessex following the discovery of a document usually denoted as the *Burghal Hidage*, so named by the scholar Frederic Maitland in 1897. The document, which originally was produced in the early tenth century during the reign of Edward the Elder (died 924), describes the system of fortifications, called *burhs* in old English, which were developed during the reigns of Aethelwulf and his four sons, particularly Alfred the Great, for the overall defence of Wessex.

Several of the thirty-three strongholds listed in the text, including the fortress city of Winchester and lesser strongholds such as Bath and Ilchester, had Roman origins. The great majority, however, were new constructions in the ninth century. The *burhs* were distributed in Wessex in a manner that allowed the king to control movement through the kingdom along the existing network of Roman roads, which continued to serve as the central arteries for overland travel in this period. Viking raiders, who carried off booty, had to use Roman roads in order to get from the interior to their ships. In addition, the fortresses were constructed at intervals of not more than 30 kilometres distance from each other, meaning that the garrisons in each stronghold, in the worst case, could reach the neighbouring *burh* in a day's travel. This close proximity made it possible to coordinate the operations of the military forces that were stationed within the *burhs*. In addition, when Viking forces sought to besiege one *burh*, the close spacing of the fortifications meant that garrisons in other *burhs* could harry the communications and supply lines of the Norse invaders.

The *Burghal Hidage* provides not only detailed information about the system of fortifications established by the kings of Wessex, but also illuminates the mechanisms by which they were able to sustain it. Each of the *burhs* was assigned a specific number of 'hides' from the surrounding area whose owners were required both to participate in the physical maintenance of the fortification and to serve in its defence in times of danger, or supply substitutes. As will be discussed in more detail in Chapter 3, a hide for assessment purposes, like the assessment manses used by the Carolingians, was an estimate of the value of the production of property rather than a geographical measurement. The number of hides assigned to each fortification was based on the length of the exterior walls of the *burhs*. The government of Wessex specified a consistent ratio of one hide for every 1.3 metres of wall in modern metric terms. The Anglo-Saxons used 'rods' for these measurements, but the Roman foot for construction purposes, as discussed earlier in this chapter.

Over the past several decades, archaeological research has added considerable additional information about the organization of the territorial defence of the kingdom of Wessex. The written sources, including the *Burghal Hidage* and the *Anglo-Saxon Chronicle*, tell only part of the story about both the extent and also sophistication of the system of fortresses established by the kings of Wessex, which modern scholars agree should be considered as a system of defence in depth. First, the royal government oversaw the construction and maintenance of many more fortifications than the thirty-three listed in the *Burghal Hidage*. This administrative document was a 'snapshot' of the particular concerns of a royal administrator at a particular time rather than a comprehensive overview of the entire system of defences in the kingdom of Wessex. In addition, excavations of the road systems that connected the

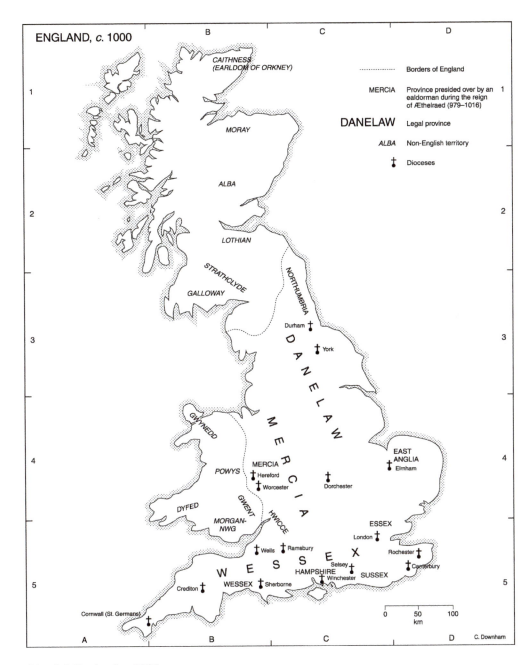

Map 2.9 England, c.1000
Source: *Atlas of Medieval Europe* © C. Downham

strongholds, as well as the surrounding territories, make clear that the kings of Wessex, like the Carolingians, maintained an extensive system of watch towers and fire beacons that served as early warning systems to provide intelligence in regard to approaching enemy forces, whether they came by land or by sea. There is no mention of these elements of the military topography of Wessex in the surviving written sources, illuminating the exceptional importance of integrating information from a broad range of disciplines, and especially archaeology, in the study of military history.

The rapid development of the mutually reinforcing systems of defence by the kings of Wessex, including fortified refuges for the population and control over the transportation infrastructure, which was maintained through the *trinoda necessitas*, saved the last of the Anglo-Saxon kingdoms from extinction at the hands of the Vikings. After the threat of the 'Great Heathen Army' receded, Alfred the Great and Edward the Elder then used their highly advanced military organization to go on the offence, and to seize control over lands throughout southern England that previously had fallen to Viking rule. The combination of a large mobile field army, which was supported by a well-organized logistical system (discussed in Chapter 4), a fleet, and the ability to construct and maintain fortresses in newly acquired lands, provided the basis not only for territorial defence, but also for conquest as they provided supply bases for offensive operations.

Post-Carolingian France

Throughout the western half of the erstwhile Carolingian Empire, various counts such as the rulers of Anjou and Normandy in the west, the counts of Flanders in the north, and the counts of Poitou south of the Loire, developed extensive complexes of fortifications. These were intended to secure the lands that they at first administered for the king and later came to rule, largely independently of the late Carolingian and early Capetian kings. In large measure, they became rulers as a result of leading the defence against foreign invaders, particularly the Vikings, as well as neighbouring magnates, and internal efforts to impinge upon their authority. Among the best studied of these great magnates, who ruled much of the west of the French kingdom with usurped regalia rights, are the counts of Anjou. In addition to their original lands situated in the region around the Roman fortress city of Angers, they also came to rule the northern part of the Poitou, most of Maine, eastern Brittany, the Touraine, the Orléanais, and finally Normandy through the conquest by Geoffrey Plantagenet. It was Geoffrey's son Henry, who ruled the Angevin Empire, which also included Aquitaine, in addition to holding office as King Henry II of England.

The most prominent of the West Frankish castle builders was Fulk Nerra, count of the Angevins (987–1040), who earned the sobriquet 'the great builder' for his construction of more than forty strongholds, many in stone. Fulk built upon the work of his ancestors, and especially of his father Geoffrey Greymantle (960–987), to create a defensive system that outlined the frontiers of the Angevin polity. To these frontier fortifications, Fulk added numerous strongholds in the interior of his realm, particularly along possible invasion routes. These included the still important system of highways, originally constructed by the Roman government, and also the numerous river valleys that crossed the territories ruled by the Angevin count. In addition to providing a powerful system of defence in depth for the Angevin lands, Fulk's construction of fortifications also gave him effective bases for projecting military force into neighbouring territories, and facilitated the conquests outlined previously.

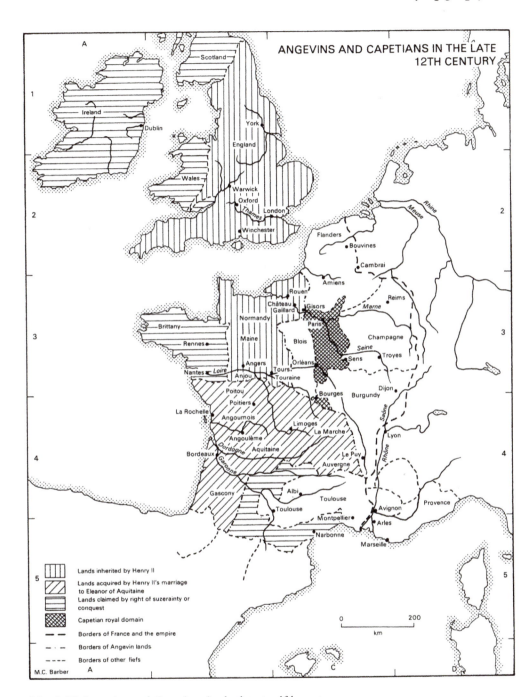

Map 2.10 Angevins and Capetians in the late twelfth century

Source: *Atlas of Medieval Europe* © M.C. Barber

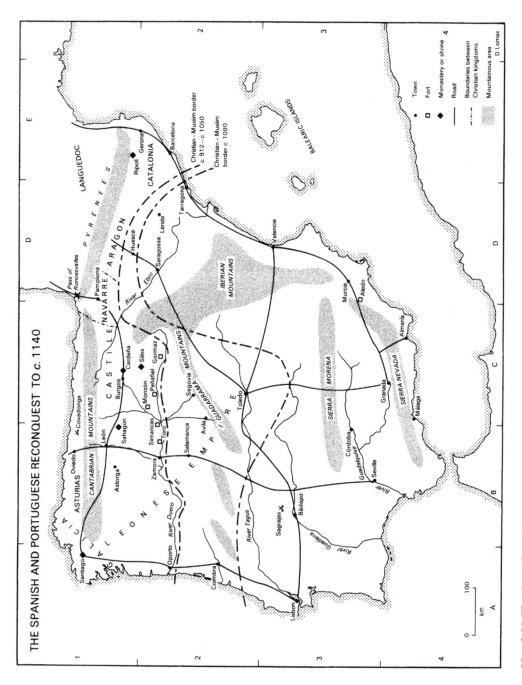

Map 2.11 The Spanish and Portuguese reconquest to c.1140

Source: *Atlas of Medieval Europe* © D. Lomax

Iberia

As seen previously in the context of the Muslim conquest of the Visigothic realm, Christian authorities in the far northwest of the kingdom utilized a range of late Roman fortifications, many of which had been maintained under the Visigoths, to preserve their independence in the region of Austurias. Gradually, the rulers in Austurias were able to expand their realm and established a new capital at the old Roman fortress of León in 910, which was located about 120 kilometres south of their previous capital in the fortified town of Oviedo. During this early period of expansion by the kingdom of León, the rulers established a military march to the east. The vast number of fortifications established in this new march gave the region its name of Castile. Eventually, the frontier march of Castile developed into the most important part of the kingdom as the Christian rulers were able to conquer additional lands to the east and south from the Muslims.

Unfortunately, archaeological investigations of the kingdom of León-Castile are still in their infancy, particularly as compared with the now robust situation in the regions comprising the medieval kingdom of Germany and her Slavic neighbours. Once excavations and analysis in Spain reach the level achieved in other parts of Europe, it is very likely that scholars will be able to tell a much more detailed story about the development of military frontiers, and the expansion of the Christian realms at the expense of the Muslims in central and southern Spain. By the latter eighth century, the authors of Muslim narrative sources were already commenting on the numerous strongholds constructed by Christians, both to defend against Muslim advances and as bases for offensive operations against the Muslims. Some of these strongholds evidently dated back to the Roman period, while others were newly built. When archaeologists have established a sufficiently dense and detailed body of knowledge about these strongholds, it will be possible, through interdisciplinary dialogue between historians and archaeologists, to develop an understanding of the thinking and planning of the Christian rulers.

Crusader states

The arrival of vast numbers of western Christian fighting men in Asia Minor during the spring of 1097 marked the beginning of a two-year military campaign that would culminate in the capture of Jerusalem on 15 July 1099, and the subsequent defeat of an Egyptian army at the Battle of Ascalon in the following month. During the course of this campaign, which has become known as the First Crusade, western Christians established new states based on the fortress cities of Edessa, located in the northwest of contemporary Iraq; Antioch, located on the Orontes River on the frontier between modern Syria and Turkey; and finally at Jerusalem. During the first decade of the twelfth century, western Christians established a fourth crusader state based on the city of Tripoli, located in modern Lebanon.

These new crusader states were constructed in a region inhabited since ancient times and that also frequently was the frontier between rival empires dating back to the second millennium BC. As a consequence, the military topographies encountered by the western settlers were heavily layered upon each other, with Egyptian, Israelite, Assyrian, Seleucid, Roman, and Muslim fortresses often sharing the same physical spaces. The newly arrived western Christians, their descendants, and periodic waves of newly arrived 'pilgrims' were heavily dependent upon the existing military topography. Of central importance were the fortress cities in the region, including such notable urban centres as Antioch and Jerusalem. However, the crusaders also made considerable additions of their own, including the

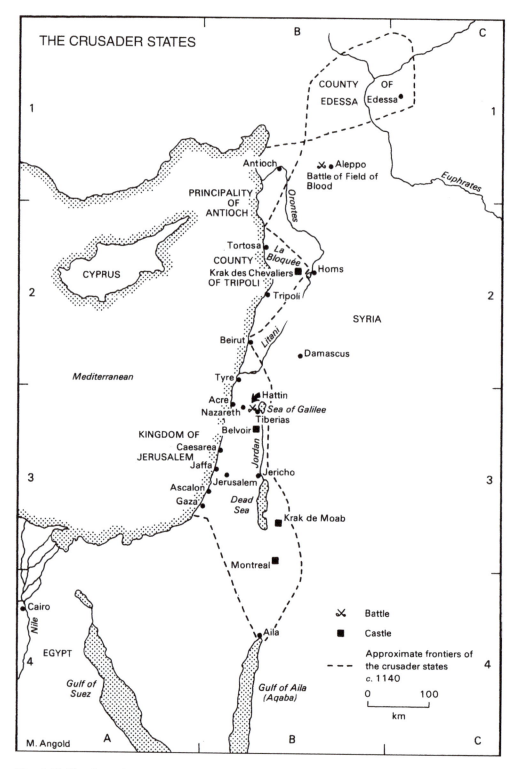

Map 2.12 The Crusader states

Source: *Atlas of Medieval Europe* © M. Angold

reconditioning of existing structures, as well as the construction of new fortifications. In these building efforts, the westerners drew upon a wide range of influences, including the contemporary models offered in Europe, as well as those by provided by Byzantine and Muslim fortifications.

The history of the crusading states can be divided into roughly two periods, one extending from the initial conquests at the turn of the twelfth century up to the fall of the city of Jerusalem to Saladin in 1187, and the second that lasted until the fall of the fortress city of Acre in 1291, and with it the last Latin Christian foothold on the eastern shore of the Mediterranean. During the first half of the crusading period, the Latin states were frequently on the offensive, and Christian forces captured all of the port cities and fortresses along the coast from Antioch in the north to the Mediterranean coast west of the Sinai desert in the south. The last Muslim strongholds at Tyre and Ascalon, in the far south, fell in 1124 and 1153, respectively. However, the crusaders were never able to extend their rule very deeply into the interior, so that the Muslim states based on the fortress cities of Mosul, Aleppo, Damascus, and in Egypt posed a constant threat to their frontiers.

In response to this geo-political situation, the rulers of Edessa in the north, and the two southern crusader states of Tripoli and Jerusalem, developed multi-layered systems of defence that were designed to protect their most valuable resources. These included most particularly the wealthy merchant cities along the coast, and the rich agricultural lands that were located to the west of the Syrian Coastal Mountain Range, the Lebanon Mountains, and the Judean Hills. In the case of the crusader state of Edessa, the rich farmlands that were located between the headwaters of the Tigris and Euphrates rivers were of prime importance, as was the capital city of Edessa itself. The rulers of Antioch developed a different strategy in this period, relying on treaties with the rulers of Aleppo to create what some scholars have described as a 'demilitarized zone' between their respective principalities. Nevertheless, the princes of Antioch did develop a series of fortifications within the immediate vicinity of their capital as part of a regional defence system.

For their part, the rulers of Edessa, Tripoli, and Jerusalem constructed numerous fortifications along their frontiers facing Mosul, Damascus, and Egypt, respectively. In addition to these fortifications along the frontiers, the rulers of the crusader states also acquired or built new strongholds along the transportation arteries, particularly in places where movement could be restricted easily, such as mountain passes, and at sources for water in desert regions. The purpose of these fortifications was not to prevent the penetration of the frontier by large enemy forces. Rather, these strongholds were part of an elaborate system of defence in depth that relied on cooperation between local garrisons and a mobile field army. Muslim generals confronted by these numerous strongholds along their line of march faced two choices, both of which had the potential to undermine the effectiveness of a campaign directed towards the wealthy heartlands of the crusader states. The Muslim forces could besiege the strongholds along their line of march. However, this process promised to slow down the advance of the army and thereby to take away from the limited time that the Muslim general could keep his large army in the field, which required significantly more logistical support than small raiding operations. Alternatively, the Muslim general could choose to bypass the fortifications, leaving their garrisons athwart his lines of communication, with the potential to disrupt his ability to move supplies. In addition, leaving these fortresses in his rear provided mobile Christian field armies with numerous bases of operation to harass the main Muslim force during the course of its march.

This multi-tiered system of defence proved quite effective for the rulers of the crusader states. However, when individual Muslim rulers acquired sufficient resources to raise very large armies over lengthy periods of time, the inherent weaknesses in the Latin strategic position, and particularly their chronic shortage of manpower, were exposed. In 1144, Zengi, the ruler of both Mosul and Aleppo, was able to capture the city of Edessa, and eviscerate the Latin state's control over the region that included the headwaters of the Tigris and Euphrates rivers. Zengi's success was due, in large part, to his ability to mobilize very large forces from both Syria and the north of what is today Iraq under his own rule. Saladin's capture of the city and most of the Kingdom of Jerusalem in 1187–1188 was due similarly to his success over the course of the 1170s and early 1180s in unifying the resources of both Syria and Egypt under his own rule.

Following the collapse of the Kingdom of Jerusalem, the rulers of Christian Europe mobilized vast military forces to participate in the Third Crusade, including armies led by Emperor Frederick Barbarossa of Germany, King Richard I Lionheart of England (1189–1199), and King Philip II Augustus of France (1180–1223). Despite some setbacks, including the accidental death of Barbarossa on the campaign, the crusader armies succeeded in stabilizing the Latin position in the east, and restoring a number of the major coastal cities to Christian rule. However, the crusader states retained a fraction of their former territory, and no longer had the resources to maintain either a frontier or a well-developed system of defence in depth. Much of the building of the military infrastructure in this period was carried out by the military orders (discussed in Chapter 3) – that is the Templars, Hospitallers, and Teutonic Knights – rather than by the rulers of the three surviving crusader states of Antioch, Tripoli, and Jerusalem. This was the case, in large part, because the military orders were able to draw upon substantial financial resources from their enormous property holdings located in Europe.

Figure 2.3 Crac des Chevaliers, Syria

Source: © Nick Ledger/Alamy Stock Photo BB5BT1

Many of the crusader fortresses built by princes and by the military orders were very impressive in scale and construction, and served as bases of Christian authority and power in the now substantially reduced areas of Latin rule. Perhaps the most famous of these strongholds is Crac de Chevaliers. The site of the fortification was given to the Hospitallers in 1142 by Count Raymond II of Tripoli (1137–1152). The Hospitallers built their first fortress here – which subsequently was destroyed by an earthquake – during the course of the 1140s. The Hospitallers developed a second and much larger fortress in the period after the collapse of the Kingdom of Jerusalem. In addition to the natural defences provided by the steep sides of its plateau that rose on three sides to a height of more than 600 metres, the Hospitallers constructed both an outer and much taller inner set of walls, both of which were studded with numerous round towers. The narrow entry into the fortress up a long and winding ramp was further protected by walls and towers, from which the garrison could inflict withering fire on would-be attackers. Crac de Chevaliers withstood ten major sieges during the course of the twelfth and thirteenth centuries, only falling in 1271 to Baibars, the Mamluk sultan (1260–1277), following an exceptionally lengthy siege.

Wales under Edward I

The Welsh frontier was a perennial source of concern and profit for Anglo-Norman and Angevin barons during the course of the eleventh, twelfth, and thirteenth centuries. Following his conquest of England in 1066, William the Conqueror established three earldoms on the Welsh frontier, Chester in the north, Shrewsbury in the centre, and Hereford in the south. Anglo-Norman earls encouraged adventurers and colonists to settle in their territories to control the frontier against raids and to establish bases of operation for expansion into Wales. The Anglo-Norman rulers also used the frontier to provide lands and opportunities for favoured military and political supporters. By the reign of Henry III (1216–1272), the baronies in the Welsh March enjoyed a well-established freedom from royal taxation and held delegated royal authority to create forests – that is, places where they were allowed to hunt – and markets. The barons in this frontier region constructed numerous small to medium-sized fortifications to secure their territories from Welsh raiders. They also developed significant military institutions that were separate from those of the royal government. In the north and west of Wales, native Welsh princes held power as independent rulers, and also constructed substantial numbers of fortifications. They also had their own military institutions, including the ability to mobilize very large numbers of fighting men at least for brief campaigns. The parallels between the Welsh and Slavic frontiers, as well as those in the crusader states, are quite striking.

The political status quo on both the Welsh Marches and within Wales itself was dramatically altered during the late 1270s and early 1280s when King Edward I (1272–1307) undertook large-scale military operations there in 1277, and again in 1282–1283. Scholars disagree about whether King Edward's initial intention in 1277 was to conquer Wales or simply to compel the Welsh prince Llywelyn ap Gruffudd of Gwynedd to recognize the English king's superior position in Welsh politics. Whatever his initial motivation, Edward's campaign that year resulted in substantial territorial gains for both the English crown and the English marcher barons at the expense of Llywelyn and his Welsh allies. The uneasy peace that resulted from the 1277 political settlement was broken in 1282 when Dafydd, the younger brother of Llywelyn, who had supported the English king in the previous war, now revolted against Edward I. Numerous Welsh leaders, including Llywelyn, joined the revolt, and forced Edward to undertake a series of very substantial military operations

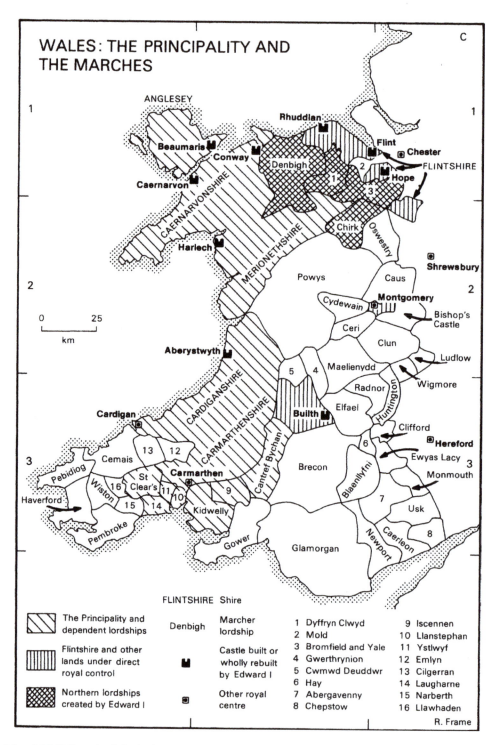

Map 2.13 Wales: the Principality and the Marches

Source: *Atlas of Medieval Europe* © R. Frame

Figure 2.4 Conwy Castle, one of Edward I's Welsh castles
Source: © robertharding/Alamy Stock Photo D1G2Y0

from June 1282 through the following June. Edward achieved a complete military victory in Wales, killing Llywelyn in battle and capturing Dafydd, who subsequently was executed for treason. Edward then reorganized the administrative and political structure of Wales, assigning significant lands to the marcher lords, and assuming direct royal rule over much of the formerly independent regions of the principalities of Llywelyn and Dafydd.

The costs involved in subduing the Welsh uprisings of 1282–1283 were very extensive, involving the mobilization of tens of thousands of fighting men, and the massive acquisition of supplies and materiel to support them. As a consequence, Edward decided to embark upon what would become one of the most extensive and expensive efforts at fortress construction in the medieval period in order to secure English rule in Wales and to thwart further Welsh uprisings before they could develop. In the south and along the marches, Edward largely relied upon existing fortifications, which were strengthened and provided with garrisons. By contrast, in the north of Wales, which had been ruled by independent Welsh princes, Edward constructed a series of fortresses that were intended both to dominate the local Welsh populations, and also provide a focus for English settlement in the region.

Over a period of twelve years between 1283 and 1295, Edward's government constructed thirteen highly sophisticated fortresses and substantially refurbished three other Welsh strongholds. Most of these fortresses, including Flint, Rhuddlan, Conwy, Beaumaris, Caernarvon, Criccieth, and Aberystwyth, were constructed along the coast so that they could be supplied by sea. In addition, these fortifications provided protected entry points and bases of operation for troops, who could be transported by ship after mobilizing at Bristol to the south of Wales or Chester to the north. Many of Edward's new castles were designed by the architect and engineer James of St. George (died 1309), who appears in hundreds of contemporary government documents, directing large-scale building projects.

In five of his new fortresses, Edward also ordered the construction of new fortified urban centres, namely at Flint, Rhuddlan, Conwy, Caernarvon, and Aberystwyth. These new 'bastide towns' may have been modelled on contemporary Gascon city-castle complexes. In addition to being king of England, Edward was also duke of Gascony, and had spent a considerable amount of time there during the early 1270s. The inhabitants of these new fortified towns were all English, and had been offered financial incentives by the royal government to move to north Wales. The crucial role that these English colonists were intended to play in the defence of the new political order is demonstrated quite clearly in administrative records detailing the garrison personnel and arsenals that were kept at Caernarvon and the other four castles with associated towns. The permanent garrisons in these fortresses ranged in size from just 20–30 men, including chaplains, smiths, and crossbow makers. However, each of the arsenals in these castles included hundreds of crossbows and many hundreds of thousands of crossbow bolts, indicating that the English settlers in the towns were expected to serve as militia troops in defence of these strongholds alongside the small permanent garrisons.

The military value of the English castles was demonstrated during the final Welsh revolt of Edward's reign in 1294–1295. Many of the strongholds, including Caernarvon, were besieged by the Welsh, but none were captured. The ability of the English to supply and reinforce these fortresses by sea, with large quantities of supplies and additional men brought from Ireland, enabled the garrisons to withstand the initial force of the uprising. In the course of the winter of 1294–1295, the English castles provided important bases of operation and fortified magazines for Edward's armies that crushed the uprising.

Late medieval military topographies

Specialists in the history of fortifications often have seen Edward I's castle building programme in Wales as the last major governmentally directed effort to use walls and garrisons as a means of territorial defence and control. A case certainly can be made that geo-political and technological factors made relatively small strongholds obsolete by the mid-fourteenth century in much of Europe. Larger armies and more sophisticated siege equipment, including gunpowder weapons, meant that small garrisons, even when supported by local militia forces, could no longer withstand sustained assaults. However, the end of the small fortress or castle as a viable unit of defence did not mean that fortifications ceased to have military significance during the late medieval period.

Rather, the scale of fortifications now increased dramatically, and drew upon the resources of entire cities. This reality helps to illuminate the nature of the military conflicts denoted by scholars as the Hundred Years' War, which were dominated not by battles in the field, but rather by the sieges of cities. At one time, scholars studying warfare during the fourteenth and fifteenth centuries tended to emphasize major battles such as Crécy (1346), Poitiers (1356), and Agincourt (1415) because of the influence of what has been called the Napoleonic or Clausewitzian doctrine that the purpose of war was to seek out and destroy the main army of the enemy. However, in recent decades, most specialists in late medieval military history have recognized the centrality of sieges to the conduct of military campaigns, particularly those that focused on territorial conquest. Avoidance of battle was usually of primary importance except under a limited set of circumstances, which are discussed in more detail in Chapter 7.

As we have seen throughout this chapter, cities had been fortified throughout Roman Europe especially from the late third century onwards, and from even earlier in the lands that were conquered by western Christians in the Levant during the crusades. However, beginning in the thirteenth century, regions throughout Europe witnessed the massive expansion of city walls to include previously 'suburban' communities, and also the construction of walls around communities that previously had been 'open' or had possessed only limited fortifications such as a local lord's castle. Many of these city walls were truly massive. The archiepiscopal cities of Mainz, in Germany, and York, in England, for example, had circuits of walls measuring almost 5,000 metres.

Many cities financed and maintained these walls through special defence taxes, often on staple goods such as grain or wine which everyone in the community consumed. The efforts of urban governments to impose these taxes universally, including on religious communities living within the walls of the city, often led to conflict and threats of or even the imposition of excommunication. In the 1250s, for example, the clergy of the city of Worms in the German kingdom threatened to leave the city and refuse any sacraments to the people if they were subjected to the sales tax on wine and grain that was used to finance the maintenance of the city's walls. Everyone wanted to be defended – that is, to be safe – but few tended to be willing to pay for the 'defence budget'. In addition to social and religious tension, the expansion and new construction of urban walls often was accompanied by increased demands on the urban populations to provide military service, particularly in the defence of these same walls in times of siege.

The development and ever-increasing accuracy and power of gunpowder weapons during the course of the fourteenth and fifteenth centuries made obsolete many of the old-style masonry walls of medieval cities. Mortar-like pieces of artillery could launch large projectiles over the walls, and the increasing size and strength of artillery meant that guns could often simply breach urban defences, which heretofore had provided exceptional protection to a city's defenders. A comparatively inexpensive response to this new technological reality was for cities to develop their own defensive artillery. The medieval military historian Kelly DeVries has shown, for example, that the decades on either side of the turn of the fifteenth century saw the introduction of artillery towers and gun-slits in city walls throughout much of England and France. This is a later incarnation of the artillery platforms for catapults that were constructed during the later Roman Empire and thereafter.

A much more expensive option for both urban and royal governments was to build newer city walls that were designed both to withstand 'modern' artillery bombardments and to force enemy guns farther from the densely settled core of the city. A first stage in this process was the construction of extra-mural fortifications, which often were comprised of massive earth-works on which artillery could be positioned. These defensive positions outside of the city walls, frequently denoted in French sources as *boulevards*, offered the defenders an advanced position to counter the artillery of besieging forces. These *boulevards* were the first step in the development of new defensive systems around cities that were intended to negate the ever-increasing effectiveness and range of artillery. In place of high stone walls, cities now were defended by low-lying earth-works that could absorb the force of projectiles. These earth-works were constructed ever farther from the city centre so as to keep the enemy forces at a greater distance from the civilian population. These earth-works also provided ample space for the deployment of both defensive artillery and support troops, equipped with missile weapons of their own.

Ultimately, the sophisticated multi-layered defences of this type were given the name *trace italienne*, because so many Italian cities developed them during the sixteenth century. In English, these are often denoted as 'starburst' fortresses, which continued to be constructed well into the modern period. Fort McHenry, for example, whose siege by British forces during the American Revolutionary War inspired the composition of the *Star Span-gled Banner*, was constructed in the starburst manner. The Italian urban and princely leaders were inspired to undertake these expensive renovations of their defences by the enormously successful invasion of northern Italy by King Charles VIII of France (1483–1498) in 1494 when he levelled numerous old-style medieval city walls with his extensive siege train of gunpowder artillery. Of course, both the construction of new fortresses and the transporta-tion of immense artillery trains required massive expenditures and had to be supported by extensive administrative systems.

Re-reading military topographies as landscapes of defence

Archaeological and written sources provide considerable information about individual strongholds, as well as groups of fortifications. Increasingly, however, scholars working with the methods of 'landscape archaeology' have been able to show that by synthesizing the findings of a broad array of fields, including archaeology, history, art history, numismatics, and onomastics (the study of place names), it is possible to 'read' human agency and inten-tion with regard to military topography into relatively broad geographical spaces.

The approach of specialists developing the model of landscape archaeology is particularly important for scholars investigating early medieval Europe. We believe that the principles of landscape archaeology thoroughly undermine the arguments of historians who present the governments of Rome's successor states in the West and their administrative institutions as primitive or pre-state manifestations of a long-supposed dark age, lacking the capacity to plan effectively. We are now long past the point where any scholar familiar with the excep-tionally large and growing corpus of archaeological studies dealing with military installa-tions can still opine about the destruction of ancient civilization and its replacement with a barbarian warrior culture modelled on epic fantasies such as *Beowulf*, or the putatively more accurate historical works such as Tacitus' *Germania*, which purports to record life in the Germanic forests of the first century AD.

There are two areas, in particular, where landscape archaeology offers the potential to revolutionize thinking about military topography. First, the material remains of a landscape of defence can be understood as illuminating planning undertaken by human agents, and the intellectual activities of early medieval rulers and their advisors in the military sphere. These men often were very well-educated not only in regard to history, but also were famil-iar with technical texts dealing with military science such as Vegetius' *Epitoma rei militari* (*Epitome of military matters*) and Frontinus' *Strategemata* (*Stratagems*), as well as Vitru-vius' *De architectura*. This process of reading systematic planning into the material record may have the most impact for those periods in which the written word is particularly scarce. Second, the inter-connected elements of military infrastructure that are illuminated through the broad, interdisciplinary approach of landscape archaeology with regard to fortifications provides a basis for the analysis of the economic, demographic, and institutional capacities of the societies that constructed them.

Defence in depth as an aspect of landscape archaeology

In 1976, the polymath nuclear arms negotiator for the United States, Edward Luttwak, rev-olutionized thinking about the deployment of military forces by the government of imperial Rome with his book *The Grand Strategy of the Roman Empire from the First Century AD to the Third*. Luttwak postulated that even in the absence of explicit and comprehensive government documents describing the thinking of the emperors and their advisors with regard to the use of military forces, it was possible to read a coherent strategic approach into the building of fortifications from what it is known regarding the deployment of Roman legions along the frontier and within the frontiers of the empire. Luttwak's argument that choices about the use of military resources, if analyzed properly, can yield insights into strategic thinking stirred enormous debate among specialists in Roman history. On one side were those who rejected categorically the idea that the imperial government had either the volume of necessary information or the analytical capacities that would permit the development of a coherent 'grand strategy' for the defence of the frontiers. Other scholars have accepted Luttwak's basic premise that it is possible to read strategic thinking into the deployment of assets, but have questioned his particular conclusions with regard to an evolving imperial strategy for the defence of the empire's frontiers and population centres located in the interior of the empire.

The latter position is now broadly accepted by specialists in Roman history. In recent years, Luttwak's insights also have been adopted by some specialists in medieval military history, including the authors of this text, to conceptualize the strategic thinking of medieval rulers through an analysis of their deployment of military resources. In particular, Luttwak's identification of a multi-level mode of defending a frontier zone, which he called a system of 'defence in depth', has proven valuable for analyzing a number of frontiers throughout the medieval millennium, including several discussed in the previous sections of this chapter. Scholars who argue that systematic thinking, building, and deployment must be rejected as incompatible with supposedly 'primitive' pre-modern polities either explicitly or implicitly take the position that the vast quantity of information that is available regarding these matters results from innumerable coincidences. In the view of the authors of this text, such an approach to human behaviour is inherently implausible.

In short, a system of 'defence in depth' is a multi-layered scheme that had a two-fold purpose: first of protecting valuable human and agricultural assets against raiders, and second of destroying raiding forces as they attempted to withdraw towards friendly territory with booty that they had collected. When a system of defence in depth functioned effectively, the local populations took refuge in fortifications which they helped to defend. At the same time, the well-equipped and well-trained military forces of the region took up their positions in pre-determined locations and prepared to harry the attackers in a number of ways. Raiders, who were denied easy access to supplies, were forced to break up into smaller groups in order to forage. At this point, the regional commander could concentrate his own forces and destroy the raiding army piecemeal. If the regional commander had sufficient forces at his disposal, he could mass his entire army and seek battle against a foe that was now exhausted by weeks of campaigning with inadequate supplies, and perhaps burdened with plunder and captives.

When combined with the insights of landscape archaeology, including analyses of available marching routes, the locations of possible sources of supply, the availability of refuges for the local population, the constraints placed upon invading forces by the local topography, and the choices made by governmental authorities about where to construct fortifications, military historians have been able to discern the strategic thinking pursued by a wide range of medieval governments. The Anglo-Saxon specialist Richard Abels, for example, has shown that the *burhs* constructed and refurbished by the kings of Wessex in the ninth century were elements of a thoroughly planned system of defence in depth, which demonstrated a coherent network of local and regional defences that included information systems such as fire beacons and watch towers. Abels, and other specialists in Anglo-Saxon history,

Figure 2.5 The fortified village of Fort Bourtange, The Netherlands, a late medieval starburst fortress
Source: © frans lemmens/Alamy Stock Photo CYF04M

rely largely on material finds rather than written sources of information to develop their models of Anglo-Saxon strategic thinking.

Recent archaeological excavations of fortifications in Scandinavia, and particularly the Danevirke in Schleswig, and the so-called Trelleborg system of fortifications, similarly permit an analysis of the intensions of their builders in the absence of contemporary written sources. The Danevirke, which consisted of a series of fortified elements that collectively defended Denmark against attacks from the south, have benefitted from extensive archaeological investigations, including the use of dendrochronological techniques, which permit a rather precise dating of their construction. It is now clear, for example, that a massive effort was undertaken in the years 736–737 to construct enormous new wood and earth ramparts, protected by a substantial ditch, in a very similar manner to the contemporary 'Dyke' built by Offa. Soon after, these earth and wooden ramparts were reinforced with a stone wall, which has been preserved into modern times up to a height of 3 metres. We learn from written sources that these defences were refurbished in the early ninth century by a 'king' named Godfred in order to respond to the threat posed by the advancing Carolingian Empire.

Through dendrochronological dating, it can be demonstrated that the system developed in the eighth century, and refurbished in the early ninth, did not receive regular maintenance for a period of over a century. It was not until the mid-tenth century that we can see through archaeological investigations that the Danevirke was reinvigorated with a massive new system of walls during the late 940s or early 950s. These new walls reached a minimum height of 4 metres and width of 14 metres. The system also gained two new elements, which were designed to incorporate the important trading centre of Hedeby into the defensive works. In contrast to the earlier phases of the Danevirke, these new walls were continuously maintained and updated over the following century. On this basis, a new scholarly consensus has developed that the Danevirke fortifications demonstrate the increasing power and sophistication of the Danish monarchy. This conclusion is supported, as well, by the appearance during the later tenth and early eleventh centuries of numerous rune stones that record the names of men bearing royal titles and holding royal offices, which indicates the consolidation of royal power and the creation of new royal institutions.

This image of increasing royal power in Denmark in the tenth century is further enhanced by recent archaeological works on a series of fortresses at Trelleborg, Nonnebakken, Fyrkat, Aggersborg, and potentially Borgeby, the last named in Sweden. Dendrochronological analysis indicates that all of these fortresses were constructed in a very short period in 980–981. Moreover, all of these strongholds were built to the exact same architectural plan, which is understood by scholars to indicate a 'master plan' by the new Jelling dynasty in Denmark. From the perspective of the development of a defence in depth strategy, it is notable that the 970s and early 980s represented a period in which King Harald Bluetooth (961–986) faced considerable danger from his powerful neighbour to the south, King Otto II of Germany. Thus, the continual strengthening of the Danevirke, and the construction of a series of strongholds that protected the approaches to Hedeby, all of which are demonstrated through archaeological research, are thoroughly consistent with a response to this threat.

John Haldon, a leading specialist in Byzantine military history, similarly has shown that on the other side of the medieval world, the East Roman emperors at Constantinople developed their own system of defence in depth against Muslim invaders in eastern Asia Minor in the difficult centuries following the loss of the Empire's eastern provinces. When an attack took place, local populations were moved into places of safety so that they could not be easily killed or carried off by Muslim raiders. Food supplies were hidden, moved, or destroyed so that Muslim forces would find it difficult to sustain themselves in Byzantine territory. Specially trained troops kept a constant watch on routes to which the largely mounted Muslim armies were limited. These scouts were able to send information about the location and movement of enemy forces with an elaborate message system that included beacon fires. The narrow passes through which enemy forces had to move were fortified and garrisoned. Finally, Byzantine forces were mobilized and concentrated so that they would enjoy a significant numerical superiority in individual skirmishes and battles, even if they were outnumbered overall by enemy forces. Haldon, and other Byzantine historians, have the benefit of significantly larger number of written sources for the period before c.900 than is true of western medievalists. However, in the case of Byzantium, material sources of information also play a considerable part in illuminating the strategic thinking of the East Roman government.

Measuring the costs of fortress construction

Just as the careful analysis of the military topography of a region can help to illuminate the strategic thinking of a medieval government, an understanding of the costs and technology involved in the construction of one or more fortifications, along with their associated infrastructure, can illuminate the administrative, economic, and technological resources available to a medieval ruler. In some instances, modern scholars have available a large volume of administrative documents that provide detailed information about all aspects of the building process for fortifications, and associated military infrastructure, including even the names and pay rates of the masons, smiths, carpenters, and other specialists involved in the project. This is the case, for example, with regard to building projects undertaken by Henry III and Edward I of England during the thirteenth and early fourteenth centuries, and also with respect to the construction of urban defences in later medieval Italy in cities such as Florence and Sienna.

In many other instances, however, and particularly with regard to military topographies that were constructed in the period before c.1200, there is very limited surviving documentary information. In fact, in many regions of Europe, there are very large numbers of fortifications about which there is absolutely no surviving written information, from any type of source. For example, as discussed previously, in the northern regions of the modern German state of Bavaria, archaeologists have uncovered more than 250 fortifications dating to the period 700–1000, of which only thirty are named in the surviving written record. As a consequence of this enormous disparity between written and material information, historians often must rely on the fortifications themselves to tell the story of their construction.

The basic method of research to determine the means of construction of a particular fortification, the labour required for the overall project, and the implications of the completion of the project for the administrative and fiscal capacities of the pertinent governmental authority is rather simple, although arriving at plausible results is considerably more difficult. The first step is to select a structure that has been thoroughly excavated, and about which specialists in archaeology and/or architectural studies have provided detailed information. From these data, a 'blueprint' can be developed that is comparable in organization, although not in detail, to documents produced by modern architects and building contractors. Then, acting much as a modern construction engineer would, the historian estimates the costs associated with each stage of the construction of the fortifications. Naturally, estimating the costs of Late Antique or medieval structures must take into account the technology that was in use at the time. In the absence of reliable figures for wages, scholars have found that estimating costs in terms of the total human and animal labour involved in a project illuminates questions regarding ability of the government to mobilize both these resources, as well as the food supplies that were required to sustain them.

This method of analysis has been used by scholars to estimate the costs involved in the construction of several very significant military projects during the early medieval period, including the imposing project known as Offa's Dyke. Constructed by Offa, the Anglo-Saxon king of Mercia (757–796), this earthwork ran for approximately 130 kilometres along the current border between England and Wales, and what was in the eighth century the frontier between Mercia and the kingdom of Powys, which was ruled by a Welsh dynasty. The width of the dyke reached up to 20 metres, and the ditch was more than 2 metres deep along its entire length. The Mercian rulers also had substantial ramparts constructed along significant portions of the dyke. In a recent publication, Richard Abels has estimated, very conservatively, that this project required a minimum of nine million man-hours requiring the labour of tens of thousands of conscripted peasants. This project, therefore, illuminates the tremendous administrative capacity of the Mercian government, for which there is only very limited written evidence.

The authors of this volume have published a similar type of analysis regarding the labour costs involved in the construction of a fortress known as Hildagsburg, which was built by King Henry I of Germany, likely during the second decade of the tenth century, about half a day's ride north of the royal complex at Magdeburg. A conservative estimate of the labour costs involved in the construction of the earth, timber, and mortared stone fortress at Hildagsburg, which also benefitted from a triple system of water-carrying moats, runs

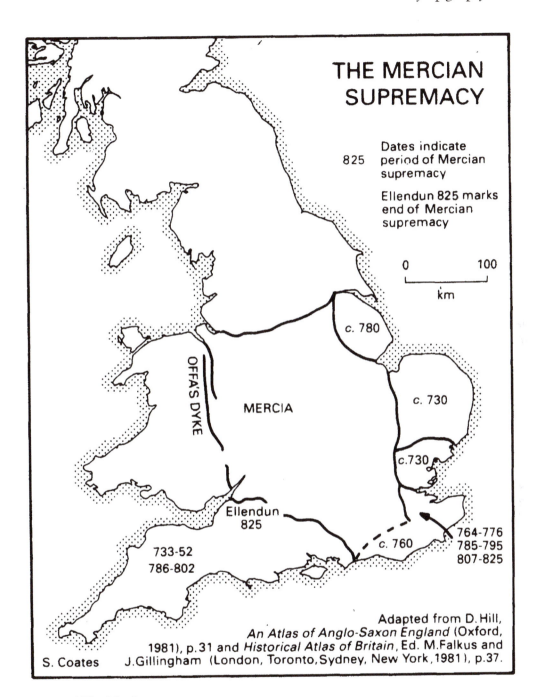

Map 2.14 The Mercian supremacy

Source: *Atlas of Medieval Europe* © S. Coates

to approximately two million man-hours. When due consideration is taken of the fact that King Henry I ordered the construction of as many as one hundred fortresses similar in size and complexity to that at Hildagsburg during the course of his reign as King in East Francia/Germany, it is clear that the first Ottonian ruler had at his disposal economic and labour resources on an astounding scale. Many of these fortifications are known only through archaeological investigation and are not mentioned in any written sources. Consequently, the descriptive reality of texts from the tenth century, discussed previously, that illuminate the authority of the king to mobilize his subjects to build fortresses can only be confirmed through excavations and subsequent historical analysis of these finds.

Figure 2.6 Offa's Dyke in Shropshire, UK

Source: © The Photolibrary Wales/Alamy Stock Photo B8W1PG

Conclusion

The central reality of medieval warfare, particularly when conducted on a large scale for the conquest of territory, was the need either to capture or defend fortifications. Even small-scale military operations, down to the level of piratical or bandit attacks that were focused on raiding and plundering, had to account for the presence of nearby fortifications and their garrisons, which were situated to minimize the threat posed to the surrounding region. Fortifications and the associated military infrastructure conditioned all aspects of military campaigns, from the need to mobilize large armies to undertake substantial sieges, to the routes that armies could travel, to the movement of supplies to keep armies fed and equipped.

Many thousands of these fortifications in medieval Europe, as well as in the eastern Mediterranean, were of Roman origin. They were connected by a vast network of roads, bridges, paved fords, canals, and ports on both rivers and seas, which also were inherited from Rome. Certainly, medieval rulers reshaped, expanded upon, and extended this military topography into regions where the Romans had only briefly ventured, or where they had never gone. However, whether medieval rulers were maintaining fortresses and other military infrastructure of Roman origin, or were constructing new military topographies, they still relied upon the technical, legal, and institutional heritage of the late empire. The knowledge that was necessary to undertake large-scale building projects came from Roman books that were assiduously copied and updated to reflect new practices and techniques. The legal authority of medieval rulers to demand a monopoly over the right to construct or license fortifications, and to demand the rendition of strongholds in private hands, was based on Roman law. So, too, was the legal authority to mobilize the entire population to participate in the construction, maintenance, and defence of fortresses for the common good.

From a broader administrative perspective, the construction and maintenance of a vast military infrastructure throughout Europe during the entirety of the medieval millennium is indicative of both widespread governmental sophistication with respect to military matters and the ability to tap considerable surplus wealth. Illiterate barbarians, who lacked effective governmental administrations and were bent on plunder and glory, could not and did not construct large fortresses, nor could they establish the logistical infrastructure necessary to besiege them. Rather, the mobilization of the human and material resources to undertake the construction of individual strongholds, and even more so systems of fortifications, is evidence of both detailed planning and effective governance. This story is relatively easy to tell for the later medieval period, as the multitude of surviving documents illuminate the entire process from initial planning to the layering of mortared stone. As a result of the insights developed by specialists in landscape archaeology, historians can now also use the material record developed through excavations to offer very similar accounts for earlier periods for which the written record is limited or even non-existent.

Finally, the ongoing obligations for the broader population to participate in the common defence, treated in Chapter 3, takes on a new urgency when understood within the context of the ubiquity of fortifications and other aspects of the military infrastructure throughout the medieval West. Despite legal requirements to serve in local militia forces, most civilians did not have very frequent experience of military action directly in their home districts because peace was far more common than war. Nevertheless, most people, of all statuses and backgrounds, were burdened with a considerable range of labour duties and other types of taxes in kind that were intended to support the government's maintenance or construction of strongholds and transportation infrastructure. It was through this system of taxes in cash, kind, and service that warfare frequently touched almost everyone.

Bibliography

A relatively small number of studies regarding the military topography of late Roman and medieval Europe have appeared in English, and most of these have dealt either with Britain or with the Holy Land.

For the physical inheritance from Rome of fortifications, see

Stephen Johnson, *Late Roman Fortifications* (Totowa, 1983);
Roman Urban Defences in the West, ed. John Maloney and Brian Hobley (London, 1983);
James Lander, *Roman Stone Fortifications: Variation and Change from the First Century AD to the Fourth* (Oxford, 1984);
War and Warfare in Late Antiquity: Current Perspectives, ed. A. Sarantis and N. Christie (Leiden, 2013).

With regard to the development of new topographies of defence in the Middle Ages, see

W. L. Urban, 'The Organization of the Defense of the Livonian Frontier in the Thirteenth Century' in *Speculum 48* (1973), 525–532;
John R. Kenyon, 'Early Artillery Fortifications in England and Wales: A Preliminary Survey and Reappraisal' in *Archaeological Journal 138* (1981), 205–240;
Michael Johns, 'The Defence of Medieval Brittany: A Survey of the Establishment of Fortified Towns, Castles and Frontiers from the Gallo-Roman Period to the End of the Middle Ages' in *Archaeological Journal 138* (1981), 149–204;
C. Coulson, 'Fortress Policy in the Angevin Tradition and Angevin Practice: Aspects of the Conquest of Normandy by Philip II' in *Battle 6* (1984), 13–38;
D. J. Cathcart, *The Castle in England and Wales: An Interpretative History* (Portland, 1988);
Matthew Strickland, 'Securing the North: Invasion and the Strategy of Defence in Twelfth-Century Anglo-Scottish Warfare' in *Anglo-Norman Warfare: Studies in Late Anglo-Saxon and Anglo-Norman Military Organization and Warfare*, ed. Matthew Strickland (Woodbridge, 1992), 208–229;
Edward J. Schoenfeld, 'Anglo-Saxon *Burhs* and Continental *Burgen*: Early Medieval Fortifications in Constitutional Perspective' in *The Haskins Society Journal 6* (1994), 49–66;
Frederick C. Suppe, *Military Institutions on the Welsh Marches: Shropshire, AD 1066–1300* (Woodbridge, 1994);
The Defence of Wessex: The Burghal Hidage and Anglo-Saxon Fortifications, ed. David Hill and Alexander R. Rumble (Manchester, 1996);
Eric J. Goldberg, *Struggle for Empire: Kingship and Conflict under Louis the German, 817–876* (Ithaca, 2006);
Gerda Bülow, 'The Fort of Latrus in Moesia Secunda: Observations on the Late Roman Defensive System on the Lower Danube (Fourth–Sixth Centuries AD)' in *Proceedings of the British Academy 141* (2007), 459–478;
Andres Siegfried Dobat, 'Danevirke Revisited: An Investigation into Military and Socio-Political Organization in South Scandinavia (c. AD 700 to 1100)' in *Medieval Archaeology 52* (2008), 27–67;
Aleksander Pluskowski, *The Archaeology of the Prussian Crusade: Holy War and Colonisation* (London, 2013);
David S. Bachrach, 'Restructuring the Eastern Frontier: *Henry I of Germany 924–936*' in *Journal of Military History 78* (2014), 9–35.

Concerning fortifications in the crusader states, see

R. Fedden and J. Thomson, *Crusader Castles* (London, 1957);

T. E. Lawrence, *Crusader Castles* (Oxford, 1988);

Hugh Kennedy, *Crusader Castles* (Cambridge, 1994);

R. C. Smail, *Crusading Warfare 1098–1193*, second edition (Cambridge, 1992);

Christopher Marshall, *Warfare in the Latin East, 1192–1291* (Cambridge, 1992);

Denys Pringle, 'Templar Castles on the Road to Jerusalem' in *The Military Orders: Fighting for the Faith and Caring for the Sick*, ed. Malcolm Barber (Aldershot, 1994), 148–166;

Thomas Biller, 'Development and Functions of Crac de Chevaliers' in *Der Crac des Chevaliers: Die Baugeschichte einer Ordensburg der Kreuzfahrerzeit*, ed. Thomas Biller (Regensburg, 2006), 374–385;

Kristian Molin, 'Teutonic Castles in Cilician Armenia: A Reappraisal' in *The Military Orders, Volume 3: History and Heritage,* ed. Victor Mallia-Milanes (Aldershot, 2008), 131–137.

With respect to medieval maps, see

Katharine Breen, 'Returning Home from Jerusalem: Matthew Paris's First Map' in *Representations 89* (2005), 59–93;

Keith Lilley, Christopher Lloyd, and Bruce Campbell, 'Mapping the Realm: A New Look at the "Gough" Map of Britain (c. 1360)' in *Imago Mundi 61* (2009), 1–28;

Kimberly C. Kowal, 'The Pembroke Map: A Medieval Sketch' in *Imago Mundi 64* (2012), 216–226;

Richard Talbert, 'Peutinger's Map before Peutinger: Circulation and Impact, AD 300–1500' in *Locating the Middle Ages: The Spaces and Places of Medieval Culture*, ed. Julian Weiss and Sarah Salih (London, 2012), 3–21;

Emily Albu, *The Medieval Peutinger Map: Imperial Roman Revival in a German Empire* (Cambridge, 2014).

With regard to Roman roads and their medieval successors, see

John W. Nesbitt, 'The Rate of March of Crusading Armies in Europe: A Study and a Computation' in *Traditio 19* (1963), 167–181;

Raymond Chevallier, *Roman Roads*, trans. N. H. Field from Voies Romaines (Berkeley, 1976);

Nigel H. H. Sitwell, *Roman Roads of Europe* (New York, 1981);

D. H. French, 'A Road Problem: Roman or Byzantine' in *Istanbuler Mitteilungen 43* (1993), 445–454;

John Bernhardt, *Itinerant Kingship and Royal Monasteries in Early Medieval Germany, c. 936–1075* (Cambridge, 1993);

Norman Hidden, 'Royal Itineraries and Medieval Routes' in *Wiltshire Archaeological and Natural History Magazine 89* (1996), 84–87;

D. F. Graf, 'Camels, Roads and Wheels in Late Antiquity' in *Donum Amicitiae*, ed. E. Dabrowa (Cracow, 1997), 43–49;

David Graf, 'The *Via Militaris*' in *Arabia in Dumbarton Oaks Papers 51* (1997), 271–281;

Ray Laurence, *The Roads of Roman Italy: Mobility and Cultural Change* (London, 1999);

Camilla Martha MacKay, *The Road Networks and Postal Service of the Eastern Roman and Byzantine Empire (First-Fifteenth Centuries AD): Social Effects on the Provincial Population* (Washington, 1999);

Hugh Davies, *Roads in Roman Britain* (Stroud, 2002);

C. R. van Tilburg, *Traffic and Congestion in the Roman Empire* (London, 2007);

Brian Paul Hindle, 'Sources for the English Medieval Road System' in *Die Welt der europäischen Strassen: Von der Antike bis in die frühe Neuzeit*, ed. Thomas Szabo (Cologne, 2009), 55–68;

Horst Barow, *Roads and Bridges of the Roman Empire*, trans. Friedrich Ragette (Stuttgart, 2013).

Conflicting perspectives

What was the effect of 'barbarian invasions' in the Western Roman Empire?

Guy Halsall, *Settlement and Social Organization: The Merovingian Region of Metz* (Cambridge, 1995);

Bernard S. Bachrach, 'Fifth Century Metz: Late Roman Christian Urbs or Ghost Town?' in *Antiquité tardive 10* (2002), 363–381;

Hugh Elton, 'Defence in Fifth-Century Gaul' in *Fifth Century Gaul: A Crisis of Identity*, ed. John F. Drinkwater and Hugh Elton (Cambridge, 1992), 167–176.

3 Military organization of medieval Europe

Introduction

Emperor Napoleon Bonaparte of France (died 1821) is once supposed to have said that God is on the side of the bigger battalions. Certainly, both Napoleon and military commanders throughout the medieval millennium were well aware that in battle, the size of the army in the field often was less important than the quality of the troops and the skill of their commander. Nevertheless, the *sine qua non* for both successful offensive and defensive military operations in medieval Europe was the recruitment and training (see Chapter 6) of substantial numbers of fighting men. As will become clear throughout the course of this chapter, military organization during the course of the long millennium between the dissolution of the Roman Empire in the West in the course of the later fifth century and the conclusion of the Hundred Years' War in the fifteenth underwent two gradual but enormously significant developments.

The military forces of the Roman Empire were dominated numerically by professional soldiers, who were paid by the central government, which levied tax revenues from throughout the empire for this purpose. The armies of medieval Europe, by contrast, were dominated numerically by various types of militia forces in governmental service, most of whom served at their own cost in lieu of paying various types of taxes. By the late Middle Ages, increasingly powerful and wealthy royal governments were again moving towards a system of recruiting professional armies, and utilizing well-developed systems of taxation to pay for them. Within this broad pattern, however, there were enormous variations that depended on a wide range of factors including the size, wealth, and administrative sophistication of the governments raising military forces.

In addition to the transition from professional to militia troops as the numerically dominant element of medieval armed forces, one continuous factor impinging on military organization throughout the period under consideration in this survey was the inheritance from Rome. This includes Roman legal and administrative practices, as well as Roman cultural norms that influenced rulers, administrators, and intellectuals throughout the medieval period, and well into the modern era. The customs of Germanic barbarians, so artfully described by the Roman writer Tacitus (died AD 117), had little to do with medieval military organization. This point must be made because of the tendency among certain scholars to use works such as those of Tacitus, or the early medieval epic poem *Beowulf*, to portray medieval Europe, and particularly early medieval Europe, as an archaic 'other' as compared with the later Roman Empire.

DOI: 10.4324/9781003032878-4

Late Roman military organization

With some notable exceptions, such as the economic historians Henri Pirenne and Alfons Dopsch, scholars from the nineteenth century up through the 1960s argued that the dissolution of Roman imperial authority in the West during the later fifth century brought with it cataclysmic devastation across a wide spectrum of social, political, and economic institutions. Particularly important was the belief that these disasters were accompanied and, in part, caused by massive demographic decline. Scholars at first argued that losses in population were due to barbarian attacks. More recently, some scholars have focused on disease, and particularly on the so-called Justinianic plague of the mid-sixth century. These arguments for demographic devastation often have been accompanied by claims that late Roman military institutions came to an abrupt end.

This image of widespread catastrophe across the western provinces of the empire began to change as historians, archaeologists, numismatists, and scholars in other disciplines developed new sources of written information, and reinterpreted previously known written sources, which largely were composed by clerics who exaggerated and even invented disasters to convince their readers that the Apocalypse was about to occur. Perhaps most importantly, scholars began to analyze in a systematic manner a massive outpouring of archaeological studies, which offered huge quantities of information about all aspects of medieval life, which demonstrated (as seen in Chapter 2) that the Roman urban centres of Gaul, for example, were not 'ghost towns' but rather Christian fortress cities with newly constructed cathedrals and numerous churches to serve large Christian populations. In a similar vein, despite the continuing claims by some historians, and most notably Kyle Harper's recent study of the impact of disease and climate on the later Roman Empire, it is increasingly clear that Western Europe was affected negligibly, if at all, by the plague that swept the city of Constantinople in 541.[1] Moreover, there is little evidence for plague activity in the erstwhile provinces of Gaul and Spain at any point during the Late Antique era.

It has become increasingly clear that the dissolution of centralized imperial rule in the West had disparate impacts across the provinces, and that the pace of change varied considerably. At one extreme, Roman Britain is claimed by many scholars to have suffered massive economic and demographic decline, which was caused, in substantial part, by large-scale out-migration to the northwestern parts of Gaul, and especially to the region that came to be known as Brittany – that is, 'little Britain'. Other provinces, including those in Gaul, Spain, Italy, and North Africa maintained a wide spectrum of Roman institutions under their new royal governments, including the Latin language, the Nicene Church, high-level educational systems, Roman law, coinage, urban centres and the accompanying infrastructure of fortifications, roads, bridges and ports (as seen in Chapter 2), economic exchange, and agricultural organization. In light of this significant pattern of continuity with late Roman traditions and institutions, understanding the organization of military forces in the period following the dissolution of the Roman Empire in the West requires a clear conception of the recruitment of the Roman army during the fourth and fifth centuries.

---

1 The main arguments regarding Harper's controversial thesis are treated in a lengthy article and response published in *History Compass Journal*. See the 'Conflicting views' section of the bibliography for this chapter.

Roman standing army

Roman military historians have accumulated a considerable body of information about the names, numbers, and locations of military units that were deployed in the western provinces from inscriptions, soldiers' discharge documents, and excavations of numerous military encampments and fortifications. However, the single most important source of information regarding the order of battle in the western provinces during the later empire is a text known as the *Notitia dignitatum*, which was drawn up c.395 and kept in use in the West for several decades after this date. Although the earliest known copy of this government document survives from the late medieval period and was based on a copy available at the court of Charlemagne c.800, the *Notitia dignitatum* provides an up-to-date assessment of the military organization and administrative system of the western half of the empire, at least in Gaul, up through c.430. The information provided in the document regarding the eastern half of the empire is accurate for the period c.390. Careful analysis of unit strengths provided in the *Notitia dignitatum*, combined with the excavations of large numbers of Roman military installations from the early fifth century, indicate that the 'paper strength' of the army in the western provinces was likely in excess of 200,000 men, and about 500,000 effectives for the empire as a whole. The majority of these troops were stationed along the frontiers as *limitanei*, who were based in permanent settlements with their families. The land that they possessed was provided by the imperial government and could be willed to a male heir, who had to be able to perform military service. The smaller of the two divisions of the regular army consisted of the highly mobile *comitatenses*, many of whom were mounted troops, who operated as both a field army and strategic reserve. These troops had no permanent bases but usually were cantoned in the environs of large cities that had well-established arrangements to bring food and other supplies to the area from the countryside and from even farther afield (see Chapter 4).

Recruitment

Although a small but significant number of men chose careers as professional fighting men and volunteered for military service, a principal method of recruitment for the imperial army from the third century onward was through conscription, and this system likely was strengthened by Diocletian (284–305) to meet the increasing needs for troops during his reign. In the late third and early fourth centuries, for example, we see the imposition of the obligation on cities to provide men for the army as well as taxes in gold to support the initial equipping of these soldiers.

The overall system of military recruitment and its ties to taxation was fundamentally revised in the East, and subsequently in the West, during the 370s by Emperor Valens. In a law issued in 375, Valens formally established the annual requirement for all landowners to provide either recruits or payment in money as a substitute for these recruits called the *aurum tironicum*. Of fundamental importance in this new recruitment system was the shifting of the responsibility to provide recruits from the *civitas* as an administrative district to the individual landowner. In order to facilitate this transition, Valens required the grouping of landowners into consortia, denoted as *capitula* or 'chapters', the members of which were jointly responsible for providing recruits or for paying the *aurum tironicum*. Those taxpayers who were wealthy enough to support this obligation on their own, including members of the senatorial class, were subject to taxation as individuals in proportion to their overall assessed wealth and might, therefore, be responsible for providing either numerous recruits or appropriate multiples of the *aurum tironicum*.

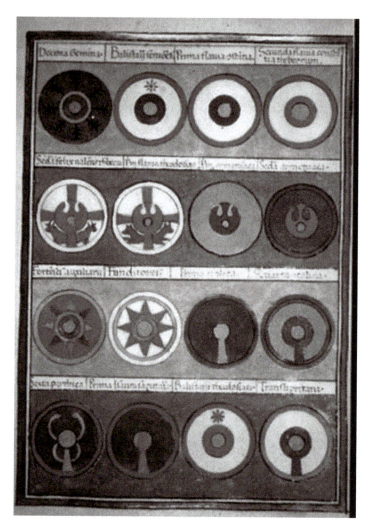

Figure 3.1 Magister Militum per Orientem 2
Source: © Jimlop collection/Alamy Stock Photo 2E366B7

The use of the tax system to provide soldiers for the imperial army worked in a rather straightforward manner, albeit one that required considerable administrative work. Approximately every five years, imperial tax assessors evaluated the economic resources of all private landowners within each *civitas* of the empire. There were, for example, approximately 100 *civitates* within the provinces comprising Gaul. After assessing all of the privately held lands, the imperial taxmen imposed a standard rate of taxation for a measurable unit of wealth, which often was designated as a *iugum*. The imperial government then decided how many of these taxable units should be combined together into one chapter, which would then be responsible for providing one recruit (*tiro*) to the imperial army. Tax assessors might assign several chapters to a single wealthy landowner. At the other end of the spectrum, a large number of small landowners could be gathered together to form a single chapter. The tax

Figure 3.2 Large numbers of Roman soldiers from the Arch of Constantine
Source: © PRISMA ARCHIVO/Alamy Stock Photo BYCE4B

rolls for each *civitas* were very detailed, and the entire process of tax assessment and collection was overseen by an official known as the *procurator tironum*. Consequently, it is unlikely that many landowners, wealthy or poor, legitimately escaped incorporation into a chapter. But, of course, there was always at least some corruption, and certainly there were complaints by landowners about large-scale corruption.

As will be seen later in this chapter, similar types of taxation in lieu of provision of military service played a significant role in the military administration of a number of medieval polities, including the Carolingian Empire, as well as Anglo-Saxon and Anglo-Norman England.

Throughout the imperial period, many Roman soldiers obtained a privileged tax status on the basis of their service in the army. Those men who were conscripted obtained freedom from the imperial head tax (*capitatio*) from the year of their conscription. In addition, members of their families – including their fathers and mothers, as well as their spouses – received freedom from the *capitatio* after the conscripted soldiers had completed five years of military service. Soldiers enrolled in the frontier units of the empire, the *limitanei*, had additional tax privileges, including the exceptionally important privileged position of their lands, which were freed from taxation.

'Barbarian' recruits in the standing army

In addition to Roman conscripts and volunteers, the imperial government also obtained substantial numbers of fighting men by conscripting a special category of 'barbarians' who lived outside the empire. In the course of numerous military conflicts across the third, fourth, and fifth centuries, almost exclusively won by the imperial army, large numbers of peoples living beyond the frontiers were compelled to surrender to the Roman government and became denoted in legal terms as *dediticii* – that is, those who have handed themselves over. These individuals were prohibited by imperial law from becoming citizens even after the grant in 212 AD of citizenship to all free people living within the frontiers of the Roman Empire by Emperor Caracalla (211–217).

Frequently, the terms of surrender of these various peoples included the conscription of some portion of their male population into the imperial army. In some cases, the negotiated settlement required a one-time delivery of a specific number of men for military service. In other cases, the defeated people, like Roman landowners, had an ongoing obligation to provide set numbers of recruits to the imperial government over a number of years. Whatever the terms of the negotiated settlement, however, the men who were chosen to serve as imperial soldiers came to enjoy all of the other benefits available to veterans upon the completion of their twenty-year tour of duty. These benefits included either money to establish a business or the grant of farm, usually on the frontier where their military skills were of continuing value for service in local militias, on which they could settle and raise their families. In addition, unlike the other members of their people who had the status of *dediticii*, the 'barbarian' veterans became Roman citizens and enjoyed the privileges associated with this status. Throughout the late imperial period, the Roman army was the primary agent for assimilation of non–Latin-speaking soldiers into the dominant culture. It was here that they learned Latin, and eventually also learned to become Christians after Christianity became the state religion of the empire during the course of the fourth century.

Yet other 'barbarian' groups, who were at peace with Rome, were permitted by the imperial government to settle within the frontiers of the empire. The settlement of these peoples had the two-fold purpose of bringing formerly empty lands into production and thereby enhancing tax revenues, and also increasing the supply of recruits for the imperial army. The peoples who were settled within the empire were denoted by imperial officials as *laeti*, and were established in colonies that were designated as public associations (*corpora publica*). Each colony was governed by an imperial functionary. In the early fifth century, there were at least twenty of these *corpora publica* in the provinces of Gaul, alone. Each of these colonies was required to provide recruits to the imperial government according to the terms of their original negotiated settlement. Consequently, the *corpora publica* functioned parallel to the chapter (*capitulum*) model noted earlier. The recruits from these colonies served in the same manner as all men in the imperial standing army, and received the same benefits upon the completion of their military service as all other veterans.

Other forces

A third source of 'barbarian' recruitment fell outside the compass of the standing army. Beginning in the third century, the Roman government made contracts or pacts (*foedera*) with some groups of 'barbarians' living beyond the frontiers. As we shall see, this strategy also was followed by various governments throughout the Middle Ages. In the later empire, these peoples were not defeated enemies, and so were not classified among the *dediticii*. Rather, the arrangements with these peoples can be thought of as types of treaties with more or less sovereign political entities. The agreements with these peoples generally were intended to secure military service to provide a temporary but stable buffer region between the Roman frontier and other 'barbarians' living even farther from the borders of the empire. The men secured for service on the basis of these *foedera* were not enrolled in the imperial army directly. They served under their own leaders, and were subject to very different standards of training and discipline, which were generally consistent with their basic customs. Thus, for example, Huns were employed as mounted archers. These 'barbarian' forces were almost always recruited to serve beyond the frontiers of the empire rather than for duty within Roman territory. However, the imperial government did provide incentives to the leaders of these peoples, along with pay, that included honours such as official imperial rank and other types of financial rewards.

By the later fourth or early fifth century, however, the imperial government instituted major changes in the *foedera* that were negotiated with various 'barbarian' peoples. These new arrangements called for the deployment of 'barbarian' military units within the frontiers of the empire, and also permitted the settlement of entire peoples within the empire. The groups settled in this manner were denoted in legal texts, such as the Theodosian Code, as *foederati*. As had been true of earlier *foedera* agreements, the 'barbarians' who settled within the empire were not required to undergo the normal training and discipline of the Roman army, and they were not incorporated as individuals into existing regular army units or auxiliary units. Instead, they served directly under one of their own leaders, who received block grants of money from the imperial government to pay their men. These *foederati* consequently appear to have much in common with mercenary units that can be seen to operate in the medieval period. Ultimately, groups of *foederati* came to include not only 'barbarians' but also Romans, and some groups even were commanded by Romans.

New Roman military institutions

Throughout the imperial period, the law known as the *lex Julia de vi publica* (the Julian law concerning public violence) banned private persons – that is, those who were neither soldiers nor veterans – from legally bearing arms for military purposes within the borders of the empire. In the early fifth century, however, this law, which was generally was not enforced, was repealed in the West by Emperor Honorius (393–423). This change in imperial law and policy led to the full legitimation of two military institutions that previously existed on the margins or even outside the Roman legal system. The first of these was the military household, whose members often were denoted in the late Roman period as *bucellarii*. Throughout the history of the Roman Republic and Empire, important people employed private military forces, often illegally, to secure their own economic and political interests. In the early fifth century, this practice ceased to be illegal, and even gained significant governmental support as the imperial administration sought to shift some of the burdens of territorial defence to the great landowners. The men who served in these military households often were volunteers, although many likely were tenants or otherwise dependents or clients and even the slaves of the great men who commanded and supported them. The members of the military households received various types of remuneration for their service, often including arms, armour, and horses, and can, in part, be understood as professional, or at least semi-professional, fighting men.

The second of the institutions that developed very rapidly in the wake of the repeal of the *lex Julia* was the citizen militia. Similar to those men who were impressed into the Roman army, civilians who were required to serve in militia forces had very little choice about whether or not to participate. They were conscripted to serve in defence of the area in which they lived, whether urban or rural, and were required by law to participate in this local defence. In many cases, these militia forces manned the walls of the hundreds of new fortifications and fortress cities that were constructed throughout the western provinces during the course of the fourth and fifth centuries (see Chapter 2). By contrast with regular army troops, *foederati*, and members of military households, the men in the urban and rural militias did not receive pay for their service.

Late Antique military organization in the West

The Roman Empire in the West dissolved into numerous kingdoms during the course of the late fifth and early sixth century. Britain had been given its 'independence', or perhaps more accurately autonomy, in 410, and splintered into dozens of tiny 'kingdoms' during the latter half of the fifth century. On the continent, the western provinces came to be ruled by Visigothic, Ostrogothic, Vandal, Frankish, Burgundian, Suevic, Thuringian, and ultimately Lombard dynasties. The replacement of imperial for royal, and distant for local, rule had important ramifications for military organization, although the administrative, social, legal, and economic institutions that undergirded much of the late Roman state remained firmly in place, as did the dominance of the Latin language and of Christianity.

The single most significant development following the end of imperial rule was the gradual, although not immediate, disappearance of large standing armies, including more than 100,000 soldiers in Gaul, that had been supported through the collection of broad-based taxes on the population living within imperial frontiers. In this context it is notable that many of the 'warlords', a term that some modern scholars have adopted to depict the leadership of the immediate post-Roman West, maintained control over important elements of the erstwhile imperial standing army. It is clear, for example, that the men who served as *limitanei* along Hadrian's Wall in the northern frontier of Britain, as well as their descendants, continued to man and defend these frontier defences for decades after the ostensible departure of Roman field forces from the province in 410. An even more obvious example of the continuing role played by regular forces of the imperial army is their use by Aegidius, *magister militum per Gallias*, to establish himself as the autonomous ruler of much of northeastern Gaul from 461 onwards, and the passing of this authority to his son Syagrius. The latter is well-known from Gregory of Tours' discussion of the defeat of Syagrius by the Frankish ruler Clovis (481–511) in the late fifth century. Clovis himself is known from near contemporary narrative sources to have incorporated troops into his army, who maintained the traditions of imperial military service, down to the level of keeping the same uniforms worn by their fathers and grandfathers. Indeed, Clovis' own father Childeric was a high-ranking officer in the imperial army in the province of Beligica Secunda, and can be understood to have been a 'warlord' in a manner similar to both Aegidius and Syagrius.

Despite the gradual nature of this process, the imperial armies in the West did dissolve as the traditional systems of pay and supply ground to a halt. However, the principle that land taxes and military service were owed to the government did not disappear, and newly established royal governments continued to assess their subjects in a variety of ways to provide 'warm bodies' for military service. First, the militarization of the civilian population for defensive purposes continued apace. A wide range of written sources, including historical works, saints' lives, letters, and legal texts from across the Latin West illuminate the universal obligation on all able-bodied men, free and unfree alike, to participate in the defence of their home districts. The mobilization of the unfree can be traced back to an imperial edict of 406, which recognized and accepted as legitimate the military service of slaves of soldiers, as well as of *foederati* and *dediticii* alongside their masters.

By contrast with this clear continuity with later Roman practice, the military forces that were recruited for offensive operations underwent significant change. Whereas the late imperial government obtained recruits for service in the standing army for a term of twenty years or more, the royal governments of Rome's rather small individual successor states no longer had either the economic or the demographic resources to maintain very large standing armies; nor, in general, did they face the types of geo-political challenges that required large military forces of this type. Instead, royal governments from across the Latin West demanded fighting men for offensive military service beyond their home districts only when these men were needed. This was especially the case when laying siege to erstwhile Roman fortress cities, which required large numbers of men to encircle or storm the walls. After the particular campaign was completed, most of these fighting men were permitted to return home. The relatively small numbers of professional fighting men serving in the king's military household (see more on this later in the chapter) remained in the royal entourage or the households of the magnates who employed them.

From the beginning of the nineteenth century, scholars recognized that a primary, perhaps the primary, public obligation of free landowners in the post-Roman world consisted of military service. Nevertheless, the origin of this service remained obscure and often was treated as a Germanic custom, ostensibly highlighted in Tacitus' *Germania* as the so-called 'nation in arms'. It is now clear, however, that a key to understanding the military organization of early medieval Europe was the conversion of the late Roman system of taxes into a personal obligation of the landowner or landholder to go on campaign when summoned by the ruler or to provide an appropriate substitute. Failure to serve, when summoned by the ruler, or the officials to whom he had delegated his royal authority (*bannum*), resulted in the imposition of a very heavy fine denoted in the ninth century as the *herribannum* and/or the confiscation of the lands that were intended to support the military service of a fighting man.[2]

The fine for the failure to perform offensive military service dates back to at least the sixth century, and was discussed by Gregory of Tours. The *Lex Ribuaria*, which dates to the early seventh century, also includes a fine for the failure to perform military service when summoned to do so, at a rate of half of the individual's wealth up to 60 *solidi*. Additional legal evidence from the Frankish kingdom in Gaul, the Visigothic kingdom on the Iberian Peninsula, and the Lombard kingdom in northern Italy makes clear that the obligation to provide military service, as had been the case in the later Roman Empire, was tied to wealth. The more land and wealth an individual possessed, the more military service that individual owed to the government. Some very wealthy landowners, who were obligated to provide correspondingly large numbers of fighting men for royal campaigns, maintained permanent military households in a manner consistent with magnates in the late Empire. As the Church grew in wealth, abbots, abbesses, and especially bishops came to play an increasingly important role in providing military forces for royal campaigns, and maintained substantial military households for this purpose. These military households also had value for ecclesiastical magnates in maintaining the local peace and protecting the assets of their churches.

---

2 The nature of the transition from standing armies to forces mobilized for individual campaigns on the basis of their wealth has been the subject of substantial and ongoing scholarly controversy. See the articles by Timothy Reuter and Walter Goffart in the 'Conflicting views' section of the bibliography.

Figure 3.3 Danish Army arriving East Anglia in 866
Source: © HeritagePics/Alamy Stock Photo 2E38YT7

The kings of Rome's various successor states were the wealthiest landowners of all as they took control over the imperial fisc – that is, the lands and other assets of the government – in the areas they came to rule. As a consequence, they had the resources to recruit and support correspondingly large military households. A significant element of these military forces, sometimes denoted in contemporary sources as the royal *obsequium*, was permanently attendant on the king, and could be mobilized to undertake military operations very rapidly. These troops may be considered the analogue of imperial household troops, broadly understood. However, many of the rulers of Rome's successor states also deployed members of the royal military household as garrison troops in significant fortresses and fortress cities, especially in areas that were newly conquered. The rank and file of the royal military households, as had been the case of soldiers in the later empire, was drawn from the lower echelons of society, and received pay for their service, both in kind and in money. These men, who were denoted in the Frankish context as *antrustiones*, were recruited not only from native Franks, but also from the indigenous Roman population, and from other peoples, as well.

A smaller sub-set of the royal military household received lands from the king. These lands provided fighting men with the economic wherewithal to support their families and also provide for their equipment, sometimes including horses, for military service. The use of lands to support fighting men who were part of the household rather than resident on the frontier can be traced back in the West to the reign of Emperor Constantius I (293–306), the father of Emperor Constantine the Great (306–337). Constantius provided lands, which were denoted as *terra Salica*, to Franks. This practice was continued by subsequent emperors throughout the late imperial period. When the Frankish king Clovis issued a legal code in Latin in 509, the *Pactus legis Salicae*, the text drew attention to the requirement that properties denoted as *terra Salica* in the land registers had to be held by men who were fit for military service. As late as the eighth century, men holding *terra Salica* were required to report, when summoned, for expeditionary military service equipped with food sufficient for three months, and clothing for six months. A similar institution played an important role in the Lombard kingdom in northern Italy, where men denoted as *arimanni* held public lands and were required to provide expeditionary military service in the armies of the Lombard dukes and kings.

In addition to mobilizing the royal military household, the military households of magnates, and the expeditionary levies of property owners, the kings of Rome's successor states also drew on military forces that might be construed as mercenaries. Gregory of Tours, for example, observed that the Frankish king Clothar I (511–561), and his son Sigebert (561–575), settled groups of Saxons, Suevi, and other unnamed peoples within their kingdom in return for military service. These ostensibly foreign peoples thus held a position quite similar to the *foederati* of the late Roman period, as they were permitted to keep their own laws and customs.

Other groups of fighting men, who might be considered mercenaries, served under their own leaders outside of an 'ethnic' context, and were employed on a cash-for-service basis by royal governments, and even by religious institutions as in the famous case of the nuns at the convent of Radegunde at Poitiers, who were roundly condemned on religious terms by Bishop Gregory of Tours. Another well-known example of the employment of mercenaries on a short-term contract concerns a Saxon named Childeric, who was employed by the Frankish ruler King Guntram (561–592) to deal with a band of marauders commanded by the Gallo-Roman magnate Vedastus. The military forces of Vedastus also may have been mercenaries.

A paradigmatic example for the military organization in Rome's various successor states in the West is provided by the Frankish 'warlord' *cum* king Clovis who, as seen previously, inherited the territories ruled by his father Childeric, an erstwhile Roman general, who seized power for himself in the province of Belgica Secunda. Clovis' military forces were drawn from disparate sources. An important element of Clovis' army was his own military household of *antrustiones*, some of whom likely were Frankish troops, originally in Roman service led by Childeric, or their sons. Clovis also drew upon formations of Roman troops or their sons originally commanded by Aegidius, and then the latter's son Syagrius, whom the Frankish leader defeated in the Battle of Soissons in 487 and subsequently murdered. Clovis also recruited the military households of numerous other Frankish 'warlords', most of whom were either former Roman officers or the sons of Roman officers, whom he defeated in battle or had assassinated, as recorded by Gregory of Tours. In addition to these professional forces, Clovis was able to draw on levies of troops from the *civitates* under his rule for expeditionary campaigns. Finally, as discussed previously, Clovis also was able to recruit various groups of soldiers as mercenaries, either directly for pay or by providing them with lands within his kingdom on which they could settle.

Late Antique developments

In the centuries following the dissolution of imperial power in the West, military organization witnessed both significant changes and important elements of continuity. The disappearance of the standing imperial army is the most significant of these changes. However, much of the equipment, including high-quality Roman breastplates, and indeed some of the uniforms or parts of uniforms possessed by soldiers c.450, continued to be available for use in subsequent generations. In addition, some elements of uniforms, including boots, were consciously copied from Roman exemplars. Nevertheless, the end of centralized control over arms and equipment factories meant that fighting men in the Late Antique West used an increasingly varied assortment weapons, some of which were old and some of which were new (see Chapter 4). Similarly, the training of professional fighting men (see Chapter 6), which had a high degree of standardization under imperial auspices, now became the responsibility of the kings and of thousands of individual aristocrats, including both secular and ecclesiastical magnates, who had to prepare their military households for undertaking military operations.

From an economic perspective, garrison towns and even fortress cities no longer benefitted from the stimulus of hundreds or thousands of soldiers spending their pay in local shops, taverns, hostelries, and brothels. On the positive side of the ledger for most landowners and proprietors of businesses, the kings of Rome's successor states gradually gave up efforts to collect the broad-based taxes on land and other forms of wealth, which were characteristic of the later empire. In large part, royal governments were able to do without these revenues, because they no longer had to bear the enormous expense of maintaining large standing armies. Consequently, a much larger portion of economic resources remained at the local level. Some scholars have pointed out that much of the revenue that once went to the imperial government likely now was claimed by landlords in the form of rents and labour dues rather than flowing back into the hands of cultivators themselves. In this context, many historians, particularly those of a Marxist bent, have significantly underestimated the number of small-scale free cultivators, who now also were freed from many imperial exactions. Nevertheless, whether kept by major landlords, free cultivators, or tenants, maintaining resources at home rather than sending them to the imperial government in Rome helped to spur economic development at the local level with concomitant demographic growth.

Despite these important changes, the end of the Roman standing army should not obscure the fact that important elements of late Roman military organization continued to play a central role in the post-Roman period. Some historians argue that the Germanic peoples, who once were thought to have destroyed the Roman Empire, brought with them a 'warrior culture', and it was this 'ethnic superiority' that enabled them to overcome the vastly larger Roman population of the Western Empire, which was protected by great fortress cities and lesser strongholds that the barbarians were unable to capture because they lacked a proper understanding of siege warfare. According to this misleading barbarian warrior model, Roman civilians with no military tradition were incapable of defending the empire, and accommodated themselves to the rule of the new 'barbarian' kings and their small 'warrior' bands.

Such a view ignores the considerable body of evidence, and most notably legal texts, which illustrate that the militarization of the civilian population, both for offensive and defensive purposes, had its origins under Roman imperial legislation and policy of the late fourth and early fifth centuries. The German-speaking peoples, who comprised only a very small minority of the population settled within the borders of the empire, were integrated into an already existing military system. The German-speaking kings who came to rule in the West not only rapidly learned Latin, as did the members of their entourages, but also made use of traditional Roman systems in the conduct of their own military operations, recruiting fighting men from their own peoples, but also from the exponentially larger populations of Romans whom they now ruled. These new kings followed such policies, not least, because of the advice that they received from advisors who were recruited from the Roman senatorial aristocracy. These men were very well-educated in the ways in which the Roman army historically had operated not only organizationally but also strategically and tactically, because of their own personal experiences.

Military service and the 'ethnogenesis' question

It is uncontested that a remarkable change took place in the north and east of Gaul between the late fifth and the late seventh centuries with respect to the composition of the population in 'ethnic' terms. At the beginning of this period, the overwhelming majority of the population was defined in legal terms as Roman, and by the end of this period, the overwhelming majority of the population was defined in legal terms as Frankish. Similar, though less drastic, developments can be identified in Spain, in southeastern Gaul, and in the southwest of modern-day Germany, where erstwhile Roman populations were transformed into Visigoths, Burgundians, Suevi, and Bavarians in terms of legal identity.

Influenced by the theories of the German historian Reinhard Wenskus, scholars once held that peoples such as the Franks, Burgundians, Saxons, and others had an ancient history based upon a core set of identifying traits (*Traditionskern*), including a common legal tradition, leadership by a charismatic dynasty, and culturally unifying traits, such as language. These peoples supposedly entered the Roman sphere of influence with fully formed cultural and legal identities, which they then maintained once settled within the Empire. In places such as northeastern Gaul, the Franks were seen to have in some way, not ever specified, replaced the vastly larger Gallo-Roman population.

It is now understand, however, that the various German-speaking groups that entered the Roman Empire were created in an active process of cooperation and co-option by imperial authorities. A traditional element of Roman diplomacy with 'barbarian' peoples was the selection of a cooperative partner, who was supported with economic and military resources, and who was expected thereafter to follow the dictates of imperial policy. Through this process, many ostensibly 'barbarian' leaders rose to positions of prominence in the late Empire, either within the structures of the Roman army and government, or as an adjunct to these structures, leading their 'peoples' in such a way as to gain both personal wealth and power, and also to serve the Roman state. Typical examples in this context are the Roman general Ricimer, his nephew, the Burgundian 'king' Gundobad (473–516), who was named *magister militum* by Emperor Anastasius (491–518), and Childeric, the father of Clovis, who also held office as a Roman general.

During the politically chaotic period in the latter half of the fifth century, many of these 'barbarian' officials of the Roman government, as well as ostensibly more Roman generals such as Aegidius, discussed previously, seized control in various provinces. As Stefan Esders, the leading scholar dealing with this question, has demonstrated, these 'warlords' imposed what amounted to military law, as well as martial law, throughout the lands they held, including on the largely Roman population. Very important in this context was the fact that these newly established rulers followed Roman practice in requiring all of their soldiers to take an oath of loyalty. In addition, an important consequence of the imposition of military law on the ostensibly civilian Roman population was that all able-bodied men also were required to take a military oath of loyalty to the ruler.

Both the law of the Salian Franks, the *Lex Salica*, and the law of the Bavarians, the *Lex Baiuvariorum*, were drawn in large part from late Roman military law. The new regime under the 'barbarian warlords' brought considerable legal and economic benefits to the military forces of the various rulers, including the continued beneficial tax status, whereby their properties were freed government imposts other than military service. Although not 'ethnically' Frankish in the sense championed by the scholars of the ethnogenesis school, the military forces of the new rulers, as well as the families of these fighting men in the northeastern regions of Gaul, were politically Frankish. Over time, the advantages of this Frankish political identity encouraged large numbers of Romans, and particularly those with property, to adopt a new identity as Franks. A very similar process played out in other former provinces of the Western Empire. However, despite these ostensible changes in 'ethnic' identity, which were really changes in legal identity, the population as a whole remained both Christian and Latin speaking.

Military organization of the Carolingian world

The sixth and seventh centuries saw rather frequent, but relatively small and brief, wars among the many kingdoms that developed on the remains of the erstwhile provinces of the Western Empire in Gaul, Spain, Italy, and Britain. The military resources of these successor states were limited both by the size and the wealth of their populations. No individual king commanded the resources to undertake wars of conquest on a scale similar to those that had been organized by some later Roman emperors, who put as many as 80,000 effectives into the field.

This reality is illuminated, ironically, by the decision of Emperor Justinian I (527–565), whose imperial seat was at Constantinople, to attempt to reunify the Roman Empire by military force and to eliminate the so-called barbarian kingdoms by reimposing direct imperial rule. The resources of the East Roman Empire, often denoted by scholars as the Byzantine Empire, dwarfed those of the individual western successor states. The Roman Empire in the East organized its military forces in the same manner as those in the late imperial period in the West, and continued to maintain a very large standing army, which was based throughout the empire and numbered in the neighbourhood of 200,000 men. In addition, the process of developing magnate military households had continued apace in the East, and many Byzantine generals, as well as wealthy landowners, augmented professional government forces with their own personal troops – that is, the *bucellarii*.

In 533, Justinian I dispatched a substantial fleet and army under his general Belisarius (died 565), who conquered the Vandal kingdom in North Africa, and brought this province once again under imperial rule. In 535, Justinian again dispatched an army under Belisarius to the West, on this occasion to conquer the Ostrogothic kingdom in Italy. Belisarius captured Rome in 536, but subsequently faced a difficult war of attrition against the Ostrogoths, whose military forces were deployed in the urban fortresses in northern Italy. After a fifteen-year stalemate, Justinian recalled Belisarius and dispatched his general Narses (died 574) in 551 to complete the conquest of Ostrogothic northern Italy and bring the entire peninsula back under imperial rule. Following his decisive victory at Taginae in 552, Narses was able to complete the destruction of the Ostrogothic kingdom. Even before Narses' victory in Italy, Justinian dispatched yet another army to the West in 551 under the aged government official (*patricius*) Liberius, which succeeded in conquering much of the southeast of the Iberian Peninsula, previously ruled by the Visigoths.

This series of campaigns in Italy, North Africa, and Spain by Justinian's generals were substantially larger and more complex than the military operations of any of the kings of Rome's successor states in the West during the Late Antique period. Similarly, the Muslim armies that began the conquest of North Africa in the early seventh century, and came to dominate the western Mediterranean from the mid-seventh into the later eighth century were far more formidable than any contemporary western forces. The Umayyad caliph Al-Walid (705–715) from his capital in Damascus ruled not only the wealthiest provinces of the East Roman Empire, but also regions stretching from Mesopotamia to India. By contrast, the *Regnum Francorum* governed by the mayor of the palace Pippin II (680–714), the great-grandfather of Charlemagne (768–814), encompassed only some parts of the Roman provinces of Gaul, as well as Belgica Prima and Secunda, a region that is less than a third the size of modern France.

By 800, however, the geo-political balance of forces in the western world had shifted dramatically. Pippin II's son Charles Martel (died 741), and his grandsons Carloman (retired from secular life 747 and died 754) and Pippin III (died 768), brought most of what is today France, Belgium, Holland, and parts of western Germany under their rule. In 751, Pippin III assumed the Frankish crown, with papal support, that previously had been held by the descendants of the first Merovingian king Clovis I (died 511) since the late fifth century. Pippin's son Charles, more commonly known as Charles the Great or Charlemagne, then used the military resources of the reunited *Regnum Francorum* to restore the Roman Empire of the West. Charlemagne's empire included the whole of modern France, Belgium, the Netherlands, Switzerland, and Austria, Germany as far east as the Elbe, northern and central Italy, Istria, Bohemia, Slovenia, and Hungary as far as the Danube, and finally the Iberian Peninsula as far south as the Ebro River, including the Balearic Islands. When he was crowned emperor on Christmas day at Rome in 800 by Pope Leo III (795–816), Charlemagne could justly claim to have restored the greater part of the Roman Empire in the West under Frankish rule. Pope Leo even described him as a New Constantine in official correspondence.

The human and material resources of this newly reconstituted empire in the West were immense. Its population of some twenty million – which was growing at a rapid rate, likely because of peace at home and a lengthy period of climatic warming known as the medieval climatic optimum – was significantly larger than that of the same area of the late empire during the fifth century. The concomitant economic activity produced enormous wealth, which was tapped by Charlemagne's government through a broad range of taxes. However, the greatest source of wealth of the Carolingian government consisted of the vast lands that were controlled directly or indirectly by the royal fisc. The enormous human and economic resources of the Carolingian Empire, which included approximately six million men of fighting age, permitted Charlemagne to mobilize armies on a scale not possible for rulers in the West since the mid-fifth century.

Although this is a much-debated topic among historians, many scholars agree that Charlemagne had the capacity to field armies numbering tens of thousands of troops, often with two or even three armies in the field at the same time, operating in different regions of the empire or converging on the same target from different directions in effectively planned pincer movements. From an institutional perspective, therefore, it is enormously important to understand that Carolingian armies, particularly those engaged in offensive campaigns, were organized on a very different basis than were those of the late Roman Empire.

Field armies

Despite his enormous wealth, including a vast income in coin derived from tolls, taxes, the sale of surpluses produced on royal estates, and the exploitation of silver mines both in the Harz mountains and in the Poitou from the mines at Melle, Charlemagne did not attempt to re-establish large standing armies of the types employed by his model Constantine the Great (died 337). Rather, Charlemagne's armies of conquest, like those of his father King Pippin I, were recruited from two main sources. The first and smaller element of the Carolingian armies that undertook the conquests of Aquitaine, Gascony, Lombardy and central Italy, Saxony, Bavaria, the Balkans and Adriatic region, and Catalonia consisted of the military households of the king, himself, and of Carolingian magnates, particularly ecclesiastical office holders. Charlemagne, following the pattern of Frankish kings dating back to Clovis and, indeed, to late Roman practice, maintained a very substantial number of fighting men numbering in the many thousands, on a permanent war footing. Whether this royal force, taken together with the military households of the magnates, constituted a 'standing army' is a very controversial matter because specialists in early modern history, who are largely unfamiliar with the early medieval period, insist that standing armies were reinvented in the late medieval or post-medieval world.

Like the Frankish kings, the abbots, abbesses, and bishops of the 1,200 or so royal monasteries and bishoprics located throughout the Carolingian Empire also maintained permanent military forces. Some of these institutions likely fielded relatively small forces of a few dozen to a few score men. However, many of the wealthier institutions supported a hundred or more professional fighting men in their military households. The royal monastery of St. Riquier, for example, which is located near the city of Amiens in northern France, provided housing for a hundred fighting men, as well as their horses, within the central complex of buildings associated with the convent. Information about these men, as well as the arms production facilities maintained by the monastery, is provided by an economic document known as a *polyptyque*, which records the revenues obtained from the monastery's properties. St. Riquier was a prosperous monastery of the middle rank in the early ninth century.

Much wealthier monasteries, such as the house dedicated to St. Martin at Tours, in the west of France, and the monastery of Fulda, located on the Thuringian frontier in the east of the empire, maintained military forces substantially larger than those of St. Riquier. So, too, did the exceptionally rich dioceses such as Rheims, Soissons, Cologne, Mainz, and Trier. To provide a sense of the wealth of some of these monasteries, contemporary documents make clear that the house of St. Martin at Tours, along with its sister house at Marmoutier, which were administered by Charlemagne's favoured advisor Alcuin, possessed 20,000 slaves. Fulda had under its control more than 12,000 agricultural units (*mansi*), each of which was inhabited by at least one nuclear family and its dependents, and in some cases many more than this.

The correlation between wealth and the military forces supported by ecclesiastical institutions illuminates the further development and solidification of the Late Antique transition discussed previously. The hallmarks of this transition were the move from the central government maintaining standing armies with resources provided by taxpayers throughout the empire, to a more locally based maintenance of military forces by those who had the wealth to support military households. Depending on the effectiveness of royal power, and looked at from a slightly different perspective, these military households, which were stationed at important points throughout the Empire, might be understood as locally based military forces, much the same as Roman military forces that were cantoned locally.

As corporate bodies at the local level, ecclesiastical institutions developed long-term relationships with the Frankish kings, spanning generations and even centuries. Bishoprics and those convents that came under direct royal control through the appointment of bishops and abbots, as happened very frequently during the reigns of Charlemagne and his son Louis the Pious (814–840), did not function independently of the king's policies, and this was particularly true in military affairs. This is illuminated quite clearly by Pippin I's order in 751, immediately after he became king, for inventories to be taken of all ecclesiastical lands so that the royal government could access them in various ways for military purposes. Consequently, the maintenance of permanent military forces by these institutions can be understood as resulting from an ongoing dialogue between the crown and ecclesiastical magnates regarding royal military needs.

This process of negotiation between the royal government and ecclesiastical institutions was by no means always harmonious. Many churchmen believed that they were unfairly burdened by the government and complained. In response to complaints of this type, in 744, Pippin's brother Carloman and co-mayor of the palace (*maior dominus*) told members of a Church council that his promise of a return of their lands was not possible at the time because of military exigency. In making this claim, Carloman was following the precedent set by his father Charles Martel, who, following the Merovingian custom, had 'borrowed' large quantities of property from the Church during the 730s for military purposes, an action for which he was roundly condemned by a number of ecclesiastical writers even long after his death.

In aggregate, Charlemagne's military household and those of his ecclesiastical magnates numbered in the many tens of thousands, perhaps even 70,000–80,000 men at any one time. If Charlemagne's entire royal military household, including those who served in constant attendance on the king and those who were established as garrison troops, numbered some 10,000 men, which is likely a significant underestimate, then the 1,200 or so bishoprics and royal monasteries needed to maintain fewer than sixty men on average to reach a figure of 70,000 fighting men. For ecclesiastical institutions, sixty men on average is likely a very conservative figure. There are references in contemporary documents, for example, to bishops employing military households of 500 men. One must also consider here the

700–800 counts who served at any one time during Charlemagne's reign and also maintained military households of anywhere from 20–50 men each.

In considering the assets devoted to military matters by ecclesiastical officials, it is useful to observe that Archbishop Hincmar of Rheims (845–882), who was a zealous protector of ecclesiastical privileges, argued during the reign of Charlemagne's grandson Charles the Bald (840–877) that under optimal circumstances, 40 per cent of ecclesiastical revenues should be devoted to the maintenance of the military household of a bishop or abbot. Hincmar was attempting to establish 40 per cent as a maximum for two reasons. First, Charles the Bald's government frequently demanded more than 40 per cent of the revenues of a monastery or bishopric for military purposes. The monastery of St. Germain-des-Prés, for example, recorded in its estate survey (*polyptyque*) that more than 50 per cent of its revenues were devoted to military affairs. Second, a number of contemporary ecclesiastical magnates chose to devote a higher percentage of their resources to military ends, rather than aiding the poor or maintaining the fabric of their churches, in order to curry favour with the king. In the later Carolingian era, these ecclesiastical magnates recruited very large military forces to overawe their neighbours.

Expeditionary levies

The tens of thousands of men who served on a permanent footing in the military households of the king and ecclesiastical magnates were not all available for offensive campaigns. First, many of these men had duties as garrison troops, and could not be withdrawn from their stations without risk. Second, ecclesiastical magnates were distributed across the Carolingian Empire, and it was often impractical to move large numbers of men 1,000 kilometres or more to undertake a campaign. This was not impossible, however, as is indicated by the deployment of fighting men from Bavaria and Lombardy for military operations south of the Pyrenees. Third, Charlemagne, and his successors, often undertook two or even three simultaneous campaigns in widely separated regions of the empire, and could not concentrate sufficient numbers of men that were drawn from military households in any one of these theatres of operation at the same time.

As a consequence of these realities, we once again see the Carolingian kings following in the footsteps of their Late Antique predecessors, by enforcing long-standing legal requirements that tied wealth to the obligation to perform military service. The great majority of the evidence that explicitly ties military service to wealth comes from royal orders that are recorded in documents denoted by modern scholars as capitularies. The name comes from the organization of these royal documents in chapters, called *capitula* in Latin. The preponderance of royal orders regarding military service generally, including the obligations inherent on property owners to provide military service for offensive campaigns, comes from the period after Charlemagne's imperial coronation in 800. However, the legal principle connecting military service to property ownership was certainly much older than this in the *Regnum Francorum*. This fact is made clear by references to this connection in earlier sources dating back to the sixth century, and also by the fact that Charlemagne's government denoted this obligation as age-old (i.e. as an *antiqua consuetudo*). This terminology in Carolingian legal usage meant that the government was drawing on much earlier precedents, often including Roman law such as the Theodosian Code, issued in 438.

The practical application by Carolingian authorities of the principle that property ownership entailed military service has much in common with the 'chapter' system of taxation in the late Roman Empire, discussed earlier in this chapter. The Carolingian government

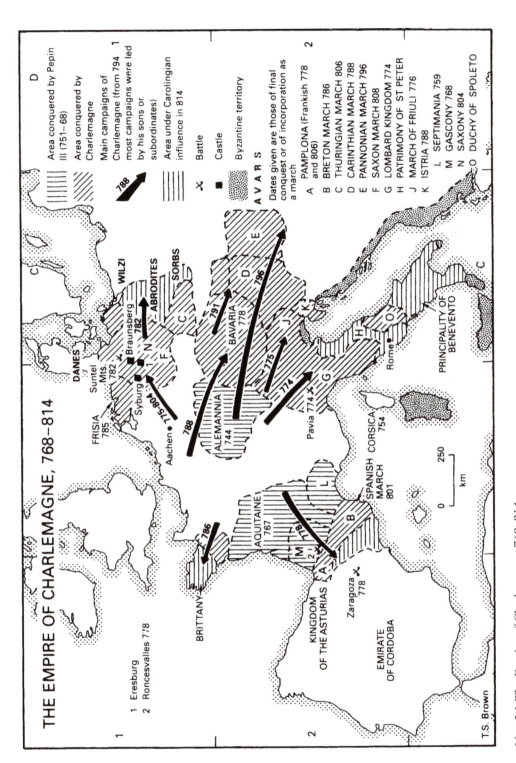

Map 3.1 The Empire of Charlemagne, 768–814
Source: *Atlas of Medieval Europe* © T.S. Brown

stipulated a measure of wealth that would obligate an individual to provide expeditionary military service. The basic measure of assessment by which obligations were determined was the *mansus*, which, in the military context, was a unit of value of production rather than a measure of surface area. A highly productive vineyard, for example, could be assessed as a *mansus*, while a much larger area of marginal farmland could be assessed at just half a *mansus*. When the imperial government required large numbers of fighting men to serve on foot, the stipulated wealth requirement was lower, in some years as low as a single *mansus*. In other years, when fewer fighting men were required, the stipulated minimum level of wealth was raised, sometimes as high as four *mansi* when bad economic conditions, such as famines, made life more difficult for everyone. The stipulated minimum wealth that would make a property owner liable for service on horseback with full armour was substantially higher, usually set at twelve *mansi*.

At the higher end of the spectrum of property owners, individuals with lands assessed in multiples of the stipulated government minimum for military service could be required to provide a number of men for the expeditionary levy – also referred to by scholars as the select levy – commensurate with their overall wealth. For example, a lay individual with 120 *mansi* might be required to send ten fully equipped mounted fighting men on campaign, or perhaps sixty men who were equipped for military service on foot. Similar to the late Roman government, Carolingian rulers put into place procedures to ensure that smaller-scale property owners did not escape the burdens of participating in offensive warfare. Individuals with properties below the stipulated minimum wealth were 'clubbed' together, when necessary, into groups of various size depending upon the current situation so that the sum of their properties added up to the governmentally mandated property minimum for service. Again, this system is quite similar in practice to the 'chapter' system of late Roman imperial taxation for military recruitment, and likely required a similar degree of administrative sophistication that could not have been much inferior to that of Rome in order to ensure that few individuals escaped their obligations.

There were, however, major differences between the Carolingian and late Roman systems of assessing property to provide military forces. First, men recruited through the *tironicum* tax were mustered into the standing Roman army, and were required to serve for twenty years. Second, the men mobilized in this manner were paid a regular salary and offered additional benefits, including land upon retirement, by the imperial government. Third, the *aurum tironicum* was assessed on property owners as a tax in cash or kind when the government did not require the provision of recruits.

In the Carolingian system, as in late Roman practice, property owners did not have to serve in person when summoned for military duty. They could provide a suitable substitute. The obligation on whoever served in the Carolingian army was for the duration of a single campaign and not a 20-year commitment. Charlemagne and his successors issued orders to government officials to ensure that the same property owners were not mobilized year after year so as to prevent them from becoming impoverished. Additionally, men serving in Carolingian armies on the basis of the military obligation inherent in owning property were not paid for this service. Rather, they were required to provide their own equipment and pay for their own supplies while on campaign, if it lasted for three months or less. Finally, the Carolingian government did not assess a tax on property owners in years when they were not summoned for military service. Despite the unfounded speculations of some scholars, the Carolingian system during Charlemagne's reign was focused entirely on the mobilization of troops, and was not a fiscal device to levy a broad-based tax on property. In effect, therefore, landowners were significantly better off financially under the Carolingian than the Roman system because they were freed from yearly taxation, and could avoid paying any monetary tax at all, even when summoned for duty, by serving in person.

Mercenaries

The Carolingian government did not have a legal vocabulary for distinguishing mercenaries from other troops, who served in the military households of magnates or the king. Undoubtedly, individuals or small groups of men were recruited for short-term contracts and could be considered mercenaries, in contrast to fighting men who made a career in the service of a single magnate. Similarly, property owners who were assessed for service on a campaign and did not wish to serve personally might find and pay substitutes to go to the army in their place. Such substitutes also might be considered mercenaries. However, the most obvious and best-recorded use of mercenaries concerns the recruitment of fighting men from outside the empire who undertook a wide range of military operations on behalf of numerous kings and emperors.

Charles Martel, Pippin III, Charlemagne, and the latter's successors established a large number of frontier regions, denoted as marches, *marchae* in Latin, which served a dual purpose of providing a defence in depth to help protect richer and more densely populated regions of the empire, and as bases of operation for raids and campaigns into lands outside the empire (see Chapter 2). Several Carolingian rulers also cultivated diplomatic and military relationships with peoples living beyond these marches for the purpose of providing yet another cordon of defence for the empire. Charlemagne and Louis the Pious, for example, provided economic and military resources to a variety of tribal leaders among the Slavic Obodrites, who lived to the east of Saxony in the region of the lower Elbe River. These Carolingian rulers hoped to use the Obodrites as a counter-weight to the aggressive aspirations of some Danish kings. Similarly, in the far southwest of the Carolingian Empire, successive Carolingian kings sought to forge short- and medium-term alliances with the Muslim emirs ruling cities in the Ebro valley, in modern Catalonia, as part of a long-term strategy, vigorously supported by the pope, to subdue the entire region and free the Christians dwelling there from Muslim rule (see Chapter 8).

In addition to establishing diplomatic and military relations with polities beyond the frontiers, in a manner similar to late Roman practice with regard to *foederati*, a number of Carolingian kings also established military colonies of foreigners within the bounds of the *Regnum Francorum*. Both Charlemagne and Louis the Pious, for example, welcomed groups of Christian immigrants from Muslim-ruled lands on the Iberian Peninsula and settled them along the Pyrenean frontier. The grants of lands to these settlers, denoted in contemporary charters as *aprisiones*, provided for a direct relationship between the colonists and the royal central government. The military colonists were not subject to the authority of the royal officials at the local level, the counts, who normally had jurisdiction over legal and other matters in the regions where the holders of the *aprisiones* were settled. Instead, these military colonists, who were settled in the region of modern Catalonia, supervised their own legal affairs. This meant, in legal and administrative terms, that they possessed immunities from the interference of the locally based comital authorities.

The West Frankish King Charles III (898–929), a grandson of Charles the Bald, made a similar arrangement with Scandinavian military colonists under the leadership of a man named Rollo. Earlier in his career, Rollo had participated in numerous raids and campaigns into the West Frankish kingdom, including the siege of Paris in 886. In 911, Rollo was defeated by West Frankish forces, and subsequently made a treaty with Charles III.

According to the terms of the pact, Rollo received a royal appointment to settle his followers in the region around the mouth of the Seine River, and received legal and military authority from the Carolingian king to govern this district. From the perspective of Charles III, Rollo's task was to guard the Seine estuary from still predatory bands of Viking raiders. This agreement with Rollo was one of many undertaken by Carolingian rulers with Viking leaders. However, Rollo's descendants were able to forge a powerful principality from their base at Rouen, eventually coming to control the broad region that came to be known as Normandy. One of Rollo's descendants, Duke William II of Normandy, conquered the English kingdom in 1066 and became more famous as William the Conqueror.

Institutions for local defence

As described earlier in the chapter, the policies of the late Roman government led to the militarization of vast numbers of erstwhile civilians for the purposes of local defence, in both rural and urban contexts. This militarization continued apace throughout the Late Antique period, and was a fact of life for virtually every able-bodied male in the Carolingian Empire, with the exception of those, such as monks and priests, who were prohibited by both canon and secular law from bearing arms and even from hunting. Numerous contemporary sources, however, indicate that prohibitions on both arms-bearing and hunting by priests and monks were largely ineffectual, so that they too sometimes played a role in the local defence.

When enemy forces entered the region, officials with the responsibility for local defence, usually the count or one of his subordinate officials, such as the *centenarii*, had the legal authority to mobilize the entire local community. In some cases, ecclesiastical office holders such as abbots or bishops were given an immunity from comital oversight, and had the authority granted to them by the king to mobilize those men living on their lands for the local defence. In most cases, these ecclesiastical officials relied upon a secular agent, sometimes denoted as an advocate, who commanded the local levies on their behalf.

During the reign of Charlemagne, there was little need for the mobilization of militia forces to undertake the defence of local regions, except on the Saxon and Muslim frontiers. However, increasingly over the course of the ninth and then the tenth century, the Carolingian Empire, and the kingdoms that emerged from it following the territorial division of 843 in the Treaty of Verdun, suffered significant attacks from raiders in the north, south, and east, at the hands of large numbers of Vikings, Muslims, and Magyars, respectively. As seen in Chapter 2, in order to meet these challenges, the Carolingian kings and their successors undertook a significant programme of fortress construction, so as to provide both refuges for the population, and constrict the movement of enemy forces using the techniques of defence in depth.

In order to effectuate these policies, the entire male population, and likely women as well, were required to participate in the military preparedness of their regions in other ways, as well. The three chief obligations which were imposed by the government were the maintenance of roads, the maintenance of bridges, and the repair and upkeep of fortifications. These duties, which also reached back to the late Roman period, were given formal and detailed enunciation in a wide range of government documents. The most famous of these is the Edict of Pîtres, issued by the Carolingian King Charles the Bald in 864. The text of this lengthy royal order (see Chapter 2) stipulates a number of universal obligations on the population living within Charles' kingdom, which encompassed the western third of Charlemagne's empire, and includes most of the territory of modern France. These included the aforementioned duties to work on bridges and maintain fortifications. Similar enunciations of these universal obligations to participate in the defence of the local region through the maintenance of the military infrastructure are found in numerous Anglo-Saxon documents, which denote these as the *trinoda necessitas*, or threefold obligation.

Impact of Carolingian military organization

As the dominant political, economic, cultural, and military power in the Latin West, the Carolingian Empire exerted enormous influence on its neighbours. This was particularly true with regard to military matters. Later Anglo-Saxon England, for example, has been described by the late James Campbell – one of the leading scholars of early English history – as a Carolingian-type state. This was certainly the case with respect to the military organization of the kingdom of Wessex as seen during the reign of Alfred the Great (died 899) and his successors, which served as the nucleus for the development of a unified Anglo-Saxon kingdom in England over the course of the tenth century.

Faced with the onslaught of Viking raids, and then armies of conquest, the kings of Wessex forged a highly integrated set of military institutions that drew heavily upon the model found across the English Channel in the contemporary *Regnum Francorum*. A key element in the defence of Wessex, as seen in Chapter 2, was the system of fortresses, which were provided with both permanent garrisons and also afforded the local population a refuge from Viking attacks. The permanent garrisons that were discussed in the *Burghal Hidage* were comprised of troops who were supported by very heavy taxes that were imposed on the populations living in the immediate region, and collected on a prescribed number of hides, which may be understood as the Anglo-Saxon version of the *mansus*. These permanent garrisons had much in common with the military colonists established by the Carolingian kings along their frontiers, who also were provided with lands to support them.

The garrison troops denoted in the *Burghal Hidage*, however, were just one element in the defensive system used by the kings of Wessex to preserve their kingdom. In addition, all able-bodied men were required to serve in the defence of their local region. This institution was denoted in contemporary sources as the *fyrd*, and is usually described by scholars as a great *fyrd* or general levy. It seems unlikely that this universal obligation for military service represents a preservation of late Roman legal practice, given the loss of so many other elements of continuity with Roman Britain during the course of the fifth and sixth centuries. It is far more likely that this institution also drew on the nearby Frankish models, whether Merovingian or Carolingian. Whatever the inspiration for establishing the universal obligation on all men to defend their home districts, this institution was destined to endure. A large part of the army commanded by Harold Godwinson at Hastings in 1066, for example, was drawn from local levies. Indeed, as will be seen in what follows, militia service for local defence retained its military viability in one or another form through the remainder of the medieval millennium.

Concomitant with the great *fyrd*, the kings of Wessex also established, or perhaps reinforced, an existing obligation on property owners to serve outside their home districts in the armies of the king, or his chosen representative. As was true in the contemporary Carolingian world, this obligation was based on the overall wealth of an individual or ecclesiastical institution. As a consequence, an individual or monastery with more property had a greater military obligation than one with less property. Those individuals with less property than the stipulated minimum were grouped together so that their aggregate property amounted to the value that was required to send one man off on campaign. This system recalls both

Carolingian and Roman models. Anglo-Saxon rulers used several different terms to denote the assessed value of property, the most common of which was the hide. This term, like the *mansus*, discussed previously, denoted, when used for military assessments, the economic productivity of a property, generally thought to be sufficient to support a single family, rather than its geographic extent.

There is some disagreement among scholars regarding the basis of the obligation on property owners to go on campaign. Some view this system as an aspect of lordship, meaning that wealthy and powerful local magnates brought their personal retainers and tenants on campaign because of the personal service that the magnates owed to the king. In turn, the retainers and tenants went on campaign because of the personal loyalty that they had to their local lord. The power of the king, in this model, was based on his position as the highest lord in the land. By contrast, other scholars argue that the system of recruitment for service on campaign, an institution often denoted as the select *fyrd* to differentiate it from the great *fyrd*, was based on the legal obligation of all subjects of the king in relation to their wealth. The connection in this system is between the king and each and every property owner in the kingdom, without the mediation of intermediary levels of lordship. In our view, the latter interpretation is correct. First, the existing written evidence in the form of both narrative texts and charters explicitly ties military service to an obligation to the king. Second, in the most likely model for the Anglo-Saxon institution – that is, the Carolingian Empire – the obligation on property owners to provide military service is clearly a legal one that is enunciated by the king, and is enforced by royal officials.

One area of likely innovation in Anglo-Saxon England is the explicit extension of *fyrd* service to the fleet. Coastal communities were given the responsibility of maintaining ships for both coastal defence and for offensive campaigns. Instead of mobilizing men to serve on campaign, properties valued in aggregate at 300 hides were grouped together, and the owners of these lands were required to build, maintain, and crew a single ship. The Anglo-Saxon kings were the only rulers in Europe who had a more or less permanent navy at their disposal. Although it should be noted that during the latter third of his reign, Charlemagne also used local and select levies, as well as household forces, in various regions of the empire to serve at sea and on rivers.

The impact of Carolingian models can also be seen on the other end of the Latin West in Moravia, which is located in regions of the modern Czech Republic, as well as in Slovakia and Austria. In contrast to the Anglo-Saxons, who maintained positive diplomatic relations with the Carolingian kings and emperors, the Moravians regularly engaged in war with the *Regnum Francorum* throughout most of the ninth century. It is not known what type of military organization the Moravians possessed before they came into contact with the Franks. However, in the course of many wars against the armies of Louis the Pious, and then his son Louis the German (840–876), the Moravians developed a tripartite set of military institutions that mirrored those of their western neighbour. All able-bodied men were required to serve in defence of their home regions. In practice, this meant in defence of the system of massive fortifications that the Moravian rulers constructed to defend their territories against Carolingian invasions. The wealthier members of society also were required to serve in the army of the Moravian rulers when they invaded Carolingian territory. The core of these expeditionary armies was comprised of the military households of the Moravian rulers, and their leading magnates. It is almost certainly the case that the Moravians, who maintained significant trading and diplomatic relationships with the Carolingian Empire alongside their regular military interactions, developed these military institutions through a process of cultural assimilation with their western neighbours.

Military organization in the post-Carolingian West

Following the Treaty of Verdun in 843, the Carolingian Empire was divided into three parts among Lothair I, Louis the German, and Charles the Bald, the three surviving sons of Louis the Pious. Subsequently, over the course of the later ninth and tenth centuries, the kingdoms in the west and central portions of the empire, inherited by Charles and Lothair I, respectively, dissolved into numerous sub-kingdoms and more or less autonomous principalities. In the east, the kingdom that was forged by Louis the German not only remained intact, but became the hegemonic power in the Latin West under Louis' descendants, and then under two new dynasties, the Ottonians (919–1024) and the Salians (1024–1124). Strikingly, throughout the lands that once comprised Charlemagne's empire, and in the new territories that were conquered by the kings of East Francia/Germany, the tripartite Carolingian military system remained the dominant form of military organization.

'Feudalism' revised

Until recently, scholarly works treating the military organization of post-Carolingian Europe presented a much different image. In the nineteenth and for much of the twentieth century, scholars described the period after the end of the Carolingian Empire as the beginning of the 'feudal' age. In this model, the large-scale participation of the male population in the local defence of their regions, and the mobilization of individuals or groups of small-scale property owners for service in expeditionary levies, came to an end. Instead, it was thought that relatively small numbers of aristocrats, with their armed followings, came to dominate warfare. These fighting men, often denoted by scholars as 'warriors' to indicate the supposed primitive nature of their combat techniques and military organization, were all mounted. Indeed, the entire 'feudal age' is depicted as an era of small-scale warfare or even feuds in which a few hundred, or even a few dozen, mounted warrior aristocrats and their so-called 'feudal' retainers fought for control over 'feudal' castles and the 'feudal' peasants or serfs who lived in the environs of these castles. Indeed, some scholars still see military campaigns as being reduced to short raids into the neighbouring lord's lands, and battles as armed scrums of mounted warriors in which individual heroics counted for far more than discipline or tactics. Scholars following this line of argument also often claim that killing one's noble opponents was frowned upon by a society that took 'chivalry', that is a sort of war model for gentlemen, quite seriously.

The feudal construct received a significant blow in the 1970s following the publication of Elizabeth Brown's enormously influential article, 'The Tyranny of a Construct', which called into question the value of feudalism as an explanatory model for any aspect of medieval history, much less military organization. Subsequently, Susan Reynolds published a highly regarded rebuttal of the feudalism model in her massively detailed and comprehensive study *Fiefs and Vassals*. Although a few scholars still hold fast to the out-dated 'feudal' concept, most scholarly debate in the Anglo-American tradition regarding the political, and particularly the military, organization of Europe in the period before the First Crusade (1095–1099) focuses on the relative effectiveness of public – that is, governmental – authority rather than on the dissolution and privatization of this power into the hands of regional or even local magnates. By contrast, many continental scholars still are mired in a 'feudal' model.

Scholarly discussion of warfare in the post-Carolingian period has benefitted considerably from the jettisoning of the intellectual straitjacket imposed by the feudal construct. The

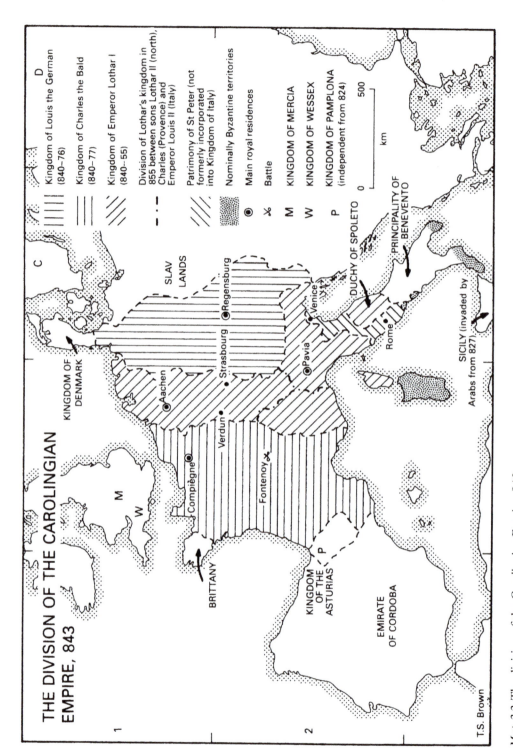

Map 3.2 The division of the Carolingian Empire, 843

Source: *Atlas of Medieval Europe* © T.S. Brown

recognition that military forces were not limited to small 'war bands' of aristocrats has permitted a re-evaluation of narrative sources that illuminate the participation of broad sections of the male population in the conduct of war, not only in the defence of their home districts, but on campaign, as well. One crucial insight has been the recognition that virtually all narrative sources were written for and/or by aristocrats, including large numbers of texts that were composed by aristocratic clerics.

As discussed in Chapter 1, the interests and biases of authors played a decisive role in the information that they chose to include and exclude from their narratives, and also the ways in which they present warfare. Consequently, the enormous emphasis on aristocrats in narrative texts and also in artistic works such as the Bayeux Tapestry is explained, in large part, by the fact that the audiences for these works desired to hear about themselves, their families, and their friends in a glorious or at least a very favourable light while significantly slighting the lower orders of society. However, even given this thorough-going bias towards including large amounts of information about aristocrats in their texts, the authors of narrative works, in order to remain plausible, nevertheless devoted considerable attention to the participation of the lower social orders in warfare. They did so because it frequently was the goal of these authors to provide a realistic frame in which to make particular claims about the aristocratic heroes of their narratives. An important goal of these authors was to persuade their audiences that these historical narratives were trustworthy and, therefore, the claims made on behalf of the heroes of these works also were trustworthy. Scholars call this stylistic device the rhetoric of plausibility.

A second, and even more important, factor leading to a re-evaluation of the nature of post-Carolingian military organization has been the enormous surge of information provided by excavations of fortifications, and the broader dissemination of this information from archaeologists to historians. Specialists in military history today have vastly more information about the number, distribution, size, and construction of fortifications in the Latin West, the Slavic lands to their east, in Britain, and in Scandinavia than was the case just thirty years ago (see Chapter 2). It has become increasingly clear that the capture and defence of fortifications dominated medieval warfare in the post-Carolingian era. Mounted forces, particularly small mounted forces of so-called warrior aristocrats, had a very limited role to play in this type of warfare. Rather, just as had been true under the Carolingians and in Late Antiquity, large armies of men on foot were required to besiege and defend strongholds whose walls ranged in size from circuits of just a few hundred metres to several thousand metres, or even more for some of the great fortress cities of Roman origin. The preponderance of the fighting men in these large armies for offensive purposes was drawn from expeditionary levies rather than from the military households of the king or magnates, while on the defence, members of local levies also participated in large numbers.

The German Kingdom

The Ottonian dynasty came to power in the eastern third of the erstwhile Carolingian Empire with the accession to the throne of Henry I (919–936), who had been the leading magnate in Saxony since 912. During his reign, and that of his son Emperor Otto I (936–973, crowned emperor 962), Ottonian armies waged war from the banks of the Seine in the west to the Oder River in the east, and from the Adriatic and Mediterranean seas in the south to the Baltic Sea in the north. In the course of dozens of lengthy campaigns of conquest, these armies defeated Lotharingians, West Franks, Danes, Obodrites, Weleti, Sorbs, Bohemians, Hungarians, Lombards, and Byzantines. These campaigns included the

Map 3.3 The Ottonian Empire, 962
Source: *Atlas of Medieval Europe* © R. Samson

sieges of hundreds of fortified sites, including more than a dozen fortress cities of Roman origin, and led to the conquest of almost the entirety of the middle kingdom acquired by Lothair I following the Treaty of Verdun, as well as the vast region between the Elbe and Oder rivers, which had never been controlled by their Carolingian predecessors.

Campaign forces

These early Ottonian armies of conquest, like those of Charlemagne, consisted of two elements. The numerically smaller element included the royal military household, and the military households of secular and particularly ecclesiastical magnates. The military households of the Ottonian kings themselves also were comprised of two elements. The majority of the men, who were drawn from the lower social orders, and indeed, some of whom were unfree (*servi*), were supported directly by the king in and around one or another royal palace, and were ready to move on a moment's notice. It is notable that the Ottonians followed Carolingian practice in recruiting unfree men to serve in this manner. These men were housed and fed as part of the royal court and travelled around the kingdom and beyond with the king. Many younger sons and nephews of aristocrats also served in this element of the military household as officers. After demonstrating their competence, some of these aristocrats went back to their families and took up command positions in the military households of their fathers or uncles. Others remained in royal service and often were granted lands, particularly in frontier regions, where they were expected to recruit and support additional fighting men for the king's military household. In some extraordinary cases, simple fighting men also could reap very rich rewards in royal service. For example, the tenth-century chronicler Widukind of Corvey recorded in his *Deeds of the Saxons* that a soldier named Hosed received twenty *mansi* from Otto I as a reward for killing the Obodrite king Stoinef in 955. Similarly, a royal charter issued by Otto I in 951 records that a soldier named Walpert received a substantial award of property for his service against the Slavs. However, such heroes were the exception rather than the rule.

When the Ottonian kings went to war, they also summoned the military households of their magnates to go on campaign. A rare surviving administrative document from this period, dating to the reign of Emperor Otto II (973–983), the so-called *indiculus loricatorum*, illuminates the process by which these magnate military households were mobilized for service in the king's army. In the spring of 982, Otto II undertook a campaign against the Muslim emir of Sicily Abu al-Qasim in southern Italy. Following his initial march over the Alps with a large army drawn from the military households of his secular and ecclesiastical magnates, as well as expeditionary levies, Otto II dispatched orders back to Germany to summon reinforcements from these and other officials. The *indiculus* was produced by the king's chancery to summarize these military summonses of reinforcements, and survived completely by chance. The *indiculus* records that just under 2,000 heavily armed mounted fighting men (*loricati*), as well as their support troops, were to be dispatched to Italy as reinforcements (*supplementum*) by the forty-seven magnates listed in the document, who provided contingents of *loricati* ranging in size from 12–100 men in addition to the men who originally had been sent the previous year.

The kings of the Ottonian dynasty were very concerned to assure that their magnates had sufficient numbers of fighting men to serve the military needs of the kingdom. As a result, the Ottonians devoted considerable economic resources to ensuring that their magnates could support substantial military households. To this end, all of the kings of this dynasty, like the Merovingians and Carolingians before them, 'borrowed' lands from individual ecclesiastical institutions, and transferred the possession of these properties, although not their ownership, to secular magnates with instructions that these economic resources were to be used to recruit and maintain fighting men. The Ottonian kings also transferred considerable landed assets to favoured ecclesiastical institutions with similar instructions that the abbots and bishops were to use their new sources of revenue to increase the size of their military households. As was the case with regard to their own household troops, when the Ottonians made property grants, these were situated in recently conquered frontier regions, so that the new landowners would have a strong interest in investing in military personnel, as well as infrastructure such as fortifications and roads. Because many of the men serving in the military households of the secular and ecclesiastical magnates in the Ottonian kingdom were drawn from the lower orders of society, they were in position to enhance their wealth by serving on the frontier and acquiring property there. However, as was true of the royal military household, officers in these magnate military households very often were recruited from among the aristocracy.

Some scholars reject the term 'officers' to denote the commanders of fighting men, arguing that this is anachronistic and suggests to uninformed readers that medieval military leaders attended military academies such as West Point or Sandhurst. In our view, however, it is far more misleading not to provide a clear term to denote the men who had the legal responsibility to command fighting men. Contemporary documents generally use the terms *principes* and *praefecti* to distinguish the leaders from the rank and file among the soldiers in the royal and magnate military households. The terms prince or prefect clearly do not have the appropriate connotation in English. It would be equally misleading to denote such men simply as magnates or aristocrats because their status as *principes militum* or *praefecti militum* was based on a position in a military organization rather than on a general level of wealth or social significance. Consequently, the term officer seems quite appropriate, particularly given the fact that the term officer is derived from the Latin word *officium* – that is, an office – which usually was military in nature.

In aggregate, the military households of the king and magnates in the East Frankish/ German kingdom numbered in the many thousands of professional soldiers, by which we mean men who earned their living serving under arms. Indeed, in light of the vast numbers of fortifications that were garrisoned by these professional fighting men during the tenth century (see Chapter 2), these forces almost certainly numbered in the tens of thousands. However, it was never possible to mobilize all of these men at one time for a single military campaign, not least because of their vital service protecting the frontiers of the kingdom, and maintaining control in newly conquered lands. Consequently, just as was true of their Carolingian predecessors, the Ottonian kings also drew very heavily on the expeditionary levies of their kingdom. For the most part, these fighting men, who continued to owe military service on the basis of the property they owned or under some type of contract, were required to serve on campaigns nearby the regions in which they lived. The men of Lotharingia, for example, frequently were deployed in the neighbouring West Frankish kingdom, while the men of Saxony were deployed against the Slavs to their east. Nevertheless, the Ottonian kings mobilized forces from throughout their realm for campaigns of extraordinary size. Otto I, Otto II, Otto III (983–1002), and Henry II (1002–1024), for example, all drew on expeditionary levies from across the entire kingdom for major campaigns south of the Alps in Italy.

Contemporary chroniclers were well aware of the distinction between the professional forces of the military households of the king and magnates, on the one hand, and the expeditionary levies on the other. To denote the professional fighting men, chroniclers used the term *milites*, which was the basic classical Latin term for soldier in the Roman Empire. By contrast, chroniclers denoted the members of the expeditionary levies as the men of a certain city or region. These authors frequently used the juxtaposition of the *milites* of the bishop, and the men of the bishop's city to make social or political observations that would be of interest to their audiences. The distinction in the terminology used to denote particular types of fighting men, particularly the use of the term *milites* to denote the professional soldiers of magnate and royal military households, is found both in narrative sources and in contemporary legal documents.

Ottonian kings occasionally augmented the forces available from military households and expeditionary levies through the employment of troops that might be considered mercenaries. One of the most notorious figures in the Ottonian kingdom during the mid-tenth century was the Saxon nobleman Wichmann Billung the Younger (died 967). Resentful of the decision by Otto I to deprive his branch of the Billung family of important and lucrative military commands in Saxony, Wichmann rebelled several times against his king. In the process, Wichmann became an important military advisor to a number of Slavic princes, and eventually came to lead a force of fighting men in his own right, against both Slavic and German adversaries.

Because of Wichmann's expertise in the political and military affairs of the trans-Elben Slavs, Otto I's celebrated frontier commander Gero (died 965) decided in the early 960s to make use of the renegade to further the king's interests. He, therefore, employed Wichmann to campaign against a number of Slavic rulers, including most notably Miesco, who was emerging in this period as the leader of the people that would later become known as the Poles in the lands east of the Oder. Wichmann successfully carried out these missions, and even succeeded in killing Miesco's brother in combat. Ultimately, however, Wichmann was released from Ottonian service following Gero's death in 965, and was defeated in battle by Miesco in 967, and subsequently killed.

King Henry II, the last of the Ottonian rulers, employed mercenaries on a far larger scale. Henry repeatedly made agreements with a Slavic people known as the Liutizi to attack the Polish kingdom, ruled by Boleslav Chrobry (967–1025), the son of Miesco I. Boleslav posed a significant danger to Henry, several times invading the eastern regions of the German kingdom, and providing diplomatic and military support to German magnates, who were opposed to Henry II's rule. What was striking about Henry II's decision to employ the Liutizi in this manner was that they were pagans, while Boleslav was a Christian king. Consequently, contemporary chroniclers, including those who were normally very positive in their portrayal of Henry II's reign, roundly condemned him for what was seen as a sacrilegious act. This condemnation was even more vehement when Henry deployed forces of Liutizi to put down a revolt in Lotharingia, which was centred on the city of Metz, whose bishop Dietrich II (1006–1047) was the king's brother in law.

Local defence

Contemporary with their extensive wars of conquest, the Ottonian kings regularly faced the need to defend their territory against both invasion from abroad and threats to their power at home. To address these military challenges, the Ottonians drew upon the institutions for local defence that they inherited from their Carolingian predecessors. Of considerable importance was the ongoing obligation on all able-bodied men to participate in the defence of their region, either under the command of the count of the district in which they lived, denoted either as a *pagus* or *gau*, or under the command of another individual to whom the king had delegated royal authority. The latter included not only ecclesiastical magnates, such as abbots, abbesses, and bishops, but also some laymen who did not otherwise hold public office.

For the most part, these local levies were intended to be deployed in defence of the wide range of fortifications that were constructed along the frontiers and within the interior of the East Frankish/German kingdom. Many of these strongholds, denoted in German as *Fluchtburgen*, provided a refuge not only for fighting men, but also the entire local population, as well as farm animals, food supplies, and equipment, such as ploughs and wagons. In order to assure that sufficient numbers of well-maintained fortifications were available for the local defence, the entire population also was subject to labour duties, which included the maintenance and even the *de novo* construction of strongholds. Once again, the authority to mobilize this labour duty rested in the hands of officials who held power delegated to them by the king. A number of royal charters issued during the tenth century make clear that these labour obligations fell not only on the poor and small landowners, but on major landowners, as well. It is likely, however, that wealthy property owners dispatched their dependents to carry out construction work rather than undertaking this labour themselves. Of course, the employment of workers in this manner was not without cost, as their labour was lost to their lord when they were called into government service.

The most well-known group of property owners who had the requirement not only to build, but also to garrison, fortifications are the *agrarii milites*, who are briefly discussed by the Saxon monk and author Widukind of Corvey. Scholars have devoted enormous attention to Widukind's comments that all of the able-bodied men along the Saxon frontier with the Slavs were organized by King Henry I into nine-man groups, with one man from each group being responsible for helping to construct fortifications, while the other eight were to support him and his family with food and supplies. Some scholars saw in these men as a special group of royal retainers designated as the king's free men, while other scholars have conceptualized these men as a remnant of old-Germanic free peasants who had not yet succumbed to aristocratic oppression. In reality, Widukind's comments almost certainly reflect the broad-based obligation of all subjects within the Ottonian kingdom to participate in the local defence, an obligation that, as we have seen, can be dated to the later Roman Empire.

Influences on the East

As discussed in Chapter 2, the eastern expansion of the Carolingian Empire, and subsequently the Ottonian kingdom, provoked profound developments in the military infrastructure of their eastern neighbours. The Moravians, Bohemians, Sorbs, Obodrites, and others built extensive networks of fortresses in an effort to block the advance of western armies and to preserve their own independence. The mobilization of the resources necessary to undertake this defensive network led to the concomitant strengthening of the rulers in these regions. As seen previously, the rulers of the Moravians were able to establish a Carolingian-style tripartite military organization during the course of the ninth century. During the tenth century, it is clear that the advances of Henry I and particularly Otto I across the Elbe and the conquest of the region between the Elbe and Oder had a similar impact on the military organization of the nascent Polish state, which was developing in the lands east of the Oder River.

A first-hand account of Polish military organization is provided by a Jewish traveller and merchant named Abraham ben Jacob, mentioned in Chapter 2, who made an epic journey from Spain through Western Europe and the Slavic lands, before ultimately arriving in

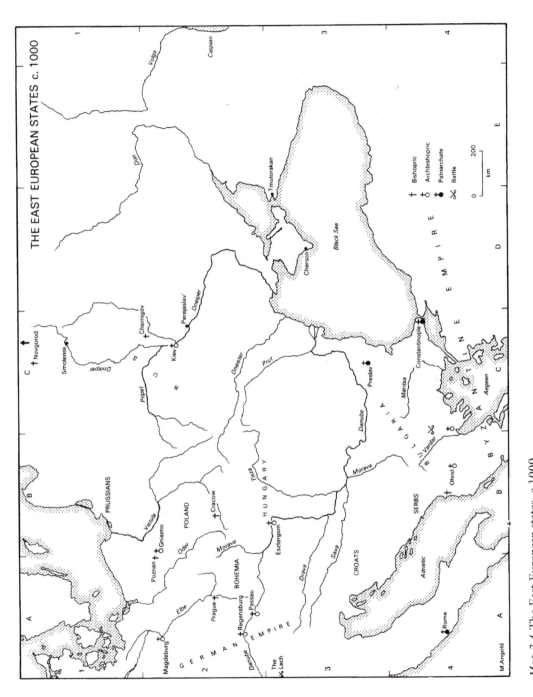

Map 3.4 The East European states, c.1000

Source: *Atlas of Medieval Europe* © M. Angold

Constantinople by way of the lands of the Rus. Abraham, who wrote in Arabic, was very positively impressed by the military household of Miesco I, which he presents as being highly organized. In his description, which treats affairs around 965, Abraham wrote, with perhaps some exaggeration, on the social customs associated with this organization:

> With respect to the land of Miesco, it is the largest of the lands and it is rich in wheat, meat, honey, and fish. He receives his taxes in minted money. He uses this to support his men. Each man receives a fixed sum every month. He has 3,000 armoured riders. These are the soldiers. One hundred of these are worth 10,000 other men. He gives the men clothing, horses, arms, and everything that they need. If one of the men has a child, he immediately orders that the child be given support whether it is a boy or girl. And when the child reaches maturity, he obtains a wife for him if it is a man and gives a dowry to the father of the girl. If it is a girl, then he marries her, himself, and gives the dowry to the father.[3]

This model of recruiting and providing for all of the needs of fighting men to serve in the royal military household closely resembles Ottonian practice, and it seems likely that Miesco borrowed very heavily from the model provided by his western neighbour.

Military organization in the post-Carolingian West

In sharp contrast with the political situation in the East Frankish/German kingdom, during the tenth and eleventh century, the power of the kings in the west of the erstwhile Carolingian Empire declined precipitously. They were reduced to controlling only a small number of territories located between the Loire and Somme rivers. They were not even in full control of the supposed centre of their power, the Ile de France. Indeed, many contemporaries marvelled that these western kings lacked the ability to compel obedience from their subjects who dwelled more than a day's ride from their capital in the late Roman fortress city of Paris.

This rapid decline in the fortune of the West Frankish kings was due, in large part, to the rapid series of deaths in the Carolingian royal family following the demise of Charles the Bald in 877. His successor, Louis II, died just two years later, in 879. Louis II's sons Louis III and Carloman II, aged just 14 and 13 at the time, were both dead by 884. Louis II's posthumous son Charles III was unable to accede to his inheritance until 898 at the age of 19. During this disastrous period for the Carolingian family, the West Frankish realm faced sustained assaults by Viking raiders. Government officials faced the necessity of opposing these depredations without effective royal support. As a result of more or less effective resistance, often based on the principle of creating a defence in depth through the construction of fortifications throughout the lands under their jurisdiction, these local government officials gained a significant degree of support from local magnates. In most cases, the officials who undertook the defence of the local districts against the Vikings, and other raiders such as the Bretons, were counts, although some were only viscounts.

When the royal government functioned effectively, these counts were supported by the king and served at his pleasure. However, as the West Frankish kings failed to fulfil their governmental responsibilities, and particularly to defend their realm, the counts, and

---

3 Georg Jacob, *Ibn Jaʿqûbs Bericht über die Slawenlande vom Jahre 973* (Kiel, 1928) in *Widukind: Sächsische Geschichten*, ed. and trans. into German by Paul Hirsch (Leipzig, 1931), 179–195.

sometimes lower ranking functionaries, usurped royal authority. These erstwhile royal officials at the local level continued to exercise government functions, including adjudicating
legal cases, collecting taxes, and above all defending the people under their jurisdiction.
Some of these former government officials established dynasties and created territorial principalities in which they usurped not only former royal fiscal assets, but also the resources of
many wealthy ecclesiastical institutions that had been under royal protection. Among the
most successful of these new regional polities were Anjou, Flanders, Normandy, and the
Poitou, whose counts were also dukes of Aquitaine.

The effective disappearance of royal power throughout the greater part of the West Frankish kingdom did not affect substantively the basic organization of the armed forces that had
been the hallmark of Carolingian military organization. In the west of France, for example,
the newly established counts of Anjou maintained a substantial military household. In fact,
they did so in a manner consistent with their previous obligations to the Carolingian kings
to provide military forces for campaign duty concomitant with their wealth. In addition, the
counts of Anjou used the long-standing legal obligation of the inhabitants of their region,
enunciated clearly in the Edict of Pîtres discussed earlier in this chapter, to provide for
the common defence by constructing, maintaining, and garrisoning scores of fortifications,
including both wooden and stone structures. Counts Geoffrey Greymantle (960–987) and
his son Fulk Nerra (987–1040) used this extensive system of fortifications, along with the
military obligations of the populations they ruled, to establish a powerful principality that
was more than twice the size of the original *pagus* centred on the Roman fortress city of
Angers, which was also an important river port on the Loire.

In contrast to the counts of Anjou, whose ancestors had long been in Carolingian royal
service, the military organization of the rulers of Normandy provides a particularly illuminating example of the enormous influence exercised by the institutions of the Carolingian
royal government. The West Frankish kings lost control to local usurpers over the five
counties along the English Channel, which ultimately would form the territorial core of
Normandy, during the later tenth century. In 911, Charles III granted the right to rule this
entire region to the Viking leader Rollo as an agent of the Carolingian king, as discussed
previously. His brief was to protect the region from further Viking attacks, and also to nor-
malize the administration of these counties in the traditional Carolingian manner, which
consisted in part of providing military support for the king. Consistent with this agreement,
Rollo made no effort to impose Scandinavian institutions in the lands that he ruled on
behalf of Charles III. Many of the higher ranking members of Rollo's army, some of whom
commanded military households of their own, were granted lands within the future duchy
of Normandy, and were assimilated into the indigenous group of lay and secular magnates.
An important element of this process was the establishment of a substantial number of
these magnates as subordinate officials (viscounts) to assist Rollo, who was given the title
of count. His descendants subsequently inflated this title to that of duke. It was these government officials, as well as other wealthy landowners, including important ecclesiastical
officials, who provided the professional core of the armies of Rollo and his successors.

Like their Angevin neighbours, Rollo and his successors built large numbers of strongholds to defend Normandy against invaders and also used this strategy to gain control of
territory outside of the original grant of five counties made by Charles III. The garrisoning
of these strongholds generally was left in the hands of the magnates and their households
of professional soldiers, usually denoted in ninth and tenth century sources as *milites*. However, when these *milites* were ordered to deploy for offensive operations in the army of
Rollo and his successors, or in the armies of the Angevin counts such as Fulk Nerra, they

were replaced by local levies, usually denoted in the sources as *rustici* (i.e. rural men) or *villani* (i.e. inhabitants of rural estates called *villae*).

Military organization in the crusading age

Beginning from a high demographic and economic base during the Carolingian period, Europe experienced a sustained period of growth in population and wealth from the eleventh through the late thirteenth centuries. These positive trends resulted from several 'virtuous cycles'. In the pre-modern West, the vast majority of wealth was produced in the agricultural sector. Each individual cultivator produced a small surplus, so that as the population grew, the aggregate surplus also grew. This relationship between population growth and economic growth only holds insofar as additional lands can be brought into cultivation, so it is telling that the period considered in this section saw the most extensive pattern of deforestation in European history to date. In human terms, having more food meant that more women had the strength to survive numerous childbirths and children had the strength to survive early diseases and grow up to have children of their own, gradually causing overpopulation in the long-settled 'core' areas of Europe. On the eve of the First Crusade, Pope Urban II (1088–1099) called attention to this situation in urging Western Europeans to recover those parts of the Byzantine Empire that had been lost to the Muslims. The population pressure identified by the pope and others both pushed and pulled people into previously unsettled regions, supporting the ongoing process of both demographic and economic growth.

Several factors contributed to the virtuous cycle of population growth and the expansion of arable lands for farming. First, a wide range of technologies for improving agricultural productivity became much more broadly disseminated throughout much of Europe. As a consequence, the model of simple production was modified by technology and increased per capita productivity. These technological advances included the three-field crop rotation system that led to higher yields, and to increasing variety of crop types, and improved harnesses that permitted the more effective use of horses as draft animals, which themselves increased in size and strength because of surplus cereal production. Other advances included improved designs for ploughs, and the great expansion of water mills, as well as the introduction of wind mills. In addition, Europe during this period experienced what historical climatologists denote as the 'medieval optimum'. This climate pattern, when temperatures averaged 2–3 degrees Celsius (3.5–5.5 degrees Fahrenheit) warmer than they are in Europe today, lengthened growing seasons and permitted the introduction of valuable crops into regions that heretofore had been untenable. This included, for example, the planting of vineyards in northern England and the cultivation of cereal crops in northern Norway.

Concomitant with these sustained and significant increases in population and wealth, Europe experienced considerable political developments that had important implications for the conduct of war and military organization. Of particular importance was the gradual rise of powerful monarchies in France, Aragon, and Castile, and the creation of a new 'Angevin Empire' with its anchor in the English kingdom. By contrast, civil wars and conflicts with the papacy led to the political fragmentation of the German kingdom, and the rise of powerful, autonomous principalities, including a group of city-states along the Rhine River such as Cologne, Mainz, and Worms, all of which were former Roman fortress cities. These centuries also witnessed a great period of urban development from Iberia in the west to Poland in the east.

However, the most striking change, and the one that gives its name to this era, was the rise of the crusading movement, which saw very large Christian armies campaign with considerable success against Muslim states across the length and breadth of the Mediterranean.

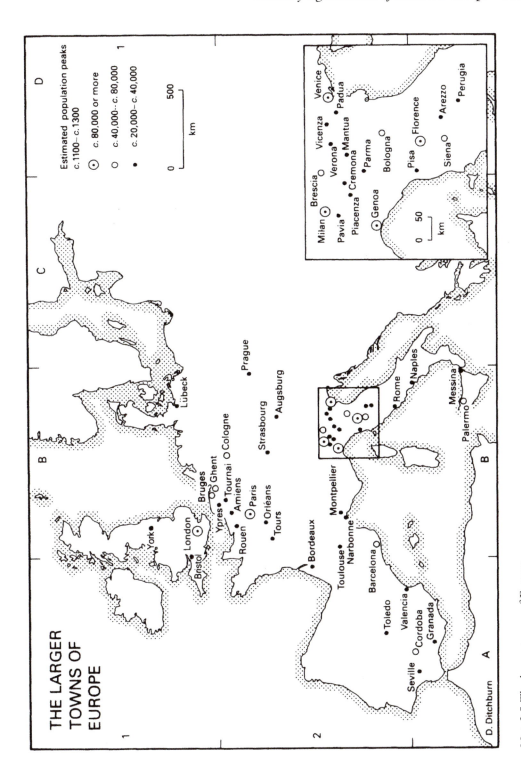

Map 3.5 The larger towns of Europe

Source: *Atlas of Medieval Europe* © D. Ditchburn

In the late eleventh century, Norman adventurers in southern Italy under the leadership of Robert Guiscard (died 1085) succeeded in wresting control of southern Italy from the Byzantines and Sicily from its Muslim rulers. Christian armies on the Iberian Peninsula made steady advances, capturing the old Visigothic capital of Toledo in 1086. The very next year, the cities of Genoa and Pisa in the Italian peninsula undertook a campaign in North Africa against the Muslim pirate haven of Mahdia. Then, in 1095, Pope Urban II launched the First Crusade that culminated in the establishment of Latin states on the eastern Mediterranean littoral. These so-called 'armed pilgrimages' to the East continued for the next two centuries.

This enormously vibrant period brought with it widespread innovation in all areas of human endeavour, and not least in the organization and conduct of war. Moreover, historians of this period have the ability to analyze these developments in considerable detail because vastly larger numbers of written sources survive than for earlier eras. To take just one eye-opening example, more administrative documents survive for just one year from the English royal government under King Edward I (1272–1307) in the late thirteenth century than for all of the governments that operated in Western Europe from the Roman Empire up to the turn of the first millennium. What these written sources – along with material evidence gained from archaeological investigations – show, however, is that traditional patterns of military organization persisted, and provided the framework in which a wide variety of military systems experienced change and new models were developed.

Military resources of kings and princes

The basic components of the military forces of the ninth and tenth centuries also predominated in both the defensive and offensive armies of kings and princes during the crusading era. In many ways, this was also true of the armies that participated in the crusading campaigns themselves. For local defence, the general obligation that required all able-bodied men, and indeed women in some cases, remained in place. In those areas where peace reigned for lengthy periods, these defensive obligations sometimes became attenuated. For the most part, however, the highly varied populations of Europe shared the common prospect, or perhaps simply the fear, of having to defend their homes at least sometime during their lives against foreign invaders or in the course of a civil war.

As a consequence, a wide range of arms and armament remained ubiquitous throughout medieval Europe in the crusading age. Even in lands where scholars have tended to see the absolute military subjugation of the peasants under a warrior aristocracy, contemporary governments recognized that their peoples continued to be armed, and prepared for some forms of combat. For example, the famous territorial peace initiatives (German *Landfrieden*) undertaken by Emperor Frederick Barbarossa (1152–1190) and his grandson Emperor Frederick II (1218–1250) in 1152 and 1235, respectively, took for granted that peasants would be armed with swords, and explicitly enunciated that they were permitted to carry them when travelling outside their home villages. It is notable that swords were 'honourable' weapons that some modern scholars claim, contrary to the relevant sources, could not be possessed by members of the lower social orders.

By contrast with the generally constant need to be prepared to undertake measures for local defence, offensive campaigns by kings and princes were highly varied in size, scope, and duration. It is certainly the case that when rulers throughout Europe and in the eastern Mediterranean undertook military operations beyond their frontiers, they drew upon traditional sources of manpower available in their own and magnate military households, mobilized the expeditionary levies of their subjects, and also recruited mercenaries. However, the

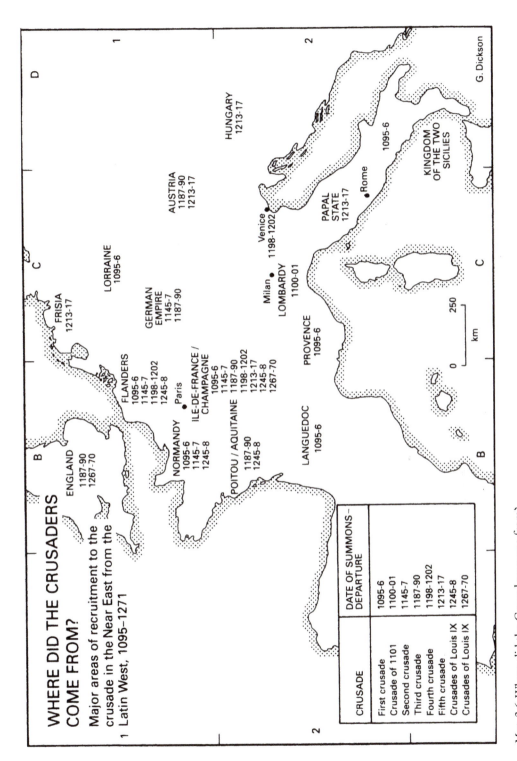

WHERE DID THE CRUSADERS COME FROM?

Major areas of recruitment to the crusade in the Near East from the Latin West, 1095–1271

CRUSADE	DATE OF SUMMONS – DEPARTURE
First crusade	1095-6
Crusade of 1101	1100-01
Second crusade	1145-7
Third crusade	1187-90
Fourth crusade	1198-1202
Fifth crusade	1213-17
Crusades of Louis IX	1245-8
Crusades of Louis IX	1267-70

FRISIA
1213-17

LORRAINE
1095-6

ENGLAND
1187-90
1267-70

FLANDERS
1095-6
1145-7
1198-1202
1245-8

Paris

NORMANDY
1095-6
1145-7
1245-8

ILE-DE-FRANCE /
CHAMPAGNE
1095-6
1145-7
1187-90
1198-1202
1213-17
1245-8
1267-70

GERMAN
EMPIRE
1145-7
1187-90

POITOU / AQUITAINE
1187-90
1245-8

LANGUEDOC
1095-6

PROVENCE
1095-6

Milan
LOMBARDY
1100-01

Venice
1198-1202

AUSTRIA
1187-90
1213-17

HUNGARY
1213-17

PAPAL
STATE
1213-17

Rome

KINGDOM
OF THE TWO
SICILIES

1095-6

0   250
km

G. Dickson

Map 3.6 Where did the Crusaders come from?
Source: *Atlas of Medieval Europe* © G. Dickson

organization, composition, and relative importance of these elements of campaign armies differed quite significantly across Europe, and often varied within the reign of individual rulers depending on the nature of the specific military challenges that he faced.

The Iberian Peninsula

In the far west of Latin Europe, the rulers of Castile and Aragon certainly relied heavily on the military resources provided by their secular and ecclesiastical magnates. However, these kings also recruited many thousands of their subjects as military colonists to establish new towns along the frontiers with the Muslims – which during this period were moving southward – offering grants of property and highly beneficial tax status to encourage migration to these potentially dangerous regions. Dozens of town charters from the eleventh through the thirteenth centuries, known as *fueros*, provide detailed information regarding the highly varied social status of these immigrants, and the wide range of their military obligations. Naturally, all of the inhabitants in the towns, as well as their hinterlands, were required to defend the walls in case of Muslim raids and invasions. However, according to the terms of their agreements with the Castilian and Aragonese kings, many of these military colonists also were required to serve in royal armies that undertook offensive campaigns into Muslim lands. Notably, military service was tied to wealth, with the more prosperous colonists required to provide mounted military service on campaign, while those less well off served as foot soldiers. In the latter case, however, some of these men owned riding horses even if they could not afford more expensive war horses. Similar to the military colonists established by Charlemagne and Louis the Pious along their Iberian frontier with the Muslims, many of the *fueros* make clear that the Castilian and Aragonese frontiersmen were subject directly to the king, and were not under the jurisdiction of local authorities, who ruled in the king's name.

The military forces provided by these frontier towns often were augmented not only by the king's military household, but also by the troops provided by major land-owning aristocrats. Perhaps the most famous of these aristocrats was Rodrigo Díaz de Vivar (died 1099), who was given the name El Cid (the Lord) by his Muslim opponents. After a successful career in the military household of King Ferdinand I of Castile (1029–1065) and the latter's sons Sancho II (1065–1072), and then Alfonso VI (1072–1109), Rodrigo was exiled from Castile in 1081. He subsequently established himself as the leader of an independent military company and sold its services to both Muslim and Christian rulers. Following Alfonso VI's defeat at the hands of the Muslim Almoravid leader, Yusuf ibn Tashfin (died 1106), who arrived in Iberia from Morocco at the head of a large army in 1086, the Castilian king recalled Rodrigo from exile. Alfonso gave Rodrigo authority to raise military forces to campaign against the Almoravids. Rodrigo was very successful and ultimately established himself as a more or less autonomous ruler of a region centred on the fortress city of Valencia, shortly before his death in 1099. We might also point here to a Muslim contemporary and counterpart of the Cid, the poet and military command Ibn 'Ammar, who not only served the crown of Castile, but led mercenaries hired from the count of Barcelona.

France

As the rulers of the Capetian dynasty (987–1328) in France gradually gained direct control over larger and larger parts of their nominal realm during the twelfth and thirteenth centuries, they also worked diligently to assert the legal obligation of their subjects to provide

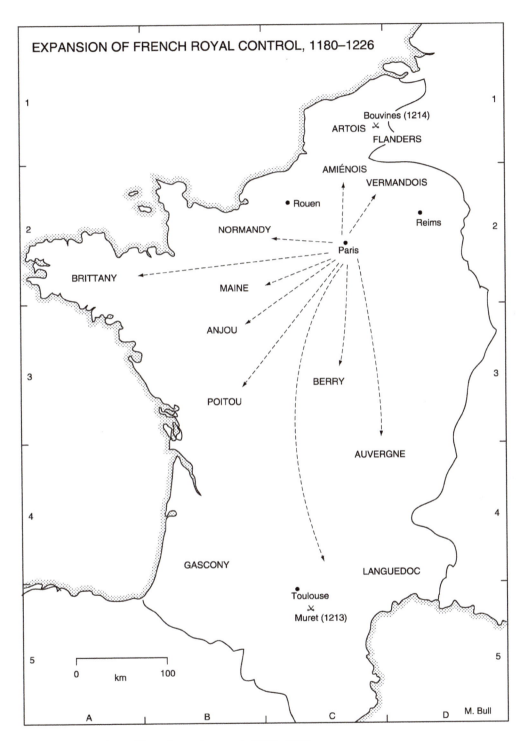

Map 3.7 Expansion of French royal control, 1180–1226

Source: *Atlas of Medieval Europe* © M. Bull

military service to the crown. Because of the weakness of the West Frankish/French kings during most of the tenth and the eleventh centuries, the royal government generally lost the *de facto* if not *de jure* right to summon both magnates and expeditionary levies throughout much of the kingdom once ruled by Charles the Bald. Consequently, under a series of successful and powerful rulers, including Philip II Augustus (1180–1223) and Philip IV (1285–1314), the French monarchy systematically sought and vindicated its legal rights over a long period of time to summon men for military service.

Ever since the reign of Louis VI (1108–1137), the French crown had become increasingly successful in obtaining military contingents from secular and ecclesiastical magnates. However, Philip II dramatically expanded the pool from which he could recruit fighting men by systematically reintroducing Carolingian military obligations based on wealth. Recognizing that the rapidly growing cities within his realm offered the most promising place to access the wealth, and concomitantly the military service of his subjects, Philip II devoted enormous effort to mobilizing urban militias for service in the royal army. A document called *prisia servientum*, first issued in 1194, lists the number of foot soldiers that the cities subject to royal rule were required to provide to the king for offensive military operations. These included the obligations on the cities in Philip's realm to provide almost 8,000 fighting men, and the additional requirement that the cities provide a wagon-load of supplies for each fifty men.

These urban military forces were approximately four times the size of the permanent military household of the king, and comprised an important component of Philip II's campaign armies. During the crucial years of 1203–1204, when Philip acquired almost all of the lands held in France by the English ruler King John (1199–1216) and thereby more than doubled the size of the French royal realm, urban militias, which were drawn largely from the northern parts of the French kingdom, took part in every stage of the campaign. At the Battle of Bouvines (1214), where Philip II decisively defeated the armies of King Otto IV of Germany (1208–1218), urban militias comprised more than a third of the French army.

Philip II's successors continued to draw substantial military forces from the cities of their rapidly expanding realm. However, Philip IV, the great-great-grandson of Philip Augustus, also secured the military service of a very broad spectrum of landowners throughout the French kingdom, including the regions in the south and southwest acquired by his predecessors in the early and mid-thirteenth century. Philip IV aggressively pursued his right to obtain military service that was tied to property ownership, utilizing legal precedents dating back to the Carolingian period. The efforts by Philip to make the maximum possible claims regarding the military obligations of his subjects provoked considerable discontent and legal challenges. In the end, however, the French kings succeeded in their efforts to vindicate their legal rights.

In 1293, Count Roger-Bernard III of Foix (1265–1302) challenged the mobilization of the men of his county for service in the king's army, claiming at the court of the royal seneschal at Carcassonne that he alone owed military service because of the lands that he held from the king. But the seneschal responded:

> for the defence of his kingdom in matters relating to the common good, no lord, count, vassal, or community in his land is permitted or ought to be excused from service, but rather is bound to set out because of the fidelity that he owes, and for the defence of the prince of his kingdom.[4]

---

4 Colonel Borrelli de Serres (ed.), *Recherches sur Divers Services Publics du XIIIe au XVIIe Siècle* (Paris, 1895), 519; and *La Collection de Languedoc* (Doat), vol. 176 folio 1.

Philip IV was very successful in imposing these military obligations throughout France, and tying military service on horseback to the possession of property, following early medieval practice. The minimum property qualification was set at fifty pounds of the city of Tours, which can be compared to the possession of twelve manses under Charlemagne 500 years earlier. In addition, Philip succeeded in broadening the pool of men subject to expeditionary service, the descendant of the select levy, even further by implementing the obligation that every 100 households, denoted as hearths (*feux*), were required to provide six fighting men on foot for service in the royal army. In this manner, small-scale property owners, and even those with only a home with a fireplace, could be mobilized in the king's service. This system recalls both the Roman *capitulum* and the Carolingian and Anglo-Saxon practice of 'clubbing'. The success of Philip's reimposition of age-old military obligations is evident in his mobilization of an army to invade Flanders in 1302. In all, more than 19,000 mounted men, and many thousands more foot soldiers, were summoned to serve in this campaign, which, however, ended in a catastrophic defeat at the hands of the urban militias of Flanders fighting on foot at the Battle of Courtrai (11 July 1302).

England

After his conquest of England in 1066, William largely kept in place the military system that he inherited, including both the universal obligation for local defence (great *fyrd*), and the requirement that property owners provide military service in the royal army for expeditionary campaigns (select *fyrd*). In fact, by the early 1070s, William deployed contingents of English soldiers drawn from men of the select *fyrd* who owned or possessed five hides in his continental campaigns, including his reconquest of the region of Maine from the Angevins. However, William overlaid this Anglo-Saxon system with an additional military obligation on the veterans of his army, who received substantial rewards of property in England. This *servitium debitum* was designed to provide William with a ready force of well-equipped and well-trained men, both mounted and foot soldiers, who could respond rapidly to military emergencies in England, such as revolts by the indigenous Anglo-Saxon nobility against the new order and uprisings by the Welsh.

Throughout his reign, William the Conqueror, and subsequently his sons William Rufus (1087–1100) and Henry I (1100–1135), recruited substantial armies for their campaigns in both England and on the continent from among those landowners owing military service for the properties they acquired during the conquest. These troops constituted, for the most part, the military households of the Anglo-Norman magnates. The new rulers of England also continued to impose on lesser landowners military obligations that were based upon the institution of Anglo-Saxon select *fyrd*. In effect, during the late eleventh and early twelfth centuries, the people of England were required to sustain the economic costs of a double-military obligation. In addition, the Anglo-Norman rulers recruited Welsh troops on an ad hoc basis.

In addition, all three of these Anglo-Norman kings used the government's exceptionally advanced tax-collecting administration to support substantial numbers of paid fighting men to augment the forces of the royal military household. Henry I of England, for example, established a contract with Count Robert II of Flanders (1093–1111) to furnish 1,000 mounted troops for service on the continent, or 500 mounted troops for service in England, to be mobilized whenever summoned by the English king. The Anglo-Norman kings were able to obtain a substantial amount of money to pay for these mercenary and

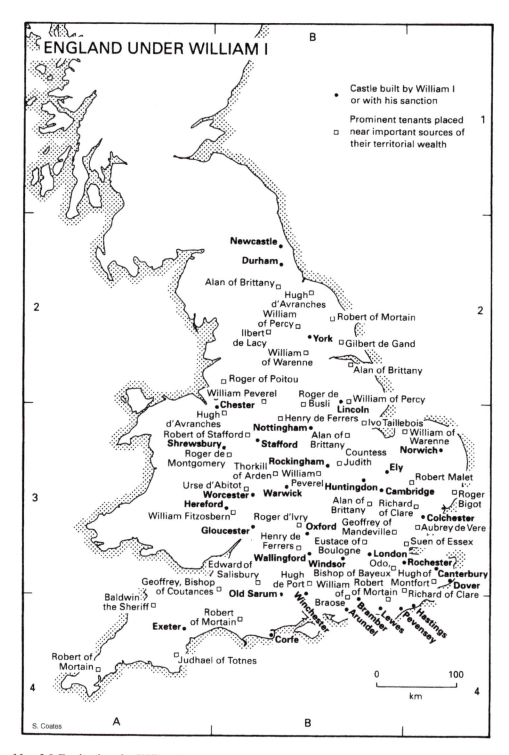

Map 3.8 England under William I

Source: *Atlas of Medieval Europe* © S. Coates

contract forces through fines, called scutage, on fighting men who held lands from the king but did not perform their military service.

Over time, the receding threat of internal revolts against Anglo-Norman rule, and a lengthy civil war between Henry I's daughter Mathilda (died 1167) and his nephew Stephen (reigned as king 1135–1154) during the 1130s and 1140s, led to a breakdown in both the Anglo-Norman and earlier Anglo-Saxon military systems. King Henry II (1154–1189), the son of Henry I's daughter Mathilda and Count Geoffrey Plantagenet of Anjou, undertook a number of steps to re-establish royal authority throughout England. This included enforcing the legal obligation of all of his subjects to provide military service in defence of the kingdom, and the broader Angevin Empire. These policies culminated in the *Assize of Arms*, issued in 1181, in which Henry II's government restated and formalized the connection between wealth and military service, and established a series of 'wealth classes' whose members were responsible for owning and training with specified types of arms. The assize of 1181 combined both the Anglo-Saxon and Norman military institutions by enunciating specific obligations for those individuals holding lands that originally were assigned by William I in the post-conquest period, and also for all other property owners in England down to those with small-scale agricultural holdings.

The 1181 *Assize of Arms* formed the legal basis for all subsequent legislation regarding the military obligations of the king's English subjects throughout the remainder of the medieval period. These include the 1252 *Assize of Arms* issued by Henry III (1216–1272), the 1285 *Statutes of Winchester* issued by Edward I (1272–1307), and the confirmation of the *Statutes of Winchester* issued by Henry IV (1399–1413) in 1404. These military obligations provided a very substantial pool of armed manpower for service in the royal army, a reservoir that was tapped very successfully by Edward I during his wars in Wales, Gascony, Flanders, and above all, in Scotland.

Indeed, Edward I was able to raise armies numbering as many as 30,000 effectives on a population base of fewer than five million men, women, and children. Armies of this size had not been seen in Britain since the days of the Roman conquest in the first century AD, and would not be seen again until the period of the American Revolution. The overwhelming majority of these troops, comprising some 90 per cent of the total, were foot soldiers recruited from the shire levies, as well as many thousands of Welshmen. Unusually for this period, these foot soldiers were paid for their service by the crown. This was far different from the French levies mobilized by Edward's contemporary and chief adversary Philip IV, who were required to serve at their own expense, much as had been true of the Carolingian expeditionary levies on whom they were modelled. By contrast, the majority of the mounted troops mobilized by Edward were not paid by the crown, but rather served at the cost of the territorial magnates, who led them to war. The exceptions were the men of the royal military household, as well as specifically recruited heavy cavalry, denoted as *solda-rii* in contemporary sources, who were paid wages by the king.

The English government was precocious in paying the king's subjects to fight in wars beyond the frontiers of the kingdom. England also was unusual in the crusading era by maintaining a royal fleet. The Anglo-Saxon kings had used the *fyrd* system to keep a fleet. The Anglo-Norman kings developed new institutions to serve the same end. A group of maritime cities in Sussex and Kent, in southern England, denoted as the Cinque Ports, provided ships and crews to the English kings in return for a range of privileges regarding the organization of their local governments, and also commerce. This association of towns and cities likely had its origins in the period before the Norman Conquest, but increased significantly in importance throughout the twelfth and thirteenth centuries. By Edward I's reign, the Cinque Ports, which now numbered in excess of thirty members, provided scores of ships and thousands of crewmen and archers for campaigns in Gascony and in Scotland.

During the course of the twelfth and thirteenth centuries, the kings of England also developed a standing fleet, consisting mostly of galleys, to patrol the English Channel, raid enemy shipping and ports, and enforce customs duties. Henry II's sons, Richard I Lionheart (1189–1199) and John, both maintained many dozens of galleys and crews, and established an extensive system of docks and warehouses to support them. John's son Henry III sold off part of this fleet, and allowed the remaining ships and infrastructure to rot in the sea and salt air of the coast. However, when Edward I found himself at war with Philip of France in 1294, the English undertook a crash programme of galley construction in an effort to fend off the fleets that the French ruler commissioned to operate against the English. The French did not establish a royal navy in this period, and instead used what were essentially pirate fleets, at least from the English perspective, operating out of the ports of Normandy. Edward I's successors drew upon a mix of naval resources for both defence and offensive campaigns, including the resources of the Cinque Ports, a small royal fleet, and also the impressment of merchant ships and crews in times of emergency. Indeed, the impressment of seamen for military service continued in England into the nineteenth century.

The German Empire

When King Henry III of Germany died in 1056, he ruled all of the lands comprising modern Germany, as well as portions of Belgium, Holland, northeastern France, southeastern France, western Poland, Austria, Hungary, and all of the Italian peninsula south to Rome. It was recognized universally that the German Empire was the most powerful political entity in Europe. However, catastrophic civil wars during the reign of his son and successor Henry IV (1056–1106) coupled with an ongoing struggle with the papacy, which involved almost every ruler of Germany from Henry IV to Frederick II (died 1250), sapped the political strength of the German kings, and led to the fragmentation royal power. By the end of the crusading era in the late thirteenth century, Germany was no longer a unified kingdom, and scores of secular and ecclesiastical magnates were well along the path to establishing themselves as more or less autonomous rulers. The situation was similar to what happened in France between c.900 and c.1100.

The cities of the German Empire, particularly those in northern Italy and along the Rhine corridor, similarly asserted control over their own destinies, and frequently established governments that represented an unprecedentedly wide spectrum of the urban population. The cities also made alliances with each other and with foreign powers in the process of maintaining autonomy from the German kings and also local territorial magnates. It was during the course of the twelfth and thirteenth centuries that the idea developed of city air making a man free (*Stadtluft macht Mann frei*) and thus posed a challenge to the landed aristocracy by attracting servile dependents to the city and its hinterland, thereby increasing the military resources of the city.

These tumultuous political events had important implications for military organization, particularly with regard to cities, as will be seen further into the chapter. Nevertheless, the systems of military organization present in earlier centuries continued to have a central role in the conduct of war. As discussed previously, all able-bodied men continued to have responsibilities for the defence of their local regions. Moreover, the German kings, including Henry IV, Frederick Barbarossa, and Frederick II, all continued to mobilize armies for offensive campaigns that drew heavily upon the royal and magnate military households, expeditionary levies of medium to small landowners, and mercenaries.

The civil war that engulfed Germany during the 1070s and 1080s saw the mobilization of all three types of forces on a massive scale by both the king and his opponents. A panegyric written for Henry IV after his spectacular victory in the Battle of the Unstrut (June 1075) over a combined army of Saxon nobles and peasant levies illuminates the array of forces that could be summoned to war. The poet recorded that as word went throughout Saxony that King Henry was coming, the peasants cast aside their farming implements, the shepherds left their flocks, and the merchants abandoned their wares. Although the author of this text certainly exaggerated in his description of the mobilization of the Saxon people, his claims permit the observation that men from every station and every profession girded themselves for war. They were joined by the professional soldiers (*milites*) of the Saxon nobles' military households. King Henry's army included the *milites* of nobles loyal to the king in southern Germany, as well as expeditionary levies drawn from Bavaria, Swabia, and Lotharingia. The German king also used mercenary forces provided by his ally, the duke of Bohemia.

Emperor Frederick Barbarossa mobilized a similar panoply of military forces for his campaigns in Italy during the 1150s and 1160s, where he faced significant opposition from northern Italian cities, who joined together in several leagues, including the Veronese league, established in 1164, and the Lombard league, established in 1167. The cities of northern Italy had grown increasingly assertive of their rights to self-government over the course of the eleventh and twelfth centuries. The leaders of these cities felt threatened by Barbarossa's effort to re-establish direct German rule throughout northern Italy, and were supported in their resistance to the emperor by Pope Alexander III (1159–1181).

The wealthy and populous Lombard cities fielded considerable numbers of urban militiamen in their struggles against the German emperor, and forced him to undertake repeated military operations to assert his rule south of the Alps. Barbarossa's ability to mobilize large armies in Germany, and to supplement these forces with both urban militias from loyal Italian cities and the military households of Italian magnates, meant that he usually had the upper hand in the time-consuming siege operations that dominated war in northern Italy. However, the Lombard league did enjoy some significant successes, including at the Battle of Legnano (29 May 1176), when an army of the Lombard league, drawn from the civic militias of its members, defeated a portion of Barbarossa's field army near the city of Pavia. Here, as at the Battle of Courtrai, noted earlier, foot soldiers defeated heavy cavalry in a pitched battle.

Southern Italy experienced a similar development of urban self-government during the course of the later eleventh and early twelfth centuries, which was manifest in revolts against King Roger I of Sicily (1071–1101) and his sons Simon (1101–1105) and Roger II (1105–1154). These cities, like their northern contemporaries, established urban governments that represented the interests of the merchant and craft elites. They also established powerful urban militias, which were intended not only to protect the city from foreign attack, but also to secure the city's interests in the local region. The composition of these militias illustrates again the importance of foot soldiers for both offence and defence.

The German kingdom witnessed a similar development of urban militias during the course of the thirteenth century. By contrast with their Italian contemporaries, however, the cities of Germany saw their economic and political interests as tied to a strong monarchy. During the civil wars that engulfed the German kingdom during the final years of the reign of Emperor Frederick II, and of his son King Conrad IV (1237–1254), urban militias provided much of the strength of royal armies. The city of Worms, for example, possessed a militia of 4,000 men who were dispatched on multiple occasions to aid Conrad IV in his campaigns. Following the death of Conrad IV, and the lengthy 'interregnum' that lasted

Map 3.9 The Hohenstaufen Empire, c.1150–1250
Source: *Atlas of Medieval Europe* © B. Weiler

until the accession of Rudolf I of Habsburg (1273–1291), the cities of Germany took an active role in the political affairs of the kingdom, deploying their militia forces, and mercenaries that they hired, to secure their own interests. About sixty of these cities gathered together in a 'Rhenish league' promising mutual military aid against territorial nobles. These cities had the capacity in aggregate not only to mobilize tens of thousands of fighting men, but also routinely deployed fleets up and down the Rhine River in support of their military operations.

Crusading armies and crusading states

When Pope Urban II preached his sermon at Clermont on 27 November 1095 about providing aid to the eastern Christians and freeing Christ's tomb from Muslim rule, he set in motion a series of military campaigns that ultimately sent many hundreds of thousands of western Christians to the eastern Mediterranean. These campaigns, which in the late eleventh and twelfth centuries were known simply as pilgrimages, eventually came to be called crusades, denoting the cross-emblazoned clothing of the participants. The term *crusignati* literally means those marked with the cross. These expeditions, both great and small, brought a cross-section of the population of Europe to the Levant. Young and old, men and women, secular and ecclesiastical of all social, political, and economic ranks participated in these campaigns. It is therefore not surprising that the armies of crusaders were a reflection of the military organizations of the lands from which they came.

Princes and other magnates travelled with their military households. These leaders, because of their wealth and prestige, also were able to recruit individuals and groups of ostensible civilians, who nevertheless were equipped with weapons of war, to serve under their command. Of the 100,000 or so armed pilgrims who are reported by the crusade leaders to have participated in the siege of Antioch throughout the autumn, winter, and spring of 1097–1098, the majority were originally simple farmers, who were motivated to go on this campaign by myriad factors, including religious fervour, religious altruism, and the hope for a place in heaven, as well as, in some cases, a desire for material gain or even adventure. The capacity of these toilers in the soil to conceptualize joining a military expedition, at their own cost and with their own equipment, is a testament to the highly militarized nature of the broader European society in this period.

This broad militarization is even clearer when considering the first group of armies to begin the armed pilgrimage to the East in the spring of 1096. These forces, collectively denoted by scholars as the People's Crusade, consisted almost entirely of the lower social orders whom Pope Urban and other secular and ecclesiastical leaders had hoped to exclude from this enterprise because of their lack of military training and the means to support themselves. It is certainly the case that the People's Crusade suffered horrific losses during its journey through the Byzantine Empire, and then was annihilated on the road to Nicaea at the hands of Kilij Arslan, the Turkish sultan of Rum, who ruled in western Anatolia (1092–1107). Nevertheless, the very fact that several tens of thousands of peasants could arm themselves, with virtually no participation by regional or even local magnates, and undertake a campaign of this magnitude speaks to the ubiquity of military experience, including the availability of arms, among the lower social orders.

The actions of the participants of the People's Crusade during the march through the Rhineland illuminate yet another facet of the militarization of the population as a whole. Consumed with hate for the Jewish inhabitants of the Rhineland cities, including Worms, Speyer, and Mainz, the crusaders launched a series of attacks against these communities, seeking to kill or compel the conversion of the Jews. However, the Jews were not helpless victims in the face of these attacks. At Mainz, Rabbi Kalonymous, the leader of the community, led his armed and armoured community in an assault against the crusaders as they sought to storm the gates of the Jewish quarter. This Kalonymous was a descendant of the Rabbi Kalonymous who had saved the life of Emperor Otto II at the Battle of Capo Colonna in southern Italy (982). Following Henry IV's return to Germany, he permitted all those Jews, who had been forced to convert to Christianity, to return to their religion. Moreover, he did so contrary to contemporary Christian teaching on this subject, which

Figure 3.4 Crusader army from a contemporary illustration; the King of France leaving for the crusades, c.1336–1455

held that although forced conversion was not acceptable, once a Jew had converted under whatever circumstances, he or she could not renounce the Christian faith. Henry IV's decision in this case illuminates the importance with which he regarded his Jewish subjects.

Throughout the history of the active crusading movement into the late thirteenth century, armed pilgrimage continued to attract broad cross sections of the population. Certainly, princes and sometimes kings dominated these campaigns, and their military households often formed the core of the armies that arrived in the Holy Land. Yet, vast numbers of ordinary people continued to participate. The army of Englishmen, Normans, and Netherlanders who captured Lisbon in 1147, during the course of the Second Crusade, were drawn from all walks of life, and included farmers, fishermen, and merchants. Similarly, the tens of thousands of Germans who followed Frederick Barbarossa on the Third Crusade in 1189 included merchants from the city of Bremen, who founded a society at Acre that eventually would become the military order known as the Teutonic Knights.

The military organization of the crusader states that were founded in the east, namely the County of Edessa, the Principality of Antioch, the County of Tripoli, and the Kingdom of Jerusalem, also reflected the experiences of their Latin rulers. The universal obligation on all able-bodied men to provide for the local defence, expeditionary militias recruited from the wealthier members of society, and the military households of rulers and magnates were all part of the mix of forces that served in both defensive and offensive operations. However, in addition to these traditional institutions, the rulers of the crusader states benefitted from the almost yearly arrival of armed pilgrims, who wished to visit the Church of the Holy Sepulchre, and then often participated in ongoing military operations, usually at their own expense. These arrivals from all over Europe varied significantly in number from year to year, from a few thousand to many tens of thousands in the case of the 'named' crusades, such as the Third Crusade (1189–1192), led by the kings of England, France, and Germany; the Barons' Crusade (1239–1241); and the Ninth Crusade (1271–1272), whose participants included the soon-to-be King Edward I of England.

Military orders

Another major addition to the military organization of the crusader states was provided by the development of a fundamentally new type of organization heretofore unknown in medieval Europe, namely the military orders such as the Templars, Hospitallers, and Teutonic Knights. The military orders combined the traditional structure of the monastery with an austere militarism that sometimes is compared by modern scholars with Sparta in Classical Greece. Members of military orders took the three traditional monastic vows of obedience, poverty, and chastity, along with a fourth vow to commit their lives to military service in defence of Christendom. The first of the military orders, officially known as the Poor Fellow Soldiers of Christ and the Temple of Solomon, and more colloquially as the Templars, was established by a minor French nobleman named Hugh de Payens (died 1136) in the early twelfth century to defend travellers along the road from the erstwhile Roman port of Jaffa to the ancient fortress city of Jerusalem, a distance of some 60 kilometres. In 1120, Hugh received official recognition from King Baldwin II of Jerusalem (1118–1131). The Templars also received an enormously important endorsement from Bernard of Clairvaux (died 1153), one of the most important churchmen of his day, who wrote a text in praise of the Templars titled *A Book to the Soldiers of the Temple in Praise of the New Military Service*. Subsequently, Pope Innocent II (1130–1143) issued a papal bull – that is, a papal encyclical – in 1139 called *Omne Datum Optimum* in which he granted formal recognition to the

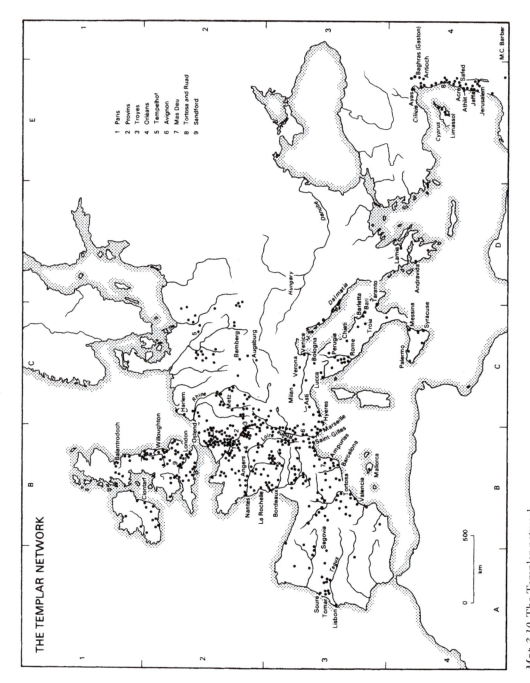

Map 3.10 The Templar network

Source: *Atlas of Medieval Europe* © M.C. Barber

Templars and exempted them from all secular and religious jurisdiction other than that of the papacy itself.

The Templars gained enormous prestige and popularity throughout Europe during the course of the twelfth and thirteenth centuries, which was manifested in vast numbers of grants of property. By the end of the twelfth century, the order possessed thousands of estates located throughout Europe, and established a highly efficient system of management that was focused on funnelling money, supplies, and men to pursue its military mission in the Latin East. This private empire of property, free from any secular or ecclesiastical jurisdiction, provided the means for the Templars to support several thousand fighting men in the Latin states, who were divided among heavy and light cavalry, and garrison troops. The latter served in the dozens of fortifications financed and constructed by the order. The Templars were widely regarded by contemporaries as an exceptionally well-trained and effective military force. This was due, in part, to their rigorous military training, as illustrated in their lengthy handbook, *The Rule of the Templars*, which was developed during the first half of the twelfth century.

The model and success of the Templars inspired dozens of imitators, including the Brothers of the Sword in Livonia (located along the eastern shore of the Baltic Sea), and the Order of Calatrava in Castile. However, the two most successful of the military orders that followed the Templar model were the Order of the Knights of Saint John, known colloquially as the Hospitallers, and the Order of Brothers of the German House of Saint Mary in Jerusalem, usually denoted as the Teutonic Order. Both of these latter orders saw their primary mission as the defence of the Holy Land. However, the Teutonic Order became involved in the crusades against the pagan Slavs in the northern tier of Central Europe during the early thirteenth century, and eventually founded their own state in Prussia, which endured into the sixteenth century.

Muslim armies of the crusading age

When the armies of western Christians arrived in Asia Minor, and subsequently campaigned along the eastern shore of the Mediterranean, they encountered a Muslim world that was divided along ethnic, religious, and political lines into a congeries of major states and relatively small 'city-states'. The Sunni Abbasid Caliphate, which at its height during the eighth century stretched from northern India to the Atlantic coast of Africa, dissolved over the course of the ninth century as a result of civil wars, rebellions, and foreign invasions. By the tenth century, large swathes of the former Abbasid Empire had been conquered by foreign powers. In the West, the Fatimids, a rival Shiite dynasty from North Africa, conquered Egypt in 969, and subsequently captured much of the Mediterranean littoral and Syria, with the intention of replacing the Abbasids as the ruling caliphal house.

In the east, the Samanids (819–999) created a powerful realm in the region of Khorasan and Transoxania, the lands east of Iran proper that stretched out to the edge of the great Eurasian steppe. The Samanids were replaced in turn, first in later tenth century by the Ghaznavid Empire, and then in early decades of the eleventh by the Seljuks. The latter led a tribal confederation known to contemporaries and modern scholars as the Oghuz Turks. Within a short period, the Seljuks conquered Transoxania, Khorosan, and Iran proper. They then extended their conquests into Iraq, and in 1055, the Seljuk confederation, led by Tughril (1037–1063), captured Baghdad and established themselves as rulers of Mesopotamia and Syria, as well as controlling their core territories in Iran.

Over the next several decades, the Sunni Seljuks competed with the Fatamids for control in Syria and the coastal lands of the Mediterranean, as well as with the Byzantine

Empire. Following the victory by the Seljuk leader Alp Arslan (1063–1072) at the Battle of Manzikert in 1071 over the Byzantine emperor Romanos IV (1068–1071), most of Asia Minor was opened up to Turkish conquest. However, the death of the Seljuk leader Malik Shah (1072–1092), the son of Alp Arslan, in 1092 led to the fragmentation of Seljuk rule. Numerous members of the Seljuk family, as well as important military officers, established more or less independent control over individual cities such as Aleppo, Mosul, and Damascus, as well as their hinterlands.

Both the Fatimids and the Seljuks conquered erstwhile portions of the Abbasid Empire with armies that were composed largely of tribal forces. In the case of the Fatimids, these were mostly Berbers from North Africa. The Seljuks, as mentioned previously, led a confederation of Turkish tribes. Very quickly, however, both the Fatimids and the Seljuks adapted to the military institutions of the regions that they had conquered. The most important of these institutions was the practice of military slavery, which dated back to the early ninth century.

The establishment of this system of military recruitment is credited by modern scholars to Caliph Abu Ishaq al-Mu'tasim (833–842). Most historians agree that al-Mu'tasim likely began purchasing significant numbers of Turkish-speaking boys during the reign of his brother Caliph al-Ma'mun (813–833), and established a corps of slave soldiers numbering 3,000–4,000 men. These troops, denoted as mamluks, played an essential role in the accession of al-Mu'tasim in 833. Over the course of the ninth century, the army of Arab tribesmen, which had been the dominant element in the early history of Islam, largely disappeared, and mamluks became the decisive element in the armies of both the Abbasids and their numerous successors.

Consequently, the Muslim forces faced by the crusaders in the field, whether fighting against the Seljuks or the Fatimids in Asia Minor and in the Levant, were comprised largely of Turkish-speaking slave soldiers (mamluks) trained in the traditions of steppe warfare. In order to maintain the level of skill expected of these elite forces, Muslim rulers continuously imported young boys from the Turkish-dominated steppe, rather than allowing the sons of the mamluks to fill the ranks left by their fathers when they retired. This tradition of keeping professional armies of slave soldiers was maintained in much of the Islamic Middle East throughout the Middle Ages, and in some places, even into the early nineteenth century.

The mamluk horse archers provided both the tactically dominant and numerically preponderant element of Seljuk and Fatimid armies. These forces, however, were augmented by a variety of other types of fighting men in some circumstances. Many Muslim cities had either official or semi-official militia forces that played an important role in the defence of their homes, much as was the case in contemporary Western Europe. Groups of volunteers also served in Muslim campaign armies, sometimes in the context of supporting the religious struggle against Christian forces – that is, as part of their obligation for *jihad* – and in other cases simply for the hope of plunder. In some cases, as in Egypt under the rule of Saladin (died 1193), we even see the conscription of men for service in the army in periods of great need. Many of these other types of troops served on foot rather on horseback, particularly in the context of siege warfare and the defence of their own homes.

Knighthood

Among the most vexed questions regarding military organization in the crusading era is the nature of knighthood. Many scholars have identified knighthood as a fundamental element of 'feudalism', and knights as the members of a warrior aristocracy that dominated military operations from the eleventh to the fourteenth centuries. As observed previously, however, feudalism as an explanatory model for medieval history, and particularly military affairs, is now regarded by most scholars as intellectually exhausted. Perhaps more importantly, it is clear that at no point from the late Roman Empire up through the end of the fifteenth century did warrior aristocrats play the dominant role in military organization either numerically or tactically, whether in the conduct of sieges or in combat in the field. Indeed, the great majority of fighting men who served on horseback during the medieval period were not aristocrats at all, but rather men from the lower social orders who sought a career in military service. Moreover, from a tactical perspective in western warfare, mounted troops, whether aristocratic or not, usually dismounted and fought on foot, both in the field and in the course in the sieges.

This is not to say that men of high social and economic status had no role to play in warfare. Some of them chose a career in military service, and took up command positions in the military households of kings, princes, and other great magnates. Some of these men were rewarded with grants of property, or other economic benefits, and ended their military careers with an enhanced economic and social position. Still other wealthy individuals were required to perform military service because of the legal obligations tied to the possession of property. Such men, however, were politically and socially important because of their wealth, not because they occasionally were summoned to serve on campaign. Moreover, in many cases, aristocrats – especially in the Angevin Empire – sought to avoid joining the army by buying their way out of service through the payment of scutage, which was treated officially as a fine. It is clear, moreover, that many Anglo-Norman and Angevin kings of England preferred to have money rather than personal service from their barons and other faithful men so that they could employ true professionals for their military campaigns.

Much of the confusion about the nature of knighthood results from a relatively modern scholarly misunderstanding of the term *miles* in medieval sources. Through a variety of complex processes, by the late twelfth century, the term *miles* had become associated with a congeries of social and legal functions that were connected with aristocratic status throughout much of Latin Europe and the eastern Mediterranean. In the German Empire, the substantive transformation of the term *miles* to mean what modern English speakers associate with the term knight took place during the 1170s, and was brought about, in large part, by the decision taken by Frederick Barbarossa to describe himself, his sons, and the members of his court as *milites*. Very quickly thereafter, courtly literature, much of it sponsored by the king and great magnates, began to use the term *miles* and its German equivalent *Ritter* exclusively to denote aristocrats. Before this point, German authors used both *miles* and *Ritter* exclusively to denote professional fighting men, whether they were aristocrats or commoners.

The process whereby the semantic field of the term *miles* was transformed in England can be seen in the way government officials, as well as contemporary chroniclers, used the term from the mid-twelfth through the mid-thirteenth century. Up through the end of the reign of King Stephen in 1154, *miles* was used by English authors to denote professional fighting men, again including both those of low social status as well as aristocrats who made a career in military service. During the reign of Barbarossa's contemporary Henry II, however, the term underwent a semantic shift, and became used increasingly to denote not professional soldiers, but rather individuals with substantial property, who were required to provide military service to the crown for this property. By the reign of Henry III (1216–1272), royal administrative documents and pay records distinguished among men providing service to the government as heavy cavalry. Those who had the social and juridical obligations that were based on property holdings valued at 20 English pounds were denoted as *milites*. Those men who provided the exact same kind of military service, but did not have the social and economic status of *milites*, were denoted by a range of terms, including *servientes ad arma*, *scutiferi*, and *armigeri*. These terms can be translated as sergeants at arms, shield bearers (squires), and arms-bearing men.

Milites, when they were paid for their service, earned 2 shillings a day. By contrast, the men of lower economic and social status, who nevertheless performed exactly the same military duties as the *milites*, were paid just half as much – that is, 1 shilling per day.

Many scholars have missed this change in the meaning of the term *miles* over the course of the later twelfth century, and consequently have read backwards the social and economic status of *milites* into earlier periods, causing serious confusion in the scholarly literature. This is due, in large part, to the fact that a vast quantity of vernacular entertainment literature from the twelfth century onward was produced for nobles and wealthy men that portrayed them at the centre of honourable military activities, and presented them as the dominant force in war. The Arthurian cycle, and particularly the knights of the round table, clearly was popular with its court-centred audience. But, in reality, very few aristocrats made a career in military service, largely because they had far better options, such as overseeing their lands. Concomitantly, the overwhelming majority of the men who did become professional fighting men were not aristocrats, but rather were recruited from the lower social orders with the hope of improving their economic and perhaps social prospects. Nevertheless, it is accurate to say that many – and perhaps most – aristocrats had an obligation to perform military service. When they did so, it was because of the ongoing tie throughout Europe between the possession of property and the obligation to provide for the common defence. However, governments recognized that aristocrats and other wealthy individuals often wished to avoid military service, and provided for this eventually by establishing a system of fines, discussed previously, such as scutage.

Military organization in late medieval Europe

Periodization – that is, the effort to divide historical time into presumably coherent blocks, often for the purpose of making it intelligible to students – tends to have the unfortunate effect of enunciating arbitrary divisions when, in reality, societies generally experienced only gradual change within an overall framework of continuity. In Europe, in the period between c.1300 and c.1500, it is possible to discern both important aspects of continuity with the military organization of previous centuries, and also significant aspects of change, some of which were carried forward into the early modern era. Indeed, it was often the case that European governments maintained long-standing institutions while at the same time experimenting with new methods of recruiting armies. Among these new methods were the employment of mercenary companies on a heretofore unprecedented scale, and the reintroduction of standing armies that were substantially greater in size and different in organization than the aggregated royal and princely households of the crusading age. In fact, these later medieval standing armies approached in size the military household maintained by Charlemagne at the height of the Carolingian Empire. In addition to these institutional developments within kingdoms and principalities, the later medieval period also saw the development of new types of political bodies that also added to the variety of military organization in the final centuries of the Middle Ages. Pre-eminent among these was the alliance of merchant cities along the coasts of the Baltic and North seas, known as the Hanse.

The Hundred Years' War: England and France

The later Middle Ages were dominated militarily by a series of conflicts that collectively are characterized by scholars as the Hundred Years' War. The primary protagonists in this struggle were the kingdoms of France and England; however, the participants and theatres of the military operations reached from Portugal in the west to Bohemia in the east, and at one time or another between 1337 and 1453 involved almost all of Europe. The conflict between England and France turned on the possession of lands in Normandy, Maine,

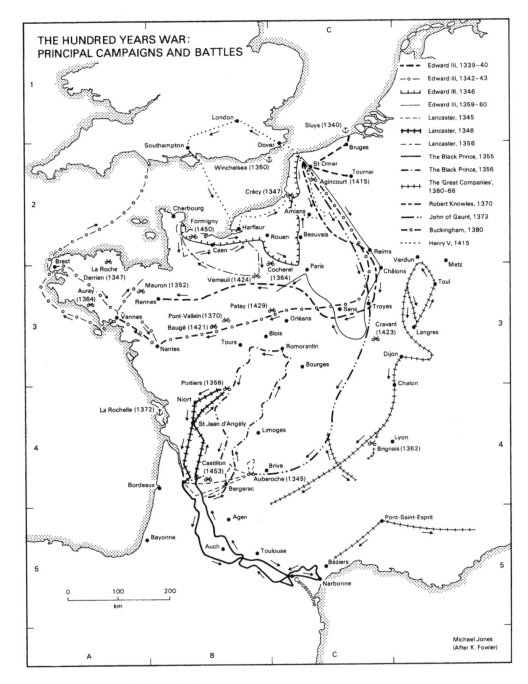

Map 3.11 The Hundred Years' War

Source: *Atlas of Medieval Europe* © Michael Jones (after K. Fowler)

Anjou, Poitou, and Aquitaine that had been lost by King John in 1204, and also, in part, on the claims of Edward I's descendants to be the rightful rulers of France. This latter claim, however, has been the subject of considerable dispute among scholars, with some arguing that Edward III (1327–1377) and his successors really had the French crown as a major war aim, while other scholars argue that this was simply a ploy to motivate the king's English subjects to support campaigns in France. The precipitating event or immediate cause for the renewed outbreak of war between France and England would appear to have been the French effort to take control of Gascony, which was in English hands.

When Edward III came to the throne in 1327, English military organization was much the same as it had been under his grandfather Edward I. The royal military household formed the core administrative centre of the army, and the bulk of the troops available for campaign were militia forces of various types drawn from the shire levies, with much smaller numbers of mounted fighting men provided by the knights and barons of the realm. For his early wars in Scotland, Edward III used these traditional military forces. However, he proved unable to convince the political community of the realm, as represented by parliament, that the universal obligation for the defence of the kingdom extended to campaigns in France. As a consequence, Edward III vastly expanded upon a model used by Edward I

Figure 3.5 Two massed opposing armies at the Battle of Crécy in the Hundred Years' War; the victorious English are on the right

Source: © Niday Picture Library/Alamy Stock Photo EGEFPD

in his Scottish campaigns in the 1290s and early fourteenth century, by offering contracts to English magnates to raise fighting forces for service at royal pay. However, whereas Edward I sought to mobilize a few hundred mounted fighting men in this manner, Edward III's contract armies comprised many thousands of men, including both heavy cavalry and mounted archers. During the long periods of war between England and France, the use of these contracts as recruiting tools led to the sustained militarization of broad swathes of the wealthier elements of the English population, with perhaps as many as 100,000 men serving overseas during the course of the fourteenth and first half of the fifteenth century. However, none of the English kings in this period sought to establish a large standing army that was permanently on duty and in royal pay. The contract companies that comprised the armies of the English kings on the continent were organized for the short term, and saw regular turnover in personnel, as one set of contracts expired and new men and new units were recruited.

A major area of study for British historians dealing with the Hundred Years' War over the past several decades has been analyzing the ways in which the contract armies mobilized by Edward III actually were recruited. A pioneer in this effort, who has exercised considerable influence over the entire field, is Andrew Ayton. He observed that during the early years of Edward III's wars in France, a substantial portion of the English army continued to consist of men levied from the shires under the traditional system of the 'commission of array'. However, the forces raised in this manner were rather unwieldy for extended campaigns overseas, and so Edward III came to rely increasingly on great 'captains' to recruit both heavily armoured troops, known as men at arms, as well as archers, many of whom were drawn from the gentry, or middling levels of society. These 'captains' developed recruiting networks in England in which they reached out to members of their own households, to tenants, neighbours, family and friends, and comrades from earlier campaigns. Eventually, Ayton argues, traditions of service built up in which many gentry families routinely provided men to serve with particular great lords for overseas service, thereby creating what he calls a 'military community'.

By contrast with the tradition-based but essentially ephemeral military formations of the English kings on the continent, both the royal navy and local militias were long-term and long lasting institutions. Throughout the late medieval period, the English royal government continued to draw upon the Cinque Ports for ships and crews, and also maintained a royal fleet to support military operations on land and to engage enemy ships at sea. The roots of these institutions are generally seen by scholars to have their origins during the Anglo-Saxon period. In addition, the English government not only maintained, but even expanded the shire-based military organization for local defence that had taken shape during the reign of Edward I. All adult males within each shire were organized into local companies according to the sub-shire district in which they lived, known as a hundred. The latter administrative district dated back to the pre-conquest Anglo-Saxon period. The property owners within these hundreds elected officers, denoted as constables, who were responsible for inspecting the arms of the men in their jurisdictions, and leading them on campaign, when summoned by royal officials to participate in military operations.

The short-lived rebellion led by a member of the Kentish gentry named Jack Cade in 1450 illustrates just how effective this military system was. Following a pattern of abuse by the royal officials appointed by the government of Henry VI (1422–1461), Jack Cade led the shire levy of Kent to London to demand redress for the grievances of the people. Almost the entire shire levy from Kent joined in the rebellion, and defeated royal troops, as well as the militia of the city of London in two separate engagements. Ultimately, the rebellion ended when the men of Kent were promised both a pardon for their actions and redress for their grievances. Many of the letters of pardon have survived, and show the organization of the rebels was exactly that of the shire levy, with each hundred represented and led by its constable. This system of local levies was maintained during the early modern period under the Tudors, and eventually was transferred across the Atlantic to North America by English colonists in the seventeenth century.

In France, during the fourteenth and fifteenth centuries, the kings of the Valois dynasty (1328–1589) drew extensively upon the military institutions that they had inherited from their Capetian predecessors. At the beginning of the Hundred Years' War, King Philip VI (1328–1350) had the legal authority and the practical ability to summon fighting men from throughout France in defence of the kingdom. This military institution, sometimes denoted as the *arriere-ban*, drew upon the vast pool of men with the minimum property qualifications for military service. The Valois kings also were able to mobilize the urban militias of the cities throughout the kingdom. These military forces were augmented, in the traditional manner, with the military households of magnates, and also mercenary forces. In the early phases of the Hundred Years' War, the French king contracted with important magnates to bring augmented military households at royal pay to the muster. Over time, however, the royal government increasingly turned to mercenary commanders, who offered the service of their companies to the crown.

This policy of employing mercenaries ultimately proved disastrous for the French people. The frequent defeats of the French at the hands of the English during most of the fourteenth and early fifteenth centuries led to extensive territorial losses, and the political and financial collapse of the French monarchy. Without the means to pay its mercenary forces, the French government was forced to cut ties with them – without, however, providing for a means of demobilization. Consequently, roving bands of mercenaries terrorized the French countryside, and even occasionally cities.

Ultimately, King Charles VII of France (1422–1461) used a truce with the English in 1445 to introduce a new model of military organization. He formally disbanded all of the mercenary companies that were in the service of the crown, and established a new standing army of 'companies of ordinance', which were under direct royal command, were officered by royal appointees, were to receive regular pay, and were assigned to specific garrisons in France. Over a six-year period of experimentation, Charles VII succeeded in establishing the first centrally organized standing army seen in Europe since the late Roman Empire, comprising twenty companies of 600 men each. The troops of these companies were kept on permanent duty, and were assigned quarters in the immediate area of their garrison. They were given a uniform rate of pay, which included both cash and in-kind allocations, such as food.

In order to manage the new military units, the royal government employed civilian officials, called *receveurs*, to oversee the pay, housing, and equipping of these troops. The history of these new units is made clearer by the development of new types of administrative documents that recorded all aspects of the service of men and officers in the *companies d'ordinance*. The effectiveness of these new military units is illustrated by the rapid success of Charles' new army in the five years after the establishment of the 'companies' in reconquering almost all of the lands held by the English in France. The companies of ordinance established by Charles VII provided the basis for the reorganization of the entire French military system during the subsequent two centuries, and lay the foundation for France's emergence as a dominant power on the continent in the early modern era.

The success of Charles VII in adding to the mix of military institutions of the French kingdom is illuminated even further by the effort and ultimate failure of Charles VII's cousin, Duke Charles the Bold of Burgundy (1467–1477), to do the same in his realm. When he came to power in 1467, Charles the Bold inherited a complex of military institutions very similar to those possessed by his Valois counterparts. The cities of Charles' lands in the Low Countries provided substantial urban levies, mostly of infantry, for his campaigns. Men holding lands in return for military service, denoted in contemporary documents as *fieffés*, were

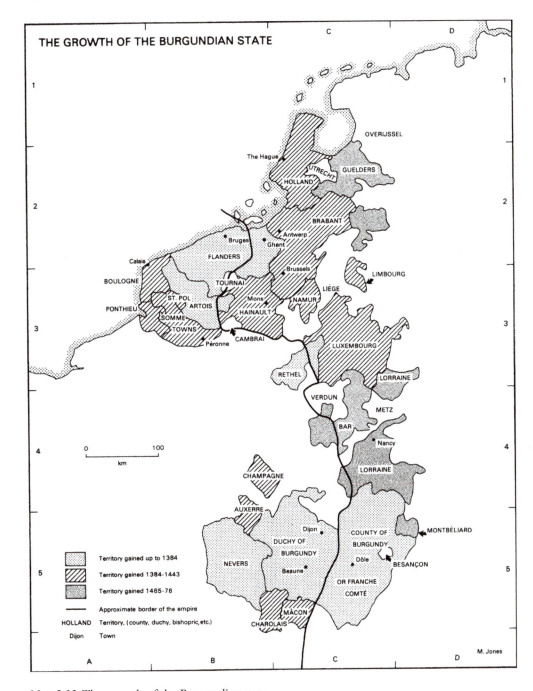

Map 3.12 The growth of the Burgundian state
Source: *Atlas of Medieval Europe* © M. Jones

mobilized by the Burgundian dukes largely to provide mounted troops for their armies. Charles also inherited from his predecessors a well-organized military household of almost 2,000 men, which included experts on artillery and siege warfare. Similarly, like his father, grandfather, and great-grandfather, Charles also employed mercenary companies. Indeed, Charles' father Philip the Good (1419–1467) employed so many mercenaries from the region of Picardy in 1452, that all of the soldiers in his army attained the sobriquet 'Picard'.

However, in the face of urban revolts in Flanders during the late 1460s and the difficulty in mobilizing sufficient military forces from his own subjects, Charles decided to reorganize the Burgundian military system and establish companies of ordinance similar to those created by Charles VII. In 1471, Charles the Bold ordered the establishment of twelve permanent companies totalling 10,800 men. The number of these companies was gradually expanded as Charles undertook a series of wars during the 1470s, until his death in battle in 1477 at Nancy. Prior to his death, however, Charles had continued to mobilize urban militias, *fieffés*, as well as mercenaries throughout the remainder of his reign. The latter included the famed companies of the Italian mercenary commander Cola de Montforte (died 1478) and Bartolomeo Colleoni (died 1475), who during his long military career became captain general of the Republic of Venice, where he was honoured with an equestrian statue.

Holy Roman Empire

During the fifteenth century, mercenary companies such as those employed by Charles the Bald played a decisive role, not only in wars north of the Alps, but in Italy, as well. Cola de Montforte and Bartolomeo Colleoni were just two of dozens of famed *condottieri* who fought the wars of Italy's numerous regional princes and autonomous city-states. These companies recruited men from throughout Europe, although the English and Germans were particularly prominent in the international mercenary community. Perhaps the most famous *condittiere* was the Englishman John Hawkwood (died 1394), whose career spanned more than thirty years of campaigns in France and Italy. In the final years of his life, Hawkwood became commander of the armies of Florence, where he was buried with full honours of the Florentine state in the cathedral of Santa Maria del Fiore in 1394. Hawkwood's career was immortalized by the contemporary French chronicler Jean Froissart (died 1405), and by the Florentine diplomat and political theorist Niccolò Machiavelli (died 1527) in his book *The Prince*.

In the German lands of the Holy Roman Empire, the process of political disintegration that began during the crusading era reduced the once powerful German kingdom in the fourteenth and fifteenth centuries to a congeries of more than 130 autonomous and sovereign polities, each with its own military organization. The basic military structures of these secular and ecclesiastical principalities, duchies, and free cities demonstrated considerable continuities with their predecessors from the twelfth and thirteenth centuries. Princes continued to employ household troops, mobilize their subjects, and recruit mercenaries for offensive campaigns, while insisting upon the obligation of all men to participate in the local defence. Imperial free cities established large-scale civic militias, and developed competencies in a wide range of military specializations, including newly introduced firearms and gunpowder artillery. In some cities, particularly in the eastern regions of the Empire, and in Slavic-speaking lands, these urban militias included Jewish contingents, much to the consternation of some vocal Christian critics.

In the north of Germany, a confederation of cities that later became known as the Hanse began to establish firm commercial ties during the later thirteenth century under the

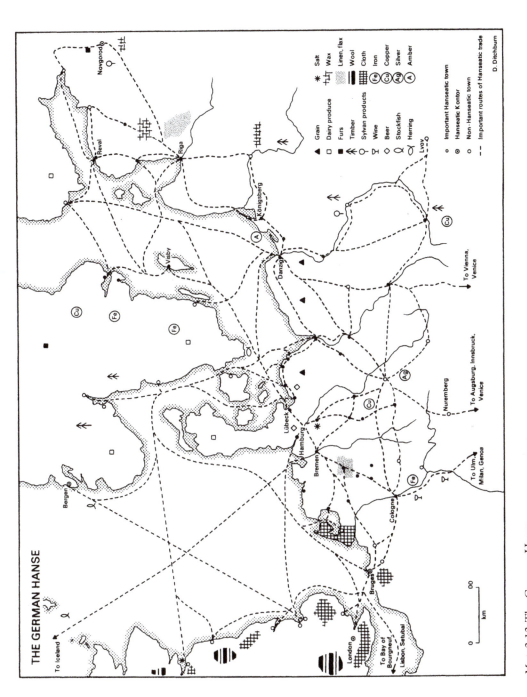

Map 3.13 The German Hanse

Source: *Atlas of Medieval Europe* © D. Ditchburn

leadership of the Baltic seaport Lübeck, which is located on the river Trave. These cities used a combination of economic strength and joint military power to free themselves from the control of nearby territorial lords, and in order to keep the sea lanes clear of both pirates and toll collectors, such as the kings of Denmark. The cities in the Hanse each enjoyed self-government within their confederation, and contributed military forces and warships to joint enterprises only when it suited their individual interests. The fighting men were drawn largely from the civic militias of the individual Hanse cities, and the warships were generally converted merchant vessels, which were equipped with a range of missile weapons, and provided with an expanded complement of archers and other combatants. Occasionally, the cities of the Hanse agreed to raise funds to recruit mercenaries, as well. Despite the relatively ad hoc nature of the military organization of the Hanse, these Baltic and North Sea cities remained a dominant power in northern Europe throughout the fourteenth and fifteenth centuries.

Conclusion

In considering the question of medieval European military organization, it is clear that the universal obligation for military service in various contexts, and particularly for local defence that developed in the later Roman Empire, played a central role in the connection between the individual, particularly the individual male, and the government throughout the medieval millennium. Wealthy and poor, aristocrats, free men, semi-free agricultural labourers, and even slaves, Christians and often Jews as well, were required by custom and law to participate in the military organization of medieval Europe.

The system of taxation developed by the Roman government to ensure a steady supply of recruits for the imperial army certainly evolved into myriad forms, shaped by regional and local demographic and economic conditions. But one constant thread throughout Europe and the Mediterranean during the Middle Ages, and even beyond to the Atlantic world during the early modern era, was the pivotal role played by militia forces in defence of their homes on the basis of the obligations they owed to the *res publica*. Similarly, between the dissolution of the imperial army in the West during the fifth century and the rise of professional armies in late medieval Europe, militia troops authorized and raised by governmental authority were the numerically dominant element of armies on offensive campaigns. The ongoing tie between wealth and the obligation to participate in military operations either personally or through paying for substitutes beyond one's local district is yet another constant throughout our period.

These militia forces served alongside the military households of kings and magnates, both secular and ecclesiastical, which provided the professional core for most armies in medieval Europe. However, these military households were by no means elements of a so-called 'feudal' order. The great majority of professional soldiers were not aristocrats, or even men of high birth, but rather were recruited from those at the lower levels of the socio-economic spectrum. The nobility was not a warrior class in medieval Europe. Quite to the contrary, nobles often sought to evade the military responsibilities that they owed on the basis of their wealth, preferring to pay fines rather than stray very far from their comfortable estates for the rigour of the campaign. Those aristocrats who sought a military career were important because of their wealth and family backgrounds, not because they were obviously more effective in wielding a sword and leading men in combat.

An additional question that has stimulated enormous scholarly controversy for more than a century is the scale of medieval armies. Resolving this issue depends on an understanding of a wide range of factors, including the administrative capacity and resources of a particular government. For example, the small kingdoms that developed in the provinces of the erstwhile Western Empire, such as the Franks in Gaul and the Visigoths in Spain, had far fewer demographic and economic resources than the empire of Charlemagne. However, the size of a kingdom was not always a clear guide to the ability of a ruler to raise large armies. Edward I of England mobilized armies numbering nearly 30,000 troops in the 1290s in a kingdom numbering fewer than five million souls. His grandson Edward III was able to raise armies in the 10,000–15,000 range even after the Black Death had killed off perhaps as much as half of England's population.

Another crucial factor in understanding the scale of medieval armies, and one that frequently is overlooked by those scholars enamoured of the idea that they were very small, concerns the objectives for which armies were mobilized. The conquest and the subsequent defence of conquered territory turned on the success or failure of siege operations, which dominated warfare throughout the medieval period. In general, the sieges of great fortress cities, and even of lesser strongholds, required the mobilization of very large armies. These armies, in turn, required vast quantities of supplies that were made available through the efforts of highly trained administrators. It is therefore fitting that we turn in the next chapter to a discussion of military logistics.

Bibliography

Some regions and periods in medieval European history have received considerably more attention than others from scholars with respect to military organization, particularly in English, and that imbalance is reflected in the bibliography which follows.

Concerning late Roman military institutions, see

A. H. M. Jones, *The Later Roman Empire 284–602: A Social, Economic and Administrative Survey* (Norman, OK, 1964), I: 679–685;

J. H. G.W. Liebeschuetz, 'Generals, Federates and Bucellarii in Roman Armies around AD 400' in *The Defence of the Roman and Byzantine East*, 2 vols., ed. P. Freeman and D. Kennedy (Oxford, 1986), 463–474;

Peter Brunt, 'Conscription and Volunteering in the Roman Imperial Army' in *Roman Imperial Themes* (Oxford, 1990), ch. 9, 188–214;

Michael Whitby, 'Recruitment in Roman Armies from Justinian to Heraclius (ca. 565–615)' in *The Byzantine and Early Islamic Near East* vol.3: *States, Resources and Armies*, ed. Averil Cameron (Princeton, 1995), 61–124;

Constantin Zuckerman, 'Two Reforms of the 370s: Recruiting Soldiers and Senators in the Divided Empire' in *Revue des études byzantines* 56 (1998), 79–139.

Concerning early military organization in the early Middle Ages, see

C. Warren Hollister, *Anglo-Saxon Military Institutions on the Eve of the Norman Conquest* (Oxford, 1962);

C. Warren Hollister, *The Military Organization of Norman England* (Oxford, 1965);

Bernard S. Bachrach, *Merovingian Military Organization* (Minneapolis, 1972), 481–751;

John Gillingham, 'The Introduction of Knight Service into England' in *Proceedings of the Battle Conference on Anglo-Norman Studies* 4 (1981), 53–64 and 181–187;

Alexander Ruttkay, 'The Organization of Troops, Warfare and Arms in the Period of the Great Moravian State' in *Slovenska archeologia* 30 (1982), 165–198;

Emily Zack Tabuteau, 'Definitions of Feudal Military Obligations in Eleventh-Century Normandy' in *On the Laws and Customs of England: Essays in Honor of Samuel E. Thorne*, ed. M. Arnold (Chapel Hill-NC, 1982), 18–59;

Marjorie Chibnall, 'Military Service in Normandy Before 1066' in *Anglo-Norman Studies 5* (1982), 65–77;

Janet Nelson, 'The Church's Military Service in the Ninth Century: A Contemporary View?' in *Studies in Church History 20* (1983), 15–30,

reprinted in Janet Nelson, *Politics and Ritual in Early Medieval Europe* (London, 1986), 117–132;

Richard Abels, *Lordship and Military Obligation in Anglo-Saxon England* (Berkeley, 1988);

Timothy Reuter, 'The End of Carolingian Military Expansion' in *Charlemagne's Heir: New Perspectives on the Reign of Louis the Pious (814–840)*, ed. Peter Godman and Roger Collins (Oxford, 1990), 391–405;

Bernard S. Bachrach, 'Grand Strategy in the Germanic Kingdoms: Recruitment of the Rank and File' in *L'Armée romaine et les barbares du IIIe au VIIe siècle*, ed. Françoise Vallet and Michel Kazanski (Paris, 1993), 55–63;

Timothy Reuter, 'The Recruitment of Armies in the Early Middle Ages: What Can We Know?' in *Military Aspects of Scandinavian Society in European Perspective, AD 1–1300*, ed. Anne Norgard Jorgensen and Birthe L. Clausen (Copenhagen, 1997), 32–37;

Simon Coupland, 'Frankish Tribute Payments to the Vikings and Their Consequences' in *Francia 26.1* (1999), 57–75;

Bernard S. Bachrach, *Early Carolingian Warfare: Prelude to Empire* (Philadelphia, 2002);

John France, 'The Composition and Raising of the Armies of Charlemagne' in *Journal of Medieval Military History 1* (2002), 61–82;

Simon Coupland, 'The Carolingian Army and the Struggle against the Vikings' in *Viator 35* (2004), 49–70;

David S. Bachrach, *Warfare in Tenth-Century Germany* (Woodbridge, 2012);

Howard Clarke, '"Those Five Knights Which You Owe Me in Respect of Your Abbacy": Organizing Military Service after the Norman Conquest: Evesham and Beyond' in *Haskins Society Journal 24* (2013), 1–39;

Leif Inge Ree Petersen, *Siege Warfare and Military Organization in the Successor States (400–800 AD): Byzantium, the West and Islam* (Leiden, 2013).

Regarding military organization in the high Middle Ages, see

J. E. Morris, 'Cumberland and Westmorland Military Levies in the Time of Edward I and Edward II' in *Transactions of the Cumberland and Westmorland Antiquarian and Archaeological Society 3* (1903), 307–327;

Daniel Waley, 'Papal Armies in the Thirteenth Century' in *English Historical Review 72* (1957), 1–30;

Michael Powicke, *Military Obligation in Medieval England* (Oxford, 1962);

Michael Prestwich, *War, Politics and Finance under Edward I* (Totowa, 1972);

John O. Prestwich, 'The Military Household of the Norman Kings' in *The English Historical Review 96* (1981), 1–35;

James F. Powers, *A Society Organized for War: The Iberian Municipal Militias in the Central Middle Ages, 1000–1284* (Berkeley, 1988);

Benjamin Arnold, 'German Bishops and Their Military Retinues in the Medieval Empire' in *German History 7* (1989), 161–183;

S. Schein, 'The Templars: The Regular Army of the Holy Land and the Spearhead of the Army of Its Reconquest' in *I Templari: mito e storia*, ed. G. Minnucci and F. Sardi (Sienna, 1989), 15–28;

G. W. S. Barrow, 'The Army of Alexander III's Scotland' in *Scotland under the Reign of Alexander III*, ed. N. H. Reid (Edinburgh, 1990), 132–148;

Timothy Reuter, '*Episcopi cum sua militia:* The Prelate as Warrior in the Early Staufer Era' in *Warriors and Churchmen in the High Middle Ages: Essays Presented to K. Leyser,* ed. Timothy Reuter (London, 1992), 79–94;

Karl-Friedrich Krieger, 'Obligatory Military Service and the Use of Mercenaries in Imperial Military Campaigns under the Hohenstaufen Emperors' in *England and Germany in the High Middle Ages,* ed. Alfred Haverkamp and Hanna Vollrath (Oxford, 1996), 151–167;

Yuval Harari, 'The Military Role of the Frankish Turcopoles' in *Mediterranean History Review 12* (1997), 75–116;

Paul Oldfield, 'Urban Government in Southern Italy c. 1085-c.1127' in *The English Historical Review 122* (2007), 579–608;

Aldo A. Settia, 'Infantry and Cavalry in Lombardy (11–12th Centuries)' in *Journal of Medieval Military History 6* (2008), 58–78;

Michael Prestwich, 'Edward I's Armies' in *Journal of Medieval History 37* (2011), 233–244.

With respect to late medieval military organization, see

H. J. Hewitt, *The Organization of War under Edward III, 1338–1362* (Manchester, 1966);

Daniel Waley, 'The Army of the Florentine Republic from the Twelfth to the Fourteenth Century' in *Florentine Studies,* ed. N. Rubinstein (London, 1968), 109–139;

Paul D. Solon, 'Valois Military Administration on the Norman Frontier, 1445–1461: A Study in Medieval Reform' in *Speculum 51* (1976), 91–111;

M. E. Mallett and J. R. Hale, *The Military Organization of a Renaissance State: Venice c. 1400–1617* (Cambridge, 1984);

Philippe Contamine, 'The Soldiery in Late Medieval Urban Society' in *French History 8* (1994), 1–13;

Anne Curry, 'English Armies in the Fifteenth Century' in *Arms, Armies and Fortifications in the Hundred Years War,* ed. Anne Curry and Michael Hughes (Woodbridge, 1994), 39–68;

David S. Bachrach, 'A Military Revolution Reconsidered: The Case of the Burgundian State under the Valois Dukes' in *Essays in Medieval Studies 15* (1998), 9–17;

Nicolas Agrait, 'Castilian Military Reform under the Reign of Alfonso XI (1312–50)' in *Journal of Medieval Military History 3* (2005), 88–126;

Bertrand Schnerb, 'Vassals, Allies and Mercenaries: The French Army before and after 1346' in *The Battle of Crécy, 1346,* ed. Andrew Ayton and Philip Preston (Woodbridge, 2005), 265–272;

Andrew Ayton, 'Armies and Military Communities in Fourteenth-Century England' in *Soldiers, Nobles and Gentlemen. Essays in Honour of Maurice Keen,* ed. Peter Coss and Christopher Tyerman (Woodbridge, 2009), 215–239.

Regarding the role of mercenaries in medieval warfare, see

Michael Mallett, *Mercenaries and Their Masters: Warfare in Renaissance Italy* (Totowa, 1974);

Marjorie Chibnall, 'Mercenaries and the *familia regis* under Henry I' in *History 62* (1977), 15–23;

Krijnie Ciggaar, 'Flemish Mercenaries in Byzantium: Their Later History in an Old Norse Miracle' in *Byzantion 51* (1981), 44–74;

Stephen Brown, 'The Mercenary and His Master: Military Service and Monetary Reward in the Eleventh and Twelfth Centuries' in *History 74* (1989), 20–38;

Michael Prestwich, 'Money and Mercenaries in English Medieval Armies' in *England and Germany in the High Middle Ages: In Honour of Karl J. Leyser,* ed. Alfred Haverkamp and Hanna Vollrath (Oxford, 1996), 129–150;

Simon Barton, 'Traitors to the Faith? Christian Mercenaries in al-Andalus and the Maghreb, c. 1100–1300' in *Medieval Spain: Culture, Conflict and Coexistence: Studies in Honour of Angus MacKay,* ed. Roger Collins and Anthony Goodman (Basingstoke, 2002), 23–45;

William Caferro, *John Hawkwood: An English Mercenary in Fourteenth-Century Italy* (Baltimore, 2006);

Kenneth Fowler, 'Great Companies, Condottieri and Stipendiary Soldiers: Foreign Mercenaries in the Service of the State: France, Italy, and Spain in the Fourteenth Century' in *Guerra y diplomacia en la Europa Occidental, 1280–1480* (Estella, 2005), 141–161;

The collection of essays in *Mercenaries and Paid Men: The Mercenary Identity in the Middle Ages*, ed. John France (Leiden, 2008).

Islamic military organization during the crusading age

H. A. R. Gibb, 'The Armies of Saladin' in *Studies on the Civilization of Islam*, ed. S. J. Shaw and W. R. Polk (Princeton, 1962), 74–90;

Yaacov Lev, "The Fatimid Navy, Byzantium and the Mediterranean Sea 909–1036 C.E./ 297–427 A. H.," *Byzantion 54.1* (1984), 220–252;

Yaacov Lev, 'Regime, Army and Society in Medieval Egypt, 9th-12th Century' in *War and Society in the Eastern Mediterranean, 7th-15th Centuries*, ed. Yaacov Lev (Leiden, 1997), 115–152;

Hugh Kennedy, *Armies of the Caliphs: Military and Society in the Early Islamic State* (London, 2001);

Reuven Amitai, 'The Mamluk Institution, or One Thousand Years of Military Slavery in the Islamic World' in *Arming Slaves from Classical Times to the Modern Age*, ed. Christopher Leslie Brown and Philip D. Morgan (New Haven, 2006), 40–78;

David Bramoullé, 'Recruiting Crews in the Fatimid Navy (909–1171)' in *Medieval Encounters 13* (2007), 4–31;

Yaacov Lev, 'David Ayalon (1914–1998) and the History of Black Military Slavery in Medieval Islam' in *Der Islam 90.1* (2013), 21–43;

Amitai Reuven, 'The Early Mamluks and the End of the Crusader Presence in Syria (1250–1291)' in *The Crusader World*, ed. Adrian Boas (London, 2016), 324–345.

Regarding naval organization, see

Timothy Runyan, 'The Organization of Royal Fleets in Medieval England' in *Ships, Seafaring, and Society: Essays in Maritime History*, ed. Timothy Runyan (Detroit, 1987), 37–52;

N. A. M. Rodger, 'The Naval Service of the Cinque Ports' in *The English Historical Review* (1996), 636–651;

John Gillingham, 'Richard I, Galley-Warfare and Portsmouth: The Beginnings of a Royal Navy' in *Thirteenth Century England 6* (1997), 78–91;

Catherine Swift, 'Royal Fleets in Viking Ireland: The Evidence of Lebor Na Cert, A.D. 1050–1150' in *Land, Sea and Home: Proceedings of a Conference on Viking-Period Settlement at Cardiff*, ed. John Hines, Alan Lane, and Mark Redknap (Leeds, 2004), 189–206;

Craig Lambert, 'The Contribution of the Cinque Ports to the Wars of Edward II and Edward III: New Methodologies and Estimates' in *Roles of the Sea in Medieval England*, ed. Richard Gorski (Woodbridge, 2012), 59–78.

With respect to the interplay between military service and social status, as well as the question of chivalry, see

Georges Duby, *The Chivalrous Society*, trans. Cynthia Postan (Berkeley, 1977);

Karl Leyser, 'Early Medieval Canon Law and the Beginnings of Knighthood' in *Instutionen, Kultur und Gesellschaft im Mittelalter: Festschrift für Josef Fleckenstein zum 65. Geburtstag* (Sigmaringen, 1984), 549–566, reprinted in *Communications and Power in Medieval Europe: The Carolingian and Ottonian Centuries*, ed. Timothy Reuter (London, 1994), 51–71;

Benjamin Arnold, *German Knighthood, 1050–1300* (Oxford, 1985);

Benjamin Arnold, 'Servile Retainers or Noble Knights?: The Medieval Ministeriales in Germany' in *Reading Medieval Studies 12* (1986), 73–84;

Janet Nelson, 'Ninth-Century Knighthood: The Evidence of Nithard' in *Studies in Medieval History Presented to R. Allen Brown*, ed. Christopher Harper-Bill (Woodbridge, 1989), 255–266, reprinted in Janet Nelson, *The Frankish World 750–900* (London, 1996), 75–87;

John Gillingham, 'Thegns and Knights in Eleventh-Century England: Who Was Then the Gentleman?' in *Transactions of the Royal Historical Society 5* (1995), 129–153;

John B. Freed, *Noble Bondsmen: Ministerial Marriages in the Archdiocese of Salzburg, 1100–1343* (Ithaca, New York, 1995);

Bernard S. Bachrach, 'The *Milites* and the Millennium' in *The Haskins Society Journal 6* (1995), 85–95;

Peter Coss, 'Knights, Esquires and the Origins of Social Gradation in England' in *Transactions of the Royal Historical Society 5* (1995), 155–178;

Eric J. Goldberg, '"More Devoted to the Equipment of War Than the Splendor of Banquets": Frontier Kingship, Military Ritual, and Early Knighthood at the Court of Louis the German' in *Viator 30* (1999), 41–78;

Richard Kaeuper, *Chivalry and Violence in Medieval Europe* (New York, 1999);

Maurice Keen, *Origins of the English Gentleman: Heraldry, Chivalry, and Gentility in Medieval England, c. 1300 – c. 1500* (Stroud, 2002);

Conor Kostick, *The Social Structure of the First Crusade* (Leiden, 2008);

Dominique Barthélemy, *The Serf, the Knight, and the Historian*, trans. Graham Robert Edwards (Ithaca, New York, 2009);

David S. Bachrach, '*Milites* and Warfare in Pre-Crusade Germany' in *War in History 22* (2015), 298–343.

Conflicting views

What were the impacts of plague and climate change in the later Roman Empire?

John Haldon et al., 'Plagues, Climate Change, and the End of an Empire: A Response to Kyle Harper's *The Fate of Rome*' in 3 parts *History Compass Journal 16.12* (2018);

Kyle Harper, 'Integrating the Natural Sciences and Roman History: Challenges and Prospects' in *History Compass Journal 16.12* (2018);

Bernard S. Bachrach, 'Some Observations on the Plague in the Regnum Francorum' in *Auctoritas: Mélanges offerts à Olivier Guillot* (Paris, 2006), 157–166.

What was the basis of military obligation in the early Middle Ages?

Timothy Reuter, 'Plunder and Tribute in the Carolingian Empire' in *Transactions of the Royal Historical Society*, 5 ser. *35* (1985), 75–94;

Idem, 'The End of Carolingian Military Expansion' in *Charlemagne's Heir: New Perspectives on the Reign of Louis the Pious (814–840)*, ed. Peter Godman and Roger Collins (Oxford, 1990), 391–405;

Walter Goffart, 'Frankish Military Duty and the Fate of Roman Taxation' in *Early Medieval Europe 16* (2008), 166–190;

Idem, 'The Recruitment of Freemen into the Carolingian Army, or, How Far May One Argue from Silence?' in *Journal of Medieval Military History 16* (2018), 17–33.

4 Military logistics

Introduction

Among the most complicated problems faced by governments and military commanders is securing food and other supplies for their troops while on campaign; that is the problem of logistics. Obtaining supplies was just as important for armies during the Middle Ages as it was for the armies of the Roman Empire, Early Modern Europe, and, indeed, of the modern period. Among many other sources, medieval commanders learned of the centrality of logistics from the commentary by the late Roman author Vegetius, whose handbook *Epitoma rei militaris* was treated as an important authority on military matters throughout the Middle Ages. In this context, Vegetius emphasized that 'armies are more often destroyed by starvation than by battle, and hunger is more savage than the sword'. He added, 'other misfortunes can in time be alleviated: fodder and grain supply have no remedy in a crisis except storage in advance'.

The fact that a medieval army was able to function on campaign, especially on extended campaign in hostile territory, is now increasingly seen by military historians as *prima facie* evidence that the fighting men and camp followers, their mounts, and their beasts of burden were supplied in a timely fashion with sufficient food and other necessary materiel. By contrast, earlier generations of historians asserted that pre-modern states in the West (excluding Rome) lacked the administrative capacity to supply armies in the field. The most prominent proponent of this view in the older scholarly tradition was Martin van Creveld, who argued with regard to pre-modern logistics in his *Supplying War: Logistics from Wallenstein to Patton*, that

> no logistic system of the time could sustain an army embarked on operations in enemy territory. Nor, indeed, was the need for such a system felt prior to our period (the seventeenth century). From time immemorial the problem had been solved simply by having troops take whatever they required. More or less well-organized plunder was the rule rather the exception.[1]

This view of the incapacity of medieval governments to supply armies, and particularly armies in the period before the First Crusade, is also an element of the 'dark age' model discussed in Chapters 2–3. If early medieval governments lacked sophisticated administration, then it follows that they lacked the capacity to organize the movement of supplies to military forces on campaign. A corollary to this argument is that because medieval governments lacked the administrative capacity to undertake sophisticated logistical operations, medieval armies necessarily were small. This second argument is sometimes denoted in the scholarly literature as logistical determinism.

---

1 Martin van Creveld, *Supplying War: Logistics from Wallenstein to Patton* (Cambridge, 1974), 7.

DOI: 10.4324/9781003032878-5

Perhaps the most influential modern historian to argue for both the limited institutional and administrative capacities of early medieval governments was Hans Delbrück. Much more recently, the late Timothy Reuter adopted Delbrück's arguments wholesale, and asserted that the Carolingian and Ottonian kings and emperors could not mobilize large armies because: 'Even the largest towns of northern Europe probably did not exceed a population of 15,000–20,000 in this period, and most were far smaller, yet even these fixed and predictable locations needed a highly developed infrastructure to survive'.[2] Leaving aside the fact that urban centres such as Cologne, Mainz, and Trier had populations in the tenth century that substantially exceeded 20,000, this argument misses a crucial point. No matter how many soldiers served on campaign under Charlemagne, Otto the Great, or, for that matter, Edward I of England, these soldiers would have to eat whether or not they went to war in the king's army. Consequently, the problem is not the quantity of supplies that was available in aggregate in a particular kingdom or principality, but rather the ability of the government to identify, acquire, and transport the necessary supplies to the troops – that is the art and science of logistics.[3]

In order to develop a clear understanding of these challenges, this chapter will first lay out the basic reality of human and animal logistical needs, as well as the transportation resources that were available to move food, fodder, and drink to soldiers and their beasts. We will then turn to a discussion of the variety of administrative and institutional structures put in place by governments from the later Roman Empire up through the late medieval period to assure timely supply for military forces in the field and in garrison. Particular attention will be given to the problem of logistics during the crusades, which were the largest and most complex campaigns undertaken by the Latin West during the medieval millennium.

The material reality of logistics

All soldiers must eat, and so too must the animals that they bring to war. Soldiers also require arms and equipment, and generally must move, as well. These realities impinge upon and shape every aspect of military operations, from the initial mobilization of troops to participate in a military operation to the final denouement of a campaign in a battle, siege, or simply with the men returning to their homes. In order to grasp the fundamental administrative challenges faced by medieval rulers when they decided to commit themselves to military action, it is first necessary to understand the caloric requirements of humans, and particularly men of fighting age, as well as of their mounts and draught animals as they undertook the labour-intensive work of military service. Although medieval planners did not have the concept of calories, they were very well aware of the food requirements for soldiers and animals on campaign. After establishing the needs of man and beast for food and drink, we can turn our attention to the transportation assets that were available during the medieval millennium for the movement of food and other supplies.

Human food consumption

A number of scholars working in a variety of fields of western military history have developed models for the food requirements of soldiers on campaign and in garrison. However, historians and, indeed, military officers vary considerably in their conclusions regarding

---

2 Timothy Reuter, 'Carolingian and Ottonian Warfare' in *Medieval Warfare: A History*, ed. Maurice Keen (Oxford, 1999), 13–35, here 30.
3 For an introduction to this debate, see the studies by David S. Bachrach, Timothy Reuter, and Guy Halsall in the 'Conflicting perspectives' section in the bibliography.

what they understand as the basic food rations that were required by soldiers. These differences are evident, for example, in terms of evaluating the types of nourishment, e.g. bread, meat, vegetables, and fruits that generally were consumed by military personnel on campaign. Moreover, specialists also disagree with regard to the total quantity of calories that were required for the soldier's diet in specific contexts (e.g. when men were on active duty in the field as contrasted to being in barracks or serving in fixed garrisons).

In his detailed analysis of the campaigns of Alexander the Great, for example, Donald Engels suggested that the Macedonian soldiers received, on average, approximately 3,600 calories a day in grain and meat. Studies of the Roman military diet indicate that government officials during the late Republic and the Principate, roughly 200 BC–AD 200, generally sought to ensure that fighting men received a daily diet of some 3,400 calories. This included a wide range of items such as grain, which could be used to bake bread or porridge; vegetables; olive oil; meat; and wine. On campaign, good wine generally was replaced by *posca*, which was a mixture of cheap wine and vinegar of the type offered to Jesus when he was carrying the cross along the Via Dolorosa. When on the march, bread and fresh meat generally were replaced by hard-baked biscuit and dried fish or meat, which sometimes was supplemented by game.

In something of an outlier, in his analysis of the food supplied to English garrisons in Scotland in the late thirteenth and early fourteenth centuries, Michael Prestwich argued that each soldier received food supplies in excess of 6,000 calories a day from the royal government. In this case, however, it is not clear whether the food was meant for the soldier alone, or for the soldier and his dependents. Somewhat later in the fourteenth century, officials of the French king planned to provide troops mobilized to serve in 1327 with approximately 3,250 calories each day, which was to be provided by wine, meat, and grain. According to government regulations, sailors in the Venetian fleets in the same period were supposed to receive a somewhat higher caloric ration of about 3,900 calories derived from biscuit, wine, and salt pork.

In the modern era, soldiers in the western armies during the First World War generally received rations that amounted to between 3,200 and 3,800 calories day. This included a wide range of items that were unknown during the medieval period, including chocolate. Today, the U.S. Army requires approximately 3,000 calories per day for soldiers younger than 30 years of age, with a declining calorie count as fighting men age into less physically intensive roles.

In many cases, scholars derive figures for pre-modern provision of food supplies from governmental administrative documents. These can, however, prove problematic in some cases because it is not always clear whether all of the food that was recorded as supposedly going to the soldiers actually found its way into their stomachs. There may, in fact, have been significant differences between 'paper' rations and what soldiers actually consumed, as in the example of the garrison troops discussed by Michael Prestwich. A separate problem that scholars must consider is that soldiers did not always subsist entirely on rations provided to them by their commanders or other governmental authorities. It is clear that while in garrison, soldiers had many opportunities to purchase 'extras' from the local population above their normal allotment of rations, and this might include delicacies that were not usually available in the normal course of affairs. While on campaign, soldiers sometimes acquired additional supplies either through purchase or through plunder, topics that will be discussed in greater depth later in the chapter.

If one takes the average of the scholarly findings with regard to the caloric needs of fighting men, and particularly those engaged in active campaigning, the figure amounts to some 3,600 calories per day. This quantity of calories was obtained in a variety of forms, including carbohydrate-laden grains, whether as bread, biscuit, or gruel; proteins and fats from meat,

fish, beans, and oil, as well as from milk-based products such as cheese; complex carbohy-
drates from vegetables; and finally alcohol in a variety of forms, including beer and wine.
Overall, however, evidence from the Roman, medieval, and early modern periods indicates
that soldiers' rations were dominated calorically by grain products.

After establishing both the caloric requirements of soldiers and the food sources that
most frequently provided these calories, the modern historian is positioned to develop models that can illuminate the logistical requirements for supplying a military force. The first
step is to establish the weight – and, to a lesser extent, the volume – of the foodstuffs and
drink that comprised a soldier's diet. In this context, 1 kilogram of bread, baked from
the types of wheat or rye that were produced in medieval Europe, provides approximately
2,000 calories. The equivalent number of calories is provided by 750 grams of biscuit. The
difference in weight between bread and biscuit is due to the fact that much of the water is
removed from biscuit during the double-baking process. One kilogram of fresh meat provides approximately 2,500 calories, while a kilogram of dried meat provides approximately
3,200 calories. Again, the drying process removes water without removing calories. Dried
peas, which formed a considerable part of the diet for English and Welsh soldiers during the
later thirteenth century, were also quite dense calorically, providing approximately 1,000
calories per kilogram. Dried broad beans, also known as fava beans, provided about 1,250
calories per kilogram. Beverages also provided considerable caloric additions to soldiers'
diets. A litre of beer ranged from 300–600 calories, dependent upon its alcohol content.
A litre of wine had about 825 calories, although red was, and is, slightly more caloric than
white. A litre of each of these liquids weighs approximately 1 kilogram.

Theoretically, a soldier receiving 3,600 calories a day in rations may have eaten 1.2 kilograms of bread, 200 grams of dried meat, 100 grams of dried peas, and 1 litre of beer.
The total weight of this soldier's daily rations comes to 2.5 kilograms. This weight can be
raised or lowered by increasing the supply of meat relative to bread or biscuit, or by replacing dried meat with freshly slaughtered animals, or replacing beer with wine. On average,
however, it is safe to conclude that in most places and times, soldiers required an average of
2.5 kilograms of consumables per day, excluding fresh water, to stay healthy and perform
their duties. To feed 1,000 soldiers, therefore, required approximately 2,500 kilograms (2.5
metric tonnes) of food supplies per day.

Animal rations

The food rations required by animals, which accompanied most pre-modern military forces on
campaign, also can and must be evaluated objectively in a manner similar to that used for estimating the food required by soldiers. A horse eats far more than a soldier, as does a mule, and
even a donkey. Animals used for military tasks also drink far more water than humans. Another
matter, which frequently does not receive attention from military historians, is that most animals connected with military operations, and especially horses, are much more fragile physically
than humans. Without adequate supplies of food and water, horses break down much more
quickly than the men who ride them or use them to carry pack loads and pull carts or wagons.

Food for horses

In the West, from the ancient world through the Middle Ages and into modern times,
horses that were used for pulling carts or wagons, for carrying heavy loads in packs, and
for riding, as well as those that were trained for combat, were stall fed, as were mules and

donkeys. These stall-fed animals can be contrasted with grass-fed ponies, which were much smaller than stall-fed horses. Ponies were used in central Asia by peoples such as the Huns, Turks, and Mongols. The process of stall-feeding means that about half of a horse's nutritional needs by weight had to be provided by grains such as barley, spelt, and oats, rather than by grass and other naturally occurring fodder. The grain used to feed horses and other animals also potentially could be consumed by soldiers, so that in cases of severe logistical problems, men could eat both their horses and the rations that would normally have been provided to their animals.

In general, the quantity of food required by a horse depends upon its weight in conjunction with the tasks that it was expected to perform under a variety of topographical and weather conditions. Most modern animals are larger than their ancient and medieval forbearers, and so an understanding of the size of horses during the course of the medieval period has depended on the research of physical anthropologists and paleo-zoologists, who have studied animal skeletons. Based on this modern scholarship, during much of the medieval period, an average-sized draft or pack horse required approximately 10 kilograms of food for its total daily ration. Horses that were trained specifically for combat purposes in the early and high Middle Ages, up to the twelfth century, generally did considerably

Figure 4.1 Eleventh-century Anglo-Saxon manuscript depiction of mounted soldiers
Source: © Smith Archive/Alamy Stock Photo WH8H2P

less work than either draft or pack horses on a daily basis. However, warhorses were probably larger than animals used for pulling wagons or carrying loads as pack animals. Consequently, most scholars agree that the daily consumption of food was likely about the same. By the later Middle Ages, however, it appears that horses that were specifically trained for combat were much larger than in previous centuries, and so the food requirements were concomitantly larger, reaching as much as 15 kilograms a day, including both fodder and grain, for some particularly large breeds.

Horses and other animals consume enormous quantities of water during the course of strenuous activities such as carrying loads and pulling wagons. Even horses that were simply ridden on campaign required approximately ten times the water of an average man. In part, this large volume of water was necessary to digest the half of the animals' diet that was composed of hay and grass. Armies that were travelling on land were incapable of transporting the water that was required by both soldiers and their animals, and so found it necessary to choose routes where fresh water was readily available from local sources. Horses and other animals are even more likely to reject brackish water than are humans.

Food for other animals

In addition to horses, pre-modern armies used mules and oxen as draft animals to pull wagons and carts. In some cases, mules, donkeys, and even camels also were used as pack animals in Western Europe. In the Muslim east, camels also were used to transport men, and even were deployed in combat. Medieval mules required, in total, about three-quarters of the rations required by horses, amounting to some 7.5 kilograms of fodder and grain. Donkeys, which generally are smaller than mules, required a total of about 5 kilograms of food per day, of which just 1 kilogram had to be grain. Camels required approximately 12 kilograms of food each day, of which 5 kilograms had to be grain. Oxen required no grain as part of their food allotment; however, they did require approximately 20 kilograms of fodder each day, all of which, in principle, could be obtained through grazing if time and conditions permitted. Considered in total, a military force accompanied by 1,000 pack and draft animals, divided evenly among horses and mules, required each day almost 9,000 kilograms of food, of which more than 4,000 kilograms was grain. If the military force were accompanied by an additional 1,000 horses that were trained for combat, then the total daily food requirements for the animals increased to almost 19,000 kilograms, of which more than 9,000 kilograms was grain.

Carrying food supplies

The soldier's pack

Detailed examinations by scholars specializing in the military history of the Hellenistic and Roman periods have made clear that soldiers were capable of carrying packs filled with approximately 45 kilograms (about 100 pounds) of rations and equipment while on the march. For a Roman legionary of the late Republic or Principate, this amounted to a minimum of seventeen days of food rations, along with his full kit of weapons and other gear. The conclusions of military historians regarding the weights of the packs carried by Roman soldiers on campaign have been tested by scholars in the tradition of cultural archaeology, who have shown, in controlled experiments, that untrained civilian men, of average size and weight, were able to carry pack loads of 43–46 kilograms over an extended period. The civilians who took part in these experiments marched for a period of twenty consecutive days, covering a distance of 500 kilometres, in the course of which they traversed an Alpine pass. During the entire course of this march, over what certainly can be considered a difficult course because of the hilly terrain and thin air, the men were able to maintain a pace that averaged 25 kilometres a day, which was about the pace expected of Roman legionaries serving under Caesar, as he made clear in his account of his army's campaigns in Gaul.

The men who took part in this experiment included a plumber, a businessman, an insurance salesman, a sanitation official, a policeman, a student, a civilian employee of the U.S. Army, and a historian. For the most part, these individuals were not engaged in professions that required the types of lengthy hard labour that would lead to the development of considerable strength and endurance. This can be understood as being in stark contrast with the farmers who comprised the vast majority of fighting men during the medieval millennium and whose daily labour was more conducive to the development of considerable bodily strength and physical endurance. It is likely for this reason that military theorists from Vegetius in the fifth century to Thomas Jefferson in the eighteenth century regarded farmers as making the best soldiers.

Food on the hoof

In considering the movement of large herds of cattle, it is clear from a wide range of sources that they could travel 25 kilometres per day if they were tended by men practiced in droving these animals. Evidence regarding the movement of large herds of cattle in the American Southwest during the nineteenth century – that is, long before the introduction of modern technology – indicates that up to 2,000 animals could be driven by no more than fifteen men. In fact, the task was really quite straightforward, despite the image presented of stampeding herds in cinema 'Westerns'. Once the herd was assembled, an experienced herder picked two of the strongest animals, which naturally move to the front of the herd, and placed a bell on each one. The cattle then followed these leaders in a docile and instinctual manner, which is often denoted as the 'herd instinct'. When the man in charge of the herd wanted the animals to stop for the night, or to stop to graze, he muted the bells. When it was time to start again, the mutes were taken off the bells.

According to the estimates of modern physical anthropologists, an average head of cattle in the medieval period weighed approximately 350 kilograms, which is about two-thirds the size of a modern animal of what might be considered the same breed. Of the total weight of 350 kilograms, about 200 could be used for food. Thus, if a commander wished to substitute fresh meat for grain in feeding his men, one head of cattle can be understood to represent some 500,000 calories, or the total caloric needs of about 140 men for one day. A herd of cattle numbering 1,000 animals, therefore, could provide the entire caloric needs of 14,000 men for ten full days. However, while on the road, the cattle tended to lose weight, so that the earlier in the march they were eaten, the more food they provided.

Vehicles

It is clear from a vast range of sources that carts and wagons were used throughout the Roman Empire and medieval Europe for the transportation of supplies. In understanding their role in military logistics, three matters are of primary concern. These are the carrying capacity of the vehicles, the speed with which they could move, and also the routes on which they could be used. In light of the considerable body of scholarly literature on the topic, it is unlikely that ox-drawn carts were capable of moving more than 15 kilometres a day, and thereby were unable to keep pace with foot soldiers or, for that matter, herds of cattle. By contrast, both carts and wagons drawn by horses and mules could travel at least 30 kilometres each day, even when fully loaded with supplies.

The research of physical anthropologists and forensic veterinary specialists has made possible an understanding of the size and strength of medieval horses and mules, and hence their hauling abilities. Similarly, the investigations by historians of technology have shed considerable light on the development of both vehicle and harness design during the medieval period. The two most crucial innovations in this regard are the gradual introduction of the shoulder harness as opposed to neck harness, during the ninth century, and the development of a pivoting front axle and moveable whippletree during the twelfth century. The first of these technological innovations allowed horses and mules to pull fully loaded carts and wagons without suffocating themselves. The latter two inventions greatly improved the manoeuvrability of wagons and provided a means of distributing equally the weight of the vehicle and its load among all of the draft animals.

In light of this research, most scholars agree that Roman wagons and carts, of the types that were in general use throughout Latin Europe up to the twelfth century, could be used to haul loads of 660 and 500 kilograms, respectively. Each of these types of vehicles was drawn by two draft animals, whether horses or mules. Thus, a wagon, if fully loaded with bread, could carry sufficient food to provide the caloric needs of 367 men for one day. A cart, by contrast, could carry enough bread to feed 278 soldiers. However, because the two horses that hauled each wagon or cart also had to eat approximately 10 kilograms of grain each day, these numbers must be reduced by about five and a half men each per day. Both carts and wagons had considerable greater hauling capacities during the thirteenth century and later because of the advantages provided by the whippletree. Many wagons had teams of 3–6 oxen or horses, each pulling an evenly distributed portion of the load, suggesting a carrying capacity of up to 1 metric tonne.

The decision by military commanders to choose to use wagons or carts to haul food supplies was affected by a number of variables. The first consideration, naturally, concerned the types of vehicles that were available. In addition, however, there were several other factors that impinged upon this decision. Wagons before c.1200 had a greater carrying capacity of some 160 kilograms as contrasted by carts, with the same cost in terms of animal transport (i.e. two draft animals for each). However, the wagon took up more space on the road, and was also more difficult to manoeuvre. This meant that there were some tertiary or even secondary routes that could be traversed by carts, but not by wagons. It was also easier to recover a cart that went into a ditch along the side of the road, or that became stuck in the mud. In general, therefore, under good weather conditions over high-quality roads, wagons were preferable. By contrast, in potentially adverse weather conditions, such as frequently occur during the spring and autumn, or along lower quality roads, carts had significant advantages.

Pack animals

As was true of draft animals, the carrying capacity of horses and mules depended largely on their size and weight. On average, horses and mules of the size available throughout the medieval period had the capacity to carry loads of about 100 kilograms. Camels, by contrast, which were used in the *Regnum Francorum* during the Merovingian period as pack animals, could carry approximately 150 kilograms. All of these beasts could easily cover 25 kilometres

Figure 4.2a Roman road surface: Via Appia Antica in Rome
Source: Licensed under the Creative Commons Attribution Share Alike 3.0 Unported license by MM.

Figure 4.2b Cobble stone at the end of the Appian Way
Source: © Panther Media GmbH/Alamy Stock Photo KRWA77

a day while carrying full loads. However, they were less efficient in doing so than draft animals pulling carts or wagons. Each pack animal consumed 5 per cent of its total potential load each day. By contrast, the two draft animals hauling a cart consumed just 2 per cent of their total load, and the draft animals hauling a wagon just 1.5 per cent. However, pack animals did provide considerably greater flexibility in terms of route, as they could travel in topographically difficult places where carts and wagons simply could not be deployed.

Water transport

Roman, medieval, early modern, and, indeed, modern military planners recognized and continue to recognize that transportation of cargo by water was and is far more efficient than overland transport. This was particularly true in pre-modern periods with regard to bulk cargoes such as grain, and exceptionally heavy objects, such as stones that were used as ammunition in artillery or for building purposes. The Romans used sailing ships for open sea transportation that could carry up to 900 metric tonnes of grain for use by the army across the Mediterranean. This is the weight equivalent of 1,800 wagons drawn by 3,600 horses. More common, however, were sea-going ships in the 30-metric-tonne range which operated in the Mediterranean Sea, Atlantic Ocean, English Channel, North Sea, and Baltic Sea. On average, each of these ships could carry the same amount of grain as sixty wagons pulled by 120 horses. The Romans also used riverboats, such as barges, for the transportation of grain inland. Many of these boats had a carrying capacity of 20 tonnes, or even more. Sometimes, ships could even sail at night, thereby increasing their relative speed vis-à-vis land-based transportation.

During the early medieval period, the very large–capacity Roman ships apparently disappeared from use in the Mediterranean as need for large-scale movement of grain, particularly to feed the erstwhile imperial capital, came to an end. By contrast, mid-scale sea-going vessels with a carrying capacity of several dozen to several score tonnes continued to be used throughout the pre-crusade period in both the Mediterranean and in the northern seas. Galleys, which were powered, for the most part, by large crews of oarsmen, often numbering well over 100 men, were a primary type of cargo ship in the Mediterranean.

There were three main types of cargo ships in the north before c.1200. These were the Nordic-type ship, the Utrecht-type craft, and the proto-cog. Both the Nordic-type and the Utrecht-type ships developed from original log-boat forms. These log-boat ships were constructed by hollowing out a large oak log and building up the sides of the ship from this base. Both the Nordic-type and Utrecht-type ships built up the sides from this oak foundation using a clinker method of overlapping planks that were held in place by rivets, often of iron, and caulked with a variety of substances, including moss and animal hair. The major difference was that Utrecht-type ships were built up from oak logs that had been expanded, using fire and water. These bases were further built up with heavy planking, which also overlapped in a manner similar to the Nordic-type ships. The Utrecht-type ships are thought by some archaeologists to have been the ancestors of the ship known as the hulk, which operated throughout the high and late medieval periods. By contrast with the other two main northern ship types, the proto-cogs and later fully developed cogs were not based on log keels, but rather had a flattish bottom with flush rather than overlapping planking. The sides of the ship used an overlapping planking system. The proto-cogs may have originated as river craft that later were adapted for ocean travel.

In addition to these sea-going ships, a variety of river boats was in use in the period before c.1200, as well. These ranged in size from simple log-boats, which had neither a stem nor

Figure 4.3 Medieval ship from excavation; an archaeologist excavating the medieval ship found during the building of a new arts centre in Newport, south Wales

Source: © Jeff Morgan 03 / Alamy Stock Photo A99D55

Figure 4.4 Anglo-Saxon view of a Viking dragon ship, tenth century

Source: © Granger Historical Picture Archive/Alamy Stock Photo FFTK7E

a stern post, to double log-boats, to flat-bottomed barges, which had planked hulls. Some of the largest of these, which shared many building characteristics with the proto-cogs, had a carrying capacity of up to 15 metric tonnes. They may also have been equipped with gates on their decks to facilitate the loading and off-loading of cargo, including animals. It is likely that further archaeological research will provide additional details about these ships and their development over time.

The twelfth century saw the rapid development of the cog into the dominant cargo ship in northern Europe. These ships had the same flat bottom of flush planks, which shifted towards overlapping edge-fastened side planking at the stem and stern, as exhibited in their earlier medieval forbearers. These vessels, like the proto-cogs, were also constructed in the clinker style on their sides, with overlapping rather than flush planks. However, the cogs of the thirteenth century and later were much larger than earlier ships, carrying cargoes a large as 300 tonnes. The main source of propulsion for the cog was a single square sail, and it used a small crew of a dozen to twenty men, as contrasted with well over 100 men who were required to row galleys, which could carry only half of the freight carried by cogs. Competition for the cogs as cargo vessels in the north came from hulks, which like the cog were both flat bottomed and clinker built. However, they lacked stem and stern posts. By the later medieval period, some hulks had a carrying capacity of 500 or even 600 tonnes. In the Mediterranean, there were also a variety of local ship types, as well as technological imports from the Muslim east, including the Red Sea and the Indian Ocean. Among these were multi-masted sailing ships. A variety of descriptions of these ships in narrative texts and depictions in a range of media indicate that many ship designs were in use at the same time.

All of these ocean-going and riverine ships had the potential to provide military commanders with great flexibility not only in the transportation of supplies, but also for carrying troops much faster than these men could march. However, the ability to make use of water transport depended on a variety of factors, including the proximity of the army to a river or the sea, the time of year, and finally the simple availability of shipping resources such as naval stores, ships, and other materials. Whenever possible, however, military commanders during the medieval period used water-borne transportation for supplies. Charlemagne, for example, used fleets of river boats on the Danube River to carry supplies for his armies that invaded the Avar kingdom in the late eighth century.

Late imperial logistics: sources of supply

In practical terms, the supply of the late imperial army had to take account of two largely separate elements. First, military forces that were stationed more or less permanently in one location, as was the case for most units along the frontier (*limitanei*) during the later empire, largely obtained provisions locally. Units that were stationed along rivers, however, could receive supplies from farther afield if necessary. Second, the mobile field units (*comatitenses*) of the later imperial army, according to imperial strategy, were not based in any one location for long periods of time, and so it was necessary to develop alternative means of supplying these forces as they were deployed in various locations throughout the empire, and even beyond the empire's frontiers. However, many of these units were encamped, especially during the winter, in the environs of large cities and benefitted from the highly developed infrastructure that fed these urban centres, which often were located along rivers.

One important source of supply for the *limitanei* consisted of the lands that were assigned directly to the military unit, often denoted as the fields of the legion (*prata legionis*). In some cases, these lands were farmed directly by the soldiers, and in others the land was leased out to civilians. In addition to these corporately held lands, over the course of the fourth and fifth centuries, as seen in Chapter 3, many *limitanei* also drew supplies from lands that were granted to them directly by the government and that were specifically intended to support their military service. These lands were intended to be sufficiently productive that they could support the fighting man, his family, and his dependents, often slaves, who actually performed the agricultural labour necessary to make the system work.

In order to augment the supplies available from these corporately and individually held lands, the Roman government relied on a variety of methods, including direct taxation on landholders, in both cash and kind; compulsory sales (*indictiones*) of goods required by the army, often at less than market rates; outright requisition; and even, perhaps as a last resort, regular purchases at the going market rate. The government appointed officials called *procuratores* who served as intermediaries between the producers of goods and merchants on the one hand, and soldiers on the other. However, there is also evidence in the form of contracts that were written on pieces of pottery (*ostraca*) that individual soldiers made arrangements with local merchants for the delivery of supplies. In Egypt, many of these contracts were written on papyrus, and a large number of these survived into the modern period and have been analyzed by scholars.

During the early empire, tax revenues in kind, as well as supplies obtained through other mechanisms, often were transported by the government from long-settled and wealthy provinces in the interior to military forces stationed along the frontier. For example, olive oil from Baetica, in south-central Spain, was transported in substantial quantities to the German frontier. Although there is very little written evidence of this pattern of distribution, distinctive oil containers (*amphorae*) from Baetica have been excavated from numerous legionary encampments that are dated through archaeological investigations to the first and second centuries AD. By the later Roman Empire, barrels replaced ceramic amphora. The wood and metal components of these storage vessels tended to break down over time, unless preserved in anaerobic conditions, so that far less material information has survived about the transportation of goods in the period after c.200. The fact that fewer barrels survive has been used by some scholars to claim that both manufacture and trade declined. However, this is, at best, an argument from silence.

Rather, it appears that by the later empire, the vast majority of supplies that were used by the *limitanei* were obtained locally. The populations living in the frontier zones, particularly along the Rhine and Danube rivers, were quite dense and wealthy, and many former legionary camps had grown into substantial cities. Among these, Trier is particularly noteworthy because it served as the imperial capital from 328–340, and again from 367–395. An important consequence of this substantial demographic and economic growth was that the frontier provinces were able to support directly the military units that had stimulated and protected their wealth.

As had been true in the early empire, during the fourth and fifth centuries, the army obtained supplies from the frontier provinces through a variety of means. Over the course of the fourth century, most taxes in kind were commuted to payments in gold. This process was far more advanced in the western provinces than in the eastern half of the empire, where taxes in kind continued to be levied in some districts well into the sixth century. Soldiers who were stationed along the western frontiers frequently were paid in cash, and were able to use this money to purchase supplies from local markets. From an economic perspective,

Figure 4.5 Amphorae, Bodrum Castle, Turkey
Source: Licensed under the Creative Commons Attribution-Share Alike 3.0 Unported license by Ad Meskens.

it is notable that soldiers were paid in low-value bronze coinage that was essentially fidu-
ciary in nature, to facilitate small-scale transactions. The commanders of military units also
used cash, including much more high-value gold coinage, to purchase supplies that were
required for the maintenance of their bases and some of the equipment of the men, including items such as leather for tents.

In many places throughout the West, it has been possible to identify, using both written
and material sources of information derived from archaeological excavations, the efforts
of local populations to engage in economic specialization to supply the needs of nearby
army bases. This included, for example, the establishment of industrial enterprises for the
production of glassware and pottery, as well as specialized smithies for the production of

high-quality armour that was superior to the equipment provided to soldiers by the government. In addition, there is a considerable amount of information to suggest that traditional trading routes were altered to provide commercial goods to army bases. This was the case, for example, in the provinces of Judea and Syria, whose garrisons of *limitanei* attracted traders in goat hides from as far away as the Arabian Peninsula. These goat skins were used to make legionary tents, and it is estimated that in excess of 60,000 goat skins were required to produce the tents used at any particular time by imperial forces in Judea alone.

The mobile field units (*comitatenses*) also benefitted from these locally based sources of supply when they were in barracks in and around one of the major cities of the empire, usually in close attendance on the emperor. Field units also had access to markets. However, when the *comitatenses* were deployed for operations within the empire, or marched towards the frontier, they often were given imperial permits to requisition supplies from the governmental officials in the provinces through which they were marching. Only grass and water could be taken legally without a permit.

In the Roman system of taxation in kind, which is sometimes denoted by scholars as the *annona militaris*, the taxpayer himself was required to transport to the local civil or military warehouse facility (*horreum*) the food, fodder, and other goods, including uniforms and leather, that were levied as taxes. These warehouses often were located in the largest local settlement of the district or *civitas*. When the taxpayer made his delivery, he received a receipt as proof of payment. The taxpayer was then, in theory, freed from any direct contact with soldiers. However, as numerous complaints by provincial taxpayers make clear, all too often, provincial officials either did not or could not provide adequate supplies for the army, and soldiers were unleashed directly on the local taxpayers to obtain their grain, oil, and wine.

When the system actually functioned in the manner that it had been designed by the imperial government, provincial officials were responsible for moving supplies from local grain storage facilities (*horrea*) to larger and more centrally located imperial *horrea*, which were established in major cities and along major transportation routes. From there, the supplies eventually would be transferred to military units. As the empire made the transition from taxation in kind to taxation in gold in the western provinces, imperial *horrea* remained important for the storage of supplies. However, food and fodder now generally were purchased by government officials rather than taken as taxes. Among the best known of these sites, from an archaeological perspective, are the great grain warehouses along the southern shore of Britain at places such as the fortified port of Pevensey (Roman Anderita).

One additional source of supply for units of both *limitanei* and *comitatenses* consisted of resources that were under direct imperial control. From at least the period of the early empire, these included substantial estates (*latifundia*) belonging to the imperial fisc that produced large quantities of grain, which could be used to supplement tax revenues in whatever ways that the emperor wished, including providing supplies to the army. A second and much more military-specific source of supply was introduced by Emperor Diocletian (284–305), who ordered the establishment of large-scale workshops (*fabricae*) that produced military equipment directly for the army. Many of the early *fabricae* were located near the frontiers to facilitate transportation to army units.

The number of *fabricae* increased steadily over the course of the fourth and fifth centuries. Forty-four of these large-scale production facilities are listed in the *Notitia dignitatum*, which was discussed in previous chapters. These *fabricae* produced bows, shields, leather and iron cuirasses, swords, spears, cavalry armour, various types of artillery, and uniforms. The individual *fabricae* were directed by officials called *praepositi fabricarum*, who oversaw the efforts of large numbers of slaves. These men and women comprised the majority of the skilled workforce in these facilities. The *fabricae* continued to function through the end of imperial rule in the West, and even beyond in some places. The Roman senator Cassiodorus, who served as the head of government offices (*magister officiorum*) to the Ostrogothic king Theodoric the Great (493–526), observed in a letter that the *fabricae* in Italy continued to function, but that it was difficult to find sufficient trained labourers. One apparent solution was to deploy soldiers, who were well acquainted with the nature of military equipment, to work in the *fabricae*.

Transportation logistics in the late empire

During peacetime, a key source of transportation resources for the movement of food supplies, fodder for horses, and also equipment both to the troops stationed along the frontier (*limitanei*) and to the mobile field forces (*comitatenses*) of the late Roman army consisted of the wagons, carts, mules, and donkeys of the civilian populations living in the provinces where these supplies were collected. Government officials at the provincial level had the overall responsibility for moving food and fodder to the military forces that required them. However, in most places, there were insufficient numbers of imperial officials to carry out these tasks in person. In addition, the imperial government did not maintain large fleets of vehicles, although there is significant evidence that there were imperial stud farms for the breeding of horses and mules, which were deployed directly with troops in the field. Rather, the supervision of the transportation process was imposed upon the members of city councils (*decuriones*). These men, who were local aristocrats, also were responsible for the collection of the taxes within their *civitates*, and so assigning to them an additional supervisory role in the service of the imperial government likely appeared both convenient and appropriate.

For the sake of convenience, transportation resources usually were mobilized from the inhabitants of the main urban centre (*urbs*) within the *civitas*. It was here that the main grain and fodder storage facilities for the district were to be found, and also where the largest concentration of wealthy landowners and merchants, who possessed substantial numbers of vehicles and animals, lived while not supervising their country estates during the agricultural season. However, if the inhabitants of the *urbes* saw the burden as too great, they could – and often did – complain to the provincial administration, and asked that the requirement to provide transportation resources as well as drivers and guards be distributed more evenly across the population of the *civitas*, and consequently be imposed on lesser centres of habitation, as well.

The obligation to provide transportation resources usually was confined to within the boundaries of the *civitates* themselves, although this might involve the transportation of goods over several hundred miles to the army, and the subsequent return home of empty wagons and carts. Moreover, the owners of the vehicles and animals were supposed to be paid for the use of their equipment and for their time and effort. The provincial government was required by the emperors to set specific rates for the use of all different types of transportation resources, and government officials were prohibited from demanding services at lower rates of remuneration. In addition, provincial governors were required to set a maximum limit on the numbers of vehicles and animals that could be requisitioned during the course of a year from both individuals and from communities. Individuals without a specific license from the government were prohibited legally from demanding the use of transportation resources. However, the great litany of complaints that were registered by provincial property owners makes clear that the regulations about payment, limitations on the number of vehicles or animals that were to be mobilized, and the prohibition on using this authority for private gain often were violated, and that the primary culprits were government officials themselves. The eighth book of the Theodosian Code includes numerous imperial commands (rescripts) to provincial governors to put an end to these abuses.

When the imperial government needed to move supplies to military units that were stationed in thinly populated frontier regions, where there were few – if any – urban centres, it was necessary to find alternative means of obtaining transportation. The most common method was to arrange contracts with private companies that used their own vehicles and animals to move government supplies at negotiated rates. Several contracts of this type have been identified by archaeologists and other specialists working on the desert frontier of the province of Egypt. Similar types of contracts also have been identified to supply remote outposts in Britain during the later empire.

Logistics in pre-crusade Europe

Just as the dissolution of imperial power in the West led to substantial changes in the organization and composition of post-imperial armies, as seen in Chapter 3, it is clear that the logistical systems that had been established by the Roman government to support a standing force of some 200,000 men in the western provinces also experienced a considerable transformation after the later fifth century. Nevertheless, in the same manner that the institutional and legal inheritance of Rome continued to play profound roles in the recruitment of medieval armies, these same factors, in addition to the military infrastructure detailed in Chapter 2, also shaped many aspects of medieval military logistics. These elements of change and continuity are illuminated most clearly in three major aspects of medieval military logistics: the acquisition of food and fodder for military forces, the production of arms and equipment, and finally, the mobilization of transportation resources.

Food and fodder in peacetime

As seen in Chapter 3, perhaps the single most important transformation in the military organization within the erstwhile Western Roman Empire from the latter fifth century onwards was the replacement of a centrally organized and sustained standing army by military forces that were dominated numerically by militia troops. From a logistical perspective, a major consequence of this transformation was that during periods of peace, the government was freed from the obligation to provide supplies of any type to the majority of the men who served in the army. By contrast with these militia troops, however, soldiers who served in the military household of the king – as well as those of secular and ecclesiastical magnates – often received food and other supplies as in-kind payment for their military service during periods of peace, as well as when they were deployed for military operations either in the field or as garrison troops. The king had to provide for his own men, but magnates were responsible for supplying their own household troops. As a consequence, the government was freed from the responsibility of supplying most of these men, as well. Overall, these medieval household troops were, in many ways, analogous to the *comitatenses* of the later empire and even more so of the military households of Roman secular officials and military commanders. As will become clear, professional soldiers in the early Middle Ages also frequently had sources of supply that were similar to those of their imperial predecessors.

During peacetime, most members of magnate and royal military households were permanently attendant on the important men who had recruited them. These fighting men received their meals, equipment, and lodging as part – and sometimes as the largest part – of their pay. The life of the mead-hall presented in the Anglo-Saxon epic poem *Beowulf*, although meant for entertainment purposes, does illuminate some of the material aspects of communal living among professional soldiers of rather low economic and social status, whose livelihood depended on the generosity of their employers. Similar insights are provided by the saga of the Jomsvikings, which is a fictional work, albeit one that drew on contemporary ideas. More accurate, although less entertaining, is the information provided by an administrative document (*polyptyque*) of the monastery of St. Riquier, which notes that the convent provided housing for 100 fighting men and stables for their horses during the early ninth century.

A more detailed account of the support of fighting men serving the military households of the king and his magnates is provided by a text titled *On the Governance of the Palace* (*De ordine palatii*). This work originally was composed by the Adalard of Corbie, a cousin of Charlemagne, during the late eighth century. It subsequently was revised and edited in various ways in the early 880s by Archbishop Hincmar of Rheims to shape the organization of the court of kings of his own day, particularly Louis III (died 882) and Carloman II (died 884). *De ordine palatii* treats a wide range of matters relating to the administration of the royal household, including many mundane issues such as the feeding of the royal family, and the obligation of the king to support the many retainers, including the fighting men, who were permanently attached to the court.

The text emphasizes that feeding the king's household troops was not to be left to chance, and the soldiers should not be required to search out their own food and drink. Rather, this task was assigned to high officials within the household. In addition, *De ordine palatii* makes clear that the queen had a particular obligation to oversee the supply of the king's household troops, and ensure that these men were well treated. She also handed out gifts in the king's name to the men in a manner similar to the *donativa* that were distributed during the later empire. The queen's role here also is reminiscent of Wealhtheow in *Beowulf*, who passed among Hrothgar's men, pouring mead into their cups. However, from an administrative perspective, the queen in *De ordine palatii* has much more in common with late Roman empresses, who received the honorific *mater castrorum* (mother of the camps) for their role in ensuring the good treatment of imperial troops.

In addition to dealing with the provision of food and drink to the king's own troops, *De ordine palatii* also considers the logistical needs of the military households of the magnates who were attending court. The treatise indicates that magnates frequently brought substantial numbers of fighting men with them when they were invited to attend court, even in peacetime. It seems likely that many magnates, including ecclesiastical office holders, employed a large and well-equipped fighting force as a means of displaying both their wealth and loyalty to the king, and as an effective means of competing with other magnates for the king's attention and largess. As a consequence, one of the challenges of palace administration was to ensure that these numerous soldiers were maintained adequately while at court. To this end, *De ordine palatii* makes clear that the king is to command his magnates to ensure the regular delivery of food and other supplies for their own men.

For the most part, in peacetime, the secular and ecclesiastical magnates drew upon the resources of their own estates to support their men. In some cases, it is clear that magnates sought to acquire estates near to royal palace complexes where kings spent a great deal of their time, and where magnates could also expect to have to find lodging and supplies for themselves and their men. During Charlemagne's reign, many magnates received permission to build permanent dwellings near the royal palace at Aachen. Similarly, the Ottonian kings of Germany gave grants of property near their royal palaces in Regensburg and Frankfurt to many bishops for the specific purpose of providing these prelates with comfortable accommodations while attending court and providing for their households.

The expenses involved in maintaining military households, particularly for ecclesiastical officials, were quite high. As was observed in Chapter 3, 50 per cent or more of the revenues of an abbot or bishop during the Carolingian period were devoted to the maintenance of his troops. In the mid-eleventh century, the chronicler Anselm of Liège looked back fondly to the pontificate of Notker (972–1008) whom he praised for being able to limit expenditures on his military household to just one-third of the bishopric's income. But this was, as Anselm stressed, an extraordinary situation, and the burdens in his own day were much higher.

During periods of peace, or at least in the absence of active offensive campaigns, the royal military household also was supported in large part through the resources of the royal fisc (discussed in more detail later in the chapter). However, many rulers in the Latin West were also able to call upon the resources of their magnates, particularly ecclesiastical magnates, for support as the court travelled through the realm. This practice was much more important for the maintenance of the royal court in larger kingdoms such as the *Regnum Francorum* under the Carolingians and in Germany during the tenth and eleventh centuries than for smaller polities such as Wessex in England or the county of Anjou in the west of France. Nevertheless, the peripatetic nature of medieval governments even during periods of peace entailed a concomitant need to supply the ruler's household troops wherever the king or lesser prince travelled, even when there were no estates of the royal fisc nearby.

Food and fodder on campaign

Concomitant with the dissolution of the imperial army in the West was the gradual but general abandonment of broad-based land and personal taxes by the governments of Rome's successor states. As seen in Chapter 3, these fiscal obligations were replaced, in large part, by the obligation on landholders to perform military service personally in expeditionary campaigns beyond their home districts, or to hire substitutes if they could not serve. The decision by Frankish, Visigothic, Ostrogothic, and other kings to commute taxation for military service meant that an important source of income, whether in cash or in kind, was no longer available to purchase or provide food and fodder for military contingents while they were on campaign. However, as will be seen in the next section, the requirement for militia troops to provide much of their own food and other supplies, such as weapons and clothing, also limited the direct expenditure by the government to provide logistic support for military operations.

Supplies carried by militia troops

One solution that many early medieval governments introduced was to require militia troops summoned for campaign duty to supply their own food, and also fodder for their animals, for a specified length of time. Carolingian edicts on this question that survive from the eighth century but which drew on much earlier Merovingian precedents, specify that members of the expeditionary levies were to supply themselves with food for three months, and with clothing and weapons for six months. When the members of the expeditionary

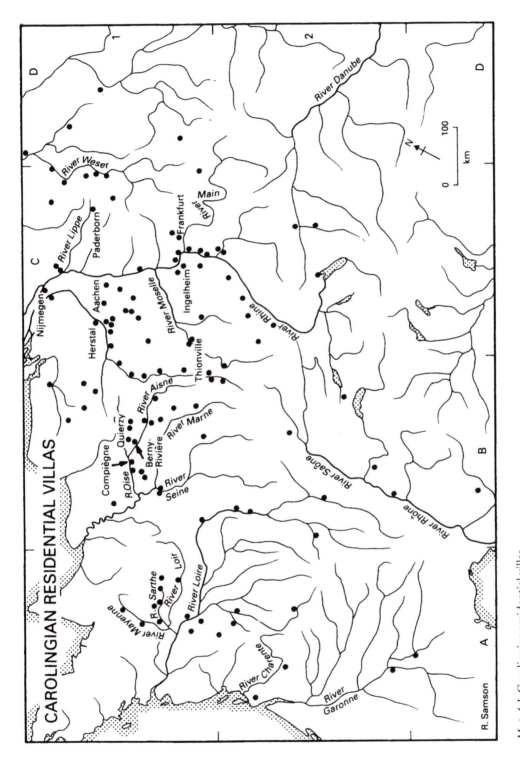

Map 4.1 Carolingian residential villas

Source: *Atlas of Medieval Europe* © R. Samson

levy had consumed their three-month ration, the government was to provide food to these soldiers free of charge. This was very important in the context of lengthy sieges that might last a year or even longer.

A similar pattern can be seen with regard to the city militias that operated along the Castilian frontiers with Muslim-ruled regions of the Iberian Peninsula. Here, many charters (*fueros*) that were granted to cities by the kings of León-Castile from the eleventh through the thirteenth centuries specified that the townsmen were to bring their own supplies when they served on campaign. Townsmen elected officials called *quadrillos*, whose tasks included overseeing the distribution of supplies among the men in their military units while on the march. In addition, many towns also had the obligation – when not called upon by the king to send contingents of fighting men to serve on campaign – to provide supplies to the militias of other towns that had been mobilized. On the other end of the Latin West, landowners in the German kingdom on the eve of the First Crusade also had the obligation to bring supplies for their own use on campaign. In his commentary on the civil war in Germany during the early 1070s, the contemporary writer Lampert of Hersfeld (died c.1088) observed that when Saxon levies marched to the frontier with Thuringia to face the army of King Henry IV (1056–1106), the expectation was that they would bring sufficient quantities of supplies to sustain themselves in the field for as long as the campaign lasted.

It should be noted that the decentralization of the obligation to provide supplies from the government to the individual soldier within the expeditionary levy was not a complete innovation in the early medieval period. As discussed previously, the *limitanei* of the later Roman Empire very frequently were granted land by the government, with which they were required to provide or to purchase with their own money many if not all of the supplies that would permit them to serve in the army. In this respect, the militia troops who were obligated to serve on campaign, although they did not hold their land from the government, nevertheless were subject to regulations that were very similar from a logistical perspective to elements of the late Roman standing army that were permanently stationed along the frontier.

Similar to the *limitanei*, members of medieval expeditionary levies also often had to leave their home districts when going on campaign. This requirement had the necessary corollary that these militia troops needed supplies while in the field. In the Frankish context, the obligation for members of the expeditionary levies to provide themselves with food supplies for three months meant that each fighting man had to bring on campaign a bare minimum of 180 kilograms of grain and other consumables, excluding beverages such as beer or wine, just for his own use. If the fighting man were mounted, he required an additional 450 kilograms of grain for each of his horses over the course of three months. The remainder of the horse's diet, comprising of 450 kilograms of grass or hay over a three-month period, might have been available at no cost over the course of the march, depending on the terrain and time of the year. One element of Roman law regarding provisioning that was enforced during the early medieval period was the right of soldiers to take water and grass at no charge from landowners.

It is self-evident that no soldier personally was capable of carrying 80 kilograms, much less an additional 450 kilograms, of grain and other food. This reality meant the government and the soldiers were compelled to find mutually agreeable methods to ensure that the supply needs of the expeditionary levies were met in an effective manner. One partial solution that is suggested by a range of narrative sources is that groups of men from the same locale pooled their resources and transported their food in a cart or wagon. Many early medieval authors drew attention to the supply carts of the army, although usually only in extraordinary circumstances such as when these were lost to enemy action.

Markets

Another solution, and one that was likely much more common within the frontiers of the kingdom, was that the government encouraged militia men to bring money with them rather than a full complement of supplies, and then facilitated the sale of food and fodder along the line of march. Several edicts issued by Carolingian kings emphasize the government's role in ensuring that merchants did not gouge customers in times of need through unreasonably high prices. This included soldiers who were on campaign. In 866, for example, Emperor Louis II (855–875), the Carolingian ruler of Italy, issued a set of ordinances for his army as it prepared to campaign in the region of Benevento in southern Italy. Among these royal commands was one focused on merchants who would bring goods to establish markets all along the army's line of march, where the soldiers could purchase food and other supplies. Louis emphasized in this command that the merchants were forbidden to sell these goods at prices that were higher than they charged to their own neighbours. As will be seen later on in the chapter, during the crusades one of the main sources of supply for the Christian army of so-called 'armed pilgrims' consisted of markets organized by the governments of the lands through which they marched, and particularly by the Byzantine imperial government.

In addition to relying on private markets, which were accorded a significant level of governmental supervision, and even encouraging local merchants to establish markets at suitable locations along the line of march, it appears that early medieval governments also sold food and other goods directly to soldiers. The rulers of Rome's successor states acquired vast landed resources when they took control of the imperial fisc, which continued to be managed by government officials on behalf of the king. The extent of fiscal resources available to governmental authorities varied considerably, both among Rome's immediate successor states and over time as kingdoms, such as the *Regnum Francorum*, waxed, waned, and waxed again in size and power. It has been estimated that Charlemagne was able to draw on the resources of approximately 2,000 fiscal complexes north of the Alps – that is, excluding those in Italy – at the time of his imperial coronation in 800.

During the tenth and eleventh centuries, the rulers of the powerful German kingdom, which comprised much of the central and all of the eastern regions of what had been Charlemagne's empire, as well as significant lands east of the Saale and Elbe rivers, which they conquered on their own, could draw upon the production of approximately 1,000 fiscal complexes, excluding imperial holdings in northern and central Italy. By contrast, the various rulers of polities on the Iberian Peninsula, Anglo-Saxon England, and the principalities that were established in the wake of the weakening of royal power in the West Frankish realm, disposed of far less extensive fiscal resources, even when they were able to draw effectively on the estates held by monasteries and bishoprics in their territories.

The fiscal resources available to powerful rulers such as the Carolingians, and their successors in the East Frankish/German kingdom, were vastly larger than would have been necessary simply to supply the needs of the members of the royal court. The kings of the Ottonian dynasty, for example, likely needed on average just about 6 per cent of their fiscal revenues to provision the court over the course of the year. However, even this small percentage was not used in most years because both abbots and bishops were required to provide extensive hospitality to the royal court as it travelled through the realm, thereby diminishing even further the need to draw on fiscal assets. Even lesser rulers, such as the kings of Wessex, possessed fiscal assets that were disproportionate to the need to supply the royal court alone. The main purpose of the fisc was to support royal policy initiatives, the most important of which were military in nature, particularly providing logistical support for military operations.

A wide range of documents attest to the uses of the royal fisc for military purposes throughout the Latin West. However, the most thorough-going description of the management of these fiscal resources is to be found in a text known as the *Capitulare de villis*, which was issued by Charlemagne before 800, and perhaps as early as the 770s. This text provides a detailed – although not exhaustive – list of instructions for royal estate managers, called variously *iudices, villici, actores*, and *maiores*. Taken as a whole, these instructions make clear that managers of royal estates were required by the government to keep active, written inventories of all assets associated with their *villae*, and also to keep detailed records of all the production of their estates over the course of the year. In addition, the capitulary indicates that the managers of the royal estates were either to keep the agricultural – as well as industrial – production of the *villae* for use by the royal government, or were to make it available for sale, depending on the instructions that they received from the king's officials. As evidenced by the numerous chapters of *Capitulare de villis* dedicated to the topic, the most important task for which estate production was earmarked was the support of the army. In some cases, this meant provision of supplies to the king's military household, and in other cases, estate managers were to sell surpluses to members of the expeditionary levy. Fragments of various government documents, such as the well-known *Brevium exempla*, which have survived accidentally even though they were highly time-conditioned, show that royal commands in regard to the *Capitulare de villis* were obeyed not only under the Carolingians, but under their successors, as well.

Roman military taxes in medieval contexts

Despite the large scale of the fiscal resources held by numerous rulers in the pre-crusade period, many governments also sought to use legal precedents from the late Roman Empire to facilitate the acquisition of additional supplies of food and fodder for the army. As discussed previously, broad-based taxation largely was abandoned by royal governments in the post-Roman period. However, some taxation in kind for military purposes did continue. Among these imposts was the government's right to take water and grass free of charge for royal officials and for the army. We see this state of affairs as early as 507, when the Frankish ruler Clovis launched an invasion of the Visigothic kingdom in Aquitaine. Clovis sent out the general order that his troops were restricted to taking only water and grass along the line of march without paying the landowner. This requirement, as discussed earlier, can be traced back to Roman law. When two of Clovis' soldiers were caught taking hay for their horses without paying for it, the Frankish king had them executed as an example to all, making clear that his orders were to be obeyed, even in regard to an item such as hay.

A second element of continuity with late Roman military taxation was the government's right to demand the provision of grain for use by the army. The anonymous biographer of Louis the Pious (died 840), who is denoted by scholars as the Astronomer, observed in his text, written during the mid-ninth century, that among the reforms for which Louis deserved praise was:

> that he prohibited the collection from the lower social orders of the *annona militares*, which colloquially was called *fodrum*. And although Louis' military commanders found this difficult to accept, this man (Louis) took account of the poverty of those who were providing the grain, and the cruelty of those who were demanding it, and the

consequent perdition for both groups. And so he judged it sufficient to provide for his own men from his own resources, rather than allow his people to fall into grave difficulties because of the enormous quantities of grain that they had to deliver.

Louis the Pious obviously had sufficient resources from the royal fisc to sustain military operations in Muslim Spain, which was the main region in which he led his armies as king in Aquitaine.

The context of the Astronomer's observations suggest that this *annona militaris* was a continuation of Roman-style taxation in kind for the support of military forces rather than the forced sale of grain. Notably, it was the king's own men who benefitted from the *annona*, and it was the king's officers who worried about the lack of supplies if the king followed through on his command. However, Louis the Pious' act did not represent a complete end to the *annona militaris*, but rather was an effort to limit what appears to have been corruption on the part of his officials, who were taking too much from those who could least afford it. Similar complaints were made regularly in the late Roman Empire and spurred similar efforts at reform, as illuminated by imperial rescripts issued by both western and eastern emperors during the fourth and fifth centuries which subsequently were recorded in the Theodosian Code. Tellingly, it was only poorer landowners, the so-called *plebei*, who were freed from the *annona* by King Louis. The obligation to pay this grain tax remained for wealthy landowners, and particularly ecclesiastical institutions, throughout the period not only up to the First Crusade but, indeed, well into the thirteenth century throughout the lands that once comprised the Carolingian Empire.

A similar pattern of taxation also can be seen in Anglo-Saxon England. The law code of King Ine of Wessex (688–726) established a standard tax, called a *feorm*, which was imposed on landowners. Royal assessors used the hide, as seen in previous chapters, as the basic unit of assessment. For each ten hides, landowners were required to pay ten vats of honey, 300 loaves of bread, forty-two measures of ale, two full-grown cows or ten castrated sheep, ten geese, twenty hens, ten cheeses, and one hundred eels, as well as butter and 20 pounds of fodder, which in this case likely meant grain in the form of rye or oats. Many scholars believe that the *feorm* was levied before Ine's reign, but that he systematized its collection. The origin of this tax is open to significant debate in light of the limited number of sources for early Anglo-Saxon history. However, it seems likely to the authors of this text that Ine or his predecessors were influenced by their Merovingian contemporaries across the English Channel, with whom they had significant cultural and economic exchange. By the later Anglo-Saxon period, the payments in kind of the *feorm* had been commuted to coin. This tax remained in force in England up through the Norman Conquest in 1066, and there are mentions of the *feorm* in the Domesday Book, which was compiled by William the Conqueror's government in 1086 in order to facilitate royal taxation.

In considering the scale of the *feorm*, it is clear that far more food was levied than was required simply for the support of the royal court, even if this was one of the original purposes of the tax. Royal charters from Wessex indicate that the king granted some of the revenues from the *feorm* to both individuals and to churches. However, it seems likely that the *feorm* also was used to support royal military forces on campaign. This supposition is supported by the observation that a very large part of the tax consisted of live animals, which, as seen earlier, could be moved relatively easily with the army. The tax also requirement the payment of honey, which was the basic sweetener used at the time, and is thought to have had a considerable positive effect on morale. In addition, one of this food's special characteristics is that it never spoils, and is a valuable source of calories for lengthy journeys.

On the continent, the key obligations imposed by the government on ecclesiastical institutions with regard to logistical matters were denoted in contemporary sources as *fodrum* and *gistum*. *Fodrum* generally entailed the provision of both food and fodder for the support of the royal court and the royal army, which often amounted to the same thing. *Gistum* was the requirement to provide lodging and hospitality to the ruler and to those of his officials who had a governmental license to demand this obligation from ecclesiastical institutions. Both *fodrum* and *gistum* often resulted in extensive costs for the monasteries and bishoprics that bore these tax burdens. It is therefore hardly surprising that just as was true of Roman military taxation, much of the information that survives regarding *fodrum* and *gistum* within the German kingdom and Italy derives from documents that record the efforts of ecclesiastical institutions either to escape from their obligations, or their complaints about abuses by government officials. These complaints are also seen in the late West Frankish and French realms, despite their relatively weak royal governments.

The most common type of source of information about the obligations for *fodrum* and *gistum* are the immunity clause of charters issued by royal, as well as princely, governments to abbots, abbesses, and bishops. These immunity clauses list the obligations from which a particular ecclesiastical institution had been freed, which sometimes included *fodrum* and *gistum*, along with other kinds of royal imposts, such as the tax on vehicles carrying goods to market (*vectigalia*), and even the obligation to provide military forces for royal campaigns. Complaints about governmental misuse of ecclesiastical assets also appear in charters when rulers addressed such abuses in the prologue of the document that was intended to demonstrate their commitment to good governance. It is more common, however, to find discussion of abuses in chronicles composed by churchmen who hoped to use their historical works as elements in a legal struggle to obtain redress from the government.

Alongside military taxes in Christian realms, the continuation of the *annona militaris* can also be seen in regions that were once part of the Western Empire but fell under non-Christian rule. The institution of the *alorines*, which operated in the Islamic Caliphate on the Iberian Peninsula during the late tenth and early eleventh centuries, also was based on the Roman military tax. Officials of the caliph's government were empowered to collect grain in areas that enjoyed good harvests in order to mitigate the effect of poor harvests in other regions. The most important use of the grain collected under the cover of the *alorines*, however, remained the support of the army. Grain that was levied by the caliph's officials in this manner was stored in government warehouses and then distributed to officials, who had licenses from the government to draw on these supplies. The system thereby resembles very closely Roman practice in the late empire. However, as was true of the *annona militaris* under the Carolingians, Merovingians, and the late Romans, the power to collect grain from the population as a tax led to a considerable level of corruption, through which a number of the caliph's officials became very wealthy.

Another important element of continuity with late Roman military taxes was the obligation to provide transportation for supplies for the army. As seen in Chapter 2, free tenants of great landlords in the later Roman Empire, denoted in legal sources as *coloni*, had a wide range of obligations to the government in the form of labour taxes. These included the obligation to provide transportation for the movement of supplies for the army. Numerous administrative documents from monasteries illuminate the ways in which these obligations were maintained by Rome's successors in the West. These obligations, denoted variously as *angaria, scara*, and *parafredus*, are listed among the obligations on tenants of great ecclesiastical estates. In times of peace, these transportation duties were at the disposal of the monasteries and bishoprics. However, in times of war, or when the royal court was passing through the region, the king was able to demand that the tenants of the great landowners provide this service to the government. Numerous ecclesiastical administrative documents also show that many of the public labour obligations imposed on tenants over time had been fiscalized and transformed into payments in money, which were owed to the government, but which often were delegated to the churches on whose lands these obligated tenants lived. The military nature of these fiscalized dues is demonstrated by the names given to them in the sources such as *hostilicium, heriscilling, herimalder, hostisana,* or payments made *ad hostem* or *in hostem,* all of which make use of either Latin or German word elements pertaining to military operations.

Foraging and plunder

Scholars enamoured of the notion that warfare in the pre-crusade period was conducted by primitive and small-scale armies of warriors modelled on Tacitus' *Germania* argue that supply was not a matter of concern for governments in an institutional sense, but rather was part and parcel of the aristocratic war band's raid-and-plunder style of fighting. According to this view, small armies of mounted 'warriors' simply looted what they required from defenceless villagers and peasants along their route, whether they were in friendly or in hostile territory. Such a model becomes untenable, however, under close scrutiny. First, from an evidentiary standpoint, there is very limited information from the sources to indicate that armies actually did plunder within their own kingdoms or territories. In the few instances in which this type of plunder is identified by authors, it is clear either that the soldiers involved were punished by their commanders, or that the writer was seeking to impugn the honour of the commander by claiming that he allowed his men to engage in clearly illegal behaviour without punishing them.

From a tactical and strategic perspective, it is clear that the vast majority of military operations directed towards territorial conquest during the medieval period focused on sieges of fortifications. These sieges, in turn, necessitated the mobilization of large armies, and concomitantly large quantities of food and fodder. The practical realities of moving an army on campaign meant that it was impossible for a large force to acquire all of the supplies that were needed simply by stripping bare the lands along their immediate line of march. In fact, to take large quantities of plunder actually requires the use of large numbers of wagons, carts, or pack animals, as well as good roads, which is contrary to the image of the small army of heroic warriors postulated by scholars who support a 'dark age' model of warfare.

With all of these caveats in mind, it is clear that both some foraging and some taking of plunder took place in the context of medieval warfare, and could, on occasion, serve as an adjunct of sorts to regular logistical supply. Among the most successful practitioners of the use of plunder and forage as an important method of acquiring provisions to continue their military operations were the Vikings. Scandinavian fleets used the extensive river systems that fed into the North Sea, English Channel, and even the Atlantic Ocean to penetrate deeply into the Frankish realms during the ninth, tenth, and even into the early eleventh centuries. They focused their attention on attacking high-value targets, such as monasteries, which were filled with precious objects, and whose inhabitants came from wealthy and aristocratic families who were able to pay high ransoms. Not coincidentally, monasteries also were the centres of rural economic networks, and held vast agricultural surpluses in their warehouses. Consequently, when Viking raiders seized control over a monastery, they also gained access to substantial stores of grain, cheese, and animals, as well as beer and wine, depending on the location. In effect, the Vikings were able to acquire supplies that already had been collected, albeit not for them, and so their foraging and plundering was simplified to a great extent.

However, even the Vikings did not go raiding without bringing some supplies with them. The Viking long ships, with their dragon heads and rows of painted shields, are well-known to modern readers through film and television. However, these narrow ships, with their shallow drafts, were not capable of carrying sufficient provisions, and especially water, to make the journey from Denmark, Norway, and Sweden to their intended targets, in England, Ireland, Gaul, and Russia. Consequently, Viking fleets were accompanied by transport vessels called *knerrir* (singular *knorr* in Old Norse), which were constructed using the clinker method of overlapping planks, discussed previously. Clearly, the Vikings required 'supply ships' not only to provide logistic support for their operations, but also to transport booty and slaves back to Scandinavia.

Moreover, when Viking leaders sought to conquer rather than simply raid territories, they found it necessary to establish permanent bases of operation that also served as gathering and storage facilities for supplies. This pattern is clearest in England, where Viking armies sought to seize control over fortifications that were located at the nexus of several communications and trading routes, where local communities were accustomed to sell their agricultural surpluses. Similarly, during large-scale military operations on the continent, such as the siege of Paris discussed in Chapter 2, Viking forces also seized control over local production and market centres in order to facilitate their logistical needs.

The Hungarians also had a reputation during the tenth century as being able to move great distances very rapidly and simply live off the land. They are depicted by many contemporary and near-contemporary writers as swarming and burning their way across vast tracks of the country, pausing only to kill. Some modern scholars have treated these tenth- and eleventh-century accounts as transparent depictions of reality. A closer examination of the written sources for this period, however, indicates that when Hungarian raiders undertook lengthy military operations, they relied on regular sources of supply in much the same manner as their western opponents. The monk Ekkehard of St. Gall (died 1056), for example, observed that when the Hungarians raided his region of Swabia during the 920s, they moved quite slowly because they were impeded by their baggage train of wagons. In fact, Ekkehard states that the Hungarians circled these wagons at night to provide themselves with a semi-fortified encampment. Three decades later, in 954, when the Hungarians launched raids as far west the Rhine River, they had been recruited as allies by the opponents of King Otto the Great, with concomitant expectations of logistical support. The Hungarians depended on these German magnates, including Otto's own son-in-law, to provide them with supplies in order to continue their operations.

For more conventional armies, and particularly those that were engaged in wars of conquest, foraging and plunder served, at most, as an adjunct to the main source of supplies for the soldiers and mounts. This reality is illuminated, for example, by the fate of the army of King Henry III of Germany (1039–1056) during his campaign in Hungary in the autumn of 1051. The previous year, the Hungarians had invaded Bavaria. Although the local Bavarian levies had defeated the invaders, King Henry desired to undertake a major retaliatory action to teach the Hungarians a lesson.

Henry III divided his army into two columns for the invasion. One, under the command of the duke of Bavaria, travelled along the Danube River. The other column, under King Henry's personal command, marched through Carinthia, likely along the Drava River. The German king organized a formidable logistical operation that would permit him to sustain a significant and lengthy military campaign. Notably, each of the columns of his army was accompanied by a fleet of ships to carry supplies. The two columns also were accompanied by large numbers of pack animals, which served to transport supplies from the ships to Henry's troops as they departed from the river valleys in order to inflict the maximum possible damage on the Hungarians. However, King Henry permitted the campaign to drag on much longer than he had anticipated because the Hungarians refused to face either of the two German columns in battle, and simply withdrew deeper into the interior rather than fight.

As Henry's forces advanced and sought to force the Hungarians to meet them in battle, the Germans ravaged the countryside, plundering as they went. However, as the contemporary German chronicler Hermann of Reichenau (died 1054) observed, King Henry's two columns eventually began to exhaust the supplies that they had brought with them by ship. Despite the withdrawal of Hungarian military forces from their immediate vicinity, the German troops were unable to take advantage of the fact they were operating in rich agricultural lands during harvest season. The threat posed by the Hungarian army in the field was simply too great to permit the division and dispersal of the German army over a wide enough area to forage for supplies or to harvest the available grain and prepare it to be eaten. In short, the Hungarians succeeded in lengthening the campaign enough so that a lack of provisions compelled King Henry to withdraw his army without achieving a significant victory in the field. It is clear that Henry III's army could not live off the land on a regular basis.

We see a very similar phenomenon in the invasion of Scotland by King Edward II of England (1307–1327) in 1322. This campaign, which has been analyzed in detail by Michael Prestwich, similarly demonstrates the inability of large medieval armies to 'live off the land'. King Edward had mobilized an army of some 20,000 men, including 2,000 mounted troops, for the campaign. In preparation for this operation, the English government, following in the traditions established by King Edward I (1272–1307), discussed in more detail in what follows, mobilized hundreds of thousands of tonnes of food and fodder, which were deployed to forward bases at Newcastle on Tyne and Carlisle. However, due to the inability of the crown to mobilize a sufficient quantity of ships to carry these supplies northward up the Scottish coast, the advance of the English army ground to a halt. The situation was made even worse as the Scottish king, Robert Bruce (1306–1329), aware of Edward II's plans, commanded that all possible sources of food along the potential lines of English advance be removed or destroyed. As a consequence, in the absence of an effective supply line and facing a veritable supply desert, the English army had to withdraw, having accomplished nothing. As Robert Bruce's actions make clear, forewarning of potential invasions (a topic discussed in more detail in Chapter 7) often led locals to protect, hide, or destroy anything that could be of value to the invader, thereby limiting even further the ability of an army to rely on plunder to support itself in hostile territory.

Arms and equipment

In terms of overall tonnage, food and hard fodder comprised the vast majority of the logistical needs of medieval armies. However, to carry out their tasks, soldiers also required a wide range of weapons and equipment. In the pre-crusade period, as will be seen in greater detail in Chapter 5, both professional soldiers and militia forces of the expeditionary levies often were equipped with helmets, shields, and a coat of mail (*brunia* or *lorica*) that protected the torso. Most members of the levies in the pre-crusade era, however, were protected by heavy leather coats rather than by mail. Wealthier members of the expeditionary levies, as well as professional soldiers who served on horseback, were equipped with swords as well

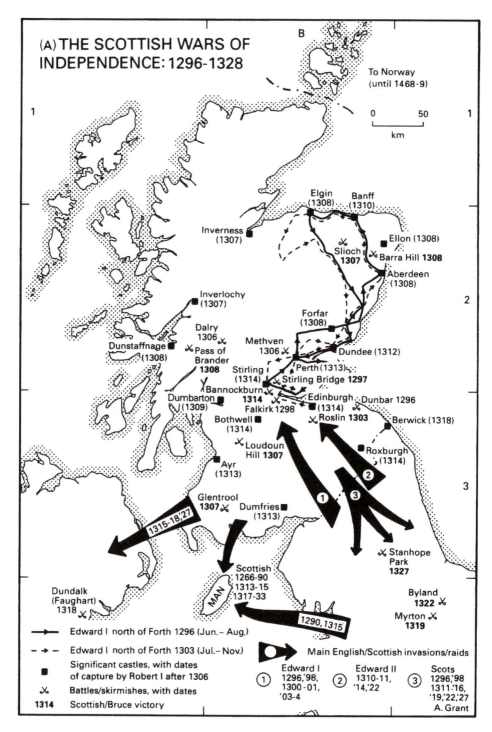

Map 4.2 The Scottish wars of independence
Source: *Atlas of Medieval Europe* © A. Grant

as spears, which could be used for thrusting or throwing. The basic hand-held weapon for foot soldiers in many regions was the spear, although Carolingian regulations from the early ninth century required that foot soldiers have swords, as well.

Many men who served on campaign also possessed missile weapons. The most common of these before the First Crusade was the bow. However, there is increasing evidence for the use of crossbows from around the turn of the first millennium. Men who lacked sufficient wealth to be mobilized for offensive military campaigns also were armed so that they could carry out their duties to defend their home regions. A number of narrative sources depict these men as being equipped with pole weapons, and also occasionally with shields. It is also likely that many of them possessed bows, as these were useful for hunting as well as for combat. Given that the vast majority of the population consisted of agricultural workers, it is also very likely that a great many farm implements were available for men engaged in local defence, including both poled tools and shorter weapons such as axes and large knives.

In addition to personal weapons, soldiers required a vast array of equipment for use in either garrison duty or on campaign. Much of this was of general use, including items such as pots, pans, knives, blankets, boots, carrying sacks, horseshoes, barrels, pitch, carts, tents, saddles, shovels, picks, and axes. Other items were much more specialized and intended specifically for military operations, including prefabricated bridges that were carried in pieces, boats, specialized water-tight war wagons (*basternae*), and siege equipment, including rams, artillery, towers, and ladders, which generally were carried in sections of about 3 metres in length.

The obligation to provide the weapons and equipment used by soldiers mirrored the obligations for the supply of food and fodder. Members of the expeditionary levies, and the broader population that had responsibilities for local defence, had to provide their own arms and other personal equipment. The requirements are illuminated in a number of governmental ordinances. The Visigothic legal code, issued during the 680s, required that men going on campaign come equipped with armour and shields. The Lombard kings of northern Italy also required that their soldiers be equipped with armour and shields, as well as arms for service in the field. The most detailed early medieval obligations were issued by Charlemagne, who specified the military equipment that members of the expeditionary levies had to bring on campaign. Men serving on foot required both a sword and shield. Wealthier men, who were obligated to serve on horseback, were required to have a mail coat (*brunia*), helmet, shield, spear, long sword (*spatha*), and short sword (*gladius*).

Information about the possession of arms by members of levies in the post-Carolingian period is found in a wide range of sources. Legal texts, including decrees for the so-called territorial peace, which were issued by kings and princes to outlaw any violence other than that specifically authorized by the government, discuss the arms possessed by men from all social strata, including ordinary farmers. The latter often had swords, which they were permitted to carry when travelling away from home, but which they were not permitted to use against their neighbours. Other legal texts that shed light on the equipment brought on campaign by militia forces are the *fueros* from the kingdoms of the Iberian Peninsula, which specify in many cases that foot soldiers were to be armed with swords and shields, as well as bows. Mounted soldiers were required to bring on campaign mail coats, shields, helmets, and swords, as well as javelins for throwing, and lances, which were thrusting weapons that could be used either on foot or on horseback. Narrative texts also provide a considerable volume of information about the equipment of militia troops from throughout the Latin West, often noting the use of swords, spears, and shields, as well as bows, crossbows, and throwing weapons such as javelins.

The vast majority of the men in the expeditionary levies of pre-crusade Europe were required to obtain their own arms, armour, and other equipment. In many cases, the items required by these militia troops were produced by craftsmen living nearby, or even those living on their own estates. Cooking utensils; travel gear; and dual-purpose items such as bows and arrows, including shafts, fletching, and heads, as well as horseshoes, saddles, and tack were produced across Europe by smiths, fletchers, carpenters, and leather workers. Similarly, the technical expertise to produce heads for lances and javelins was widely diffused. By contrast, some specifically military equipment such as shields, swords, helmets, and armour required considerably greater technical expertise to produce, and were beyond the capacity of many smiths and carpenters. To obtain this equipment, men in the local levies had to purchase items directly from specialized craftsmen, or from merchants who carried military equipment as part of their stock in trade.

The production of arms for sale was an important industry in pre-crusade Europe, and manufacturers, or the merchants who acquired their products, sought markets beyond their local regions. The sale of weapons and armour beyond the frontiers of the *Regnum Francorum* was such a problem, for example, that Charlemagne prohibited the sale of both swords and mail to the Slavs who lived beyond the eastern frontier. This prohibition appears to have had limited effect, however, because very large numbers of Frankish arms, including both spears and swords, have been identified by archaeologists excavating sites in Poland, Hungary, the Czech Republic, and Scandinavia. Some of these weapons, particularly those in the northern lands, may have been acquired through plunder. But given the very large numbers of finds, it is clear both that weapons and arms were exported to the east, and that eventually they began to be produced there by local manufacturers using Frankish models.

The most famous of the arms manufacturers of the Carolingian and Ottonian eras was the production facility where craftsmen inscribed the name Ulfberht on the swords that were produced there. The earliest weapons from this manufacturer are dated to c.800, and the latest to c.1000. The majority of the swords inscribed with the Ulfberht name have been found in the lands east of the Carolingian and Ottonian empires, which is another sign of the export of arms despite governmental prohibitions. In general, the Ulfberht-inscribed swords were very high-quality weapons. However, a large number of swords of inferior quality with the Ulfberht 'signature' also have been found by archaeologists. Some scholars have suggested that these blades are evidence of a type of 'trademark infringement', meaning that some producers sought to take advantage of the good reputation of the Ulfberht weapons by passing off their inferior quality swords as the real thing. Some arms manufacturers or dealers – that is, middle men – even sought out armies on campaign rather than simply waiting for soldiers to come to them.

Equipment for professional soldiers

The military equipment of professional soldiers was broadly similar to that used by the men in the expeditionary levies. However, whereas poorer men in the expeditionary levies may have lacked mail coats and swords, or at least high-quality long swords, most professional fighting men were equipped with high-quality arms, as well as armour, and almost always had mounts, even if they did not actually own them.

It is clear that some of the men serving in the military households of the magnates and rulers of pre-crusade Europe did own their horses, as well as their arms. This is almost certainly true of all of the higher ranking *milites* who held command of units of soldiers in the field or in garrison. Other soldiers benefitted from gifts given by their employers, or acquired equipment and mounts as booty during the course of military campaigns. For the most part, however, the men recruited from the lower social and economic strata of society for service as professional soldiers in military households did not own their own high-quality swords, armour, and other equipment, much less warhorses, which were necessary to do their jobs. In fact, as discussed in Chapter 3, unfree men and even slaves (Latin *servi*) were recruited in substantial numbers by magnates to serve in their military households, and were provided with the equipment that was required for effective military service. Such *servi* are denoted in the sources as having been honoured with vassalage, and were required to swear an oath of faithfulness both to their employer and to the king or emperor. Men with sufficient wealth to purchase this equipment generally did not volunteer for service as professional soldiers. As a consequence, the employers of professional fighting men faced the necessity of acquiring large quantities of military equipment, repairing broken or ageing arms and armour, and replacing items that were lost or captured on campaign. It is noteworthy that the employers had to provide the same array of equipment for their paid troops as men who possessed twelve *mansi*, of the type noted in Chapter 3, had to provide for themselves.

As seen previously, the governmental arms and equipment factories of the late empire, the *fabricae*, largely disappeared in the West following the dissolution of the Roman government in the late fifth century, although some continued to function into the sixth century. However, the end of this centralized and centrally funded system of production did not lead to a complete privatization of the manufacture of arms in early medieval Europe. Rather, royal governments, as well as ecclesiastical and secular magnates, took control over the production of this equipment on a much more decentralized basis. On both the continent and in England, excavations of royal palaces have made clear that throughout the pre-crusade era, they were centres of industrial production of all kinds of goods including, cloth, pottery, glass, leather, and pitch, as well as iron goods, including arms. The material information developed through excavations provides a helpful framework for understanding legislation, such as the *Capitulare de villis*, discussed previously, which required each estate manager of the royal fisc to employ smiths and carpenters who could produce weapons. In fact, this capitulary specifies that each estate was to have on staff a shield maker (*scutarius*). The ordinances in *Capitulare de villis* also included the requirement for each estate to maintain an arsenal of weapons and tools for use on military campaign, as well as for wagons to haul this equipment.

It is likely that the shields produced on royal estates were intended to be of a consistent size and weight. In *Capitulare de villis*, Charlemagne insisted that other types of military equipment produced by his estates be of uniform construction and size, including both war wagons (*basternae*) and the barrels that were to be loaded into the wagons. In his updated version of the late Roman military manual *Epitoma rei militaris*, Archbishop Rabanus Maurus of Mainz (died 856) notes explicitly that in his day, there was a *scutum publicum* – that is, a standard issue governmental shield – which was supposed to be used by all soldiers on campaign. In light of Rabanus' discussion of the training of men who were equipped with these shields to serve shoulder to shoulder in an infantry phalanx, it seems certain that these *scuta* were to be uniform in size and weight.

Ecclesiastical institutions also produced large quantities of arms and other equipment for the members of their military households, and perhaps also for their tenants and dependents who served in the expeditionary levies. For example, the famous early ninth-century visualization of a monastic building complex, which was drawn up at the monastery of St. Gall, included a workshop for shield makers, which is similar to the *scutarium* that was supposed to be established at every royal estate, as well as a workshop for the repair of swords. *Polyptyques* and charters from the ninth and tenth centuries indicate that many other monasteries, as well as bishoprics, had workshops for the production and repair of weapons.

Large-scale weapon systems

One particularly specialized aspect of military supply concerned the production of large-scale weapons systems, including various types of artillery and siege engines. Lever-action, torsion, and tension-powered artillery, discussed in greater detail in Chapter 5, were employed throughout the pre-crusade period to cast both sharps – that is, poled missiles – and stones. Lever-action engines were the most widely diffused stone-throwing technology, and were deployed by Avars, Vikings, and Saxons, as well as by the more advanced governments of the Latin West. These weapons, which used a lever principle similar to that employed by the piece of modern children's playground equipment known as a see-saw or teeter-totter, were powered by companies of pullers. The construction of these types of engines was complex and required training, but could be accomplished at the sites of sieges with comparatively little preparation.

Spear-casting *ballistae* and torsion-powered stone-throwing engines required even more technological expertise to construct, as well as many more specialized materials and parts. As a consequence, the carpenters and smiths who built these engines required highly specialized training, and it is not an accident that these weapons systems were deployed almost exclusively by the royal and princely governments of the Latin West, rather than by their 'barbarian' opponents, whether Slav, Viking, or Magyar. By contrast, Muslim forces were well-equipped with a wide range of siege engines, and likely acquired the expertise in building them directly from late Roman – that is, Byzantine – engineers, who converted to Islam or simply used their skills in the service of their new masters.

Even greater technical expertise was required for the construction of siege towers. The earliest detailed description of a siege tower in the post-Roman West comes from the cleric Richer of Rheims, who wrote c.1000 that King Lothair IV of West Francia ordered the construction of a two-storied siege tower during his siege of the erstwhile Roman fortress city of Verdun in 984. Of particular interest is that this tower not only was intended to give the West Frankish troops the ability to shoot their bows and crossbows at the defenders from an equal height, but also was designed so that it could be rolled up to the walls of the fortress city. Richer's description of the process of constructing the tower makes clear that the designers of this siege engine were fully aware of the danger posed by wobbling and tipping. In order to combat these potential problems, they added external supports along the frame of the engine at right angles to the horizontal frames of the two fighting platforms, which modern engineers recognize as the appropriate solution to assure the stability of the entire structure.

The authors of numerous narrative sources indicate that siege engines, particularly towers and stone-throwing engines, were constructed on site rather than being transported over great distances. Thangmar of Hildesheim (died c.1022), for example, observed that Emperor Otto III built a large number of engines once he arrived to begin his siege of the fortress of Tivoli, located 30 kilometres northeast of Rome. Similarly, the West Frankish monk Raoul Glaber (died 1047) noted that when Emperor Henry II undertook his siege of Troia, in southern Italy, in 1022, he also constructed his engines once he arrived outside the walls of the fortress city. The practice of building siege engines on site suggests that many western rulers maintained craftsmen in their military households who had the technical skills that were necessary for the highly specialized tasks that were involved in the construction of various types of large-scale weapons systems, although the construction of battering rams likely required less skill.

Although most large engines were built, or reconstructed, on site, there were still significant logistical challenges involved in their construction. In many cases, it was necessary to disassemble existing engines, such as stone-throwers, and load them onto wagons or barges in order to transport them from storage facilities to the site of the siege. We are best informed about the logistical challenges in moving siege engines in the later Middle Ages, when we have significantly more administrative documents. In England, for example, during the reign of Edward I, government officials produced at least eight separate documents to move even a single engine from its storage facility to the site of a siege. These documents illuminate the obligations of various royal officials, such as sheriffs and castle commanders, as well as ship and barge captains, to take possession of the disassembled engines and to move them, often in several different stages, by land and by sea to where they were needed.

In those cases when completely new engines were constructed on site, it was necessary to bring in huge volumes of building materials. These included wood, ropes, sinew, iron, and brass. In the case of large counter-weight stone-throwing engines, which will be discussed in more detail in Chapter 5, it was also necessary to bring vast quantities of lead to the building site to make counter-weights. During Edward I's siege of Stirling castle in 1304, for example, engineers and builders used scores of wagon loads of lead, weighing many tonnes, from well over 100 miles away. As a consequence, the building of siege engines was a test not only of the engineering skill available to medieval governments, but to their logistical capacities, as well.

Transportation and the infrastructure of supply

As seen earlier in the chapter in the discussion of late Roman logistics, the supply of the army depended, at least in part, on the ability of governmental authorities to move food, fodder, and equipment to soldiers, whether they were in garrison or on campaign. This was particularly true when conditions made it difficult to establish markets along the line of march. In pre-crusade Europe, governments faced the same basic requirement of transporting military supplies, although usually to forces in the field rather than to those in garrison. However, the scale of this endeavour varied considerably in the period between the late fifth and late eleventh centuries. The rulers of small kingdoms and principalities such as the Romano-German successor states of the fifth to seventh centuries, Wessex and Denmark during the eighth to tenth centuries, or Anjou and León-Castile during the tenth and eleventh centuries, undertook relatively small military operations within narrowly confined geographical limits. By contrast, the Carolingian kings and emperors in the eighth and ninth centuries, and the East Frankish/German kings of the tenth and eleventh centuries, undertook lengthy campaigns with very large armies over great distances. As a consequence, there were considerable differences in the scale and scope of the administrative systems that rulers developed to ensure the adequate provision of their armies. This can be seen most clearly in the mobilization of transportation resources and the establishment of storage and distribution facilities for supplies.

Vehicles, pack animals, and ships

Each of the estates of the Carolingian royal fisc, as noted earlier, was required to maintain a fleet of vehicles that were specifically designed and constructed for the movement of supplies to the army. These wagons, denoted as *basternae* in the *Capitulare de villis*, had to be constructed to an exacting standard that required them to be water-tight so that they could be floated across rivers without leaking. These carts also were to be of standard size so that each one could carry twelve barrels of flour or wine, each of which also was of a standard size and designed to withstand the rigours of travel and remain water- and largely air-tight in order to reduce spoilage.

The principles of estate management, including the requirement to maintain standard-ized transportation resources, were maintained by the successors of the Carolingians both east and west of the Rhine. The counts of Anjou, for example, required that the estates of the comital fisc provide wagons and animals for the transport of supplies for the army on campaign, as well as for transporting supplies to garrison troops. In the east, the Ottonian kings of East Francia/Germany, as well as their Salian successors, also used vehicles main-tained on royal estates to move supplies to the army. The transportation resources from royal and princely fiscal estates, however, were not the only ones available to rulers as they went on campaign. As discussed previously, just as ecclesiastical institutions had an obliga-tion to provide *fodrum* to the royal army, they also were required to provide carts, wagons, and even barges and ships to move these supplies where they were needed. As seen earlier in the chapter with regard to Henry III's invasion of Hungary in 1051, the demand for ships could be quite considerable, particularly when large armies were mobilized for extended campaigns beyond the frontiers.

Advanced supply bases and magazines

In the pre-industrial age, it was usually easier to move large numbers of men to food than it was to move the large quantities of food that were required on campaign to men. This was one reason why markets had such value and entrepreneurial habits were encouraged by gov-ernments. It was also for this reason that late imperial authorities pre-positioned large quan-tities of grain and other foodstuffs in public *horrea*, so that these supplies would be available nearby to the military forces that used them. As discussed previously, the prepositioning of supplies by the government in peacetime generally was not necessary in pre-crusade Europe, because most fighting men – that is, militia forces – lived at home. Professional fighting men in the military households of magnates were supported directly by their employers through-out the kingdoms and smaller states of the Latin West. However, large-scale campaign armies required very large quantities of supplies, both as the soldiers marched to join the army and as the army advanced towards the frontier. It was for this reason that the rulers who engaged in large-scale military operations, such as the Carolingians, Ottonians, and Salians, established advanced bases, often at monasteries, where supplies could be stored in anticipation of the arrival of the army.

This process is illuminated by a series of actions taken by Charlemagne during the winter of 772–773, when it became clear that he might need to undertake a major military opera-tion across the Alps into the Lombard kingdom. The best route available for the Carolin-gian armies went through the Mont Cenis pass, which connects Lanslebourg in the modern French department of Savoy to the city of Susa in northern Italy. This pass was a primary invasion route for Frankish armies heading towards the Lombard plain from the west since the sixth century, and had been used by Charlemagne's father King Pippin I in both 754 and 756, when he invaded Italy and subsequently besieged and forced the surrender of the Lombard capital at Pavia.

The dominant magnate who controlled the environs on both sides of the Mont Cenis pass was the abbot of the monastery of St. Peter at Novalesa, which was located at its southern terminus just 8 kilometres from Susa. The abbots of Novalesa had been among the faithful supporters of the Carolingians since the days of Charles Martel, Charlemagne's grandfather. In preparation for his invasion in 773, Charlemagne summoned Abbot Frodoenus of Novalesa to the winter court being held at the royal palace of Quierzy in what is today the Picardy region of northern France. Here, Charlemagne gave a wide-ranging grant of immunity to Frodoenus freeing all of the monastery's lands and all of its dependents in Provence, Burgundy, and northern Italy from the authority of comital officials with regard to all public obligations, including the duty to provide *fodrum* and transportation. The practical effect here was to give Frodoenus full authority and responsibility for mobilizing all of the resources of the monastery of Novalesa in all of the dozens of counties in which they were located on behalf of the king's army. These preparations served Charlemagne well as his army advanced towards and marched through the Mont Cenis pass from its mustering point at Geneva during the summer of 773.

The immunity granted to Novalesa by Charlemagne provides a 'snapshot' image of the administrative reorganization initiated by the royal government under the exigencies of an impending military operation. However, numerous Carolingian and East Frankish/German kings also undertook long-term measures to ensure the proper provisioning of their armies over well-established campaign routes. For example, over the course of the 950s and 960s, Otto I undertook extensive efforts to ensure that the bishops of the city of Chur, strategically located along the Septimer pass through the Alps, had control of sufficient resources to provision royal armies marching from Germany either to Milan or Pavia in northern Italy. Between 951 and 967, Otto I made seven grants to the bishops of Chur establishing them effectively as administrators over royal fiscal property throughout the Alpine valleys connected to the Septimer, Splügen, and Reschen passes, as well as lands in the foothills of the

Figure 4.6 Col du Tourmalet mountain pass in the Pyrenees

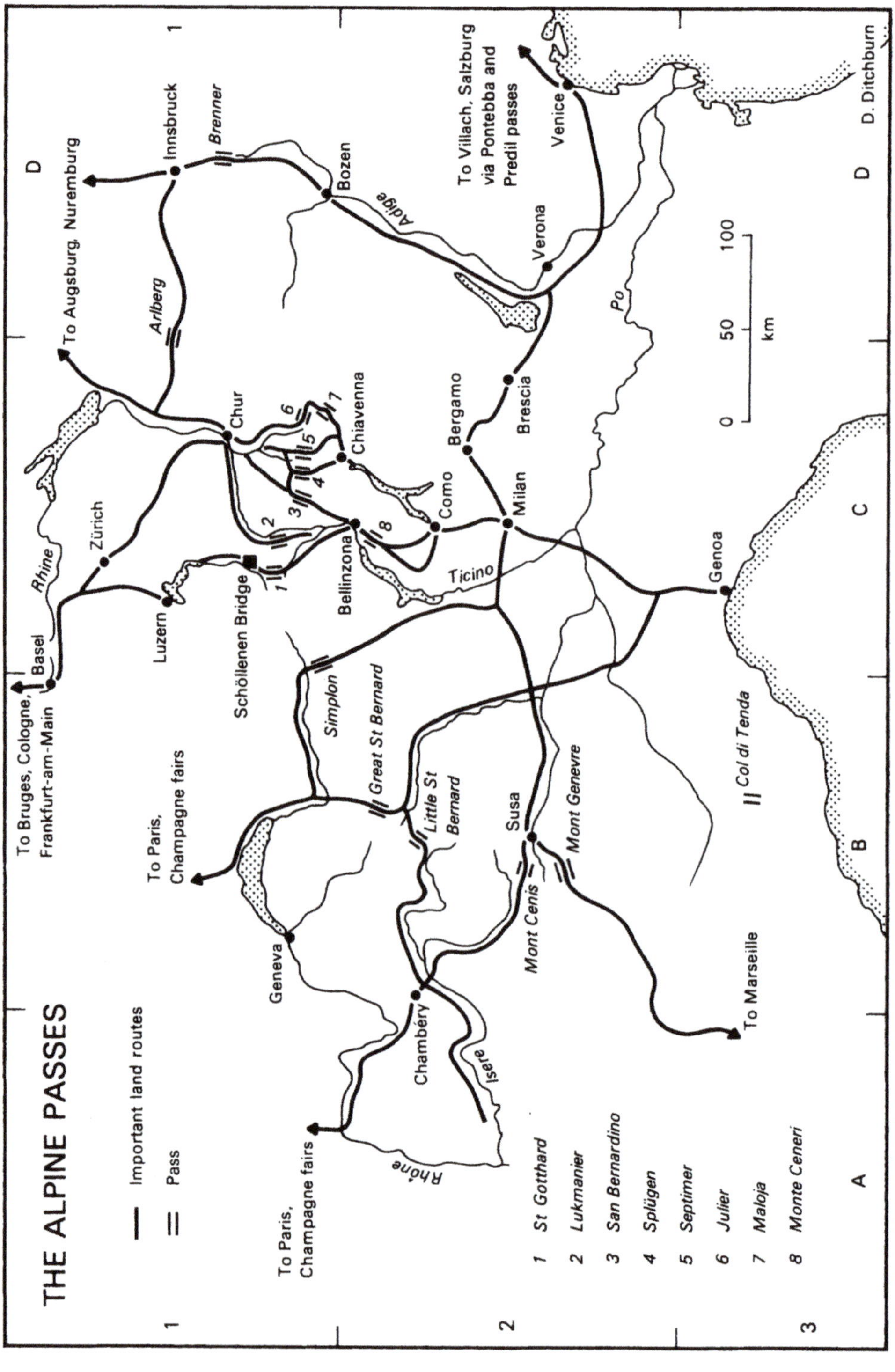

THE ALPINE PASSES

Legend:
— Important land routes
= Pass

1 St Gotthard
2 Lukmanier
3 San Bernardino
4 Splügen
5 Septimer
6 Julier
7 Maloja
8 Monte Ceneri

Map 4.3 The Alpine passes

Source: *Atlas of Medieval Europe* © D. Ditchburn

Alps in what is today the region of Alsace in France. Otto I's heir and successor Otto II further enhanced the ability of the bishops of Chur to provide supplies for royal armies heading to northern Italy by granting them control over lands at the terminus of the Splügen pass at Chiavenna in northern Italy. Otto's efforts in regard to establishing the bishops of Chur as major figures in ensuring supply for royal armies built upon earlier initiatives dating back to the reign of Charlemagne.

Logistics while campaigning in enemy territory

Logistical operations within one's home territory – although requiring well-developed administrative systems, a high degree of sophisticated oversight, and detailed planning for each operation – were relatively straightforward when compared with obtaining sufficient supply when an army was campaigning in enemy territory. Viking raiders, as seen earlier in the chapter, solved this problem by focusing their military operations on wealthy monasteries where supplies already had been collected. This logistical strategy was possible because of the highly developed economy of the Latin West, where considerable concentrations of wealth were easily accessible by river, and were, at least originally, only lightly defended.

By contrast, Carolingian and German armies operating in Slavic lands and in Hungary faced populations that had learned the technique of creating military topographies to sustain a strategy of defence in depth. When faced by western armies, populations took refuge in fortifications and either brought their food supplies – including livestock – to safety, hid them, or destroyed them. As a consequence, narrative accounts of military campaigns undertaken by Carolingian and German armies routinely observe that they were forced to withdraw, without having made significant contact with the enemy, after running out of supplies. This was very similar to the situation that faced the army of Edward II in Scotland in 1322, as seen previously.

Western armies operating in what is today East-Central Europe usually only found success when they had limited campaign objectives and focused on the capture or establishment of strongholds, which could then be used as bases for further military operations. This was the method used by Otto I, for example, to conquer the region between the Elbe and Oder rivers during the course of the 950s and 960s. By employing armies of conquest year after year, Otto was able to capture all of the major strongholds of the Slavic peoples living in this region. In addition to either destroying these fortresses or establishing royal garrisons in them, the German ruler added an additional system of fortifications, located along the course of the Havel River, which provided a well-defended water route for the movement eastward of both troops and supplies.

The situation was rather different in Italy, where both Carolingian and German rulers operated in a land filled not just with strongholds but also scores of fortress cities of Roman origin. But in Italy, as contrasted with the east, these rulers could count on local allies to provide logistical support, and were not required to undertake the arduous task of moving thousands of tonnes of supplies over long distances, especially through the Alps. During his campaign against the Lombards in 773, for example, Charlemagne received enormous quantities of supplies from Pope Hadrian I (772–795), at whose request the Carolingian ruler had invaded Lombardy. In a similar manner, Emperor Conrad II (1024–1039) relied largely on supplies provided by Archbishop Heribert of Milan (1018–1045) for his campaign in northern Italy, which included the siege and capture of the fortress city of Lucca in 1027.

Logistics in the crusading age

Feeding crusader armies

As we saw in Chapter 3, the masses of armed pilgrims who took part in military campaigns to the eastern Mediterranean from the late eleventh through the late thirteenth centuries often had the same profile and, in many cases, were the same men who served in contemporary military operations within Europe. However, the crusades were no ordinary wars, and the provision of supply to western troops, who travelled many hundreds or even thousands of miles from home, required the organization of new logistical systems. Certainly, princes and kings were able to manage the logistics for their own military households in a manner consistent with ordinary warfare, while still in their home territories. Similarly, individual armed pilgrims could carry food with them as they marched to join larger crusader groups, much as they would have done if called up to perform expeditionary military duty in a war being conducted by their legitimate ruler. However, once these crusaders, whether as individuals, small groups, or entire military households, departed their home territories and began to run low on supplies that they could carry in packs, on animals, or even in vehicles, they required access to new sources of food, fodder, and potentially various types of equipment, as well. Moreover, these armed pilgrims faced the need to replenish their supplies without having any legal access to pre-existing or institutionalized systems of distribution. The logistical difficulties facing the crusaders were exacerbated by the vast number of people involved. Although scholars disagree about the overall number of pilgrims participating in all phases of the First Crusade (including the so-called People's Crusade), the minimum figure presented by historians is in the range of 100,000, and some scholars argue for as many as 150,000 armed participants, which does not include many thousands more camp followers.

In order to deal with the logistical needs of their men, all of the major magnates involved in the First Crusade made preparations long in advance of their scheduled departures in July 1096. The first step was to make agreements with the rulers of the territories through which they intended to travel. For Duke Robert of Normandy, Count Robert of Flanders, and Count Stephen of Blois, this meant making arrangements with the king of France; with a series of city-states along the Mediterranean coast of the Italian peninsula, including Genoa and Pisa; with the papacy; and with the Norman rulers of southern Italy and Sicily either to provide supplies or establish markets where supplies could be purchased.

In the case of Duke Godfrey of Lotharingia (1087–1100), matters were complicated by the ongoing civil war in the German kingdom between King Henry IV, who was trapped in northern Italy, and the latter's son Conrad, who had allied with various rebel factions in Germany, including Duke Welf of Bavaria. As a consequence, Godfrey, who also was hostile to Henry IV, made arrangements with Welf and also with King Colomon of Hungary (1095–1116) to establish markets to supply the Lotharingian duke's troops. Once they arrived in the territory of the Byzantine Empire, supplies were provided by prearrangement by the government of Emperor Alexios Komnenos (1081–1118) until the fracture of the alliance between the crusaders and the Byzantines in the summer of 1098. Even Bohemond of Taranto, who had waged a war of conquest against the Byzantine Empire from 1080–1085, made arrangements with his erstwhile antagonist Emperor Alexios I Komnenos to provide supplies for his troops.

The efforts of the crusader leaders to seek sources of supply along their routes, and particularly to ask for the establishment of markets, were quite successful. This is made clear by

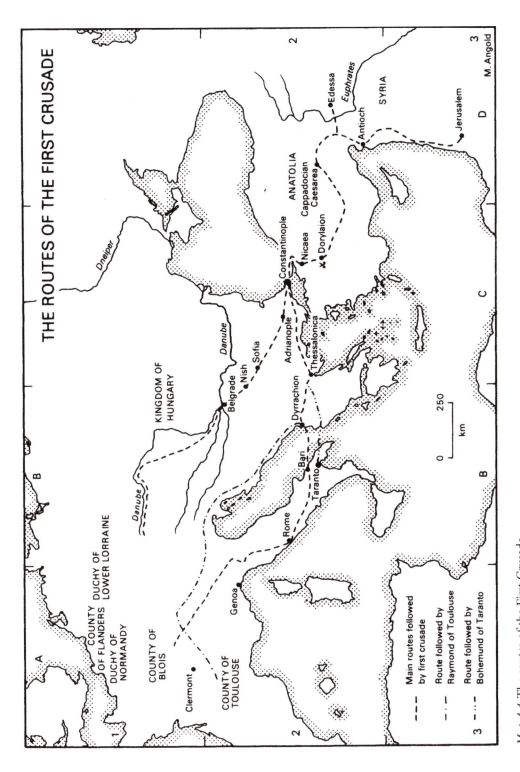

Map 4.4 The routes of the First Crusade
Source: *Atlas of Medieval Europe* © M. Angold

the rather small number of complaints in contemporary chronicles about violent foraging by the crusader armies led by western princes, or failures of supply leading to the collapse of the various crusader groups. As powerful princes, men such as Duke Robert of Normandy and Duke Godfrey of Lotharingia, had political and diplomatic connections that gave them the opportunity to write to other European rulers to explain their needs and ask for appropriate supply to be made available. This was not the case for individual pilgrims, or even groups of pilgrims, drawn from the minor nobility or especially the land-owning peasantry. It is therefore not surprising that from the beginning of the First Crusade, the great majority of the men from the lower social and economic ranks in society who actually survived the first leg of the journey to Constantinople did so by attaching themselves to the army of one or another of the princes. In effect, they became members of extended military households for the duration of the campaign, because this was the only way to survive.

There was one major instance during the First Crusade when a substantial number of pilgrims set out for the Holy Land without a significant magnate as a leader, and without significant logistical planning. These were the participants in the so-called People's Crusade, who departed in several groups during the spring of 1096, several months before the crusader armies were scheduled to begin their journeys to Constantinople, the capital of the Byzantine Empire. Two separate elements of the People's Crusade, under the leadership of the charismatic preacher Peter the Hermit and the minor French nobleman Walter Sans Avoir, respectively, negotiated at several points with the king of Hungary and several local magnates along their line of march to establish markets.

Neither of these leaders was consistently successful in his efforts, and the armed pilgrims turned to plunder to obtain food and other supplies. These acts of pillage and plunder were met with stiff retribution by local military forces in Hungary. When the two forces crossed the imperial frontier into what is today Bulgaria, both Walter and Peter separately negotiated with Byzantine officials to establish markets, and these were duly organized. However, further acts of plunder by both groups of pilgrims led to renewed attacks, in this case by imperial troops, who inflicted heavy casualties on the untrained and poorly armed crusaders. Ultimately, the remnants of both groups made their way to Constantinople, and subsequently across the Bosphorus with imperial aid to Asia Minor, where they were annihilated almost to the last man by the forces of Kilij Arslan, the Seljuk sultan of Rum, whose western capital was at the ancient Christian city of Nicaea.

After the First Crusade

The First Crusade, from a Christian military perspective, was a major success. It led ultimately to the capture of Jerusalem and the establishment of four Latin states, stretching from the headwaters of the Tigris and Euphrates rivers in the north to the Sinai desert in the south. The biggest winner, however, was not the crusaders, but rather Emperor Alexios, who used his control over the logistical support of the Latin armies to compel the western princes to recover Byzantine territory that had been lost to the Turks, and restore them to the Byzantine Empire. The *realpolitik* approach taken by Alexios led to significant resentment among the crusaders, which ultimately came to characterize western attitudes toward the Byzantine Empire more generally. Nevertheless, it was clear to many participants that Byzantine logistical support in the form of both direct grants of supplies and through the organization of markets had made possible the crusaders' march from Constantinople through Asia Minor to the fortress city of Antioch more than 1,100 kilometres to the east, and ultimately to Jerusalem itself.

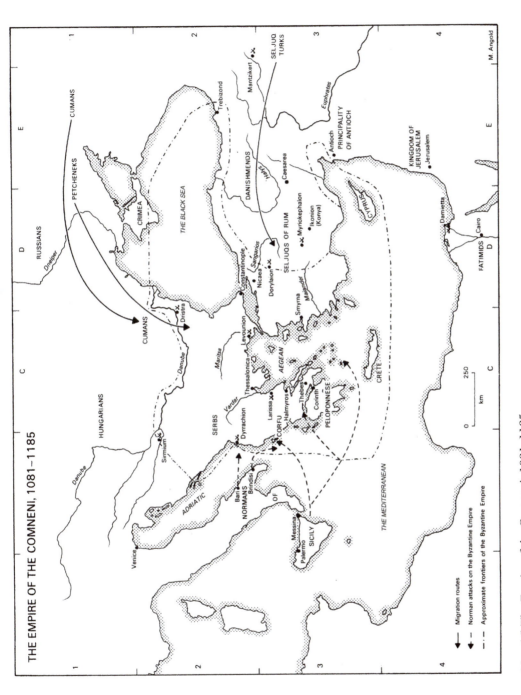

Map 4.5 The Empire of the Comneni, 1081–1185

Source: *Atlas of Medieval Europe* © M. Angold

As a consequence, it is not at all surprising that the leaders of the Second Crusade, King Conrad III of Germany (1138–1152) and King Louis VII of France (1137–1180), made arrangements with Emperor Manuel I Komnenos (1143–1180) to establish markets for their armies as they marched through Byzantine territory toward the Holy Land. Both of the major royal armies were well supplied in their own kingdoms in the traditional manner through support of ecclesiastical institutions and the royal fisc. The formal starting point for their journey east was the city of Regensburg. It was here, according to the historian Odo of Deuil (died 1162), who also served as King Louis' chaplain on the Second Crusade, that representatives of Emperor Manuel waited for the French army to guide them on their way, and assure the provision of supplies through markets along their route. The army of Conrad III had preceded the French by several weeks, and constructed a number of bridges over rivers that the French army was able to use on its march. The German army also obtained substantial logistical support from the Byzantine Empire. However, bad weather conditions, which the crusaders could not predict, hampered the speed of their march, which meant that they needed more food and fodder than they originally had estimated.

Following the failure of the Second Crusade outside the walls of Damascus, German crusaders still relied heavily on the Byzantines. For the Third Crusade, Emperor Frederick Barbarossa (1152–1190) decided to follow the same route used by his uncle Conrad III four decades earlier when Frederick, as a young man, had first participated in an armed pilgrimage to the east. Barbarossa sought to replicate the arrangements for supplying his vast army, which likely numbered well in excess of 20,000 men, not including camp followers, by making arrangements with both King Béla III of Hungary (1172–1196) and Emperor Isaac II Angelus (reigned 1185–1195 and again from 1203–1204). A full year before setting out on campaign, Barbarossa dispatched emissaries to Constantinople to negotiate with Emperor Isaac in order to establish markets and to provide a route through his lands where the Germans' horses would have plenty of grass and water, and where hay and grain could be purchased. These emissaries were able to conclude a treaty whereby the Byzantine emperor promised to establish both markets and to have his guides lead the German army along routes that were appropriate for large numbers of mounted troops and draft animals.

A second group of German emissaries was in Constantinople in 1189 to make final arrangements, including permission to dispatch a small force under the command of Barbarossa's close confidant Archbishop Conrad of Mainz (1183–1200) to scout out the road system in Bulgaria and arrange for the storage of food and other supplies for the main army. For his part, King Béla of Hungary provided a corridor through his lands for the German army, established markets with set prices to avoid any problem that might be caused by gauging the German crusaders, and even joined Barbarossa's army with a substantial military contingent. By contrast, the Byzantine Emperor Isaac reneged on his promises and even sent forces to attack the German army. Ultimately, Barbarossa was forced to occupy the Byzantine city of Philippopolis (modern Plovdiv in Bulgaria) to compel the Byzantines to provide the supplies and establish the markets that they had promised.

By contrast with their German fellow crusader, both King Richard I of England and King Philip II of France (1180–1223) decided to avoid Byzantine entanglements by sailing directly to join the Christian forces besieging Acre on the Mediterranean coast. In this manner, they bypassed imperial territory completely. Travelling by ship considerably reduced the travel time of the crusaders, and particularly the French, who had a much shorter route from Marseille than did Richard's fleet, which had to sail around the Iberian Peninsula and through the Strait of Gibraltar before joining Philip on the southern French coast. In order to prepare for his crusade, Richard hired and purchased a very large number of ships,

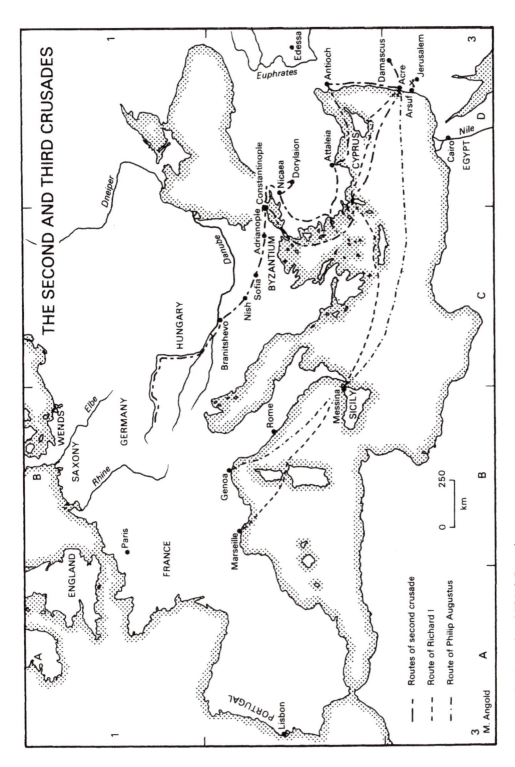

Map 4.6 The Second and Third Crusades
Source: *Atlas of Medieval Europe* © M. Angold

Figure 4.7 Medieval bridge: Pont Vieux over the River Tarn in Albi, southwest France
Source: Released to public domain by Marion Schneider and Christoph Aistleitner.

including both oared galleys and what appear to have been early cogs of the type discussed previously, which were heavy sailing ships common to the North Atlantic, Baltic Sea, and North Sea. The English fleet numbered more than a hundred ships, and included vast quantities of supplies, such as more than 60,000 horseshoes and 14,000 cured pigs, according to one contemporary chronicler.

The crusade campaign of 1189–1190 was the last one in which a large army sought an overland route to the eastern Mediterranean. The Fourth Crusade (1202–1204), which was organized by Pope Innocent III (1198–1216), was planned as an entirely amphibious operation. One of the leaders of the crusader army recruited by Pope Innocent, Geoffrey of Villehardouin, provides a detailed – albeit substantially biased – account of the vast logistical preparations that were undertaken in preparation for the Fourth Crusade. Geoffrey was part of a team of negotiators who travelled to Venice in 1201 on behalf of the leaders of the Fourth Crusade to negotiate the terms for moving their army to the eastern Mediterranean. In his chronicle, Geoffrey reports that in return for a payment of 85,000 marks, the leader of Venice, the doge, promised to build transports to carry 20,000 foot soldiers, 13,500 mounted soldiers, and 4,500 horses, as well as sufficient food to support these men and mounts for nine months. Ultimately, this army never reached the east, and instead undertook a siege of Constantinople, capturing the city in 1204.

The Fifth (1218–1221), Sixth (1228–1229), and Seventh (1248–1254) Crusades also saw the deployment of armies from the West by ship. Jean de Joinville (died 1317), a participant in the Seventh Crusade, also known as the Crusade of King Louis IX of France (1226–1270), provides an exceptionally detailed account of his experiences in this campaign in his *Life of Saint Louis.* Jean devotes enormous attention to the vast fleet that the French

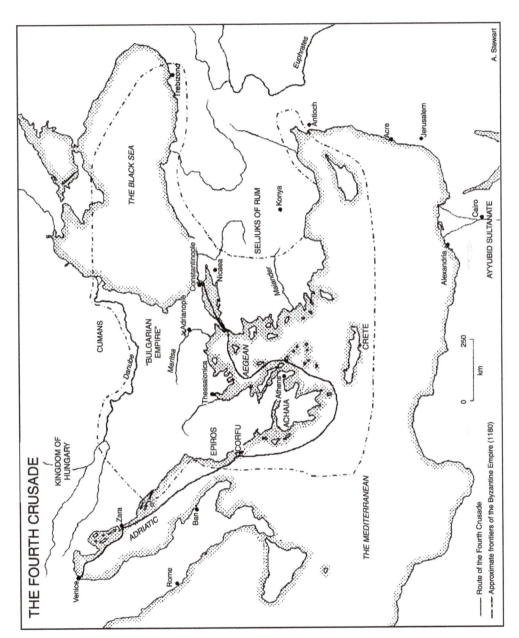

Map 4.7 The Fourth Crusade

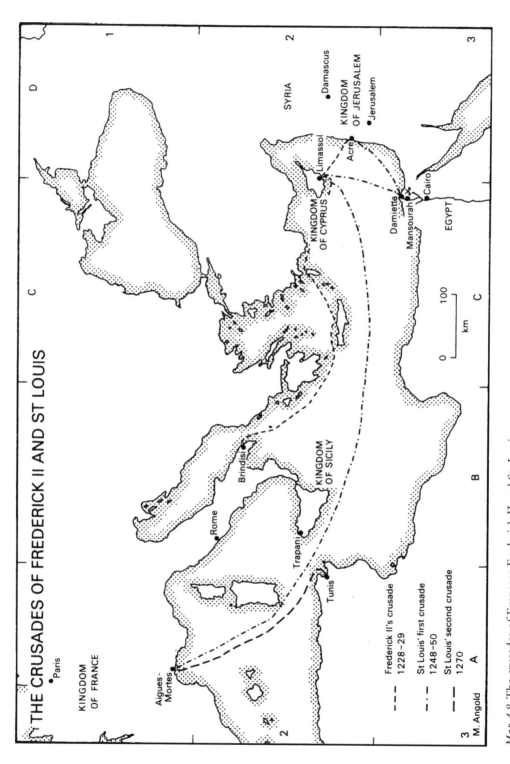

Map 4.8 The crusades of Emperor Frederick II and St. Louis

Source: *Atlas of Medieval Europe* © M. Angold

king mobilized to bring his forces to besiege the Nile Delta city of Damietta, which also had been the focus of the Fifth Crusade. Among Louis' primary concerns was bringing sufficient supplies to support a lengthy siege. The king hoped to avoid the costly errors that had led to the premature abandonment of the siege of Damietta thirty years earlier, including the inability to feed the besieging Christian army. As part of this effort, Louis spent two full years reorganizing the entire system of trade in the Rhône river valley to ensure that merchants brought their goods to the French army's port of embarkation at Aigues-Mortes, which is located some 30 kilometres east of Montpellier and 130 kilometres west of Marseilles. Louis suppressed all tolls in the region, and even secured a papal bull that prohibited the establishment of any new tolls on goods that were destined for the army going on crusade.

Logistics within Europe during the crusades and in the later Middle Ages

Much as had been true in the pre-crusade period, governments during the later medieval era were able to draw upon the same basic sources of supply and transportation as they had in earlier centuries, including the resources of the Church and lands and other economic assets under direct governmental control. Similarly, the men serving in militia forces, which continued to provide the majority of the manpower in medieval armies from the twelfth to the fifteenth centuries, also remained responsible for supplying or purchasing most of their own food and equipment while on campaign. However, beginning in the twelfth century, royal, princely, and urban governments also began to reintroduce or, in some cases, simply expand existing broad-based taxation in coin, as well as in kind, to support military operations. The types of taxation, and the success of governments in raising resources in this manner for military purposes, varied greatly across Europe. In many cases, however, these fiscal experiments led both to the increasing sophistication of governmental institutions, and in some to the development of representative bodies and proto-parliaments, where the king's subjects gained a voice in the affairs of state through the power to withhold approval of taxation.

Campaign supplies

France

As seen in Chapter 3, the urban militias, which comprised a large part of the military forces of King Philip II of France, were required to bring wagon loads of supplies with them on campaign. This obligation was consistent with military practice dating back to the early medieval period, and remained generally in force up through the mid-fifteenth century when King Charles VII established both a regular standing army and a centralized system of military supply for his newly minted professional military units. Many French rulers from the thirteenth to the fifteenth centuries used the expedient of issuing a general summons to war, the *arrière-ban*, for the defence of the *patria*, which then was commuted for many communities into a grant of supplies or of cash that could be used to purchase supplies in regions closest to where military operations were planned. In general, these requisitions in lieu of service fell heaviest on the magnates who were understood to hold their lands directly from the king, and from the cities. However, cities also faced heavy burdens. In 1340, for example, King Philip VI summoned the citizens of Toulouse for military service, but then commuted this demand in return for a 'gracious gift' of some 6,500 pounds of Tours – that is, the weight of money minted at Tours.

Iberian kingdoms

A quite similar system for the provision of supplies for royal military campaigns was in place in the Christian kingdoms of Iberia. This can be seen clearly, for example, during the reign of King James I (1213–1276) of Aragon, who also ruled Valencia, Majorca, Catalonia, and the region of modern France around the city of Montpellier. He routinely required his magnates to supply their own military households and the cities to supply their militias for campaigns, both within his realm and along his frontiers with the Muslim polities to his south. In general, three or four weeks before the impending campaign, James' government issued written mobilization orders to all of the magnates and city councils, which had an obligation to serve in a particular theatre of war. These mobilization orders generally included information about when and where the military forces that had been summoned were to meet, and the equipment and supplies that they were to bring with them on campaign. The supply burden varied considerably from campaign to campaign, and the quantity of supplies that these magnate households and urban militias were required to have on hand when the campaign began varied from as little as three days' worth of food to as much as three months' supply.

On those occasions when the duration of the military service demanded of the soldiers outlasted the supplies that they had been ordered to bring on campaign, the burden for resupply was taken up by royal quartermasters, as had been the case in the Carolingian Empire and many other governments during the pre-crusade period. To this end, James' government sought subsidies of food, as well as of cash, from both nobles and towns at the beginning of campaigns. King James also sought to arrange markets while marching within his kingdom. When campaigning beyond his frontiers, the Aragonese king also sought to extend his supplies through the capture of Muslim strongholds or by extorting supplies from Muslim-held towns.

For his campaigns along the coast, King James routinely demanded the use of privately owned merchant vessels to carry supplies that had been acquired through purchase, taxation, or compulsion. While conducting campaigns inland, James' armies made extensive use of pack animals. Christian armies on the Iberian Peninsula very rarely made use of wagons or carts to transport supplies, particularly when campaigning against Muslim forces in regions where Roman roads were in poor repair or never had been constructed. On the Iberian Peninsula, war was not a stimulus for infrastructural development, as had been the case among the Romans and many of the early medieval polities that succeeded them.

German Empire

In contrast to the situation in the kingdom of France and to the Christian kingdoms of the Iberian Peninsula, the kings of Germany did not enjoy a gradual but steady increase in royal power and central control of their realm. Despite the efforts of a number of powerful German rulers, including Rudolf of Habsburg (1273–1291) and Louis IV (1314–1347), the kings of Germany during the later Middle Ages were unable to harness the resources of the great territorial magnates and cities for use by the royal government in a manner consistent with their predecessors in the period before c.1200. Rather, over the course of the thirteenth century, the German Empire, including the subordinate kingdoms of Italy and Burgundy, began a process of political dissolution that resulted in the creation of more than 100 sovereign polities by the end of the Middle Ages. When considering logistics, therefore, it is necessary to analyze not only royal military campaigns, but also those undertaken by both secular and ecclesiastical princes, as well as by powerful cities, which came to resemble the city-states of northern Italy.

The dissolution of royal power within Germany was due, in no small part, to a series of debilitating civil wars that led, among other results, to the loss of considerable portions of the royal fisc, from which the king could mobilize both supplies and financial resources. These included the conflicts of Henry IV from the 1060s up through the first decade of the eleventh century, and the civil war in 1235–1254, noted in Chapter 3, between the adherents of Emperor Frederick II and his son Conrad IV on the one hand, and the adherents of the papacy on the other hand. As a consequence, the rulers of Germany depended to an even greater extent on contributions of supplies by the great magnates and the cities than was the case, for example, for the rulers of France, Aragon, and Castile.

This reliance on the contributions of supplies was particularly evident during yet another civil war in Germany that took place in the period 1199–1208 between Philip IV, the son of Frederick Barbarossa, and Otto of Brunswick, the son of Duke Henry the Lion of Saxony and Mathilda, who was the daughter of King Henry II of England. The authors of the *Annals of Cologne* observed with regard to the beginning of military operations between the two sides in 1199 that Otto IV came to the region of the middle Rhine near the town of Boppard at the invitation of local nobles who promised to join his side and, more importantly, to provide the royal contender's army with supplies. However, when these local nobles failed to appear, Otto was forced to withdraw because he could not maintain his army without their logistical support. Otto's opponent Philip IV received intelligence regarding the precarious position of his adversary and advanced into the same region to attack Otto's ally, Archbishop Adolf I of Cologne (1192–1205). The chronicler emphasizes that in preparation for this military operation, Philip IV mobilized both large numbers of wagons and a fleet of ships to carry supplies for his army as he marched down the Rhine River. Many of these supplies were provided by the cities that were loyal to Philip, as the current leader of the Staufen royal family, as they would later be loyal to his nephew Emperor Frederick II (1216–1250) and the latter's son Conrad IV (1250–1254) in the civil wars that again wracked Germany during the 1240s and 1250s.

The fracturing of royal authority in Germany during the course of the thirteenth century also made possible a considerable number of regional wars involving secular and ecclesiastical princes, as well as a numerous cities. One of these substantial regional conflicts was recorded in detail by the author of *The Deeds of the Bishops of Utrecht*, which was intended as a post-mortem of the disastrous military campaign undertaken by Bishop Otto II of Utrecht (1216–1227) into the region of Drenthe, located in the northeast of the modern Netherlands. Throughout the first half of the 1220s, Bishop Otto sought to maintain his control over the regions of Groningen, Overijssel, and Drenthe which his predecessors had ruled as the representatives of the German kings since the mid-eleventh century. In both 1226 and 1227, Bishop Otto made military agreements with several of his fellow bishops, local secular magnates, and also with the city of Utrecht to provide substantial contingents of soldiers for an invasion of the Drenthe region, and particularly to capture or kill Count Rudolf of Coeverden, the principal opponent of the bishop of Utrecht.

Bishop Otto II prepared for both campaigns by purchasing large quantities of supplies and arranging for the provision of substantial numbers of wagons and, particularly, ships to carry the food and fodder, as well as arms and siege equipment, required by his army. Unfortunately for Otto, his army was soundly defeated by the forces commanded by Rudolf of Coeverden at the Battle of Ane (1227), and the bishop of Utrecht was killed after being captured by the enemy. In the aftermath of his victory, Rudolf and the men of the region of Drenthe raided the region around the episcopal fortress of Groningen and caused considerable damage. In response, the author of the *Deeds* proudly recounted, the citizens of the city of Utrecht provided a force of 400 soldiers as well as all of their supplies, at their own expense, to go to the aid of the lord of Groningen, who was attempting to defend the district against Rudolf and the latter's allies.

The English exception

As we have seen, the procurement and transportation of supplies in most of Europe in the period after the First Crusade was highly decentralized. The situation in England, however, was far different. From the Anglo-Saxon period onward, the kings of England had available an extensive apparatus of institutions that enabled them to maintain a high degree of centralized control over both the mobilization and the transportation of supplies for royal armies in the field and in garrison. Throughout much of the twelfth and thirteenth centuries, the scale of royal military operations was relatively small. One important exception was King Henry II's campaign in Ireland in 1171–1172, which involved some 10,000 troops and required an enormous logistical undertaking, which left considerable traces in the Pipe Rolls, which recorded, among other matters, the expenses undertaken by the sheriffs in England to purchase and transport supplies for King Henry's army. These included thousands of tonnes of grain, beans, peas, and other foodstuffs, as well as vast quantities of iron goods, including 1,000 shovels that would be used for constructing earth-works and other engineering projects. The Pipe Rolls also include costs for hiring shipping and paying crews to transport supplies from England across the Irish Sea.

Henry II's Irish invasion would not be matched in scale by an English king until the reign of Edward I, whose logistical preparations for campaigns in Wales, Gascony, and above all in Scotland dwarfed those of his great-grandfather. In 1296, 1298, and 1304, Edward I sent armies numbering between 25,000 and 30,000 men to conquer Scotland and establish his rule there. Rather than seeking to have these troops, the vast majority of whom were foot soldiers of the shire levies, provide their own supplies, King Edward's government set in motion a well-developed plan that led to the mobilization of enormous quantities of food, fodder, and equipment from throughout England, amounting to hundreds of thousands of tonnes, and also secured transportation for all of these supplies to the king's troops.

Several months before mobilization orders went out to the counties to raise troops, the royal government issued writs to each sheriff in England notifying these officials about the quantities of specific types of supplies that were to be purchased within their counties. Royal commissioners were then dispatched to each county to work with the sheriffs to purchase these foodstuffs and other supplies, and to arrange for their transportation to regional population centres for storage. Still other royal officials then arranged for the shipment of these supplies, at the cost of the royal government, to major ports, where these supplies were unloaded and placed in large warehouses that were provided with guards at royal expense. From these ports, food was then transported by ocean-going ships to forward supply depots, and particularly to the royal fortress at Berwick-on-Tweed, which served as the central storage and distribution centre for the king's forces in Scotland, and continued in this role until its capture by the Scots in 1318. The very extensive logistical preparations by Edward I's government were supplemented, to a limited extent, by merchants who saw opportunities for profit among the vast numbers of soldiers mobilized by the king, and also by some magnates who either brought or procured supplies for themselves and their men from their own resources.

This centralized control by the royal government over supply had the enormous advantage of ensuring that military operations would not come to an end prematurely because the soldiers ran out of food, although there were failures in execution, as seen in the previous discussion of the campaign of 1322 under Edward II. However, the purchase and transportation of such huge quantities of food and equipment was exceptionally expensive. When the royal government sought to reduce the costs of its logistical preparations during the reigns of Edward II (1307–1327) and Edward III (1327–1377) through the use of compulsory purchases at fixed prices, a system denoted by contemporaries as a *prise* (the French for taking), there was tremendous popular opposition. Ultimately, the use of the *prise*, and the more general system of royal mobilization of supplies, was abandoned after 1351. From this point onward, the English kings relied almost exclusively on contracts with merchants to obtain supplies for campaigns, particularly in France.

Warfare and institutionalized taxation

Through much of the Middle Ages, centralized control over the conduct of war did not lead to the re-establishment of the types of broad-based taxation that financed the army and military infrastructure of the late Roman Empire. Rulers such as Charlemagne and Otto the Great were able to raise large armies and carry out wars of conquest on a scale similar to the late Roman emperors without the need for substantial taxation. This was due to a number of factors, including the replacement of direct taxation with personal military service by landowners and the concomitant requirement for militia troops, as well as magnates with military households, to pay for their own supplies. Another crucial factor, and one that often is not appreciated by scholars, is the enormous wealth of the powerful rulers of the Carolingian and German empires, which was derived from the assets of the royal fisc. In essence, they were able 'to live off their own' rather than seek revenues from their subjects.

The most important driver of increased governmental expenses during the later medieval period was warfare. However, the wars waged by the kings of France in the fourteenth and fifteenth centuries, for example, were smaller in an absolute sense than those waged by Charlemagne in the eighth and early ninth centuries. Even taking into account the substantial decline in population brought about by the arrival of the Black Death in 1347, it is clear that the armies operating during the Hundred Years' War were relatively modest in size. The impetus for the renewal of institutionalized taxation, therefore, was not the scale of the military burdens of the government, but rather the scarcity of economic resources under direct governmental control. Kings could no longer 'live off their own', much less wage war with the limited resources available from the fisc.

One of the early efforts to re-impose broad-based taxation, drawing upon both Carolingian and Ottonian, as well as Roman, precedents, was undertaken by Frederick Barbarossa. However, he did not look to his German domains for taxes, but rather to northern Italy. In 1158, after his siege and capture of the fortress city of Milan, Barbarossa summoned both German and Italian magnates to an imperial assembly at Roncaglia, located near the city of Piacenza, with the goal of defining and laying claim to all imperial rights in Italy. Barbarossa called upon four legal scholars from the law school established at Bologna in 1088, to analyze all legal texts pertaining to taxation and other support that were owed to the imperial authority by the northern Italian cities. These legal scholars confirmed that the imperial government had the right to levy taxes amounting to some 30,000 pounds of silver per year in support of the emperor's governance of the *res publica*, which included the waging of war. Ultimately, the emperor's numerous opponents in Italy refused to accept the judgement of the jurists and assembly, and Barbarossa was only able to establish his claims to taxes when he had his army *in situ*.

By contrast with the situation in the empire, the kings of Aragon benefitted from some regular taxes within their realms, the most important of which, from a military perspective, consisted of payment in lieu of performing military service. However, from the late twelfth century onwards, the Aragonese kings also summoned representative assemblies (*cortes*) from which they asked for special subsidies in support of the needs of the kingdom. The centrality of these assemblies to providing funding for the king's wars is made clear by the statement of King James I of Aragon, made in 1264, that 'without the *Cortes*, this business of war cannot be settled'.

This same view is evident in the actions of James' contemporary, King Alfonso X of Castile (1252–1284). *Cortes* had been summoned by Alfonso's predecessors from the late twelfth century onward. Aside from the resources of the royal fisc, Alfonso had income that was directly related to military operations in the form of fines collected in lieu of military service (*fonsadera*) and the *tercias reales*, which was the royal third of the tithes received by churches, which the Castilian rulers claimed was due to the crown for its role in the reconquest of lands from the Muslims. Under Alfonso, however, a substantial increase in military operations in Andalusia, a planned invasion of North Africa, ongoing border warfare, and an effort by the Castilian king to gain election as the king of Germany, all increased the government's expenses far beyond the level that could be accommodated by normal royal revenues. In response, Alfonso summoned *cortes* several times during his reign to request additional taxation from his subjects. However, in return, the Castilian monarch was required to confirm many traditional privileges of the nobility and towns, and also made other concessions, including promising to refrain from imposing a uniform law over the entire kingdom. In effect, Alfonso X was required to recognize local traditions that stood in the way of centralized power.

The kings of France also enjoyed a number of regular taxes in addition to income from the royal fisc. As was true of their contemporaries in the Iberian kingdoms, the most important of these was the substitution of payments in cash or kind in lieu of military service. Beginning in the 1340s, however, the French kings, who now faced increasing pressure from English armies operating on French soil, began to seek ever-increasing sums of money from their subjects. However, they did so in a piecemeal manner, because the various regions of France maintained their distinctive local customs and rights vis-à-vis the royal government. As a consequence, the French kings were obligated to summon regional assemblies of magnates and representatives of towns to ask for special war subsidies. In addition, many high-ranking nobles were able to negotiate their own terms with the king. The difficulty of raising taxes in this manner meant that French kings from Philip IV (1285–1314) through the mid-fourteenth century found it easier to enforce royal rights, such as control over the silver content in the money supply, rather than levy new taxes. As a consequence, the royal government established extensive bureaucracies at both the central and local levels to enforce as rigorously as possible all royal rights that could generate income.

However, following their disastrous defeat at the Battle of Poitiers (1356) and the capture of the French King John II (1350–1364) by the English, the French royal government embarked on a new course. In 1357, an effort was made to institute a national hearth tax, with a fixed rate for each hearth in the kingdom. The royal government built on this initial experiment, and by the early fifteenth century, royal officials held the view that 'the king can levy *tailles* (taxes) and *aides* (special subventions) on his kingdom as an emperor, for its defence and guardianship; nor may any lord whoever he be levy anything without the king's consent'.[4] In practice, however, the ability of the French royal government to levy taxes, even for war, was limited by numerous factors, including a lack of knowledge regarding the number of taxpayers in France, very sparse information about their wealth, and an absence of a cadre of professional administrators to oversee the process of assessment and collection of revenues. These problems were exacerbated by the very different systems of tax collection in force in the various regions of the kingdom and the exemption of large numbers of powerful magnates from the royal tax structure. This multi-regional system of highly variegated taxation would endure up to the French Revolution at the end of the eighteenth century.

The English kingdom was once more an outlier with regard to centralized taxation. From the tenth century onward, the kings of England had the ability to impose a kingdom-wide tax, called *gelds*, to serve the needs of the state. These *gelds* were used for a variety of purposes, including paying for wars and also paying off armies of Viking invaders with tribute – that is, the so-called *Danegeld*. The ability of the English kings to tax their subjects in this manner was due to a highly effective system of assessing the value of the property of both ecclesiastical and secular landowners. The famed Domesday Book of 1086, whose compilation was ordered by William the Conqueror to facilitate the taxation of England, was simply one in a long line of similar wealth surveys.

Over the course of the second half of the twelfth century, and particularly during the period 1189–1199, the property and financial assets held by the royal government shrank precipitously as King Richard sold or pawned vast tracts of land and mortgaged future revenues to pay for his wars in France and for his crusade. In an effort to make up for these shortfalls, Henry II of England had introduced the so-called Saladin Tithe of 1188, which was collected by King Richard throughout England, and raised significant sums. Despite the Saladin Tithe, however, Richard's brother John was compelled to enforce royal rights and remaining sources of income with a heretofore unknown vigour in order to make up for shortfalls in royal revenue. The financial situation of the crown became even worse after John's loss in 1204 of almost all of the lands that had been held by Henry II and Richard I on the continent. The resulting financial pressure placed on the English baronage by the royal government led to a rebellion and the imposition of the *Magna Carta* on John in 1215, which was intended to limit the abuses by the king and to require the agreement of the king's subjects to extraordinary taxation.

Over the course of the thirteenth century, the demands enunciated in the first Great Charter (*Magna Carta*) with regard to taxation became the accepted model for raising tax revenues. Henry III, Edward I, and the latter's successors throughout the fourteenth and fifteenth centuries, regularly summoned representatives of the people to hear the rationale of the king for taking his people to war, and his pleas for their financial support. In contrast to the *parlement* in France, which was a self-selecting advisory body to the king, the English parliament was comprised of elected representatives from the counties. These men, who were leaders in their local communities, demanded and received reasoned arguments from the king before they were willing to agree to taxation. In return, they facilitated the efficient collection of the taxes to which they had agreed by working with royal officials to develop accurate financial assessments of the property throughout the kingdom.

---

4 For the quotation, see D. Potter, 'The King and His Government under the Valois' in *France in the Later Middle Ages, 1200–1500*, ed. D. Potter (Oxford, 2003), 172.

Conclusion

All men and animals need to eat if they are to survive. The very fact that soldiers, their mounts, and their beasts of burden functioned effectively on campaign is irrefutable evidence that they had adequate supply from one or another source. While it is certainly true that humans can survive without food for rather extended periods without dying, this does not mean that they have the capacity to march long distances with heavy packs and undertake all of the other aspects of campaign life without adequate caloric support. Physiologically, horses are much more fragile than humans, and the failure to provide them with an adequate supply of food and water leads quickly to their breakdown and death.

The governments that mobilized fighting men for military service were well aware of the logistical needs of their troops, and put in place systems for the purpose of ensuring their supply needs. These systems varied considerably, and were based on a wide range of factors, including the wealth and sophistication of the governmental polity, the types of troops who were mobilized for service, and the duration of the campaign. When considered over the long term, it is clear that the transition from the standing army of the Roman period to largely militia-based armies that dominated during the Middle Ages shifted much of the burden of acquiring and transporting supply from the government to the individual soldier or his immediate employer. Nevertheless, many medieval governments continued to play active roles in the logistical operations of armies, particularly for long campaigns, by prepositioning large quantities of supplies along the main routes that were to be taken by the army and along the frontiers, and by mobilizing transportation assets to carry additional supplies into enemy territory. Moreover, medieval rulers and the commanders of armies also routinely sought to organize markets along their lines of march in order to facilitate the purchase of food and other necessities. This aspect of supply was particularly crucial during the crusades, when the armies of armed pilgrims were operating in the friendly territory of the Byzantine Empire, but otherwise had no claim to logistical support. By contrast with these governmentally organized sources of supply, plunder and 'living off the land' played a very small role in the logistical operations of armies, particularly for large armies over lengthy periods of time.

The planning for the logistical needs of armies that were to go on campaign, and the execution of these plans, required a highly trained and well-organized cadre of governmental officials, and sophisticated administrative systems. The vast quantity of 'paperwork' that was necessary to move a barrel of wine or a bushel of grain to soldiers in the field is illuminated, for example, by the hundreds of thousands of surviving government documents relating to the campaigns of Edward I in Scotland between 1296 and 1307, or the English siege of Calais in 1346. As a consequence, the large scale of the administration required to organize these military operations is unquestioned. By contrast, some scholars, who hold a 'dark age' view of Europe in the pre-crusade period, suggest that similar logistical operations 'simply happened' when a ruler mobilized an army. It is quite clear, however, that the same kinds of information had to be developed and placed in the right hands to organize the procurement and transportation of food for 30,000 men during Charlemagne's invasion of Italy in 773 as was necessary for Edward I's invasion of Scotland in 1296. Consequently, a proper understanding of logistics helps to illuminate the sophistication of governmental operations throughout the medieval millennium in a manner that might otherwise be missed by scholars not focused on the 'nuts and bolts' of the conduct of war.

Bibliography

With regard to the basic models for logistics in pre-modern warfare, see

Donald Engels, *Alexander the Great and the Logistics of the Macedonian Army*, second edition (Berkeley, 1980).

For the early imperial Roman background on logistics, see

Jonathan P. Roth, *The Logistics of the Roman Army at War (264* B.C – A.D. *235)* (Leiden, 1999).

For the later empire, see

Ramsay MacMullen, 'Inscriptions on Armor and the Supply of Arms in the Roman Empire' in *American Journal of Archaeology 64* (1960), 23–40;

R. W. Davies, 'The Roman Military Diet' in *Britannia 2* (1971), 122–143;

Stephen Mitchell, 'Requisitioned Transport in the Roman Empire: A New Inscription from Pisidia' in *The Journal of Roman Studies 66* (1976), 106–131;

W. S. Hanson, 'The Organisation of the Roman Military Timber-Supply' in *Britannia 9* (1978), 293–305;

J. M. Blázquez, 'The Latest Work on the Export of Baetican Olive Oil to Rome and to the Army' in *Greece & Rome 39* (1992), 173–188;

Colin E. P. Adams, 'Supplying the Roman Army: "Q. Petr"' in *Zeitschrift für Papyrologie und Epigraphik 109* (1995), 119–124;

Roger Kendal, 'Transport Logistics Associated with the Building of Hadrian's Wall' in *Britannia 27* (1996), 129–152;

Peter Kehne, 'War and Peacetime Logistics' in *A Companion to the Roman Army*, ed. Paul Erdkamp (Malden, MA, 2007), 323–338;

Patricia Crone, 'Quraysh and the Roman Army: Making Sense of the Meccan Leather Trade' in *Bulletin of the School of Oriental and African Studies 70* (2007), 63–88;

The collection of essays in *Feeding the Roman Army: The Archaeology of Production and Supply in NW Europe*, ed. S. Stallibrass and R. Thomas (Oxford, 2008).

For the early medieval period, see

Bernard S. Bachrach, 'Animals and Warfare in Early Medieval Europe' in *Settimane di Studio del Centro Italiano di Studi sull'alto Medioevo 31* (Spoleto, 1985), 707–764, reprinted with the same pagination in Bernard S. Bachrach, *Armies and Politics in the Early Medieval West* (London, 1993);

Carroll Gillmor, 'Naval Logistics of the Cross-Channel Operation, 1066' in *Anglo-Norman Studies 7* (1985), 221–243;

Bernard S. Bachrach 'Some Observations on the Military Administration of the Norman Conquest' in *Anglo-Norman Studies 8* (1986), 1–25, reprinted with the same pagination in Bernard S. Bachrach, *Warfare and Military Organization in Pre-Crusade Europe* (London, 2002);

Michael Jones, 'The Logistics of the Anglo-Saxon Invasions' in *Naval History: The Sixth Symposium of the United States Naval Academy*, ed. D. M. Masterson (Wilmington, 1987), 62–69;

William Ziezulewicz, 'The Fate of Carolingians Military Exactions in a Monastic Fisc: The Case of Saint-Florent-De-Saumur (ca. 950–1118)' in *Military Affairs 51* (1987), 124–127;

Bernard S. Bachrach, 'Logistics in Pre-Crusade Europe' in *Feeding Mars: Logistics in Western Warfare from the Middle Ages to the Present*, ed. John A. Lynn (Boulder, 1993), 57–78, reprinted with the same pagination in Bernard S. Bachrach, *Warfare and Military Organization in Pre-Crusade Europe* (London, 2002);

David Beougher, '"More Savage Than the Sword": Logistics in the Medieval Atlantic Theater of War' in *Studies in the Medieval Atlantic*, ed. Benjamin Hudson (New York, 2012), 185–206;

Abels, Richard, 'The Costs and Consequences of Anglo-Saxon Civil Defense, 878–1066' in *Landscapes of Defence in Early Medieval Europe*, ed. John Baker, Stuart Brookes, and Andrew Reynolds (Turnhout, 2013), 195–222.

For the later medieval period, see

Frederic C. Lane, 'Diet and Wages of Seamen in the Early Fourteenth Century' in *Venice and History*, ed. Frederic C. Lane (Baltimore, 1966), 263–268;

H. J. Hewitt, *The Organization of War under Edward III* (Manchester, 1966);

Michael Prestwich, 'Victualling Estimates for English Garrisons in Scotland during the Early Fourteenth Century' in *The English Historical Review 82* (1967), 536–543;

Joseph F. O'Callaghan, 'The Cortes and Royal Taxation during the Reign of Alfonso X of Castile' in *Traditio 27* (1971), 379–398;

John F. Guilmartin, 'The Logistics of Warfare at Sea in the Sixteenth Century: The Spanish Perspective' in *Feeding Mars: Logistics in Western Warfare from the Middle Ages to the Present*, ed. John A. Lynn (Boulder, 1993), 109–136;

Yuval Noah Harari, 'Strategy and Supply in Fourteenth-Century Western European Invasion Campaigns' in *The Journal of Military History 64* (2000), 297–333;

Bryce Lyon and Mary Lyon, 'The Logistics for Edward I's Ill-Fated Campaign in Flanders (1297–1298)' in *Handelingen der Maatschappij voor Geschiedenis en Oudheidkunde te Gent 55* (2002), 77–91;

David S. Bachrach, 'Military Logistics in the Reign of Edward I of England, 1272–1307' in *War and Society 13* (2006), 421–438;

Michael Prestwich, 'The Victualling of Castles' in *Soldiers, Nobles and Gentlemen: Essays in Honour of Maurice Keen*, ed. Peter Coss and Christopher Tyerman (Woodbridge, 2009), 169–182.

For logistics of the crusading armies, see

William C. Jordan, 'Supplying Aigues-Mortes for the Crusade of 1248: The Problem of Restructuring Trade' in *Order and Innovation in the Middle Ages in Honor of Joseph R. Strayer*, ed. William C. Jordan (Princeton, 1976), 165–172, reprinted with the same pagination in William C. Jordan, *Ideology and Royal Power in Medieval France: Kingship, Crusades and the Jews* (Aldershot, 2001);

John Pryor, 'Transportation of Horses by Sea During the Era of the Crusades: Eighth Century to 1285 A.D.: Part I to c. 1225 and Part II: 1228–1285' in *The Mariner's Mirror 68* (1982), 9–27 and 103–125;

M. Barber, 'Supplying the Crusader States: The Role of the Templars' in *The Horns of Hattin*, ed. Benjamin Kedar (London, 1992), 314–326;

Alan V. Murray, 'Finance and Logistics of the Crusade of Frederick Barbarossa' in *In Laudem Hierosolymitani: Studies in Crusades and Medieval Culture in Honour of Benjamin Z. Kedar*, ed. Iris Shagrir, Ronnie Ellenblum, and Jonathan Riley-Smith (Aldershot, 2007), 357–368;

John Haldon, Vincent Gaffney, Georgios Theodoropoulos, and Phil Murg-atroyd, 'Marching across Anatolia: Medieval Logistics and Modeling the Man-tzikert Campaign' in *Dumbarton Oaks Papers 65/66* (2011–2012), 209–235;

Elena Koytcheva, 'Logistics of the Early Crusades in the Balkans on Via militaris' in *Die Vielschichtigkeit der Strasse: Kontinuität und Wandel im Mittlelalter und der früher Neuzeit*, ed. Kornelia Holzer-Tobisch and Gertrud Blaschitz (Vienna, 2012), 209–232;

Bernard S. Bachrach, 'The Crusader March from Dorylaion to Herakleia' in *Shipping, Trade and Crusade in the Medieval Mediterranean: Studies in Honour of John Pryor*, ed. Ruthy Gertwagen and Elizabeth Jeffreys (Aldershot, 2012), 231–254.

Also see the collection of essays in John H. Pryor, *The Logistics of Warfare in the Age the Crusades* (Aldershot, 2006).

For the impact on the development of military logistics on governmental and economic institutions, see

John B. Henneman Jr., 'Financing the Hundred Years' War: Royal Taxation in France in 1340' in *Speculum 42* (1967), 275–298;

Edmund Fryde, 'Royal Fiscal Systems and State Formation in France from the 13th to the 16th Century, with Some English Comparisons' in *Journal of Historical Sociology 4* (1991), 236–287;

Jeffrey H. Denton, 'Taxation and the Conflict between Philip the Fair and Boniface VIII' in *French History 11* (1997), 241–264;

Kelly DeVries, 'Gunpowder Weaponry and the Rise of the Early Modern States' in *War in History 5* (1998), 127–145;

The collection of essays in *The Roman Army and the Economy*, ed. Paul Erdkamp (Amsterdam, 2002);

David Potter, 'The King and His Government under the Valois, 1328–1498' in *France in the Later Middle Ages*, ed. David Potter (Oxford, 2002), 155–181, 226–229;

Erica Schoenberger, 'The Origins of the Market Economy: State Power, Territorial Control, and Modes of War Fighting' in *Comparative Studies in Society and History 50* (2008), 663–691;

Andrew Wareham, 'Fiscal Policies and the Institutions of a Tax State in Anglo-Saxon England within a Comparative Context' in *The Economic History Review 65* (2012), 910–931.

Conflicting perspectives

Were early medieval governments capable of supplying large armies on campaign?

Timothy Reuter, 'Carolingian and Ottonian Warfare' in *Medieval Warfare: A History*, ed. Maurice Keen (Oxford, 1999), 13–35;

Guy Halsall, *Warfare and Society in the Barbarian West 450–900* (London, 2003), particularly chapter 6;

Bachrach, David, 'Feeding the Host: The Ottonian Royal Fisc in Military Perspective' in *Studies in Medieval and Renaissance History*, third series, *9* (2012), 1–43.

5 Military technology

Introduction

The increasingly rapid tempo of technological change in the modern world has led to a widely held view that might be termed the theory of technological replacement, whereby newer and arguably better technologies drive earlier technologies from the marketplace. For example, tapes replaced records, compact discs replaced tapes, and digitally stored music replaced compact discs, all within a very short time. Economists and sociologists point to the phenomenon of early adopters of new technologies, followed by the great mass of consumers, leaving only a small remnant to cling to the older technology until it becomes too difficult to find replacement parts. In the military sphere, the ongoing effort by industrialized societies, and particularly the great powers, to improve upon and then replace older ships, armoured vehicles, airplanes, and artillery, including various 'generations' of missiles, as well as small arms, has been understood by a number of military theorists and historians as axiomatic of modern warfare, which is seen to be dominated by the cliché 'evolve or die'.

However, this model of 'in with the new and out with the old' is a relatively recent phenomenon in the history of warfare. In her enormously important study of artillery in the classical Greek and Roman worlds, *The Catapult: A History*, Tracey Rihll observes that governments constructed and deployed many types of artillery, which originated in very different areas of the Mediterranean world and the Middle East throughout a period of several centuries, all at the same time. This same conservative phenomenon can be seen in all types of arms and weapons used during the medieval millennium, largely as a result of the inability in economic terms of governments to mobilize the resources that were necessary to undertake consistent and rapid revolutions in military technology, even when innovative ideas and prototypes were available. Instead, we see a pattern that is very different from that of the wealthier nations in the contemporary world. In medieval Europe generally, it was 'in with the new when possible but conserve the old because of necessity'. The invention or development of a new type of helmet, sword, or ship did not mean that all or even a great majority of the older models became obsolete. A range of factors came into play when consumers of military technology chose what to purchase or order to be constructed, including not least, the cost of the new technology relative to the old. This was especially the case when old equipment not only was already available, but also was still usable and generally easy and inexpensive to repair.

In this chapter, we will discuss the wide range of military equipment utilized by combatants over the course of the medieval period, including personal arms and armour, as well as large-scale siege equipment, ship design, and fortress construction. The investigation of military technology also opens up discussions of cultural transmission, both across time

DOI: 10.4324/9781003032878-6

and space. For example, one can see the continued use of Roman equipment and manuals during the Middle Ages, as well as the transfer of technology, such as winched crossbows and counter-weight traction artillery, from the Muslim East – which often benefitted from developments in China – to the Christian West. Similarly, technological knowledge regarding ship design can be seen passing from Europe's northern seas to the Mediterranean, and in the reverse direction, as well.

Personal arms and armour in the late empire

As seen in Chapter 3, over the course of the fourth century, the Roman imperial government introduced a range of military reforms that created two distinctive administrative divisions in the regular army. The relatively stationary frontier forces (*limitanei*) were composed mostly of foot soldiers, while the elite units of the field army (*comitatenses*) were organized largely as mounted troops, although the latter also were trained to fight on foot. This division between foot and mounted soldiers led inexorably to differences in the armaments of the two elements of the army. Foot soldiers continued to be equipped with spears (*pila*), as well as with short swords similar in both form and use to the *gladius* of the early empire. The *pilum* remained a missile weapon, and the fifth century Roman author Vegetius described methods for training Roman soldiers in its use, focusing on building up sufficient arm strength and throwing technique so as to increase the range at which the *pilum* would be effective. The short sword used by Roman foot soldiers was a thrusting weapon, and was provided with a sharp point. Slashing weapons with sharp edges, which were longer than the *gladius*, were unsuitable for late Roman foot soldiers, who continued to be trained for deployment in a traditional late imperial phalanx formation. A soldier in a phalanx who attempted to slash at his enemy was just as likely to injure his mate next to him in line as he was an opponent.

Roman mounted troops were equipped with long swords (*spathae*) and with pole weapons (*conti*) used for thrusting, some of which were rather lengthy. Other shorter pole weapons called *lancea* were used for throwing. The *spatha*, in contrast to the short swords used by foot soldiers, was intended as a slashing weapon, and was equipped with two cutting edges, which enabled the wielder to cut the enemy both with forehand and backhand strokes. It is likely that Roman mounted troops also were equipped with short swords. This was true because the elite units of the field army could be deployed on both foot and on horseback. As a consequence, it was necessary to provide these men with swords that were suitable for thrusting at the enemy while serving within a standard infantry phalanx.

Most Roman swords were produced using a process known as pattern welding. The smith forged the sword using several rods of iron, hammering and twisting the bars around each other to create a single bar and then blade. The differing mineral content of the iron bars, including substantial quantities of impurities, created patterns in the metal, giving the process its name. The Celtic contemporaries of the Romans used a similar process, which was intended specifically to create attractive patterns in the metal. Smiths continually improved the process of pattern welding throughout the Roman period and in Rome's various successor states. By the sixth century, smiths had learned how to construct blades with a thin outer layer of carburized iron, meaning iron with a higher carbon content, that were forged over a core of softer iron. This process gave the blades both an attractive patterned surface and the advantages of a stronger structure. The carburized iron provided greater hardness on the cutting surface, while the softer core gave the blade greater flexibility. The harder surface meant that both the edges and the point of the sword could hold their sharpness for a longer period of time than was possible using a softer metal.

The basic armour for both foot soldiers and mounted troops consisted of mail. During the early fourth century, the Roman government decided to abandon the production of the type of armour that had been in use for most of the previous hundred years. This was the *lorica segmentata*, which consisted of overlapping strips of iron or bronze that were held together by a variety of mechanisms, including buckles, straps, and hooks. In place of the *lorica segmentata*, the government owned and administered arms and equipment factories (*fabricae*) began to produce iron mail coats, which covered the torso, arms down to the elbow, hips, and lower back. Each mail coat consisted of tens of thousands of rings. These were produced through two basic methods. The first was to stamp out rings from sheets of iron, usually with hand-held punches. The second method was to convert iron ingots into wire and then turn the iron wire around a dowel with a diameter of the desired dimensions, and then clip off the rings with metal cutters.

In the pre-modern period, there were two basic methods of making iron wire. The first was to cut thin strips from sheets of iron, and then hammer these strips to the correct shape and diameter. The second method for producing iron wire was to draw thin, heated bars of iron through drawing plates. These devices were iron plates with holes drilled in them, through which the heated iron bar was pulled with tongs. As the bar grew thinner, it was pulled through increasingly more narrow holes, ultimately producing the wire with the diameter required by the armourers.

There is some controversy among specialists regarding the methods used by Roman and medieval armourers to produce iron wire. One school of thought holds that the only method utilized for this task, up through the late Middle Ages, was the cutting of thin strips from metal plates. Scholars asserting this view have argued that impurities in iron made it impossible to draw it through plates.

The transition to mail armour by the Roman government was to have an enormous impact on the history of protective equipment for the next 1,000 years. Throughout most of the medieval millennium, mail remained the dominant form of metal armour, worn by men from every social and economic status. As will be seen later in the chapter, it was not until the fourteenth century that medieval armourers began to produce a new type of

Figure 5.1 Norman armour from the Bayeux Tapestry, depicting the Battle of Hastings
Source: © GL Archive/Alamy Stock Photo C1A3JF

defensive equipment that was based on plates of iron, and later steel, rather than on mail. Some of these suits of armour were still supplemented with mail elements, however.

In addition to mail armour, the defensive equipment of Roman soldiers also included helmets and shields. The basic helmet for foot soldiers during the late empire generally consisted of two iron plates, which were hammered into a concave form and held together by a central strip of metal to which they were riveted. This formed a bowl-shaped covering over the head to which additional plates were added to protect the cheeks and back of the neck. However, in some cases, infantry helmets lacked these side and back plates, and the additional protection for the soldier's head was provided by a coif of mail, which was worn under the helmet. In all cases, fabric linings were required to keep the metal from bruising the wearer or causing

Figure 5.2 Image of late Roman mail: Ludovisi Battle sarcophagus; soldiers wearing mail in battle scene between Romans and Goths, Altemps Palace, Rome

Source: © Lanmas/Alamy Stock Photo EKM913

even deeper injuries. These linings also provided some degree of cushioning when a direct hit was suffered. Roman cavalry helmets had a similar design, with plates of metal riveted together to provide protection to the top, sides, and back of the head. Some Roman cavalry helmets also had nose guards, which consisted of a strip of metal that came down over the centre of the soldier's face. More elaborate and expensive cavalry helmets had a complete covering or mask for the face, and some of these were designed to a high artistic level.

Roman infantry shields in the late empire were rectangular-shaped, taller from top to bottom and shorter from side to side. These were formed from overlapping wooden strips, which were riveted together, and bound in leather that was held in place by broad-headed rivets or nails. The edges of the shields were given a thin iron covering, and many shields also had an iron or bronze metal protrusion on its front, called a boss, at the centre. The grip on the shield, which was constructed of wood with a leather cover, was horizontal rather than vertical, and the shield was meant to be gripped by the hand rather than held on the forearm. Often the grip extended from within the shield to the boss. Images of these shields have survived in large numbers on late Roman reliefs, and some pieces of shields – particularly the hollow bosses from the front – have been discovered in archaeological excavations. Roman cavalry shields were oval rather than rectangular, but their construction was similar to infantry shields, utilizing wooden strips covered with leather and iron. Cavalry shields were much smaller than infantry shields and were provided with a strap so that they could be worn on the rider's back when not in use.

Earlier medieval personal arms and armour

Among the most common misconceptions regarding the fate of the late Roman Empire in the West is the view, often propagated by historians wedded to the notion of the 'dark ages', that vast numbers of barbarians overwhelmed imperial defences. In fact, the total population of barbarians settling within the frontiers of the western half of the empire during the course of the fifth century comprised somewhere between 4 per cent and 8 per cent of the indigenous Roman population. In terms of raw numbers, the confederations of peoples denoted by the Romans as Burgundians, Goths, Vandals, Suevi, Franks, Angles, Saxons, and Jutes who settled within the empire from the late fourth through the late fifth century may have numbered one million souls, including men, women, and children. This can be compared with the approximately one million men who served in the Roman army in these same western provinces over this same century-long period, although not all at the same time! In sum, the total quantity of arms brought into the empire by the so-called barbarians was dwarfed by those produced by the imperial government for its soldiers within the frontiers.

Vast quantities of state-manufactured arms, armour, helmets, and shields were in circulation in the western provinces, in the hands of Roman soldiers, Roman veterans, and barbarians who were equipped by the Roman government in various types of military units. In addition, the private manufacture of equipment, following governmental specifications, for the military households of great magnates, and for militia forces further increased the reservoir of standardized arms and armour that was in circulation. Certainly some fighting men from the barbarian peoples kept the arms that they had brought with them into the empire. However, there is very little evidence of what might be thought of as typically 'barbarian' equipment, as contrasted to Roman equipment used by 'barbarians'.

In light of the enormous cultural and economic influence of the empire beyond its frontiers, it is not surprising that excavations of sites in the lands outside the Western Empire, such as in 'Free Germany', reveal that copies of Roman-style equipment were being produced there, as well. The one truly distinctive barbarian weapon would seem to have been the *francisca*, a throwing axe which was associated with the Franks. However, an illustrated page from the *Notitia dignitatum* indicates that axes of this type also were being produced in state *fabricae* early in the fifth century by the Roman government.

In fact, the arms utilized by the late Roman army remained the basic weapons of fighting men in the period up through the reign of Charlemagne (768–814). For foot soldiers, these were the spear and short sword. For mounted troops, the personal weapons were the lance and long sword, although most mounted fighting men also had short swords, as well, likely for the same reasons that these weapons were carried by Roman cavalry: namely, the need to dismount and serve in an infantry phalanx. The continuity in the basic form of weapons utilized in the three and a half centuries after the end of imperial rule in the West does not mean, however, that the early Middle Ages were marked by technological stasis or decline. Rather, the opposite was the case. As mentioned previously, master craftsmen throughout the Latin West continued to experiment with new methods of forging iron to produce higher quality weapons with improved strength and flexibility. A wide range of types of both short and long swords were produced in this period, which varied considerably in length and breadth, as well as in their ability to hold a sharp edge and point.

As discussed in Chapter 1, much of the information about swords from the early medieval period is derived from weapons that were elements of the grave goods in burials from the later period of the Roman Empire into the eighth century. Typical are the numerous 'row graves' in which Roman soldiers, barbarian allies, and militia troops were buried. It was not until after c.700 that Christian leaders, who had been teaching that the inclusion of material goods in graves was a pagan custom, began to have a significant impact on burial practices in the former provinces of the Western Empire. Up until this point, it was common for the Christian inhabitants of the former Roman provinces to bury their dead, including women and children, with grave goods.

The burial of swords is not indicative, as once thought, of ongoing pagan influence in the ostensibly Christian kingdoms of the Latin West. Nor are sword burials elements of a supposed heroic culture. It is clear that very large numbers of men were buried with swords, and relatively few of these men are likely to have been professional soldiers of barbarian origin, much less members of an aristocratic warrior elite. The possession of a sword, as well as a spear and shield, was required of virtually all male property owners throughout the post-Roman world, because of the obligation to serve in the expeditionary levy as discussed in earlier chapters. Somewhat more ambiguous is the inclusion of arrows in the burials, as these were used both for hunting and for military purposes. As a consequence, the burial of men with swords should be understood as the normal practice of providing everyday household items for the deceased as standard elements of the goods placed in graves. Other such everyday items included ceramic tableware, knives, and belt buckles.

From the perspective of the archaeologist and historian, the burial of these items is important because they provide important insights into the everyday life of ordinary laypeople who do not otherwise appear in written sources. In addition, the burial of swords in such large numbers indicates that the families who made the decision to give up possession of this 'tool' of war were sufficiently wealthy that they could afford to do without it and had the ability to purchase a new one if needed. This reality, in turn, makes clear that swords were not simply tools of the elite, but rather were ubiquitous throughout society. The large-scale production and possession of swords, even to the extent that they could be taken out of circulation by placing them in graves, is also an indication of the wealth of this society as a whole, as well as the wide availability of both raw materials and trained craftsmen.

Nevertheless, there are important distinctions between the simple and comparatively low-cost iron and low-carbon steel swords found in most graves, and the weapons that accompanied elite burials. The latter swords often were very well constructed of reasonably high-quality steel, and their hilts were encrusted with valuable jewels and inlaid with silver and gold. In this manner, they were consistent with the other grave goods found in elite burials, which included gold jewellery, gems, and high-value ceramics, as well as vessels constructed of precious metals and expensive glass. Indeed, high-quality long swords also were found in graves with either horse skeletons or stirrups, indicating the connection between wealth, the possession of a mount, and the possession of expensive arms.

Although swords and spears were the primary weapons throughout most of post-Roman Europe, the situation was somewhat different in Scandinavia. Here, long-handled axes, sometimes denoted by scholars as battle axes, were an important adjunct to the armament of northern fighting men. Battle axes appear prominently in both the grave goods of Scandinavian men, and also in descriptions in Latin sources, which depicted axe-wielding Vikings as bloodthirsty murderers. Following the conquest of much of England by Scandinavian invaders during the course of the ninth century, the axe also was adopted by many professional Anglo-Saxon fighting men, as well as by the professional military households of the kings of Wessex, the *huscarls*, who were recruited largely from Scandinavia. Good examples of this weapon are depicted in the Bayeux Tapestry, which is discussed in greater detail later in this chapter.

The defensive equipment of soldiers in the post-Roman period included mail, which was similar in construction to late Roman military equipment. Armourers continued to punch out rings and also to cut them from wire. The open ends of the wire-cut rings were flattened with a hammer, and then riveted together. Each ring was connected to four other rings. Depending on the size and thickness of the mail coat, it weighed 7–10 kilograms. Roman-style helmets also continued to be produced in this period, and it is likely that helmets constructed in imperial *fabricae* remained in use long after the end of the empire. However, it is also clear that by the sixth century, a new type of helmet construction had been developed in the Latin West, which likely was inspired by trade contacts with the Slavs. Many scholars believe that the Slavs, in turn, obtained this knowledge from the Middle East.

These new helmets are called *Spangenhelme* by scholars because of their method of construction. The German word *Spangen* (singular *Spange*) refers to the strips of metal that provided the structure to these conical-shaped helmets. Two strips of metal, one running from the front of the head to the back, and a second running from one ear to the other, were riveted to a third strip of metal that had been beaten into the shape of a circle. Four plates then were riveted to this frame to cover the entire head. A crest or ornament at the top of the helmet served to deflect a direct stroke to the crown of the head. The process of building up the helmet from strips was less labour intensive than hammering out large sheets of iron that were necessary to produce Roman-style bowl helmets, noted earlier. Over time, the relative ease with which the *Spangenhelm* could be produced led to its adoption throughout much of the West. Some of these helmets were fitted with face masks, as was the case with the famous helmet buried with a military leader at Sutton Hoo in the early seventh century. Nevertheless, helmets that were produced from a single sheet of iron also continued to be produced throughout the early medieval period. One famous example is the so-called St. Wenceslaus helmet, which is associated with Duke Wenceslaus of Bohemia, who was murdered by his brother Boleslav c.935. The helmet is dated by many scholars to the first quarter of the tenth century.

Many professional soldiers and members of the expeditionary levies were equipped with mail and helmets, but all men in the expeditionary levy were required to have shields. New shield designs began to develop during the late Roman period for mounted troops. These oval shields, which were convex in construction, continued to evolve and took on a variety of forms, including the round shield that appears in Carolingian legislation during the eighth century, and in the military manual of Rabanus Maurus in the ninth century, which was a modern adaptation of Vegetius *Epitoma rei militaris*. Shields were relatively inexpensive equipment, and legal texts indicate that a shield and spear together were valued at just a third of the price of a helmet. A coat of mail was valued as much as six shields and six spears.

Carolingian developments

Spears and swords remained the primary weapons of foot soldiers in the *Regnum Francorum*, the Ottonian kingdom, as well as with their Danish and Slavic adversaries through the end of the tenth century. The most common type of spear was the so-called 'winged lance' (*Flügellanzen* in German) that had its origins in the *Regnum Francorum* in the eighth century. In contrast to the Roman *pilum* and spears that developed from it during the early medieval period, the winged lance was equipped with a crossbar at the point where the lance head was connected with the shaft of the weapon. There is considerable disagreement among scholars regarding the origin of the winged lance, with some arguing that it

Figure 5.3 Flügellanz
Source: © UtCon Collection/Alamy Stock Photo M0J2A2

originally was a hunting weapon, particularly for wild boar. This type of lance was typical for boar hunting in the late imperial period and is depicted in a variety of artistic media. Other scholars argue that the lance was developed primarily for warfare, observing that the crossbar would have limited the penetration of the head into the body of the opponent, thus making it easier to withdraw and reuse. In our view, it is likely that both hunting and warfare played a role in the development of this weapon.

From the Carolingian Empire, the winged lance rapidly spread through trade and war into Scandinavia, England, and the Slavic East. Close examination of winged lance heads that have been recovered from excavations indicate that they were attached to poles, likely made of ash, and had a variety of lengths ranging from 150–250 centimetres. The shorter versions probably were used by foot soldiers, while the longer lances were employed by mounted troops. The primary function of the winged lance for foot soldiers was in the thrust and parry of hand-to-hand combat on foot, and the 150-centimetre version of this weapon could be used one-handed by foot soldiers equipped with shields. The longer winged lances employed by mounted soldiers also were used for stabbing the enemy, whether mounted or on foot.

There is no evidence, however, to suggest that the winged lance was ever intended to be held in a couched position by a rider thundering down the field at his opponent. It was once a commonly held view among scholars that the introduction of the stirrup during the course of the eighth century made cavalrymen equipped with lances well-nigh invincible against foot soldiers. The argument, which was set out in considerable detail by the historian of technology Lynn White Jr., was that with the stirrup, the mounted fighting man could keep himself firmly in the saddle and on his horse using only his legs, and thereby freed both arms for battle. When equipped with a lengthy lance, this 'centaur', combining both man and horse, could drive down the field of battle against his opponents and skewer them. This tactic was denoted as mounted shock combat.[1]

However, other specialists in military history disputed White's theory, pointing out from a technological perspective that stirrups alone would not permit this kind of charge with a couched lance. A high wrap-around cantle was required to keep him from being pitched off the back of his horse on contact, and a high wrap-around pommel was required to keep the rider from being thrown over the head of his horse as the result of an equal and opposite reaction to striking an opponent with a couched lance. These, as well as the double-girthed saddle to keep the seat in place, were not developed until the twelfth century. Consequently, it is not surprising that there is no evidence in narrative or archaeological sources to suggest that any foot soldiers in the period before the First Crusade were deployed with long pole weapons to ward off attacks at a distance by heavily armed warriors who were engaged in the tactics of mounted shock combat.

In addition to the development of the winged lance for combat purposes and not merely for hunting, the Carolingian period also saw the development of a new kind of sword which would come to be the dominant type throughout the *Regnum Francorum*, and all of its neighbours, into the eleventh century. Up through the mid-ninth century, foot soldiers in the Carolingian Empire were armed primarily with short swords of various types, often denoted as a *seax* or *gladius*. By contrast, mounted troops possessed both a short sword, for dismounted combat in a phalanx, and a long sword, the *spatha*, which was a slashing weapon for mounted combat.

---

1 See the scholarly works brought together in the 'Conflicting views' section of the bibliography regarding the role played by stirrups in bringing about change in medieval combat.

However, the *spatha* underwent substantial improvement over the course of the ninth century as sword smiths experimented with tapering blades from hilt to tip. The result was that the centre of gravity of the weapon moved backwards towards the hand-grip, making the weapon much more manoeuvrable for use in the cut, parry, and thrust of hand-to-hand combat. As a consequence, the *spatha*, with its longer reach and increased manoeuvrability, made the short sword redundant for use on foot. Because these weapons had a sharp point, they could be used effectively in a phalanx as a thrusting weapon, whereas slashing was more likely to hurt friend than foe. Increasingly from the mid-ninth century, therefore, professional soldiers and wealthier members of the expeditionary levy came to be equipped with the improved *spatha*, and only those poorer soldiers who served exclusively on foot continued to carry only short swords until they could afford to purchase or acquire the new longer weapons in other ways.

Towards the end of the Carolingian period, smiths also developed new methods for constructing swords and began to abandon pattern welding in favour of a type of a technique denoted by specialists as 'piling' or 'laminating'. In this new method of forging, several pieces of iron or steel were forged into a bar without utilizing the type of twisting that produced designs in the pattern-welded swords. In addition to 'piled' swords, smiths also produced some weapons from a single bar of iron. From the ninth century onward, smiths also developed much better techniques for carburizing iron, thereby giving it greater hardness. Among the most important techniques was the process of case carburization that involved packing the iron sword in a carbon-rich substance, such as charcoal, and heating the package so that the carbon migrates into the iron. The migration process is followed by a rapid quenching of the treated iron in cold water. The hardened surface is then tempered by heating it in the forge and allowing it to cool so as to increase its toughness and reduce its brittleness. Carolingian innovations in metallurgy built upon a centuries-long process of experimentation in the post-Roman period, which should serve as yet another nail in the coffin of the supposed technological 'dark ages' in early medieval Europe.

Developments in protective equipment up through the crusading age

As discussed earlier in the chapter, the basic metal armour of the entire period up through the end of the eleventh century, and beyond, was mail. Nevertheless, in some regions, such as in Scandinavia and among the Slavs in eastern Europe, small quantities of armour were produced using a type of construction denoted by modern scholars as lamellar, after the plates or scales (*lamellae*) from which the armour was constructed. This style of body protection, which had much in common with earlier Roman armour, utilized hundreds of small metal plates, often of iron but sometimes also of bronze, that were pierced and laced together on a leather shirt to fit over the wearer's torso. A similar type of armour, consisting of overlapping plates, known as scaled armour, was also produced in limited quantities, and is best known from Scandinavia, and particularly among the Vikings. These may have been modifications of Roman army equipment, although there is some archaeological evidence to suggest that scale armour may have come from the Middle East.

The vast majority of men equipped with metal armour, however, continued to use mail. There were some gradual changes in different regions of Europe and over time with regard to the size of the rings. More important were developments in the length of the mail coats, and the extension of the arm and leg coverings to afford the wearer greater protection over a larger percentage of his body. However, greaves, which were used by the Romans, also were available to the Franks in the sixth century and are noted as late as the ninth century in redactions of the Ripuarian Frankish law code. Perhaps the most famous and extensive depiction of mail armour comes from the Bayeux Tapestry, which was commissioned by Bishop Odo of Bayeux (1049–1097), the half-brother of William the Conqueror, to commemorate the Norman victory at Hastings in 1066.

Odo arranged for the manufacture of the tapestry in the first half of the 1070s, and it depicts large numbers of both Norman and Anglo-Saxon fighting men. Most of the Normans are depicted wearing mail coats that extend down to the knees and with sleeves that go down to the soldiers' elbows. Some scholars have argued that replacement of oval shields with kite-shaped shields, with which the Norman troops are depicted on the Bayeux Tapestry, came about because it was no longer necessary to provide full protection to the legs, which now were covered by mail *chausses*. However, Carolingian mounted troops in the eighth and ninth centuries had metal greaves for their legs and still utilized oval shields, so the explanation for the transition to the kite shield remains unresolved.

From the late eleventh century onwards, the pattern in armour development appears to have been to increase the coverage offered to the soldier. Reliefs in sculpture and also illustrations from manuscripts indicate that by the late eleventh century, the sleeves of mail coats extended to the wrist. By the mid-twelfth century, mail leg coverings appear to have become increasingly common. These *chausses* took two main forms. One was a strip of mail that covered the front of the leg and was held in place by ties around the back of the leg and over the foot. The second type consisted of a type of stocking that covered the entire leg and sometimes the foot, as well. By the end of the twelfth century, the sleeves of mail coats came to cover the back of the hand, although not the front. All of these developments are evidence for the refinement of the armourer's craft consistent with the steadily growing economy of the medieval West that produced the wealth that was necessary for consuming higher-quality goods. This advanced mail armour found a ready market among the growing numbers of mercenaries, and other types of military specialists, who were employed by princes and magnates throughout Europe.

Helmets also continued to evolve over the post-Carolingian period. *Spangenhelme* continued to be produced in very large numbers throughout Europe. In order to provide better protection to the wearer's face, these helmets acquired a nosepiece that extended from the lip of the helmet over the centre of the face. These helmets are ubiquitous on the Bayeux Tapestry for both the Anglo-Saxon and Norman soldiers. This type of helmet also was common in contemporary Germany. In his history of the civil war in Germany during the 1070s, Bruno of Merseburg observed that during one battle: 'Markgrave Udo struck his cousin Duke Rudolf so hard in the face with his sword that he would have cut off the entire upper part of his head if the nose guard on Rudolf's helmet had not faithfully defended him'. These nasal guards are similar in structure and purpose to some types of Roman helmets.

The second half of the twelfth century saw the development of several new types of helmets that were used alongside the conical *Spangenhelme* with nose guards that were so prominent in the Bayeux Tapestry. These included a rounded version of the *Spangenhelm*, often without a nose guard, and also a flat-topped helmet, which in the next century often was topped by a plume or crest, which also had been the case with many styles of Roman helmets. These crests helped to protect the top of the head from slashing strokes. The first quarter of the thirteenth century saw the introduction of the helmet denoted by contemporaries as a *cerveillière* in French texts and also a *bascinet* in some French, as well as Latin, works. This was a relatively small helmet, which was shaped like a skull cap. It was easy to produce and therefore inexpensive because it was produced from a single small plate. Over the course of the thirteenth century, all of these types of new helmets gradually evolved to include both a permanent neck guard, and also a fixed face guard. The culmination of this process was another new type of helmet that completely enclosed the head. It came to be known as the great helm.

Yet another type of helmet that came into use during the twelfth century was the so-called kettle-hat, denoted in many contemporary sources as the iron cap (*chapel-de-fer*). This was an iron hat with a wide iron brim. It was similar in design to both late Roman helmets, and also to the well-known depictions of the helmets worn by Carolingian soldiers in the ninth century. This helmet, which was structured in the manner of a *Spangenhelm*, was very inexpensive to produce, and became the standard head protection for foot soldiers and other poorer elements of medieval armies up through the sixteenth century.

Later medieval developments

The sword and spear remained the basic weapons for both foot soldiers and mounted troops throughout the Middle Ages. In part, this was due to the fact that armour had not changed significantly over this period. During the later thirteenth century, however, and increasingly thereafter, there were significant developments in the production of armour that led, in turn, to developments in hand-held arms, including both thrusting and projectile weapons.

The major change in armour was the reintroduction of plates in place of mail. The use of plates had never fully ended in the medieval West. As noted earlier, Scandinavian armourers produced both lamellar and scale armour, albeit in limited quantities, during the pre-crusade period. It is, therefore, not surprising that the earliest reference to plate armour in a narrative source concerns a force of Danish fighting men. In his text *The Topography and Conquest of Ireland*, which was written in about 1188, Gerald of Wales (died 1223) described an attack by a Danish army against the city of Dublin in 1171. The Danish soldiers are described as wearing armour that consisted of iron plates that were carefully sewn together. This type of armour appears to have been a continuation of the lamellar construction that was known from the Viking age and even earlier.

A rather different tradition of plate armour appears to have developed during the late twelfth century, as plates of armour were added to mail to protect key points of the body. These included the legs, elbows, and knees. The first depictions of these additional plates appear during the mid-thirteenth century. The lag in time between the introduction of plates and their artistic representation is not surprising, however, as manuscript illustrations were marked by a considerable level of conservatism in depicting new types of images. The earliest reference to plates utilized in conjunction with mail comes from the pen of the French author William the Breton, whose position at the court of King Philip II of France gave him access to considerable information about the most recent developments in all types of fields, including military technology. In his text *Philippidos*, William, who wrote during the early thirteenth century, observed that when King Richard I of England fought in a battle, he was protected by iron plates (*fera fabricate patena*) on his knees and elbows.

From the mid-thirteenth century onwards, armourers began a steady process of increasing the quantity of plate that was used to cover the body. By 1250, knee plates seem to have been very common, and were depicted regularly in contemporary manuscripts. The second half of the thirteenth century saw the increasing development of plate protection for arms and also for the trunk. A development that was concomitant with the attachment of plates to mail suits was the introduction, during the late thirteenth century, of a body defence denoted by modern scholars as a coat of plates. This armour, which was the most common type of plate protection during the fourteenth century, consisted of a cloth or leather garment that was lined with plates. Its construction, therefore, was similar to the lamellar armour, noted previously. Armourers experimented with a large variety of materials for these coats of plates, including not only iron, but also whalebone, horn, and boiled leather.

During the fourteenth century, armourers also began to experiment with solid plate armour, producing a wide range of pieces that ultimately would develop into a complete suit that covered the soldier from head to toe. By 1350, armourers had succeeded in producing a complete fitted breastplate, and by the end of the century, wealthy soldiers or their patrons could purchase a solid plate cuirass, which consisted of both a chest and a back covering held together by means of straps or hooks, constructed of leather or metal. It remains unclear whether Roman moulded breastplates, made of bronze or boiled leather, which were well-known from a variety of sculptures and reliefs during the later Middle Ages, had any impact on contemporary designs.

By the early fifteenth century, armourers produced entire suits of plate armour, which included numerous pieces that protected the torso, hips, legs, inner thigh, groin, knees, feet, arms, elbows, hands, and neck. The head was protected by variants of the great helm, which had developed over the course of the thirteenth century. All of these pieces of equipment had to be fitted personally to the wearer, meaning that they could not be mass produced and were therefore very expensive. Many of the armourers were artists who consistently developed and refined their techniques and tools while teaching the next generation of craftsmen as apprentices.

Partly in response to changes in armour, the primary hand-held weapons of soldiers also began to change during the later thirteenth century. High-quality steel swords became increasingly narrow and were provided with a sharp tip for thrusting, to penetrate gaps in the opponent's armour. Foot soldiers had always been equipped with thrusting swords, but now swords that were intended for mounted combat were produced in this manner, as well. The considerable protection afforded by plate armour and the rider's shield was sufficient to ward off slashing blows. By using a thin blade with a sharp point, the attacker sought to strike a point that was not protected, such as the gaps between the various pieces of armour. In this case, one can marvel at the hand-eye coordination of the attacker if such a thrust were to be effective against a skilled opponent. By contrast, maces and ball-and-chain weapons were designed to smash rather than penetrate the armour.

By the later fifteenth century, some swords also were being produced for a market of aristocrats and wealthier merchants, the latter who wished to copy the elites. These swords were intended to be worn on a daily basis. Consequently, the weapons were constructed so as to be comfortable when worn during the course of a normal day's activities, and developed into very slender blades, which were not useful for the battlefield, but which could be used in duels by men who were not wearing armour. Many of these blades, as well as their hilts and scabbards, were decorated to such a degree that they can be considered works of art. As was true of highly decorated armour, such swords were outward markers of high social status.

During the later medieval period, smiths also continuously experimented with alloys and forging techniques to create harder yet tougher edges and points, while maintaining the internal flexibility of their weapons. Perhaps the most striking development with respect to the production of swords in the later Middle Ages was the two-handed long sword utilized most famously by German mercenary troops known as *Landsknechte*. These swords were almost 2 metres long, and required prodigious strength, as well as extensive training, to use effectively.

Pole weapons also underwent significant developments during the late thirteenth century and throughout the subsequent centuries. Although throwing and thrusting spears of various types continued to be produced during the later Middle Ages, foot soldiers, in particular, increasingly were equipped with arms that were an amalgamation of the spear and the axe. These weapons gave foot soldiers the option of either thrusting or slashing at an opponent, particularly a mounted opponent, before he had a chance to strike with his sword. The halberd, which was well-known as the most effective pole arm used by Swiss infantry, was the model for such weapons. In addition, the continuing development of the infantry phalanx to stop charges by heavy cavalry equipped with long lances, and riding nestled in saddles with high pommels and cantles, led to the broad introduction of the long pike. This weapon extended up to 10 feet beyond the front of the phalanx as, for example, at the Battle of Bannockburn in 1314, where Scottish infantry defeated a cavalry charge by the heavily armed horsemen of the army of King Edward II of England. This late medieval development can be seen as a type of 'back to the future' phenomenon, in which infantry formations of the fifteenth century resembled those of the Macedonian phalanxes that served under Alexander the Great in the fourth century BC.

Hand-held missile weapons

At the most basic level, anything thrown by a combatant that can hurt humans, animals, or equipment can be considered a missile weapon. Throughout the medieval millennium, the defenders of city and fortress walls, aided by the force of gravity, utilized small and large stones, boiling oil, boiling water, and even wagon wheels to injure or kill attackers. However, combatants also had available a wide range of specialized weapons that were intended to strike the enemy at a distance.

Thrown projectiles

The purported national weapon of the Franks during the later Roman Empire was the throwing axe known as the *francisca*. This weapon fell out of general use during the early Middle Ages, but throwing axes of various types with various potential ranges continued to be produced and utilized on a sporadic basis throughout the medieval period. Much more common, however, was the spear, which remained an important missile weapon for foot soldiers during the early medieval period, and for mounted troops, particularly light cavalry, well into the thirteenth century. Grave goods from the fifth through seventh centuries indicate that most fighting men were equipped with two or three spears, including a type denoted by contemporaries as an *ango*. This weapon had a relatively short haft, but an iron tang that was at least two feet in length so that when it struck an enemy shield, it could not be cut off easily and made the shield useless for combat. The Byzantine historian Agathias, who wrote during the second half of the sixth century, observed that Frankish forces operating in Italy were equipped with spears of this type and hurled them at the enemy before advancing into combat in order to nullify the value of their enemies' shields.

Mounted troops also used short spears as missile weapons. The early tenth-century author Regino of Prüm observed, for example, that Breton mounted troops caused havoc when fighting against the Frankish infantry phalanx of King Charles the Bald during his invasion of the region in 851 when they rode in close to the tightly packed Carolingian soldiers and hurled spears at them, before darting away again. Welsh mounted troops in the twelfth century and Irish hobelars in the thirteenth century were equipped in a similar manner, and also were effective in operations against both foot soldiers and slower moving heavy cavalry. Muslim cavalry from the Iberian Peninsula, North Africa, and the Middle East used throwing spears, as well as short reflex bows, to great effect in various tactical situations.

Mechanically cast projectiles

The earliest known and simplest mechanical projectile is the sling. The sling works by extending the reach of the human arm, thereby adding velocity and range to what can be achieved by arm strength alone. The basic form of the sling consists of a small pouch, to which two strings are attached. The projectile, which was often simply a smooth stone but which could be a manufactured lead pellet, is placed in the pouch. The slinger then takes hold of the ends of the two strings, swings the pouch in an arc, and releases one of the two strings to let the projectile free. In order to increase the range and striking power of the projectile, the sling also could be mounted on a staff. Scholars have offered differing views about the range of slings, however, there is a consensus that staff slings could strike targets at a distance of more than 200 metres with deadly force.

The sling was well-known to Christians, as well as Jews and Muslims, from the passage in 1 Samuel 1:17, where the story of David and Goliath is told. David was able to fell the giant because of his enormous skill with this weapon, which he had developed over the course of his youth as a shepherd to kill predators such as lions. As the biblical story indicates, the sling was a weapon that had a range of uses beyond the battlefield, both for driving off wild animals and for hunting, which meant that considerable numbers of men and boys living in the countryside were proficient in its use.

Figure 5.4 Slingers
Source: © Florilegius/Alamy Stock Photo EG7NE8

The sling as a weapon of war is discussed by Vegetius in his *Epitoma rei militaris*, and also by Rabanus Maurus in his ninth-century redaction of this work. Legal sources from the late eighth century indicate that Charlemagne's foot soldiers used slings of the type attached to staffs, and had wagon loads of these arms, along with pre-cast lead ammunition brought on several campaigns. There are several references in narrative sources to the use of slings by soldiers in the armies of the Ottonian kings. An image from a gospel book belonging to Otto III, commissioned in the period 998–1001, includes a depiction of two soldiers armed with slings who are participating in the siege of a city, meant to illustrate Jerusalem. A manuscript illustration in Matthew Paris' *History of the English*, from the mid-thirteenth century, shows two men equipped with staff slings on the deck of a ship casting projectiles at the defenders of a coastal fortification. Pay records from the early fourteenth century indicate that Edward I of England deployed slingers from Sherwood Forest during his siege of Stirling castle.

Bow and arrow

Similar to the sling in terms of its multi-purpose nature was the bow and arrow. The bow is perhaps only slightly less ancient than the sling, and was ubiquitous in the ancient world. Roman armies routinely included large contingents of auxiliary archers. The bow remained an important weapon throughout the medieval period, and was only gradually replaced by hand-held gunpowder weapons during the early modern period. In the context of the Revolutionary War by the British colonies in North America, Benjamin Franklin in a letter to General Charles Lee in 1776 suggested that it would be advisable to arm soldiers of the Continental Army with bows rather than the less accurate musket. Indeed, as late as the nineteenth century, Cossacks equipped with bows were deployed by the Russian army. The excavation of vast numbers of different types of arrow heads from throughout Europe testify to the use of the bow both for hunting of various types of animals and for military purposes throughout the medieval millennium.

The Salian-Frankish law code, which was redacted in the eighth century, also provides considerable information about the importance of archers where very high fines were imposed for damage to or loss of an archer's fingers that made him incapable of using the bow. Carolingian capitularies issued in the early ninth century required some fighting men to bring bows and arrows on campaign. By contrast, narrative sources from the early medieval period rarely comment on the use of bows by the 'home side' particularly in battles in the field, in part, because it was not seen as an aristocratic weapon. It is generally agreed by scholars that Charlemagne was not able to develop a corps of mounted archers, but the Byzantine Empire did develop units of this type, often by recruiting nomadic peoples into imperial service.

By contrast with the relative silence of narrative sources regarding their use in battles in the field, bows are mentioned quite frequently in the context of sieges as being used by both attackers and defenders. Similarly, during the pre-crusade period, the authors of narrative sources also tended to emphasize the use of bows by the enemies of the Christian West, including the Avars and Hungarians, who had come into Europe from the steppes of central Asia. During the crusading era, Muslim foot soldiers, as well as cavalry, are described by the authors of chronicles as archers, a description that is depicted in numerous manuscript illustrations from this period. Of course, the use of bows was entirely consistent with the warfare of the Eurasian steppe from where many Muslim rulers imported boys to serve as slave soldiers (mamluks) in their armies.

A wide range of bows were utilized by military forces from the late Roman period up through the late Middle Ages. From a technological perspective, these can be divided into two broad categories. The first, and more common among western armies, consisted of wooden bows, with ash and yew among the favoured species used for their construction. The second type of bow, known as a composite bow, was produced through a process of laminating thin strips of wood, glue or sinew, bone, and/or horn. The wooden bows were relatively easy to construct, as contrasted with composite weapons, and were produced by professional bowyers from materials that were found throughout Europe. Wooden bows also were able to withstand the damp climate that predominated in much of Europe during the medieval period. The major advantage of composite bows was that they stored much more potential energy in the bow than a wooden bow of comparable length. It is the potential energy in the bow, rather than the draw of the string, that provides the force to drive the projectile. Thus, inch for inch, a composite bow is much more powerful than a wooden bow. However, composite bows are very susceptible to damage from moisture, even when properly stored in fur-lined cases, and are also much more complex to construct, expensive to produce, and difficult to repair.

The composite bow was the primary missile weapon of both the steppe peoples, such as the Huns, Avars, and Hungarians, and of the Arabs, Egyptians, and Turks of the Middle East whom Christian armies met in battle from the sixth through the thirteenth centuries. However, it is not clear whether composite weapons ever became popular in the West. Many westerners were aware of these weapons, either from personal experience in combat or from images in books or, more likely, sculpted reliefs on churches, which depicted Ishmael, the brother of Isaac and the supposed father of the Arabs, using this weapon. Part of the problem in determining the use of the composite bow in the West is that the weapons themselves have left no trace in the archaeological record, and illustrators of manuscripts and the artists who carved stone reliefs on church facades usually did not stray from the *topos* that the short composite bow was a weapon of the 'other'.

There is a similar lack of clarity regarding the question of whether there was a 'long bow revolution' during the fourteenth century. Many scholars in the first half of the twentieth century argued that the success of the English in battle during much of the Hundred Years' War was due to their adoption of a new super weapon, namely a longer and more powerful bow that could be used to penetrate the plate armour of their French opponents. More recently, other scholars, notably Kelly DeVries, along with Matthew Strickland and Robert Hardy, have argued that there was no long bow revolution, and that bows used by foot soldiers always had been relatively long and powerful. In our view, it seems likely that the length of the bow was relative to the size, skill, and strength of the men who used them, and that bows of varying lengths were used throughout Europe during the entire medieval period. In addition to the length of the bow, further variables that affected the hitting power of the weapon were the length and weight of the shaft and head of the arrow.

The effective range of bows depended largely on the potential energy that could be stored in the bow stave. Relatively few bows have survived from the medieval period that would provide an opportunity to undertake an analysis of their potential energy storage capacity. One exception from the early Middle Ages is a cache of bows that were excavated from an eighth century merchant settlement on the frontier between Denmark and Germany at Hedeby (German Haithabu). An examination of these bows, and replicas that were made using wood of the same type and dimensions, suggests that these weapons had an effective killing range of 200 metres against men wearing mail when the length of the arrow, the quality of its fletching, and the pull of the bow were optimized. Archaeologists have found similar bows in Alamanic graves from the sixth century in the southeast of Germany, although these have not been modelled by scholars for range and striking power. Another important find of so-called long bows was made for the late medieval period from the wreck of the *Mary Rose*, which sank in 1545 while carrying a cargo of military equipment, including hundreds of wooden bows and staves that were to be turned into bows. Analysis of these staves indicates that many of them had 100–120 pounds of torque available as potential energy when fully drawn. A number of tests have been performed on bows that have been modelled on those found in the *Mary Rose*. The conclusions vary considerably, but the maximum range of the weapons appears to have been close to the 200-metre distance postulated for the ninth century bows found at Hedeby, which suggests that powerful bows had an important place on European battlefields many centuries before the supposed long bow revolution of the Hundred Years' War.

Crossbows

In contrast to the simple bow, the bow of the crossbow was on a horizontal plane relative to the man using the weapons rather than a vertical plane. In addition, the drawstring on a crossbow, once pulled into position, was held in place by a nut, and did not release its projectile until a trigger mechanism was pulled, releasing the bolt. Crossbows were well-known in the Roman period, and numerous reliefs show Roman soldiers using these weapons. They also were widely used by civilians for hunting. It seems very likely that crossbows continued to be employed during the immediate post-Roman era, but there is not significant evidence for their use in either written sources or illustrations until the turn of the first millennium. The first medieval author to devote considerable attention to the weapon was Richer of Rheims, at the end of the tenth century, who repeatedly mentions the use of *ballistae*, by which he meant crossbows, alongside bows in his discussion of the wars in the French kingdom. At about the same time Richer was writing, the illustrator of the *Gospel Book of Emperor Otto III*, noted earlier, included an image of soldiers using crossbows alongside slingers in defence of the city of Jerusalem.

The weapon drew increasing attention in all forms of visual media, as well as narrative sources, over the course of the eleventh and twelfth centuries, suggesting to some scholars that its use was becoming more widespread. In her discussion of the western armies that participated in the First Crusade, Anna Komnena, the daughter of the Byzantine ruler Emperor Alexios Komnenos, describes the crossbow as a specifically western weapon. However, in 1139, the bishops who assembled in Rome for the Second Lateran Council banned the use of the crossbow against Christians in a measure that clearly was aimed at the King Roger II of Sicily (1130–1154), who employed large numbers of Muslim soldiers, many of whom were equipped with crossbows. At the time of the Second Lateran Council, Roger was the primary enemy of the papal government at Rome.

The crossbow became the weapon of choice for urban militias and mercenary companies throughout Europe during the course of the twelfth century, and retained an important role among both groups through the end of the Middle Ages. One important reason for the adoption of this weapon by militia forces was that a crossbow was far easier to master than a bow. In addition, the crossbow could be held cocked until the archer had picked out his target. Furthermore, the crossbowman could take cover while searching for a target, and even discharge his weapon from a kneeling position in order to decrease his exposure to enemy action. Archers did not have either of these latter two advantages. The one major

Figure 5.5 Man loading a crossbow
Source: © Album/Alamy Stock Photo R5E6TX

limitation of a crossbow as contrasted with the bow is the slow rate at which it could be loaded and shot. Scholars have estimated that a well-trained crossbowman could get loose two well-aimed shots in minute, while an equally well-trained archer could discharge five carefully aimed arrows in the same time.

The ability to keep the crossbow cocked while under cover offered significant advantages in the context of sieges, which dominated warfare throughout the Middle Ages. The same virtues which made the crossbow well suited for siege warfare also made it very useful at sea. No later than the end of the twelfth century, for example, Genoese ships were provided with large complements of crossbowmen who filled the fighting platforms of their ships during battles. Within a few years, all other maritime powers had followed suit. The contemporary perception that the crossbowman was superior to the archer was reflected in the higher rates of pay received by the former throughout Europe. This was even the case in England, where archers formed a very significant part of all armies.

The importance of the crossbow as a weapon led many medieval governments to purchase them in large numbers, and even to establish centralized production under governmental auspices. The city of Genoa, on the Mediterranean coast in northern Italy, became one the largest international centres for the production of crossbows, for use in its own fleets and for export around Europe. Genoese crossbowmen also became famous as mercenaries during the later medieval period, and were recruited in substantial numbers by the kings of France during the Hundred Years' War. Thousands of Genoese crossbowmen served on the French side at the Battle of Crécy in 1346.

Ironically, during the twelfth century, one of the main markets for Genoese crossbows – if not the actual crossbowmen – was England. Both King Henry II and his son Richard I imported very large numbers of these weapons. However, following John's loss in 1204 of most of the English royal possessions in France, obtaining Genoese crossbows became more difficult because of the efforts of the French crown to discourage trade between England and Italy. In addition, the supply of crossbows from manufacturers in northern France disappeared entirely. John's response was to organize a crossbow industry in England, establishing half a dozen production centres between 1204 and 1212, including one in the Tower of London.

Royal investment in the production of crossbows continued throughout the thirteenth century so that by the time Edward I began his wars of conquest in Wales and Scotland during the late thirteenth century, dozens of crossbow makers were in direct royal employ, producing many thousands of weapons. In addition, employees of the royal government produced millions of crossbow bolts, with the most important production facility located in the royal forest of Dean, where rich iron ore deposits were exploited. The government also purchased very substantial numbers of crossbows and bolts on the private market, which is evidence of the diffusion of this highly complex craft, as well as the entrepreneurial spirit of the English people.

As was true of the bow, there were a variety of types of crossbows in use in Europe. The earliest form of the crossbow was spanned by placing one's feet on the belly of the bow in order to hold it steady, and then pulling the cord into place. Many crossbowmen kept a hook on their belts for this purpose, so that much of the strength for lifting came from the thigh muscles and back rather than the arms. By the end of the twelfth century, many new crossbows were fitted with an iron stirrup on the back of the bow, into which the crossbowman could place his foot for leverage. These crossbows came to be known as *ballistae ad unum pedem* – that is, crossbows for one foot. A larger and more powerful weapon, which likely came into use right around the turn of the thirteenth century, was the *ballista ad duos pedes*, or crossbow for two feet. Detailed administrative documents from England indicate that as early as the first decade of the thirteenth century, one-foot and two-foot crossbows were being produced not only entirely of wood, but also using a method similar to that used for composite bows. In order to produce the composite bows, the royal government purchased large quantities of horn and also glue that was made from fish bones. These materials were then fabricated by royal crossbow makers (*attilliatores*) into composite weapons.

Human strength was the main limit imposed on the power of crossbows of the one-foot and two-foot varieties. The thicker and larger the wooden or composite bow of the weapon, the greater the range and the striking power of the bolt would be. However, there are clear limits to the ability of a single man using his bodily strength alone to span this bow and draw its string into place. This problem was solved in England by borrowing technology that had been in use in the Muslim East since at least the 1180s, if not earlier. An arms treatise composed for the Sultan Saladin, dated to c.1190, clearly makes reference to such a mechanical device for spanning crossbows, although scholars have failed to agree whether this mechanism was a crank, a windlass, or a winch. The first reference to a mechanical spanning device in the Christian West appears in 1213, when King John sent a letter to Engelard de Cigogné, one of the royal officers in charge of crossbow production, asking about the safe delivery of crossbows by Engelard's men, including four *ballistae de cornu ad turnas* – that is, four composite crossbows that were equipped with a mechanical spanning device (*turnus*).

Numerous administrative documents from the reigns of John, Henry III, and Edward I indicate that the *turnus* was a detachable metal device, which could be used on any powerful crossbow to span it. Some scholars argue that the *turnus* was a device known as a goat's foot lever, which consists of a hook attached to an arm. Once the hook was placed on the string, the arm could be levered backwards, pulling the string into a locked position. However, this explanation seems unlikely. A letter issued by King Henry III to the office of the exchequer ordering payment for military supplies used in his siege of Bedford Castle in 1224 includes a charge for the production of 'two circles of iron used in a *turnus*' which was a spanning device for a piece of torsion-powered artillery known as a mangonel. The two circles of iron that were part of the *turnus* construction indicate that it was type of winch or windlass device, rather than a simple lever.

The answer to the question of how the *turnus* technology made its way to England is suggested by King John's recruitment of two crossbow makers named Peter the Saracen and Benedict the Moor to join the staff at the royal production facility at the Tower of London. The names of these men suggest their connections with, if not their origin in, the Middle East. These two men were paid at a much higher rate than the other crossbow makers employed by the crown, and the appearance of the *turnus* post-dates their arrival in England. It seems likely, therefore, that these men either brought the knowledge of constructing these spanning devices, or facilitated the transfer of this knowledge, to England. The next mention of this spanning device outside of England comes from the island of Majorca after its conquest from its Muslim ruler in 1232 by King James I of Aragon. In this case, the *turnus* was utilized on a piece of spear-casting artillery, called a *ballista*, which was, in effect, a giant crossbow. Peter of Portugal, then serving as the Aragonese governor of Majorca, issued a charter in 1240 in which he commanded that the town of Palma maintain stationary artillery for its own defence including spear-casters (*ballistae*) with the spanning devices attached.

Over the course of the fourteenth century, crossbow makers experimented with new materials for making their weapons, and developed steel crossbows, with ranges of up to 400 metres, doubling what was possible with wooden or composite weapons. The metal for these weapons was produced in a manner similar to that used to produce steel for swords and armour. However, the traditional methods of spanning the crossbows were no longer adequate, so new mechanical devices were developed, including the cranquin, which used a rack-and-pinion system, and the windlass, which employed a series of pulleys in place of gears. However, the development of newer and more powerful crossbows did not lead to the abandonment of earlier types. The very simplest 'one-foot' wooden crossbows were still being used well into the fourteenth century.

Artillery

The two methods for propelling large-size projectiles that were available from classical Antiquity up through the early Middle Ages were tension and torsion. For the most part, tension engines, which drew their power from the potential energy stored in the bow of the weapon, fired long 'sharps' that looked like spears. These engines, often denoted as *ballistae* in the early medieval period, had, as noted previously, the appearance of very large crossbows, and could be aimed and held cocked until the artilleryman had picked out his target. Tension engines were ideal anti-personnel weapons for both attackers and defenders in sieges. Depending on their size, they were relatively easily transportable in carts or wagons, and could also be mounted on walls. In addition, they had a considerable advantage in range over hand-held bows, so that the operators of these engines were relatively free to pick their targets without worrying about being struck by arrows shot by opposing archers or crossbowmen. Some medieval chroniclers somewhat playfully suggested that men using *ballistae* could skewer several enemy soldiers with one shot in the manner of a shish kabob.

Torsion artillery in the Roman Republic and Principate frequently comprised complex two-armed engines. Some of these engines hurled stones, and others were designed to cast spears. These weapons launched their payloads in a horizontal trajectory. By the Late Antique period, however, the two-armed stone-throwing engines had given way to the much simpler design of the one-armed engine that launched its payload of stone in a high parabolic arc. The one-armed torsion engine, known as the *onager* or wild ass because its tremendous recoil seemed to be like a powerful kick. This weapon was relatively easily transportable in ox carts. In addition, this type of artillery could be mounted on a wall for the defence of a fortification. The maximum range of these weapons, discharging a 2–4-kilogram stone, was about 450 metres. Like the spear-caster, this torsion engine was primarily an anti-personnel weapon, and also had excellent value in destroying enemy wagons, carts, and artillery.

During the nineteenth and much of the twentieth century, there was considerable debate among scholars about whether the design or use of any types of artillery survived from the Roman period. One of the major problems faced by scholars, who have tried to identify the types of artillery actually deployed in Late Antiquity and the Middle Ages, is the lack of precision in the use of terminology in contemporary narrative sources. Many of the authors of historical narratives, in which artillery is discussed, were personally unfamiliar with military technology and used generic terms, such as *instrumentum* (instrument), *machina* (machine), *ingenium* (engine), and *catapulta* (catapult) to describe the weapons that were deployed. Many authors of narrative sources also used terms such as *tormentum*, *scorpio*, *petraria*, and *onager*, which may have had a technical meaning as a particular type of artillery. The general lack of description for these weapons, however, makes it virtually impossible to determine the source of their power, much less their specific characteristics, such as whether they were one-armed or two-armed, wheeled or stationary.

Two of the early leading specialists in the history of medieval artillery who wrote in the nineteenth century were Rudolf Schneider and Gustav Köhler. Relying on the same body of narrative sources, Köhler and Schneider came to diametrically opposed conclusions. Köhler argued that medieval armies continued to use torsion engines into the twelfth century, while Schneider – who saw the Middle Ages, and especially the early medieval period, in terms of a 'dark age' – asserted that engines of this type were far beyond the capacity of the supposedly primitive technology available in the post-Roman world. In place of the ostensibly complex torsion engine, Schneider argued that medieval artillery consisted entirely of traction engines, which worked on the lever principle.

Today, many scholars agree that both torsion and tension technology were used in the post-Roman West, and that they were joined in the sixth century by the traction engine, which appears to have come west from China through the Middle East, and to have been used by the Byzantines from the late sixth or early seventh century. By 617, the Avars had learned to construct and use this equipment from captured Byzantine engineers. By the eighth century, tension technology was known even farther west and used by the relatively backward Saxons in their wars against the Franks.

The traction engine was essentially a long beam fixed to a fulcrum. The shorter end of the beam faced the target, and the longer end had a sling attached into which the projectile was set. Energy was generated by the rapid descent of the target end and the concomitant rapid rise of the projectile end. The power for this descent was provided by a well-trained crew of pullers, who pulled down in unison on ropes attached to the target end of the engine's central beam. Because of its design, the traction engine was much larger than contemporary torsion artillery. In particular, it required a very long beam and space along its sides for the crews of pullers, thus limiting its use on the walls of fortifications unless these had been expanded specifically to support them.

By contrast with the relatively light payload of the torsion engine, traction engines had the capacity, if they were sufficiently large, to throw very heavy stones. The late ninth-century writer Abbo of Paris, for example, describes engines called *mangana* that stand out because of the enormous stones that they could throw. These are in marked contrast to the various *catapultae* that were deployed by both the Franks defending Paris and the Vikings who were attacking the city. The *catapulta* were used, for example, to throw pots of melted lead rather than large stones. A traction engine deployed from within the walls of a fortification had to be used in a manner similar to that of a modern mortar – that is, without a direct line of sight to the enemy – because it was too large to be mounted on the walls.

Debates concerning the type of propulsion employed in stone-throwing engines have turned largely on the modern interpretation of the terms used by contemporary authors to denote these weapons. What has been missing from this discussion has been an assessment of the deployment of these engines, and particularly a recognition that traction engines, with their long rotating beams and teams of pullers, simply could not have been stationed atop narrow walls. As a consequence, when the authors of narrative texts describe the placement of engines in this manner, it is clear, regardless of the terms that are used by chroniclers, that we are dealing with a small torsion-powered stone-thrower rather than a traction engine. Thus, for example, when Abbo notes the deployment of *catapultae* on the walls of Paris, the necessary conclusion is that these were torsion engines. Similarly, the author of the early eleventh-century *Deeds of the Archbishops of Trier* observed that during King Henry II of Germany's siege of this city in 1008, the defenders made extensive use of engines in defence of the archiepiscopal palace, launching stones out from this strong point at the royal troops as the latter began their assault. The limited space within the archiepiscopal palace, and the use of the artillery specifically to target attacking troops indicates that the stone-throwers were smaller rather than larger, and designed as anti-personnel weapons. Both of these considerations point to the deployment of torsion rather than traction engines.

There were two major developments in artillery technology in the West during the course of the thirteenth century. The first of these was the introduction of the counter-weight traction engine, which is the only type of artillery that is properly called a trebuchet. There is considerable disagreement about whether the transmission of the trebuchet into the West from China was through the Byzantine Empire or the Islamic East. In our view, it is far more likely that the counter-weight engine came to the West through contacts with Muslim forces in the eastern Mediterranean during the late twelfth century. The entry point of the trebuchet into the West was the French kingdom, where these engines were being produced no later than the second decade of the thirteenth century. Prince Louis of France brought several with him for his invasion of England in 1216.

It is clear that the technology for producing counter-weight engines was very complex, and that without a clear understanding of what today would be called the engineering principles in its construction, these machines could not be built. There were no trebuchets constructed in England, for example, for almost a decade after the defeat of the French invasion in 1216. It was not until 1225, when King Henry III's government recruited a man named Jordan to come to England that trebuchets were constructed there. Jordan, who was given the title *trebuchetarius*, was very active in England between 1225 and 1230, overseeing the construction of trebuchets at several construction sites, and transmitting to English engineers the knowledge of how to build this complex engine.

The most distinctive element of the trebuchet was its counter-weight, which provided all of the thrust for the throwing arm and, in effect, replaced the pullers who had provided the energy for the earlier traction engines. It is, therefore, not surprising that following the arrival of Jordan the *trebuchetarius*, English royal administrative documents begin to record the purchase of vast quantities of lead to be used specifically for counter-weights. The introduction of the trebuchet into England is one of the few examples during the medieval period when one technology completely superseded another. Up through 1225, the English royal government produced large numbers of traction engines that were powered by pullers. However, this type of engine, denoted by royal officials as a *petraria*, ceased to be built within a few years of Jordan's arrival in England, and was never built again by the government. By contrast, trebuchets continued to be produced and used in England and throughout Europe into the fifteenth century, until they were finally superseded completely by gunpowder weapons (discussed in what follows).

The second type of artillery innovation in the thirteenth century concerned a spear-caster denoted by contemporary government authorities in England as a springald. Unlike the existing spear-caster, the *ballista*, which was a tension-powered engine, the springald used torsion power to cast a spear, or in some cases round stones or lead balls, on a horizontal trajectory. The springald had two torsion-powered arms, and marks the first use of a two-armed torsion device since the second century AD. It is not clear why royal artillery engineers decided to experiment and reintroduce this weapon during the late 1270s. They were more difficult to build and expensive than the existing *ballistae*, which carried out the same function. Nevertheless, the springald became quite popular in both England and in France, and was produced in large numbers during the later thirteenth and fourteenth centuries. However, the springald never replaced the *ballista*, and both engines appear side by side in arsenal inventories up through the late fourteenth century.

Gunpowder artillery

Scholars disagree about whether gunpowder was invented in India or China, although the preponderance of opinion rests with the latter. By the tenth century, gunpowder was used as a weapon in incendiary devices in the Far East, and by the thirteenth century, if not earlier, Chinese armies were equipped with firearms whose explosive charge was provided by gunpowder. The route by which gunpowder came to the West also is unclear, with some scholars arguing for transmission through the Muslim Near East and the Byzantine Empire, and others by way of Spain. The earliest known reference to gunpowder in the West comes from the pen of Roger Bacon in his *Third Work (Opus Tertium)*, which was composed in 1267, in which he set forth his ideas about experimental science. He observed that a compound of saltpetre, sulfur, and charcoal (from hazelwood) could bring about a considerable explosion when ignited. Several other authors mention recipes for gunpowder in the late thirteenth century, but none of them discuss the practical uses of the product for weaponization.

The earliest dates suggested by scholars for gunpowder weapons in the West are in the last two decades of the thirteenth century. However, most specialists in the history of gunpowder weapons point to the fourth decade of the fourteenth century as the first point when specific and credible evidence can be demonstrated for their use. Narrative sources describing the sieges of the cities of Metz in 1324 and Friuli in 1331 mention the use of gunpowder artillery. The earliest image of a gunpowder weapon comes from William de Milemete's text *Concerning the Majesty, Wisdom and Prudence of Kings*, produced in 1326, which depicts a vase-shaped container lying on its side, firing a spear as a projectile. From the 1330s onwards, references to gunpowder weapons become much more frequent, not only in narrative sources but also in inventories of arsenals.

The artisans who created the first gunpowder weapons appear to have conceptualized their new devices in a manner consistent with contemporary non-gunpowder artillery, and provided them with traditional projectiles, including both spears and stones. Within a few decades, however, gunpowder weapons began to be produced that utilized metal balls as well as large stones. A vast range of types and shapes of gunpowder artillery were produced, some with long barrels that fired on a horizontal trajectory, and others that were squat, opened-mouthed and shaped much like mortars that were used in the nineteenth century, and fired ammunition on a parabolic trajectory.

Gunpowder artillery was produced from two different types of metal during the medieval period: bronze and forged iron. The processes for producing non-brittle cast iron effectively were not developed until the mid-sixteenth century. Bronze, which is an alloy of copper and tin, has a lower melting point than iron, which made it quite suitable for pouring into moulds. In addition, bronze is more flexible than iron, and thus is less likely to burst when firing. However, it is more expensive than iron, and so significantly increased the cost of producing artillery. Wrought iron artillery was produced using a technique known today as hoop and stave construction. Iron strips were set side by side in a circular form. Iron bands, which had a diameter somewhat smaller than the diameter of the circle formed by the staves, were then heated to white heat and forced over the staves. As the bands cooled, they contracted and bound the staves together. Modern tests of medieval guns produced with the hoop and stave method have demonstrated that these weapons were air-tight and well able to contain the explosive gases released by the ignited gunpowder.

As was true of non-gunpowder artillery, the gunpowder weapons were used largely for siege warfare. The sound of the explosion after their fuses were lit was often as much a factor in terrifying the defenders of a city or fortress as was the projectile launched by such a weapon. However, it is clear that these weapons also were deployed in the field as well as on ships. The slow rate of fire of most gunpowder artillery meant that the weapons had to be well-defended on the battlefield by other soldiers and often by earth-works. At sea, the slow rate of fire was less of a factor, particularly if the ships on which the artillery was mounted were engaged in bombardments of stationary land-based targets, such as coast fortifications or cities. When used in naval battles, artillery largely was deployed against men rather than ships, and fire from the guns was intended to sweep the decks before boarding. It was not until the sixteenth century that artillery could be used reliably against the ships themselves for the purpose of penetrating the hull.

The value of gunpowder artillery was readily recognized by a number of medieval rulers, although exploiting this new technology required significant wealth both for the purchase of materials and the recruitment of specialists in their construction. Among the first rulers to develop a siege train that included gunpowder artillery was Edward III of England (1327–1377). The Burgundian allies of the English during the Hundred Years' War also developed an impressive artillery train under four successive archdukes from the third quarter of the fourteenth century to the third quarter of the fifteenth century. The last of the Burgundian archdukes, Charles the Rash (1467–1477), amassed a vast arsenal of gunpowder weapons, although they did not ultimately help him achieve his dream of becoming a king when he was defeated and killed by an army of Swiss pike men at the Battle of Nancy on 5 January 1477.

Siege technologies

Artillery of all types played an important role in siege warfare during the course of the medieval millennium. However, a wide range of other technologies was employed by military commanders to compel the surrender of fortresses, or to capture them by storm. In terms of saving lives of both attackers and defenders, the most efficient strategy was to appear at the gates with such a large army that the inhabitants immediately realized that they could not hope to hold the fortress. If the defenders chose to resist, then the costs in men could be minimized best by undertaking a siege and starving the inhabitants of the fortress or fortified city into submission. If it became necessary to assault the defences, attacking armies had options of going over, through, or under the walls.

Starving a city into submission

Medieval military commanders had a vested interest in preserving the lives of their men, not only because this was their duty as Christians, but also because the majority of the men under their command were property owners – that is, people who mattered in society. Getting them killed without reasons that were acceptable to the soldiers' families was liable to have significant negative political consequences, as well as cause morale problems both in the present and in the future. For economic reasons, medieval rulers often also had a vested interest in preserving the lives of the inhabitants of the substantial urban centres, as well as the physical infrastructure of the cities that they were besieging. As a consequence, when time and resources were available, besieging armies often settled in for a long conflict in the hope of starving the enemy into submission.

There were four crucial factors that a medieval commander had to take into account when deciding whether he was in a position to undertake a lengthy siege: his lines of communication and supply, his ability to deny the besieged population access to supply, the ability of the besieged forces to launch attacks against him, and finally, the ability of other forces in the field to attack his army as it was deployed for the siege. The logistics of the besieging army depended on a variety of factors that were discussed in the previous chapter. However, the other three issues facing the besieging army could be accounted for through the construction of effective field fortifications.

There were two primary methods used to establish counter-fortifications by the besieging army in order to prevent a besieged enemy force from sallying forth, and to keep relief forces from attacking the besieging army. The first, and relatively less expensive in terms of time and resources, was to establish fortified camps or even full-scale strongholds directly opposite the gates of the fortress or fortress city that was being besieged. This was the strategy employed, for example, by King Pippin I, the father of Charlemagne, during his siege of the fortress city of Bourges in 763, when he established *castella* – that is, fortifications – in front of each of the gates. In a similar manner, King Otto I of Germany constructed fortified encampments outside the gates of fortress city of Regensburg in Bavaria during his siege of this city in 954. By occupying the area immediately outside the gates, the besieging army was able to interdict most supplies arriving into the city and prevent most of the population from escaping. In addition, the besieging army was protected from assaults by forces stationed within the city or by a relief force.

The fortified encampments and even counter-fortifications utilized a relatively straightforward technology that was widely known throughout Europe during the entirety of the medieval period. Encampments usually consisted of a trench some 2 metres deep and 2–3 metres wide. The earth from the excavation was piled up on the inner side of the trench, thereby creating a barrier of 4–5 metres in height. This earthen berm was then often provided with a palisade of sharpened poles some 65–100 centimetres in length. These camps were constructed in a manner that provided ample space for the men to set up their tents and cooking areas, as well as latrine facilities, and also afforded them the ability to move quickly to any portion of the wall that was threatened by enemy action. The continuous wall of the rampart was broken at regular points with gates that permitted easy entrance and egress. Fortified encampments of this type were constructed by Roman troops throughout the imperial period, and their construction was well-known in the post-Roman West, both through practice and from manuals, including illustrated handbooks, such as Pseudo-Hyginus' *Regarding the Fortification of Encampments*, that circulated widely. The acute observer may even have noted the remains of these Roman marching camps in the local countryside, such as those that were described by the early eleventh-century author of the *Deeds of the Bishops of Cambrai* in the context of discussing the operations of Julius Caesar in Gaul.

Castella of the type constructed by King Pippin at Bourges also followed a relatively straightforward plan. They usually were constructed of wood, although an earth and timber construction of the type later associated with motte-and-bailey castles also is likely in some circumstances. The basic form of the *castella* was a palisade that was equipped with platforms for the deployment of troops with missile weapons, and perhaps also platforms for artillery. The accounts of Pippin's siege, for example, emphasize that he employed a variety of engines against the defences of the city.

The advantage of constructing simple *castella* or field fortifications outside the gates of the besieged stronghold was that this work could be accomplished relatively rapidly, the technology was not complex, and it was inexpensive to build in terms of labour and material. The major drawback of only blocking the gates of a fortress, however, was that the defenders were not sealed off completely from the outside and could sneak in small quantities of supplies and men over the walls, or send out messages in the same manner. For example, when William the Conqueror besieged the fortress of Alençon in 1050 using only field fortifications, he found it necessary to keep elements of his mounted forces at the ready by riding along the roads leading to the city in order to cut off relief forces and supplies.

In order to impose maximum pressure on the defenders, medieval commanders sometimes constructed a *vallatio* – that is, a wall – around the entire city. This sealed in the defenders and prohibited anyone from exiting the fortress or any food or other supplies from getting in. The *vallatio* also protected the besieging army from sorties carried out by the defenders. In addition to the *vallatio*, military commanders also frequently constructed a *contravallatio*, which was a second wall that faced outwards from the siege, and which was intended to protect the besieging army from attacks by relief forces. Perhaps the most famous set of besieging walls in Antiquity were those constructed by Julius Caesar during his siege of the Celtic ruler Vercingetorix at Alesia in 52 BC, which was well-known in medieval Europe from the numerous texts of Caesar's *De bello Gallico* that were produced and circulated throughout the Latin West.

The construction of the two sets of besieging walls required a major investment of time and resources, and usually was only possible when the besieging army was both very large and had an exceptionally secure line of communications and logistical support. This was the case during Otto I's siege of Rome in 964. The monk Benedict of the monastery of St. Andrew on Monte Soratte, some 45 kilometres north of Rome, wrote c.968 that the emperor's army completely surrounded the Eternal City during his siege in this year, so that no one could enter or depart. The *Liber Pontificalis*, which was written for the papal curia, confirms this, noting that the emperor surrounded the entire city with a wall.

A somewhat different model of surrounding a fortified city with fortifications can be seen during the crusader investment of Nicaea in the spring of 1097. In this case, the various crusader contingents, as well as the Byzantines, established fortified encampments that were contiguous to each other and encompassed the three landward sides of the city. The fourth side of Nicaea was protected by Lake Ascanius, which had an area of some 300 square kilometres. It was not until Emperor Alexios Komnenos ordered the transportation of ships overland to Nicaea and deployed them on the lake that the city was fully encircled and cut off from supplies. At both Nicaea and at Rome, it is likely that the investing armies utilized similar technologies as those employed by the Carolingians and Ottonians during their sieges of Bourges and Regensburg, respectively.

Figure 5.6 Reconstruction of a motte-and-bailey castle
Source: © Heritage Image Partnership Ltd/Alamy Stock Photo HT3KPR

Over the walls

When a commander decided that it was preferable to assault a city rather than starve it into submission, he had a variety of options available, which could be employed singly or together. In conceptualizing 'going over the top', the most important tool for any medieval army was the storming ladder. These usually were brought on campaign in sections (they were too long to be carried in wagons) because building ladders from scratch in the field was often a very difficult proposition, requiring both trained carpenters and smiths, as well as sufficient quantities of wood that was often difficult to find. This was the case for the crusaders at the siege of Jerusalem in 1099 who required a miracle, according to the chronicler Ralph of Caen, to find enough wood for just one assault ladder.

Of particular concern when constructing assault ladders is determining the height of the wall to be assaulted. Ladders that are too short, for example, will not reach the top of the wall, but ladders that are too long provide an opportunity for defenders to push them away more easily. Illustrated surveying texts (*agrimensores*) that circulated widely in Europe provided detailed information about the use of the astrolabe and other surveying tools. These tools made it possible to measure the height of the tower or wall in the same manner that one measures the height of the sun.

Vegetius' military handbook, discussed earlier in the chapter, also included two techniques for measuring the height of walls and towers. The first was to take a length of rope, which was marked like a measuring tape, and attach it to an arrow, which was shot into the top of the wall. Then a man was to run to the base of the wall and note the measurement on the rope. This obviously was quite a dangerous method if utilized when the defenders were watching. A second method was to measure the length of the shadow cast by the wall, again a very dangerous task in the face of enemy action. Once this measurement was taken, a pole 10 feet in length was to be placed in the ground and the length of its shadow was to be measured at the same time of day as the measurement was taken of the shadow produced by the wall. A ratio between the two shadow lengths then provided the height of the wall. A similar means of calculating heights was provided by the monk and author Bede of Jarrow in the early eighth century, and was widely disseminated throughout the Latin West.

After ladders, the most important tools for carrying men over the walls were siege towers. These engines were well-known in Antiquity and were widely employed by the Romans during the late empire, particularly in the east where they faced opposition from the Parthian and Persian empires. It was once argued by scholars who held a 'dark age' view of the early Middle Ages that the art of building siege towers was lost throughout the Latin West in the post-Roman period, and was not rediscovered until the First Crusade brought western armies into more direct contact with Byzantine military technology. However, it is now widely accepted that various types of siege towers were in use in Europe long before the late eleventh century, not least because western armies in Rome's successor states regularly encountered Byzantine military technology in Italy from the sixth century onwards.

It is likely that many of the *ingenia* that appear in narrative sources from the sixth–eighth centuries referred to towers. Procopius, for example, observed that towers of this sort were used by the Ostrogoths at the siege of Rome in 537, and some scholars have argued that they were used by the Avars at the siege of Thessaloniki in 597. However, the first clear mention of a siege tower north of the Alps concerns the Viking army that invested Paris in 885, which was mentioned by Abbo, an eyewitness to the siege, in his epic poem *On the Battles for the City of Paris*. As seen in the previous chapter, Richer of Rheims mentioned the deployment of a rolling tower by King Lothair IV of West Francia in his siege of Verdun in

985. In the next decade, Emperor Otto III deployed mobile towers in 998 during his siege of Castel Sant'Angelo near Rome. During the First Crusade, the western armies deployed a number of siege towers, including several in the assault on Jerusalem in July 1099.

By the later Middle Ages, some of these towers were very elaborate and included rams on the lower level and artillery on the upper levels. Froissart (died c.1405), the famed chronicler of the Hundred Years' War, records the use of a mobile tower at the Siege of Breteuil in 1356 that had three levels, each of which he claims could hold 200 men. Froissart's account may have been an exaggeration, as 600 men with equipment likely weighed sixty tonnes and would have required a herd of 100 oxen to move the load carried by the tower, not counting the weight of the tower itself.

Mobile siege towers were not only used on land, but also on ships. Alpert of Metz (died 1024), who wrote his chronicle *On the Variety of our Times* between 1021 and 1023, records the deployment of a ship-borne siege tower by the German magnate Balderich of Drenthe (died 1021) in the second decade of the eleventh century. In this case, transport ships were hauled into a swamp where the enemy had constructed a wooden palisade on a small hill. Two of Balderich's ships were lashed together and a tower was built on their decks that would reach over the wall of the island fortification. Once the men inside the fortification realized that the attackers could reach the top of their walls, they surrendered. Much more complex ship-borne towers were deployed by the Venetians during the siege of Constantinople in 1204, when the participants on the Fourth Crusade were diverted to the capital of the Byzantine Empire in order to help install Alexios IV Angelos (1203–1204) on the throne from which his father Isaac II Angelos (1185–1195) had been driven in the previous decade. The participants in the Fifth Crusade also deployed ship-borne towers against the Egyptian fortress of Damietta in 1218.

Building a tower, in itself, was not an uncommon technological feat, as simple two- and three-storey wooden structures could be found in great numbers in most urban centres throughout Europe, and even taller structures were known. The major difference in the construction of siege towers was that, in addition to withstanding bombardment, they had to be designed in such as a manner that they could be moved up to the wall of a fortification. There were two major engineering problems involved. The first was the question of actually making the tower mobile. The second was designing the tower so that it would not wobble and tip over when it was moving. To deal with the first of these issues, towers often were equipped with rollers rather than wheels. Rollers permitted a tower to traverse somewhat uneven ground, and also helped to prevent the heavy structure from sinking into soft ground. In order to deal with the problem of tipping, towers were provided with diagonal braces that connected the upper stories of the tower to the lower stories, and provided substantial external support to the structure. The difficulties of moving the towers often were exacerbated by the necessity of moving men and equipment across water-filled moats, or filling up dry moats along their path, as was the case, for example, during Count Geoffrey Plantagenet's siege of Montreuil-Bellay in 1150.

The propulsion for the tower generally came from pushing rather than pulling so that the men and animals moving the structure could be afforded some protection from the defenders stationed atop the walls of the fortress that was being besieged. However, Richer of Rheims describes a rather ingenious method for advancing a tower using a series of pulleys that allowed a team of oxen that was moving away from the walls of the city of Verdun to pull the siege tower forward. The oxen were on the far side of the tower, from the perspective of the city walls, and thus were protected from direct fire from archers stationed there. In order to construct this pulley system, Richer explained, King Lothair IV's men, under the cover of night, drove heavy wooden posts into the ground near Verdun's walls, and then hammered in metal brackets through which they ran ropes. These ropes then were connected to brackets at the top and bottom of the siege tower, and from there to the harness holding the team of oxen.

Constructing siege towers on ships solved one set of problems in terms of moving them into position next to a city's walls; however, these structures raised an entirely new set of technological challenges, as well. The greatest difficulty faced by the military engineers was constructing the tower so that it would not capsize the ship, even in relatively rough water. In many cases, as happened at the siege of Damietta for example, two or more ships were lashed together to provide a broader base on which to construct the towers. At the siege of Constantinople, however, the Venetians did not use this technique, but rather built upward extensions onto the high fore and aft decks of their great round ships. These ships were designed with elevated fighting platforms for naval combat, so that the towers did not need to be very tall in order to reach the top of the walls at Constantinople.

Through the walls

The weakest point of any fortification is its gate or gates, where the circuit of the walls necessarily is broken to permit ingress and egress. A basic tool for exploiting this weakness was the battering ram (*arietes* in Latin), which was widely used in the Latin West throughout the medieval period. The physics involved in making a ram swing with maximum effectiveness is very complex, and the equations for determining this motion were not developed until the seventeenth century. However, constant practice, including trial and error, clearly made these tools of war very effective. Nevertheless, defenders often were able to blunt the effectiveness of rams through the use of a variety of counter-measures, including hanging quilted mats or bales of hay in front of the rams to absorb some of the shock of the blows, and also by attempting to hook the rams and pulling them out of position.

Rams are described in numerous narrative sources, and medieval commanders seeking additional information about their use and construction could find it in various technical manuals. Vegetius describes, for example, a timber frame construction, covered with fire-retardant hides and mats that provided a protective covering for the operating crew of the beam while they repeatedly rammed the gate. The collection of technical descriptions and manufacturing recipes known as the *Little Key to the World* (*Mappae clavicula*) also provides a description for the construction of a ram, although the surviving text appears as if it were intended to serve as a set of rubrics for an experienced builder rather than as a blueprint for constructing the engine.

The simplest types of rams were simply felled trees that were stripped of their branches and had ropes attached them to provide grips for the men to facilitate hammering the trunk into the gate of a fortification. More complex rams, equipped with wheels and housing to protect the men, were deployed widely throughout Europe from the early Middle Ages up through the early modern period. The basic design of this equipment was relatively constant over the entire medieval period, and is illuminated quite well by Abbo in his description of the Viking siege of Paris. He observed that Vikings constructed a number of very large wheels from heavy oak, which were grouped together in threes. The large size of the wheels meant that when they were connected together within a frame, the battering ram would be able to swing freely rather than drag on the ground. These wheeled engines were protected by a rectangular housing. Abbo then notes that the battering rams had crews of sixty men to swing the log that comprised the majority of the ram. Parenthetically, there were often sixty rowers on a Viking ship, and so it is possible that the ship's crew formed the basic unit for manning a ram, as these men had long practice of undertaking physical activities in unison.

Under the walls

Among the most difficult technological options facing a besieging army was attempting to bring down the walls, or rather a part of a wall of a medieval city or fortress through mining. The basic process was to dig a tunnel from a point within one's own encampment, preferably out of range of enemy missiles, to a point underneath the fortress walls. Once this initial mine shaft had been constructed, the sappers excavated a large area underneath the wall. As part of this process, the sappers had to construct temporary wooden supports to hold up the wall while the mine was being dug, in order to prevent the premature collapse of the wall while they were in the mine. After a suitably large section of the wall had been undermined, combustible material was transported into the excavated area and set ablaze. The wooden supports then burned and the wall collapsed.

Although quite straightforward in conception, in practice, the mining of an enemy fortification usually was a very difficult undertaking. Digging a mine shaft that was several hundred metres in length required a detailed understanding of mining techniques, including the construction of supports all along the mine shaft and the inclusion of adequate ventilation. The undermining of a city wall that often extended in excess of 3 metres underground, and was 5 metres or even more in width, required a vast investment in labour and in time, not to mention expertise. It is likely that military commanders recruited men with mining experience in commercial enterprises, such as silver, tin, and salt mines. For example, the English royal government frequently employed Welsh tin miners in this capacity. Additional information could be found in Roman manuals, which provide information about digging and supporting mine shafts.

The defenders usually were well aware that mining operations were being undertaken, particularly when the tunnel drew close to the walls and the sounds of picks and shovels could be heard above. When possible, the defenders took active counter-measures, including digging counter-mines or tunnels through which they could engage the miners in combat, or even flood the 'attack shaft' with water from a nearby river or lake. There are many hundreds of accounts of the mining of city and fortress walls in medieval narrative sources. In his history of the reign of Emperor Frederick I of Germany, the ruler's uncle Bishop Otto of Freising observed that the German forces were thwarted in their efforts to mine the towers at the fortress city of Tortona in northwestern Italy because of the counter-mines dug by the defenders. Narrative reports can sometimes be corroborated through archaeological excavations, as for example at Bungay Castle in Suffolk, England, which was besieged by King Henry II of England in 1174. In this case, both the mine and the counter-mine have been excavated.

Less sophisticated sapping operations also were undertaken by medieval commanders who lacked the time or resources for thorough-going mining. At the simplest level, men equipped with picks and other tools assaulted the base of the wall attempting to dig out the stones and create a gap. One account of the Siege of Acre (1189–1191) by the Christian forces during the Third Crusade records that King Richard of England offered a reward of two gold coins for any man who could pry a stone from the walls, which is an indication of just how difficult and dangerous a task this was. A variety of devices were available to protect men as they advanced to the wall and strove to take it apart stone by stone. These included large wooden screens with an overlay of leather or fire-retardant mats, which were carried on wheels. These protective engines had a variety of names, including *plutei* and *vinea*, and are often denoted in English as mantlets.

Incendiary devices

The defenders of fortifications had a variety of defences against all types of siege equipment ranging from hand-held missiles, weapons, and artillery to counter-mines and sorties from within the walls. However, the most effective counter-measure against siege towers, mantlets, and rams tended to be incendiary devices. There are numerous reports in narrative sources from throughout the medieval millennium of siege equipment being destroyed by fire. In 1017, for example, during his siege of the fortress of Glogau, located in southwestern Poland, King Henry II of Germany suffered the catastrophic loss of all of his siege equipment after the Polish defenders launched incendiaries at them from engines stationed on the walls of their stronghold.

At Glogau, it is likely that the incendiaries were delivered in unfired clay pots, which were fitted with wicks and lit before being launched. When they struck their target, the pots shattered and spread their flammable, and burning, contents over the wooden structure of the siege engine. The multiple layers of sand and wetted leather that covered many siege towers, mantlets, and other equipment were intended as a counter-measure to incendiaries of this type. These defensive techniques are discussed in both Vegetius' text and in *Mappae clavicula*. Vegetius suggested the use of animal skins and fire-retardant mats, and the *Mappae claviculae* indicates that alternating layers of felt, leather, and sand are to be used. Gregory of Tours, writing in the late sixth century, described the Gallo-Roman general Calomniosus fitting out his battering rams with this latter type of anti-incendiary technology.

The incendiaries used in the West were different in kind from the flammable material often denoted by modern scholars as Greek fire. This liquid substance was used initially on Byzantine ships, and provided the Byzantine fleet with a decisive advantage over the Arab fleet that besieged Constantinople in 673. The Byzantine ships were equipped with a pump and hose, which sprayed the Greek fire at enemy ships in a manner similar to a modern flame thrower. One of the most important characteristics of Greek fire for naval warfare was that it could not be extinguished with water, and had to be smothered with sand. The exact recipe for Greek fire remains a mystery, but knowledge of its production spread from the Byzantines to their Muslim adversaries, who used it to devastating effect both at sea and on land. In his account of Louis IX's crusade to Egypt (1249–1254), Jean de Joinville reports with great horror the enormously effective incendiary devices hurled by the Muslims at Christian siege works, which continued to burn even after being doused with water. It appears that although a wide range of petroleum-based materials were used to make incendiaries similar to Greek fire, the technology for projecting this liquid through a hose was lost.

Fortifications

One of the central conceits of the 'dark age' model of early medieval history is that the technology developed by Roman engineers for the construction of high-quality stone fortifications was simply lost during the so-called barbarian invasions. According to this model, erstwhile Roman fortress cities were turned into ghost towns and their walls served as quarries for nearby building projects at the few religious institutions that maintained the knowledge and wherewithal to construct buildings in stone. However, as illustrated in Chapter 2, many Roman stone fortifications and fortress cities not only were maintained during the early medieval period, but were modified and even expanded to meet the needs of the current population. In short, the technological know-how of the late empire with regard to construction in stone was not lost. It is likely that Roman manuals, such as Vitruvius' *De architectura*, continued to provide important information about constructing different types of fortifications.

However, in conceptualizing the technological inheritance of Rome, it is also important to understand that the Romans themselves did not always build in stone. Rather, they chose building materials that were appropriate for the purpose at hand, and which, in many cases, were easily and economically accessible. Many of the frontier fortifications in Britain, for example, were constructed of turf and timber, with some receiving stone fronts at a later date. Roman fortifications along the Rhine and Danube frontiers frequently were constructed of wood, or earth and timber, rather than from stone. These included not only the walls that marked the frontier, but also the so-called mile castles, which were placed at intervals of approximately one Roman mile along the wall. These were often wooden block houses that were similar in construction to those used in Britain's American colonies during the seventeenth and eighteenth centuries.

All of the basic types of construction that were utilized by the Romans also were employed throughout Europe during the entirety of the medieval millennium. These included solid masonry walls that were held together by a combination of gravity and mortar, earth, timber, and stone fortifications, earth and timber structures, and finally simple earth/turf field works. The men charged with designing these fortifications utilized these materials in a wide variety of ways and developed a broad range of designs which were intended to meet the perceived military threat that the specific fortifications were intended to address. Even when fortifications also served as residences, the military purpose was paramount.

'Frankish' fortifications

Archaeologists specializing in the history of fortifications identify two broad zones of fortress construction in the post-Roman world from the mid-sixth to the mid-eleventh centuries. The first of these encompassed much of the Latin West, with the exception of Britain, from the mid-sixth century up to the beginning of the crusading age. The other broad region is often denoted as the Slavic fortress zone, which extended from the Elbe River eastward and the Danube River northward and encompassed much of East-Central Europe and Eastern Europe, which gradually was brought into contact with and then influenced by the Frankish zone from the late eighth century onwards.

As discussed in Chapter 2, along the frontiers of the *Regnum Francorum*, and particularly in the marches against the Muslims, Saxons, and later the Slavs, Merovingian and Carolingian rulers from the sixth through the ninth centuries built a considerable number of stone fortifications. These were constructed of cut stone, excavated from quarries, and held together with mortar. One early example is the fortification at Büraburg, near Fritzlar in Hesse, Germany, which was established in 723 as a missionary centre by the Anglo-Saxon missionary Winfrid, who later became known as St. Boniface. By 742, this frontier missionary centre had been raised to the status of a bishopric and was provided with a mortared stone wall by the two Carolingian mayors of the palace, the brothers Carloman and Pippin III, who later became King Pippin I.

The fortification at Büraburg was constructed in a rectangle. The total circuit of the wall measured 1,300 metres. The walls along each side were approximately 4 metres wide, with the exception of the north wall, which was just 2 metres wide. The wall was constructed of some 15,000 cubic metres of stone, most of which was quarried in the immediate vicinity of the fortress. In addition to the protection afforded by the wall itself, the designers put in place around the fortress a series of ditches that averaged 4 metres in depth and had berms piled up on their inner sides, meaning that attackers had to scale heights of 6 metres or more in order to pass this obstacle and reach the wall.

In constructing this fortification, the Carolingian builders made use of mortar, which required both a considerable investment in equipment and materials, and a high level of technological expertise, to produce. The first major expenditure was the capital investment in the construction of kilns to 'cook' limestone in order to produce lime. A wide range of lime kilns were produced in Antiquity and during the early medieval period, and these required skilled workers who knew not only how to build the kiln, but also understood the design principles when a new apparatus was to be built under new circumstances. Once the limestone was cooked, and the lime was produced, it had to be mixed with clean sand at a ratio of one-quarter lime to three-quarters sand. At Büraburg, this amounted to some 5,250 cubic metres of clean sand and 1,750 cubic metres of lime. Two cubic metres of limestone were required during this period to produce 1 cubic metre of lime, so the builders had to bring to the site for cooking some 3,500 cubic metres of limestone, which weighed 3,500 tonnes. To this can be added the weight of the sand that had to be brought to the site, which had a total weight of 5,000 tonnes, or 10,000 cart loads drawn by 20,000 oxen. The technological knowledge for building in this manner came from Rome and was not used by people living beyond the frontiers prior to contact with the empire.

In addition to the transportation costs for the raw materials required to produce limestone, the kilns required very large quantities of wood to operate. These kilns had to be heated to 1,000 degrees Celsius to cook the lime, which is about 200 degrees hotter than what is needed to manufacture pottery. For each kilogram of lime produced, the kilns required 2 kilograms of wood, amounting to some 3,500 cubic metres. The cutting and transportation of this wood required an enormous investment in time and materials. Assuming a forest cover of mixed sizes of trees, with a preponderance of oak, it would require clear-cutting some 60 hectares (150 acres) of forest to acquire sufficient wood to fire the kilns at Büraburg. This area is approximately sevenfold larger than the area enclosed within the walls of the fortress. To put it another way, an oak tree with a diameter of 56 centimetres contains approximately one cord of firewood, which is equal to 3.6 cubic metres. So, in order to fire the kilns at Büraburg, the builders required about 1,000 oak trees with this average diameter. However, a fully grown oak tree has a diameter of approximately 2.5 metres, and so only 200 trees of this size would be required to fire the kilns.

Combinations of building materials

Mortared stone construction of the type identified by archaeologists at Büraburg was used throughout the Latin West during the entirety of the medieval period. However, under both the Carolingians and in the post-Carolingian period, stone fortifications often were paired with additional defences that were constructed of other types of materials. Typical of multi-material fortifications is the stronghold at Rosstal, located 20 kilometres south of Nürnberg. Archaeological excavations, primarily undertaken by Peter Ettel, have demonstrated that the fortification there was already in place by 800, although the first surviving mention of the site in a written source is by Widukind of Corvey, who composed his *Deeds of the Saxons* during the third quarter of the tenth century. During Charlemagne's reign, Rosstal was a densely settled site that was protected by an earth and timber wall that was further strengthened by a dry stone front, meaning that the stone was held in place by gravity rather than by mortar. This late eighth–century fortification had walls that were 4.4 metres wide, and a dry stone front of some 0.8 metres in width. This wall was further protected by a series of ditches, one of which was 12.5 metres wide and 3.5 metres deep, with a berm that raised the inside edge of the ditch by several additional metres.

In the early tenth century, perhaps in response to the threat of Hungarian raids, the fortification was improved, so that the dry stone frontage was replaced by mortared stone, utilizing the ashlar construction technique that was standard for Roman fortifications. The ashlar method of wall construction creates two parallel, mortared stone walls. The space between these walls is then filled with rubble, which sometimes was 'drowned' in mortar and sometimes left dry. The stone front of the wall at Rosstal tripled in width to some 2.5 metres during this period of improvement. In addition, the earth and timber portion of the wall also was expanded, doubling its width. The new walls of the early tenth century were approximately 10 metres in width. Parenthetically, the vast expansion of the width of these walls made it possible to deploy traction engines, powered by pullers, on top of them. These strengthened mural defences were further improved with the construction of a wooden tower that had a base measuring 10 × 8 metres, and which likely reached a height of not less than 20 metres. Finally, the ditches protecting the walls were increased to a width of 15 metres. The resulting complex was so well designed that when King Otto I of Germany sought to put down a rebellion in Bavaria in 954, his first assault against Rosstal failed and he decided to bypass the stronghold rather than invest it, believing that it would take too long to capture. Instead, he devoted his energies to the ultimately successful six-week siege of the erstwhile Roman fortress city of Regensburg.

Earth, timber, and stone

When making the decision to construct a fortification, medieval rulers and military commanders did not always choose to use stone. Earth and timber fortifications of a variety of types were produced in vast numbers, with thousands of sites across the Latin West, as well as in Slavic lands and Scandinavia. However, the majority of the excavations of these sites have been carried out in Central, Northern, and Eastern Europe, and so much remains to be learned, particularly about construction techniques by both Christians and Muslims on the Iberian Peninsula, as well as in much of Italy and substantial regions of France.

In their most basic form, earth-works consisted of little more than a trench, a berm, and a palisade resembling a Roman or medieval marching camp, or the fieldworks established at sieges. Very few of these sites have left behind sufficient remains to be identified by archaeologists, but there are numerous references to earth-works of this type in both narrative sources and legal codes, such as the *Customs* of Normandy issued by Robert Curthose, the son of William of the Conqueror, before 1106, as discussed in Chapter 2. Much more substantial earth and timber structures, however, have been excavated across much of Europe and show several prominent patterns in their construction.

Traditionally, archaeologists working in the pre-crusade era have described fortifications according to three different schemata. The first is the location of the stronghold: high point, plateau, valley, or island. The second type of classification concerns the shape of the fortification: round/elliptical, rectangular, plateau wall (*Abschnittsbefestigung* in German), and bipartite, which consisted of a citadel (*Hauptburg* in German) and a bailey (*Vorburg* in German). The third type of classification concerned the purpose of the fortification: governmental control, refuge, fortified church, or aristocratic centre. Typically, the method of construction of these fortifications has not been used by archaeologists as an organizing principle for categorization, largely because there was no consistent pattern in the ways that particular types of strongholds, using these three schemata, were constructed. From a technological perspective, however, the method of construction takes precedence in our discussion here.

An early type of earth and timber fortification, which had much in common from a structural perspective with Roman walls constructed along the Rhine and Danube frontiers, consisted of two parallel timber walls, with an earthen fill between them. The vertical poles comprising the walls were driven into ground to provide greater stability. This type of fortification, which was common in the eighth and ninth centuries along the Frankish-Slavic frontier, was relatively easy to construct, and was inexpensive in terms of labour and materials because most of the body of the wall consisted of earth, which could be dug nearby, and of trees, which were plentiful all along the frontier. However, from a structural perspective, the earth exerts considerable outward pressure on the thin wooden frame. In order to combat this, the front surface of the walls often had a berm to reinforce the bottom third of the wall, and wooden supports on the inner surface. The fortress of Gars-Thunau, which was constructed in the late eighth century in northeastern Austria by the Carolingians in the course of their numerous campaigns against the Avars, utilized this type of construction. The berm on the outer wall did not provide an attacker with an easier path to go over the top because the berm itself was protected by a ditch. Usually, the berm extended from the inner edge – that is, the defender's side – of the ditch to the bottom of the wall, thereby forcing the attacker to climb from the bottom of the ditch to the top of the berm. The back wall of these types of structures usually was supported by a 'counter-wall', which was an angled support constructed of wood that provided counter pressure to the earthen fill within the wall.

Even with the external supports provided to the wooden walls, earth and timber fortifications of this type could not be built to a width of more than 3–4 metres because the earthen fill in a wider structure would exert too strong an outward pressure and buckle the wooden retaining walls. In order to construct wider earth and timber structures, builders utilized a lattice-work type of interior structure in which logs were set both facing the front and back sides of the wall, and also horizontal to the front and back of the wall, creating large numbers of individual rectangular cells. These cells were then filled in with earth. The entire structure had considerable internal cohesion as the wooden framework within the wall held the earth in place. In some cases, the logs were notched in the manner of 'Lincoln logs' in order to provide a stronger connection. In other cases, natural protrusions on the logs, including notches where branches had been cut off, served the same purpose. A typical example of a fortress utilizing this type of construction is Wiprechtsburg at Groitzsch in Saxony, which was constructed by King Henry I of Germany during the 920s. The clay soil that was used for this fortification preserved the imprint of the individual logs in their lattice-work pattern, which made it possible for archaeologists to reconstruct the building technology in substantial detail.

The wide walls of these earth and timber fortifications, often 12–20 metres in width, made it possible to deploy a range of artillery on them, including traction engines that required a long beam and also room for teams of pullers. The other major advantage of a wider wall was that it made it possible to construct higher walls, as well. The average height of the lattice-work earth and timber walls along the frontier between the German kingdom and its Slavic neighbours during the tenth and eleventh centuries was 10 metres. This gave the defenders significant advantages against attackers, not only by presenting greater challenges to storming the walls, but also increasing the range at which the defenders' missile weapons might be effective. Concomitantly, the high walls made it more difficult for opponents to shoot arrows over the defensive works into the stronghold, itself. This was particularly important when facing opponents, such as the Hungarians, whose main weapon was the composite bow.

Building earth and timber walls to a height of 10 metres or more required considerable technical expertise. An oak log, which was the basic building material throughout much of the eastern frontier regions of the Ottonian kingdom, measuring some 40 centimetres in diameter and 12 metres in length, weighed some 800 kilograms. Such a log could not be carried up scaffolding to the top of a 10-metre wall. Rather, it had to be hauled up using ropes and pulleys. First, a large wooden frame had to be constructed over which a rope and pulley system was installed. Teams of oxen then pulled the log slowly up into the air. Once the logs were at the correct height, they were then hooked and guided into position by men stationed on top of the wall. This task was both physically taxing and very dangerous, as a log weighing almost a metric ton could not be easily brought to a stop once it began to swing. This construction was made easier when the individual cells of the wall were filled in with material and tamped down before each additional layer of logs was lowered into position. In light of modern practice by which log cabins can be constructed to a height of three storeys using non-mechanized means, it is likely that a team of eight men and four oxen could manoeuvre into position one log of the size noted here in the course of an hour.

Towers and curtain walls

Because of the vast wealth of the Carolingian and Ottonian kings and emperors, they were able to construct enormous numbers of fortifications throughout the course of the ninth and tenth centuries. This was particularly the case along their eastern frontiers where constant conflict with Saxons and Avars, and then Slavs and Hungarians, made it imperative to develop both fortified systems of defence in depth and topographies of conquest. There was no fortress building on this scale in the West. However, individual rulers were able to develop the economic and material resources to construct significant numbers of fortifications, as seen, for example, with regard to Count Fulk Nerra of Anjou (987–1040) in Chapter 2. Wealthy rulers such as Fulk tended to follow a particular pattern of fortress construction that included a rectangular tower of cut and mortared stone, which was then further protected by a wooden palisade, often denoted by scholars as a curtain wall. These stone towers, such as the one constructed by Fulk at Langeais in 993–994, utilized the same building techniques as the Carolingian fortification at Büraburg in the early eighth century, and, indeed, late Roman fortifications from the fourth and fifth centuries. The wooden palisade at Langeais and the dozens of other strongholds constructed by Fulk over the course of his fifty-three–year period of rule would have been familiar anywhere in Europe throughout the Middle Ages, and indeed, to soldiers serving in the U.S. Army in the West during the nineteenth century.

Wealthy rulers – such as the counts of Anjou and Flanders, and the dukes of Normandy and Aquitaine in the kingdom of France – had the economic wherewithal to construct numerous towers in stone during the eleventh century. In the German kingdom, as well as in Italy and on the Iberian Peninsula, important secular and ecclesiastical magnates also built in stone, but often were constrained by their limited resources to construct one or perhaps two fortifications. Many lesser magnates throughout the Latin West could not afford to build even one stone stronghold, and relied on less expensive fortifications to secure their political and military interests at the local level. The basic type of inexpensive fortification consisted of a wooden tower, usually constructed on a natural or artificial hill, which was surrounded by a wooden palisade, which was further protected by a ditch. These strongholds often are denoted by scholars as motte-and-bailey castles, although the term castle has not been defined adequately.

The motte-and-bailey fortifications did not involve a new technology or even a new design. In form, they were very similar to earth and timber fortifications that were common throughout the Carolingian Empire, and which also had been employed by Scandinavians, both at home and during their extended raids. Perhaps the best-known example of the widespread use of motte-and-bailey fortifications came in the wake of Duke William of Normandy's conquest of England in 1066. He established scores of wooden towers with wooden curtain walls throughout the kingdom to serve as temporary bases for his army of occupation, and to secure his control over the local population. At the same time, however, William also began construction of the White Tower in London. The new English king imported stone and Norman masons from across the channel to undertake the construction project. The result was a massive stone edifice with a ground floor of 1,170 square metres that rose to a height of more than 27 metres. It should be noted that the White Tower represented the introduction of an internal citadel within a city, which was quite common in much of the Roman West as well as in the Near East, but was previously unknown in England.

Concentric castles and fortresses: from wood to stone?

It appears that during the twelfth century, the men responsible for constructing fortifications replaced many of the wooden elements with stone, although wooden fortifications continued to be built through the end of the Middle Ages. Indeed, as seen in Chapter 2, cheaper earth and timber fortifications, which could be constructed very rapidly, became very important again during the course of the fourteenth and fifteenth centuries as gunpowder artillery gradually made many high and comparatively thin mortared stone walls obsolete.

In addition to a broad pattern of replacing wooden fortifications with stone, another notable aspect of fortifications from the twelfth century onward was the increasing complexity of these strongholds. One of the most famous of the great castles of the new type is Château Gaillard, located 95 kilometres northwest of Paris, which was constructed by King Richard I of England in just two years between 1196 and 1198. The massive fortress, which was located on a promontory overlooking the river Seine, included a keep, which was reached by passing through three concentric fortified baileys, each of which was separated from its neighbour by both a stone wall and a dry moat. In addition to the massive stone walls, each of the baileys was equipped with several round towers.

These towers are illustrative of the reintroduction of round towers into fortress construction in the later eleventh century after a hiatus stretching back to the late Roman Empire. Although churches during the early and high Middle Ages frequently were built with curved walls and round towers, this design element was absent from stone fortifications until the late eleventh century. By contrast, wood and timber strongholds, including those with dry and mortared stone facings, often were constructed as circles or ellipses. The inspiration for the reintroduction of the round tower may well have been the Roman arch, which when set on its side provides the basic structure for a tower with a round shape. The major advantage of a round tower as contrasted with a flat stone wall is that it better deflects the blows from battering rams and also heavy stone-throwing artillery, such as the traction engine and the trebuchet.

Figure 5.7 Château Gaillard in Les Andelys, France, a twelfth-century fortress built by Richard the Lionheart

Source: © Hemis/Alamy Stock Photo CN1E0W

Concentric fortifications with large numbers of round towers, massive stone walls, and highly complex designs that afforded the defenders overlapping fields of fire were never very common during the later medieval period, not least because they were very expensive to construct. Krak de Chevaliers in the Latin East and the castles of Edward I in Wales, discussed in Chapter 2, are important examples of fortress building at the height of its art. Their construction was possible because of the vast wealth of their builders, namely the Hospitaller military order and the king of England, respectively. However, despite their impressive structure, these thirteenth-century concentric fortifications were not an entirely new phenomenon, in either construction technology or design. The basic method of building with mortared stone walls had remained unchanged for the past 1,000 years. From a design perspective, a central keep protected by two or even three fortified baileys was also known during the ninth and tenth centuries. Most of the royal palaces and major fortifications constructed by the Ottonian kings of Germany were organized in this manner, and the keeps, at least, often were protected by mortared stone walls.

Later medieval fortifications

The *trace italienne*, discussed in Chapter 2, incorporated many of the design principles of the most advanced concentric fortifications of the thirteenth century, but utilized a technology that was in use during the early Middle Ages, and in the pre-historic past of Europe, as well. Late medieval cities developed layered defences that were intended to keep enemy artillery – and particularly large gunpowder weapons – as far from the densely inhabited portions of the urban centre as possible. To this end, engineers constructed ever-expanding networks of earth and timber barbicans on which defensive artillery and soldiers could be stationed. In order to prevent these outer works from being overrun, engineers designed their defences to provide overlapping fields of fire on the flanks of all of the barbicans. Eventually, the defences evolved into the classic 'starburst fortress' in which numerous triangular-shaped bastions provided mutual defence to the barbican on either side, and offered an exceptionally small area upon which the attacker could launch direct fire against the defenders.

Another innovation that took place during the later medieval period with regard to fortifications was the widespread construction of fortified residences and towers within cities, particularly in Italy and in the German kingdom. During the course of the later eleventh century and thereafter, many secular magnates constructed private fortifications in regions that lacked strong central authority. As discussed previously, these tended to be of mortared stone construction. However, during the course of the thirteenth century and then for the remainder of the medieval period, many aristocrats established their main base of operations within cities. One of the most famous of these buildings is the Golden Tower, which was originally constructed in the city of Regensburg in Bavaria during the second half of the thirteenth century, and was continually enlarged and strengthened up through the sixteenth century. Although marking a new trend in urban architecture, from a technological perspective, these new urban towers – which can still be seen in many cities in Italy and Germany today – utilized the same mortared stone construction that was employed by fortifications since the late Roman Empire.

One of the most distinctive forms of fortifications during the later medieval period is the red brick castles of the Teutonic Knights in Prussia. Brick had been used in fortifications since the Roman period, especially in places where obtaining sufficient quantities of stone was difficult and hence very expensive. Many of these late imperial structures can still be seen today. Brick also was used as adjunct or replacement for stone in many places in Europe when there was a lack of suitable stone and also a substantial brick-making industry. This was the case for the Teutonic Knights, who produced massive quantities of bricks in industrial facilities. Most of their castles throughout Prussia were constructed of this material, including the vast fortress at Malbork, which was named Marienburg (Mary's Fortress). Similar to other strongholds utilizing a concentric design, the fortification at Malbork consisted of multiple baileys, each of which could be defended independently, but which also provided mutual support. The fortification enclosed some 21 hectares (52 acres), and was constructed entirely of red brick, making it the single largest all-brick stronghold built in Europe. From a technological perspective, however, mortared brick functioned in the same manner as quarried stone, and utilized the same types of mortar to hold the individual pieces of the wall in place.

Warships

During the late Roman Empire, the basic warship for blue-water service was the light galley, which was powered by both oars and a single square sail. River patrols along the Rhine and Danube in the West utilized a range of river craft that were similar in structure to the poled and sailed barges discussed in previous chapters. The Romans did not face any significant opponents in the Mediterranean or in the north who had the wherewithal to develop and maintain large fleets for naval combat. However, various groups of the migrating peoples, such as the Jutes, Angles, and particularly the Saxons, were quite avid pirates, and utilized their own light coastal ships for extensive raiding anywhere they could put into shore. As seen in Chapter 2, this was the genesis of the system of defence in depth of the so-called Saxon Shore. It was certainly possible for several of these light and low coast raiders, which were powered by oars, to attack a slow-moving sailing ship in the waters of English Channel; however, the main purpose of these craft was to land men for quick hit-and-run raids against unfortified places near the coast.

In the east, the rise of the Islamic Caliphate as a military power during the course of the seventh century brought with it the development of a substantial maritime capacity. By the mid-seventh century, Muslim fleets were operating in the Mediterranean and took part in significant sieges of Constantinople in 673 and again in 717–718. In response to the growth of the Caliphate as a naval power, the Byzantine Empire substantially improved the quality and size of its fleet by constructing large numbers of galleys that were equipped with two decks of oars (biremes). These are generically denoted as *dromons* in the sources. These new warships were significantly larger than those deployed by the late empire, and had larger crews. The *dromon*, which moved very fast (the name means racer), remained the basic fighting ship in the Byzantine and Muslim arsenals up through the twelfth century. They also were copied and modified in the western kingdoms, as well. The Italian city of Amalfi, on the west coast of the peninsula, is credited with developing a sail rigging that improved the speed and manoeuvrability of the *dromon*.

From a technological perspective, the most important changes between the galleys of the fifth century and those of the eighth were the addition of a full deck, which provided space for a second bank of rowers, the replacement of the square sail with the triangular lateen sail, and the replacement of the ram with a spike. The lateen sail permitted a skilled crew to sail closer to the wind than did a square sail, meaning that if the wind were blowing due east, the ship could sail on an angle closer to due east. The addition of the spike may have been intended to wreck the oars of the enemy ship and thus render it immobile. Unlike the ram, the spike was not intended to strike the enemy below the water line and sink it.

The elimination of the ram has been explained by some scholars as resulting from the greater internal strength of Mediterranean ships in the post-Roman period, which was brought about by the introduction of a new method of constructing these vessels. Throughout the classical period and well into Late Antiquity, the standard method of construction in the Mediterranean (and in the north) was to build the shell of the ship first and then provide some internal bracing. In the Mediterranean, the planks of ships fit together flush and were held together using a mortise-and-tenon joint. In its basic form, this joint consists of a groove (mortise) and tongue (tenon) that fit together and would be pinned or wedged together, and/or held in place with an adhesive. By the seventh century, however, some ships in the Mediterranean were being constructed skeleton first, meaning that an internal structure was built and external planks were fastened to them. The transition to skeleton-first construction was largely complete by the end of the tenth century. This type of construction gave much greater rigidity and strength to ships, making them far less susceptible to attacks by rams, although sacrificing some flexibility in handling in rough water as a result. In addition, building ships skeleton first was both faster and less expensive than the older methods.

Shipping in the north

As had been true in the Roman period and remained the case in the Mediterranean, warships in the north were powered largely by oars rather than sails, although most medium- and large-size craft were equipped with a single mast that continued to utilize a square rather than a lateen sail. Following the end of Roman rule, centralized naval operations declined significantly, as rulers of the smaller western kingdoms did not have sufficient resources to maintain standing fleets. Coastal traders, powered by both oars and a single sail, continued to operate throughout the early medieval period, as did riverine craft that operated using oars and poles.

The major new development in warship design came not from within the frontiers of the former Roman Empire, but rather from Scandinavia. The peoples living along the extensive coasts and fjords of this region improved the Late Antique ship designs by adding a keel, which was a continuous wooden strip along the bottom of the ship, and ribs that were placed low in the ship to provide structural support to the sides without giving up flexibility in manoeuvres. The sides of the ships were built up using a clinker method, meaning that the planks were overlapping, rather than flush, as was the case in the Mediterranean. The individual planks were held together by iron fasteners and were made water-tight through the addition of a caulking of moss and hair. These Scandinavian ships were propelled by both oars and a single square sail. Warships were distinguished from trading ships, the knar, by their greater length, lower sides (freeboard), and the placement of a larger number of holes (tholes) along the sides for oars. Trading ships generally had places for oarsmen at the front and back of the ship, leaving the space in the middle for cargo. Both trading and war-ships had exceptionally shallow (low) draughts, meaning that they could land on beaches anywhere and go up rivers. The primary purpose of Scandinavian warships was to land troops rather than to engage in combat at sea.

The so-called longships, which were the primary warship of the Scandinavians, changed very little structurally from the eighth through the early eleventh centuries. The major development at the turn of the millennium was the permanent fixing of the planks at the sides of the ships to the internal elbows, which gave the ships a stronger structure, albeit with the sacrifice of some flexibility. Eventually, the competition for naval superiority in the North Sea and the English Channel among the various Scandinavian kingdoms, as well as the kings of England, led to the development of longer and larger warships that most scholars denote as galleys, which were equipped with fighting platforms on both the front and rear of the ship. Whereas Scandinavian ships of the ninth century normally had comple-ments of 40–60 oarsmen, the galleys of the twelfth and thirteenth centuries often had as many as 120 oarsmen, as well as complements of soldiers who were trained for combat at sea. By contrast with Mediterranean galleys, however, those in the northern seas utilized only a single bank of oars, with two or even three men sitting on the same bench, rather than fitting their ships with a complete upper deck.

Naval response to the Vikings

The term Viking is derived originally from the word *wicman*, which meant merchant or trader, indicating the overlap between trade and piracy in the centuries following the end of Roman rule in the west. The emergence of large numbers of Vikings in the early ninth century and the subsequent three centuries of raiding and conquest by Scandinavians throughout the northern tier of Europe led to a range of naval responses by their intended victims. In the early ninth century, Charlemagne established naval squadrons and bases in the English Channel to deter Viking raids; however, there is no archaeological evidence or clear description in narrative sources to indicate what types of ships were deployed.

During the later ninth century, King Alfred the Great of Wessex is reported by his court biographer Asser to have developed a new type of warship that was intended to engage the Viking raiders at sea. There are no archaeological finds, as of yet, of these late ninth-century

Anglo-Saxon ships. However, Asser's contention that these warships were distinguished by their great length has led some scholars to conclude that they were galleys and were equipped in a manner similar to ships in the Mediterranean that were designed to grapple and then board the enemy. This conclusion is given credence by the fact that Alfred the Great, as well as many of the leaders of Wessex, likely had an opportunity to see galleys of this type during their journeys to Rome. It remains an open question whether the ships built by Alfred and his successors were in the overlapping clinker style, or had the flush Mediterranean style of construction. The latter would have provided both greater speed and manoeuvrability, qualities of the ships that are stressed by Asser. However, to date, the only ships from this period discovered in England were constructed using overlapping planks. Moreover, clinker-built galleys remained standard in England well into the fourteenth century, suggesting that if flush-planked ships were introduced in the ninth century, they did not displace the northern style for very long.

Later medieval developments

The galley, in its various forms, remained the dominant warship in both the northern and southern seas up through the thirteenth century. They were produced or purchased in large numbers by the rulers of Aragon on the Iberian Peninsula; by the powerful Italian maritime city-states, including Genoa, Pisa, and Venice; and by the kings of France and England. Many of the Mediterranean states, such as Venice, utilized galleys that were equipped with two banks of oars (biremes). However, in the late thirteenth century, the Genoese reintroduced the trireme, which had been the dominant warship of Classical Greece. The Genoese used these larger and taller ships to great effect against their Venetian rivals in a series of naval conflicts during the course of the last decade of the thirteenth century.

Cargo ships, which were propelled primarily by sail, often were converted into warships for brief periods through the addition of fighting platforms, artillery, and above all, fighting men. The latter, equipped with crossbows, were able to rain deadly storms of bolts on opposing ships from a considerable distance. Moreover, the conversion of merchant ships to a military footing can be seen not only on the high seas, but also on the rivers of Europe. During the mid-thirteenth century, for example, the merchants of the Rhineland cities converted their trading vessels into warships by adding fighting platforms and paying the wages of crossbowmen to serve on them. The term utilized by contemporary chroniclers for these fighting decks, *propugnacula*, is the same word that is used to denote the wooden platforms that were added to the stone walls of fortifications to facilitate the deployment of additional forces atop these mural defences.

The basic pattern of galley dominance in the northern seas was broken decisively during the course of the thirteenth century through the development of the cog, discussed in Chapter 4. This exceptionally high-sided ship gave its crew an enormous advantage in naval combat over the comparatively low-riding galleys. Men equipped with missile weapons were able to stand on the high decks of the cog and shoot down into the galleys, whose defenders were significantly handicapped by the need to shoot upwards. Moreover, the traditional style of sea combat in which the enemy ship was grappled and then boarded was impossible for a galley that encountered a cog. In effect, cogs were immune from galleys, and could not be hindered in their progress. Only another cog could engage a cog in direct combat at sea. However, the cogs were far less manoeuvrable than galleys, and could not force a confrontation if the commander of the galley did not wish to engage. The latter could simply row into the wind to escape.

As a consequence of the very different strengths of the galleys and cogs, the kings of France and England, as well as Scotland – the dominant naval powers in the northern seas from the thirteenth through the fifteenth centuries – utilized both types of ships for military operations. Cogs were essential for the transportation of troops and supplies, and could engage enemy cogs at sea. Galleys retained their value for coastal raiding because they could penetrate into shallow waters that were inaccessible to the cogs with their deep draughts. In addition, galleys could and did engage each other in combat at sea.

The cog also was introduced into the Mediterranean in the thirteenth century, and the first evidence for the building of cogs there is in the early fourteenth century. However, the cog was never as widely used in the south as it was in the north. This is likely because the single mast of the cog, with its square sail, was less useful in the comparatively light winds of the Mediterranean. However, as was true in the contemporary northern seas, sailing ships did come to play an increasingly important role in naval warfare in the Mediterranean in the course of the thirteenth century and thereafter. Larger, high-sided sailing ships, which often were equipped with three masts and lateen sails, largely were immune to assault by galleys for much the same reason as the cogs were in the north. The galleys usually could not overcome the height difference and board high-sided sailing ships, and the defenders were able to use their height advantage to deadly effect in the exchange of missiles. However, galleys remained important in Mediterranean naval warfare well into the sixteenth century because of their greater manoeuvrability and their ability to land virtually anywhere on the coast. This was very important, not only for raiding purposes, but also because the heavily manned galleys frequently had to stop to bring aboard supplies of fresh water.

By the early fifteenth century, several Mediterranean building techniques made the transition to the northern seas, which had a revolutionary impact on ship development. The first of these was the introduction of two-masted ships to the north, with the concomitant addition of lateen sails to complement the traditional northern square sail. The second innovation in northern ship-building was the introduction of the skeleton-building technique, which had become standard in the Mediterranean by the turn of the first millennium. The new type of northern ship built in this skeleton-first manner was called a caravel. The first caravel that is known to have been built in England was the *Edward*, which was constructed in the 1460s.

Horse transports

The horse transport was a highly specialized type of ship. Men and material could be transported on virtually any vessel; however, horses are notoriously prone to seasickness and can come to considerable harm if not properly treated when transported over water. In part, this is because horses are not capable of vomiting to relieve their seasickness. The two most crucial factors that had to be considered when moving horses by sea was providing easy access into and out of the ship, and having proper facilities for keeping the horses quietly in place during transit. Of particular concern was ensuring that the horses moved as little as possible, so as to keep them from damaging themselves or the ship, as a broken leg bone could not be repaired and meant that the horse had to be put down.

The Byzantine Empire maintained the Roman imperial tradition of constructing specialized horse transports for the movement of military mounts to theatres of operation across the sea. These ships were equipped with specialized stalls in which the horses were supported with canvas wraps under their bellies to hold them in place. The ships also were outfitted with ramps so that the horses could enter without having to jump over the side, and also disembark in a safe manner. By the tenth century, the Muslims also had acquired the technology to build similar types of horse transports, and used them in a variety of operations throughout the Mediterranean.

During the course of the eleventh century, adventurers from Normandy established a series of principalities in southern Italy, and then began the conquest of Sicily from the Muslims during the 1060s under the leadership of Robert Guiscard, the father of Bohemond of Taranto, who played a key role during the First Crusade. The emergence of the Normans led to a three-way struggle among them, the Byzantines, and the Muslims for control in the central Mediterranean. It is during this period that the Normans developed the naval capacity to move their horses on short-haul routes in southern Italy and across the Tyrrhenian Sea to Sicily. There is some scholarly controversy about whether the Normans copied task-specific Byzantine horse transports, or rather converted merchant vessels for this purpose by retro-fitting them with stalls as well as access ramps.

The expertise developed by the Normans in the transportation of horses became important in the context of William the Conqueror's invasion of England in 1066. Between the end of Roman rule and the mid-eleventh century, there had been little or no need for substantial numbers of horse transports in northern Europe, and the skills for building these specialized vessels or even retro-fitting merchant ships to carry horses appears to have been lost. As a consequence, when William planned his invasion of England, which was to include a very substantial mounted force of several thousand men, he found it necessary to recruit Norman ship designers and builders from southern Italy to help him. Some scholars, including one of the authors of the present volume, have argued that these Norman shipwrights from southern Italy introduced Byzantine-style task-specific horse transports into the north. Other scholars have contended that this is unlikely and that the Norman experts from southern Italy provided the know-how to retro-fit existing merchant ships with appropriate sea-going stalls and ramps. The famed Bayeux Tapestry, which depicts horses jumping over the sides of ships, almost certainly does not provide an accurate image of the transportation of these animals, because the absence of stalls would have made movement over water requiring almost a full day at sea impossible. Similarly, the failure to depict ramps for embarkation or disembarkation makes clear that the designers of the tapestry did not understand the transportation of horses by ship. The type of construction used for the Norman horse transports, however, almost certainly will remain unresolved until archaeologists unearth one of these ships.

Up through the early twelfth century, Mediterranean designs for horse transports had two significant drawbacks. The first of these was the limited number of animals that could be transported at any one time. Most Byzantine and Norman ships carried about a dozen horses. The second significant technological hurdle was designing ships that could carry horses over long distances. Both of these challenges were overcome during the 1120s when new ship designs, which included longer and higher hulls, made it possible to carry as many as forty horses across the length of the Mediterranean. Ships of this type were used by the Italian maritime republics of Venice and Genoa to carry substantial numbers of mounts and riders to the Holy Land from the third decade of the twelfth century onwards.

The next major design improvement in horse transports in the Mediterranean was the introduction of stern ports – that is, gateways in the backs of ships – which allowed horses to be loaded and unloaded directly onto a beach or prepared pier. The ship transports with this mode of ingress and egress were all powered by oars, rather than primarily by sail, because it was necessary to back up the ship to the shoreline, something which was not possible using sails alone. The common name for horse transports of this type was *tarida*. There were also sailing ships with stern ports, but these required docking facilities to load and unload their cargoes of horses. In theory, a *tarida* could launch an attack of mounted troops directly onto the shore in the manner of a modern landing craft. However, in practice, this was rarely possible because most of the horses were not fit for immediate service after a long journey at sea. The earliest mention of a horse transport equipped with a stern port comes from the pen of Leo the Deacon (died c.992), who described a military operation by a Byzantine fleet in 969. Ships of this type also were used extensively by western armies operating in the Levant, including Richard the Lionheart's fleet that included fourteen oared horse transports, which had the capacity to deliver forty horses each onto the shore. This type of ship remained in service for the remainder of the medieval period, and figured prominently in naval operations that involved amphibious operations throughout the Mediterranean.

In light of the use of *tarida* by crusader forces from northern Europe, it seems likely that ships of this type also were used in the northern seas under a variety of names, including the *buss*. However, it is also clear that northern fleets made use of retro-fitted merchant ships to carry horses to their destinations across the sea. For example, during his lengthy series of campaigns in Scotland in the period 1296–1307, Edward I of England routinely impressed merchant shipping for this purpose, with very large numbers of ships coming from the busy ports of Ireland, including Dublin. Numerous administrative documents from the English royal chancery that were issued during the first years of the fourteenth century mention the purchase of vast numbers of boards for the purpose of building stalls and ramps on these merchant ships to accommodate the horses. The English government also purchased substantial quantities of rope and canvas in order to produce slings to hold the horses in position for the voyage across the Irish Sea to Scotland.

Conclusion

One of the striking features of medieval warfare is the extent to which older technologies were recycled on a regular basis to serve contemporary needs, as was the case with earth and timber fortifications in the later Middle Ages, when it became clear that these withstood gunpowder artillery better than much taller and thinner mortared stone walls. A second noteworthy element of medieval military technology was the persistence of specific types of equipment over many hundreds of years, or indeed, over the entirety of the Middle Ages. This was the case, for example, with mail, which continued to be produced and utilized in vast quantities even after plate armour became rather widely diffused in the fourteenth and fifteenth centuries.

Within these broad patterns of continuity, however, medieval craftsmen continually experimented with new techniques and styles. The refashioned *spatha* – that is, the long sword – of the ninth century was made possible by this type of experimentation, as was the Viking longship with its special keel. However, even as new and improved weapons and equipment were developed, it is clear that the diffusion of this new technology was neither rapid nor even. The trebuchet was not constructed in England, despite its use on English soil by the French, until a master craftsmen with detailed knowledge of the system, Jordan *trebuchetarius*, could be induced to come to serve King Henry III. Similarly, the skeleton-first construction of ships, which was well-known throughout the Mediterranean by the turn of the first millennium, was not widely used, if at all, in Northern Europe until the fifteenth century, despite the fact that it was faster and the result was a stronger and less expensive ship.

Finally, it should be emphasized that even when medieval rulers and decision makers were aware of the newest military technologies, they did not always choose to use them, or to use them exclusively. The Carolingians and Ottonians employed numerous specialists who were competent to construct mortared stone walls, and built considerable numbers of fortifications using this technology. However, they also used other, less expensive, building techniques when these were sufficient to meet the perceived military threat. On a smaller scale, the kings of England in the thirteenth century produced in their own workshops very high-quality and powerful composite crossbows, which were spanned with mechanical devices. However, despite the obvious advantages of these weapons in terms of both range and striking power, the royal government did not cease production of lower-quality and correspondingly weaker wooden bows. Rather, the opposite was true, and upwards of 70 per cent of all the crossbows produced by the royal government during the thirteenth century were of the weakest 'one-foot' variety. Once again, considerations of cost and the expected opponents against whom these weapons were to be used, such as the Welsh and Scots, who did not possess much 'modern' armour, likely played a significant role in making decisions about what to produce.

The arms and equipment that we denote under the rubric of military technology were tools – or perhaps more appropriately, 'tools of war'. One of the tasks of a military planner in the medieval period, which is similar to the task of planners today, was to determine the right range of tools that were required to accomplish a particular task. The retention of certain technologies over long periods, as was the case with mail, indicates that it served its purpose very well. The development of new technologies largely was driven by current needs, as these were perceived both by political and military leaders, and by the craftsmen they recruited to implement their vision.

Bibliography

For the Roman background on arms and armour, see

H. Russell Robinson, *The Armour of Imperial Rome* (New York, 1975);
M. C. Bishop and J. C. Coulston, *Roman Military Equipment from the Punic Wars to the Fall of Rome, second edition* (Oxford, 2006).

For a broad overview of medieval military technology, see

The collection of essays in A Companion to Medieval Arms and Armour, ed. David Nicolle (Woodbridge, 2002);
Kelly DeVries and Robert Douglas Smith, *Medieval Military Technology*, second edition (Toronto, 2012).

With regard to helmets and armour in the early medieval period, see

E. M. Burgess, 'The Mail-Maker's Technique' in *The Antiquaries Journal 33* (1953), 48–55;
Alan R. Williams, 'The Manufacture of Mail in Medieval Europe: A Technical Note' in *Gladius 15* (1980), 105–134;
Dominic Tweddle, 'The Coppergate Helmet' in *Fornvännen: Tidskrift för svensk antikvarisk forskning 78* (1983), 105–122;
Ian Pierce, 'The Knight, His Arms and Armour in the Eleventh and Twelfth Centuries' in *The Ideals and Practice of Medieval Knighthood*, ed. C. Harper-Bill and R. Harvey (Woodbridge, 1986), 152–164;
Geoffrey Lester, 'The Anglo-Saxon Helmet from Benty Grange, Derbyshire' in *Old English Newsletter 21* (1987), 34–35;

Theodore F. Monnich, 'Construction of the Knightly Shield' in *Chronique: The Journal of Chivalry 8* (1994), 34–38, 74;

Erik Schmid, 'Link Details from Articles of Mail in the Wallace Collection' in *Journal of the Mail Research Society 1* (2003), 2–20;

Michael Lewis, 'Questioning the Archaeological Authority of the Bayeux Tapestry' in *Cultural and Social History 7* (2010), 467–484;

Graham N. Askew, Federico Formenti, and Alberto E. Minetti, 'Limitations Imposed by Wearing Armour on Medieval Soldiers' Locomotor Performance' in *Proceedings of the Royal Society B 279* (2012), 640–644.

With respect to helmets and armour in the later medieval period, see

Bengt Thordeman, *Armour from the Battle of Wisby,1361,* 2 vols. (Stockholm, 1939);

Ewart Oakeshott, *European Weapons and Armour: From the Renaissance to the Industrial Revolution* (London, 1980);

David Nicolle, *Arms and Armour of the Crusading Era, 1050–1350* (White Plains, 1988);

Charles Ffoulkes, *The Craft of the Armourer* (London, 1988);

Thom Richardson, 'The Introduction of Plate Armour in Medieval Europe' in *Royal Armouries YearBook 2* (1997), 40–45;

Frédérique Lachaud, 'Armour and Military Dress in Thirteenth and Early Fourteenth-Century England' in Armies, Chivalry, and *Warfare in Medieval Britain and France*, ed. Paul Watkins (Stamford, 1998), 344–369;

Alan Williams, *The Knight and the Blast Furnace: A History of the Metallurgy of Armour in the Middle Ages and the Early Modern Period* (Leiden, 2003).

Concerning hand-held arms, see

Ewart Oakeshott, *The Sword in the Age of Chivalry* (New York, 1964);

Alan R. Williams, 'Methods of Manufacture of Swords in Medieval Europe: Illustrated by the Metallography of Some Examples' in *Gladius 13* (1977), 75–101;

Simon Coupland, 'Carolingian Arms and Armour in the Ninth Century' in *Viator 21* (1990), 29–50;

Vytautas Kazakevicius, 'One Type of Baltic Sword of the Viking Period' in *The Balts and Their Neighbors in the Viking Ages*, ed. Vytautas Kazakevicius and Vladas Zulkus (Vilnius, 1997), 117–132;

Bert S. Hall, *Weapons and Warfare in Renaissance Europe* (Baltimore, 1997);

E. E. Astrup, 'The Construction of Viking Age Sword Blades' in *Proceedings of the 16th IAMAM Congress 2002*, ed. Carl Olsson (Oslo, 2003), 105–113;

John Waldman, *Hafted Weapons in Medieval and Renaissance Europe* (Leiden, 2005).

Concerning bows and crossbows, see

Jim Bradbury, *The Medieval Archer* (New York, 1985);

Bernard S. Bachrach and Rutherford Aris, 'Military Technology and Garrison Organization: Some Observations on Anglo-Saxon Military Thinking in Light of the Burghal Hidage' in *Technology and Culture 31* (1990), 1–17, reprinted with the same pagination in Bernard S. Bachrach, *Warfare and Military Organization in Pre-Crusade Europe* (London, 2002);

David S. Bachrach, 'Crossbows for the King: Some Observations on the Development of the Crossbow during the Reigns of King John and Henry III of England, 1204–1272' in *Technology and Culture 45* (2004), 102–119;

Matthew Strickland and Robert Hardy, *The Great Warbow: From Hastings to the Mary Rose* (Stroud, 2005);

Russell Mitchell, 'Archery *versus* Mail: Experimental Archaeology and the Value of Historical Context' in *Journal of Medieval Military History 4* (2006), 18–28;

David S. Bachrach, 'Crossbows for the King Part Two: The Crossbow during the Reign of Edward I of England (1272–1307)' in *Technology and Culture 47* (2006), 81–90;

Clifford Rogers, 'The Development of the Longbow in Late Medieval England and "Technological Determinism"' in *Journal of Medieval History 37* (2011), 321–341.

With respect to artillery from the late Roman Empire, see

E. W. Marsden, *Greek and Roman Artillery: Historical Development* (Oxford, 1969);

E. W. Marsden, *Greek and Roman Artillery: Technical Treatises* (Oxford, 1971);

Tracey Rihll, *The Catapult: A History* (Yardley, 2007).

For medieval artillery, including gunpowder weapons, see

J. R. Partington, *A History of Greek Fire and Gunpowder* (Cambridge, 1972);

Donald Hill, 'Trebuchets' in *Viator 4* (1973), 99–114;

Carroll Gillmor, 'The Introduction of the Traction Trebuchet into the Latin West' in *Viator 12* (1981), 1–8;

D. J. Cathcart-King, 'The Trebuchet and Other Siege-Engines' in *Château Gaillard 9/10* (1982), 456–470;

Randall Rogers, *Latin Siege Warfare in the Twelfth Century* (Oxford, 1992), 251–273;

Paul E. Chevedden, 'Artillery in Late Antiquity: Prelude to the Middle Ages' in *The Medieval City Under Siege*, ed. I. A. Corfis and M. Wolfe (Woodbridge, 1995), 131–173;

W. T. S. Tarver, 'The Traction Trebuchet: A Reconstruction of an Early Medieval Siege Engine' in *Technology and Culture 36* (1995), 136–167;

Kelly DeVries, 'Gunpowder and Early Gunpowder Weapons' in *Gunpowder: The History of an International Technology*, ed. Brenda Buchanan (Bath, 1996), 121–135;

Paul E. Chevedden, 'The Invention of the Counter-Weight Trebuchet: A Study in Cultural Diffusion' in *Dumbarton Oaks Papers 54* (2000), 71–116;

Paul E. Chevedden, Zvi Shiller, Samuel R. Gilbert, and Donald J. Kagay, 'The Traction Trebuchet: A Triumph of Four Civilizations' in *Viator 31* (2000), 433–486;

Robert Douglas Smith, 'The Technology of Wrought-Iron Artillery' in *Royal Armouries Yearbook 5* (2000), 68–79;

Robert Douglas Smith and Kelly DeVries, *The Artillery of the Dukes of Burgundy, 1363–1477* (Woodbridge, 2005).

David S. Bachrach, 'English Artillery 1189–1307: The Implications of Terminology' in *English Historical Review 121* (2006), 1408–1430.

For an introduction to naval technology, see

R. C. Anderson, 'English Galleys in 1295' in *The Mariner's Mirror 14* (1928), 220–241;

J.T. Tinniswood, 'English Galleys 1272–1377' in *The Mariner's Mirror 35* (1949), 276–315;

Richard W. Unger, 'Warships and Cargo Ships in Medieval Europe' in *Technology and Culture 22* (1981), 233–252;

Richard W. Unger, 'The Archaeology of Boats: Ships of the Vikings' in *Archaeology 35* (1982), 20–27;

Ian Friel, 'The Building of the Lyme Galley, 1294–1296' in *Proceedings of the Dorset Natural History and Archaeological Society 108* (1986), 41–44;

Richard H. F. Lindemann, 'The English *Esnecca* in Northern European Sources' in *The Mariner's Mirror 74* (1988), 75–82;

John Pryor, 'The Naval Architecture of Crusader Transport Ships and Horse Transports Revisited' in *The Mariner's Mirror 76* (1990), 255–273;

Michael Swanton, 'King Alfred's Ships: Text and Context' in *Anglo-Saxon England 28* (1999), 1–22;

John Pryor, 'Types of Ships and Their Performance Capabilities' in *Travel in the Byzantine World*, ed. Ruth Macrides (Aldershot, 2002), 33–58;

Aleydis Van de Moortel, 'Medieval Boats and Ships of Germany, the Low Countries, and Northeast France: Archaeological Evidence for Shipbuilding Traditions, Timber Resources, Trade and Communications' in *Settlement and Coastal Research in the Lower North Sea Region* (Köthen, 2011), 67–105;

The collection of essays in *War at Sea in the Middle Ages and the Renaissance*, ed. John B. Hattendorf and Richard W. Unger (Woodbridge, 2002).

With respect to the development of fortifications, see

Derek Renn, 'The Anglo-Norman Keep, 1066–1138' in *Journal of the British Archaeology Association*, third series *23* (1960), 1–23;

R. A. Brown, H. M. Colvin, and A. J. Taylor, *The History of the Kings's Works: The Middle Ages* (London, 1963);

J. R. Hale, 'The Early Development of the Bastion: An Italian Chronology, c. 1450–1534' in *Europe in the Late Middle Ages*, ed. J. R. Hale, J. R. L. Highfield, and B. Smalley (Evanston, 1965), 466–494;

Beric M. Morley, 'Aspects of Fourteenth-Century Castle Design' in *Collectanea historica: Essays in Memory of Stuart Rigold*, ed. A. Detsicas (Maidstone, 1981), 104–113;

Bernard S. Bachrach, 'The Cost of Castle-Building: The Case of the Tower of Langeais, 992–994' in *The Medieval Castle: Romance and Reality*, ed. K. Reyerson and F. Powe (Dubuque, 1984), 46–62, reprinted with the same pagination in Bernard S. Bachrach, *Warfare and Military Organization in Pre-Crusade Europe* (London, 2002);

Sidney Toy, *Castles: Their Construction and History* (New York, 1984);

Bas Aarts, 'Early Castles of the Meuse-Rhine Border Region and Some Parallels in Western Europe c. 1000: A Comparative Approach' in *Château Gaillard 17* (1996), 11–23;

Ronnie Ellenblum, 'Frankish Castle Building in the Latin Kingdom of Jerusalem' in *Medieval Warfare, 1000–1300*, ed. John France (Aldershot, 2006), 487–491;

John Goodall, 'The Baronial Castles of the Welsh Conquest' in *The Impact of the Edwardian Castles in Wales*, ed. Diane Williams and John R. Kenyon (Oxford, 2007), 155–165;

David S. Bachrach and Bernard S. Bachrach, 'The Costs of Fortress Construction in Tenth-Century Germany: The Case of Hildagsburg' in *Viator 45* (2014), 25–58.

Also refer to the publications discussed in the bibliographic essay for Chapter 2.

For the development of transportation technology with relevance to the conduct of war, see

Marjorie Nice Boyer, 'Medieval Pivoted Axles' in *Technology and Culture 1* (1960), 128–138;

Albert C. Leighton, *Transport and Communication in Early Medieval Europe AD 500–1100* (New York, 1972);

John Langdon, *Horses, Oxen and Technological Innovation: The Use of Draught Animals in English Farming from 1066–1500* (Cambridge, 1986);

James Masschaele, 'Transport Costs in Medieval England' in *The Economic History Review 46* (1993), 266–279;

Paul Gans, 'The Medieval Horse Harness: Revolution or Evolution? A Case Study in Technological Change' in *Villard's Legacy: Studies in Medieval Technology, Science, and Art in Memory of Jean Gempel*, ed. Marie-Thérèse Zenner (Aldershot, 2004), 175–188.

Conflicting views

What was the impact of the stirrup on medieval Warfare?

Lynn White, Jr., *Medieval Technology and Social Change* (Oxford, 1962);

R. H. Hilton and P. H. Sawyer, 'Technological Determinism: The Stirrup and the Plough' in *Past and Present 24* (1963), 90–100;

J. D. A. Ogilvy, 'The Stirrup and Feudalism' in *University of Colorado Studies: Series in Language and Literature 10* (1966), 1–13;

Donald A. Bullough, ' *Europae Pater.* Charlemagne and his Achievement in the Light of Recent Scholarship' in *English Historical Review 85* (1970), 59–105, here 84–90;

Bernard S. Bachrach, 'Charles Martel, Mounted Shock Combat, the Stirrup, and Feudalism' in *Studies in Medieval and Renaissance History 7* (1970), 49–75, reprinted with the same pagination in Bernard S. Bachrach, *Armies and Politics in the Early Medieval West* (Aldershot, 1993);

Alex Roland, 'Once More into the Stirrups: Lynn White Jr., Medieval Technology and Social Change' in *Technology and Culture 44.3* (2003), 574–585.

6   Medieval combat

Introduction

Dust, smoke, the crashing of weapons, the blaring of horns and beating of drums, as well as the screams of wounded men and animals, assaulted the senses of men on the battlefields and ramparts of medieval Europe. These soldiers were, themselves, filled with a mixture of emotions ranging from paralytic fear to rage as they faced the need to kill or be killed. The chaotic press of the battlefront often meant that the perspective of the individual fighting was limited to the man on his left and right, and the enemy to his front. But as the historian gazes back on the battle from the perspective of the army commander and the military planners around the ruler, certain important patterns emerge that make it possible to understand the experience of the individual soldier within a broader context.

Medieval battles did not, with certain very limited exceptions, consist of individual combat in the heroic tradition of an Achilles and a Paris fighting on the plains of Troy or Beowulf and Roland against dragons and Muslims as numerous as the fish in the sea. Rather, medieval combat, much as had been true of the late Roman Empire, and would continue to be true throughout the early modern and modern eras, was predicated on the preparation of men to cooperate in large groups. As will become clear in this chapter, foot soldiers and mounted troops, as well as mariners and fighting men deployed on ships, fought as units and were deployed in consistent ways throughout the medieval millennium.

In order for fighting men to learn how to stand their ground in battle, advance against the enemy, and withdraw from combat, as well as how to use their weapons and equipment, they required training, sometimes rudimentary, but in other cases quite extensive. Training, although necessary for an effective military force, is not, however, sufficient for victory on the battlefield or in sieges. Men with low morale, with little trust in their follow soldiers, and for whom fear of death overwhelmed the desire for glory, honour, or even the defence of their homes, usually did not serve effectively in combat. Investigating the ways in which medieval military commanders sought to maintain high morale is, therefore, also crucial to understanding combat in our period.

Battles in the field

The main arms used by combatants in battles in the field over the course of the medieval millennium were the sword, spear/lance, and bow/crossbow. Certainly, as seen in Chapter 5, these arms saw regular – although relatively gradual – changes in various characteristics over time, but their basic purposes and uses remained essentially the same. These weapons were augmented to some degree by other types of arms, such as war axes and slings that served

DOI: 10.4324/9781003032878-7

the same purpose of killing and wounding the enemy but never attained a central role in combat in medieval Europe. Toward the end of the Middle Ages, some new types of arms, including gunpowder weapons, were introduced, but these were insufficiently developed to bring about significant changes to combat in the field. An important consequence of the overall continuity in military technology from the late Roman Empire up through the end of the Middle Ages is that the 'face of battle', to use the evocative phrase popularized by the military historian John Keegan to describe the experiences of soldiers in combat, was not driven by technological change.

In the American Civil War (1861–1865), more accurate and faster loading firearms, and vastly improved communications and transportation technology, meant that the experiences of soldiers in battle differed significantly from those of their grandfathers who had fought in the American War of Independence (1775–1783), or in the War of 1812. These later developments in technology brought about substantial changes in tactics and in training. By contrast, the slow technological development of arms and the uneven diffusion of technological innovations in medieval Europe, as well as among all of the adversaries of the Latin West in Scandinavia, the Slavic East, Central Asia, North Africa, and in the Middle East meant that there was no impetus to introduce radically new tactics, or to teach large numbers of fighting men to use new weapons systems.

The battlefield tactics used by the armies of the late Roman Empire to confront their adversaries were quite similar to those used by combatants in the field for the next 1,000 years. As we will see, there were some developments within this paradigm of continuity, such as the heavy cavalry charge with couched lances, which although not unknown in the ancient world was made more deadly by the introduction of new types of saddles, which in turn made possible the more efficient use of stirrups. However, a Swiss soldier who was deployed in a phalanx during the Burgundian wars of the late fifteenth century possessed similar weapons and served much the same tactical function as the Anglo-Saxon spearmen at Ashdown in 871.

Foot soldiers in combat

As seen in Chapter 1, throughout the nineteenth and the early twentieth centuries, retired military officers dominated the writing of medieval military history. From their perspective, 'real' armies were those in which highly trained and thoroughly drilled infantry were the numerically dominant element, with cavalry and artillery forces playing a complementary but ancillary role. The heavy infantry legions of the Roman Republic, Principate, and early Empire held a lofty position in historiography of pre-modern warfare. By contrast, modern military historians decried what they saw as the decline of military science following the dissolution of the professional Roman army in the fifth century AD.

Foot soldiers in the Middle Ages, in this older historiographical school, were nothing more than a poorly equipped, untrained rabble. Medieval mounted troops, who will be discussed in greater detail later in this chapter, fared little better in the historiography up through the end of the nineteenth century. However, they were rehabilitated to a significant degree by scholars over the course of the first half of the twentieth century. In the period after the Second World War, the view generally emerged that mounted forces not only dominated warfare, but also that the individual cavalrymen were both well-equipped and well-trained as soldiers. In the following sections, it will become clear that the historiographical traditions dealing with both the fate of foot soldiers and the tactical dominance of cavalry in the medieval period were misguided. Although mounted troops often were both well equipped and well trained, foot soldiers remained both the numerically preponderant and tactically dominant element on the battlefields of Europe and of western armies on the eastern shores of the Mediterranean during the entirety of the medieval millennium.[1]

The phalanx in battle

Throughout the Middle Ages, the most common and certainly the most effective tactical deployment of foot soldiers for battles in the field was in a phalanx. The dense formation of the phalanx meant that each soldier was protected on his left and right side by a comrade, and only had to be concerned about dealing with the enemy in front of him. In fact, the cliché developed that medieval foot soldiers were so tightly packed that the dead had no place to fall and were held upright by the men around them. In order to protect the overall phalanx from attacks on its flanks and from the rear, military commanders often positioned their cavalry forces on the left and right of the formation. Depending on the size of the army and the terrain, military commanders frequently sought to anchor at least one flank on a topographically secure position such as a swamp or river. Phalanxes usually were at least five ranks deep, and often were even more dense. During the later Middle Ages, the Swiss pike men, who engaged the armies of the dukes of Burgundy at battles including Nancy in 1477, deployed in formations up to sixteen ranks in depth.

Phalanx on defence

The phalanx was an important formation for commanders who sought to remain on the defensive on the battlefield. This was the case, for example, at the Battle of Rimini (AD 554), in which a Frankish army faced an East Roman/Byzantine army under the command of Narses some 350 kilometres northeast of Rome. The Frankish corps at Rimini had been detached from the main Merovingian army that invaded Italy, and amounted to some 2,000 men, including both foot soldiers and mounted troops. The Franks were attacked while engaged in foraging and plundering operations in the valley near the fortress of Rimini. When the Byzantine general Narses saw that the Frankish troops were dispersed throughout the valley, he ordered a cavalry unit of 300 men to attack the foragers. In response, the Frankish commander used a variety of signals to recall his troops. When his men had reformed, the Frankish commander deployed the foot soldiers in a phalanx that was five ranks deep, positioned his mounted troops on both of the flanks, which were protected by forest, and waited to see what Narses' next move would be. This deployment provided a defence against efforts by the Byzantines to turn the flank of the Frankish force. This deployment also gave the Frankish commander the option of going on the offensive, should the Byzantine forces focus all of their attention on the infantry, and expose their own flanks to attack by the Frankish mounted troops, who could execute either a single or double envelopment of the enemy, meaning that they might attack the flank and rear on one or both sides.

At Rimini, the Franks, despite their effective initial deployment that repulsed several assaults by the Byzantine cavalry, suffered a significant defeat. This was due, in large measure, to the successful deployment of the tactic of the feigned retreat by Narses. The

---

1 Regarding the role of mounted forces in combat, see the conflicting views of Clifford Rogers, Charles Bowlus, and Matthew Strickland in the 'Conflicting views' section of the bibliography.

feigned retreat had the goal of luring enemy foot soldiers out of their close defensive formation by attacking and then pretending to flee. An insufficiently disciplined force would then pursue, and consequently lose the cohesion of the phalanx that was necessary for effective defence against more mobile mounted troops. Once the enemy was sufficiently extended from their original position, the ostensibly fleeing mounted force would then wheel about, and inflict heavy losses on the now disorganized foe. The ruse was successful at the Battle of Rimini in fooling many of the Frankish foot soldiers, who broke formation and charged after the apparently routed Byzantine forces. Once the Franks were, themselves, in a disordered state and the cohesion of their phalanx was broken, the Byzantine cavalry wheeled about and slaughtered many of the foot soldiers, who were no match for mounted troops one on one.

By contrast, the Frankish army under the command of Charles Martel achieved an overwhelming victory over its Muslim opponents at the Battle of Poitiers in 732 while also deployed in a defensive phalanx. Charles positioned his army astride the road that the Muslim army had to use in order to advance northwards towards the fortress city of Tours. A contemporary Christian writer living in Spain described the Frankish troops as holding their positions in the phalanx 'like a glacier from the frozen north'. The Muslim army at the battle was comprised exclusively of mounted troops, who hurled themselves into the Frankish phalanx and sought to break their formation using both the momentum of their charging horses and the advantage of striking at the foot soldiers from above. However, the Muslims were unable to break the Frankish phalanx. Rather, the Franks decisively defeated the Muslims in hand-to-hand combat, causing them to retreat in disorder as night began to fall. Charles Martel, however, did not order his troops to pursue the fleeing Muslims, fearing that he would lose command and control of the army and perhaps snatch defeat from the jaws of victory.

Similar to Charles Martel, Harold Godwinson deployed the Anglo-Saxon army at Senlac on 14 October 1066 in what is perhaps the best-known use of the infantry phalanx to halt the advance of the enemy army during the entire medieval period. Harold's goal was to keep William the Conqueror's army pinned to the coast, and only to engage in battle if he could maintain a strong defensive position. To this end, Harold deployed his army of professional household troops (*huscarls*) and local levies, including men from the select *fyrd*, in a dense formation atop a ridge at Senlac. This position made it impossible for the Normans to outflank the Anglo-Saxon army, and forced William the Conqueror's army to attack uphill, giving the Anglo-Saxon forces all the advantages of height. In particular, the position of the Anglo-Saxon troops on the heights at Senlac negated any advantage that Duke William may have hoped to gain by launching a shock attack with his cavalry against the enemy infantry.

In Harold's view, which was an accurate assessment of the strategic situation, William's invasion could not proceed unless the Norman duke succeeded in dislodging the Anglo-Saxon forces from their position athwart his line of march toward London. As a consequence, Harold's primary military objective was to keep his army intact and viable. The logic of Harold's tactical decision is borne out by the fact that the Anglo-Saxon army still held the ridge at Senlac after a day of assaults by William's army, including the famous feigned retreat that led many of the Anglo-Saxon soldiers to break ranks, as the Franks had done at Rimini. What Harold had not included in his calculations was his own death and the deaths of his two brothers, Gareth and Leofwine, who were his main sub-commanders, during the course of the battle. It was the loss of their leaders rather than defeat in battle that led the Anglo-Saxon troops to abandon their phalanx and the position along the ridge at Senlac after night fell. The retreat after darkness fell enabled many of the Anglo-Saxons to escape, particularly those who had 'parked' their horses during the battle and had fresh mounts, as contrasted with the Normans, whose horses were exhausted from the day's battle.

In contrast to the outcome at Hastings, the Flemish levies that mobilized outside the town of Courtrai in July 1302 not only held the field of battle, but inflicted a significant defeat on the French mounted forces that assaulted their phalanx. The 10,000 or so Flemish militia troops from the cities of Bruges, Ghent, and Ypres included archers and crossbowmen. However, the majority of the men were equipped with pikes or with the Flemish weapon known as the *goedendag*, which was wooden shaft topped with a metal spike. On 11 July, the Flemish troops took up their position on a field near the town of Courtrai, which they had prepared ahead of time with ditches that were intended to break the momentum of the enemy charge. The French army, which was about the same size as the Flemish force, was comprised of two-thirds foot soldiers and one-third mounted troops. The initial charge by the French foot soldiers failed to break the Flemish phalanx. A second charge by French cavalry was hindered to a significant degree by the pits and trenches dug by the Flemings. Once they reached the Flemish phalanx, the French cavalry also was unable to break the foot soldiers' formation, and the mounted troops withdrew in some disorder. During this disorganized retreat, the Flemish troops advanced in good order and killed many hundreds of noble French mounted troops who had become bogged down on the muddy field. They took as booty large numbers of expensive spurs, which gave rise to the name of the clash, the Battle of the Golden Spurs.

At the battles of Tours, Hastings, Courtrai, and likely at Rimini as well, the commanders deployed their foot soldiers in a fixed defensive position, and did not intend for the soldiers to move, except perhaps if the enemy withdrew in disorder, and then only when ordered to do so and in formation. In all of these encounters, one key to victory was maintaining command and control. However, the phalanx also was used by military commanders as a defensive formation in situations where it was necessary for the foot soldiers to move while keeping in their ranks. At the Battle of Andernach (876), for example, the East Carolingian King Louis the Younger (876–882) used a moving phalanx against the army of his uncle, the West Carolingian ruler Charles the Bald (840–877). In this battle, Louis the Younger deployed his foot soldiers, consisting largely of levies from Saxony, in a phalanx several hundred yards in front of his fortified encampment, which was located in a large clearing in a forest near the village of Andernach. Louis kept his mounted forces out of sight on the edge of the woods on both flanks of his infantry.

As the army of Charles the Bald, which consisted largely of mounted troops, advanced toward Louis the Younger's foot soldiers, the latter withdrew step by step in their phalanx formation, drawing the West Frankish forces after them in a deployment technically known as a refused centre. The Saxon troops halted their withdrawal in front of the ramparts of their encampment and engaged with Charles the Bald's troops in close-order combat as the horsemen closely pursued the 'retreating' foot soldiers. At this point, Louis the Younger gave the signal for his mounted forces to attack both of the flanks and rear of Charles' army, a deployment denoted by specialists in military science as a double envelopment. The result was an overwhelming victory for the East Frankish forces. As some contemporary writers may have been aware, the engagement at Andernach replicated the victory achieved by Hannibal over the Romans at the Battle of Cannae in 216 BC.

An even more impressive example of deploying a moving defensive phalanx is provided by the crusader army under the command of King Richard of England at the Battle of Arsuf (7 September 1191) during the Third Crusade. After the capture of the fortified port

The Battle of Roosebeke.

Figure 6.1 Battle of Roosebeke, 1382, French against Flemish militiamen

Source: © Florilegius/Alamy Stock Photo DKP2CW

of Acre, Richard led a substantial army from Acre along the coast of the Mediterranean towards the port of Jaffa, which it was necessary for him to capture in order to facilitate a campaign against Jerusalem itself. During the entire march, the Muslim ruler Saladin (died 1193) shadowed the crusader army looking for an opportunity to bring Richard to battle and thereby end the threat to Jaffa. As Richard's army reached a wooded region along the coastal plain near the town of Arsuf, about 25 kilometres – that is, about a day's ride – north of Jaffa, Saladin was able to bring his entire army within striking distance of the Christian forces by hiding his troops in a forest that came within about 1,500 metres of the coast. Saladin's plan is a good example of a classic ambush, which much improved the odds of victory for light cavalry – the dominant element in Saladin's army – against more heavily armed forces.

Because of effective scouting, Richard was well aware of Saladin's intentions, and also understood the likelihood that he would face an assault by the Muslims once his army came into the narrow strip of flat land between the Mediterranean Sea and the forest of Arsuf. He therefore deployed his forces so as to be able to keep advancing while also presenting a defended left flank against Saladin's army. To this end, the English king arranged his forces in three columns, with his foot soldiers, including men equipped with spears and crossbows, on his left flank, which was the part of his column that was the most exposed to attacks by the Muslims. The middle column consisted of his mounted troops, and the third column closest to the sea included the baggage train. Richard assigned the forces of the Templars and Hospitallers to the vanguard and rear guard of his army, respectively.

Saladin launched his attack while the entire crusader army was on the march. The first wave of assaults was directed against Richard's infantry forces, which were deployed in a marching column and then redeployed into a dense phalanx formation along the left flank. The Christian troops responded to the arrows and javelins launched by Saladin's soldiers with crossbow bolts, as the spearmen provided protection to the crusaders armed with missile weapons by establishing a hedgehog deployment with their spears. Wave after wave of Muslim assaults against the marching Christian phalanx failed to break their formation. The ability of the Christian troops to march in close order, defend themselves when attacked, and then resume their march in the lulls between Muslim assaults is a testament to their training, discipline, and bravery.

Preparing the battlefield for a defensive phalanx

When commanders had the benefit of choosing the battlefield on which they planned to make a defensive stand with their men formed up in a phalanx, they often prepared the field in an effort to maximize their defensive position, and also make the enemy's advance as difficult as possible. One tactic regularly employed by commanders of infantry forces on the defensive was to construct fieldworks that afforded them some limited protection against archery, and significantly greater protection from mounted troops. In addition, when the nature of the field and time permitted, defenders also sought to create obstacles in the field to impede the ordered advance of the enemy, and particularly enemy mounted forces, as was the case at Courtrai. This practice had a long pedigree in western warfare.

In 531, the Merovingian King Theuderic (511–533) undertook an invasion of the kingdom of Thuringia, located in the east of the contemporary Federal Republic of Germany. The Frankish army, which included a large mounted contingent, advanced as far as the Unstrut River, where the Franks were confronted by a substantial host of Thuringians, who were deployed on foot. As discussed in previous chapters, the Thuringian commander had considerable intelligence regarding the advance of the Frankish army, and positioned his forces so as to block access to an important ford across the Unstrut River. The Thuringians also prepared the field in front of their position by digging ditches and covering these over with sod, so that they would be barely visible, unless closely reconnoitred, until enemy troops were right on top of them. In the initial phase of the battle, the Franks sought to break up the Thuringian infantry phalanx with a cavalry charge. However, as the Frankish horsemen advanced rapidly across the field, many of them fell into the ditches prepared by the Thuringians and were injured or killed. However, King Theuderic prudently had kept a substantial reserve, and was able to advance more cautiously with these troops, once his cavalry had been extricated from their difficult position. In the end, the numerically superior Frankish forces were able to achieve the victory by enveloping the smaller enemy force.

A very similar situation can be observed in the Battle of Conquereuil in 992 between an army under the command of Count Fulk Nerra of Anjou and a Breton army under the command of Count Conan of Rennes. In the spring of 992, Fulk managed to gain control over the fortress city of Nantes, which was strategically located on the frontier between Angevin-held lands and Brittany. In response, Conan undertook a siege of Nantes. Fulk then mobilized a substantial army, which included a large number of mounted troops, some of whom were mercenaries, to relieve the siege. As the Angevin forces approached Conan's position, the two counts agreed to fight a battle at the field of Conquereuil to settle their dispute.

Conan arrived at Conquereuil several days before Fulk, and prepared the field with a substantial number of traps, including ditches covered with sod, similar to those employed by the Thuringians noted previously. Conan also constructed field works across his end of the field at Conquereuil, which were anchored on the two flanks by impassable swamps. When the Angevin army arrived at Conquereuil, Fulk divided his forces into two parts, with a lead unit and a reserve unit. However, surveying the preparations made by Conan, Fulk refused to initiate combat. Conan then resorted to a ruse in an attempt to draw Fulk's men into a precipitous charge. Utilizing a type of feigned retreat, Conan had his Breton troops make a great show of retreating from their defensive positions behind the earth-works.

Conan's ruse was successful because the Angevin lead unit undertook a pursuit of the apparently fleeing Bretons. These mounted troops acted without the orders of Count Fulk, who temporarily lost command and control over his men. However, when he realized what had happened, Fulk joined in the attack with his personal bodyguard and standard bearer. The pits dug by the Bretons were very effective, and many of the Angevin horsemen fell into them. Fulk, himself, lost his horse in this manner. As the Angevin charge was disrupted and many of the men were unhorsed, the Bretons wheeled about, and charged the field. Many of Fulk's men were killed, although the Angevin count himself was saved from serious injury by his heavy coat of mail. Fulk's standard bearer was killed, and when the Angevin banner fell, the remaining Angevin horsemen withdrew from the field. Fulk himself managed to retreat with his men.

At this point, the Bretons believed that they had won the battle. They broke formation and began the process of looking after their wounded, and claiming the spoils of victory by stripping the enemy of their arms and equipment. However, Fulk still had his reserve unit intact, and launched a counter-attack against the now disorganized Bretons. This second Angevin attack was very successful, and they killed large numbers of Breton troops, as well as Count Conan. From a tactical perspective, the initial advantages gained by the Bretons through the use of a field enhanced with traps and the feigned retreat were overcome by Fulk's use of a reserve force.

The preparation of the field by defensive forces also can be seen in the later medieval period. For example, at the Battle of Loudon Hill in 1307, the Scottish King Robert Bruce (1306–1329) shaped the battlefield to funnel the English cavalry under the command of Aymer de Valence (1276–1324) onto a narrower front so that the Scottish infantry phalanx could be deployed in a denser formation. The field where King Robert Bruce positioned his force was bordered on both sides by swampy areas that could not be traversed effectively by men on horseback. However, the dry level area between the two swamps was still too wide to cover with the forces that the Scottish ruler had at his disposal. He therefore commanded his troops to dig three long trenches parallel to each other on both edges of the field. The intention of the Scottish king was to force the English cavalry through a narrow funnel directly towards the Scottish phalanx, and protect his flanks and rear from attack. Despite the obvious impediments placed on the field, the English commander ordered an attack, but the cavalry was unable to break the infantry phalanx, and large numbers of the attackers were killed at the hands of the Scots, who were wielding long spears with which they pierced both horses and men. Robert Bruce used a similar deployment of a phalanx of pikemen who were protected by streams and a swamp during the Scottish victory at the Battle of Bannockburn in 1314.

BATTLE OF STIRLING BRIDGE, 1297.

Figure 6.2 Battle of Stirling Bridge, 1297; nineteenth-century illustration

Source: © Timewatch Images/Alamy Stock Photo B7EDWN

The phalanx deployed on offence

The numerical dominance of foot soldiers on the battlefields of Europe during the Middle Ages entailed that they were involved not only in defending themselves from attack, but also went on the offensive, as well. At Courtrai, noted earlier in this chapter, the French foot soldiers, who were involved in the initial assault, were deployed in a phalanx. They were able to maintain a steady advance across the trenches and pits of the field that had been prepared over the previous day by the Flemish defenders, but ultimately were not able to break the numerically superior enemy phalanx. The lack of success of the French infantry can be contrasted with the successful operations of the army of King Arnulf of East Francia (887–899), which defeated an entrenched Danish force at the Battle of the Dyle in 891.

In the spring of 891, a large Danish army, which included both foot soldiers and mounted contingents, began operations in the region between the Meuse and Rhine rivers in what is today the border region between modern Belgium and Germany. King Arnulf dispatched an army to confront them, but these East Frankish forces were defeated on 26 June near a stream called the Geule. Arnulf, who was occupied elsewhere in his kingdom, was not able to deal with the Danes until the autumn of 891, when he led a very substantial army to dislodge the enemy from the fortified positions that they had established at Louvain, in modern Belgium, 25 kilometres east of Brussels. The Danish fortifications were protected on one flank by a swamp, and on the other by the Dyle River, which also protected the rear of the fortifications.

In order to attack this position, Arnulf ordered most of his cavalry to dismount and join the foot soldiers in a phalanx to advance over the open field leading up to the Danish field works, which consisted of earthen walls topped with palisades. The East Frankish king commanded a rear guard of mounted troops, who were positioned to protect against the chance of his infantry phalanx being taken unaware by any Danish forces lurking on his flank in the nearby swamp. The victory of Arnulf's infantry phalanx was overwhelming. Once the East Frankish forces drove the Danes back from their fortifications, they had no place to retreat, and the majority of the enemy were killed, either at the point of Frankish spears and swords, or by drowning in the Dyle River as they attempted to flee.

As a post-script to the battle of the Dyle, the phrase used by the author of the *Annals of Fulda* to describe the advance by King Arnulf's troops became a central piece of evidence in the scholarly argument during the nineteenth century that warfare came to be dominated by mounted warriors. The annalist stated in Latin that the Franks advanced against the Danes *pedetemptim*, although they were unused to doing so. The Latin term *pedetemptim* means advancing in step, much like soldiers marching in cadence. However, the great German medievalist Heinrich Brunner mistranslated this passage in his classic essay 'Mounted Military Service and the Origins of Feudalism', first published in 1887, to state that the Franks were unused to fighting on foot, hence his argument that the Frankish army had been transformed sometime earlier into a cavalry force. Brunner clearly misunderstood that the intention of the author was to explain that the Franks were unused to marching slowly in step over muddy ground under a hail of enemy missiles. It was not until the 1970s that one of the authors of this text illuminated Brunner's error and its implications for the German scholar's broader argument, including his claim that infantry no longer had any importance in warfare during the medieval period.

Before the 1970s, it was only with regard to England that scholars accepted that foot soldiers played a central role in combat, including in taking the offensive. Anglo-Saxon sources emphasized the importance of infantry phalanxes advancing against the enemy, as for example, at the Battle of Ashdown (871) when Alfred the Great led his troops, employed in a dense phalanx, in a victory over the Vikings. In the days preceding the battle, the Anglo-Saxon army under the joint command of Alfred and his elder brother Ethelred, the king of Wessex, had been defeated at Reading and retreated northwest to a place called Ashdown. The Vikings pursued and established a fortified position on a hill above the Anglo-Saxon encampment. Realizing that this tactical position was untenable, Alfred, according to his biographer Asser, did not wait for his brother Ethelred to bring up his forces, but rather decided to drive the Vikings from their position using only the men under his direct command. Alfred consequently ordered the half of the army that he commanded to form into a dense phalanx, and charge up the hill towards the Viking camp, driving them from their positions and inflicting heavy casualties.

At both the Battle of the Dyle and at Ashdown, the infantry phalanxes advanced without cavalry support against infantry in fixed positions, who likewise lacked cavalry support. Arnulf deployed his mounted forces as a reserve rather than committing them immediately to battle for two reasons. First, these troops would not be able to operate effectively against the flanks of the Danes, which were protected by a swamp and the Dyle River. The mounted forces also could not operate effectively when faced with a fortified palisade. Second, Arnulf was concerned that the Danes may have had concealed cavalry forces of their own, and he wanted his mounted troops to protect the advancing East Frankish phalanx against possible attacks on its flanks or rear. At Ashdown, Alfred did not commit mounted troops to the battle for the simple reason that the Anglo-Saxons did not possess any cavalry.

By contrast, at the Battle of Lenzen in September 929, the Saxon army dispatched by King Henry I of Germany (919–936) under the command of two counts named Thietmar and Bernhard included both infantry and mounted forces. Their Slavic opponents, the Redarii, had only foot soldiers. Bernhard and Thietmar were operating in Slavic-held territory because they had been commanded by the German king to capture the fortress at Lenzen in reprisal for an earlier attack on a German fortress called Walsleben. Bernhard and Thietmar began their siege of Lenzen in late August. However, a relief army that was composed mostly of fighting men from the Redarii arrived on the fifth day of the siege, and the Saxon commanders realized that it would be necessary to defeat the relief force before continuing their investment of the fortress of Lenzen.

In the early morning of 4 September, the Saxon and Redarii infantry phalanxes faced each other across a field that had been drenched the previous night by a powerful rainstorm. In the first stage of the battle, Bernhard launched an attack on the Slavic phalanx with his mounted forces, intending to use the tactic of the feigned retreat to cause the Redarii to break ranks. As mentioned previously, the Byzantines had used this tactic successfully at Rimini, as had Conan at Conqerueil and William the Conqueror at Hastings. However, the Saxon mounted forces had no such luck against the Redarii at Lenzen, in part because the wet ground prevented the Saxon cavalry from manoeuvring effectively.

Following the failure of his probing attack with the cavalry, Bernhard ordered the Saxon infantry phalanx to advance to attack the Redarii, while keeping his mounted forces in reserve. The two infantry forces engaged for a lengthy period, and many men were killed on each side. The Saxon historian and near contemporary, Widukind of Corvey, who provides considerable details about the conduct of the battle, indicates that the fighting took place along the entire front line of the two phalanxes, but that there were also occasions on which small groups of men were cut off from their fellows, surrounded, and killed to the last man. Eventually, however, Bernhard saw the opportunity for which he had been waiting. A gap appeared along the flank of the enemy phalanx. The Saxon commander immediately signalled Thietmar, who was in command of the mounted forces that were being held in reserve. Thietmar led a charge into the flank of the Redarii, and this surprise assault, after a hard day of fighting, utterly shattered the enemy phalanx and threw the Slavs into a panic, leading very rapidly to a rout. The Saxon foot soldiers and mounted troops mercilessly pursued the fleeing Redarii, and killed almost all of them as they fled. The fortress at Lenzen surrendered the next day.

The important complementary role played by mounted forces in a battle dominated by combat between two infantry phalanxes is also illuminated by the Battle of Tinchebrai that was fought between the armies of King Henry I of England (1100–1135) and his elder brother Duke Robert of Normandy (1087–1106) on 28 September 1106. King Henry was seeking to wrest control of the Norman duchy from his brother and was besieging the fortress of Tinchebrai, which was held by Count William of Mortain, who was loyal to Robert. Much as had been true of the Redarii at Lenzen, Duke Robert advanced with his army to break the siege, and the result was that King Henry redeployed his forces for a battle.

As was typical of Norman battle tactics throughout the eleventh and twelfth centuries, both Henry and Robert ordered a significant number of their well-trained, professional soldiers (*milites*) to dismount and form up into infantry phalanxes alongside the militia levies that the two rulers had mobilized for the campaign. In addition, however, Henry kept a mounted reserve under the command of Count Elias of Maine out of sight of Robert. This force was to prove decisive on the battlefield. Duke Robert initiated combat by ordering his men, who were deployed in a column, to charge against Henry's troops, who were arrayed in two dense lines. The levies of the Norman towns of Bayeux, Avranches, and Coutances were deployed in the first line of Henry's army, reinforced by some dismounted professional troops. The English king himself, as well as his barons and most of the men of their military households, were deployed in a second line. The decision by Henry I to avoid direct participation in conflict will be addressed in more detail in what follows.

Duke Robert's initial assault failed to break King Henry's first line, and the battle between the two infantry forces was hotly contested. Once King Henry saw that Robert's men were fully engaged, the English king then signalled the cavalry forces, which had been kept in reserve up to this point, to attack Robert's infantry in the flank. During the course of the battle, most of Duke Robert's mounted forces, who were under the command of Robert of Bellême, fled, thereby leaving the Norman ruler without a sufficient cavalry reserve of his own to halt or even slow down King Henry's mounted attack, which was led by Count Helias. The result was that the king's mounted forces disrupted the formation of the defenders, and caused a general panic. In contrast to Lenzen, however, Henry I's men did not mercilessly pursue their enemies, but rather accepted their surrender, including that of Duke Robert himself.

As the examples provided here – and many more could be adduced – make clear, soldiers deployed on foot in a dense formation posed a virtually insurmountable obstacle to mounted forces operating on their own. To defeat an infantry phalanx that was positioned on the defensive required either a substantially larger force of foot soldiers, who were themselves operating in a cohesive manner, or the effective use of combined arms – that is, men on foot, mounted troops and missile weapons. Conversely, dense formations of foot soldiers generally were ineffective against an enemy deploying mixed arms, unless also supported by mounted forces and troops equipped with missile weapons.

Missile troops on the battlefield

With very limited exceptions, the commanders of western armies never purposefully deployed soldiers equipped with missile weapons on the battlefield without support from either infantry or cavalry. This was because men equipped with bows, crossbows, slings, and javelins lacked both the velocity and quantity of projectiles to stop the advance of a large enemy force with their resources alone, whether these opponents were deployed on foot or on horseback. Consequently, soldiers equipped with missile weapons who lacked the ability to protect themselves with hand-held weapons, or were unprotected by other forces equipped with swords, spears, and shields, would be overrun by the advancing enemy. Such was the fate, for example, of the English archers at the Battle of Bannockburn in 1314 who were overrun by the cavalry of the Scottish King Robert Bruce when the English cavalry, which had been ordered to provide them with protection, was completely engaged in a losing effort against the Scottish infantry phalanx.

Although very rarely deployed on their own, archers, crossbowmen, and other soldiers equipped with missile weapons did serve very important roles as an adjunct to infantry phalanxes, both in defending a position and on the attack. The deployment of mixed forces of archers and men equipped with spears has received considerable attention in the context of the English armies of the Hundred Years' War, although the role and effectiveness of archers in these English formations has been the subject of some dispute.[2] The standard deployment of English troops at battles from Halidon Hill in 1333 up through the mid-fifteenth century, including at Crécy (1346), Neville's Cross (1346), Poitiers (1356), Nájera (1367), and Agincourt (1415), consisted of a central phalanx of dismounted men at arms with archers stationed on each of the flanks. The men at arms generally were equipped with full suits of mail during the early period of the Hundred Years' War and gradually acquired far more expensive plate armour over the course of the fourteenth century. These men at arms were equipped with lances that they used in the manner of foot soldiers holding pikes, although the latter were often much longer and easier to wield than cavalry lances. The archers generally wore significantly less armour, and were equipped, at best, with short swords.

When the English had time to prepare their defensive position, the archers constructed earth-works and palisades to offer some protection against enemy troops equipped with missile weapons, and also most importantly against charges by enemy cavalry. In addition, armies on the tactical defensive frequently spread caltrops across the potential battlefield as another means of hindering the mounted forces of the enemy. All of the soldiers in England's armies during the Hundred Years' War were mounted for transportation purposes. However, they almost never deployed as mounted forces in combat. It was only after achieving a victory that the English men at arms mounted their horses and pursued the retreating enemy forces when they were at their most vulnerable because it was very difficult to defend themselves while running away.

The regular deployment by English commanders of archers alongside dismounted men at arms who were positioned in a phalanx has been described by a number of military historians, including most prominently Clifford Rogers, as marking a revolution in military affairs. In numerous articles and books, Rogers has identified what he describes as a particularly English approach to combat in the field, whereby English commanders undertook the tactical defensive in battle while maintaining the strategic offensive in the various theatres of the Hundred Years' War in Scotland, in France, and on the Iberian Peninsula. English commanders, and particularly Edward III, inculcated the imperative among their subordinates that it was crucial to force the enemy to attack them, after the English army had established a sound defensive position. It certainly is appropriate to observe the enormous success enjoyed by the English armies during the course of the fourteenth and fifteenth centuries; however, it also is important to understand that Edward III was not the inventor of the tactical deployment of a phalanx supported by troops equipped with missile weapons.

In March 1262, more than two full generations before Edward III successfully deployed the mixed formation of armoured pike men and archers against the Scots at the Battle of Halidon Hill, the city militia of Strasbourg inflicted a significant defeat on the bishop of their city Walter von Geroldseck (1260–1263) using the very same deployment at the Battle of Hausbergen. During this battle, the great mass of the city's militia was deployed on foot approximately 1 kilometre from Strasbourg. They were supported by a small number of mounted troops, drawn from among the wealthier citizens and their aristocratic allies from the nearby region. Nicholas Zorn, a local aristocrat whom the citizens had chosen as their commander, then deployed 300 of the city's archers along the flank of the Strasbourger army.

---

2 In this regard, see the studies by Kelly DeVries and Clifford Rogers regarding the importance and effectiveness of the 'long bow' in the Hundred Years' War in the 'Conflicting views' section of the bibliography.

Figure 6.3 Battle of Formigny, 1450; after a fifteenth-century miniature

Source: © INTERFOTO/Alamy Stock Photo CP1C8M

Bishop Walter's army included a substantial contingent of 300 heavily armoured mounted troops, as well as 5,000 foot soldiers. As it turned out, the bishop did not wait for his infantry to arrive before launching an attack on the Strasbourg militia, believing that he could break up their formation before the foot soldiers were fully in formation. However, before the bishop's heavy cavalry could engage with the city militia, a young aristocrat named Marcus of Eckwersheim rode out from the Strasbourger lines and challenged one of the bishop's men to engage in single combat. This challenge temporarily halted the advancing heavy cavalry and allowed the Strasbourg militia, including the archers, to get into position. Marcus won his single combat and killed the bishop's knight, which was the signal for the small mounted force from Strasbourg to charge against the bishop's cavalry. The bishop's more numerous heavy cavalry quickly surrounded the mounted forces from Strasbourg, but the phalanx of foot soldiers of the militia quickly advanced and enveloped the cavalry from both sides. The vastly superior numbers of foot soldiers quickly overwhelmed the bishop's men, almost all of whom were killed or captured. In the meantime, the archers from Strasbourg had been given strict orders to direct their fire at the bishop's approaching infantry. In order to keep up a steady barrage, their commanders divided the archers into two groups, and instructed them to engage in volley fire, so that as one group loosed their arrows, the second group was to be pulling back on their bows. The archers were so effective that the bishop's infantry was delayed and did not arrive in time to join the fighting and save the bishop's cavalry from complete defeat.

Among the dead in the battle was Bishop Walter's brother Hermann, the royal governor in the Rhineland appointed by Richard of Cornwall, who had been elected king of Germany in 1257. Richard was the younger brother of King Henry III of England, and it may well be the case that he shared with his brother and members of the English royal court the remarkable success enjoyed by the Strasbourg city militia, with its deployment of a phalanx that was accompanied by a substantial number of archers. Richard certainly was aware of the battle and its outcome, because shortly after its conclusion he attempted to mediate between the bishop and the city of Strasbourg.

However, it is very unlikely that Richard had any need to bring word back to England about the value of deploying an infantry phalanx and archers together while maintaining the tactical defensive. The deployment of an infantry phalanx with support from archers was already well-known in England during the century before the Battle of Hausbergen. It was used, for example, at the Battle of the Standard (22 August 1138), by an Anglo-Norman army that was composed of militia troops mobilized from throughout the archdiocese of Yorkshire and the military households of a number of northern Anglo-Norman barons. This army was opposed by King David of Scotland (1124–1153), whose forces included not only the military households of the great Scottish magnates, but also militia levies from the district of Galloway, who were famed for their ferocious nature in battle.

When the Battle of the Standard began, the Anglo-Norman army was deployed in a dense phalanx with most of the professional soldiers of the baronial military households serving on foot among the troops of the militia levies. The archers were stationed off to the side of the infantry phalanx. In the first phase of the fighting, David ordered an assault by the troops mobilized from Galloway. Some chroniclers suggest that the men of Galloway insisted on charging in the first wave, and were permitted to do so by David. As the Scots charged, they were cut down in large numbers by concentrated barrages of arrows loosed by the English levies. Once the Galwegians reached the English lines, they were unable to penetrate the defensive front and retreated. Following this failed assault, the English army began an advance on foot. King David's son Henry launched a mounted assault against the advancing English phalanx. This attack was met by the English mounted reserve and turned back. Following these two failed assaults, one on foot and one on horseback, the Scottish army retreated in the face of the English advance, suffering considerable numbers of casualties in the process.

Missile troops deployed on the offensive: breaking the phalanx

The most important offensive role of archers, crossbowmen, and troops equipped with other missile weapons on the battlefield was to disrupt the enemy phalanx so that infantry – and sometimes cavalry, as well – could close in for the kill. At the Battle of Rimini, noted earlier, when the Byzantine general Narses saw the strength of the Frankish position, he halted his troops within missile range of the enemy phalanx and ordered his archers and javelin throwers to target the men in the front ranks. Narses purposefully refrained from a fruitless effort to 'rain death' upon the mass of the phalanx because he was aware that well-trained fighting men could protect themselves by holding up their shields over their heads in a formation denoted by Roman military writers as the *testudo* or tortoise, in which the overlapping shields of the infantry present an impenetrable barrier to arrows and other projectiles coming from above. Ultimately, however, Narses' decision to direct arrows and javelins at the front rank also proved ineffective, and the Byzantine commander employed the tactic of the feigned retreat against the Franks, discussed previously.

The Battle of Hastings also featured an impressive effort to break an infantry phalanx that was deployed in a fixed position through the use of a sustained barrage of arrows that some contemporary accounts recorded lasted longer than an hour. Many tens of thousands of arrows plunged down onto the English army massed atop the hill at Senlac. However, very few found their marks during the first phase of the battle. The soldiers crouched down under the protection of their shields and waited out the storm. When William ordered his infantry to advance up the hill, they were met by a ferocious response that threw them back in disorder. In one of the ironies of the battle, the Anglo-Saxons inflicted far more casualties on the advancing Norman infantry with their own thrown axes and javelins than they had suffered from the Norman archers. It was only during the last phase of the battle, when William ordered a renewed barrage from his archers, that one arrow found its way into the eye of Harold Godwinson, and thus determined the outcome of both the battle and William's campaign in England.

A far more effective use of arrow barrages against a phalanx that was deployed in a fixed position can be seen at the Battle of Falkirk on 22 July 1298. King Edward I of England mobilized a substantial army, numbering close to 15,000 men as revealed by the surviving pay records, including more than 12,000 foot soldiers and at least 2,000 heavily armed mounted troops. The Scottish commander William Wallace (died 1305) sought to evade Edward's army as it advanced into central Scotland, but made the mistake of concentrating his forces within a few hours' forced march of the English near Falkirk. When William Wallace learned that Edward had undertaken a rapid advance towards his position, he deployed his infantry into four dense phalanxes denoted by the Scots as *schiltrons*. He deployed his limited number of archers among the *schiltrons*, and kept his even more limited force of cavalry in the rear as a reserve.

When the English army arrived at the field selected by Wallace, two of Edward's cavalry commanders began an assault against the *schiltrons* without receiving authorization from the king, who had not yet arrived. They had some limited success against the Scottish archers, but made no impact at all on the *schiltrons*. When Edward finally reached Falkirk, he ordered his cavalry to withdraw immediately, and held them in reserve. He then deployed thousands of archers against the *schiltrons*. Wallace ordered his limited cavalry forces to attempt to drive off the English archers, but Edward's cavalry easily swept away the Scottish mounted troops, who retreated from the battle completely. The English and Welsh archers in Edward's army were thus free to direct murderous volleys of arrows at the Scots, whose lack of defensive equipment, including shields, now proved disastrous. Once the *schiltrons* began to break under the continuous archery assault, Edward ordered his cavalry to attack, and they completed the destruction of the Scottish army.

Cavalry on the battlefield

As a number of the battles discussed previously illustrate, cavalry often was deployed effectively alongside infantry, including phalanxes and missile troops. Mounted troops served valuable complementary functions by protecting the flanks and rear of the phalanx, as well as the archers from assaults by enemy cavalry. In addition, cavalry sometimes played a decisive role at a crucial point in the battle by exploiting weaknesses in the enemy force that had been created or exposed by soldiers fighting in the phalanx or by archers. This was the case, for example, at Lenzen and Tinchebrai. In western armies, however, cavalry forces very rarely operated independently of infantry and missile support against foot soldiers who were deployed in a defensive phalanx. In the instances when they did so, the western cavalry generally suffered a significant defeat, although there were some exceptions to this general pattern, as will be seen later. In this context, it is noteworthy that western armies never developed a significant component of mounted archers. This is the case despite considerable evidence that at least some mounted forces were equipped with bows. The capitularies of Charlemagne, for example, required that men coming to the host on horseback with arms appropriate for equestrian warfare also were to bring with them a bow and a quiver full of arrows. The absence of a significant missile component is one of the reasons why mounted forces in the western tradition very rarely were successful on the battlefield against well deployed and commanded soldiers on foot.

The failure of an independent column of cavalry against an infantry force is illustrated by the Battle of Süntel Mountain that was fought between Frankish and Saxon forces in 782 in an early phase of Charlemagne's thirty-year war to subdue Saxony. Two Carolingian military commanders named Adalgis and Gailo were given the responsibility of leading a column of mounted troops to undertake a reconnaissance in force of the Saxon positions near Süntel Mountain. The remainder of the Carolingian army, comprised largely of foot soldiers, was following behind. However, rather than wait for the rest of the army to arrive, Adalgis and Gailo led their column in a charge against the Saxon phalanx that they had discovered, and suffered extensive losses. Both of the commanders, as well as twenty-two high-ranking officers, and many hundreds of rank-and-file Frankish horsemen, were killed in the course of the battle.

The author of the contemporary *Royal Frankish Annals* provided significant details about the battle and condemned the two Carolingian commanders for two reasons. First, Adalgis and Gailo led their troops in an assault against the plan of the campaign in the hope of gaining personal glory. Readers familiar with the story of U.S. Army Col. George Custer and the fate of the Seventh Cavalry at the Battle of the Little Bighorn in 1876 may seem important parallels here. Second, the two commanders led their troops in a disorganized charge, with each man riding as fast as he could. As a consequence, rather than striking the Saxon phalanx all at once, which offered the best opportunity to have a significant impact, the Carolingian soldiers each faced overwhelming odds as they crashed individually into the Saxon line. The ultimate result at Süntel, as would be the case 500 years later at the Battle of Hausbergen near Strasbourg, discussed previously, was that the cavalry was surrounded by infantry once the momentum of their charge was broken, and were killed almost to the last man.

The successful deployment of cavalry against an infantry phalanx usually involved the extensive use of missile weapons to 'soften up' the dense formation of foot soldiers. As discussed previously, there is no indication in the sources that western armies included mounted archers, although the Byzantine Empire did employ substantial numbers of steppe nomads as horse archers in its army. The missile weapons employed by western mounted troops were limited to javelins. These were employed, for example, by William the Conqueror's troops at Hastings in the context of their charge into the Anglo-Saxon shield wall. However, the large horses that were necessary to carry the heavily armed and equipped Norman troops were not very manoeuvrable, and many of them were killed by the Anglo-Saxons as they came in close to their lines. Duke William himself had at least two horses killed under him and he had to be rescued from the field.

At Hastings, the Norman cavalry — like the Norman foot soldiers who comprised the first assault — used javelins as missile weapons as an adjunct to their intention of directly engaging the Anglo-Saxon infantry in hand-to-hand combat. The Normans understood that whatever 'shock' value their mounted troops may have had under better conditions was eliminated by the fact that they had to charge uphill. This not only eliminated any serious shock effect, but greatly tired the horses. The main value of the Norman cavalry at Hastings was the fact that they could strike down on the Anglo-Saxon foot soldiers from above, while the defenders were forced to thrust upwards at their attackers. Of course, in this situation, the Normans' horses were exceptionally vulnerable.

By contrast with armoured Norman mounted troops, the rulers of some economically and administratively backward regions of Europe, such as Brittany in the ninth century, and Wales and Ireland in the eleventh–fourteenth centuries, did employ cavalry specifically as missile troops, with the expectation that these mounted forces would be able to engage directly with foot soldiers who were deployed in organized defensive formations. One of the few times when an exclusively mounted army from western Europe had significant success against foot soldiers deployed in a defensive formation involved light cavalry from Brittany equipped with javelins who defeated a Carolingian army under the command West Frankish King Charles the Bald in 851. At the beginning of the battle, Charles ordered his infantry to deploy in a phalanx and sent out a small unit of Saxon mounted troops as skirmishers to screen the infantry as they transitioned from their marching column into the desired line formation. As the main force of the Breton army, which was comprised of light cavalry, approached, the Saxon horsemen retreated behind the infantry phalanx, which had now completed its deployment. From a tactical perspective, from their position behind the phalanx, Saxon cavalry were in position to undertake a close pursuit of the Bretons if the latter were routed.

However, the Breton commander, who understood the limitations of his own force, did not engage in a direct assault against the Frankish phalanx. Instead, he launched wave after wave of horsemen who came into missile range of the infantry, hurled their javelins, and then retreated before the foot soldiers could engage. The Franks, apparently, lacked at this battle missile troops of their own who could counter the light cavalry. According to early tenth-century author Regino of Prüm, who provides the most detailed account of the battle, the Franks were unaccustomed to fighting against this type of foe, and consequently lost the disciplined organization that made infantry phalanxes so effective against cavalry. After numerous assaults by the Bretons, Charles the Bald lost command and control over some of his troops, who charged after the withdrawing Bretons. At this point, with the phalanx disrupted, the Bretons wheeled about and inflicted numerous casualties on the pursuing Franks. Regino does not explain the failure of King Charles to deploy his mounted Saxons against the Bretons, other than to say that the Saxons were terrified of them.

Cavalry battles among western armies

Because of the lack of missile capacity of most western cavalry, the relatively small number of battles between mounted forces of necessity involved combat at close range. But for cavalry, unlike for infantry, waiting to receive an enemy charge was a recipe for disaster because men on horseback are not able to establish the kind of cohesive counter-push against an onrushing enemy that is possible for a dense formation of men on foot. This is true for two reasons.

First, mounted troops cannot be deployed in a deep formation because horses required a considerable amount of space behind them to operate effectively. Second, even well-trained riders cannot control their horses as effectively as men on foot can control their own movements. Consequently, battles between western mounted forces almost always involved the two sides advancing towards each other.

On the advance, it was very important for mounted men to maintain a dressed line, meaning that all of the troopers advanced at the same pace and kept even with the man on the right and on the left. An undressed or uneven line would mean reaching the enemy in a disordered state, which often had the result that one attacker had to face two or more of the enemy at the same time. In his commentary on the Battle of Süntel Mountain, mentioned earlier, which featured cavalry against infantry but makes clear the point nevertheless, the author of the *Frankish Royal Annals* condemned the attackers for attacking as if 'they were chasing runaways and going after booty instead of facing an enemy lined up for battle'.

Some scholars have argued that western cavalry used two basic cavalry formations, namely deployment in an open or closed line. In the former, troops were positioned at intervals of 4–5 feet. Troopers positioned with this open formation had the space that they required to wheel about in position if this became necessary. By contrast, in close formation, troops were packed in knee to knee. Cavalry deployed in this dense formation could not wheel about, which reduced their manoeuvrability on the battlefield. However, the densely packed force was particularly useful for the purposes of creating the maximum possible shock against the enemy force. This shock, however, also ensured that there were forceful collisions with enemy horsemen, which resulted in many horses breaking their legs and collapsing. Until the development of saddles with high cantles and pommels in the twelfth century, the deployment of mounted troops in a dense line did not involve charging with a couched lance, because the impact would throw the rider off of his own horse. Rather, combat consisted of thrusting with a javelin or sword in the initial charge. Thereafter, as the battle devolved into a series of individual combats, or two or three against one, the fighting consisted of forehand and backhand slashes with the sword, or perhaps an axe or mace.

Cavalry battles against non-western armies

The military forces of the steppe peoples faced by western armies within Europe from the late Roman period onwards, namely the Huns, Avars, Hungarians, and Mongols, were comprised primarily of light cavalry, who were equipped with bows for combat at a distance, as well as with swords and spears for hand-to-hand fighting. The same was true of the Arabs, Berbers, and Turks whom Christian armies faced in Spain, North Africa, and in the Middle East. There is very little evidence up through the end of the ninth century that rulers of the Frankish kingdom, who were the primary opponents of the Arabs and Avars, ever deployed mounted forces against them without support from infantry. Indeed, in most battles, the light cavalry of the Arabs and Avars faced foot soldiers deployed in infantry phalanxes, with little or no cavalry support. There is also no evidence for cavalry battles between the Visigoths and their successors against the Muslims on the Iberian Peninsula during the eighth or ninth centuries.

By contrast, during the tenth century, western armies fought a number of cavalry battles against mounted Muslim forces in Italy, and against Hungarians (Magyars) in the East Frankish/German kingdom. The cavalry forces of both the Hungarians and Muslims posed significant tactical challenges to western mounted troops. First, the lack of a significant missile capacity among the cavalry in western armies meant that they were subject to attack from a distance by opposing horse archers, and could not respond in kind unless supported by missile troops of their own who were deployed on foot in range of the enemy. Additional important advantages of the Hungarian and Muslim cavalry were the greater manoeuvrability of their horses within confined spaces, and their greater speed over distance as compared with the larger and heavier western mounts. However, western cavalry had some significant advantages in close combat. The larger size and weight of their horses allowed western cavalrymen to 'bowl over' the smaller mounts of their opponents when coming into close contact, and also often gave them a significant height advantage in hand-to-hand combat. In addition, western cavalry troopers were usually much better equipped with heavier armour and shields than their Hungarian and Muslim adversaries. In the one on one combat of cavalry battles, this extra protection often gave Christian soldiers important advantages.

From a tactical perspective, therefore, a western commander had to position his mounted forces in such a manner that they were able to reach and engage the enemy before the latter could flee. In addition, western commanders also had to devise methods for protecting their mounted troops from enemy horse archers. The tactical imperative in combat between western and Hungarian cavalry is illuminated quite clearly in the battle between East Frankish/German and Hungarian forces at Riade in 933. The fundamental tactical problems that King Henry I faced were the speed of the Hungarian horsemen and their ability to inflict heavy casualties on his troops at a distance with their bows. Henry's plan, therefore, had to negate these two advantages of the enemy, while still giving the Hungarians sufficient enticement to commit to a battle.

To achieve these ends, the East Frankish/German king conceived a *ruse de guerre* so that his heavily armed mounted troops could engage the Hungarians and bring to bear their bigger horses, as well as their better weapons and armament in hand-to-hand combat. At the first stage of the battle, King Henry deployed a force of light cavalry with only a handful of heavily armoured troopers mixed in with orders to attack the Hungarians and then withdraw to give the impression that they were running away. In effect, they were to use the tactic of the feigned retreat. The objective was to bring the Hungarians within range of the mass of the Henry's heavy cavalry, who had been concealed at a distance from the Hungarian army. Once the Hungarians had reached a position that was sufficiently close to the heavy cavalry, Henry intended to undertake a charge against the enemy, and strike them before the mounted archers could take flight.

As the situation developed, the German light cavalry managed to attract the attention of the Hungarians, briefly engaged, and withdrew. The Hungarians took the bait and pursued them. Unfortunately for King Henry, however, the Hungarians caught sight of the Saxon heavily armoured horses and, realizing that a trap had been set, they fled. Widukind of Corvey, one of the main sources for this battle, reports that Henry's force pursued the Magyars for a distance of about 8 miles before the latter escaped largely unhurt. Not only were the horses – or perhaps more accurately, steppe ponies – of the Hungarians much quicker than the larger horses ridden by Henry's troops, but they also had considerably greater endurance and could easily stay far ahead of the pursuing horsemen.

Another contemporary observer, Liudprand of Cremona (died 972), also commented on the events at Riade and offers a description of King Henry's pre-battle rules of engagement that demonstrates important insights regarding contemporary thinking about how to deal with an enemy force of mounted archers. Liudprand wrote:

> Before the beginning of the battle, King Henry gave wise and salutary advice to his men. 'When you advance into the game of Mars, no one should attempt to go as fast

as he can, but rather advance at an even pace. Catch the first volley of arrows from the other side on your shields, and then rush upon them in a gallop and with the strongest possible attack so that they will not have time to launch a second volley against you before they feel the wounds of your arms upon them'.

Notably, Liudprand's words echo those of the author of the *Royal Frankish Annals*. It was crucial to keep a dressed line when attacking, in this instance enemy horsemen rather than an infantry phalanx. A compact formation was essential both for heavy cavalry and for infantry to strike a decisive blow. These tactics required not only bravery, but – as will be discussed later – extensive training, as well.

At Riade, Henry I's heavy cavalry was supported not only by light cavalry, but also by a large force of infantry, which was deployed out of sight and out of range of the Hungarians. As a consequence, if the cavalry battle had gone poorly, Henry I's men had a place to which they could retreat. By contrast, at the Battle of Capo Colonna (14 July 982), Henry I's grandson Emperor Otto II (973–983) suffered a major defeat in a cavalry battle at the hands of Muslim forces in southern Italy because his mounted troopers on their large and heavy horses became overextended and then were cut off and defeated in detail by swifter and better organized Muslim light cavalry.

The battle actually began auspiciously for the western emperor when Otto II's German and Italian heavy cavalry engaged with the army of Abu al-Qasim, the emir of Sicily. During the first phase of the battle, Otto II's cavalry overwhelmed the forces positioned in the centre of the Muslim battle array and killed the emir. However, rather than regrouping, Otto led his forces in a hot pursuit of the remainder of the contingents that they had just defeated. In doing so, Otto does not appear to have taken into account that the mounts of the Muslims, like those of the Hungarians, had greater endurance than the horses used by the Germans and Italians. In response to the German king's reckless decision to continue his pursuit of the defeated forces in the centre of the Muslim line, the commanders of the units along the flanks of the Muslim army withdrew from the battlefield and shadowed the German and Italian heavy cavalry. Once the latter were worn down by their long chase, the Muslims launched a counter-attack beginning with barrages of arrows, and then closing on the disorganized enemy. Otto II's heavy cavalry could not respond effectively, not only because their horses were exhausted but also because they lacked infantry and missile support. A large number of German magnates, as well as thousands of men, were killed. Otto II barely escaped the battlefield. He was rescued by a prominent local rabbi named Kalonymous, who escorted the emperor along little-known local paths to the coast, where Otto had to swim out to sea to be rescued by a nearby Byzantine warship.

Cavalry battles on crusade

As seen in Chapter 3, western armies fighting in the eastern Mediterranean were, for the most part, very similar in composition to those in Europe, and included mounted forces alongside infantry and missile troops. By contrast, light cavalry equipped with bows comprised both the numerically and tactically dominant element in the armies of their Turkish, Arab, Kurdish, and Egyptian opponents. Consequently, it was necessary for the crusaders and the Latin inhabitants of the crusader states to develop tactics for cavalry battles that allowed them to maximize the advantages provided by their own heavily equipped horsemen, and to blunt the advantages of their adversaries. In general, western commanders used tactics similar to those employed by Henry I against the Hungarians at Riade, which was to hold their cavalry in reserve until they could be deployed for a short charge against a massed force of the enemy that was deployed in such a way that it was difficult for them to disengage and escape. In this manner, the enemy's ability to lose multiple volleys of arrows would be limited, as would their ability to escape before the western horsemen were able to close in on them.

In the Battle of Arsuf, noted earlier, King Richard of England did not originally plan to commit his forces in battle against Saladin while marching toward Jaffa. However, the English king's hand was forced by an unauthorized charge by the Hospitaller cavalry unit that was deployed at the rear of the crusader marching column. Rather than leave the Hospitallers to the fate that they deserved because of their violation of orders, King Richard ordered a halt and began a general engagement against the Muslims. In the course of the battle, Richard consistently employed tactics that allowed him to maximize the effectiveness of his heavy cavalry. Saladin, for his part, was unable to overcome the topographical situation whereby the Muslim forces were essentially pinned between the crusader army and the forest of Arsuf. The forest initially concealed Saladin's army and made possible an ambush. However, because Richard was able to anticipate this attack and placed his men in a strong defensive position, the narrow stretch of land now was problematic for Saladin's forces because they had insufficient room to manoeuvre and thus avoid direct physical contact with the enemy's heavy cavalry.

As soon as the Hospitallers launched their attack against the mass of Saladin's light cavalry at the rear of the crusader column, Richard ordered all of his mounted forces to reinforce this attack. However, once the Muslim forces succeeded in extricating themselves from close-order combat, Richard ordered his cavalry to withdraw behind the infantry and cavalry units that the English king had kept in reserve. The Muslim forces along the centre of their line, which had not been involved in the first phase of the attack, then closed in to participate in the battle. As they came in close to the crusader lines to launch their arrows, Richard ordered his mounted troops to undertake a second charge against the enemy flank. This attack again succeeded in bringing the Muslim light cavalry into close-order combat in which Saladin's troops suffered significant casualties. The Muslim cavalry forces once more extricated themselves from the *mêlée* and retreated, but Richard, who led his men in this attack, refused to pursue, and again withdrew his heavy cavalry to the protection of his infantry and archers. The Muslims then renewed their attack for a third and final time, and Richard once more dispatched his heavy cavalry in a charge as soon as the Muslim horsemen were in range. This final charge broke the will of the Muslim forces, which scattered and did not regroup. However, rather than pursue them, Richard once more withdrew his cavalry towards the infantry lines, and avoided making his men vulnerable to the kind of counter-attack that destroyed Otto II's army at Cap Colona. Having defeated Saladin's army, Richard continued his march towards Jaffa, the port of Jerusalem, which was his primary objective.

Richard's tactical decisions about the deployment of his heavy cavalry at Arsuf were based on hard-learned lessons by western commanders in numerous battles against the Muslims over the previous century of warfare. In particular, Richard obtained detailed information from both the Templars and Hospitallers, who had long experience of cavalry warfare against the Muslims. A similar sharing of tactical knowledge between experienced easterners and newly arrived westerners can be seen at the Battle of Dorylaeum (1–2 July 1097) during the First Crusade. In this encounter, Christian forces under the command of Bohemond of Taranto and Duke Robert of Normandy faced the army of Kilij Arslan, the sultan of the Rum, in western Asia Minor (1092–1107).

Following their capture of the fortress city of Nicaea in June, the crusader army divided into two parts for the march towards the fortress city of Dorylaeum, which was located at the junction of several military highways in western Asia Minor. The vanguard of the crusader army under the command of Bohemond and Duke Robert marched at night in order to protect their men from the scorching summer heat, and arrived in the early morning hours in a valley near Dorylaeum, which provided a source for fresh water. They stopped here for the day and dispatched a cavalry force under the command of Tancred, Bohemond's nephew, to reconnoitre the area.

Tancred discovered that Kilij Arslan's force was in the immediate vicinity, and so the crusaders quickly established a fortified perimeter for their camp, utilizing their wagons and other vehicles. The crusaders then spent the remainder of the day resting and improving the initial improvised fortifications by adding an earth and timber palisade. Towards dusk, the Muslims advanced across a small river that ran through the valley at Dorylaeum, and approached the crusader camp, which they assaulted with missile weapons. Bohemond and Duke Robert then sought the advice of the Byzantine general Tatikios, who had been dispatched by Emperor Alexios to accompany the crusader vanguard because of his long experience of fighting against the Turks in Asia Minor. After consulting with Tatikios, Bohemond and Robert decided on an attack which was intended to dislodge the Muslim forces from their positions near to the crusader camp and protect their men from a nearly constant barrage of arrows. Two columns of heavily armed cavalry were formed up under the command of Bohemond and Robert, and they advanced out from the camp. They were followed by a dense formation of infantry equipped with spears, who were intended to provide protection to the horsemen if they were forced to retreat.

Once all of the men were in position, Bohemond and Robert led them in a two-pronged attack against the Muslims and had significant initial success, killing many of the enemy horsemen in hand-to-hand combat. However, the great numerical superiority of Kilij Arslan's mounted forces, and especially their ability to rain arrows on the westerners from a distance, eventually turned the tide, and the crusader cavalry was forced to retreat. The foot soldiers were able to cover this retreat. However, due to a lack of training, there was some confusion as the mounted forces attempted to withdraw through the phalanx. Not all of the foot soldiers knew where they should go in order to allow the mounted troops to pass through their formation. As a result of this confusion, the Muslims were able to press home their attack and kill a number of the Christian foot soldiers and cavalry. Nevertheless, in the end the entire crusader force was able to withdraw back into the fortified encampment. The deployment of the cavalry with an infantry force as a reserve indicates that Bohemond and Duke Robert understood the tactical difficulties of combatting light cavalry with heavier mounted forces that lacked a missile capacity.

Commanders in battle

As several of the previously discussed examples indicate, medieval military commanders had to make the choice about where they would be stationed on the battlefield, and whether they would put themselves in a position where they would likely face the need to engage in combat directly. Roman military tradition – with which, as we will see in the next chapter, many medieval commanders were quite familiar – offered two very different models for the proper role of the military commander. The Roman commander Scipio Africanus, who defeated Hannibal at the Battle of Zama (202 BC), is famously reported by the Roman general and author Frontinus to have said 'my mother bore me as a general not a warrior'.

By this, Scipio meant that his task was to command men in battle, not to fight himself. On the other hand, Julius Caesar presented himself as frequently leading from the front in his account of his conquest of Gaul, even going so far as to wear a conspicuous red cloak so as to hide the blood from any wounds he might suffer in battle.

For the most part, medieval military commanders, and particularly those of very high rank, followed the model of Scipio Africanus rather than that of Caesar. In the immediate post-Roman world, kings such as Clovis and his descendants in the Merovingian dynasty very rarely placed themselves in danger on the battlefield, although many of them were assassinated. Similarly, Charlemagne does not appear to have participated directly in any battle during the entire course of his reign. The same appears to be true of his descendants, as well, although the authors of contemporary narrative texts did sometimes try to create a sense of the direct participation in battle by one or another Carolingian king or emperor. For example, the erstwhile courtier Ermoldus, who sought reinstatement at court by Louis the Pious, presents the then king of Aquitaine hurling his spear at the walls of the city of Barcelona during the siege of 801–802. Even here, however, there is no indication that the Carolingian ruler was involved in combat. None of the Ottonian, Salian, or Staufen rulers of the East Frankish and subsequently German kingdom led their men into battle, and none of them were ever killed in battle. Indeed, one of the consistent criticisms of King Henry IV by his political enemies is that he was always among the first to flee from the numerous battlefields where he had deployed troops.

When we consider the Anglo-Norman and French rulers, we see a very similar pattern in which kings led armies to the battlefield but did not engage directly in combat. Henry I of England, whose victory at Tinchebrai was discussed previously, positioned himself in the second battle line of his army rather than the first. His grandson Henry II did not engage in personal combat, nor did the latter's son John, grandson Henry III, or great-grandson Edward I, with the exception of the Battle of Evesham (1265) while Edward was still a prince. The rulers of the Capetian dynasty similarly avoided putting themselves in immediate risk in battle.

There are, however, counterexamples that should be considered. William the Conqueror famously had multiple horses killed under him as he participated in an assault on the Anglo-Saxon forces atop the hill at Senlac. In this case, however, it is clear that William only joined in the assault after his initial attacks had failed and had to provide a boost to the morale of his men. Richard Lionheart also led the counterattacks against Saladin's mounted forces at the Battle of Arsuf, discussed previously, at least once, and perhaps twice. In this case, it is clear that the English king was seeking to avoid the problem of having his mounted troops engage in pursuit of the fleeing Muslims and believed that exercising command and control required his personal presence.

Overall, the task of the military commander was to direct his forces in battle, maintain open communications with his subordinate commanders, and understand how the overall course of the battle was developing. A commander directly engaged in combat lost his ability to direct the army as a whole. This was particularly problematic in those situations when large armies were engaged in fighting over a large area. The anomalous situation pertaining in early medieval England, where numerous Anglo-Saxon kings were killed in battle, can be explained, in part, by the fact that they were commanding relatively small armies that were fighting within a relatively small area, so that maintaining communications was not of central importance. In the context of major battles between large armies commanded by powerful rulers, the active decision by a military commander to take part in fighting, as contrasted with the fighting coming to him unexpectedly, usually was based on a pressing need that outweighed the general's normal obligations. In short, Scipio's dictum generally won the day in medieval Europe. Nevertheless, Caesar's brash style of command, based upon his own overriding goal of gaining political power, also had its place, however rare, in medieval warfare.

Sieges

Some elements of combat in the course of a siege were largely the same as battles in the field. This is particularly the case when forces sallied from the besieged stronghold. This type of combat is illuminated by events at the siege of the fortress city of Regensburg in 954. Here, the defenders launched a two-pronged attack against the army of King Otto I of Germany, which was positioned in a fortified camp in front of the west gate of the city. The mounted forces of the defenders burst out of the gate in a diversionary attack, while the majority of the men from Regensburg were loaded onto boats for an amphibious assault against Otto I's encampment that was located along the Danube River. Unfortunately for the defenders of Regensburg, Otto I was aware of their intentions. He deployed his mounted forces to screen his camp, and moved his foot soldiers to face the river. The foot soldiers were, there-fore, in position to thwart the amphibious landing undertaken by Regensburg's defenders, and inflict numerous casualties on them. The king's mounted troops similarly emerged victorious in their engagement, and the city subsequently surrendered.

Impact of artillery

Although there were some similarities to battles between armies in the field, combat dur-ing sieges also differed significantly in a number of ways. As seen in Chapter 5, many sieges involved starving the enemy into submission, with little actual combat between the two sides. However, even when the soldiers did not engage directly in hand-to-hand fighting, missile weapons, and particularly artillery, played an important role in sieges. A number of sieges during the pre-crusade era were decided, at least in part, when the artillery of the attackers broke the will of the defenders to resist further. This was the case, for example, during Otto I's siege of Rome in 968, when after just a few days of bombardment, the citi-zens of the Eternal City were convinced to surrender.

As engineers designed ever more powerful engines, including trebuchets during the twelfth century and gunpowder artillery during the fourteenth, artillery came to play an increasingly important role in deciding the outcome of sieges. For example, in his discussion of the siege in 1137 of the castle of Montferrand by Imad ad-Din Zengi, the Turkish atabeg of Mosul (1127–1146), Bishop William of Tyre (died 1186) describes the terror induced in the defenders by the Muslim commander's use of trebuchets. These counter-weight traction engines hurled large stone blocks over the walls of the castle. The projectiles crashed down on top of buildings, destroying them and crushing the people inside. In face of this savage bombardment, the large garrison, which very likely could have repulsed an effort to storm the walls, quickly negotiated surrender terms, despite having ample provisions to endure a lengthy investment.

As the technology for trebuchets made its way to Europe, western military command-ers eagerly deployed these engines. One of the first westerners to grasp the psychological value of the trebuchet for defeating the will of defenders was Simon de Montfort, who led the northern French crusading effort in the region of Occitania in southern France. This effort, called the Albigensian Crusade, had the putative goal of ridding the region of the heretical Cathars. During the period 1209–1218, Simon's armies carried out scores of sieges of castles and fortified cities, utilizing the newly introduced trebuchets, and had remarkable success in reducing these strongholds. In some cases, Simon's troops merely had to assemble their trebuchets, which had been carried in pieces in wagons, in front of the stronghold to convince the defenders to surrender. It is therefore ironic that Simon himself was killed by a stone cast by an engine emplaced on the walls of the city of Toulouse, which he was besieging in 1218.

As discussed in Chapter 5, the trebuchet was first introduced to England in 1216 during the invasion by the future King Louis VIII of France. In 1225, King Henry III of England invited an artillery engineer named Jordan, with the illuminating nickname of the 'Trebuchet Maker', to construct a large number of these engines for the royal government. By the late 1220s, trebuchets were the dominant type of stone-throwing artillery in the royal arsenal. Henry III's son, Edward I, used these engines during his wars in Wales in the 1270s and 1280s. However, Edward I's most famous deployment of trebuchets, and the clearest example of the psychological impact that these weapons could have on defenders, occurred during the siege of Stirling castle in 1304.

During the course of a four-month siege from April–July, the English army bombarded the defenders with stones cast by at least a dozen trebuchets. These engines did not succeed in compelling the Scottish garrison to surrender. However, at the beginning of the siege, Edward authorized the construction of a massive new trebuchet, which the administrative documents make clear was much larger than any of the others currently in the royal arsenal. One of the king's chief military engineers named James of St. George (died 1309) began construction in April, and by mid-July, the new engine, christened Warwolf, was ready for action. When he saw the massive siege engine was ready for operation, the Scottish commander requested surrender terms. However, Edward would not allow the surrender until he had tested out his new trebuchet, which hurled stones weighing some 130 kilograms. A contemporary chronicler claimed that when these stones struck Stirling castle, they took down sections of the curtain wall. It was only after he had had a chance to test out his new 'super weapon' that King Edward permitted the Scots to surrender.

Gunpowder artillery sometimes had an equally powerful psychological effect on defenders. The military historian Kelly DeVries has shown that by the last quarter of the fourteenth century, gunpowder weapons not only had the capacity to inflict considerable physical damage on the defences of castles and fortress cities, but also terrified the defenders. In his account of the siege of the castle of Odruik in 1377 by Duke Philip the Bold of Burgundy (1363–1404), for example, Froissart, the famed though highly romantic historian of the Hundred Years' War, stressed that once the defenders saw the strength of the Burgundian artillery, they surrendered rather than fight. Froissart also recorded that during the siege of Oudenaarde by the city militia of Ghent, it was the artillery of the attackers that decided the outcome. The projectiles fired by the Ghentenaars not only broke down sections of the wall of Oudenaarde, but also flew over the walls and set fires within the city. The inhabitants compelled Louis de Male, the count of Flanders, who was leading the defence of the Oudenaarde, to surrender before everything within the walls was consumed by fire.

Storming the walls

Artillery often proved to be a valuable tool in sieges; however, in many cases, military commanders calculated that they had to storm the walls of a fortress in order to secure its capture. These attacks differed from battles in the field in a number of significant ways.

First, the men assaulting the walls often were subject at a considerable distance to withering attacks from troops stationed atop the walls who were equipped with defensive artillery and hand-held missile weapons such as bows and crossbows. At closer range, stones, boiling oil, and even scalding water were dropped from the heights upon those attempting to scale the walls. The sources suggest men attacking fortifications faced significantly greater barrages of missile weapons than was the case for soldiers on the tactical offensive in battles in the field between western armies. This was likely due to the more confined area in which the attackers were concentrated and the larger number of defenders who were equipped with missile weapons. An additional advantage for defenders of fortifications was that men stationed atop the walls of strongholds had better angles of fire and could achieve greater ranges than opposing troops, who were deployed at ground level.

The open fields that surrounded many strongholds were intended by the defenders to be killing grounds. At a distance of 400 metres from the walls, the advancing soldiers came into range of stone-throwing and spear-casting engines. Once the advancing troops were within 200 metres, archers and crossbowmen were able to pick out their targets. Even if the defenders were not trained, their commanders could direct barrages of arrows and bolts that fell like showers of hail on the attackers. Within the last few dozen metres of the wall, the assaulting troops came into range of defenders equipped with spears, as well as stones and anything else that could be hurled from the walls. Attackers without effective counter-measures against these missile attacks could expect to suffer casualties amounting to 40 per cent of the entire force by the time they reached the base of the wall.

In order to protect themselves from the hail of enemy missiles, military commanders used a military formation that was well-known from the Roman army and was recorded in a number of historical works, as well as military manuals – namely the *testudo*, which was noted earlier in this chapter with respect to infantry phalanxes on the battlefield. Liudprand of Cremona notes, for example, that when the East Frankish king, Arnulf of Carinthia, assaulted the walls of Rome in 896, his troops advanced against the walls of the city unit by unit with each group gaining protection not only from their shields, which they held above their heads, but also from specially constructed wicker screens (*crates*). Similarly, during his siege of the fortress city of Senlis in 949, Duke Conrad the Red of Lotharingia (945–953) ordered his troops to use the *testudo* formation, and hold up their shields in an overlapping pattern to protect themselves from the spears and arrows launched by the defenders. Moreover, it was not only troops from the *Regnum Francorum* who were accustomed to using the *testudo* when assaulting the walls of a fortress. When the Vikings attacked Paris in 885, they also advanced with 'painted shields held up above to form a life-preserving vault', in the evocative phrase of the eyewitness Abbo of St.-Germain-des-Prés. Both the shields and the large wicker screens described by these early medieval authors are a standard element of assaults on walls throughout the medieval period. In addition to narrative sources, which describe their use, the purchase of these items is recorded in numerous financial accounts, such as those for Edward I's previously mentioned siege of Stirling castle.

The soldiers advancing in formation toward the walls, although providing a large target for the defenders, at least had the benefit of being able to protect themselves. By contrast, the men who were given the responsibility of carrying assault ladders to the base of the walls were exceptionally vulnerable during the entire journey across the 'killing field'. Assault ladders often weighed hundreds of kilograms and were carried by teams of 12–16 men who had to step or jog in unison in order to make effective forward progress. Obviously, these men were not in a position to defend themselves against incoming arrows, javelins, and stones, and had to rely on the limited protection that could be provided by men running alongside them with shields. If several men in a ladder-carrying party were killed or wounded, it was necessary to insert replacements who also were trained in the proper techniques for carrying a heavy ladder.

Once the assault ladders were set in place at the bottom of the wall of a stronghold, the soldiers had to climb up holding weapons or a shield in one hand, as the defenders attacked them with missile weapons from close range. The defenders also tried to knock the ladders backwards off the wall with long pole devices with hooks at the end, which were pushed against the top of the ladder until the 'tipping point' was reached. The task of climbing these ladders must have been exceptionally daunting for even the bravest of men. Modern firefighters receive extensive physical and psychological training to undertake this task, and they do not have to worry about slings, arrows, and javelins, much less boiling pots of oil, as they make their ascent, only fire, which also was faced by medieval soldiers. It must have been that much worse for medieval fighting men, most of whom never had any cause to climb a tall ladder under normal circumstances in the course of their daily lives. Consequently, it is obvious that men who were selected to climb these ladders required considerable training.

When they reached the top of the wall, the attackers faced the most dangerous situation of all, as one or two men bore the assault of all of the defenders who could immediately converge on the point of attack. Ralph of Caen describes the fate of the first man up the ladder during the siege of Jerusalem in July 1099:

> a young man came forward. He was worthy of rejoicing if fate favoured him and even worthier of being mourned if fate cast a jealous eye upon him. He was seen as lucky by every class from lowest to highest. But he was unlucky in this final task. For as he reached the top of the wall with his left hand, the sword of an adversary fell upon him. He who had climbed up quickly using both hands was hardly able to climb back down bereft of his sword and hand.

These dangers were diffused, to a certain extent, when armies attacked with numerous assault ladders at the same time, often at different points along the wall, thereby preventing the defenders from concentrating all of their strength in one place. In addition, the use of storming towers, discussed in Chapter 5, with drawbridges that allowed men to charge straight onto the wall, gave attackers a better chance at success. Finally, missile troops on the attacking side also had an important role in forcing the defenders to take cover rather than to engage with the men storming the parapets of the walls.

Fighting within the walls

Once the attackers were within the walls of the city or stronghold, it became very difficult for most medieval commanders to retain command and control over their troops. Fighting no longer was confined to soldiers, but rather now involved the entire population of the city or fortification. The decision by the defenders to resist meant that they were legally – insofar as we may speak of the then unwritten 'laws of war' – subject to any reprisals that the commander of the attacking forces thought appropriate, and that they had no right to mercy. Moreover, even if the commander of the attacking forces wished to spare non-combatants or even maintain the infrastructure of the city for future use, the confused and chaotic nature of house-to-house fighting made saving anything very difficult.

The chaotic situation that resulted from urban combat is illuminated by the early eleventh-century chronicler Wipo (died 1048). In his discussion of a battle within the walls of Ravenna between the forces of King Conrad II of Germany (1024–1039) and the populace of the city, Wipo wrote:

> One day the wretched Ravennese provoked a struggle with the army of the King, and, trusting in their great number, they strove to expel the army from the city. Taking advantage of the narrowness of a certain gate, they prohibited those who were outside the walls from succouring those within. Once the rebellion had been stirred up, the battle began to grow serious in all quarters. Some assailed those billeted in their houses; others fought in the streets, still others obstructed the gates. Many from the walls, many from the high turrets, were guilty of a dastardly kind of battle, with stones and sharpened stakes. On the other side, the German resisted with arms and ingenuity, and, pairing off detachments, beset the Ravennese from the front and from the rear. Making their way toward each other with raging swords, they left them who were between them dead, wounded or fleeing.

This battle took place after Conrad had already occupied Ravenna peacefully, but because the citizens had been aroused by the bad behaviour of the German troops, the former revolted.

Ralph of Caen's description of the capture of the city of Ma'arra by the forces of the First Crusade in 1098 paints a very similar picture:

> They undermined Ma'arra, which was now surrounded by troops. Arrows flew over Ma'arra, stones struck the walls, and mines made them tremble. There was noise everywhere and assaults. Everywhere there were blows. The townsmen gave back equal to what they received. Their stone throwers reverberated. From far off they shot javelins and from up close they dropped ploughshares and marble statutes. They caused many wounds and suffered many as well. Some died as others lived, some sickened while others remained healthy, some weakened while others remained strong. It was the aim of the townsmen to disrupt the siege, which had begun and was only half completed, to bring an end to this great labour. They strove to overcome glory, and to overcome fortune through their patience. But as more and more blows of the hammer on an anvil, or strikes on the threshing floor, the walls were overcome by an inexhaustible supply of stones. The tower crumbled, the wall collapsed, the bastions fell away. Thus, both the ruins and the walls offered and raised up a path.

Ralph then turns in some detail to the situation within the walls:

> There was sorrow for the supporters of Mohamed and joy for the supporters of Christ. Certainly all things now prospered for one side and everything, even their hopes, turned against the other. However, even when the way was open, there was no delay in finding a defender. The city rose up to resist. They placed whatever strength they had to oppose those coming in. But while the struggle went on, one side grew stronger and the other weaker. This side was fervent and that side saw its defence weaken. The shields of the Christians rang less and less now when but a short time earlier they had almost drooped under a hail of stones. Therefore, the attackers placed the ladders against the wall. A climber topped the tower and jumped into the captured city. When this sound was heard and he was seen running back and forth, the morale of the defenders was broken. Their feet sought refuge in the shadows and they hoped to live by throwing down their

arms. But, once the city was captured, some of our men spent their time killing while others sought riches. Some sought out victims and others seized booty. With this victory in hand, it was possible to remember more joyfully the achievements of their harsh labours. And I, who was once a hunter, see a crowd of hunters joyful and yet worn thin from exhaustion of a labour that lasted from the last hour of the previous night to the third hour of the following day.

Battle at sea

Individual ships and fleets played an important role in military operations from the late Roman period up through the end of the Middle Ages, and certainly beyond. However, as seen in Chapter 5, this role predominantly involved the transportation of men and supplies. Ship-to-ship encounters, particularly those involving pirates and merchant vessels, were a fact of life throughout the medieval millennium. However, battles between fleets at sea were much less common even than those between armies in the field. The naval engagements between the fleets of the Byzantine Empire and their Avar and Arab opponents in the seventh and early eighth centuries were notable exceptions during the early medieval period. It is noteworthy that these fleet actions all took place in the context of sieges of the East Roman capital of Constantinople, where the Byzantine fleet acted as a 'wooden wall' greatly aided by Greek fire, protecting the great city from being encircled and cut off from supplies and military support from the sea.

In the pre-crusade period, when oared ships of a variety of types provided the great majority of all warships in both the Mediterranean and in the northern seas, those seeking battle at sea faced largely insurmountable challenges. The large crews of oared vessels, such as the Byzantine dromon and western galleys, required larger quantities of fresh water than could be carried on board for lengthy journeys. A typical warship could carry no more than 3–4 days' supply. Fleets had to hug the coast where they could gain access to fresh water supplies on a regular basis. The need for water also meant that a fleet could only advance along the coast if there were secure locations for taking on additional fresh water. As a consequence, fleets of warships rarely were used to secure even a coastal base deep in enemy-held territory. Instead, as was the case at Constantinople, the Avars and Arabs deployed their fleets as adjuncts to land-based campaigns, just as the Byzantines deployed their fleet in support of the soldiers who were defending the city.

There is some evidence to suggest that early medieval rulers considered the possibility of deploying fleets of warships against opposing fleets. In the early ninth century, for example, Charlemagne ordered the construction of a fleet of purpose-built warships, perhaps of the galley type, as part of a broader system of maritime defence against the emerging Viking threat. An important part of this defensive system was the establishment of a large number of signal stations, including at least one originally a Roman lighthouse, which could transmit information quickly up and down the coast of the English Channel and North Sea to alert local commanders that a Viking fleet had been sighted, or even that an attack had taken place. As part of this system, each royal estate was required to keep materials on hand to set up signal fires, including both dry wood and accelerants such as oil.

With this information in hand, the commanders of the Carolingian naval squadrons had the opportunity to catch the Viking fleets close to shore, or perhaps trap them by taking up position between the Viking ships and the open sea. However, there are no contemporary reports of naval battles between Carolingian and Viking fleets, and consequently no information about what types of tactics were employed by the two sides. Although it is very unlikely that the Carolingians planned to seek out and engage the Vikings at sea or even in the estuary of a river, Frankish warships were positioned to trap the slower-moving knarrs that the enemy used to carry booty and slaves, and thereby strip the raiders of their profits and rescue captured Christians. This was a defence in depth on water and, therefore, an analogue of the defensive systems used on land to prevent raiders from escaping with loot and prisoners.

Alfred the Great of Wessex and his successors also constructed a fleet of purpose-built warships during the late ninth and early tenth centuries to confront the Viking fleets that were raiding the coasts of England, as well as transporting troops for operations inland. In his discussion of this construction programme, Alfred's court biographer Asser suggests that the Anglo-Saxon warships were significantly larger than the contemporary Viking ships, which were intended primarily as troop transports rather than as combat vessels. The soldiers who were transported in this manner doubled as rowers. A number of scholars have suggested that the larger Anglo-Saxon ships, therefore, had the capability of running down the smaller Vikings vessels and smashing their oars, thereby rendering them immobile. However, victory in such a battle ultimately would have turned on combat between the crews, rather than the sinking of the enemy ship, except perhaps by setting it on fire, by using arrows that had been dipped in pitch and then set ablaze.

In contrast to the Carolingians, there are some indications that Anglo-Saxon fleets may have met Viking fleets in battles at sea in 851, 875, and again in 882. However, it is not clear how the Anglo-Saxons managed to find Viking fleets in the great expanse of water between Scandinavia and England. It is probable that the Anglo-Saxon fleets stayed close to shore at the likely landing points for an invasion fleet and waited there in ambush. As noted in Chapter 5, ramming did not play an important role in naval combat during the early medieval period in either the northern or southern seas because improvements to naval architecture had made it difficult to stave in the sides of ships. Northern ships had the added defensive advantage of being constructed of oak, which was even denser than the wood types employed in the construction of ships in the Mediterranean.

Naval combat in the crusading age and Hundred Years' War

Among the earliest recorded fleet actions in the northern seas was a battle between King Harald Hardrada (1046–1066) of Norway and King Sweyn II (1047–1074) of Denmark in 1062, which is recounted by the Icelandic poet Snorri Sturluson (died 1241). Snorri's account was composed in the thirteenth century and, therefore, often is discounted by historians as providing an accurate depiction of combat in the earlier period. However, Snorri does likely provide insights about contemporary naval combat in the thirteenth century because of his need to maintain rhetorical plausibility. Moreover, because the types of warships used by the Scandinavian kings in the second half of the eleventh century were similar to the types used by their successors in the thirteenth, there is good reason to believe that the tactics were similar, as well.

According to Snorri, the two Scandinavian kings arranged their ships in opposing lines, with the king's own ships in the centre. The best captains in each fleet were placed at the ends of the lines to help keep the ships in order. Snorri then recorded that the ships in the middle of the two lines were connected to each other with ropes, while the ships at the ends of the line remained free. The two lines advanced against each other, propelled by their oars, which suggests that the ships in the centre were connected loosely enough to permit the rowers to operate. The purpose of connecting the ships with ropes was to keep the ships close together in rough seas, and allow the commander to concentrate the maximum number of archers and other missile troops, who were stationed on the forecastles of the ships, against his opponents. Combat took place initially with missile weapons, and then hand-to-hand, with most of the fighting concentrated on the prows of the ships.

The anonymous author of the early thirteenth century *Journey of the Pilgrims*, which focuses on the events in the Holy Land following Saladin's victory at Hattin in 1187, provides a similar image of combat at sea in a detailed description of a naval battle between western crusaders and Saladin's fleet off the coast of the city of Acre in 1190. According to the anonymous author of the *Journey*, once it became clear that Saladin's fleet of fifty galleys was coming out of the protected harbour at Acre to fight, the western galleys withdrew out to sea so that they could form up for battle without danger of running aground. The crusader ships were deployed in a crescent formation, with the most powerful ships at the ends of the line, so that if the Muslims attacked the centre of the formation the ships on the ends of the Christian line could attack them from the flank. The author specifically mentions that this tactic was used by the Romans, and is an example of a double envelopment in naval warfare.

Just as was the case in the battle described by Snorri Sturluson, the fleet action at Acre began with an exchange of missiles between the two sides. Once the ships closed, the men engaged in hand-to-hand combat. The goal on each side was to board the enemy ship and take control of it. The anonymous author mentions that the Muslims used incendiary devices, which he called Greek fire, and managed to burn several of the crusader ships. However, the crusaders also were able to capture several of the Muslim ships. In the end, the Muslim fleet was forced to withdraw back into the harbour at Acre. The Muslims failed either to scatter or defeat the crusader fleet, and thereby lift the blockade of the city that prevented additional men and supplies to enter the besieged fortress.

The battle at Acre involved galleys on both sides, which meant that the ships, by and large, were evenly matched in terms of size and capability. By contrast, the anonymous author of the *Journey* provides a vivid description of the difficulty faced by the crews of galleys when they sought to engage a sailing ship with a high freeboard. As King Richard of England was sailing with a squadron of galleys from Cyprus to join the crusader siege of Acre in 1190, he caught sight of a very large, three-masted sailing ship which was attempting to enter the port of Acre. When it became clear that this was a Muslim ship, Richard ordered his galleys to attack. The lower and faster oared vessels surrounded the sailing ship but, according to the anonymous author, they could not find any way to attack it. At the same time, the Muslim crew used their bows and crossbows to deadly effect against the Christians.

According to the chronicler, in an effort to get on board the Muslim ship, a number of the Christian sailors jumped into the sea, and swam over to the sailing vessel, and scaled the sides using the cables that held the rudder in place. However, this assault was unsuccessful. In a last desperate attempt to take the Muslim ship, King Richard ordered his galleys to ram the ship along its sides with their prows. The more manoeuvrable Christian ships withdrew a suitable distance, and then the rowers drove their ships as rapidly as possible into the sailing ship on both its sides, and managed to break holes in its timbers. Richard's ships did not possess sub-surface rams to bear the brunt of the force engendered by the crash, so this manoeuvre was very dangerous both to the attackers as well as to the defenders. As the Muslim ship began to take on water, the Muslims abandoned ship. Most of them either drowned or were killed by Richard's men. However, the English did take as prisoners a number of skilled artisans, who knew how to construct siege engines.

Sailing ships and galley tactics

As the battle between King Richard's galleys and the Muslim ship outside the port of Acre in 1190 illustrates, the development of much larger, high-freeboard sailing ships over the course of the twelfth century had important implications for the deployment of low-lying, oared warships in naval combat. By the late twelfth century, it had become common to deploy mixed fleets of galleys and sailing vessels with a high freeboard, which gave naval commanders tactical flexibility in deploying their ships. However, when one side in a conflict enjoyed a monopoly on large sailing ships, this offered an exceptional advantage.

During the thirteenth century, German crusaders operating against Slavic peoples living along the eastern shore of the Baltic Sea enjoyed complete naval superiority because the Christians had cogs, which towered over the small-oared ships available to their opponents. The Teutonic Knights, as well as the kings of Denmark, used cogs to transport large numbers of troops, as well as equipment and supplies, including fresh water when necessary, to naval bases along the Baltic coast. Each of these cogs carried with it several smaller oared vessels, so that when the crusader fleet came into contact with Slavic naval forces, the oared ships were deployed against them. The cogs advanced behind, if the wind permitted, and served as mobile fortresses with large numbers of crossbowmen, archers, and even stone- and spear-casting engines providing missile support to the smaller crusader ships. In addition to their role in combat, the cogs in the Baltic also were used to blockade ports. The great size of these ships made it possible to store sufficient supplies, including water, to stay at sea for many weeks, and even months.

In most regions of Europe, the naval forces of competing powers were more evenly matched than was the case in the Baltic. In the wars between the French and English, as well as their allies, from the early thirteenth to the mid-fifteenth century, it was common to find both sailing ships and galleys on both sides. In most cases, however, fleets still did not meet in the open sea. Rather, most engagements took place within close proximity to the coast, and very frequently near a port. The main reason was that without modern navigation, communications, and tracking technology, it was exceptionally difficult to determine where an enemy fleet would be at sea. In addition, even with actionable intelligence, contrary winds and rough seas made it difficult to move a fleet to a specific place at a specific time. Consequently, fleet actions usually took place when one commander was able to position his fleet near the coast where he knew the enemy would likely be, or had to go.

This was the situation, for example, in August 1217 when a fleet departed from the port of Calais in the French kingdom to bring supplies and reinforcements to Prince Louis of France who, as discussed earlier, had invaded England the previous year. The English fleet, which was composed largely of converted merchant ships from the Cinque Ports mentioned in Chapter 3, was positioned in the harbour at Sandwich, some 60 kilometres as the crow flies northeast of Calais. Both fleets included large sailing ships and smaller oared and sailing vessels, with twenty support ships on the English side, and as many as seventy on the French side. In order to reach the Thames estuary and then move upriver to London to reach the army of Prince Louis, the French fleet had to sail past Sandwich. Hubert de Burgh (died 1243), the commander of the English fleet, recognizing this reality, kept his fleet in port until the French had sailed past, thereby ensuring that he would not be caught with his fleet half in and half out of the harbour. After the French had made their way beyond Sandwich, Hubert then deployed the English fleet so that his ships had the wind behind them. When the French commander realized that the English were behind him, he was compelled to turn about to face the threat.

As the two fleets closed in on each other, the English archers enjoyed a great advantage over their French counterparts because the wind was at their backs, and gave added range to their missile weapons and conversely hindered the French archers. The English inflicted very heavy casualties before the French could even reach the English fleet with their bows. One contemporary chronicler even claims that the English opened up pots of lime dust, which was carried by the wind to the French fleet and burned the eyes of the French sailors and fighting men. Once the fleets closed with each other, several English ships surrounded the French flagship, called *The Great Ship of Bayonne*, which was commanded by the famous pirate Eustace the Monk. The English soldiers and sailors then boarded the *Bayonne* and succeeded in capturing her. At this point, the French fleet withdrew, and most of the large ships, carrying troops and supplies, escaped. However, the English captured more than fifty of the smaller vessels. Eustace was then executed by the English for piracy and treason.

Although the ships involved in the initial phase of the sea battle off the coast of Sandwich were all sailing vessels, it is clear that the commanders used the same basic tactics as were used in battles between fleets composed exclusively of galleys. The opposing lines of ships exchanged various types of missiles at long range, and then sought to overwhelm the opposing crews in hand-to-hand combat. The offensive strength of the fleet lay in its fighting men, including archers, crossbowmen, and men at arms, rather than in the ships themselves. Sailing ships with a high freeboard did offer their crews significant advantages in battle over men stationed on galleys that rode much lower in the water. Notably, missile troops and heavily armed fighting men retained their central role in naval battles during the course of the remainder of the medieval period.

The dominance of what might be thought of as a land battle at sea is illustrated very clearly by the most famous naval battle of the Hundred Years' War, which was fought at Sluys on 24 June 1340. King Philip VI of France (1328–1350) had prepared a large fleet during the spring of 1340, and it was in anchorage in the calm waters outside the port of Sluys. French administrative records put the size of the French fleet at somewhat more than 200 vessels, including large sailing ships, galleys, and numerous smaller support craft. A fleet of this size could not be hidden from spies, and King Edward III of England was fully informed about both the mobilization of the French fleet and its location. In preparation for landing a large army in Flanders, King Edward also had mobilized a substantial fleet, which consisted of merchant ships that were converted for military use by the addition of fighting platforms for the use of crossbowmen and archers. The English king then loaded these ships, most of which were cogs, with large numbers of archers and heavily armed foot soldiers.

The English fleet set sail from the port of Ipswich, located some 120 kilometres west-northwest of Sluys as the crow flies, on 22 June, and came into sight of Sluys the following day. On the evening of 23 June, Edward sent out a scouting party in small, oared vessels to learn the disposition of the French fleet. They reported back to the king that the French were at anchor and chained together in three tightly compressed lines. On the morning of 24 June, Edward manoeuvred his fleet so that the ships approached the French with the wind at their backs. According to the contemporary chronicler Froissart, King Edward used the greater mobility of his fleet to dispatch groups of three of his ships against individual target ships in the French fleet. Each of these three-ship English squadrons included two that were filled with archers and a third that carried a large unit of heavily armed troops. In each of the individual actions within the battle, two English ships with archers pulled alongside a French ship, and poured arrows onto the men on the decks. When the French had suffered significant casualties, the English ship filled with foot soldiers came alongside and the English troops boarded the French vessel, killing or capturing the remaining crew and defenders. The battle did not go entirely the English way, and several English vessels also were captured. However, after a battle that continued throughout the day on 24 June and into the night and the next morning, the English emerged victorious and captured or destroyed almost the entire French fleet.

Training

No child is born knowing how to use a sword or advance in either column or line against an enemy force. Just as was true of Roman soldiers and of combatants in the modern world, medieval fighting men had to learn how to use their equipment and weapons, how to march, and how to deploy in formations. In the Roman context, when professional armies were equipped and paid by the imperial government, this training was an ongoing focus in soldiers' lives throughout their military careers. They engaged in weapons drills, marching drills, and combat drills on a daily basis when deployed in their bases. Detailed information about the nature and scope of this military training has survived from the Roman Republic and Empire. These sources include discussions in narrative texts, administrative documents, manuals, the layout of legionary fortresses with their extensive training fields (traditionally called fields of Mars), and also in visual media, such as carved stone reliefs.

For the late Roman period, the military manual by Vegetius, noted in previous chapters, provides insights into training during the fourth and fifth centuries. As will become clear, this text also provides crucial insights regarding the training of at least some types of fighting men during the Middle Ages, as well. This is because Vegetius' manual was constantly copied, revised, and updated for use by military commanders throughout the medieval millennium. In fact, it was one of the most copied non-religious texts from Late Antiquity during the entirety of the Middle Ages, and continued to be copied and translated into many of languages into the modern period. When printing was invented, Vegetius' text was introduced to an even wider audience and became a 'best seller'.

Nevertheless, it must be noted at the outset of this discussion of military training in the Middle Ages that far less information survives than for the armies of Rome. This dearth of source material is one of the factors that has led some scholars to assume that medieval military forces were a rabble not even meriting classification as armies. Our view is very different and is based upon both a careful assessment of the admittedly limited surviving positive evidence, and also on the understanding, noted previously, that soldiers are made and not born. Thus, for example, when the contemporary sources make clear that fighting men advanced in step and in order against the enemy, particularly when the enemy was inundating them with arrows, stones, and other projectiles, it is clear that the men in the attacking force had been taught what to do. Similarly, when mounted forces carried out complex manoeuvres on the battlefield, such as the feigned retreat, it is necessarily the case that both men and horses had been trained to carry out these tasks. The same deductions must be made when the sources discuss the successful use of hand-held arms, projectile weapons, and artillery, even if there is no other positive evidence of military training. In fact, it is likely that the more effectively soldiers performed in action, the greater the training they had received.

Training in arms

Medieval commanders could and often did look for models of behaviour from the Bible, which provided much of the basic education for aristocratic youth, whether or not they were designated for a career in the Church. Among the important lessons taught by the

Bible was the necessity of training to develop effective fighting men. A number of the Psalms speak directly to this issue. Psalm 18, echoing 2 Samuel 22:35, presents King David as thanking God for training his hands for battle so that he has the strength to draw his bow. Psalm 144:1 calls blessings upon God who 'teaches my hands for war and trains my fingers to fight'. This particular psalm seems to have had particular resonance with military men. In the early eleventh century, a north Italian count named Ragenardus had the text of this passage stitched into a battle flag that also featured images of the archangels Michael and Gabriel. Many medieval writers also stressed the importance of effective training for military success. For example, Nithard, a grandson of Charlemagne, wrote in his *Histories* that a small but well-trained army usually would emerge victorious in a battle against a larger but poorly trained foe. This observation also is found in the text of Vegetius, with which Nithard undoubtedly was familiar, as copies were available in the courts of his grandfather Charlemagne and cousin Charles the Bald, where Nithard spent considerable time both as a youth and as a grown man.

As seen in the previous sections, throughout the medieval millennium, most foot soldiers fought in the context of a phalanx, whether they were on offence or defence and whether the opponent was on horseback or on foot. This meant that the highly complex and intricate 'dance' of the duel that is illustrated in late medieval fencing manuals surviving in great numbers from Italy and Germany had little relevance to the battlefield experience of most medieval soldiers. Duels, whether fought for judicial purposes or in the context of tournaments, demanded an exceptionally high level of skill from an individual fighter, who operated within a rigorously enforced system of rules. By contrast, men serving in a phalanx with a sword or short spear had to work in cooperation with the men on their right and left within the chaotic tumult that characterized the front lines as two phalanxes came into contact with each other.

Widukind of Corvey provides a sense of this experience in his account of the Battle of Lenzen in 929, discussed previously:

> Then the signal was given, and the legate urged on the legions that charged with a great shout against the enemy. When it became clear that the great number of the enemy would not allow the Saxons to drive through them, they struck them on the left and right with their weapons. Whenever the Saxons were able to separate some of the Slavs from their fellows, they killed them all. As the battle intensified, with many dead on each side, and the barbarians still managing to maintain their formation, the legate ordered his colleague to provide support to the legions.

In this type of combat, it was not individual excellence with a sword or spear that mattered, but rather doing one's job and keeping track of one's comrades in arms on the battle line.

In the mid-ninth century, Archbishop Rabanus Maurus of Mainz (848–856) wrote an updated version of Vegetius' military manual for use, as he put it, in 'contemporary times'. Rabanus included a lengthy section about training soldiers to serve in the phalanx with swords. The archbishop recommended that individual posts, which were the height of an average man, be set up in a line as if they were enemy soldiers in formation. Both new recruits and established soldiers were then to attack the posts, thrusting with their swords first at the 'face' of the enemy, and then at what would be his side, then at his knee and lower leg. While attacking the posts, the soldiers and recruits were to practice lunging forward, stepping backward, and thrusting upward. The men participating in the training were to take care, at all times, to cover themselves with their shields so as to avoid exposing themselves to the enemy's weapon while moving in and out on the attack. In each case, the men engaged in training were to thrust with their swords, and avoid any slashing motion. Rabanus stressed that a slashing stroke would not have sufficient power to penetrate the enemy's armour. In addition, a slashing stroke, as contrasted with a thrusting motion, opened up the right side of a soldier's body to the enemy, which substantially raised the risk of suffering a wound. Just as importantly, a slashing stroke posed a risk to a fellow soldier in the phalanx.

In discussing the training of both new recruits and soldiers, Rabanus adopted the regimen of Roman military authorities of recommending that the men use double-weight practice weapons so that men would find their actual arms easier to bear when faced with real opponents. The practice swords were to be constructed of wood, and the shields were to be made of wicker. The practical value of this recommendation is illustrated in the eleventh-century historical text, *The Happenings at St. Gall*, which was written by one of the resident monks named Ekkehard. In this work, Ekkehard observed that Abbot Engilbert of St. Gall had training weapons constructed for his household troops, including wicker shields with a heavy core of closely fitted wooden boards, and felt armour for protection. It is likely not a simple coincidence that one of the surviving tenth-century manuscripts of Vegetius' *Epitoma rei militaris* was copied at St. Gall and preserved in the library there into modern times.

Training militia troops

The extensive training provided to the professional fighting men serving in military households throughout the medieval millennium is illustrated in hundreds of chronicles that comment on the skill with which these men used their arms and manoeuvred in the field. These soldiers often were described as 'picked men', 'highly skilled in the knowledge of arms', and 'most excellent soldiers'. By contrast, there is virtually no information about the of training of militia troops to use the swords, shields, spears, or other weapons with which they were equipped for close combat. Indeed, when commenting at length on the competence in the use of arms by militiamen, contemporary commentators generally sought to denigrate them. For example, in describing a battle that took place in 882, the monk Regino stressed that the Vikings defeated the local levy from his monastery of Prüm because these farmers 'lacked military training'. Similarly, the eleventh-century author Berthold of Reichenau emphasized that when farmers from the region of Franconia in Germany, who were loyal to King Henry IV, faced real soldiers in battle, the militiamen were defeated despite being equipped with the weapons of war, as contrasted with farm implements such as pitchforks and scythes. Berthold went on to say that the farmers, who were captured, were castrated rather than killed, which the author depicted ironically as an act of mercy to these men of low social station.

As discussed in Chapter 1, however, the negative portrayal of militia troops by aristocratic authors writing for aristocratic audiences must be understood within the context of their broader agenda of emphasizing the inherent superiority of aristocrats in all aspects of life, and the corollary inferiority of the commoners who made up the vast majority of the militia troops in medieval Europe. Nevertheless, even hostile aristocratic authors often had to admit that military levies fought effectively in hundreds of military operations, including many of those discussed previously. In doing so, these militiamen necessarily were able to handle their swords, spears, shields, and other arms effectively. Such part-time fighting men were particularly effective when they were deployed to defend the walls of fortifications, or when in the field they were supported by well-trained professional soldiers.

Because of a lack of sources, however, the ways in which the men of the military levies obtained this training in arms remains very obscure. At one level, it is almost certainly the case that militiamen required similar types of training to professional soldiers simply to learn to handle their weapons. It seems likely that in realms with strong central governments, such as the Carolingian and German empires, as well as the English kingdom, the obligation to train with swords and shields was imposed by royal officials. In fact, the well-known English ordinances, such as the 1252 Assize of Arms, which required able-bodied men to practice shooting with bows at least once a week, might be understood as the basic model. Such training tended to reinforce the ability of many men to use the bow and arrow for military purposes. The lower social orders generally were not permitted to hunt big game such as deer, bear, or aurochs. But they were permitted to hunt smaller game such as rabbits and birds that, of course, are much more difficult to hit with an arrow than a man, a horse, or a man on a horse.

In areas with strong urban militias, such as the German kingdom from the eleventh century onwards, most of Italy both south and north of Rome from the tenth century onwards, the French kingdom from the twelfth century onwards, and the Iberian kingdoms from the eleventh century, it is also likely that military training took place as a communal activity. In many cities, such as Worms in the German Rhineland and Sienna in northern Italy, urban militias were organized by parish, and it may be that religious festivals provided the leisure time that was necessary for men to gather and train together with their arms, including not only bows but also swords, spears, and shields. The repeated ecclesiastical legislation against carrying arms in churches or on church property may be understood as a reaction to this type of gathering. Similarly, the establishment of military organizations associated with craft and merchant guilds in cities such as Nürnberg, Florence, Paris, and London during the course of the fourteenth century also likely provided both the organizational structure and venues for the organization of training in arms for militia troops.

Training mounted troops

Historians studying nomadic peoples, such as those of the Eurasian steppes and the Native Americans of the western plains, often make the argument that mounted warriors are born rather than made. By this they mean that in nomadic societies, children often learn to ride at the same time, or even before, they can walk. As young boys grew into youths and men, they had the intrinsic skills as horsemen that permitted them to perform feats such as shooting at a full gallop and even shooting their bows over their shoulders while riding away from the enemy – that is, the famous 'Parthian shot' which appears in a bastardized version in the English idiom as 'parting shot'. It is for this reason, as discussed in Chapter 3, that many Muslim rulers purchased boys from the Eurasian steppe to serve as slave soldiers in their armies once the youths had achieved basic competency in equestrian skills.

A corollary to this idea in medieval Europe is the notion that aristocratic youths began learning to ride by the age of 7 in order to acquire the equestrian skills that supposedly allowed them to dominate medieval warfare with the tactics of 'mounted shock combat'. As we have argued throughout this work, cavalry did not dominate warfare, and even men trained to fight on horseback generally fought on foot throughout the medieval period, whether on the battlefield or in sieges that were far more common. Nevertheless, it was necessary in medieval Europe to train both men and horses to perform the particular set of skills that were required of mounted troops.

Rabanus Maurus, discussed previously, devoted a chapter in his updated version of aspects of Vegetius' *Epitoma rei militaris* to the training of mounted troops entitled 'How they are to be trained to mount horses'. Rabanus observed that in his day:

> In winter time, wooden planks (saw horses) were set up at an equal height under cover in a field. The trainees attempted to mount these first while unarmed. Then, they mounted them while wearing their helmets and holding a shield. Then, they mounted wearing a helmet, holding a shield, and holding a very long spear. They took such great care in this matter, that the trainees were ordered to jump on and off with their drawn swords from the right, but also from the left, and from the rear. In this manner, they learned how to mount in many different ways. Thus, the practice of mounting a horse was very vigorous among the Frankish people.

This skill in managing one's horse while also managing one's arms had a natural corollary in the proper training of the horses themselves. These animals had to be taught not to fear the noise and smell of blood and smoke of the battlefield, and also to charge towards danger, all of which are against their instincts. In horses, the fight-or-flight response is heavily weighted towards the latter. In addition, horses had to be trained to shift their bodies instantly at the commands of their riders, who used the bit, stirrups, and their knees, as well as verbal cues, with their animals so as to carry out the various movements that were necessary for combat. As Carroll Gillmor, a medieval historian and trained equestrian, has shown, this training required a detailed understanding of the mechanics of a horse's movement. In particular, the individuals responsible for training warhorses had to understand the individual motions of each of the horse's legs, and to develop cues for the horse to alter its orientation, not only at a trot but also at a gallop when all four feet were off the ground at the same time. This manner of training horses with an understanding of the need to have the animal change the front foot that landed first – that is, the right or the left – while galloping dates back to the fourth century BC, and was discussed by the Athenian general and author Xenophon. During the medieval period, however, the training of horses relied largely on oral traditions passed down from masters to apprentices at stud farms that specialized in the production of warhorses. It was not until the sixteenth century that we again see specialized works dealing with the training of these animals.

Training for the attack

Among the many challenges faced by a military commander is ensuring that his men not only are properly deployed on the field at the beginning of the battle, but that he is able to move his units where they are required during the course of the fighting. For Roman military commanders, the movement of troops in the field was predicated on extensive and ongoing training. Roman foot soldiers were deployed in loose phalanx formations, and were able to advance, withdraw, slide to the side, and charge the enemy while keeping their places in the formation, even when facing difficulties such as incoming missiles from the enemy or rough terrain. By contrast, most medieval fighting men – that is, the men of the various levies – likely had very limited training for battlefield conditions as members of large units. For this reason, many medieval commanders sought to remain on the defensive in battle and to deploy their infantry in tight formations, where little was required of the men other than to hold their ground. Infantry phalanxes of this type, as previously discussed, were deployed at battles such as Poitiers (732), Hastings (1066), Courtrai (1302), and Crécy (1346).

However, in many battles throughout the Middle Ages, infantry phalanxes also advanced into combat. Professional soldiers likely learned to advance step by step in a manner consistent with the recommendations made by Rabanus Maurus, beginning slowly and gradually increasing their speed as they approached the enemy formation. The well-trained professionals of the military households also likely learned to make brief period checks so as to dress their lines. In order to keep in order, the fighting men chanted or sang songs that had a clear beat. Songs of this type survive from the pen of the sixth-century writer Venantius Fortunatus. A number of crusade chronicles also record that Christian soldiers sang as they went into combat. A corollary to this is the use of instruments such as pipes and trumpets to keep the marching beat for the advancing soldiers. In the late thirteenth century, the pay records for the English armies invading Scotland included invoices for trumpeters attached to large infantry units. Just a few decades earlier, the city militia of Limoges was accompanied to war by drums, trumpets, and other musical instruments to attack Viscountess Margueritte of Aixe-sur-Vienne.

For militia troops, who lacked the opportunity to practice marching and advancing in step, particularly in large formations, banners played a crucial role in helping men to keep their places in line. In his military manual, Vegetius drew attention to the effectiveness of training men always to maintain their stations relative to their unit banner. Apropos this point, in his discussion of the battle at Geule in 891, Regino of Prüm emphasizes that Frankish troops were organized in the phalanx by their commanders so that each man took his place under his own unit banner. Regino's description is consistent with the regulations in Carolingian capitularies from the late ninth century requiring that every unit have a standard bearer. In a similar manner, the military ordinances (*fueros*) for the frontier towns of the Christian kingdoms of Castile and Aragon in Iberia emphasized that the militias were to have banners, and that each man was to know his place in battle by reference to these standards. On a larger scale, the commander's banner served to signal the subordinate commanders. As long as the banner was on the field, the troops were to continue to fight. But when the banners were lowered or withdrawn from the field, this was a general signal to retreat.

Training cavalry to attack

As this section has highlighted, cavalry tactics required considerable precision by both men and horses. After the men were taught to use their arms while on horseback, and the animals had been taught how to function on a battlefield, it was necessary to train both man and beast to cooperate with each other, and with all of the other pairs in their unit. As is true of training in general, there is limited information about how soldiers gained the skills that they required for mounted combat. However, one detailed discussion does survive in the *Histories* written in about 843 by Nithard, discussed previously, who had significant experience in his own right as a military commander.

When Charles the Bald, for whom Nithard wrote his *Histories*, and Charles' elder brother, Louis the German, joined together their armies in 842 against their eldest brother Lothair I, the two allied kings organized war games in order to train their men to work together effectively. Nithard explains that Louis and Charles divided their mounted forces into units of equal size, and had two units at a time face off against each other across a large open field. When their turn came, the individual units raced towards each other across the field at full speed, according to Nithard, who was an eyewitness to these war games, as if they were going to close with each other. But then before they came into contact, one unit received a signal to wheel about as if in retreat, with their shields shifted to their backs. At another signal, the unit that initially had retreated then wheeled back around to the attack, and the other unit turned in retreat. The mounted forces spent considerable time in this exercise, getting used to their new allies, and also practicing wheeling about on command. Nithard commented that the exercises were a remarkable sight, because of the high level of skill demonstrated by the riders, as well as their discipline. It should also be noted that the spears with which these troops exercised had their steel tips removed so that no one would be injured in this inherently dangerous activity. It is noteworthy, as well, that this type of training exercise was well-suited to preparing men to engage in a feigned retreat.

For the later medieval period, many scholars argue that tournaments provided a similar function to the war games described by Nithard. This view gains credence from the comments of some late medieval writers, such as the author of the *Song of Lewes*, written shortly after the victory of Simon de Montfort and the English barons over King Henry III of England at the Battle of Lewes (1264). The *Song of Lewes* emphasizes that many of the men in the battle had received military training in tournaments. In these artificial or mock battles, individuals with sufficient wealth to purchase and maintain armour and warhorses had the opportunity to work as members of teams, and had to practice to fight effectively alongside one another during the course of *mêlées*, which featured groups of men, both on horseback and on foot, facing off against each other. This exercise, which had considerable value for training purposes, should not be confused with the joust – that is, mounted men charging each other with couched lances on a tournament enclosure, which likely did not have much value on the battlefield.

Morale

The motivation to fight, to risk one's life, and to accept the rigours of a military campaign played a central role in combat in medieval Europe, just as had been true in the ancient world and up through the present day. Tactics and training are of no avail when the men refuse to fight or even to serve on campaign. The importance of good morale to military success can be seen, for example, in the context of Edward I's effort to conquer Scotland in the late thirteenth and early fourteenth centuries. During the first years of the war, Edward sought to overwhelm the Scots by mobilizing very large armies of foot soldiers, who largely were conscripted from the northern counties of England. However, the morale of these soldiers, as recounted in both letters sent by government officials and in contemporary chronicles, was abysmal. The result, as illuminated by pay records, was that between half and three-quarters of the conscripts deserted at the first opportunity.

By 1303, the English king had learned his lesson, and sought volunteers, whom he paid and fed well. He augmented the material rewards given to his troops by offering substantial spiritual support to his men, ensuring that they had chaplains to hear their confessions and to preach uplifting sermons. In addition, Edward sought to gain the support of the English people as a whole for his wars by organizing a thorough-going propaganda campaign to portray Scots as the enemies not just of England, but of all Christians. Edward went so far as to command the archbishops of York and Canterbury to offer indulgences – that is, remissions of sin – to those English men and women who prayed for the success of the king's army in Scotland. The results were very positive, and in the course of a lengthy campaign in 1303–1304, Edward was able complete the conquest of Scotland, in large part because he was able to keep substantial forces there over the winter. As will be made clear in the next sections, the various elements of the morale-building programme developed by Edward I are part of a lengthy pattern of morale building and maintenance in Christian medieval Europe.

Defeating fear and promoting courage

In Chapter 4, we discussed the crucial role of supply in keeping armies in the field. Hungry men are unhappy men who rarely are highly motivated to fight. However, even well-fed soldiers can still suffer from low morale when living through the realities of a campaign that was characterized by lengthy periods of tedium and drudgery interspersed with short periods of intense emotion, and particularly the fear of injury or death. For many Christian soldiers, these worries about their own physical fate likely were exacerbated by the fear of what would happen to their souls after their death. Would they go to heaven, even after committing the mortal sin of homicide? Even if the soldiers believed that they were fighting in a just cause, and that killing the enemy was necessary, would their other sins permit them everlasting peace in the Kingdom of Heaven? In order to combat these fears, Christian rulers and military commanders from the late Roman Empire up through the end of the Middle Ages – and indeed, into the present – have developed a broad range of rites and ceremonies to provide fighting men with the confidence that they required for combat.

Military religion

Following the conversion of the Roman Empire to Christianity during the fourth century, small numbers of bishops and priests accompanied armies into the field for the purpose of invoking divine support on behalf of the emperor and his men. These bishops and priests carried sacred relics (such as the bones of saints), celebrated intercessory masses asking for God's aid, led soldiers in prayer, and preached to the troops in order to encourage them to be worthy of God's support. Constantine the Great (died 337), the first Christian emperor, even had a special chapel outfitted to bring with him on campaign so that he could pray while in the field. These religious ceremonies within the army had their counterpart on the 'home front', where congregations throughout the empire prayed for the success of the army, and asked for God's aid. The Hebrew Bible likely had a significant influence in the development of this aspect of the Christian military religion.

Individual pastoral care for soldiers developed very gradually in the post-Roman West. It was not until the sixth century that Christian thinkers, particularly in Ireland, began to develop the notion that individuals could confess their sins more than once in their lifetimes and obtain absolution each time they confessed. In the early Church, confession usually had been reserved for the death bed, and was intended to cleanse the soul of sin just before an individual faced eternal judgement. This penitential system, however, did not work well for soldiers who did not know when or if they would die on the battlefield. In addition, because homicide was a mortal sin, once a soldier confessed, he could no longer be a soldier and still be a member of the Christian community. A number of sources from the fourth, fifth, and sixth centuries attest to the conundrum faced by soldiers and their desire for a more flexible system of penance. The ultimate solution was the development of a regime of repeatable confession and penance whenever a sinner felt the need for spiritual cleansing. The idea and practice of repeatable confession developed first in Ireland, and from there spread to England and then to the rest of the Latin West. This new religious practice led to the development of penitential manuals, sometimes called tariff books by scholars, which provided priests with a list of standard penances for particular sins, such as adultery, theft, and homicide.

The practice of repeatable confession had very important consequences for the religious care of soldiers. Soldiers could now confess their sins before going into battle, and thereby cleanse their souls before risking their lives in combat. In addition, soldiers could confess their sins after battle for having killed their fellow men, who also often were Christians. This meant that armies had to recruit much larger numbers of priests than ever before to provide direct pastoral care to fighting men. These pastoral tasks included hearing soldiers' confessions and assigning penances, as well as the traditional duties of leading soldiers in prayer, celebrating intercessory masses, and caring for relics. The first surviving evidence for the regular practice of recruiting priests in large numbers to serve as military chaplains for the particular purpose of hearing confessions comes from 742, when Carloman, the Carolingian co-mayor of the palace, along with his brother Pippin, the future king of the Frankish realm, issued a command that every unit commander in his army must have on staff a priest capable of hearing confessions and assigning penances to the fighting men under his care.

From this point onward, almost all Christian armies both within Europe and those engaging in operations across the Mediterranean were accompanied by large numbers of chaplains. It is often possible to see these men in government records because they were paid directly by rulers to provide pastoral care to soldiers in the field and in garrisons. The pay records of Edward I, for example, show that the government employed chaplains both for militiamen from the county levies and for garrisons in Wales, Scotland, Gascony, and the Channel Islands. Strikingly, these government records emphasize that military commanders were to recruit chaplains who spoke the same language as the men under their care so that there would be no obstacles to providing pastoral care. Both secular and ecclesiastical magnates also employed chaplains within their military households. Some of these priests, such as William of Poitiers and Ralph of Caen, have become quite well-known to scholars because of their subsequent literary efforts, writing the histories of the men whom they originally had served in a pastoral role – William the Conqueror and the First Crusade commander Tancred, respectively.

Army-wide rites and public religion

The pastoral care provided to soldiers on campaign and often immediately before battle was combined with numerous other elements of military religion that dated back to the late Roman Empire. Most people in medieval Europe believed that God could and often did intervene in human affairs. In order to gain this divine support, they believed, it was necessary to have a worthy and just cause, and also to conduct themselves so that they as individuals would be worthy of God's aid. Governments throughout the Latin West during the entirety of the medieval period, therefore, organized army-wide religious rites and ceremonies, and also sought to mobilize the entire realm religiously on behalf of the army. Within the army, military commanders had priests preach to the troops to urge them towards proper and moral behaviour so that God would look kindly upon them. Armies also engaged in religious processions, prayer, and fasts in order to purify themselves before battle. To put it simply, there was a widespread belief that God would support – indeed, give victory – to those who followed His laws as made clear in both the old and new testaments.

In the prelude to the Battle of the Standard (1138), for example, Archbishop Thurstan of York (1114–1140) organized an entire programme of religious rites for the Anglo-Norman army. All of the soldiers were required to confess their sins to their unit priests. All of the men then undertook a fast as a penance for their previous sins. Following the conclusion of the three-day fast, which required that the men not eat during the daylight hours, Archbishop Thurstan granted a general remission of sin, meaning that all of the men were spiritually cleansed, and offered his blessing. From the perspective of morale, these religious rites and ceremonies provided comfort to the men, by demonstrating that they were right with God, and that He would be on their side in the coming battle, or at the very least, that their souls would go to heaven if they died in battle.

In conjunction with the religious programme carried out in the field by armies, medieval rulers often mobilized the 'home front' in order to beg God to intervene on behalf of their side. Special intercessory masses were developed, which included additional prayers during the course of the standard Christian service asking for the support of patron saints and of God. For example, a tenth-century intercessory mass from Germany included a prayer begging God to support the Christian army in its war against the pagans (probably the Slavs to the east) and to give aid to the soldiers just as He had aided the Israelites fleeing from Egypt. A similar prayer, which was said in masses held throughout Germany in 960 on behalf of the army of Emperor Otto I asked of God: 'give triumph to Your servant our emperor' and 'let us have the power to rule which Joseph had in the armed camp, and which Gideon held in battle'. King Philip IV of France (1285–1314) ordered the bishops of the French Church to organize very similar intercessory masses on behalf the royal army before the campaign that ended in disaster at Courtrai in 1302.

These intercessory masses on behalf of the army in the field often were accompanied by further religious rites, such as processions, public prayers, fasts, and the giving of alms. This was particularly widespread during the crusades. One of the earliest surviving requests for such prayers came from the crusader Anselm of Ribemont in a letter to Archbishop Manasses of Rheims written from the siege camp at Antioch in November 1097. Anselm asked first that the archbishop, and whoever else received the letter, pray for the souls of those who had died during the siege of Nicaea. Then Anselm requested that the archbishop and all the others reading his letter pray for the crusading army. He followed this by requesting that the archbishop order all of the bishops within his province to authorize such rites, as well. A very similar example can be seen 300 years earlier during Charlemagne's Avar campaign of 791. The great Frankish king sent a letter to his wife Fastrada, letting her know that the army was engaged in penitential rites, and commanding her to organize a programme of ceremonies throughout the kingdom on behalf of the soldiers in the field, including prayers, masses, almsgiving, and fasts.

The religious ceremonies held by armies and by the families and communities of soldiers back home helped to instil the idea that the men were fighting for a just cause and that God was on their side. The result was that most fighting men had the comfort of 'knowing' that if they committed the sin of homicide, this would be forgiven, whether on crusade or in 'secular' wars. Moreover, if they fell in battle, they could be assured of a place in heaven. In addition, their families, friends, and members of the communities in which they lived shared these same understandings, and were able to provide comfort to soldiers as they prepared to go off to war, and when they returned.

Orations

In addition to the ongoing support provided to soldiers through the mobilization of religious rites and ceremonies, including sermons, large numbers of contemporary sources emphasize the importance of pre-battle orations by military commanders in lifting the spirits of their men before combat. These public addresses are described or 'quoted' in a wide variety of narrative works, and were delivered by both laymen and clerics. The most widely attested addresses in the surviving sources were those delivered by laymen, usually either an officer or the commander of a military force. These orations, sometimes denoted by scholars as harangues, often included a combination of secular and religious themes. Common *topoi* in these orations included reminding the soldiers of their victorious military tradition, the fact that they had defeated the enemy many times in the past, and the promise of glory in this world and eternal life in the next.

For example, the crusade chronicler Albert of Aachen, writing in the early twelfth century, described an oration delivered during the First Crusade by Duke Godfrey of Lotharingia to his troops in the early morning hours of 3 June 1098 before they began their successful assault on the walls of the fortress city of Antioch. The duke began his harangue by reminding the Christian troops that they were fighting for Christ and had devoted themselves to divine service. Godfrey expanded upon this point by insisting that the soldiers should have no fear of death because each man had a place prepared for him in heaven to live for eternity alongside Christ. Godfrey then added that the soldiers were worthy of such divine protection and aid because they fought for the promise of eternal salvation rather than any earthly reward. The oration concludes by combining this promise of salvation with the assurance that the army would be victorious over its foes so that the men should have no fear of risking their lives in the Lord's service.

Perhaps the most famous exemplar of a battlefield oration, although fictional, is the one delivered by King Henry V of England (1413–1422) in Shakespeare's *Henry V* on the morning of the great English victory at Agincourt. In response to the lament by Ralph Neville, the Earl of Westmorland, that the English lacked sufficient troops to face the French, Henry V responded:

> What's he that wishes so?
> My cousin, Westmoreland? No, my fair cousin;
> If we are mark'd to die, we are enow
> To do our country loss; and if to live,
> The fewer men, the greater share of honour.
> God's will! I pray thee, wish not one man more.
> By Jove, I am not covetous for gold,
> Nor care I who doth feed upon my cost;
> It yearns me not if men my garments wear;
> Such outward things dwell not in my desires.
> But if it be a sin to covet honour,
> I am the most offending soul alive.
> No, faith, my coz, wish not a man from England.
> God's peace! I would not lose so great an honour
> As one man more methinks would share from me
> For the best hope I have. O, do not wish one more!
> Rather proclaim it, Westmoreland, through my host,
> That he which hath no stomach to this fight,
> Let him depart; his passport shall be made,
> And crowns for convoy put into his purse;
> We would not die in that man's company
> That fears his fellowship to die with us.

This day is call'd the feast of Crispian.
He that outlives this day, and comes safe home,
Will stand a tip-toe when this day is nam'd,
And rouse him at the name of Crispian.
He that shall live this day, and see old age,
Will yearly on the vigil feast his neighbours,
And say 'To-morrow is Saint Crispian'.
Then will he strip his sleeve and show his scars,
And say 'These wounds I had on Crispin's day'.
Old men forget; yet all shall be forgot,
But he'll remember, with advantages,
What feats he did that day. Then shall our names,
Familiar in his mouth as household words –
Harry the King, Bedford and Exeter,
Warwick and Talbot, Salisbury and Gloucester –
Be in their flowing cups freshly rememb'red.
This story shall the good man teach his son;
And Crispin Crispian shall ne'er go by,
From this day to the ending of the world,
But we in it shall be remembered –
We few, we happy few, we band of brothers;
For he to-day that sheds his blood with me
Shall be my brother; be he ne'er so vile,
This day shall gentle his condition;
And gentlemen in England now-a-bed
Shall think themselves accurs'd they were not here,
And hold their manhoods cheap whiles any speaks
That fought with us upon Saint Crispin's day.

As was true in many medieval orations, Henry V explicitly rejects plunder as a reason to fight. Rather, his emphases – on honour, glory, and perhaps most importantly, that the men would survive to tell their tale into old age – each tap into a lengthy medieval tradition.

Unit cohesion

One of the most telling lines in Henry V's speech was the description of the English army as a 'band of brothers'. The notion of a band of brothers is central to unit cohesion, which entailed the bonding of the individual soldiers within each small group, so that they had faith and trust in each other to carry out their common goals. Religious rites and orations by commanders served important roles in raising the morale of individual soldiers and giving the army, as a whole, a sense of purpose and commitment. However, in the chaos of battle, particularly on the point of the clash between phalanxes or as squadrons of cavalry met in a *mêlée*, soldiers had to be able count on the man on the left and the man on the right. For militia forces, this sense of unit cohesion often was reinforced by pre-existing ties based on family and community.

Fathers, sons, uncles, nephews, and cousins stood side by side in the phalanx, and to fail to do one's duty meant betraying one's own family and leaving them to die. Similarly, the personal ties among men in units drawn from the tenants of a local magnate, or from among the medium and smaller landowners in a district, imposed powerful social controls over these soldiers on the battlefield. Running away rather than fighting could mean being ostracized from the local community and social oblivion, leading perhaps to prosecution by the government. As city militias grew in importance following the turn of the first millennium, units drawn from among masters, journeymen, and apprentices in various crafts created similar social controls whereby personal failure on the battlefield could mean expulsion from the guild and exile from the city. This same pattern can be seen in the contract companies that were recruited to serve in the English armies of the Hundred Years' War. As seen in Chapter 3, virtual 'military communities' emerged in many regions of England where families produced volunteer soldiers to serve in the retinues of the same magnate family generation after generation.

The professional fighting men serving in the military households of magnates also developed unit cohesion through long association, as well as common experiences of training and war. However, it was also often the case that the magnates who were summoned on campaign by kings and other rulers were hostile to each other, and even engaged in violence against each other. In fact, it was not uncommon for soldiers who had fought against each other in earlier private conflicts to find themselves on the same side on a large-scale campaign organized by a prince or king. As a consequence, medieval rulers used a variety of methods to damp down these previous animosities and to build a sense of trust among former adversaries so that there would be unity among the fighting men in the army as a whole.

Military codes and discipline

The late Roman state had a complex of rules and regulations regarding the behaviour of soldiers that can be understood as a corpus of military law. This body of law treated a number of topics that relate to the broad question of *ius in bello* – that is, the law of battle – including prohibitions against unauthorized violence against non-combatants, and taking supplies and other property without payment, i.e. plundering, without authorization from their commanders. As was true of many other aspects of Rome's military legacy, these legal norms and requirements did not come to an end with the dissolution of the Empire in the West, but rather were maintained by Rome's early medieval successor states.

An early example of this continuity with Roman legal tradition can be seen in the sixth-century *Lex Baiuvariorum* that lays out penalties for soldiers who committed a *scandalum* within the army while serving on a campaign organized by the king or duke; the perpetrators of such a *scandalum* had to pay a fine of 600 *solidi*. In addition, any soldier who struck someone, wounded someone, or committed homicide without authorization by the commander would be compelled to make proper restitution. The Bavarian law also set out penalties for any soldier engaged in plundering, taking fodder or grain, or committing arson without the command of his military leader. Each count leading a contingent within the army was to ensure the proper behaviour of his men, and was to establish commanders of a hundred men (*centuriones*) and commanders of ten men (*decani*), each of whom was required to ensure that the men under his direct command did not act contrary to the law. Counts were responsible for investigating crimes committed by soldiers and, if they failed in this task, were held personally responsible for all of the damages caused by their men. The Bavarian law also set out even more specific penalties for the theft during a campaign of horseshoes, horse tack, or harness, so that a slave guilty of this crime would lose his hands, and his master would be responsible as well for replacing the equipment. A free man convicted of this crime could redeem his hands for a payment of 40 *solidi*.

The sixth-century Frankish government also drew upon late Roman law to define the conduct of men on campaign. For example, as seen in Chapter 5, as part of his preparations for the invasion of the Visigothic kingdom in 507 that culminated in the Battle of Vouillé, Clovis issued a circular letter to all of the bishops through whose dioceses his army was to march emphasizing to them that he had issued orders to his men that they were not to take anything from the bishops or from their people. He also promised that if any damages were done, he would immediately make restitution. Commenting at a remove of three generations from this campaign, Gregory of Tours recorded that Clovis issued strict orders to his army that nothing should be taken from the people of the Touraine other than grass and water. When two of Clovis' men seized some hay from a local without payment, the ruler immediately had them executed. Gregory notes similarly harsh punishments imposed by other Merovingian kings. Sigibert I (561–575) had troops, whom he had recruited from across the Rhine, stoned to death for plundering villages around Paris. Chilperic I (561–584) had the count of Rouen executed for failing to keep his men from plundering the area around Bourges following a peace agreement with Chilperic's brother Guntram (561–592).

Charlemagne and his Carolingian successors also issued legislation on the eve of military campaigns regulating a wide variety of behaviours, including forbidding the pursuit of private vendettas against fellow soldiers. Each military commander was held responsible for the behaviour of his men and was required to punish publicly any breaches in the peace of the army. Repeated prohibitions against getting drunk were intended to prevent the breakdown of discipline, as inebriated soldiers often acted violently against each other, especially in the pursuit of vendettas. It was widely understood that alcohol, in excess, undermined discipline in the camp and on the battlefield, although 'liquid courage' did have an important role to play in preparing men for combat. In addition, it was very important to the Carolingians that their men behaved properly on the march and did not engage in unauthorized violence.

Charlemagne, for example, commanded that if anyone in the army took more supplies than those required by the king's command, he would be compelled to pay three times the value of these goods to the victim. Additionally, if a free man committed this crime while in the army, he was to pay the fine required by the royal *bannum*, while a slave who committed this crime was to be subject to physical punishment. Louis the Pious, Charlemagne's heir, similarly commanded that all military commanders were responsible for the behaviour of the men in their units (*obsequie*), whether they were their own dependents or *alieni*. Each of these commanders was to be held responsible for providing restitution for any damages that these men had caused, as well as presenting them either to the emperor or one of his *missi* for judgement. Moreover, any office holder who failed in his duty to curb the misbehaviour of his men would be deprived of his office.

A very similar set of ordinances was issued by Louis II, the grandson of Louis the Pious, in the context of his campaign against the Muslims in the region of Benevento in 866. In order to maintain peace within the army, Louis commanded that men were to leave all of their personal enmities (*fagidis*) at home, and that anyone who caused a disturbance – either coming from or going to the army – would lose his life. The next regulation stated that because it was the period of Lent when God's precepts are particularly to be followed, anyone who broke into a church, or committed adultery on campaign, or set a fire, was to lose his life. He added that whoever stole a horse, cow, clothing, or arms was to pay three times their value in compensation. In addition, if a free man committed this crime, he was to be subject to the humiliation of the *hamiscara*, in which the guilty party had to crawl on his hands and knees wearing a saddle. If a slave committed a theft of this type, he was to be whipped and beaten, and his owners, who permitted the crime to take place, were to make compensation in his place. Moreover, Louis decreed that if military commanders learned of crimes that were committed by their men and did not take remedial action, then they would be compelled to make compensation to the victims personally, and they were to be subject to the *hamiscara*.

In the East Frankish/German kingdom of the tenth–twelfth centuries, rulers frequently required all of the fighting men to take oaths of peacefulness towards each other, and to do their duty in the battle. Frederick Barbarossa went so far as to issue a code of conduct for his army during a campaign in Italy in 1158. The first clause of this code was that no soldier was to provoke strife in the army or in the camp. Similar ordinances were issued by groups of crusaders. Among the more famous of these was the ordinance that was developed in the course of the campaign in 1148 that led to the capture of the fortress city of Lisbon. One of the participants on the campaign, a priest named Raol, emphasized that the various contingents of the crusading army, each of which spoke a different language, pledged to maintain peace and concord among themselves. Raol added that these pledges of friendship were to be guaranteed by a series of regulations that were intended to reduce friction among the units and end conflicts with the least possible violence. These regulations included forbidding the display of costly garments, requirements to keep women out of the public eye, and a strict rule providing that all injuries had to be compensated for on a one-to-one basis, so that a life had to be repaid with a life.

Similar regulations were issued by many of the armies operating in Europe during the later Middle Ages, including King Henry V of England and Archduke Charles the Bold of Burgundy. Two of the late medieval ordinances that have received the most attention are the code of conduct issued by King Richard II on 17 July 1385 for the army that he led in an invasion of Scotland, and the ordinance drawn up that same month for the Franco-Scottish army that mobilized at Edinburgh to oppose the English invasion. In her examination of these two documents, Anne Curry, a specialist in late medieval military history, shows that there were important common elements that is suggestive of an 'international code' of military discipline. Many of the elements of this 'code', such as the need to maintain peace in the camp and in maintaining proper behaviour toward civilian populations, demonstrate considerable continuities with military practice dating back to the high and early Middle Ages and, indeed, to the later Roman Empire.

The problem of chivalry and the treatment of enemy combatants

Among the most contested topics in the history of medieval combat concerns the role of 'chivalry', which is often defined as a code of secular military conduct for the elite members of society in medieval warfare. A leading figure in the study of chivalry is the British historian John Gillingham, who argues that there were two fundamental phases of warfare with regard to the broad question of the development of chivalric tradition. In the first phase, he argues, medieval armies engaged in a type of total war that focused on the killing of elite prisoners, the sale into captivity of captured rank and file, and, when possible, the capture and sale into captivity of enemy non-combatants. In phase two, according to Gillingham, we see a transition away from the enslavement of non-combatants, efforts to capture and hold for ransom elite prisoners, but the concomitant wholesale slaughter of the rank and file. It is this second phase that Gillingham calls, somewhat tongue in cheek, the 'damsels in distress' period.

Gillingham's emphasis on the role of 'chivalry' in conditioning the thinking of elite men about warfare is echoed by many other scholars, and particularly those who have sought to demonstrate a connection between positive treatment of elite enemy combatants and the origins of medieval knighthood. For example, the early medieval historians Karl Leyser and Janet Nelson argued for the development of proto-chivalric and 'knightly' concepts of Carolingian fighting men as early as the ninth century. With regard to the high Middle Ages, Matthew Strickland similarly has argued for the development of a code of conduct, which he identifies as already well-developed in the ninth century among the Franks, and transmitted through them to the Normans, that led to better treatment of elite enemy combatants. Strickland, like Gillingham, argues that these 'chivalric' values were imported into England following the conquest of 1066, thereby transforming the conduct of war – at least for elite combatants – there, as well.

The leading figures with regard to the matrix of questions connecting chivalry and warfare in the late Middle Ages are the late Maurice Keen and Richard Kaeuper. The first of these scholars took a largely romanticized approach to the study of late medieval warfare, in which knights followed rules of chivalry as outlined in contemporary entertainment literature. Kaeuper, by contrast, has trained a rather jaundiced eye upon the claims that later medieval fighting men, including knights, refrained from using ambushes or killing their enemies from afar. However, he does hold to the notion that elite men sought guidance about the proper conduct of soldiers in war through reference to manuals of chivalry.

In our view, the emphasis by scholars on accounts provided in narrative works regarding the treatment of both enemy combatants and non-combatants is certainly justified in light of the absence of surviving treatises from the early Middle Ages that discuss the appropriate treatment of enemy soldiers, limitations on the abuse or exploitation of enemy non-combatants, or even a definition of a non-combatant. However, we do not find credible the various models of chivalry presented by these and other scholars as these have been connected with medieval warfare. Indeed, we reject as a false premise the idea that military affairs in medieval Europe were organized around an aristocratic warrior elite or that knighthood was an essential element in the conduct of war. Rather, we argue that chivalry, in all of its manifestations, has its origins as a series of literary tropes derived from popular entertainment literature, and that entire model has value only insofar as it provides some insights regarding the ways in which some individuals in some places sought to make life resemble art.

Those scholars arguing for the supposedly ameliorative effects of chivalry on medieval combat have tended to ignore that early medieval rulers and their advisors had available a considerable corpus examples from both classical historical works, as well as the Bible, that provided a variety of models for dealing with of the enemy, whether soldiers or non-combatants. Both classical and biblical traditions dealing with the conduct of war did provide a warrant for the wholesale annihilation of both enemy combatants and ostensibly non-combatant populations, or their enslavement. However, the Bible and classical histories also provided contrary examples that encouraged a more lenient treatment of enemy combatants, and even the conceptualization of a category of non-combatants. The text of Deuteronomy 20:19–20, for example, called upon the Israelites to offer lenient terms to the defenders of cities, and also prohibited the destruction of fruit-bearing trees. In a similar vein, Cicero, whose works both in the original and mediated through Isidore of Seville played a significant role in the education of early medieval rulers, argued in *De Officiis* 1.35, 'when victory has been achieved, the enemy must be spared, unless he has shown that he is cruel and uncivilized'.

These admonitions for the lenient treatment of both combatants and ostensible non-combatants frequently were followed by medieval rulers. For example, Charlemagne provided for the peaceful surrender of Pavia in 774 and Muslim-ruled Barcelona in 801, despite the fact that both fortress cities had resisted for the better part of a year. The latter case is particularly interesting, given the general consensus among scholars that inter-cultural warfare led to even greater excesses of violence against both combatants and non-combatants than intra-cultural warfare, even after the putative development of a chivalric ethos. As these examples indicate, a teleological approach to the question of the treatment of both enemy combatants and non-combatants based on the supposed development of a chivalric ethos offers a misleading impression of medieval attitudes and behaviours. It was rather the case that medieval rulers and military commanders adopted a variety of approaches to the treatment of the enemy combatants and non-combatants, which were influenced not only by current conditions but also by broader conceptual models that were transmitted through the Bible and classical texts.

Conclusion

Contrary to the romantic nineteenth-century view of medieval warfare, which is unfortunately shared by some scholars even today, medieval battlefields and sieges were not scenes of chaos in which knights galloped around the field and engaged in heroic single combat to gain glory, renown, and the hand of a fair damsel. The reality was far more prosaic. Fighting men, including both professionals and militia troops, were deployed in formations, most frequently the phalanx, and moved as they were directed by military commanders with an overall plan for the battle. Indeed, the general view that military science was at a low ebb during the Middle Ages is belied by the complex manoeuvres undertaken by armies, such as advancing in a phalanx up hill, assaulting fortifications in a *testudo* formation, and undertaking double envelopments of enemy forces.

As has been true throughout the history of warfare, the factor that modern military planners call friction also played a role in medieval combat. Battle plans rarely could be followed after the two sides had their first encounter. It is in part because of friction that not every military deployment during the Middle Ages was effective, and there are numerous examples of men – as well as their commanders – failing to perform effectively, and even running away before fighting had begun. But these very same circumstances also can be shown in historical periods that enjoy a far superior military reputation among scholars. Indeed, from the perspective of writing history, it is methodologically unsound to use 'mistakes' to characterize medieval warfare in general, just as it would be misleading to use George Custer's failed campaign in 1876 as evidence for the training and effectiveness of U.S. military forces in the decade or so following the American Civil War.

The frequent effectiveness of medieval fighting men in combat, both on the battlefield and the far more numerous sieges, cannot be explained by reference to an innate warrior spirit, whether this is attributed to the primitive nature of medieval man, or to some old-Germanic holdover putatively attested in literary fantasies such as *Beowulf*. Rather, the effective use of arms and equipment, as well as the ability to manoeuvre on the battlefield, required training. In short, no man is born a soldier. Soldiers must be made. Our admittedly limited sources point to the ongoing training of professional soldiers in a manner similar to that employed by Roman officials. By contrast, we have very little information at all about the training of militia men to use their arms, other than bows. Nevertheless, if we accept the testimony of our sources that both professionals and militia troops were able to use their arms effectively and that they were able to perform complex manoeuvres on the battlefield and in sieges, then it is a necessary corollary that this training did take place. Men are not born knowing how to thrust with a sword, climb 10-metre ladders under enemy attack, work with the men to their left and right in the phalanx, march in step up hills, over broken ground, or across killing fields surrounding fortresses unless taught how to do so.

Finally, soldiers in medieval armies, as has been and continues to be true of soldiers in armies in all times and places, must be provided with aid in suppressing fear and augmenting bravery. As Widukind of Corvey said about the Saxon troops before the Battle of Lenzen in 929: 'The fighting men moved between hope and fear according to the nature of their personalities'. Fear of death, fear of killing, and fear of damnation all played their roles in undermining morale. Military commanders from Constantine the Great to Henry V sought to alleviate these fears by showing their men that God was on their side and that they would have victory because they always had been victorious in the past. To win was glorious, but to die in a just cause was even more glorious, bringing renown to a man's name and eternal life in the Kingdom of Heaven. Individual soldiers sought reassurance through the mechanisms of pastoral care, such as confession. Armies gained a renewed sense of mission and strength from both religious rituals and battlefield orations. Families and communities on the home front gained comfort by supporting their men with prayers and religious rites such as almsgiving and fasts. As a group, consequently, the morale-building efforts of military commanders encompassed the entire society.

Bibliography

With regard to the conduct of siege warfare, see

Bernard S. Bachrach and Rutherford Aris, 'Military Technology and Garrison Organization: Some Observations on Anglo-Saxon Military Thinking in Light of the Burghal Hidage' in *Technology and Culture 31* (1990), 1–17, reprinted with the same pagination in Bernard S. Bachrach, *Warfare and Military Organization in Pre-Crusade Europe* (London, 2002);

Randall Rogers, *Latin Siege Warfare in the Twelfth Century* (Oxford, 1992);

Jim Bradbury, *The Medieval Siege* (Woodbridge, 1992);

Bernard S. Bachrach, 'Medieval Siege Warfare: A Reconnaissance' in *The Journal of Military History 58* (1994), 119–133, reprinted in Bernard S. Bachrach, *Warfare and Military Organization in Pre-Crusade Europe* (London, 2002);

Michael Toch, 'The Medieval German City under Siege' in *The Medieval City under Siege*, ed. Ivy A. Corfis and Michael Wolf (Woodbridge, 1995), 35–48, As well as the other essays in this volume;

Laurence W. Marvin, *The Occitan War: A Military and Political History of the Albigensian Crusade, 1209–1218* (Cambridge, 2008);

Peter Purton, *A History of the Early Medieval Siege c. 450–1200* (Woodbridge, 2010);

Peter Purton, *A History of the Late Medieval Siege, 1200–1500* (Woodbridge, 2010);

Leif Petersen, *Siege Warfare and Military Organization in the Successor Sates (400–800): Byzantium, the West and Islam* (Leiden, 2013).

Concerning medieval battlefield tactics, see

Karl J. Leyser, 'The Battle at the Lech, 955: A Study in Tenth-Century Warfare' in *History 50* (1965), 1–25, reprinted in Karl J. Leyser, *Medieval Germany and Its Neighbours, 900–1250* (London, 1982), 43–67;

Bernard S. Bachrach, 'The Feigned Retreat at Hastings' in *Medieval Studies 33* (1971), 344–347;

Nicholas Hooper, 'Anglo-Saxon Warfare on the Eve of the Conquest: A Brief Survey' in *Proceedings of the Battle Conference on Anglo-Norman Studies 1* (1978), 84–93 and 211–213;

Jim Bradbury, 'Battles in England and Normandy, 1066–1154' in *Anglo-Norman Studies 6* (1984), 1–12;

Bryce Lyon, 'The Role of Cavalry in Medieval Warfare: Horses, Horses All around and Not a One to Use' in *Mededelingen van de Koninklijke Academie voor Wetenschappen, Letteren en Schone Kunsten van Belgie 49* (1987), 77–90;

Stephen Morillo, 'Hastings: An Unusual Battle' in *Haskins Society Journal 2* (1990), 95–103;

Richard Abels, 'English Tactics and Military Organization in the late Tenth Century' in *The Battle of Maldon, AD 991*, ed. Donald Scragg (Oxford, 1991), 143–155;

Kelly DeVries, *Infantry Warfare in the Early Fourteenth Century: Discipline, Tactics, and Technology* (Woodbridge, 1996);

Charles R. Bowlus, 'Tactical and Strategic Weaknesses of Horse Archers on the Eve of the First Crusade' in *Autour de la Première Croisade: Actes du Colloque de la Society for the Study of the Crusades in the Latin East*, ed. Michel Balard (Paris, 1996), 159–166;

Clifford J. Rogers, 'The Offensive/Defensive in Medieval Strategy' in *XXIInd Colloquium of the International Commission of Military History: From Crécy to Mohacs: Warfare in the Late Middle Ages (1346–1526)* (Vienna, 1997), 158–171;

Bernard S. Bachrach, 'Verbruggen's "Cavalry" and the Lyon-Thesis' in *Journal of Medieval Military History 4* (2006), 137–163;

John Gillingham, 'Fontenoy and after: Pursuing Enemies to Death in France between the Ninth and Eleventh Centuries' in *Frankland: The Franks and the World of the Early Middle Ages, Essays in Honour of Dame Jinty Nelson*, ed. Paul Fouracre and David Ganz (Manchester, 2008), 242–265;

John France, 'A Changing Balance: Cavalry and Infantry, 1000–1300' in *Revista de História das ideias 30* (2009), 153–177;

Bernard S. Bachrach and David S. Bachrach, 'Ralph of Caen as a Military History' in *Crusading and Warfare in the Middle Ages: Realities and Representations, Essays in Honour of John France*, ed. John Simon and Nicholas Morton (Aldershot, 2014), 87–99;

Benjamin Z. Kedar, 'King Richard's Plan for the Battle of Arsuf/Arsur, 1191' in *The Medieval Way of War: Studies in Medieval Military History in Honor of Bernard S. Bachrach*, ed. Gregory I. Halfond (Farnham, 2015), 117–132.

For an introduction to naval tactics and combat, see

F. W. Brooks, 'The Battle of Damme, 1213' in *The Mariner's Mirror 16* (1930), 264–271;

James Sherborne, 'The Battle of La Rochelle and the War at Sea, 1372–1375' in *The Bulletin of the Institute of Historical Research 42* (1969), 17–29;

Federico Foerster Laures, 'The Warships of the Kings of Aragon and Their Fighting Tactics during the 13th and 14th Centuries AD' in *The International Journal of Nautical Archaeology and Underwater Exploration 16* (1987), 19–29;

M. J. Swanton, 'King Alfred's Ships: Text and Context' in *Anglo-Saxon England 28* (1999), 1–22;

Susan Rose, *Medieval Naval Warfare 1000–1500* (London, 2002);

Ian Friel, 'Oars, Sails and Guns: The English and the War at Sea, c. 1200–1500' in *War at Sea in the Middle Ages and Renaissance*, ed. John B. Hattendorf and Richard W. Unger (Woodbridge, 2003), 69–79;

William Sayers, 'Naval Tactics at the Battle of Zierikzee' in *Journal of Medieval Military History 4* (2006), 74–90;

Kelly DeVries, 'God, Leadership, Flemings and Archery: Contemporary Perceptions of Victory and Defeat at the Battle of Sluys, 1340' in *Medieval Ships and Warfare*, ed. Susan Rose (Aldershot, 2008), 131–150, as well as the other essays collected in this volume.

For the use of naval forces in support of land-based armies, see

Daniel P. Waley, 'Combined Operations in Sicily AD 1060–1078' in *Papers of the British School at Rome 22* (1954), 118–125;

W. Stanford Reid, 'Sea-Power in the Anglo-Scottish War, 1296–1326' in *The Mariner's Mirror 46* (1960), 83–103;

Michael Weir, 'English Naval Activities 1242–1243' in *The Mariner's Mirror 58* (1972), 85–92;

Donald Queller, 'Combined Arms Operations and the Latin Conquest of Constantinople' in *Changing Interpretations and New Sources in Naval History*, ed. R. W. Love (New York, 1980), 45–57;

Matthew Bennett, 'Amphibious Operations from the Norman Conquest to the Crusades of Saint Louis c. 1050 – c. 1250' in *Amphibious Warfare 1000–1700: Commerce, State Formation and European Expansion*, ed. D. J. B. Trim and Mark Charles Fissel (Leiden, 2006), 51–68;

Louis Sicking, 'Naval Warfare in Europe, c. 1330 – c. 1680' in *European Warfare, 1350–1750*, ed. Frank Tallett and D. J. B. Trim (Cambridge, 2010), 236–263;

Craig L. Lambert, 'Edward III's Siege of Calais: A Reappraisal' in *Journal of Medieval History 37* (2011), 245–256.

Regarding fear among soldiers and efforts to maintain high morale, see

John Keegan, *The Face of Battle: A Study of Agincourt, Waterloo, and the Somme* (New York, 1978);

W. R. Jones, 'The English Church and Royal Propaganda during the Hundred Years' War' in *Journal of British Studies 19* (1979), 18–30;

Michael McCormick, *Eternal Victory: Triumphal Rulership in Late Antiquity, Byzantium, and the Early Medieval West* (Cambridge, 1986);

John Bliese, 'Aelred of Rievaulx's Rhetoric and Morale at the Battle of the Standard 1138' in *Albion 20* (1988), 543–556;

John Bliese, 'The Battle Rhetoric of Aelred of Rievaulx' in *The Haskins Society Journal 1* (1989), 99–107;

D. W. Burton, 'Requests for Prayers and Royal Propaganda under Edward I' in *Thirteenth Century England 3* (1989), 25–35;

Christoph T. Maier, 'Crisis, Liturgy, and the Crusade in the Twelfth and Thirteenth Centuries' in *Journal of Ecclesiastical History 48* (1997), 628–657;

David S. Bachrach, *Religion and the Conduct of War c. 300–1215* (Woodbridge, 2003);

David S. Bachrach, 'The Organisation of Military Religion in the Armies of Edward I of England (1272–1307)' in *Journal of Medieval History 29* (2003), 265–286;

Steven Isaac, 'Cowardice and Fear Management: The 1173–74 Conflict as a Case Study' in *Journal of Medieval Military History 4* (2006), 50–64;

Stephen Morillo, 'Expecting Cowardice: Medieval Battle Tactics Reconsidered' in *Journal of Medieval Military History 4* (2006), 65–73;

Robert W. Jones, *Bloodied Banners: Martial Display on the Medieval Battlefield* (Woodbridge, 2010).

With respect to military discipline, see

Elisabeth Magnou-Nortier, 'The Enemies of the Peace: Reflections on a Vocabulary, 500–1100' in *The Peace of God: Social Violence and Religious Response in France around the Year 1000*, ed. Thomas Head and Richard Landes (Ithaca, 1992), 58–79;

Anne Curry, 'Disciplinary Ordinances for English and Franco-Scottish Armies in 1385: An International Code?' in *Journal of Medieval History 37* (2011), 269–294.

With respect to training, see the suggested further reading in Chapter 7

With regard to the supposed relationship of chivalry and warfare, see

John Gillingham, '1066 and the Introduction of Chivalry into England' in *Law and Government in Medieval England and Normandy: Essays in Honour of Sir James Holt* (Cambridge, 1994), 31–55;

Robert C. Stacey, 'The Age of Chivalry' in *The Laws of War: Constraints on Warfare in the Western World*, ed. Michael Howard, George J. Andreopoulos, and Mark R. Schulman (New Haven, 1994), 27–39;

Maurice Keen, *Chivalry* (New Haven, 2005);

Richard Kaeuper, *Medieval Chivalry* (Cambridge, 2016).

Conflicting views

What was the role of mounted forces in early medieval warfare?

Charles R. Bowlus, 'Two Carolingian Campaigns Reconsidered' in *Military Affairs 48* (1984), 121–125;

Matthew Bennett, 'The Myth of the Military Supremacy of Knightly Cavalry' in *Armies, Chivalry and Warfare*, ed. Matthew Strickland (Stamford, 1990), 304–316;

Clifford Rogers, 'Carolingian Cavalry in Battle: The Evidence Reconsidered' in *Crusading Warfare in the Middle Ages: Realities and Representations. Essays in Honour of John France*, ed. Simon John and Nicholas Morton (Farnham, 2014), 1–11.

What was the value of longbows in combat during the Hundred Years' War?

Kelly DeVries, 'Catapults Are Not Atomic Bombs: Towards a Redefinition of "Effectiveness" in Premodern Military Technology' in *War in History 4.4* (1997), 454–470;

Clifford Rogers, 'The Efficacy of the Medieval Longbow: A Reply to Kelly DeVries' in *War in History 5.2* (1998), 233–242.

7 Strategy

Introduction: what is strategy?

Military theorists and military historians tend to divide the topic of strategy into two parts: grand strategy and campaign strategy. The first of these concepts has benefitted from considerable discussion, but there remains no consensus about how to define the term. Instead, both theorists and historians tend to use a bundle of characteristics when discussing grand strategy. The first characteristic about which there is some agreement is that grand strategy involves the long term, which has been described as anything longer than a single campaign to a period of decades. In addition, grand strategy generally is presented as encompassing not only the planning of military operations, but also as involving the mobilization of economic and perhaps ideological resources, the establishment of extensive infrastructure elements, and also as possessing diplomatic and political components. Grand strategy is, therefore, not primarily about winning battles or even about winning wars, but rather concerns the mobilization over the long term of a polity's overall assets, including its military resources, in order to define its place among its neighbours.

As discussed in previous chapters, perhaps the best known and certainly the most controversial treatment of a supposed grand strategy in the pre-modern West is Edward Luttwak's book *The Grand Strategy of the Roman Empire from the First Century* A.D. *to the Third*, originally published in 1976. In this work, and in subsequent essays, Luttwak postulated that the Roman government envisioned and carried out a strategy of frontier defence for the entire empire over a period of three centuries. Moreover, Luttwak argued that this grand strategy evolved over time in order to meet the changing geo-political situations in which the empire found itself, with the eventual development of three entirely different schemes for territorial defence. Numerous scholars have disputed Luttwak's basic premise that the Roman imperial government had the capacity to undertake planning on an empire-wide scale, and the concomitant administrative and material resources to put these plans into action. By contrast, other specialists in Roman history – while arguing against the notion that any single strategy encompassed the entire empire – nevertheless accept the model that the imperial government had both the inclination and capacity to make and execute long-term plans involving a range of military, political, economic, and ideological assets.

In a similar vein, in Chapters 2–3 of this text, we have made the case that Luttwak's premise regarding the development of a grand strategy by the Roman imperial government is applicable to numerous polities in the Latin West and Levant throughout the medieval millennium. On a societal scale, the organization of medieval Europe for war, although divided over time in a kaleidoscopic array of kingdoms and lesser polities, was marked by the construction and maintenance of a systematic and ubiquitous military topography of

DOI: 10.4324/9781003032878-8

fortifications, with the associated transportation infrastructure, alongside the institution of universal military service by all able-bodied secular men for the purpose of defending the homeland.

During most of the medieval period, this military service was determined by wealth so that richer individuals and ecclesiastical institutions bore heavier military burdens in a gradated manner down to the level of the *pauperes*. At the scale of individual kingdoms, it is clear that numerous medieval governments envisioned long-term plans for territorial conquest, often with a strong ideological component. The intellectuals at the court of Charlemagne, for example, developed a model of hegemonic imperial rule based on the re-establishment of the Roman Empire in the West. This ideological model strongly influenced Charlemagne's strategic thinking throughout his reign of forty-six years. Similarly, over a period of twenty-five years, King Edward I of England developed and executed a grand strategy for the conquest of Wales and Scotland, thereby bringing under his control almost the entirety of the island that later would become known as Great Britain.

By contrast with grand strategy, both scholars and military theorists typically use the term strategy *tout court* to describe the approach taken by a polity to the conduct of war, and particularly to the conduct of an individual campaign. In our view, campaign strategy remained relatively stable across the entire Middle Ages. This reality, in large part, was a consequence of the slow and uneven development and diffusion of both military and transportation technology throughout the medieval millennium, as seen in Chapters 4 and 5. As a result of these factors, both territorial defence and territorial conquest depended upon the control of fortress cities, as well as lesser fortifications. For offensive warfare directed at conquest, the need to capture fortresses entailed both the mobilization of large armies capable of undertaking sieges, and the concomitant development of an administrative system that was able to keep these forces supplied with food and materiel for lengthy periods.

By contrast, raiding operations that were focused on capturing booty and taking prisoners as slaves and for ransom were relatively short-term efforts and small scale in nature. As will be discussed later in the chapter, the one major exception to this pattern in the Middle Ages was during the period of the Hundred Years' War, and particularly after the advent of the Black Death in the mid-fourteenth century and its recurrence throughout the next century. The death of between one-third and one-half of the population across much of Western Europe had profound effects on the organization of society for war generally, and the conduct of military campaigns directed towards territorial conquest in particular.

The focus in this chapter is on those elements of campaign and grand strategy that were not developed fully earlier in the text. The initial stage of any campaign and its conceptualization as part of a polity's longer-term political, diplomatic, and military interests was the gathering of information not only in regard to adversaries or potential adversaries, but also in regard to one's own resources. Despite the image presented in popular media, and even by some scholars, medieval rulers did not simply wake up in the morning, decide to invade a neighbouring principality, and rouse their 'warriors' for a gallop down the road. Just as is the case with respect to modern military operations, a vast quantity of information first had to be gathered, synthesized, and then analyzed so that the ruler could conceptualize his goals in a reasonable manner and make an informed decision about his range of options. Determining what these options were required an accurate accounting of the resources available to him and to his opponent, including military, economic, and diplomatic assets, and the likely consequences of a particular set of military operations. In addition, even the most powerful rulers found it necessary to convince many of their subjects – both among the magnates, as well as the rank and file of the army – that the military option not only was desirable, but also likely to be successful. The first two sections of this chapter, therefore, deal with the issues of military planning and the acquisition of intelligence.

We have already discussed at length in previous chapters the roles played by military topography, military organization, and military technology and transportation resources in the development of both campaign and grand strategy, and will not rehearse these in detail here. Rather, in the second half of this chapter, we will focus on the ways in which medieval rulers conceptualized and used diplomacy and calculated destruction, or the threat of destruction, as elements in campaign strategy, and also, to some extent, in grand strategy, as well. Finally, all aspects of the development of both grand strategy and campaign strategy required an infrastructure of educated military commanders and trained staff who were capable of planning and carrying out military operations in both the short and long term. As a consequence, we will conclude this chapter with a discussion of military education in the medieval millennium.

Military planning

All military operations, whether offensive or defensive, require planning. The depth and detail of the planning that is required today and was required during the Middle Ages depended upon three factors: the complexity of the military operations that were to be undertaken, the quantities of material and number of men involved, and the potential duration of the campaign. For the most part, medieval rulers developed military plans either in support of an ongoing strategy or for the initiation of a new strategy. For example, the development of plans at the royal court of Mercia during the later eighth century that led to the construction of the massive defensive work now known as Offa's Dyke, which divides Wales from Mercia, can be understood as an element in an ongoing strategy to defend the western frontier of the kingdom. By contrast, the military planning that preceded King Henry I of Germany's conquest of the lands to the east of the Saale and Elbe river systems and the concomitant construction of several layers of fortifications there during the 930s can be understood as the initiation of a new strategy of territorial defence against the Hungarians (which is discussed in greater detail in Chapter 8). Indeed, this new strategy was a marked deviation from the strategy of Henry I's Carolingian predecessors, who assiduously avoided attempting to conquer these eastern lands.

In a similar vein, Thomas Asbridge recently has discussed the military planning undertaken by King Baldwin II of Jerusalem (1118–1131) to alter fundamentally the strategic status quo facing the nascent crusader state, which comprised a narrow strip along the Mediterranean littoral. Baldwin understood that in order to create strategic depth for his realm as well as for the Principality of Antioch, it would be necessary to push Latin Christian rule into the interior of Syria. As a consequence, Baldwin, who possessed important sources of intelligence from within the Muslim realms to his east, developed a complex plan to capture the fortress city of Aleppo, located 100 kilometres to the east of Antioch, in alliance with the disaffected Bedouin leader Dubais ibn Sadaqa, as well as other Muslim magnates. The siege of Aleppo, which was carried on throughout the fall and early winter of 1124–1125, ultimately failed when the city was relieved by an army from Mosul commanded by the atabeg Aksungur al-Bursuqi.

Despite the failure of this enormous military operation, King Baldwin maintained his view that the long-term success of the Kingdom of Jerusalem required the establishment of territorial depth. As a consequence, in 1129, Baldwin undertook another major military operation, this time directed at Damascus. The Christian army is estimated by Asbridge to have numbered more than 12,000 men, including forces from all four crusader states, as well as additional troops brought by Count Fulk of Anjou, Baldwin's new son-in-law and future king of Jerusalem. This invasion also failed, in large part, because of the ability of the ruler of Damascus to kill the Muslim magnates, who had agreed to aid Baldwin in his siege of the city.

It is difficult to exaggerate the great masses of detail that it was necessary for military planners such as King Baldwin II to gather and to analyze in the course of their work. This includes information about all of the variables relating to the mobilization of one's own military forces, as well as their supply and transportation. Just as important is information about the physical and military topography of the region or regions where military operations are to take place, as well as the numbers, types, and dispositions of enemy military forces and defensive assets. To these factors must be added information regarding the strategic and tactical doctrines of the enemy, their military organization, the potential political vulnerabilities of the enemy, and the likely actions of ostensibly allied and neutral rulers once a campaign has begun. The success of any particular military strategy depends, in very large part, on the ability of a government to develop accurate information with regard to all of these questions. A second necessary step is the analysis and effective distribution of this information to military commanders so that they can use it when planning their own operations in a more localized context or in responding to impending enemy action. The acquisition of this information is treated in the next section. Here, the focus is on the evidence for military planning during the Middle Ages.

Military planning groups

It is sometimes argued that medieval rulers, particularly in the period before the First Crusade, lacked the intellectual framework or inclination for long-term planning of any sort, but particularly in the conduct of war. A corollary argument, which has also been made with respect Luttwak's model of Roman grand strategy, is that there is no term in Latin or in any medieval vernacular language for an institution that might be understood as having similar functions to a planning or general staff as this concept is used in modern military contexts. As will become clear, this latter claim is factually incorrect, at least with regard to the Carolingian Empire. However, with respect to the broader question about the failure of most medieval governments to coin specific terms to denote a staff with responsibility for military planning, it is worth noting that Great Britain lacked both the term and the specific institutional structure of a general staff until the late nineteenth century. Nevertheless, it is quite clear that substantial military planning was carried out by officials within the British government to deploy both armies and fleets for operations across the globe before this point. Britain's continental competitors, France and Prussia, were somewhat more precocious in this area, introducing a formal general staff structure in the late eighteenth and early nineteenth centuries, respectively. Both nations, of course, also demonstrated considerable capabilities in military planning before the introduction of these formal institutions and the coining of terms to denote them.

Perhaps the clearest theoretical – as well as practical – discussion of the function of a military planning staff in the early medieval period comes from the pen of Adalhard (died 826), a cousin of Charlemagne and abbot of the prestigious and wealthy monastery of Corbie. As we have discussed in previous chapters, in the late eighth century, Adalhard wrote a handbook on the governance of the kingdom entitled *On the Organization of the Palace* (*De ordine palatii*), which provides insights, garnered from personal experience, regarding both the proper functioning of the royal household and the administration of the kingdom as a whole. In this text, Adalhard observes that the Frankish kings generally had two military assemblies each year. The second, which often took place late in the spring, involved the mobilization of the army for campaign. The first meeting took place four or five months earlier in November or December, and involved a small number of senior advisors and knowledgeable specialists. These men, who were summoned by the king, worked together to plan the campaign(s) for the forthcoming year. According to Adalhard, the specialists who attended the earlier, winter assembly included those who were familiar with affairs within the kingdom, and those who had special expertise regarding one or another of the neighbouring peoples against whom the Frankish kings might need to wage war. In fact, Adalhard used specific terms to identify these men, such as special advisors (*praecipui consiliarii*).

The planning staff were required to develop detailed reports, denoted by Adalhard as *capitula*, which were to be used by the king in determining whether he would launch a campaign, and if so, what actions were required to carry out these military operations. The assembled planning group also had a common designation, which was known to members of Charlemagne's court, and is recorded c.805 by the anonymous author of the *Earlier Metz Annals*, whose audience consisted of members of the court. The term used by the author of the *Metz Annals* to denote this planning staff was the *magistratus*. This term is otherwise known from the Carolingian period in ecclesiastical legislation issued by the council of Ravenna in 877, where a body of specialists denoted as a *magistratus* was to be convened to hear complaints made by bishops and other clerics, and see to it that they were remedied.

Adalhard's enunciation of a programmatic model for planning by the Frankish government to undertake military operations finds its 'real-time' counterpart in numerous commands issued by Carolingian rulers for the organization of men and supplies for campaigns that were to take place months in the future. These commands are discussed in detail in Chapters 3–4, and clearly are indicative of planning that took place before the royal commands were issued. For example, Emperor Louis II's issuance of ordinances for a campaign towards Benevento in 866, discussed in Chapter 4, is only understandable if detailed logistical planning for this campaign already had taken place.

A somewhat less detailed – but nevertheless revealing – discussion of military planning can be seen in Henry of Huntingdon's (died c.1157) account of the assembly of Norman magnates that took place at Lillebonne in Normandy in early 1066. According to Henry, whose twelfth-century chronicle is informed by earlier and now lost oral and written testimony, once Duke William learned in the first weeks of 1066 about Harold Godwinson's decision to take the English crown, he ordered his magnates to join him in an assembly at Lillebonne for the specific purpose of offering the duke their counsel. Once there, William asked his magnates to support his prospective campaign to England, and then had William FitzOsbern (died 1071), his close advisor, make a presentation to the assembled men. FitzOsbern then, according to Henry of Huntingdon, made the case to the assembled Norman magnates about the ways in which they would be able to undertake this dangerous campaign and emerge victorious. Following this presentation, the Norman magnates are all reported to have agreed to support their duke. Henry then emphasizes that as soon as William had confirmed the support of his magnates, he undertook the construction of a fleet to transport an army to England and assigned additional quotas of ships that his magnates were to supply for the campaign.

Henry of Huntingdon's presentation of the events at Lillebonne makes clear that even before the death of King Edward the Confessor of England and Harold's succession, William and his advisors had been hard at work developing plans for an invasion. The success of William FitzOsbern in galvanizing the support of the Norman magnates for their duke's exceptionally ambitious military operation should certainly be understood as resulting from the ability of the duke and his close advisors to answer all of the practical questions raised by the men at Lillebonne regarding how the campaign would unfold. Hard-headed Norman magnates, who had a great deal to lose in this gamble, including their lives, surely would not have been persuaded by airy promises of divine intervention on their behalf or have been blinded by greed to the dangers inherent in an amphibious invasion of a powerful kingdom. Moreover, Henry of Huntingdon's emphasis on Duke William's subsequent and immediate construction of a fleet makes clear that all of the necessary preparatory planning already had taken place, including the acquisition of timber and the recruitment of carpenters and other specialists in ship construction, perhaps including Normans from southern Italy.

There are numerous other examples of references in pre-crusade narrative sources of rulers meeting with their advisors for the purpose of planning military operations. The eleventh-century German historian Berthold of Reichenau, for example, notes that King Henry IV of Germany announced at his winter court at Strasbourg in 1074 that he was intending to undertake a campaign the next year against Hungary, and that planning for this military operation was under way. King Henry's enunciation of this plan, in the presence of the assembled princes of the kingdom, who would be responsible for leading military contingents, is similar to the winter planning session described by Adalhard with regard to the Carolingian court. However, Berthold wryly observes that the announcement was a ruse, and that the king intended to use the army that he mobilized against the Saxons rather than against the Hungarians. Similar discussions of advanced planning for military operations can be seen in numerous narrative accounts, as well as letters from the high and late Middle Ages. Edward III, for example, enunciated his plan to undertake a battle-seeking strategy against the French in a letter to the English parliament in 1346.

In addition to the mention of planning in various narrative texts and letters, however, the vast increase in the survival of administrative documents from the later Middle Ages makes it possible to trace out the specific actions undertaken by members of the ruler's staff as they developed plans for military operations. The best documented actions that were taken as a result of military planning come from the considerable surviving archives of the English royal government, particularly from the reign of Edward I. As these texts make clear, Edward I worked with a council of military, financial, and administrative advisors who offered their expertise over many years and even decades of service. The results of their advice and advanced planning can be seen in thousands of surviving orders dispatched by the chancery to sheriffs, constables, and other royal officials at the local level.

In response to the failure of peace negotiations with the French in 1294, for example, Edward I's council planned to send substantial military forces and supplies to Gascony to counter an expected French invasion. To this end, as revealed in surviving administrative documents, dozens of royal clerks were dispatched to the counties throughout England, where they successfully collaborated with sheriffs to acquire, transport, and store thousands of tonnes of food supplies and substantial quantities of arms, including hundreds of thousands of crossbow bolts, for subsequent shipment to Gascony. The execution of the plans developed by the king's council for mobilizing supplies was placed in the hands of John de Maidstone, who had been employed as a military administrator by Edward I for well over a decade. Indeed, it was John de Maidstone who organized the successful provisioning of English forces during their invasion of Wales in 1282. It is consequently fitting that it was also John de Maidstone who was given the task of redirecting all of the men and materiel that had been mobilized to deal with the French in Gascony towards Wales in response to the rebellion there against English rule late in 1294.

Military intelligence

The previous section indicates the extensive work that was necessary to develop a coherent strategy for the conduct of military operations. The foundation for this planning work was information. In many cases, information necessary for military planning was made available to medieval rulers through the normal processes of governance. For example, the regular auditing of fiscal, secular, and ecclesiastical resources by the government of the Carolingian Empire and its successors east and west of the Rhine provided considerable information to the court about both the quantities and locations of militarily useful resources such as food and equipment. In the Christian kingdoms of Iberia, these auditing procedures were complemented by the ongoing obligation of frontier towns to keep detailed records of their own military resources. The kings of England maintained up-to-date lists of all property owners who owed military service for their lands. In addition, royal clerks such as John de Maidstone, noted previously, and his officials cooperated with sheriffs at the county level to assess the number of men, tonnes of food supplies, as well as the ships, carts, and pack animals that were available for military operations. In considering the enormous administrative efforts that were required to mobilize military forces during Edward I's reign, it is worth considering that the population of England c.1300 was approximately one-fifth the size of Charlemagne's empire in c.800.

Different types of efforts, however, were required to develop sound intelligence regarding matters that were not under the direct control of the government. These external factors can be divided into categories. Information about the intentions and goals of enemy rulers and commanders, the location of roads, sources of fresh water, and fortifications in enemy territory as well as the campaign and combat doctrines of the enemy might be termed strategic military intelligence. For example, it was necessary to know that Arabs and Hungarians used light fast horses, while western opponents used heavy warhorses for combat purposes. By contrast, the specific location of enemy forces at any given time, their numbers, and their deployment in the period before a potential battle can be thought of as tactical military intelligence.

Strategic intelligence

Medieval Christians had an easily accessible account of the importance of strategic intelligence for military operations in the biblical Book of Numbers (13:1–31), where the story is told of the exploits of Joshua and Caleb. As the Israelites were planning their entry into Canaan, Moses asked twelve spies, one from each of the Israelite tribes, to bring back information about the topography of the land, the location and size of the cities, the population, their military strength, and their political organization, i.e. the basic information that was required for satisfactory military intelligence. According to the biblical account, ten of the spies were ineffective in their task because their fear prevented them from providing an accurate assessment, overstating the military strength of the Canaanites. By contrast, Joshua and Caleb were effective in gathering intelligence because they provided accurate information that allowed Moses and his advisors to plan effectively.

In his path-breaking study of military intelligence from the late eleventh through the early thirteenth centuries, J.O. Prestwich, who served as an intelligence analyst in Britain during the Second World War, illuminates the existence of a veritable intelligence service under the Anglo-Norman and Angevin kings of England. William the Conqueror, for example, possessed a highly placed operative or operatives within the Danish royal court who provided considerable advance warnings about the planned invasions of Yorkshire by Danish fleets in both 1075 and 1085. In the first case, Archbishop Lanfranc of Canterbury (1070–1089), after receiving instructions from King William, issued orders to the garrison commanders in the region to ready their forces and fortify their castles because 'the Danes are coming for certain, as the king has informed us'. In 1085, King William had sufficient advance warning of the planned Danish invasion that he was able to muster an army in France and transport the troops to the north of England to counter the Danish landing.

In this context, when William conquered the Anglo-Saxon realm, he learned that his new subjects had a highly developed intelligence system, as well as messenger systems for the rapid transmission of information. This was particular true along the Welsh frontier, where the Anglo-Saxon rulers frequently found it necessary to undertake military operations to retaliate for Welsh raids across the frontier into the valley of the Wye River, with its major city at Hereford. The men of this messenger and scouting system were called *radmanni* in contemporary Anglo-Saxon documents. The Domesday Book records 665 *radmanni* also known as *radchenishtri*, who held estates of considerable value along the Welsh frontier, indicating that William the Conquer kept this system in place once he gain power throughout England.

William the Conqueror's descendant Henry II also actively sought to place agents in courts throughout Europe. One royal clerk named John of Oxford undertook missions in the German kingdom, as well as in Rome and in Sicily. The detailed accounts of the topography, political organization, and culture of Ireland and Wales written by Gerald of Wales, a royal chaplain at Henry II's court, also might be understood as elements in Henry II's intelligence-gathering operations. Gerald's activities take on increasing importance as evidence of intelligence gathering in light of John Gillingham's argument that Henry II was not really interested in contemporary history at all, and so would not have patronized works that were merely of scholarly interest. In this context, Gerald's histories are akin to many such previous works dating back to the ancient Greeks and Romans that provided basic information about the enemy. Texts of this sort are discussed later in the chapter in relation to the education of military leaders.

Naturally, neither Henry II nor William the Conqueror was the first ruler to understand the crucial importance of strategic intelligence for the purposes of military planning. In addition to discussing the military planning staff at Charlemagne's court, Adalhard of Corbie also emphasized the necessity of obtaining intelligence so that the military planners could do their jobs. Narrative sources and government documents, as well as letters from the reigns of Charlemagne and his successors, indicate that the information analyzed by the *magistratus* was derived from numerous sources. Among these were detailed itineraries, often Roman in origin, such as the so-called Peutinger Table, discussed in Chapter 2, which provided details about the location of roads, cities, towns, and villages throughout the Latin West. Carolingian authorities also consulted historical works that could provide insights regarding topographical features that remained stable over long periods such as the location of mountain passes and large river valleys. In one case, on the eve of his invasion of Saxony in 777, Charlemagne commanded Abbot Gundelandus of Lorsch to come to the royal court and bring with him a copy of Lucius Annaeus Florus' *Epitome*, written in the first century AD, because it provided information about the roads, marching routes, and fortifications that the Romans had established during their campaigns in the region between the Rhine and Weser rivers.

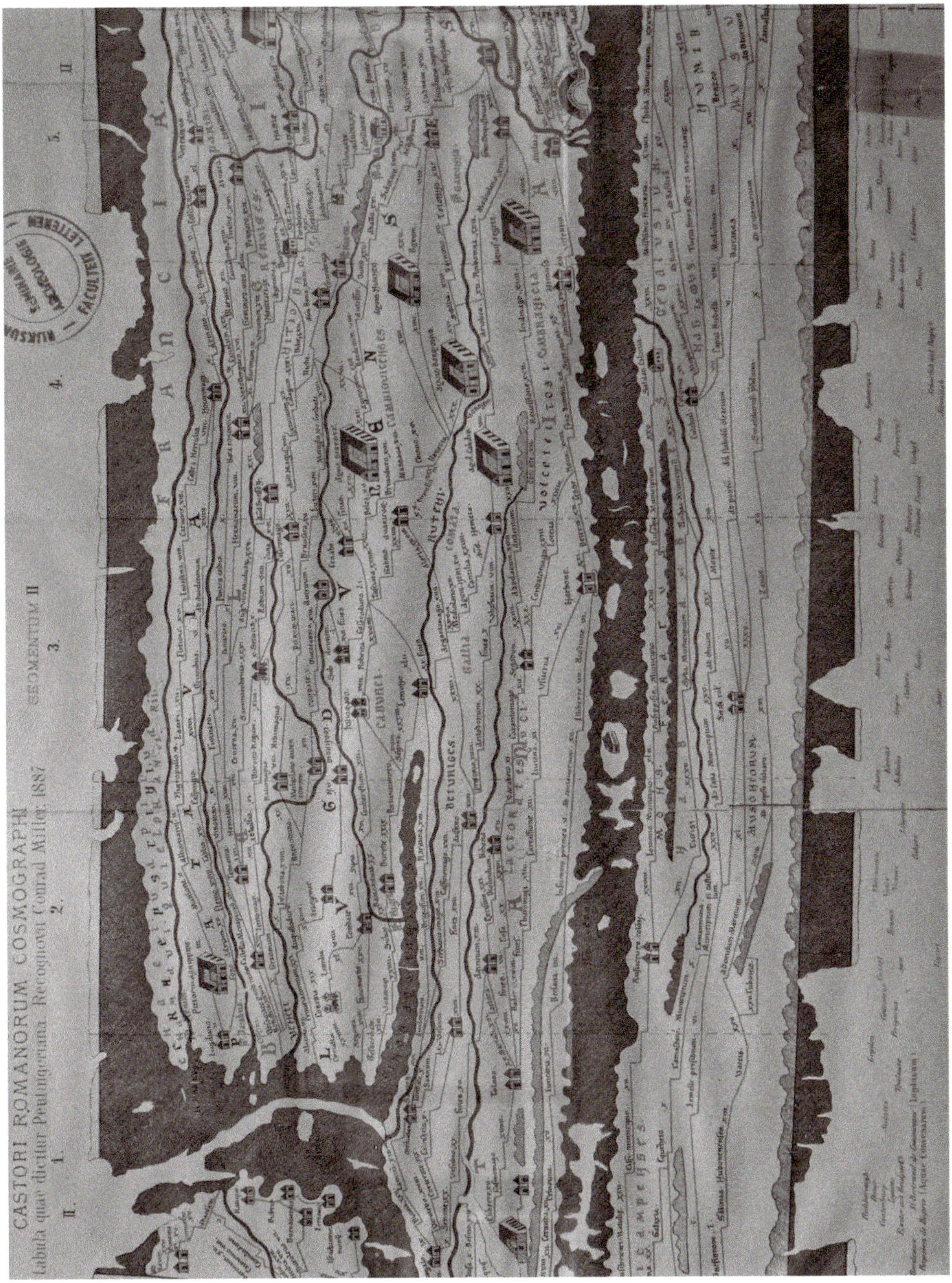

Figure 7.1 Francia on the Peutinger Map

Source: © Arterra Picture Library/Alamy Stock Photo W7H42T

In addition to 'old books' that provided historical intelligence, Charlemagne's officials routinely debriefed merchants and missionaries who had travelled to the lands beyond the frontier of the Frankish kingdom in order to gain fresh information. In some cases, information obtained in this manner played decisive roles in Carolingian campaigns. Charlemagne's intense interest in intelligence gathering is further evidenced by the command for all royal officials in frontier regions to take the initiative in finding out as much as they could about the lands beyond the kingdom's borders and to pass this information to the royal court expeditiously. Official documents issued by Charlemagne, denoted as capitularies, refer to the ongoing work of government officials throughout the empire to gather intelligence about problems both beyond the frontiers and at home.

The practical results of such intelligence gathering are illuminated in a report commissioned by Charlemagne's grandson, Louis the German, sometime between 846 and 862. The *Description of the Fortresses and Regions along the Northern Banks of the Danube* provides extensive and detailed information about the number of fortifications that had been constructed by Louis' adversaries, and potential opponents, in the Slavic lands between the North Sea and the Danube. Considerable archaeological work undertaken during the past fifty years has made clear that Louis the German's intelligence network was quite competent in providing an accurate assessment of the military situation beyond the eastern frontier of his kingdom. As more excavations are pursued by archaeologists, it likely will be learned that Louis the German's intelligence sources were even more effective than the as-yet-incomplete survey of Slavic fortifications has unearthed.

In addition to obtaining strictly military intelligence about their adversaries, the Carolingians also were concerned to gain political intelligence that impinged on long-term military concerns. For example, the author of the court-based *Annales regni Francorum* recorded that in 823, Louis the Pious dispatched two counts to Denmark to learn 'all that

Figure 7.2 King and court

they could about these lands'. Louis also dispatched Archbishop Ebo of Rheims ostensibly to preach in the Danish kingdom, but also to engage in intelligence gathering. A similar example of political intelligence gathering is revealed in a fortuitously surviving letter sent by Margrave Aribo of the Pannonian frontier to King Arnulf of Carinthia, a grandson of Louis the German. The letter informed Arnulf that Aribo's agents had returned from the east and brought news about what was happening in the Slavic border lands of his march. In particular, Aribo reported that the Slavic people, whom he denotes as the Marahoni, which should be taken to mean the Moravians, were prepared to subordinate themselves to Arnulf's rule, and to reject the rule of their current leader Svatopluk, who held power in Moravia (c.870–c.894). Aribo's letter also makes clear that Wiching, who later served as Arnulf's chancellor and as bishop of Passau, also was operating in the Slavic lands and had obtained additional intelligence for the royal court.

Despite the rise of supposed 'chivalric values' during the course of the later Middle Ages, discussed in Chapter 6, and their putative role in affecting military affairs (i.e. the idea that gentlemen do not read each other's mail), medieval rulers from the thirteenth century onwards also recognized the pressing need for strategic intelligence in order to prepare for war. The remarkable case of Thomas Turberville, for example, illuminates the efforts of King Philip IV of France to gain information about the military plans of Edward I of England. Thomas made a long career in the service of the English kings, participating in several campaigns as a member of Edward I's military household. In 1294, Thomas led a substantial contingent in the royal army in Gascony, but was captured along with his sons by the French in April 1295. A few months later, Thomas reappeared in England, where he insisted that he had escaped from the French. In fact, however, Thomas had agreed to spy for King Philip in return for the continued safety of his sons, who were kept in Paris, and also for a substantial payment. Thomas provided considerable strategic intelligence to the French including the location of English military forces, and King Edward's diplomatic plans with regard to Scotland and Germany. Thomas' position as a member of the king's personal military household certainly facilitated his access to this information. Unfortunately for Thomas, his messenger to the French court was captured, and all was made known to Edward. Subsequently, Thomas was tried and executed, and the details of his case were distributed broadly within England as propaganda against the French and as a deterrent to anyone else who might choose to spy against his king and country.

In the next century, the use of spies during the course of the Hundred Years' War was discussed in detail by numerous contemporary chroniclers, and payments to spies can be found in royal records from both England and France. As Christopher Allmand has observed, the French soldier and writer Philippe de Mézières (died 1405) claimed that all prudent rulers sought information about the enemy before making any military plans. Jean Froissart, the prolific historian of the Hundred Years' War, who died in the same year as Mézières, also observed that princes and kings routinely employed spies. In fact, Froissart even made recommendations about the best individuals to recruit, emphasizing that those men who spoke numerous languages, such as French, German, and English, often were the most effective agents. Moreover, it was not only men who served as spies. The leaders of the city of Orléans dispatched a woman to join the household of King Henry V in 1417 in order to gain information about his military plans regarding their city. In view of the role that women played in intelligence gathering, late medieval commanders also issued ordinances alerting their men to the danger of accidentally providing sensitive military information to local prostitutes.

Secrecy

Indeed, maintaining secrecy was of paramount importance with regard to strategic intelligence. Medieval rulers were well aware that their enemies also were attempting to gain information about their plans and strategies. This point was emphasized, for example, by Charlemagne in several texts where the doctrine of sharing information on a 'need-to-know basis' was laid out very clearly. The practical implication of this concern for secrecy also is illuminated by Bishop Thietmar of Merseburg in his *Chronicon*, written in the early eleventh century. Thietmar, who worked closely with King Henry II of Germany in the development of military plans, emphasized this ruler's efforts to keep his intentions secret from the enemy. In one example regarding the planning of military operations in the spring of 1004, Thietmar records that Henry was well aware that his enemy Duke Boleslav of Poland had spies at the royal court. In order to mislead them and hence Boleslav, King Henry publicly issued orders for the mobilization of an army for the invasion of Poland. The German ruler even went so far as to pre-position a fleet on tributaries of the Elbe River in order to strengthen the impression that the operation would be directed at Poland. In response, Boleslav, who received warning from his spies, deployed his own forces in Poland to defend against the German invasion. However, Henry II's plan all along had been to march south to Bohemia rather than east to Poland, and he was able to achieve strategic surprise, leading a substantial army to Prague before Boleslav could respond. The element of misdirection used by Henry II in 1004 can be compared to the decision by Allied commanders in the Second World War to station a 'ghost' army under the command of U.S. Army Gen. George S. Patton at the logical crossing point to Calais in order to disguise the real invasion sites in Normandy in 1944.

A similar concern for maintaining secrecy regarding operational plans is discussed by William of Poitiers, the chaplain and biographer of William the Conqueror. As seen earlier in this chapter, William as king actively sought and used strategic intelligence regarding matters such as the military plans of the kings of Denmark. It is not surprising, therefore, that even before 1066, Duke William, according to William of Poitiers, was well informed about the intention of King Henry I of France to invade Normandy in 1054. William's successful defence of Normandy in that year led, however, to the extensive effort made by the French king to keep his planning and mobilization of forces secret from the Norman duke as he planned a renewed invasion of Normandy in 1057. William of Poitiers makes clear the success of the French forces during their invasion in this latter year was due, in great measure, to their ability to frustrate the efforts of Duke William's spies.

However, it was not only clandestine spies who obtained secret information. Members of embassies to foreign courts, as seen with regard to Henry II of England, also often provided exceptionally valuable intelligence. This point certainly was not lost on astute contemporary observers. Philippe de Mézières, mentioned previously, recommended that when foreign envoys were welcomed at court, they should always be given an escort and be prevented from speaking with anyone not pre-approved by the king. This is precisely what happened to Liudprand of Cremona when he was dispatched in 968 by Emperor Otto I of Germany as an ambassador to the court of the Byzantine emperor Nikephoros Phokas (963–969). Liudprand's detailed account of his visit, entitled *Report on my Legation to Constantinople*, describes the close confinement – indeed, house arrest – of himself and his entire staff, who were charged with attempting to spy and also to foment discord in the Byzantine court. A similar strategy was used in the eighth century by King Pippin I, the father of Charlemagne, when dealing with envoys to the Carolingian court from the Abbasid caliph in Baghdad.

The effort to keep military plans secret also led to the development of numerous devices and codes to hide the content of written messages. One technique used in the Merovingian period was to carve out hiding places in wooden tablets into which messages were placed that were written on either papyrus or parchment. These secret messages then were covered with a thin layer of wood, which, in turn, was covered with a layer of wax. As a last step, an innocuous message was inscribed in the wax that purported to be the entirety of the communication. This method of keeping information secret was employed, for example, by two messengers sent by the Merovingian Prince Gundovald during his effort to seize control of the kingdom of Burgundy from his uncle Guntram in 585. Unfortunately for Gundovald, the messengers were captured by Guntram's men, who discovered the hidden messages, and then jailed and beat the two messengers in order to obtain additional information.

More complex methods of maintaining the security of secret dispatches included using encryption codes and even entire secret languages. In other instances, the information was not committed to writing at all. Rather, the messenger was given a sealed letter of introduction that included details about his identity and appearance so that the recipient could be sure of his identity. These letters of introduction, some of which still survive today, then made clear that the messenger would provide the detailed information orally. Of course, there was a considerable danger that the messenger would be captured and tortured to obtain the information that he possessed. Torture during the Middle Ages tended to be very effective in getting victims to talk, especially when the information that was being divulged could be verified easily.

The danger of not using a secret code or other means of protecting a written message is illustrated by the failure of King Philip II of France's planned invasion of England in 1193. In preparation for this invasion, Philip first successfully plotted to prevent King Richard from returning to England after the Third Crusade. Richard had been captured by the duke of Austria while attempting to make an overland journey to his territories in Normandy without passing through lands ruled directly by the king of France. The duke of Austria then handed Richard over to King Henry VI of Germany, an ally of Philip, who encouraged the German ruler to hold Richard for a large ransom. Henry VI agreed, and Philip then put into action the next stage of his plot by supporting Prince John's revolt against his elder brother Richard in an effort to usurp the throne of England.

It was in support of this revolt that King Philip prepared a fleet and invasion force to join with John's supporters in southern England. However, according to the contemporary writer Gervase of Canterbury (died 1210), agents working for Richard's chief official in England (justiciar), Bishop Walter of Coutances (died 1207), captured messengers who were carrying the plans for the invasion, and gave up this information to the English government officials who interrogated them. In response, Walter mobilized extensive resources to refurbish and garrison fortifications along the coast in order to block the intended invasion. When he received word of the English preparations, King Philip stood down his fleet. Detailed information regarding the military expenditures authorized by Bishop Walter is to be found in the reports made by the royal sheriffs to the exchequer.

Strategic intelligence by the enemies of the Latin West

It was not only rulers of the Latin West who understood the vital importance of strategic intelligence for military planning. Their opponents also actively sought detailed information regarding political affairs, military topography, and the disposition of enemy forces. For example, many monastic chroniclers from the ninth and tenth centuries marvelled at the ability of the Vikings to attack a region precisely when the local rulers were at odds with each other and were therefore not able to provide a united defence. In part, the success of the Vikings in anticipating where they might attack with the least resistance can be explained by the fact that Frankish kings and magnates made a habit of employing Viking bands in their own internecine wars. However, it is clear that Scandinavian merchants also proved to be excellent sources of information to their pagan brethren regarding port facilities, the location of local fortifications and garrisons, and above all, the location of monasteries themselves. These religious houses, filled with treasures and members of noble families, were natural targets for Viking bands, and their precise locations and systems of defences were well-known to the raiders through diligent intelligence efforts.

A similar pattern of strategic intelligence gathering can be seen in the military planning of the Hungarians (Magyars), who raided extensively in the German kingdom, northern Italy, and even as far west and north as modern Belgium and northwestern France during the course of the first half of the tenth century. As was the case for the Vikings, the Hungarians first were introduced into Western Europe as mercenaries, employed by one or another king or magnate in pursuit of political control within his region. By the first decade of the tenth century, however, the Hungarians were undertaking independent military operations for their own purposes. These extensive raids, which often involved several thousand men, were made possible by the detailed knowledge that Hungarian leaders had gained during the course of the previous twenty years regarding the location of roads, including their state during various times of the year, and fortifications, as well as likely sources of plunder and supply for themselves and their numerous mounts. The last large-scale Hungarian penetration deep into the West, which took place in the spring of 954, saw thousands of mounted raiders reach the densely fortified region along the middle course of the Rhine River. Numerous contemporary chronicles make clear that this Hungarian raid into lands that previously had been free from their scourge only was made possible by the provision of guides by rebels against the German ruler Otto I, such as the duke of Lotharingia.

In Southern Europe and across the Mediterranean, Muslim forces throughout the medieval millennium also sought to obtain strategic intelligence about their Christian foes. As seen in Chapter 3, the Muslim conquest of Iberia and their successful military operations in southwestern Gaul during the early eighth century were facilitated to a significant degree by the military support and intelligence provided by the Jewish populations in numerous fortress cities, who had been persecuted by several of the recent Visigothic kings. In addition, Jews who had fled from Iberia to North Africa provided information to Muslim leaders there, which was passed on to the generals who led their armies into Spain.

In the period following his capture of Jerusalem in 1187, Saladin also was quite successful in obtaining strategic intelligence regarding military planning by the kings of France, England, and Germany as they prepared for the Third Crusade to re-establish the Kingdom of Jerusalem by retaking control of the capital. Indeed, it is clear that western rulers, including both Richard I and Frederick Barbarossa, believed that Saladin worked diligently to establish cordial diplomatic relations with the Byzantine Emperor Isaac II Angelos, in large part, to frustrate the movement of western armies through Asia Minor and to deny them access to Byzantine ports and sources of supply. Western chroniclers who provide information about the lengthy siege of Acre also record that Saladin had information about the death of Barbarossa in Asia Minor in June 1190 and the subsequent dissolution of the German army long before this news reached the Christian besiegers of Acre directly.

However, it is also the case that the Muslims were no more infallible with regard to the acquisition of strategic intelligence than were their Christian adversaries. It is clear, for example, that Kilij Arslan, the sultan of Rum, was poorly informed regarding the nature of the expedition being organized at Constantinople during the winter months of 1096–1097. He at first mistook the so-called People's Crusade, noted in earlier chapters, as a poorly equipped Byzantine army. Second, following his victory over the People's Crusade in the autumn of 1096, Kilij Arslan incorrectly believed that his realm would be free from further invasions from the west for the foreseeable future. As a consequence, he led his field army of mounted archers 1,000 kilometres to the east to campaign against his fellow Turkish ruler Danishmend Gazi (died 1104) in the region of Commagene. This decision allowed approximately 50,000 Latin and Byzantine troops to undertake a siege of Kilij Arslan's western capital at Nicaea largely unopposed during the spring of 1097.

Tactical intelligence

The collection of tactical intelligence by medieval commanders is a matter of some dispute among modern scholars. For example, in his survey of early medieval warfare, Guy Halsall asserts, consistent with his view that western military science was at a nadir in this period, that commanders dispensed with scouts. He concludes that these commanders allowed chance to determine whether or not they blundered blindly into an enemy force. By contrast, the later medieval historian Clifford Rogers has made the case that scouts played a consistent role in providing tactical intelligence to commanders throughout the medieval period. In this context, Rogers approvingly quotes the comment by the Burgundian soldier-turned-historian Waurin that the duke of Bedford, an English general, 'had a good watch kept in the army and scouts sent out for fear of surprises'. Indeed, Waurin, whose history covers the late fourteenth and early fifteenth centuries, observed that all good commanders were in the habit of using scouts for this purpose. We agree with Rogers' conclusion that scouts were ubiquitous in military operations throughout the medieval millennium, although we dispute his suggestion that there is limited information about their use and the development of tactical intelligence, more generally, in the period before c.1000.

Where is the enemy?

On 9 August 378, the field army of the eastern half of the Roman Empire, under the command of Emperor Valens, was defeated and all but annihilated in the Battle of Adrianople. Valens himself lost his life in the aftermath of the battle when the mill into which he fled was set on fire by Gothic troops. The likely outcome of the battle, the first and only time in which a Roman field army was defeated by an ostensibly 'barbarian' opponent in the later Roman Empire, appeared quite different during its initial phases. At the beginning of the battle, the seasoned Roman troops gained the upper hand against their Gothic adversaries. However, Emperor Valens' scouts failed to identify and give warning about the presence of a significant force of enemy mounted troops, composed primarily of Alans. As a consequence, the assault by the Alans against the flanks and rear of the Roman army came as a complete surprise, and the Roman troops fled the field in disorder. The most detailed account of the battle was provided by the Roman military officer and historian Ammianus Marcellinus (died c.391). Separately, memory of the disaster was preserved in numerous briefer accounts, and appears in many early medieval historical works. These texts gave ample opportunity, as will be seen in the following section on military education, for military commanders to learn from the epic failure by Valens to obtain accurate tactical intelligence about the location of enemy forces in the field.

Scouts

Numerous historical works from the early medieval period make clear that military commanders worked assiduously to obtain tactical intelligence regarding the location of enemy forces. For example, as seen in Chapter 6, the scouts employed by the Thuringian king Hermanfrid provided timely and accurate information in 531 about the approach of a Frankish army under the command of King Theuderic I. It was because the Thuringians had access to information about Theuderic's line of march and the composition of his forces that they had time to prepare the field of battle with traps for the Frankish cavalry. A similar example of the development of accurate tactical intelligence can be seen in the case of the Gallo-Roman general Mummolus (died 585), who played a major role in the effort of the Merovingian Prince Gundovald, noted earlier, to seize control of the kingdom of Burgundy in 585. Despite some initial successes against his uncle, King Guntram of Burgundy, Gundovald's army under the command of Mummolus was forced to retreat to its stronghold in the fortress city of Avignon. However, Mummolus continued to use his scouts to keep close track of the army of King Guntram. These scouts effectively delayed the advance of Guntram's army by seizing, burning, and especially sabotaging all of the ships along the Rhône River, which the army needed in order cross to reach Avignon.

The use of scouts to obtain tactical intelligence also is well attested during the Carolingian period. For example, the Carolingian military commander Nithard, discussed in earlier chapters, repeatedly refers to the use of scouts by all of the Carolingian kings during the course of the civil war that raged across the *Regnum Francorum* in the period 840–843. In one case, Nithard observes that Lothair I, the king in Italy, purposely advanced north from his base at a very deliberate pace in June 840 because 'he wished to know the state of affairs before he crossed the Alps'. Similarly, Nithard observes that in the spring of 841, Lothair 'quickly sent out men because he wished to know the state of affairs, that is where Charles (King Charles the Bald) was, and with whom'. The adversaries of the Carolingians also were aware of the imperative of gaining tactical intelligence. At the Battle of Geule in 891, discussed in Chapter 6, the Northmen sent out scouts to determine the strength and location of the army dispatched by the East Frankish King Arnulf to drive them from the lower Rhineland.

The use of scouts also is well attested in numerous narrative sources from the post-Carolingian period. In the early eleventh century, for example, Bishop Adalbold of Utrecht (1010–1026) recorded in his *Life of Henry II* that in 1002, the German ruler dispatched scouts to locate the army of Arduin, margrave of Ivrea (died 1015), who contested the northern king's claims to rule in Lombardy. King Henry II's enemies also used scouts to good advantage as happened, for example, when the Frisians were able to obtain extensive tactical intelligence regarding the German royal army that was invading their territory in 1018. The contemporary observer Alpert of Metz recorded that as a result of the advance warning that they obtained from their scouts, the Frisians were able to withdraw to prepared positions and ultimately defeat the royal army at the Battle of Vlaardingen on 29 July 1018.

The use of scouts continued, as one would expect, during the later Middle Ages, as well. It was a standard element in urban military ordinances (*fueros*) in Christian Iberian kingdoms of the eleventh–thirteenth centuries that scouts were to be recruited and paid by the town government for each campaign. These men obviously had both skills and knowledge that justified their recruitment. The use of scouts remained the norm in Iberia in later periods, as well. Clifford Rogers draws attention, for example, to the use of scouts by King Pere III of Catalonia (1336–1387). Pere, who wrote a historical account of his own reign called the *Chronicle*, recorded that he dispatched a unit of twenty-five light cavalry who shadowed the enemy army and sent back detailed reports about its movements every few hours, during the day and night.

In some cases, however, military commanders dispensed with scouts and undertook military reconnaissance on their own. Perhaps the most famous ruler to have done this was William the Conqueror. In his study of the generalship of William the Conqueror, John Gillingham emphasizes that it was the duke's practice to go on patrol himself rather than rely on intelligence provided by others. Consequently, shortly after his landing at Pevensey on 29 September 1066, William rode out with just twenty-five men to reconnoitre the surrounding district. The early twelfth-century historian Orderic Vitalis (died 1142) noted in his history that William also personally scouted the terrain and walls at the city of Exeter as he prepared to put down a revolt there in 1068. William the Conqueror's descendant, King Richard I, also undertook personal reconnaissance missions. While the English king was preparing to attack Philip Augustus of France in 1198, for example, Richard's scouts provided significantly different estimates regarding the size of the French army, so Richard, according to the memoir of the prominent English military commander William Marshall, went personally to reconnoitre before ordering an attack that led to his victory at the Battle of Gisors.

As discussed previously, obtaining strategic intelligence often required the services of individuals with extensive language skills and knowledge of the local conditions. The same conditions often prevailed with regard to obtaining tactical intelligence when operating in foreign lands. The anonymous author of the *Journey of the Pilgrims and Deeds of King Richard* recorded, for example, that the English ruler recruited a western Christian named Bernard, who was fluent in Arabic, to provide information about supplies being sent from Egypt to Saladin's forces in the region around the fortified port city of Ascalon. Bernard then recruited two native Egyptians to aid him in this work. These three Arabic-speaking agents provided intelligence regarding the location and routes of Egyptian supply caravans, information that Richard used to capture the enemy's supplies. In a similar vein, King Edward I of England employed Welsh scouts during his invasion of Wales in 1282–1283 to provide information about the location of enemy forces. These scouts were under the command of one of Edward's Welsh officers, a constable named Llewelyn ap Philip. In contrast, however, to information about Richard's Arabic-speaking scouts, which is recorded in a narrative source, we know about Edward's native scouts from royal pay records issued in 1283.

Captured information

In addition to sending out scouts from an army's main column, tactical intelligence also was acquired through the interrogation of prisoners, such as the capture of two messengers dispatched by Prince Gundovald, discussed earlier. In yet another case involving this Merovingian prince, two of Gundovald's envoys to King Guntram of Burgundy were denied diplomatic status and treated as spies. Guntram then ordered the two erstwhile envoys to be tortured in order to discover information about the location of his enemy's army, and also what they may have known regarding Gundovald's plans. Guntram subsequently used this information effectively to thwart his nephew's efforts to conquer Burgundy.

A somewhat different example of obtaining information from prisoners is illuminated in Orderic Vitalis' account of the prelude to the Battle of Ascalon in August 1099. After their capture of Jerusalem on 15 July, the crusader commanders received intelligence, perhaps from paid spies, that a large Egyptian army had entered the region with the intention of taking back the Holy City. A small reconnaissance force was dispatched under the command of Tancred, the nephew of the crusader prince Bohemond, and the magnate Eustace of Boulogne. The crusaders captured some men from the vanguard of this Egyptian relief force from whom they obtained precise information regarding the composition of the Egyptian army, its size, and the commanders' plan of action. With this information in hand, the crusader army, under the command of Godfrey of Bouillon, Eustace's elder brother, was able to launch a surprise attack on the Egyptians near Ascalon and win a decisive victory, thereby securing the Christian hold on Jerusalem at this time.

Similarly, in his autobiography, *The Book of Deeds*, King James I of Aragon (1213–1276) recorded that he sent out a patrol of mounted troops to scout in the region of Valencia in preparation for a raid. In addition to obtaining useful intelligence from their own observations, these raiders also carried back sixty prisoners, whom James and his staff interrogated to gain further actionable intelligence. In particular, the Aragonese king wished to know whether the military commander in the Valencia district had mobilized men and supplies to be brought to the fortification at Puig, which was located approximately 15 kilometres north of the city of Valencia.

Strategic role of diplomacy

The acquisition of intelligence regarding the political and military intentions of both hostile and ostensibly friendly polities had considerable potential to shape the thinking of a ruler as he conceptualized his operational and strategic goals. In addition, however, medieval rulers frequently sought to shape the geo-political terrain to facilitate the realization of their strategic goals. Of the utmost importance in this context was the use of diplomacy to gain new allies and to neutralize actual or potential opponents. In both the Roman and Byzantine contexts, it is well understood that Roman emperors actively sought to engage the rulers of so-called 'barbarian' peoples beyond the frontier in an effort to encourage them to wage war against other 'barbarian' peoples. The effort by Gundovald to seize power in Burgundy can be understood as this type of Byzantine diplomatic operation in that the erstwhile Merovingian prince received significant political and financial support from imperial backers in Constantinople. Western medieval rulers were no different in this regard than their imperial predecessors and contemporaries. They also actively sought to use diplomacy to gain new allies and to neutralize enemies so as to facilitate the execution of large-scale military operations. The first example considered in what follows sheds light on the exceptionally important and complex role played by strategic diplomacy in shaping the political history of the Frankish kingdom, the Lombard kingdom in northern Italy, and the papal state during the period between 768–774.

In May 772, Charlemagne began a major military operation east of the Weser River as the first stage in what he intended to be a systematic conquest of the region inhabited by the Saxons. By enforcing the formal surrender of elements of the Saxon people and establishing numerous fortifications and garrisons within their homeland, Charlemagne was engaging in a significant departure from the policy of his father and grandfather. By contrast with Charlemagne, both Charles Martel and King Pippin had sought to maintain peace along the frontier through occasional punitive expeditions against the Saxons. However, instead of renewing his efforts in the spring of 773 to conquer and integrate the Saxon region into the Frankish realm, Charlemagne mobilized and deployed two substantial armies to invade the Lombard kingdom in northern Italy. One result of Charlemagne's decision to deploy the greater part of his offensive military forces south of the Alps was that the Saxons were able to reverse much of the Carolingian success of the previous year. So how can this extraordinary change in military strategy by the normally cautious Frankish ruler be explained? The answer is that Charlemagne's invasion of Italy in 773 was the culmination of five years of diplomatic manoeuvring by Charlemagne, the Lombard King Desiderius, Charlemagne's younger brother Carloman, Duke Tassilo of Bavaria (748–788), and perhaps most importantly, the papal curia and particularly Pope Hadrian (772–795), which led to a war that no one wanted.

Since the emergence of the Lombard control of northern Italy in the decades following their invasion of 568, they had posed a considerable threat to the territorial integrity of the lands controlled and ruled by the papal government. Throughout most of the late sixth, seventh, and first decades of the eighth century, the imperial government based in Constantinople had provided for the military defence of Rome, but also had maintained a tight control over the papacy. The papal curia sought to gain independence from Byzantine control in the mid-eighth century by soliciting the military protection of the newly strengthened Frankish kingdom under the leadership of the Carolingian mayors of the palace. In fact, the papal government had offered the keys to the palace of St. Peter in Rome to Charles Martel, the grandfather of Charlemagne, if he would be their protector so that they could abandon their reliance on Constantinople.

In 751, Pope Zachary (741–752) gave his support to the usurpation of the Frankish crown by Pippin I (751–768). Three years later, Pope Stephen II (752–757) travelled north to the monastery of St. Denis, near Paris, where he consecrated Pippin along with his sons Charles (the future Charlemagne) and Carloman as kings of the Franks. For the previous two and half centuries, this office had been held by members of the Merovingian dynasty. Pippin, in turn, twice invaded the Lombard kingdom to force the withdrawal of Lombard troops from papal lands. Pippin's defence of papal interests marks a transition away from the Lombard alliance of his father Charles Martel, who had rejected the deal, noted above, offered by the papal government, and recruited Lombard troops to serve in his army that ejected Muslim forces from parts of southern Gaul.

Following the death of Pippin I in 768, the Lombard King Desiderius (756–774) actively sought to reshape the diplomatic balance among his neighbours in his favour. Desiderius previously had negotiated the marriage of one of his daughters to Duke Tassilo of Bavaria, who controlled the eastern Alpine passes into the Lombard plain. Complicating matters from a diplomatic point of view was the fact that Tassilo had been estranged from his kin, the Carolingian royal family, since 763. From Desiderius' point of view, the situation in the Frankish kingdom was problematic because Pippin's younger son Carloman, who according to his father Pippin's will monopolized access to all of the northern and western Alpine passes into Lombardy, appeared inclined to continue his father Pippin's policies in protection of the papacy.

Charlemagne, for his part, was displeased about his exclusion from Italian affairs that was the practical corollary of Carloman's control of the Alpine passes. Charlemagne was motivated not least because he held jointly with his brother Carloman the office of *patricius Romanorum*, which had been awarded by the pope and brought with it a leading role in Roman affairs. This office included especially the obligation to protect the Holy City and papal lands from foreign attack. Desiderius and Charlemagne, therefore, had common interests in ensuring that Carloman was not the only Carolingian king with access to and potential involvement in Italy, although Charlemagne was not in favour of a hyper-aggressive approach by Desiderius toward the papacy. In order to facilitate cooperation with Charlemagne in their mutual interest, Desiderius offered another of his daughters, named Gerperga, in marriage to Charlemagne.

Desiderius hoped that by tying both Tassilo and Charlemagne to himself through marriage, he would have a free hand in dealing with the papacy, and particularly with the efforts of the papal court to regain territories lost to the Lombards over the past several decades. Desiderius understood that Charlemagne, although interested in protecting papal interests, also had to balance this goal against gaining access to Italy despite his brother Carloman's territorial monopoly on Frankish access through the Alps. Carloman, for obvious reasons, opposed this alliance involving his brother, King Desiderius, and perhaps Duke Tassilo. In order to ensure his own strong position in Italy, Carloman supported a faction at the papal curia, led by an aristocrat named Christopher with the tacit approval of Pope Stephen III (768–772), who feared an alliance between Desiderius and Charlemagne. Christopher argued that Pope Stephen, with the promise of military support from Carloman and possibly the Byzantines as well, should take an aggressive stance towards King Desiderius, and make maximalist demands for the return of territories taken decades earlier by the Lombards.

However, Charlemagne, in cooperation with Desiderius through diplomatic negotiations led by Charlemagne's mother Bertha, convinced Pope Stephen that an alliance among the three of them was not harmful to papal interests. Bertha even succeeded in gaining the agreement of Desiderius to some of the papacy's lesser territorial and political demands. The result of Charlemagne's intervention was a factional conflict among the high officials in the papal court, which led ultimately to the blinding and death of Christopher, the imprisonment or exile of his chief supporters, and the significant diminution in the ability of Carloman to influence events at Rome.

The diplomatic situation radically changed, however, in 771 following the death of Carloman, likely of natural causes, and the flight of his wife and children to the papal court. Charlemagne now controlled the entire Frankish kingdom, and therefore, direct access to Italy. Desiderius, for his part, saw the unification of the *Regnum Francorum* as posing a potential threat to Lombardy, but also hoped to retain the alliance among himself, Charlemagne, and Duke Tassilo on the basis of the marriages with his daughters mentioned previously. Charlemagne, for his part, was focused at this point on the conquest of the Saxon region and had no desire to become any more entangled in Italian affairs than was absolutely necessary. This meant that Desiderius had a largely free hand vis-à-vis the papacy now that the threat of direct intervention from the north had receded with the death of Carloman. This free hand, however, was contingent upon Desiderius acting reasonably with respect to his territorial ambitions in the papal state because of Charlemagne's ongoing obligation to the Holy See based upon his possession of the office of *patricius Romanorum*, and his hope ultimately of being named emperor by the pope.

Pope Stephen, who ultimately decided to maintain a positive diplomatic position with regard to the alliance between Desiderius and Charlemagne, died in February 772. His death was followed by a struggle between those who accepted that the alliance between Charlemagne and Desiderius could be managed effectively, led by a papal official named Paul Afiarta, and those who sought to weaken the ties between the two kings. This latter group hoped to restore the Frankish protectorate, which had existed during the reign of Pippin, Charlemagne's father, and was needed to thwart Lombard aggression. The papal officials seeking to maintain the status quo ante that prevailed under King Pippin were led by Hadrian, who was elected as pope on 9 February 772, just a week after Stephen III's death. However, Hadrian's election was contested and he did not inform Charlemagne of his elevation as pope as normally was required.

The newly elected pope had several diplomatic cards to play if he wished to cause trouble for Charlemagne. The first of these was the option to consecrate the young sons of the

Charlemagne's deceased brother Carloman as Frankish kings with a claim to a portion of the *Regnum Francorum*. The second option was to intensify his relationship with Duke Tassilo of Bavaria, who was seeking papal recognition for an independent Bavarian kingdom, in opposition to the Franks. However, Pope Hadrian had to tread very carefully, because his ultimate goal was to cause a rift between Charlemagne and Desiderius and not give them reason to take action together against the papacy, as had happened just two years earlier when the two kings had brought pressure to bear on Pope Stephen to accept the pact negotiated by the queen mother Bertha. In order to effect this break between the kings, Hadrian decided that he had to provoke Desiderius to act in such an exceptionally aggressive manner that Charlemagne would be compelled to intervene to stop the Lombard king's military adventurism. The end result would be a breakdown in the alliance between Charlemagne and Desiderius. Hadrian hedged his bets, however, by also opening negotiations with the Byzantine imperial court, which had the resources and perhaps the inclination to play a military role in northern Italy. At this very time, the Byzantine emperor Constantine V was operating in the Balkans with a large army.

Maintaining the alliance with Desiderius remained very important for Charlemagne because he wished to retain a free hand to operate against the Saxons without having to worry about Italian affairs. However, this became more complicated for the Frankish ruler as it became increasingly clear that his wife Gerperga, the daughter of Desiderius, was barren and could not give him the male heir that he desperately needed. This problem was even more acute in light of the presence of his nephews in Italy, and the potential that the magnates in the Frankish kingdom would demand their recall as Charlemagne's natural heirs. At the same time, Charlemagne's concubine Hildegarde, a noblewoman from a very powerful Frankish family, gave birth to a son late in 772, who had the potential to become Charlemagne's legitimate heir. Not long thereafter, Charlemagne repudiated his marriage to Gerperga and sent her back to her father at Pavia. However, Charlemagne also sent a large sum of money with Gerperga as recompense for his actions, which is clear evidence of his desire to maintain the alliance with Desiderius.

Pope Hadrian, in the meantime, continued to make provocative demands of the Lombard king, and even moved papal troops into territories that were disputed between the two sides. Ultimately, Desiderius, who now had reason to question the commitment of Charlemagne to the continuance of their alliance, decided that a full-scale invasion of papal lands was a necessary response to the hostile policies of Hadrian. It is likely that Desiderius hoped to remove this recalcitrant pope and secure the election of a more pliable candidate from among the supporters of Paul Afiarta. Over several months, Lombard forces undertook a series of military operations against papal assets, setting the stage for a siege of Rome itself. At this point, Hadrian sent an embassy to Charlemagne, begging him to intervene and save the papacy from the Lombards, just as his father Pippin had done two decades earlier.

This was not a request that Charlemagne had wished to receive. He thoroughly disapproved of Hadrian's actions over the course of 772 in provoking the Lombards. However, he also could not ignore the obligations inherent in his office as *patricius Romanorum* or the precedent set by his father. For his part, Desiderius certainly had no desire for Charlemagne to bring an army south of the Alps, but he could not continue to tolerate the provocations of Pope Hadrian. In the course of the tense standoff between the papacy and the Lombards, several embassies were sent back and forth across the Alps among Frankish and Lombard royal courts and Rome.

Ultimately, Pope Hadrian's diplomatic manoeuvring had the desired result, in terms of the papal effort to cause a rift between the Lombard and Frankish courts, and Charlemagne decided that he had to intervene. In the spring of 773, two Frankish armies invaded the Lombard kingdom in a giant pincer movement, capturing the capital of Pavia and King Desiderius himself after an eight-month siege. However, Hadrian did not emerge unscathed from the war. The pope had used all of his diplomatic skills to foment discord between Desiderius and Charlemagne for the purpose of breaking up their alliance and re-establishing the Franks as the protectors of the papacy against the Lombards. Hadrian's main goal was to ensure the independence of the papal state. However, having committed such extensive military forces to the invasion of Lombardy, Charlemagne decided to annex the northern Italian kingdom and thereby established himself as a powerful neighbour of the papal state. Far from emerging with its independence intact, the papacy now became a *de facto* dependent of a much more powerful empire. In the bargain, the papacy also lost control of the key city of Ravenna, whose archbishop became a close dependent of Charlemagne.

The complex diplomatic negotiations and strategies involving numerous political leaders, such as those that led ultimately to Charlemagne's invasion of the Lombard kingdom in 773, were replicated on numerous occasions throughout the Middle Ages. For example, the civil wars in Germany during the reign of King Henry IV over the course of the 1070s and 1080s were accompanied by extensive diplomatic efforts by Henry IV's government, the secular and ecclesiastical leaders of the Saxons, the papacy, and ultimately the 'anti-king' Rudolf of Rheinfelden (1077–1080) to secure political and military support for their respective causes in this multi-sided conflict. In the early phases of the civil war, King Henry sought to mobilize a coalition of foreign powers to help him conquer the recalcitrant Saxons. To this end, the German ruler offered territorial concessions in Saxony to the Danish king and also to the Liutizi, who were a pagan Slavic people and the traditional enemies of the Saxons. Henry reportedly also sought additional military support from as far afield as his maternal kin, the dukes of Aquitaine in southwestern France, and William the Conqueror. None of these diplomatic negotiations bore fruit, and King Henry was only able to secure the military support of the Bohemian duke, who readily accepted territorial concessions offered by the German ruler in the southeast of the Saxon duchy.

After their initial military defeat at the hands of Henry IV at the battle of the Unstrut in 1075, the leaders of the Saxons desperately sought both political and military support within Germany and from outside the kingdom, particularly from the papacy. The Saxon political leadership, and particularly the ecclesiastical leaders including the bishops and archbishops of the region, wrote letters and made personal pleas to their fellow magnates in other regions of Germany, claiming that the king was acting overly harshly, and that they wished to make peace on honourable terms, but that Henry had refused. These diplomatic entreaties were quite successful, and many princes, including the dukes of Bavaria and Swabia in southern Germany, switched sides and joined forces with the Saxons against their king. The success of the Saxon leadership in persuading many other magnates to join their side was due, in large part, to the growing hostility between Henry IV and Pope Gregory VII (1073–1085), which led to the German king's excommunication in February 1076.

Even before his elevation as pope in 1073, Gregory VII was a leading figure in the ecclesiastical reform movement, which sought, among other matters, to free the Church from secular control. Central to this effort was excluding secular rulers from a role in appointing ecclesiastical office holders, including abbots and bishops. This reform agenda was entirely antithetical to the established political system throughout Europe, and nowhere more so than in Germany, where imperial bishops and abbots controlled vast economic and military assets that had been granted to them by earlier rulers. Gregory VII's excommunication of Henry IV was directly connected to their dispute over the appointment of bishops, but the pope also was aware of the king's delicate political position in Germany, and hoped to use this reality to push the ruler onto a path that was acceptable to the ecclesiastical reformers.

The pope's action gave the cover of legitimacy to the Saxons and their allies in Germany to withdraw their obedience from King Henry despite having sworn oaths of loyalty to him as their ruler. The political and military pressure of the rebels within Germany offered significant leverage to Pope Gregory to negotiate with Henry IV. However, the interests of the Saxons and other rebels were not identical with those of the papal government. The rebels within Germany wished to replace Henry with a new king — and, in fact, a new dynasty — and elected Rudolf of Rheinfelden, whom Henry IV had removed as duke of Swabia, as their king in 1077. Pope Gregory, however, was not invested in the removal of Henry IV, but rather his main interest was the imposition of ecclesiastical reform in the German kingdom.

A series of letters from the Saxon leaders and also from Rudolf of Rheinfelden to Pope Gregory from 1077–1080 indicate that they felt betrayed by the pope, who had promised them his blessing and support if they endured in their rebellion against Henry IV. However, in January 1077, less than a year after excommunicating the German king, Gregory met with him at Canossa and absolved him, thereby undercutting the justification of the rebels within Germany to continue their revolt and opposition to Henry. However, the pope had to take into account the political and military realities in Italy, and particularly the strong support for King Henry among the political leadership in northern Italy. Making peace with Henry was imperative if Gregory were to remain in control as pope in Rome.

Ultimately, Pope Gregory excommunicated Henry IV again, in 1084, but by this time, the military situation in Germany had been transformed. Rudolf of Rheinfelden died as a result of wounds he suffered in battle in 1080. Henry not only defeated the Saxons, but also all of his opponents outside of the Saxon duchy. As a result, most of the Saxon magnates made peace with him. In response to this second excommunication, Henry invaded Italy again, captured Rome, and drove Pope Gregory into exile among the Normans of southern Italy, where he died in 1085. Gregory's diplomatic efforts had failed because in the longer term, he lacked the military force under his direct control with which to oppose the German king, or for that matter, the aggressive and acquisitive Normans, who controlled the south of Italy.

In the end, Pope Gregory VII failed in all of his diplomatic initiatives. The betrayal of the Saxons in 1077 did not lead to the institution of ecclesiastical reform in Germany. By contrast, one of Gregory's successors, Pope Urban II (1088–1099), was far more successful in dealing with Henry IV, and succeeded for a time in depriving him of effective rule in Germany, but only by obtaining the support of the emperor's disloyal son Conrad. However, it is another diplomatic coup by Urban II that we consider here, namely his success in placing an army of at least 50,000 western Christian soldiers under the walls of Constantinople in the winter and spring of 1096–1097 as part of his policy of reuniting the western and eastern churches.

This story begins in 1054, when the clumsy diplomatic efforts of Cardinal Humbert of Silva Candida (died 1061) led to the schism between the Catholic and Orthodox Churches, a schism that still endures to the present day. A major policy of the popes, as the leaders of the western Church, was to restore the previous relationship with the eastern Church. However, from the papacy's perspective, this reunification was to be carried out on the basis of their superior position vis-à-vis the patriarchs of Constantinople. Pope Gregory VII had envisioned restoring this relationship by leading a western army to the aid of the Byzantines following the military disaster at Manzikert in 1071 that opened up most of Asia

Minor to Turkish occupation. Like so many other of Gregory VII's schemes, this plan came to nothing. However, the renewal of diplomatic relations with the papacy by the Byzantine Emperor Alexios Komnenos (1081–1118) provided Pope Urban II with the means to renew Gregory VII's initiative in a new form.

The Byzantines and the papacy had a shared enemy in the Normans of southern Italy, who threatened the territorial integrity of the papal state, and also regularly attacked Byzantine interests. In fact, Robert Guiscard, the Norman ruler of southern Italy and Sicily, and his son Bohemond of crusading fame, undertook a five-year campaign (1080–1085) with the objective of conquering the Byzantine Empire as a whole. However, following the death of Robert Guiscard in 1085, Alexios was focused far more on affairs in Asia Minor and in the Balkans than he was in southern Italy. By the early 1090s, the stable political and military position that Alexios had established in both regions began to crumble, and the Byzantine emperor grew increasingly desperate for additional military forces particularly to strengthen his position against Kilij Arslan, who had become the sultan of Rum – that is, western Asia Minor – with his capital at Nicaea, located just 140 kilometres southeast of Constantinople.

Beginning in 1092, Alexios sought to reinvigorate the lapsed diplomatic relationship with the papacy by sending several groups of legates to Pope Urban II asking the bishop of Rome to encourage western soldiers to come to Constantinople to fight in the Byzantine army. Alexios already had a contract of this type with the count of Flanders, who provided several hundred soldiers for this purpose. Urban, who was in a difficult military situation in Italy because of the presence of Henry IV with a large army in the region of Lombardy, was not able to respond immediately. However, in late 1094, Urban lay the groundwork for a major ecclesiastical council to be held at the city of Piacenza, which was held in early March 1095. Alexios dispatched envoys to this council, and after meeting with them, Pope Urban took the first steps in mobilizing a western army to go to the aid of the Byzantines.

This process reached a crescendo at the council of Clermont in November 1095, where Pope Urban famously preached a sermon calling upon all western Christians to take back Jerusalem from the Muslims, who not only desecrated the most holy city in Christianity, but also abused and persecuted Christians throughout the Middle East. As a minor theme, he also advocated that Christians in the West were to aid their eastern brothers in freeing themselves from the Muslim yoke.

For centuries, scholars have argued about the goal of this campaign that came to be known as the First Crusade. The ultimate arrival of the crusading army at Jerusalem in June 1099, and the considerable contemporary focus on Jerusalem as the centre of the world and the most important pilgrimage site for Christians, has led most scholars to conclude that Pope Urban intended the army that he summoned at Clermont to recapture the Holy City, and bring Christ's final resting place back under Christian – that is, Catholic – control. However, from a military perspective, it would have been simply absurd for the papacy to mandate that the crusading armies muster at Constantinople if the goal, in fact, were Jerusalem. Moreover, the employment of the western armies for the better part of eighteen months in the reconquest of territories on behalf of the Byzantine Empire also cannot be reconciled with Jerusalem as the primary goal of the army.

Rather, it is far more likely that Alexios and Urban, each for his own reasons, negotiated for the papacy to mobilize very substantial western military forces to go to Constantinople, where the soldiers would be provided with supplies by the imperial government. Why would Pope Urban undertake such a negotiation? The answer is that he hoped to succeed where Gregory VII had failed. He intended to use the reality of a large western army at Constantinople under the command of his own faithful men, namely Bishop Adhemar of

Le Puy and Count Raymond of Toulouse, to bring about a reunification of the western and eastern churches on western terms. Alexios' reasons for participating in these negotiations are obvious, as these western troops would reconquer the Byzantine lands that had been lost to the Muslims. What is less appreciated is Alexios' enormous success in making use of these western troops for his own purposes, without having to make any concessions on ecclesiastical issues, or bringing about a reunification of the two churches.

As the preceding examples illustrate, diplomatic relations in the medieval period had the potential to be quite complex, and the strategy of one participant could affect the options of several others. In the final example considered here, the diplomatic relations between just two partners also had the potential to have far-reaching consequences for polities that were not party to the negotiations at all. King Philip IV of France and King Edward I of England confronted each other militarily across a range of theatres for almost a decade on both land and on sea. In addition to this primary strategic struggle, each of these kings also faced a significant additional opponent: Flanders in the case of France, and Scotland in the case of England. Both Edward and Philip were well aware of – and exploited – the opportunity to discomfit their main opponents by giving financial, material, and even military support to Flanders and Scotland, respectively. Edward led a major military expedition involving more than 10,000 men to Flanders in 1297, and Philip regularly sent naval forces to aid the Scots during the late 1290s and into the next decade. Overall, Edward's support of Flanders can be understood as an effort to protect Gascony, which was possessed by the English, from the French, by compelling Philip to undertake a 'two-front' war. Philip's support of the Scots can, in turn, be understood as intended to compel the English to devote resources to the north that otherwise could be deployed in either Gascony or Flanders.

The strategic balance of power between France and England was altered to a significant extent, however, following the substantial victory by the Flemish communes over the French at the Battle of Courtrai in July 1302. The death of thousands of French soldiers, including large numbers of nobles, brought with it a loss of confidence in the French king among his own people. An additional result of the victory was to raise the confidence of the people of Flanders in their policy of aggressive defiance towards the French king. Consequently, the defeat at Courtrai convinced Philip that he should undertake a new policy vis-à-vis the English. To this end, the French ruler made diplomatic overtures to Edward, and the English king responded positively, dispatching a legation to Paris. The two sides negotiated a peace agreement that went into effect in May 1303. One of the major elements in the treaty was that both Philip and Edward would cease providing military support to Scotland and Flanders, respectively. Both the French and English benefitted significantly from the negotiated truces, to the great disadvantage of the smaller powers. Edward used the respite from French military operations in the English Channel, and the absence of French support for the Scots, to complete his conquest of central and northern Scotland in a lengthy campaign from the summer of 1303 through the spring of 1304. The last surviving redoubt of Scottish resistance, at Stirling castle, surrendered in the summer of that year.

Following through on his agreement with the French king, Edward I in April 1304 dispatched his trusted clerk Peter of Dunwich to mobilize a fleet of twenty ships to aid Philip in his renewed campaign in Flanders. The French naval victory at Zierikzee on 11 August 1304, combined with the substantial losses suffered by the Flemish army one week later at the Battle of Mons-en-Pévèle, convinced the Flemings that they had to sue for peace. The transformation of the English from allies to enemies undoubtedly also played a role in their thinking. In the treaty of Athis-sur-Orge with King Philip, signed by the French ruler and Count Robert III of Flanders on 23 June 1305, the Flemings secured their *de jure* independence, but were forced to give over control of the cities of Lille, Douai, and Orchies, and pay a very heavy war indemnity. Both Philip IV and Edward I would appear to have adhered to the view enunciated by Lord Palmerston, prime minister during the reign of Queen Victoria of England, that 'Nations have no permanent friends or allies, only permanent interests'.

Devastation as a strategic tool

Whereas the strategic role of diplomacy in medieval warfare has received relatively little attention from historians, it is a common theme in popular and even scholarly discussions of medieval warfare that military operations largely were focused on plunder and destruction. Scholars have adduced three basic reasons for this interpretation. The first, which draws its inspiration from the *Beowulf* poem, a poetic epic fantasy rather than a historiographical work, is that rulers had to promise booty to 'warriors' in order to motivate them to go on campaign, or conversely 'warlords' required a constant flow of plunder in order to maintain the loyalty of their followers on the 'warpath'.

The second ostensible reason for taking plunder and causing damage was to obtain supplies for the invading military force. Indeed, some specialists in medieval military history have erroneously argued that such a strategy was recommended by Vegetius in his *Epitoma rei militaris.* They point to Vegetius' admonition that a winning campaign strategy required assuring supplies for one's own army and denying them to the enemy. This passage does not, however, recommend that a commander commit his army to live off the land. In fact, Vegetius advocates the opposite. Nevertheless, the misapplication of Vegetius' advice also has led to the third argument for the centrality of plunder and devastation to the conduct of medieval warfare, which is that by wrecking the economic infrastructure of the enemy, a military commander could also undermine an opponent's ability to project force in the future.

As we have seen in the previous chapters, there is a kernel of truth to each of these three suggestions, but they cannot either singly or collectively explain large-scale destruction by armies on campaign. For example, military morale certainly was enhanced by the prospect of making a profit, or at least recouping some of the costs of a campaign, from plunder or the capture of individuals who could be sold as slaves or held for ransom. However, the overall costs of even small-scale campaigns rarely could be made good through plunder. Moreover, most men who participated in offensive wars, whether large or small, did so because of their legal obligation to serve, not because of the lure of booty. This was true both of the members of military households, who were professional soldiers, and of militia levies, who were not professional soldiers.

In a similar vein, plunder could, on occasion, provide an adjunct to the provision of regular supply through a well-orchestrated logistical system. However, as made clear in Chapter 4, even relatively small armies of a few thousand men could not 'live off the land' in an effective manner for very long. Finally, it is possible to identify many instances in which the military capacity of a polity was damaged to a significant extent by the efforts of an enemy to destroy its economic infrastructure. For the most part, however, the limits imposed by the transportation infrastructure and technology made it virtually impossible for an invading army to inflict extensive devastation within the context of a military campaign that was focused on either the capture of enemy strongholds or the defeat of an enemy force in the field. Significant devastation could not be an effective adjunct to a campaign, but rather had to be the focus of a military campaign.

Why choose devastation?

King Frederick the Great of Prussia (1740–1786) is credited with the saying that 'diplomacy without arms is like music without instruments'. The concept that military force was an essential adjunct to diplomacy certainly was well-known to medieval rulers. However, when considering what type of force was to be employed, medieval rulers first had to determine the nature of the goal that they intended to achieve. The direct conquest of territory, as seen in the previous chapters, usually was accomplished over the long term through the capture of enemy strongholds, the establishment of garrisons, and the imposition of taxes on the subjected population. By contrast, medieval rulers were able to achieve some political objectives short of territorial conquest through the use of force in a different manner, and in particular by inflicting large-scale damage to the economic infrastructure of the enemy.

In his detailed studies of the wars of King Edward III of England, Clifford Rogers has argued that the English ruler's political objectives in France were achieved not through the systematic capture of enemy fortifications and strongholds, which he lacked the military reserves to sustain, but rather through the use of large-scale raids known as *chevauchées*. For a number of reasons, including the political incompetence of his father Edward II, as well as the demographic and economic devastation wrought by the Black Deaths of the mid-fourteenth century (the Black Death), Edward III did not have the military resources that had been available to his grandfather Edward I. As a consequence, whereas Edward I regularly mobilized armies numbering in the tens of thousands for campaigns of territorial conquest in Wales and Scotland, most of the armies of Edward III numbered fewer than 10,000 men, and often only a few thousand men. Recognizing these limitations over much of his reign, Edward III's primary objective was not to conquer foreign lands, but rather to prevent the conquest by the French of English-held lands in the west of France, and particularly in Gascony. Despite the plague, the population of the French kingdom was a great deal larger than that of the English kingdom, and the concomitant economic and military resources of the French kings also were, at least potentially, greater as well.

Faced with the challenge of having inadequate resources, especially manpower, due to the impact of the plague, to undertake a systematic campaign of conquest, Edward III instead sought to undermine the political legitimacy of his French opponents, Philip VI (1328–1350), John II (1350–1364), and Charles V (1364–1380), and thereby hinder their current offensive military operations, and deter future military operations. Edward's tool of choice to thwart the French was the *chevauchée*, in which several thousand mounted English fighting men purposefully devastated a region, burning towns, killing civilians, and destroying important economic assets such as mills and bridges. The primary obligation of a ruler was to protect his people and their material assets. Consequently, the success of Edward III's raiding columns was a testament to the failure of the French kings to carry out this basic duty. As a consequence, in addition to wrecking the ability of a particular region to provide men and supplies to the French king's army in the short term, the English *chevauchée* had the longer-term effect of undermining the legitimacy of the French king in the eyes of his subjects.

Rogers also has argued that Edward III's additional goal in carrying out these *chevauchées* was to compel the French kings to fight battles on unfavourable terms, as happened at both Crécy and Poitiers. In this manner, the English could achieve the same result through a decisive victory in the field that would otherwise require the systematic reduction of numerous fortresses over a lengthy period. This view of Edward III's strategic thinking, however,

GEOFFREY WITH THE GREAT TOOTH BURNING THE ABBEY OF MAILLIÈRES.

Figure 7.3 Medieval woodcut from the story of Melusine: Geoffrey with the great tooth burning the Abbey of Maillieres

Source: © Walker Art Library/Alamy Stock Photo C3YNC3

recently has been called into question by Michael Livingston and Kelly DeVries in their mammoth new study of the Battle of Crécy.[1]

Whether or not Edward III did pursue a particular battle-forcing strategy, the capture of the French King John II at the Battle of Poitiers in 1356 did indeed dramatically change the political balance between France and England, and gained major territorial concessions for Edward III. These would otherwise have required long campaigns focused on lengthy and expensive sieges using large numbers of soldiers, whom Edward could not mobilize, and would have significant difficulty in sustaining even if he were able to raise large armies with the aid of allies.

The use of devastation to compel an adversary to fight a battle also played a significant role in William the Conqueror's invasion plan in 1066. In order for the Norman duke to achieve victory and secure his conquest of England in a timely manner, Harold Godwinson had to either be captured by the Normans or die. This reality compelled William to undertake a battle-seeking strategy. However, William needed a way to force Harold to accept battle rather than harrying the Norman invaders throughout the English countryside. If the Anglo-Saxons refused battle, the Normans ultimately would run out of supplies and suffer failure. The denial of supplies and allowing an enemy army to starve in this manner was, far and away, the most common strategy employed by a defending army during the eleventh century.

William, who fully understood these realities, chose to provoke Harold into choosing battle by undertaking extensive raiding operations in the area around the port of Pevensey, which was located within the ancestral lands of the Godwin family in the Sussex region. Several contemporary chronicles make clear that news of these raids was brought to Harold as he marched south from his victory over Harald Hardrada at the Battle of Stamford Bridge. Allowing William to burn and pillage at will had the potential to undermine the legitimacy of Harold's rule as king, something that the Anglo-Saxon ruler could not afford less than a year into his reign. It is in this context that Harold raced from London to Senlac in an effort to pin the Norman army to the coast, and gave William the battle that the Norman duke required if he were to win the kingdom of England.

Punishment and deterrence

In addition to using devastation of an enemy's lands in order to obtain a political or military objective, many medieval rulers also laid waste the lands of their adversaries as both punishment for and deterrent against future attacks or, in the case of domestic opponents, rebellions. According to Bruno of Merseburg, a contemporary and critic of Henry IV of Germany, this was precisely the goal of the German ruler when he mobilized an army for the invasion of the Saxon duchy in the autumn of 1075. Just a few months earlier, on 9 June, Henry had won a decisive victory over the Saxons at the battle of the Unstrut. Nevertheless, despite the fact that the Saxons had been thoroughly defeated, Henry was not able, as Bruno put it, to do 'the only thing that he wanted to do, namely immediately to subject them all to servitude'. Bruno goes on to explain:

> He was not able to capture all of the princes because they were dispersed in several places, nor could he keep his army in this land for very long because hunger, for once, was useful to us this year, and in the month of July the crops were not yet ripe.

---

1 See the opposing views by Livingston and Rogers in the 'Conflicting views' section of the bibliography.

Consequently, after withdrawing from the Saxon duchy in July, Henry IV raised yet another army to invade the region again in October. During his earlier invasion, the king had observed the crops growing in vast abundance in the fields. Now that the crops had been harvested, Henry IV planned to use them to feed his own troops and burn them to deny them to the Saxons. Bruno claims, in fact, that if the king had been successful in this plan, 'he would either devour the entire people with his sword, or subject them as humble petitioners to perpetual servitude'.

Bruno, who was exaggerating for effect, used the potential devastation of the Saxon countryside to explain the decision of the Saxon leaders to surrender rather than face this destruction. From a practical perspective, the Saxon duchy was the home to numerous royal estates that generally had the obligation to support royal military operations directed eastwards against the pagan Slavs and against the Poles. It is likely, therefore, that although King Henry's army had the potential to inflict considerable devastation in the region, the troops also were in a position to obtain supplies from the king's own estates, which were organized for this purpose. Consequently, rather than living off of the land, the royal army would be supplied, when necessary, by government assets. Henry had no intention of trying to live off the land in enemy territory.

William the Conqueror used a similar policy just a few years earlier and far more successfully in the winter of 1069–1070. In the autumn of 1069, William faced a rebellion in northern England and invasion launched from Scotland by Edgar Aetheling, the last surviving member of the old dynasty of Wessex, who was supported by King Sweyn II of Denmark. The rebels, led by Edgar, captured the city of York from the Norman garrison there. However, William successfully recaptured York and drove Edgar back into exile in Scotland. William also made an agreement with Sweyn, which led to the departure of the Danish fleet. In this case, we see diplomacy at work, supported by the threat of military force.

Following his defeat of the main military forces of his enemy, William took the strategic decision to make an example of the 'North' and also to make it virtually impossible for the region to support another uprising. Over a period of several months, thousands of William's troops systematically burned villages, killed livestock, destroyed stored grain supplies, and killed large numbers of men, women, and children. Thousands more died in the subsequent famine. This 'harrowing of the north' had a profound effect on the local economy. A decade and a half later, the Domesday Book, compiled in 1086 as a register of the economic assets of the English kingdom, recorded that large swathes of the region all around Yorkshire were still wastelands. While these lands ultimately were part of William's kingdom, he concluded that teaching the rebels, and others, an unforgettable lesson was what modern strategists would consider a sacrifice that was 'cost effective'.

A similar policy of destruction can be seen in an earlier period when Charlemagne sought to inflict widespread devastation on the Saxons in retaliation for their invasion of the Rhineland during the summer of 773. The previous year, Charlemagne had invaded the Saxon region and imposed oaths of faithfulness on a number of local and regional leaders. However, the Saxons obtained intelligence that the Carolingian ruler was leading several large armies in an invasion of the Lombard kingdom in the spring and summer of 773. The Saxons then reneged on their agreements and initiated large-scale raids, many of which resulted in the destruction of newly established churches. Much as would be true of the German King Henry IV, Charlemagne waited until late autumn – that is, the harvest season – of 774 to retaliate. The Frankish ruler dispatched four large mounted units with orders to burn, pillage, and loot as extensively as possible, over as broad an area as possible. Unfortunately for these units, the Saxons again appear to have enjoyed substantial success in gaining strategic and tactical intelligence, and deployed forces to deny them easy access to stored grain supplies and other assets. Three of the Carolingian units faced the necessity of fighting their way out of Saxon territory without achieving their goals. However, the fourth mounted force did succeed in burning, plundering, and killing large numbers of Saxons, and returning with considerable quantities of booty, which may have included captives to be sold into slavery.

Waste zones

In addition to punishing or discouraging attacks and rebellions, premeditated devastation also served defensive purposes in frontier regions through the creation of an uninhabited district facing the potential enemy. During the first decades of the tenth century, much of the territory comprising modern Austria was overrun by the Hungarians and, for all practical purposes, was lost to the East Frankish kingdom. The resident Christian populations were enslaved or fled, and the region was left as a waste. Despite the reconquest of much of this region under ducal and royal auspices during the course of the 930s and 940s, resettlement was not permitted by either Duke Arnulf of Bavaria (907–937) or by his successors, who were appointed by King Otto I of Germany. The purpose for keeping this region a waste was to make it more difficult for the Hungarians to attack Bavaria, by denying them easy access to supplies or even local guides along their potential line of march.

Ultimately, it was the defeat of the Hungarians at the Battle of the Lechfeld near Augsburg and its aftermath in 955, and the subsequent projection of German power to the east, that brought peace to the frontier. Nevertheless, it was not until 979 that King Otto II of Germany permitted Bishop Wolfgang of Regensburg (972–979) to establish agricultural settlements in the region between the Ybbs and Erlaf rivers in the modern district of Lower Austria, which had been overrun by the Hungarians two generations before. Even with the Hungarians quiescent, however, the German king only permitted the establishment of the new settlements with the proviso that the bishop also had to undertake the construction of a fortification there to protect the colonists from potential enemy raids. This resettlement and the requirement to construct a fortification formed an eastern extension of the frontier defences that already were in place.

The rulers of the Christian kingdoms in Iberia also created regions of 'no-man's land' as part of their system of territorial defence during the course of the ninth and tenth centuries. Muslim *razzias* (Arabic for raids) from the south often had the two-fold purpose of destroying the economic infrastructure of the Christian kingdoms along the frontier and of taking captives who could be sold as slaves, thereby making the raids economically profitable. In response, as discussed in Chapter 2, the rulers of León-Castile ordered the withdrawal of their populations farther north, and established a series of fortifications in mountain passes to provide a system of defence in depth for the Christian populations even farther to the north. During the period of Christian southward advance during the mid-eleventh century, rulers such as Alfonso VI of León-Castile resettled the frontier regions with populations from the interior and rehabilitated abandoned settlements and even towns. These newly established Christian centres of population were heavily fortified, and, as seen in Chapter 3, the urban militias of these new towns provided a crucial element to the Christian royal armies of conquest during the eleventh–thirteenth centuries when they joined the king's army for offensive military operations.

The experience of the Christian rulers in northwestern Iberia in dealing with Muslim advances, and the creation of a no-man's land, also can be seen in the contemporary

Byzantine-Muslim frontier in Anatolia. Following the loss of its eastern provinces, the rulers of the East Roman Empire were compelled to develop strategies that allowed them protect the civilian population from endemic Arab raids, many of which were exceptionally large, and led to the siege of the capital of Constantinople on several occasions in the seventh and early eighth centuries. As the Byzantine historian John Haldon has argued, defence was no longer predicated on keeping Muslim armies out of Christian territories or meeting them in battle, but rather on providing early warning systems so that the rural population could make their way to the fortifications that increasingly dotted the landscape. Byzantine military operations were focused on getting civilians and their livestock out of the way of marauding Arab forces, and engaging in guerrilla operations when the opportunity presented itself. In order to provide earlier warnings to widely scattered rural populations that were still under Byzantine rule, and theoretically governmental protection, the East Roman emperors mandated the abandonment of a broad zone to the west of Muslim-held lands, which were patrolled on a regular basis by small groups of Roman troops. The role of these forces was not to engage the Muslims, but to send word that hostile forces were organizing for another raid.

A similar process of developing a 'no-man's land', but one focused on offensive rather than defensive warfare, can be discerned in the military strategy of the Sword Brothers, and later the Teutonic Knights, during the course of the Livonian crusade of the thirteenth century and the Lithuanian crusade of the fourteenth and fifteenth centuries. The German priest Henry of Livonia, an eyewitness and participant in the Livonian crusade, describes the efforts of the Sword Brothers and their native Christian allies to annihilate the pagan populations along the frontiers of their territory, kill their livestock, and burn their settlements. The crusaders left these frontier regions as barren wastes for the two-fold purpose of denying easy access to supplies for their opponents, and also keeping native pagans from infiltrating the lands of the Sword Brothers and influencing the local populations that had been converted to Christianity. During the course of the fourteenth century, the Teutonic Knights, who absorbed the order of the Sword Brothers, also used the policy of establishing wastes along the frontier to inhibit raids, and also to establish a *cordon sanitaire* against the infiltration of pagan ideas into recently Christianized areas. Today, the wastelands can be identified through pollen analysis, developed through archaeological research, that shows periods of several decades in which no agricultural activity was undertaken.

Strategy of restraint

Large-scale devastation clearly could be effective in achieving both political and military goals. However, contrary to the commonly expressed view that warfare was all about plunder, it is clear that many medieval rulers also consciously eschewed inflicting damage on the economic assets of the enemy. This strategic choice ironically is particularly evident in the early Middle Ages when putatively 'Germanic' warlords are presented as seeking booty to feed the insatiable greed of their 'warriors'. One of the most important reasons for showing restraint was to ensure that the region in which the campaign is taking place can provide economic value to the invader in the future, whether in the form of tribute or direct exactions following conquest.

An exceptionally clear statement of the rationale for instituting a strategy of restraint with regard to the economic resources of the enemy is articulated by Aridius, a Gallo-Roman magnate from the Burgundian kingdom in the context of the siege of the fortress city of Avignon by the Frankish king Clovis I discussed in previous chapters. From his vantage point in the late sixth century, Bishop Gregory was drawing a comparison between the late Roman imperial view, on the one hand, that economic resources were to be husbanded, that tribute frequently was preferable to conquest, and on the other hand, the supposed 'barbarian' – and particularly 'pagan' – concept that wholesale destruction was an acceptable adjunct to military operations.

Gregory claims that Clovis followed the advice of the Gallo-Roman senator, and refrained from further destruction of the region around Avignon. Instead, he accepted an annual tribute. Moreover, Clovis adopted a strategy of restraint with regard to economic assets for the remainder of his career, a fact that Gregory implies was connected with the king's conversion to Christianity. During his campaign against the Visigothic kingdom in 507, for example, Clovis issued strict orders to his army that the men were to take nothing along their line of march, even in enemy territory, other than grass and water. These items were permitted, as seen in Chapter 4 on logistics, by late Roman law. According to Gregory, Clovis went so far as to order the execution of soldiers who violated these orders. Separately, in surviving letters from Clovis to Catholic bishops, including Archbishop Remigius of Rheims (459–533), the king explicitly states that he will protect Church lands from the ravages of war, and in return expected both the spiritual and material support of these ecclesiastical magnates.

Collateral damage

The employment of a strategy of devastation or of restraint by a particular military commander is properly understood as resulting from decisions made at the beginning of a campaign and as contingent on detailed planning efforts. However, many matters relating to the actual execution of military operations are not today, and were not in the Middle Ages, actually intended or planned. The killing of civilians by soldiers of Western armies in the period after the Second World War is, for example, almost always accidental and not related in any way to the planned conduct of a particular raid, missile strike, or bombing attack. These accidents are due to the factor denoted by many military professionals as the 'fog of war'. The accidental nature of such damage is evidenced both by the heroic efforts made by contemporary Western armies to avoid civilian casualties, even to the extent of putting their own soldiers in greater danger as result of their restraint, and by the punishment of Western soldiers by their own governments for the direct use of violence against civilians when this is deemed intentional and therefore criminal. Nevertheless, it is still the case that civilians are killed and civilian infrastructure is destroyed in the conduct of contemporary Western military operations. In many cases, this is due to equipment failures, errors in intelligence, or errors in judgement.

In the medieval period, as seen in the discussion of the affirmative use of devastation as a tool of war, rulers and military commanders generally did not draw the same very strict distinctions between combatants and non-combatants that are drawn today. In the course of a lengthy sieges, which were the predominant type of large-scale military action during the entire medieval millennium, both attackers and defenders were aware that residents who were primarily non-combatants, including women, children, old men, and clergy, were at significant risk even if they did not take up arms personally or aid those who did. These non-combatants were subject to artillery bombardments, to shortages of food, and very likely would die at the hands of attackers in a frenzy of close-quarter combat if a fortress were stormed successfully rather than surrendered. This was the case even when military commanders did not make the affirmative decision to slaughter the population or to destroy much or all of the capital infrastructure.

During the course of an army's march through enemy territory, it was also the case that non-combatants and their property were subject to assault and destruction even when this was not an element of the commander's strategy. As seen previously with regard to Clovis' invasion of the Visigothic kingdom in 507, even when the ruler gave explicit orders that private property was not to be taken, some soldiers violated this command. The tendency of well-armed fighting men to take what they wanted from the population in the lands through which they marched was recognized by military leaders throughout the medieval millennium. Capitularies issued by Charlemagne and his successors, *fueoros* issued by the Christian kings of Iberia to frontier towns, and military ordinances such as the one promulgated by Frederick Barbarossa for his Italian campaign in 1158, discussed in Chapter 6, all point to the ongoing efforts to curb such behaviour. Nevertheless, violence against non-combatants remained a constant possibility, particularly in the absence of a strong government with a record of vigorous enforcement of standing orders, which today are denoted as 'rules of engagement'.

Problems caused to the civilian population can be seen very clearly, for example, in the behaviour of demobilized military companies that ravaged the French countryside during much of the Hundred Years' War. It should be noted that whatever rules of engagement governed their behaviour before being discharged from royal service, these no longer applied when the soldiers were operating on their own initiative. By contrast, in periods and places where there were strong governments, collateral damage was often kept to a low level because fear of punishment helped to restrain the violent and acquisitive tendencies of some fighting men. For example, the chronicles during Charlemagne's reign are remarkably silent about the violence of his troops, except when they were given commands to engage in strategic destruction. In fact, Charlemagne and several of his Carolingian successors agreed to pay compensation to civilians who were unjustly subjected to loss due to military operations of his forces.

Military education

The development of strategic thought regarding political and military goals and options, with all of the concomitant elements necessary for this process, required the service of men with a great deal of expertise in a wide range of pertinent matters. Despite this reality, there remain today numerous scholars, including even those who focus on military history, who argue that medieval military commanders did not require anything resembling a formal education because warfare was quite simple, and that leadership demanded little more than the use of 'common sense'. By contrast, the leaders charged with training the next generation of officers in the armed forces of the United States, for example, do not share or endorse the idea of leaving the execution of even the simplest military operations to so-called common sense. To take just one small example, the military manual *FM 7–8: Infantry Rifle Platoon and Squad, 3.20*, dealing with the topic 'Point Ambush', emphasizes that the officer in charge is to instruct his men: 'Take weapons off SAFE. Moving the selection lever on the weapon causes a metallic click that could compromise the ambush if the soldiers wait until the enemy is in the kill zone'.

To an armchair general sitting at his desk in the university, such an injunction may seem superfluous or even an egregious example of the tendency of military officials to belabour obvious details. In reality, however, the training of officers is intended to remove, as much as possible, the element of human failure through education by foreseeing and addressing potential errors that can arise during the course of a complex or even a simple military campaign and in the confusion of battle. As this and previous chapters have illuminated, medieval warfare was far from simple, and it was no more possible for either medieval commanders or their subordinates simply to rely on their 'common sense' than it is for military officers today.

Among the numerous tasks that had to be undertaken by medieval commanders in the context of preparing and executing military strategy were the development of strategic intelligence, the organization of supply, and the mobilization of military forces. While on campaign, military commanders had the responsibility for overseeing the construction of marching camps and fortifications, establishing sieges, overseeing the construction and emplacement of siege equipment, defending fortifications against sieges, overseeing the construction of mines and counter-mines, choosing a battlefield, deploying their troops in formation, choosing the appropriate tactics for mounted and foot soldiers as well as missile troops under a variety of conditions, providing leadership on the march and in the field, maintaining high morale among their men, training men in the use of their arms, and training men and horses how to deploy in formations and to fight in concert on the battlefield. Every one of these duties, and many more, had to be learned by young men before they were in a position to participate in the development of military strategy or could be entrusted with the command of soldiers in the field. Those commanders who were ignorant generally failed and rarely got a second chance.

Military education in Rome

In the ancient world, there were three main sources of information for aspiring military commanders. Polybius, a Greek historian who spent seventeen years as a hostage in Rome (167–150 BC), observed that in both the eastern and western Mediterranean, it was common for successful military leaders to have studied handbooks, to have obtained the advice of men who were knowledgeable about war, and to have learned by experience in the field. By contrast, the Roman historian Sallust (died 35 BC) wrote that Marius, a leading general of the late Roman Republic (died 86 BC), preferred practical experience and action as contrasted with learning from books. Other Roman generals, such as Julius Caesar (died 44 BC), Sextus Julius Frontinus (died AD 103), and Lucius Flavius Arrianus (died c.160), wrote historical accounts and military handbooks expressly for the purpose of providing information to future military leaders regarding the proper means to proceed in myriad situations. As Frontinus points out in the introduction to his book *Stratagems*, commanders will learn how to act by studying how others acted in similar situations.

Some specialists in Roman history have made the case that the training of future military commanders during the Republic, Principate, and early Empire largely was left to private initiative. Young men, according to this model, were groomed by older relatives, who brought them on campaign, discussed military matters in informal settings, and recommended appropriate historical works and manuals for them to read. By contrast, other scholars suggest that there was a much more rigorous process for selecting and training young aristocrats for a military career. It seems to us that the education of young men for command likely combined both models at various times up to the end of the second century AD.

By contrast, it is beyond dispute that during the course of the later third and early fourth centuries, emperors Diocletian (284–305) and Constantine the Great (306–337) created the foundations for a professional and, in theory, a hereditary officer corps. By the second half of the fourth century, the imperial government had in place a formal system of military education that began in childhood. Boys who were too young to serve under arms were enrolled in official registers, according to an edict issued by Emperor Valentinian in 365, and attached to units of the imperial guard. These boys began receiving allowances for food and clothing from the time of their enrolment. In addition, following an initial period of training, the 'cadets' – who were now youths – received a military commission and began to earn an annual salary that was four times a regular soldier's pay. The formal institutional structure for the education of the future imperial military officers was provided by the military units attached directly to the emperor's person, the so-called *scholae*. During the course of the later fourth and early fifth centuries, numerous 'barbarians', including Franks and Goths, were enrolled in the imperial *scholae*. Many of them subsequently rose to high ranks in the imperial army, including as generals and even as the overall military commanders in one-half of the empire – that is, as *magister militum* for the East or West. Not only were these supposed 'barbarians' members of the imperial elite, but many of them were literate in both Latin and Greek.

The court as military academy

As illuminated in the previous chapters, the dissolution of Roman imperial authority in the West did not lead to the abandonment of traditional Roman institutions. Rather, as had been the case with respect to military topography, technology, recruitment, and logistics, late imperial practices with regard to training future army officers played a central role in shaping military education throughout the medieval period. Many of the leading 'barbarian' military commanders and rulers during the fifth century had received a formal military education under Roman auspices; so, too, had their Roman senatorial counterparts. For example, Sidonius Apollinaris (died 489), a Roman aristocrat from the Auvergne region of modern France, bragged in his copious surviving collection of letters that he and his friends had received extensive military educations in their youth. Among other matters, Sidonius commented knowledgeably about important military texts such as M. Terentius Varro's now lost manual about military logistics entitled *Libri logistorici*, a copy of which he possessed. He also had another copy of the text made for a fellow Gallo-Roman senator who served as a military commander in the Visigothic army.

It is hardly surprising, therefore, that the rulers of the kingdoms that grew up in the former provinces of the western half of the Roman Empire established their own versions of the imperial *scholae* of the type that had been established during the fourth century in Constantinople. The Frankish king Theudebert I (511–548), for example, recruited a Roman aristocrat named Parthenius, whose grandfathers were Emperor Avitus (455–457) and Bishop Ruricius of Limoges (485–510), to serve as a chief official (*magister officorum*) at his court. Among his many duties, Parthenius was responsible for overseeing the military education of the youths serving at Theudebert's court. Theudebert's fellow Frankish kings, as well as their Visigothic and Ostrogothic counterparts in the erstwhile Roman provinces of Spain and Italy, also maintained the traditional pattern of providing a formal military education to young men – both Romans and 'barbarians', usually aristocrats, who were sent or summoned to serve at the royal court.

The early medieval pattern of court-based education of future military leaders was replicated during the eighth and ninth centuries on a far grander scale at the Carolingian imperial courts of Charlemagne and Louis the Pious. The formal structure of this military education was quite similar to that of the *scholae* in Constantinople of the fourth and fifth centuries. Abbot Adalhard of Corbie, noted earlier in the chapter, described the military school at the imperial court in his practical handbook, *On the Organization of the Palace*.

The students, denoted as *discipuli*, were divided up among a number of instructors called masters (*magistri*). These *discipuli*, like the youths in the imperial *scholae*, were enrolled among the emperor's household troops.

In the wake of the dissolution of the Carolingian Empire during the ninth century, Charlemagne's grandsons and their successors continued to use their courts as a central place of military education both for the sons of aristocrats and to talented young men from more modest backgrounds. In a well-known passage in his *Deeds of Charles the Great*, the monk Notker of St. Gall (died 912) told the story of Charlemagne visiting the palace school after returning from a long military campaign. In this story, which provides more information about the time of Charlemagne's great-grandson than his own, when the emperor saw what was going on there, he praised the boys from middling and low status backgrounds for their hard work. However, he warned the aristocratic youth that if they continued in their lazy habits, they would never receive any offices, military or administrative, from him.

The Ottonian rulers in Germany continued the Carolingian, and ultimately Roman, norm of establishing court-based schools to provide military educations to future army commanders. The Ottonian system is illuminated by the career of Adalbero, the nephew of Bishop Ulrich of Augsburg (923–973). As a child, Adalbero was sent by his uncle Ulrich to get a basic education in the liberal arts in a monastery. In this context, fundamental to the study of grammar, which formed a central focus of the liberal arts, was the reading of historical works, including not only the Bible but also classical texts such as Caesar's commentary on his Gallic wars. After Adalbero had spent several years at the monastery, Ulrich summoned his nephew home to Augsburg and then sent him to serve in the court of King Otto I. Adalbero remained at the king's court for many years, where he was enrolled in Otto's military household and learned how to be a military officer, as well as to carry out the types of administrative duties that were required of men of his status. Following this apprenticeship, Adalbero was again summoned back to Augsburg by his uncle and was appointed to serve as commander of Ulrich's military household. Two of Bishop Ulrich's other nephews, named Manegold and Hupold, similarly had served in the royal military household before returning home and taking command positions at Augsburg.

The courts of numerous other rulers throughout the medieval period served a similar function by providing a setting for the training of young men for a career in military service. Perhaps the best studied of these institutions over a long period is the military household of the Anglo-Norman kings from the reign of William the Conqueror to that of his descendant Edward I. In a landmark essay, J.O. Prestwich traced out the careers of dozens of aristocrats who joined the courts of the Anglo-Norman and Angevin kings of England, where they learned the skills of military leadership and went on to serve as high-ranking officers. Henry I and his grandson Henry II, in particular, were renowned for recruiting able young men from throughout Europe whom they enrolled in their military households and started on successful careers for which they had been well prepared by their education at court.

Learning from books

The practical education in military matters provided to youths and young men at the courts of rulers, and likely also in the households of many lesser magnates, involved extensive hands-on training. What is often discounted by modern medieval historians, however, and particularly with regard to the period before c.1200, is the crucial role played by the written word in military education. The case against learning from books has been made most forcefully by the early medieval historians Timothy Reuter and Guy Halsall. They have asserted that the copying of military treatises, particularly in the period before the First Crusade, represents nothing but the antiquarian interests of monks, and that these works were not read by leaders of plunder-seeking war bands, who, in any event, had no need of a sophisticated military education. This argument is based on a model of the primitive nature of medieval warfare, and of early medieval society in general. In our view, as elucidated in the previous chapters, such a model of medieval society is untenable. Instead, learning from books, including both manuals and histories, played a central role in military education. The importance of such books, including manuals and works of history, is illuminated both by the very large numbers of texts that were produced and the comments by leading figures in society about the role that they were intended to play.

The ubiquity of military manuals among medieval leaders is illuminated, for example, in the comments made by the twelfth-century chronicler William of Malmesbury (died c.1143) about Henry I of England. William wrote that this king embodied the statement, discussed in Chapter 6, by the great Roman general Scipio Africanus (died 183 BC): 'My mother bore me for command, not combat'. The comment reportedly made by Scipio survived into the medieval period because of the decision by another Roman general, Sextus Julius Frontinus, mentioned earlier, to include it in his military manual, *Stratagems*. Frontinus was making clear that Scipio's claim referred not to some inborn body of knowledge about military command, but rather to Scipio's fitness for the role of general rather than being relegated to serving as a simple soldier in a phalanx. In the introduction to his manual, Frontinus asserted that the knowledge gained from his text would help readers 'to develop their own ability to think out and carry out operations successfully that are similar in nature [to those that they have studied]'. Frontinus went on to emphasize that 'the commander' who is so educated, 'will have an added benefit insofar as he will not be worried concerning the likelihood for the success of his plans because he has learned that similar plans have already worked in practice'.

William of Malmesbury appreciated the practical importance of Frontinus' text, and it is for this reason that he drew upon it when describing the military knowledge of the English king. An even more direct impact of Frontinus' text on contemporary military thinking is evidenced two centuries earlier, by the decision of Archbishop Brun of Cologne (953–965) to have a presentation copy made of *Stratagems* for his elder brother King Otto I of Germany. In the dedicatory poem in Latin that accompanied the gift to Otto, Brun wrote that the state (*res publica*) has suffered the ravages of barbarian savagery, 'but where your right hand holds the sceptre, the state enjoys safety provided by you'. Brun clearly believed that Frontinus' work would help Otto to continue to succeed in his military endeavours. Indeed, the gift illuminates the value of such texts in informing the military thinking of commanders during the course of their careers and not simply during their initial education.

The ongoing use of books is illuminated, for example, by the account in the *History of Geoffrey, Duke of the Normans and Count of the Angevins* regarding the siege of the stronghold of Montreuil-Bellay by Geoffrey Plantagenet in 1150. According to the text, Geoffrey faced a significant tactical problem. Although his siege engines knocked holes in the walls of the enemy fortification each day, he could not take advantage of the situation because the defenders were able to patch up the holes each night with wooden timbers. In order to find a solution to this problem, the author states that Count Geoffrey consulted his personal copy of Vegetius' *Epitoma rei militaris*. The author goes on to state:

> Some monks from Marmoutier were present [at the siege] because they had brought dispatches from their church to the count. Thus, the respectful count, because of his

esteem for the monks, put down the book that he had in his hands so that he might listen to them more attentively. One of the monks, the head of the delegation who was named Walter of Compiègne . . . picked up the book and began to read. He found the place where Vegetius Renatus explains fully how a tower that has been repaired with joined oak beams may be quickly laid open to capture. The thoughtful count eyed the exceptional monk who had demonstrated such skill and care in reading, and said: Brother Walter, beloved of the Lord, just as you have discovered in the reading, so tomorrow you will see demonstrated in practice.

In evaluating this text, it should be noted that the extant version of Vegetius' original work does not include the passage described here. However, it was common practice throughout the medieval period to annotate books with additional information and commentary. It is likely that the monk Walter read aloud this commentary, which provided Geoffrey with an effective course of action that led to the capture of Montreuil-Bellay.

The ongoing practical value of Vegetius' text, as indicated in the account about Geoffrey, is echoed by numerous writers throughout the medieval period, including the early Middle Ages, who discussed the impact of reading manuals on the military thinking of rulers and commanders alike. In the mid-ninth century, for example, Frechulf of Lisieux (died c.850), royal chancellor of the West Frankish kingdom, provided King Charles the Bald with a specially revised edition of Vegetius' *Epitoma rei militaris*. In his preface to the book, Frechulf stated that the text was intended to provide guidance in both strategy and tactics when dealing with the Viking menace.

Moreover, Charles the Bald was not the only member of his family to possess and draw on Vegetius' work for insights regarding military affairs. When writing to Charlemagne, the great courtier and churchman Alcuin of York (died 804) quoted extensively from the *Epitoma* without even mentioning Vegetius' name. This is a clear indication that Alcuin knew that Charlemagne was very familiar with the text. As seen in previous chapters, Archbishop Rabanus Maurus of Mainz composed his own revised version of Vegetius' text, a copy of which he sent the Carolingian ruler Lothair II (855–869). Charles the Bald's elder brother Louis the German also possessed a copy of Vegetius' text, as did King Odo of West Francia (888–898), who acquired a copy of the handbook from the monastery of St. Denis. Abbot Engilbert of St. Gall, as mentioned in Chapter 6, had a copy of Vegetius' text and followed the instructions regarding the use of double-weight weapons for training fighting men.

Indeed, during the Middle Ages, Vegetius' *Epitoma rei militaris* was among the most copied secular texts dating from the Late Antique world. By the later Middle Ages, Vegetius' work was described by both secular and ecclesiastical writers as 'the authority' in regard to military matters. Today, more than 300 manuscripts of the *Epitoma* survive, most in Latin but also in many vernacular translations. It is likely that many hundreds more have been lost, in part because these texts, as handbooks, were used and worn beyond repair. Many of the surviving manuscripts of the *Epitoma* were the subject of very detailed commentaries, and some were even illustrated in an effort to illuminate various points Vegetius makes. In addition, wills and other accounts indicate that men with a strong interest in military matters collected a small library of texts that pertained to warfare and had them bound together in book form. The text that was most commonly bound with the *Epitoma* in the later Middle Ages was Frontinus' *Stratagems*. Many writers also assumed that their readers were so well versed in Vegetius' text that they quoted liberally from it in their own works without providing attribution to the *Epitoma*. Two of the more famous writers to have drawn extensively from Vegetius in the later Middle Ages were Giles of Rome and Machiavelli, although neither writer mentions Vegetius by name or the title of his work.

During the period of the Hundred Years' War, numerous authors, particularly in France, sought to expand upon the advice offered by Vegetius in new military manuals that were focused on 'modern times'. Among these perhaps the most prominent, at least in terms of scholarly attention, are Honoré Bouvet (1340–1410), who wrote a volume entitled the *Tree of Battles* (*L'arbre des batailles*), and Christine de Pizan (1364–1430), whose most systematic treatment of warfare is found in *Book of Deeds of Arms and Chivalry* (*Livre des fais d'armes et de chevalerie*). Christine is famous for arguing that France should undertake a radical reform of its military organization in the face of defeats at the hands of the English in which the army served as the agent of the ruler in protecting the realm and people. As much a moral guide as a military manual, *Book of Deeds of Arms and Chivalry* argued for the revitalization of a 'Roman' model of military organization, that was based on a well-trained and professional army of volunteers, who received a regular salary. Christine's view was that this type or professionalization was necessary to avoid the mistreatment of civilians by soldiers.

Reading history

All too often, the discussion of military education in the early Middle Ages has turned solely on the question of military manuals. However, works of history also played a central role in the military education of aspiring commanders, as well as in the ongoing learning of military men during the course of their careers. In his *Etymologies*, a handbook of unrivalled popularity in the early Middle Ages, Bishop Isidore of Seville (died 636) emphasized that men who wished to be effective rulers had to read history. He specifically argued that historical works would help men in public life by allowing them to learn from the successes and failure of leaders from the past. Of course, this was the same point made by Frontinus, whose *Stratagems* was almost entirely a collection of historical examples that were arranged in categories. During the Carolingian period, the prodigious thinker and writer Ardo Smaragdus (died 843) observed: 'that it was the most ancient practice, customary for kings from then to now, to have deeds written down in annals for posterity to learn about'.

Alcuin, noted earlier, also emphasized the importance of reading history, particularly in the context of military affairs. In 798, Alcuin wrote a letter to Charlemagne, who was then campaigning in Saxony, in which he stressed

> that it very important for us to read in ancient books of history about the kind of strength that fighting men had so that the kind of wise temperament, which ought to be acted upon, shall guide and rule us in all things.

According to Charlemagne's contemporary biographer Einhard, the great Carolingian ruler relished the learning of history, and had historical texts read out loud during meals at court. These sessions likely included some of the numerous historical writers, such as Livy, Caesar, and Suetonius, whose books were assiduously copied and disseminated throughout the Carolingian Empire. Charlemagne's descendants also devoted considerable attention to gaining knowledge through the reading of history. In a letter to Rabanus Maurus, for example, Emperor Lothair I (840–855) made clear that he carried his works of history with him when he went on campaign.

Numerous rulers in the post-Carolingian period commissioned historical texts both to record the successes of their dynasties and to provide models for their descendants.

Widukind of Corvey's *Deeds of the Saxons*, for example, was commissioned by a member of the German royal court, and likely King Otto I himself, to provide instruction to his daughter Mathilda as she prepared to serve as regent in Germany in the absence of her father and brother in Italy. In the West, we have the *Life of Robert the Pious*, written by Helgaud, a chaplain of King Robert II of France (996–1031), which was intended to provide practical guidance in the art of government to future rulers of the Capetian dynasty.

Below the level of kings and princes, both ecclesiastical and secular magnates commissioned historical works so that past events could be used to provide guidance for future policies. The rulers of Normandy were particularly assiduous in their patronage of historical works. Duke Richard II of Normandy, for example, commissioned the monk Dudo of St. Quentin to write the *History of the Normans*, which was focused largely on military operations. Duke William II of Normandy similarly commissioned historical works, both before and after his conquest of England in 1066. These included William of Poitiers' *Deeds of Duke William of the Normans and King of England*. William's successors on the English throne also commissioned numerous historical works.

Numerous ecclesiastical writers also composed historical works to provide instruction regarding the conduct of secular affairs. Perhaps the most famous and influential historical writer in the Anglo-Norman tradition is John of Salisbury (died 1180), whose historical and political tracts include the *Policraticus* and *Metalogicon*, both of which offer extensive models of good and bad decision making to the author's intended audience in the court of King Henry II of England. Parenthetically, King Henry II, was reported by a contemporary writer to have memorized a vast quantity of historical texts that he believed were of great importance for governing his realm. In addition to writing for an appreciative Henry II, John of Salisbury also wrote hundreds of letters to leading political figures of his day, including Archbishop Thomas Becket, offering advice about military – as well as political and ecclesiastical – matters, advice that drew upon historical events. It is notable that John of Salisbury also relied heavily on Vegetius when offering military advice to leading magnates of his own day.

Similar historical works were commissioned in the German kingdom by ecclesiastical princes. For example, Bruno of Merseburg commented on the value of historical writing, and particularly his *Saxon Wars* in a dedicatory letter to his patron Bishop Werner of Merseburg:

> Therefore, I wish to write briefly and truthfully about the war that King Henry waged against the Saxons just as I have been able to learn about it from those who participated in these events. I do so because this war was quite remarkable for its great scale as well as for the mercy shown by God during its course as we, ourselves, experienced. Anyone who wishes to read the following pages will be able to learn about these matters. For just as in castigating us, God mixes in the oil of compassion with the wine of severity, so too we happily recognize that the prophet spoke truly when he said: 'when you are wrathful, remember your mercy', and the apostle said: 'God is faithful who does not permit you to be tempted beyond what you can bear'.

Bruno's claim that he was preserving information about the past so that others could learn from these events in the future is echoed in the anonymous history entitled *The Deeds of the Bishops of Utrecht*, which was written in 1232–1233. The author observed that Bishop Wilbrand of Utrecht (1227–1233) summoned both laymen and clerics with knowledge of events of the past decade to attend the episcopal court so that he could hear and have recorded their testimony about the events that led up to the death of his predecessor, Bishop Otto II (1216–1227), in battle against the rural levies from the region of Drenthe. According to the author, Wilbrand carefully questioned all of these individuals to find out all of the mistakes that had been made, and subsequently had this information compiled into a history of the diocese for the purpose of learning from these past events. During the later Middle Ages, historical works continued to be read assiduously at royal and princely courts for the information that they provided about earlier successes and failures. Froissart, the famed historian of the Hundred Years' War, enjoyed considerable noble patronage for the production of his historical texts as the nobility undoubtedly found his detailed accounts of military events to be of value in conceptualizing their own military operations.

Conclusion

A primary purpose of this chapter has been to illuminate the complexity of strategic thought in the Middle Ages, both in regard to the organization of military operations in the short term and with respect to broader geo-political issues inherent in grand – or, perhaps more accurately, long-term – strategy. The considerable range of problems that rulers had to confront with the help of dedicated and well-educated staffs as they conceptualized their military, political, and diplomatic options should put to rest for good the idea that medieval warfare was in any way primitive, or that successful military operations could be conducted in a haphazard manner on the basis of 'common sense'.

In the first stage of planning, all offensive military operations, and some defensive operations that rose above the level of small-scale raids conducted at the local level, required detailed planning before any fighting men, supplies, and transportation resources could be mobilized. This planning, in turn, depended on the acquisition and analysis of a broad range of information, including but not limited to military intelligence. Military planners needed to know how many fighting men were available for service and where they were located, the location and availability of supply and transportation assets, the likely responses of supposedly uninvolved neighbouring realms to the allocation of these forces for campaign duty, and the likely responses of the enemy to attack. Governments obtained this information for their military planners through a combination of the normal practices of governance, as well as active intelligence gathering by formal and informal agents, such as merchants.

Once in the field, military commanders also required regular fresh and accurate intelligence in order to acquire up to date and accurate information about such matters as the location of enemy forces and the most suitable line of march, which would provide adequate fresh water, defensible campsites, and other resources for the army. The need for such tactical intelligence was no less imperative for armies in early medieval Europe than it was during the later Middle Ages. Clovis and Charlemagne were just as active in dispatching scouts, debriefing captured prisoners of war, and interrogating members of the local population as were Philip IV of France in the fourteenth century or Henry V of England in the fifteenth century.

The lack of sophistication associated with medieval warfare in popular media and also by some scholars is further belied by the ways in which medieval rulers used both diplomacy and destruction as adjuncts to both campaign and grand strategy. Aside from the Hundred Years' War, the role played by diplomacy in medieval military strategy has received limited attention from scholars. However, the multi-sided diplomatic negotiations such as those among the Lombard King Desiderius, Charlemagne, and the papal curia in the period 768–774, or those between Edward I and Philip IV in 1303, which are treated in this chapter, reveal the ability of these governments to develop long-term plans in order to define their places among their neighbours. This, in large part, is the essence of grand strategy.

By contrast with diplomacy, the destruction caused by medieval armies has received considerable attention from scholars, who argue that thoughtless violence and devastation were the hallmark of warfare in the medieval period. This is of a piece with the conceit that military science was at its nadir in this period. However, a careful analysis of the sources, as contrasted with prior assumptions about a supposedly backward age, reveal that medieval rulers and military commanders had quite complex ideas regarding the use of both destruction and restraint in the conduct of military campaigns. There certainly was collateral damage, as this term is used today, in medieval warfare. For the most part, however, when armies caused destruction, this was an element in a purposeful military strategy, not simply haphazard violence characteristic of a brutal age.

Finally, it bears repetition that successful rulers and military commanders in the medieval millennium not only had to be intelligent; they also had to be well-educated. As David Bates recently has argued with respect to William the Conqueror, it is no longer possible to understand him as an 'ill-educated soldier'. William, like all other successful military leaders, benefitted from a lengthy practical education in leadership that was complemented by the study of books. Moreover, this study continued over the course of a lifetime, as evidenced by the career of a ruler such as Geoffrey Plantagenet, who actively consulted Vegetius' *Epitoma rei militaris* as a practical guide to carrying out a siege.

Bibliography

For a discussion of the concepts of strategy and grand strategy, see

Edward Luttwak, *The Grand Strategy of the Roman Empire* (Baltimore, 1976);
Everett Wheeler, 'The Methodological Limits and the Mirage of Roman Strategy' in *Journal of Military History 57* (1993), 7–41 and 215–240;
Kimberly Kagan, 'Redefining Roman Grand Strategy' in *Journal of Military History 70* (2006), 333–362.

For the practice of long-term strategy by medieval polities, see

Bernard S. Bachrach, 'The Angevin Strategy of Castle Building in the Reign of Fulk Nerra, 987–1040' in *American Historical Review 88* (1983), 533–560;
Paul E. Chevedden, 'Crusader Warfare Revisited: A Revisionist Look at R. C. Smail's Thesis: Fortifications and Development of Defensive Planning' in *Journal of the Rocky Mountain Medieval and Renaissance Association 14* (1994), 13–31;
Roger Turvey, 'Defences of Twelfth-Century Deheubarth and the Castle Strategy of the Lord Rhys' in *Archaeologia Cambrensis 144* (1997), 103–132;
Paul E. Chevedden, 'Fortifications and the Development of Defensive Planning during the Crusader Period' in *The Circle of War in the Middle Ages: Essays on Medieval Military and Naval History*, ed. Donald J. Kagay and L. J. Andrew Villalon (Woodbridge, 1999), 33–43;
Matthias Hardt, 'Hesse, Elbe, Saale and the Frontiers of the Carolingian Empire' in *The Transformation of Frontiers from Late Antiquity to the Carolingians*, ed. Walter Pohl, Ian Wood, and Helmut Reimitz (Leiden, Boston, Cologne, 2001), 219–232;
John E. Dotson, 'Foundations of Venetian Naval Strategy from Pietro II Orseolo to the Battle of Zonchio' in *Viator 32* (2001), 113–125;
Bernard S. Bachrach, *Early Carolingian Warfare: Prelude to Empire* (Philadelphia, 2002);

Charles R. Bowlus, 'Italia–Bavaria–Avaria' the Grand Strategy Behind Charlemagne's *Renovatio Imperii* in the West' in *Journal of Medieval Military History 1* (2002), 43–60;

Valerie Eads, 'The Geography of Power: Matilda of Tuscany and the Strategy of Active Defense' in *Crusaders, Condottieri and Cannon: Medieval Warfare in Societies around the Mediterranean*, ed. Donald J. Kagay and L. J. Andrew Villalon (Leiden, 2003), 355–386;

Bernard S. Bachrach, 'Dudo of Saint Quentin and Norman Military Strategy' in *Anglo-Norman Studies 26* (2004), 21–36;

John France, 'Thinking about Crusader Strategy' in *Noble Ideals and Bloody Realities: Warfare in the Middle Ages*, ed. Niall Christie and Maya Yazigi (Leiden, 2006), 75–96;

Gyorgy Szabados, 'The Hungarian National Defense during the German Wars 1030–1052' in *Chronica 6* (2006), 72–81;

John Baker, 'Warriors and Watchmen: Place Names and Anglo-Saxon Civil Defence' in *Medieval Archaeology 55* (2011), 258–267;

David S. Bachrach, *Warfare in Tenth-Century Germany* (Woodbridge, 2012);

Bernard S. Bachrach and David S. Bachrach, 'Early Saxon Frontier Warfare: Henry I, Otto I, and Carolingian Military Institutions' in *Journal of Medieval Military History 10* (2012), 17–60;

Concerning campaign strategy, see

John Gillingham, 'Richard I and the Science of War in the Middle Ages' in *War and Government in the Middle Ages: Essays in Honour of J. O. Prestwich*, ed. John Gillingham and J. C. Holt (Totowa, 1984), 78–91;

John Gillingham, 'William the Bastard at War' in *Studies in Medieval History Presented to R. Allen Brown*, ed. Christopher Harper-Bill, Christopher J. Holdsworth, and Janet Nelson (Woodbridge, 1989), 141–158;

John France, *Victory in the East: A Military History of the First Crusade* (Cambridge, 1994);

M. Barber, 'Frontier Warfare in the Latin Kingdom of Jerusalem: The Campaign of Jacob's Ford, 1178–9' in *The Crusades and Their Sources: Essays Presented to Bernard Hamilton*, ed. J. France and W. G. Zajac (Aldershot, 1998), 9–22;

Clifford J. Rogers, 'The Vegetian "Science of Warfare" in the Middle Ages' in *Journal of Medieval Military History 1* (2002), 1–19;

John Gillingham, '"Up with Orthodoxy": In Defense of Vegetian Warfare' in *Journal of Medieval Military History 2* (2004), 149–158;

Clifford J. Rogers, 'The Bergerac Campaign (1345) and the Generalship of Henry of Lancaster' in *Journal of Medieval Military History 2* (2004), 89–110;

Clifford J. Rogers, 'Henry V's Military Strategy in 1415' in *The Hundred Years War: A Wider Focus*, ed. L. J. Andrew Villalon and Donald J. Kagay (Leiden, 2005), 399–428;

L. J. Andrew Villalon, '"Cut Off Their Heads, or I'll Cut Off Yours": Castilian Strategy and Tactics in the War of the Two Pedros and Supporting Evidence from Murcia' in *The Hundred Years War (Part II) Different Vistas*, ed. L. J. Andrew Villalon and Donald J. Kagay (Leiden, 2008), 153–184.

With regard to the gathering of military intelligence and military planning, see

John R. Alban and Christopher Allmand, 'Spies and Spying in the Fourteenth Century' in *War, Literature and Politics in the Late Middle Ages: Essays in Honour of G. W. Coopland*, ed. Christopher Allmand (Liverpool, 1976), 73–101;

Reuven Amitai, 'Mamluk Espionage among the Mongols and Franks' in *Asian and African Studies 22* (1988), 173–181;

Christopher Allmand, 'Intelligence in the Hundred Years War' in *Go Spy the Land: Military Intelligence in History*, ed. Keith Neilson and B. J. C. McKercher (Westport, 1992), 31–47;

John O. Prestwich, 'Military Intelligence under the Norman and Angevin Kings' in *Law and Government in Medieval England and Normandy: Essays in Honour of Sir James Holt*, ed. George Garnett and John Hudson (Cambridge, 1994), 1–30;

Pamela O. Long and Alex Roland, 'Military Secrecy in Antiquity and Early Medieval Europe: A Critical Reassessment' in *History and Technology 11* (1994), 259–290;

Brian Catlos, 'To Catch a Spy: The Case of Zayn al-Din and Ibn Dukhan' in *Medieval Encounters: Jewish, Christian and Muslim Culture in Confluence and Dialogue 2* (1996), 99–113;

Bernard S. Bachrach, 'Charlemagne and the Carolingian General Staff' in *The Journal of Military History 66* (2002), 313–357;

David S. Bachrach, 'Military Planning in Thirteenth-Century England' in *Nottingham Medieval Studies 49* (2005), 42–63;

Bryce Lyon, 'The Failed Flemish Campaign of Edward I in 1297: A Case Study of Efficient Logistics and Inadequate Military Planning' in *Handelingen der Maatschappij voor Geschiedenis en Oudheidkunde te Gent 59* (2005), 31–42;

Susan B. Edgington, 'Espionage and Military Intelligence During the First Crusade' in *Crusading Warfare in the Middle Ages: Realities and Representations, Essays in Honour of John France*, ed. Simon John and Nicholas Morton (Aldershot, 2014), 75–85.

Concerning the importance of diplomacy in the conduct of medieval warfare, see

Malcolm Vale, 'The Anglo-French Wars, 1294–1340: Allies and Alliances' in *Guerre et société en France, Angleterre et en Bourgogne: XIVe – XVe Siècle*, ed. Philippe Contamine, Charles Giry-Deloison, and Maurice Keen (Lille, 1991), 15–35;

Michael Mallett, 'Diplomacy and War in Later Fifteenth–Century Italy' in *Lorenzo de'Medici*, ed. Giancarlo Garfagnini (Florence, 1992), 233–256;

Richard Abels, 'King Alfred's Peace-Making Strategies with the Vikings' in *The Haskins Society Journal 3* (1992), 23–34;

John France, 'Thinking about Crusader Strategy' in *Noble Ideals and Bloody Realities: Warfare in the Middle Ages*, ed. Niall Christie and Maya Yazigi (Leiden, 2006), 75–96;

David S. Bachrach, 'Making Peace and War in the "City-State" of Worms, 1235–1273' in *German History 24* (2006), 505–525;

Jelle Haemers and Frederik Buylaert, 'War, Politics, and Diplomacy in England, France and the Low Countries, 1475–1500: An Entangled History' in *The Yorkist Age: Proceedings of the 2011 Harlaxton Symposium*, ed. Shaun Tyas (Donington, 2013), 195–220;

Also see The collection of essays published in *War and Peace in Ancient and Medieval History*, ed. Philip de Souza and John France (Cambridge, 2008).

For scepticism of the specialized military education in the Middle Ages, with particular regard to the use of books by future military commanders, see

Timothy Reuter, 'Carolingian and Ottonian Warfare' in *Medieval Warfare: A History*, ed. Maurice Keen (Oxford, 1999), 13–35;

Richard Abels and Stephen Morillo, 'A Lying Legacy? A Preliminary Discussion of Images of Antiquity and Altered Reality in Medieval Military History' in *Journal of Medieval Military History 3* (2005), 1–13.

With regard to both military education and training in the Late Roman and medieval contexts, see

Richard I. Frank, *Scholae Palatinae: The Palace Guards of the Later Roman Empire* (Rome, 1969);

John Marshall Carter, 'Sport, War and the Three Orders of Feudal Society, 700–1300' in *Military Affairs 49* (1985), 132–139.

Bernard S. Bachrach, 'The Practical Use of Vegetius' *De re militari during the Early Middle Ages*' in *The Historian 47* (1985), 239–255;

J. Brian Campbell, 'Teach Yourself How to Be a General' in *Journal of Roman Studies 77* (1987), 13–29;

Matthew Bennett, '*La Règle du Temple* as a Military Manual, or How to Deliver a Cavalry Charge' in *Studies in Medieval History Presented to R. Allen Brown*, ed. Christopher Harper-Bill, Christopher J. Holdsworth, and Janet L. Nelson (Woodbridge, 1989), 7–19;

Caroll M. Gillmor, 'Practical Chivalry: The Training of Horses for Tournaments and Warfare' in *Studies in Medieval and Renaissance History*, new series *13* (1992), 5–29;

Alan J. Forey, 'Literacy and Learning in the Military Orders during the Twelfth and Thirteenth Centuries' in *The Military Orders 2: Welfare and Warfare*, ed. Helen Nicholson (Aldershot, 1998), 185–206.

Conflicting views

Did Edward III engage in a battle-seeking strategy?

Clifford J. Rogers, 'Edward III and the Dialectics of Strategy, 1327–1360' in *Transactions of the Royal Historical Society 4* (1994), 83–102;

The Battle of Crécy: A Casebook, ed. Michael Livingston and Kelly DeVries (Liverpool, 2015).

8 Two campaigns in focus

Introduction

In the course of conversations with our students and colleagues, and also based on reviews and reports regarding the first edition of the book, it became clear to us that it would be helpful to readers for the numerous topics addressed in the previous seven chapters to be tied together in the context of a particular campaign. In thinking about adding this chapter, we considered a wide range of possibilities for possible campaigns to highlight. Ultimately, we decided on two early medieval campaigns. The first of these is Charlemagne's operation in the spring and early summer of 778 that was intended to take control over the Muslim-held fortress cities of Pamplona, Saragossa, Tarragona, Barcelona, and Gerona, and establish a new frontier along the Ebro River. The second is the campaign by King Henry I of East Francia/Germany in the winter of 928–929, which brought under his control several dozen fortresses beyond his eastern frontier, including the 'capitals' of the Hevelli at Brandenburg and the Sorbs at Gana.

The first of these campaigns provides considerable scope for examining several important factors that we have highlighted throughout the text. These include understanding the role of diplomacy on the international stage in the conduct of military operations, military planning, intelligence gathering, and, not least, the ongoing and central role played by Roman military topography in medieval military history. The second campaign allows us to discuss in considerable detail the methodological approaches to examining military operations in contexts when we have only very limited written sources of information. In particular, we draw on more than six decades of archaeological research to fill in the numerous gaps in the written sources, and to develop a coherent understanding of Henry I's campaign objectives, his route, the size of his army, and the scale of his military achievement.

Charlemagne's Spanish campaign of 778

In the spring and early summer of 778, Charlemagne undertook a major military intervention in Iberia for the purpose of securing control over the fortified cities along the valley of the Ebro River, located south of the Pyrenees Mountains, including Pamplona, Saragossa, Huesca, and Lérida. An equally important objective was securing control over the fortress cities that dominated the Mediterranean coast of Iberia north of the Ebro River, including Gerona, Barcelona, and Tarragona. This campaign, which took a year to plan and drew upon military forces from throughout the Carolingian Empire, provides an opportunity to examine a range of topics considered in this volume, including international diplomacy, strategic planning, intelligence gathering, campaign planning, military organization, and

DOI: 10.4324/9781003032878-9

logistics. The following discussion will provide an overview of the international status of forces and diplomatic relationships before Charlemagne's campaign, an analysis of the planning required for the campaign, a treatment of the campaign strategy employed by the Carolingians, and finally an examination of the decisions made by Charlemagne in the wake of his failure to achieve the objectives set out above.

The diplomatic state of play (711–778)

In the course of just three years (711–714), Muslim armies operating from North Africa under the command of Tariq ibn Ziyad and Musa ibn Nusayr conquered almost the entirety of the Visigothic kingdom in Iberia, with the exception of a small region in the far northwest of the realm, which eventually developed as the kingdom of Asturias. After establishing themselves firmly in lands south of the Pyrenees, Muslim forces, under the leadership of the Umayyad governor Al-Samh ibn Malik al-Khawlani, penetrated north of the mountains in 719 and captured the fortress city of Narbonne, the capital of the rump Visigothic realm. Subsequent military operations brought under Muslim rule most of Septimania, which is the region along the Mediterranean coast in the southwest of modern France.

In 732, another large Muslim army, under the command of the Umayyad governor of Spain, Abdul Rahman Al-Ghafiqi, headed northward toward the fortress city of Tours but was defeated by Charles Martel, the grandfather of Charlemagne, near the city of Poitiers. Despite the death in battle of Al-Ghafiqi, just two years later, in 734, another Muslim army under the command of the new Umayyad governor of Narbonne, Yusuf ibn 'Abd al-Rahman al-Fihri, captured the fortress cities of Arles and Avignon. The latter of these two cities was located almost 200 kilometres east-northeast of Narbonne, and its conquest represented a major expansion of Muslim power along the Mediterranean coast. It is likely that the Christian ruler of Avignon, a Christian count named Maurontius, sought the military intervention of al-Fihri to ward off the looming threat posed by Charles Martel (Carolingian Mayor of the Palace 718–741). Despite this pact between Maurontius and al-Fihri, Charles Martel was able to capture the city of Avignon in 737 after a lengthy siege. However, the further campaign by Charles against Narbonne was unsuccessful.

Charles Martel and then his son Pippin (Mayor of the Palace 741–751, King of the Franks 751–768) maintained a tense peace along their frontier in the Rhône Valley with the Muslim rulers of Septimania in the later 730s and throughout the 740s. The Christian rulers of Gascony, in the southwest of modern France, with their capital at Toulouse, also maintained the peace with the Muslim rulers to their south. However, in the early 750s, Pippin, who had claimed the Frankish royal title in 751, began a series of military operations against the Muslims. In 752, Pippin secured control over the eastern regions of Septimania and subjected the fortress city of Narbonne to a siege. However, this siege failed because the Muslim garrison there was supplied by sea, and it was not until 759 that Pippin finally secured control over Narbonne and ended Muslim presence north of the Pyrenees. Subsequently, during the course of the 760s, Pippin and then his son Charlemagne subjected the Christian-ruled regions of Aquitaine and Gascony to their rule and absorbed them into the Frankish realm.

In the same period that Pippin began offensive operations against Septimania, the Muslim Caliphate, as a whole, was thrown into chaos by the Abbasid revolution. This revolt against Umayyad rule culminated in 750 with the massacre of almost the entirety of the ruling Umayyad dynasty, and its replacement by the Abbasid dynasty. The one surviving adult male member of the Umayyad family, the 20-year-old Abd al-Rahman ibn Mu'awiya ibn Hisham, fled first to Egypt and then to North Africa before finally landing in Iberia in 755. Abd al-Rahman's efforts to seize control in this far western province of the Caliphate were opposed by al-Fihri, mentioned previously, who had become the *de facto* ruler of Muslim Spain in the period since the Abbasid revolution. Abd al-Rahman was victorious in the subsequent struggle with al-Fihri, but faced numerous threats to his own rule, both from internal revolts and attacks by the Abbasids, including an invasion of Spain in 763. As a consequence of Abd al-Rahman's efforts simply to stay alive and preserve his rule in the south, the Muslim-ruled cities in the north of Spain were able to retain significant autonomy, if not outright independence.

Despite the ongoing challenges faced by Abd al-Rahman, King Pippin recognized the potential danger to his newly won position in Septimania posed by Abd al-Rahman gaining full control in Spain and leading armies north of the Pyrenees as had happened in the 720s and 730s during the rule of Pippin's father Charles Martel. Indeed, Pippin likely also worried about the Christian rulers of Aquitaine and Gascony seeking Muslim support against him, just as Count Maurontius had done against Charles Martel. As a consequence, from 763 at the latest, Pippin assiduously developed diplomatic contacts with the new Abbasid rulers of the Caliphate, who also saw the last of the Umayyads as significant adversaries. Charlemagne, who succeeded his father in 768 as co-ruler of the Frankish realm with his brother Carloman, maintained the diplomatic contacts with the Abbasid caliphs. The famous story of Charlemagne receiving an elephant from the Abbasid caliph Harun al-Rashid in 801 represents just one episode in this long and fruitful diplomatic relationship.

In the mid-770s, the strategic situation began to develop in the direction forecast and feared by Pippin and Charlemagne as Abd al-Rahman consolidated his rule in the southern part of Spain and cast his eyes to the north. The autonomous rulers of the fortress cities in the north, such as Pamplona, Saragossa, and Barcelona, also now worried that the Umayyad ruler would seek to impose his authority throughout the peninsula, and they sought for ways to protect themselves from this threat. It is in this context that sources from the Frankish kingdom reveal that representatives of these autonomous Muslim-ruled cities travelled to Charlemagne's court to invite him to intervene militarily on their behalf in Spain.

Negotiations and planning the campaign

When the first group of Muslim ambassadors arrived at the Frankish royal court, probably in the spring of 776, they encountered a ruler in Charlemagne who just three years earlier had conquered the Lombard kingdom of northern Italy. Charlemagne also, so he thought at this time, had subdued the Saxons and incorporated their lands in the Frankish realm after campaigning there for the better part of seven years. As a result of his military successes, particularly in Italy, the papal government had begun denoting Charlemagne in official correspondence as the 'New Constantine' with the implication that he had a claim to the imperial title. In short, Charlemagne was riding a wave of military success unparalleled since Emperor Justinian's conquests of the erstwhile provinces of the Western Empire in the mid-sixth century.

Charlemagne and his advisors were sufficiently intrigued by the proposal of the Muslim ambassadors, and confident in their own abilities, to invite the Muslim leaders to travel to the Carolingian court to negotiate a formal pact. Consequently, in the winter of 776–777, a delegation headed by Sulayman ibn Yaqzan al-A'rabi, ruler of cities of Gerona and Barcelona, travelled to Charlemagne's Christmas court at Paderborn located some 1,500 kilometres to the northeast, in the Saxon region. According to reports from Carolingian

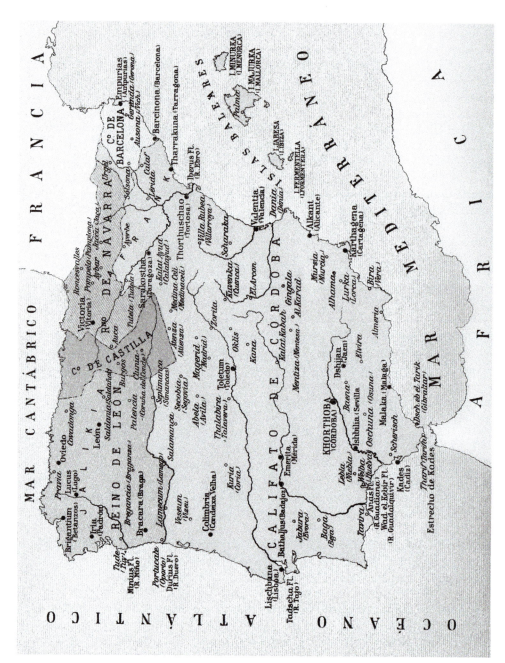

Map 8.1 Muslim Spain

Source: © Classic Image/Alamy Stock Photo H6E7PP

court sources, Charlemagne was offered the opportunity to extend his rule to the fortress cities of the Ebro valley, as well as those on the Mediterranean coast, including Gerona, Barcelona, and Tarragona.

The logic of the pact was similar to that orchestrated in 734 between al-Fihri and Count Maurontius for the surrender of Arles and Avignon to Muslim control, when Charles Martel, Charlemagne's grandfather, posed a threat to conquer the entire southern coast of modern France. Like Maurontius, Sulayman was willing to give up some of his autonomy to a ruler of the opposing religious faith in order to ward off conquest by his co-religionist; in this case the Umayyad, Abd al-Rahman. In the context of the Muslim embassy in 776–777, Charlemagne saw an opportunity to expand his power south of the Pyrenees, which would bring him closer to the goal of reuniting under his own rule the provinces of the old Western Roman Empire. He was encouraged in this goal by the papacy. In addition, by denying these cities, and their resources, to Abd al-Rahman, Charlemagne sought to avoid the threat posed by large Muslim armies operating north of the Pyrenees, as had happened during the reign of his grandfather.

Once Charlemagne and his advisors made the decision to make a pact with Sulayman, as well as his ally al-Husayn ibn Yahya ibn Sa'd ibn 'Ubada, the governor of Saragossa, it became necessary to set in motion several different planning groups. The first of these groups, which was part of the Carolingian 'general staff' denoted in contemporary sources as the *magistratus*, had to collect all available information about the man-made and natural topography of the lands south of the Pyrenees through which the Carolingian armies were to march. This body of royal advisors had access to information from a wide range of sources, including Christian and Jewish merchants, who had travelled to Spain; updated itineraries and 'word maps' derived originally from Roman sources, such as the well-known Peutinger map; and perhaps even information from the Abbasid court. Additional information likely was made available by the papacy, which was in close contact with the Catholic bishops in the Muslim-ruled cities of northern Spain. The Carolingians' new allies Sulayman, al-Husayn, and the other Muslim notables in their group, also could be counted on to provide important information about matters such as the location of roads, bridges, fords, and the marching distances between cities. Equally important was detailed information about the size of the fortress cities that the Carolingian troops were to occupy, so that Charlemagne would know how many men to mobilize for this campaign. Concomitantly, another group within the *magistratus* had to develop pertinent intelligence information about potential dangers along the other frontiers of the Frankish realm, whether in Italy, the Saxon region, or the Balkans, which might pose a threat while Charlemagne and a large army was operating in the far west in Spain.

Yet another planning group from the *magistratus* had to develop a plan of march for the Carolingian forces within the Frankish realm so that contingents from all over the empire would arrive in a timely fashion for the 'invasion' south of the Pyrenees. A crucial element in this part of the campaign plan was ensuring that adequate food supplies were made available to the individual contingents as they marched – in some cases more than 1,000 kilometres, as was the case for the troops from Bavaria – to join the royal army.

In this context, the Carolingian royal government ensured that it had fresh information about the types and quantities of supplies that were available on estates of the royal fisc – that is, those estates held directly by the government – by requiring each of its estate managers to submit detailed reports three times each year. This information was collected and analyzed at the royal court by the king's officials, who were responsible, under routine circumstances, for planning the royal itinerary, and in times of war, for ensuring that supplies were available for the army. Information about these administrative practices comes to us from a variety of contemporary sources. One of these is known by scholars as the capitulary *de villis*, which was a royal edict detailing the proper management of the king's estates. This lengthy document lays out a series of requirements for estate managers for stockpiling both equipment and food, as well as for sending reports to the royal government. Another important text that describes these types of preparations is a handbook known as *De ordine palatii* (*On the Administration of the Palace*), which also provides detailed information about organizing supplies. This text was written by Charlemagne's cousin Adalhard, who intended the handbook to provide guidance to Charlemagne's son Pippin, who had been installed as king in northern Italy.

In addition to providing supplies to the army from its own estates, as well as the estates of bishops and abbots, who were required by the king to support royal military efforts, Charlemagne also organized markets along the line of march for his army to provide his men with food. As discussed in previous chapters, we are fortunate to have a detailed description of the organization of this type of market from the reign of Louis II, the great-grandson of Charlemagne, who ruled northern Italy in the mid-ninth century (844–875). In preparing for a campaign against Muslim forces in Benvento in 866, Louis II issued a detailed set of commands to ensure that his men had supplies along their line of march. Louis commanded the men mobilized for this campaign to bring with them a few weeks' worth of supplies, which were to last until the spring crop was harvested. He also sent orders to all of the communities along the line of march of his army to be prepared to hold markets to supply his men. This Carolingian ruler insisted that his men 'were to pay the same price for necessities as those who live in the neighborhood'. However, he also added that those selling food at these markets 'shall not presume to sell for a higher price to our men than they do their own neighbors'.

Campaign strategy and Charlemagne's armies in action

After collecting and analyzing information about a vast range of matters, including routes of march, sources of supply, and the topography of fortress cities and lesser strongholds that were to be occupied, Charlemagne's planning staff developed a strategy and determined the manpower that would be required for the campaign. The contemporary Frankish sources indicate that Charlemagne's staff recommended, and Charlemagne decided, to mobilize a very large army that included contingents from throughout his empire. The purpose for mobilizing such a large force was to engage in a strategy denoted by modern scholars as one of using 'overwhelming force'. The key concept of this strategy was to deploy such a powerful army that no opponent was willing to face it in battle, or to attempt to hold a city against it.

Key to mobilizing and supporting an army of this size was to deploy multiple columns, which would converge on the target from different directions. This was the successful strategy that Charlemagne had deployed in his invasion of the Lombard kingdom several years before. From a logistical perspective, a great advantage of deploying multiple columns was that each one could draw upon a separate supply system, and thereby increase the overall number of men who could be deployed in a single campaign. From a strategic perspective, deploying multiple columns prevented the enemy from concentrating his forces, and kept the initiative with the attacker, whose 'pincer' could close upon the enemy at a time of the attacker's choosing. For the 'invasion' of Spain in 778, Charlemagne decided to employ two separate armies.

The first of these armies, which included troops from Austrasia, Burgundy, Bavaria, Provence, Septimania, and northern Italy, was directed to follow a route along the Mediterranean coast with its mobilization point at the fortress city of Narbonne in the early spring of 778. For most of the troops from Septimania, Provence, and Burgundy, this required journeys of just a few days to perhaps two weeks, following the well-maintained Roman road system in the south of modern France. Troops coming from Austrasia, located in the northeast of modern France, as well as Belgium and the Netherlands, had a rather more substantial distance to go, requiring several weeks. This was also the case for the Lombard troops coming from northern Italy. The Bavarians, who had to come the farthest distance, marching approximately 1,000 kilometres from their starting point at Augsburg, likely required more than a month to arrive at Narbonne.

Once the various contingents had arrived, this army followed the Roman imperial highway along the Mediterranean coast called the Via Augusta. Their line of march took them through the cities of Ampurias, Gerona, Barcelona, and then finally Tarragona, which was located at the mouth of the Ebro River, where it emptied into the Mediterranean Sea. None of our contemporary sources reveal that this army faced any obstacles as it marched along the Via Augusta, and it seems clear that Sulayman lived up to his agreement by opening the gates of the cities under his control to the Christian forces. After securing Tarragona, this army marched up the valley of the Ebro River to meet the second invasion force, under Charlemagne's direct command, at Saragossa. Over the entire line of march, the army following the Via Augusta could be supplied quite easily by ships sailing along the coast. Similarly, once the army headed up the Ebro River, poled barges could carry supplies, thereby obviating the need for a long and exposed baggage train.

The second army, under Charlemagne's direct command, was composed of forces drawn from Neustria, the region around Paris, Aquitaine and Gascony. This army mustered at the city of Bayonne, located on the Bay of Biscay, and from there followed the Roman road along the coast to San Sebastian before heading down the Ebro valley to the fortress city of Pamplona. This city was held by the Banu Casi family, which had joined in the pact made by Sulayman and al-Husayn with Charlemagne. The contemporary accounts indicate that as had been the case along the Mediterranean coast, Pamplona surrendered to Charlemagne without any difficulty. Charlemagne then led his army down the valley of the Ebro to Saragossa, where he joined forces with the Carolingian army that had come upriver. Supply for Charlemagne's army was facilitated first along its march along the Bay of Biscay and then downstream along the Ebro by the use of ships.

The contemporary sources do not provide any specific numbers for the size of the two armies that Charlemagne mobilized for the 'invasion' of Spain in 778. However, they do consistently present the Carolingian forces not simply as large, but as very large. This description is at odds with the typical approach of early medieval writers, who tended to downplay the size of the army on the 'home side' and the to exaggerate the size of the forces on the opposing side so as to enhance the honour achieved in victory and provide an excuse for defeats. However, the depiction of Charlemagne's armies in 778 as very large is consistent with the overall discussion by contemporary sources of the military forces that the Carolingians deployed for the siege of large fortress cities. This was the case, for example, in the context of King Pippin's siege operations in Aquitaine in the 760s, and Charlemagne's siege operations in Italy in 773.

But we are left with the question of what a 'very large' army entailed in the context of the operations along the Mediterranean coast and the valley of the Ebro River in 778. As we have discussed in earlier chapters, there are some scholars who insist that the armies of the Carolingians were very small, by comparison with those deployed, for example, by the Romans in their military operations in the western half of the Empire. However, armies of 2,000–3,000 men would have been incapable of undertaking the siege of large-scale fortifications, or of garrisoning those strongholds that they captured.

The walls of the fortress city of Saragossa, for example, measured 2,700 metres and likely had a garrison in excess of 2,000 men, not including the local militia forces. As discussed in Chapter 6, to undertake a successful assault on a fortress required an army numbering 5–6 times as many attackers as defenders. It is not clear whether Charlemagne envisioned having to assault the walls of Saragossa when he made the pact with Sulayman and al-Husayn. Nevertheless, he surely would have considered it prudent to have sufficient forces with him not only to provide a garrison for Saragossa, and the numerous other fortress cities that were to be handed over to the Franks, but also to maintain a sufficiently large army to deter attacks by potential enemies, including Abd al-Rahman, himself. In sum, it is likely that the two armies that came together at Saragossa in June 778 numbered in excess of 25,000 effectives, as compared with the 40,000 men whom Charlemagne deployed in two columns for his invasion of the Lombard kingdom in 773.

Failure at Saragossa

Throughout the spring of 778, Charlemagne's two armies achieved remarkable successes, taking control of numerous fortress cities along the Mediterranean coast and the Ebro River without facing any noteworthy opposition. These achievements are a testament to the sound planning and strategy developed by the Carolingian planning staff, the efficient logistical system that they put into place, and the well-organized military administration of the Frankish kingdom, which successfully mobilized military contingents from throughout the territories ruled by Charlemagne. However, the effective planning and execution of the movement of two armies in a pincer, meeting at Saragossa, ultimately ended in failure when al-Husayn reneged on his agreements and refused to open the gates of his city to the Carolingian forces.

Charlemagne's initial response was to establish a siege camp outside the walls of Saragossa, in an effort to convince al-Husayn to honour his commitment. When the Muslim ruler refused to do so, Charlemagne faced several unpalatable alternatives. He could prepare to storm the walls of Saragossa, after preparing appropriate siege equipment including rams, ladders, and perhaps stone-throwing engines. Such an assault, although likely to succeed, would take significant time to prepare and probably lead to thousands of his men being killed or suffering significant, life-threatening wounds. In addition, once his forces entered the city, it is likely that the civilian population, much of which was Christian, would be subject to massacre, which was the typical fate of the populace of a city captured by storm.

Alternately, Charlemagne had the option of settling into a lengthy siege of Saragossa, with the intention of starving the city into submission. But such a strategy entailed its own risks. First, Charlemagne would have to establish a logistical support system for his army for a siege that might well last a year or more. Moreover, he would have to do so without local allies. By contrast, when Charlemagne undertook a lengthy siege of the Lombard capital at Pavia in 773, he had material support of the papacy, which supplied the Frankish army for the better part of a year. An additional danger of a lengthy siege was the chance that Abd al-Rahman would be able to attack Charlemagne's besieging army or cut off his line of communications and supply, or both. In a worst-case scenario, Charlemagne's army might be trapped south of the Pyrenees. Another factor that may have weighed in

Charlemagne's decision was news from the far eastern frontier of his empire that some groups of Saxons had violated their oaths of loyalty to him, and had engaged in extensive raids in the Rhineland.

In the end, Charlemagne decided that neither an assault nor a lengthy siege were in his long-term interests. He commanded his armies to return along the same routes by which they had marched to Saragossa. The army heading down the Ebro River to the Mediterranean arrived back at Narbonne without any mishap. However, the rear guard of Charlemagne's army, as well as the baggage train, were ambushed by Basques in the Roncevaux pass through the Pyrenees, approximately 45 kilometres northwest of Pamplona. The commander of the rear guard, Count Roland, was killed and the baggage train was lost. This battle gave rise to the epic poem *The Song of Roland*, in which the Christian Basques were replaced by Muslims for propaganda purposes.

A new plan

Charlemagne's decision to make an agreement with Sulayman and al-Husayn at his winter court at Paderborn in 776–777 likely was influenced by his recent military successes, which gave the Frankish ruler as sense of momentum, if not invincibility. The deployment of two large armies beyond the frontiers of the Frankish kingdom on the basis of promises made by the non-Christian rulers, without any local allies to support his troops, was considerably at odds with Carolingian military doctrine up to this point, as practiced by Charlemagne, his father Pippin, and his grandfather Charles Martel. Carolingian grand strategy over the previous four decades had been focused on the methodical step-by-step conquest of neighbouring lands, and their incorporation into the Frankish kingdom, before moving on to the next target. The decision making by Charlemagne with regard to Spain over the decade following the debacle at Saragossa makes clear that he learned his lesson in 778.

First, Charlemagne now understood that in order to establish his southern frontier along the Ebro River, he would have to take full control over the fortress cities and lesser fortifications between the Pyrenees and the Ebro valley. To undertake this objective first required that he had far tighter control over Aquitaine, Gascony, and Septimania. As a first step, Charlemagne established his 3-year-old son Louis as king in the newly created kingdom of Aquitaine, which included Gascony. This new kingdom was staffed by Charlemagne's officials, whose task was to build up the network of fortifications along the frontier and provide the context for the development of new population centres. These would serve both to provide logistical support to Carolingian forces and provide additional manpower for Carolingian armies operating in Spain.

Charlemagne also created a frontier march under a *dux* named Chorso, based at Toulouse, whose task was to build up the frontier region between this city and the Pyrenees. Within a year of returning from the Saragossa campaign, Charlemagne began the process of recruiting Spanish Christians living under Muslim rule to settle along this southwestern frontier on empty lands owned by the royal fisc. These settlers were established in a privileged position, directly under the supervision of their king, as military colonists. Over the next twelve years, Charlemagne's officials in Aquitaine and on the march developed a substantial military infrastructure that in 801–802 provided the basis for the conquest of the fortress city of Barcelona and laid the foundation for the new march of Catalonia south of the Pyrenees.

King Henry I of Germany's winter campaign of 928–929

A methodological introduction

In the winter of 928–929, King Henry I of East Francia/Germany (919–936) undertook a lengthy campaign beyond his eastern frontiers that led to the capture of dozens of fortifications and the conquest of the lands of the Hevelli, located east of the middle course of the Elbe River, and of the Sorbs, located between the Saale and Elbe rivers. He also imposed tributary status on the Bohemians, with their capital at Prague. Despite the enormous importance of this campaign, in the course of which Henry I substantially enlarged his realm and conquered territories never held by his Carolingian predecessors, modern scholars have only limited information about it from contemporary written sources. Widukind of Corvey, a court historian under Henry's son King Otto I (936–973) provides an outline of the campaign of 928–929 that amounts to a short paragraph in the published version of his work. Two brief accounts in the anonymous *Annales Ratisponenses* and *Auctarium Garstense*, which provide a Bavarian perspective, shed some additional light on the presence of Duke Arnulf of Bavaria (died 937) at the siege of Prague in support of King Henry's army. One royal charter, issued by King Henry on 30 June 929 at the royal estate at Nabburg in Bavaria, some 55 kilometres northeast of Regensburg, provides a terminal date for the campaign.

By contrast with the relatively limited material provided by contemporary written sources, archaeological excavations over the past sixty years have revealed vast quantities of information regarding the military topography of the regions conquered by Henry I. This information includes details about the number, size, and construction of fortifications by both Henry's Slavic opponents, and by the German ruler, as well as the location of roads and fords. Many of these fortifications have been dated quite closely through the use of the techniques of dendrochronology. These data, when analyzed in the context of *Sachkritik* – that is, the material reality within which military operations were carried out – provide exceptionally important insights regarding King Henry's likely campaign route and strategy, as well as the scale of his undertaking. The following discussion of Henry I's campaign, therefore, sheds light on the crucial role that material sources of information, developed through archaeological excavations, can play in our understanding of military history, in general, and military campaigns, in particular.

Background to the campaign

As discussed in Chapter 2, the first decade of the tenth century saw the entry of the Hungarians as a major power in Central Europe. From their base in the Carpathian Basin, the Hungarians undertook large-scale military operations throughout the southern regions of the East Frankish realm, as well as in northern Italy. In 907, the Hungarians defeated a large Bavarian army at the Battle of Pressburg (Bratislava). Three years later, in 910, an army nominally under the command of the East Frankish King Louis the Child (899–911) was defeated by the Hungarians near Augsburg. Following these victories, the Hungarians seized control of large parts of what had been eastern Bavaria, which comprised much of the former Roman province of Pannonia, and established a hegemonic position over the Bohemians and Sorbs. Subsequently, the Hungarians were able to launch substantial raids into the regions of Thuringia and Saxony in the northern part of the East Frankish realm.

In response to the increasing tempo of Hungarian raids in the period after 910, Count Otto the Illustrious, the father of Henry I, began to strengthen the frontier defences in Saxony by building new fortifications. Henry I, after he succeeded his father as the leading magnate in the Saxon region in 912, continued the policy of building new fortifications. As part of this process, Henry constructed a new stronghold at a place called Püchau on the Mulde River, some 60 kilometres east of the Saale River, which had been the frontier under Carolingian rule. Information about this stronghold comes from the pen of Bishop Thietmar of Merseburg (died 1018), who relied on oral histories about the origins of Püchau.

Henry, who was elected king by the leading magnates of East Francia in 919, successfully defended Saxony and Thuringia from Hungarian raids on several occasions. In 924, after local forces defeated a Hungarian raiding party and captured its leader, Henry negotiated a peace agreement with the Hungarians. The peace agreement gave Henry a respite to strengthen his rule elsewhere in the East Frankish realm. Over the next four years (924–928), Henry successfully established his control over the wealthy and populous region of Lotharingia, in the west of his realm, which had been the heartland of the old Carolingian Empire. After achieving this major goal, which added considerable resources to the royal fisc, Henry turned his attention east once more and began planning for his long-cherished goal of establishing a major defensive bulwark against future Hungarian raids.

The campaign of 928–929

The very extensive campaign undertaken by Henry I in the winter and spring of 928–929 required considerable preliminary planning, very similar to that undertaken by Charlemagne for his Spanish campaign of 778, discussed previously. The three main objectives of Henry I's campaign, as described by Widukind, were the fortresses at Brandenburg, Gana, and Prague. These three strongholds were separated by a distance of some 300 kilometres from north to south, along the eastern frontier of the East Frankish realm. Each of the three strongholds was protected by numerous additional fortifications, many of which also were quite large and strongly built.

Fundamental to Henry I's planning and preparation was the gathering of intelligence regarding the matrix of questions relating to the man-made and natural topography through which his army was to travel. Very important, in this context, was the diligent questioning of merchants who travelled the busy trade routes between the East Frankish and its neighbours to the east. Henry's fortress and palace complex at Magdeburg, located on the eastern edge of his realm along the Elbe River, sat at the nexus of several important trade routes. One of these went northeast to Brandenburg and ultimately toward Poland and the Baltic Sea. A second major route went southeast toward Prague. In addition to debriefing merchants, the numerous military operations carried out by Otto the Illustrious, Henry's father, and by Henry himself before becoming king, also were an important source of intelligence regarding the location of enemy fortifications, and usable marching routes.

These military operations in the decade before 928 had led to the capture of a series of Slavic strongholds at Biederitz, Schartau, Burg, Grabow, and Dretzel, all east of the Elbe River in the region around Magdeburg. Farther north along the middle course of the Elbe River, Henry I established fortifications at Tangermünde, Osterburg, and Walsleben, as well as Havelberg and Klietz, located near the confluence of the Elbe and Havel rivers. These building efforts undoubtedly were accompanied by extensive scouting of the nearby districts. Not coincidentally, the fortresses constructed by Henry I marked the re-establishment of

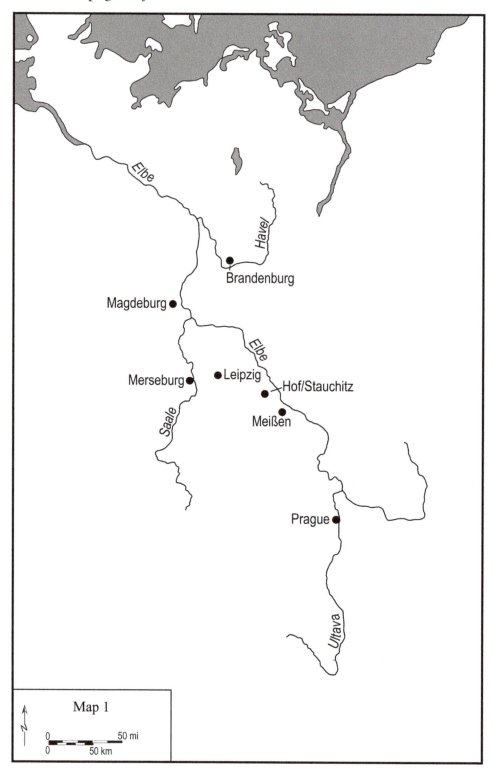

Map 8.2 Map of 929 campaign objectives

Source: © Bernard S. Bachrach and David S. Bachrach

the defensive line along the course of the middle Elbe, which Charlemagne had organized a century earlier in the decades around the turn of the ninth century.

In addition to debriefing merchants and other travellers, as well as obtaining information from earlier military operations, Henry I almost certainly followed the well-established Carolingian practice of dispatching scouts to obtain current information about the state of the roads, defensible camping sites for the army, sources of water, and the location of enemy bases. Henry certainly was familiar with the maxim set out by Vegetius in his handbook *Epitoma rei militaris* that a good military commander had itineraries made of all regions where war was to be waged so that he would know the distances between places, the qualities of the roads, and the potential difficulties posed by the terrain.

Objective Brandenburg

Based on all of these factors, it is almost certainly the case that Henry I was well-informed that the main seat of the Hevelli in the fortress at Brandenburg was protected by two sets of walls, measuring approximately 870 metres in circumference. Henry also knew that the walls at Brandenburg were protected by a ring of ditches, and most importantly, also were protected by the waters of the Havel River itself because the fortress was constructed on an island. Moreover, Henry and his planning staff understood that Brandenburg was defended by five other fortifications located within a day's march to the west and northwest. These defences were matched by a series of powerful fortifications to the south of Brandenburg in the Fläming Hills, at Belgiz, Niemegk and Mörz. To the east, the Hevelli prince at Brandenburg controlled a series of fortifications along the banks of the Havel River that extended 80 kilometres to Spandau, the location of the notorious twentieth-century prison. As a group, these numerous Hevelli strongholds provided a system of defence in depth for Brandenburg that Henry's army would have to neutralize before a close siege of the island fortress could be undertaken.

All of these fortifications are known to modern scholars through archaeological investigations. However, none other than Brandenburg itself are mentioned in any contemporary written sources. Widukind's report of the first part of this campaign, which almost certainly drew upon information provided by members of the royal court, laconically indicates that Henry began operations against these subsidiary fortifications before beginning his siege of Brandenburg, without providing any mention of Henry's specific actions. Rather, Widukind merely observed that Henry wore out the Slavs in numerous attacks, in the course of which the East Frankish/German ruler almost certainly worked diligently to capture many, if not all, of the fortifications in the immediate vicinity of his main objective.

With German garrisons in the erstwhile Hevelli fortresses, Henry could ensure that his operations at Brandenburg would not be disrupted by an intervention of the allies of the Hevelli to the northeast of the Havel River. Among the most important of these allies were the Redarii, another people of the Slavic Weleti confederation. The Redarii demonstrated the danger that they posed in the summer of 929 with the capture of the Ottonian fortification at Walsleben, located approximately 80 kilometres north of Brandenburg, and the slaughter of both the garrison and local population that had taken refuge there.

In addition to protecting his forces from intervention from the northeast, Henry also had to ensure that his besieging forces would not face an attack from the east and south from the garrisons of the Hevelli fortifications along the Havel River and in the Fläming Hills.

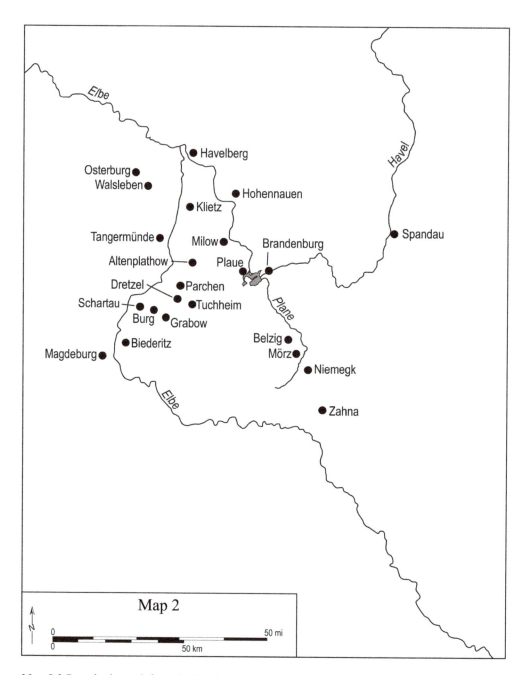

Map 8.3 Brandenburg defence in depth

Source: © Bernard S. Bachrach and David S. Bachrach

In this context, excavations of the Hevelli fortress at Spandau, mentioned previously, indicated that it was destroyed in a catastrophic fire in the first half of the tenth century, before being rebuilt, likely during Henry I's reign. In light of this archaeological evidence, there is a strong possibility that Spandau was destroyed by Henry I's forces in the context of his siege of Brandenburg.

As Widukind makes clear in his brief account, Henry I's forces undertook a close siege of the fortress at Brandenburg in the winter of 928–929. In particular, Widukind emphasizes that by the time Henry was ready to undertake direct action against the main seat of the Hevelli ruler, the coldest part of winter had arrived. As a consequence, the German army was forced to makes its camp on the ice. One major benefit, of course, of a winter campaign against an island fortress was that the German troops could pass over the frozen surface of the Havel River to get to the fortification itself and did not have to rely either on boats or a temporary bridge.

Once he arrived at Brandenburg, Henry decided to take the stronghold by storm rather than attempting to starve the defenders into submission. Henry was aware that this course of action would lead to very substantial casualties among his men. He decided, nevertheless, that the logic of a winter campaign that was directed at achieving numerous strategic objectives mandated pursuing the fastest possible resolution to each phase of his operation.

As we have discussed in previous chapters, the contemporary Anglo-Saxon Burghal Hidage, which was developed at the royal court of Wessex, established an optimum minimum ratio of one defender for approximately 1.3 metres of wall. Given the broadly similar technology across Europe in this period, it is likely that the Hevelli princes came to the same general conclusions regarding the number of men required to defend their fortifications, as well. Given the length of the wall at Brandenburg, 700 men, at a minimum, were needed for its defence. However, given that the siege of Brandenburg followed upon numerous previous engagements with Henry's forces, it is likely that the regular garrison of the island fortress was augmented by refugees from the nearby area. In order to capture Brandenburg by storm, Henry required an advantage of 5 or 6 to 1. Henry's assaulting force, therefore, likely was in the range of 3,000–3,500 men. This was not, however, the entirety of Henry's army, but rather the minimum number required to assault the walls of Brandenburg itself.

In describing the successful siege and capture of Brandenburg, Widukind does not belabour the casualties suffered by Henry I's forces. He notes merely that once the fortress fell, Henry acquired the entire territory that had been subject to the Hevelli prince. In order to secure his gains, however, Henry had to leave behind a substantial garrison at Brandenburg itself, as well as at several other fortresses in its vicinity. These men served the double function of beginning the integration of Havelland into the German kingdom, and also providing a secure base of operations for the next stage of the campaign against the Daleminzi Sorbs. Notably, excavations – as well as later written sources, particularly royal charters – have revealed that many of the strongholds that provided a defence in depth for Brandenburg subsequently were held by German garrisons.

Objective Gana

After capturing Brandenburg, Henry began the second phase of his campaign, which was directed toward the important Daleminzi fortress which Widukind calls Gana. For more than a century, scholars disputed the actual location of Gana. However, recent excavations at the site in the valley of the Jahna River, a tributary of the Elbe, about 11 kilometres southwest of the modern Elbe River town of Riesa, appear to have demonstrated that this

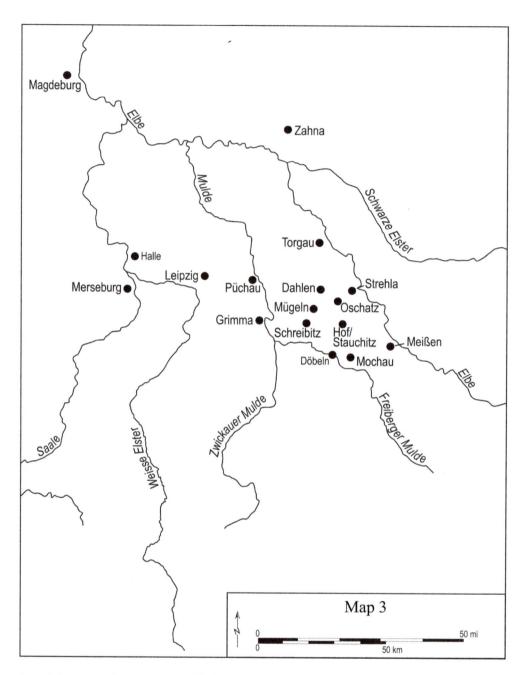

Map 8.4 Fortifications constructed by Henry I in context of the 929 campaign

Source: © Bernard S. Bachrach and David S. Bachrach

was the fortress discussed by Widukind. This massive stronghold was protected on three sides by marshes created by the Jahna River. The one dry approach to the fortress was from the south. During the final stage of its construction, which has been dated by archaeologists to the reign of Henry I, the walls of the main fortress were approximately 15 metres wide at their base and 6 metres high. The wall was protected by a 15-metre-wide and 5-metre-deep ditch. The earth and timber main wall was further protected by a dry stone front. The walls of the fortress measured some 700 metres and enclosed an area of four hectares, which is 40,000 square metres. This was the heart of the fortress, which may have been protected by a further outer wall, although this has not been conclusively established through excavations.

To its north, Gana was protected by a series of fortifications that were constructed along the Elbe River. Another series of fortifications protected Gana from approaches to the west. The size and strength of the fortress at Gana itself, as well as the groups of other fortifications around it, were known to Henry and his commanders from campaigns against the Daleminzi over the previous two decades. This detailed but historical information almost certainly was updated through the work of Henry's scouts as he approached from the north, after the successful capture of Brandenburg.

In conceptualizing the line of march of Henry I's army from Brandenburg to Gana, we benefit from a wealth of archaeological material regarding both the existing road system and also the location of numerous Slavic-held fortifications which were destroyed and then replaced by the German king in rapid succession in the context of this campaign. Excavations at Auberg, Torgau, Fichtenberg, and Görzig, for example, make clear that all four Slavic strongholds were destroyed and rapidly replaced by German fortifications in the immediate vicinity of the original Slavic sites. At the same time, we have evidence for the construction of three additional German fortifications, at Leipzig, Dahlen and Strehla, which sat astride the main transportation artery, later known as the Hohenstrasse, which led eastward from the Ottonian fortress at Merseburg on the Saale River to Silesia in modern Poland. Perhaps the most important archaeological finding, based on dendrochronological analysis, is that Henry I also immediately began construction on the fortress at Meißen, located on the Elbe River 25 kilometres southeast of Gana. This construction effort required, at a minimum, that the German ruler had control over the course of the Elbe River from Meißen downstream to Magdeburg.

Based on these archaeological findings, it seems likely that Henry's operations against Gana were based on the employment of a pincer movement of two columns. The first of these, probably under Henry's direct command, marched up the valley of the Plane River into the Fläming Hills, and then to the Elbe River. It is notable that at this time Henry established a fortification at Pratau which protected a ford over the Elbe River on the route from the Fläming Hills. Once his army reached the Elbe, Henry's forces likely marched south along the river valley, neutralizing Slavic fortifications on their route, until reaching the confluence of the Jahna and Elbe rivers. The second column in the pincer movement likely came east from its starting point in the vicinity of Merseburg and followed the protected route of the Hohenstrasse through the mentioned previously fortifications at Leipzig, Dahlen, and Strehla.

The deployment of multiple columns to reach the enemy target had been a hallmark of Carolingian warfare throughout the ninth century, and was practiced regularly by Henry I's Carolingian predecessors in East Francia. There are two important reasons why Henry would have chosen to mobilize a second column for the phase of the campaign directed at Gana. First, the troops moving east from the Ottonian fortresses along the Saale River could provide support to the column under Henry I's command as it marched south through enemy-held territory. Any Slavic army that attempted to mobilize in the valleys of the Mulde or Elbe rivers would face attack from both the west and north. Second, when the two German columns converged at Gana, the German garrisons in the fortifications along the Hohenstrasse helped to ensure a secure line of communications and supply.

Upon arriving at Gana, Henry's forces faced a very difficult task. Widukind, in his brief account, recorded that the siege lasted for twenty days before the German troops successfully stormed the walls. As a first stage in the operation, the massive protective ditch, measuring 15 metres in width and 5 metres in depth, had to be filled in, almost certainly while under attack from the missile weapons of the Slavic defenders stationed atop the walls of Gana. Otherwise, Henry's troops would have found it very difficult to reach the walls of the main fortress. To fill in just one 200-metre section of the ditch would have required 15,000 cubic metres of earth, weighing approximately 15,000 metric tonnes. Under ideal circumstances, an experienced digger could excavate 3 cubic metres of earth from the surface level in the course of a ten-hour work day. Consequently, simply to excavate the earth needed to fill in a 200-metre section of the defensive ditch at Gana would have required 50,000 man-hours under ideal conditions. Of course, conditions in wintertime, when the ground is frozen solid, were far from ideal.

Once the earth was removed from a surface area measuring 1.5 hectares, this material had to be carried to the defensive ditch and dumped in, while under enemy fire. Under ideal circumstances, Henry I's men would have used carts, perhaps brought from the Ottonian fortress at Merseburg, to load, carry, and unload the earth. Carts available in the early tenth century had a carrying capacity of half a metric tonne. Loading the earth onto carts and then unloading the earth required, at a bare minimum, ninety minutes under idea circumstances, which certainly were not present in the winter siege at Gana. Consequently, loading and unloading the approximately 30,000 cart loads of earth likely required, at a minimum, 60,000 man-hours of labour.

Presumably, the site from which the earth was excavated was a sufficient distance from the walls of Gana that the diggers were not subject to enemy missile weapons, but were close enough to limit the overall time of transporting the material to the defensive ditch. Horse-drawn carts operating under difficult circumstances, such as those that prevailed in the wintertime, could travel at approximately 3.2 kilometres per hour. If the earth were excavated at an average of 1 kilometre from the edge of the defensive ditch, each cart that was deployed could make three trips, in a best-case scenario, in the course of the eight hours or so of daylight available in January and February in northern Germany. This includes two hours for loading and unloading the carts, as well as forty minutes for the carts simply to travel 2 kilometres.

In the course of the twenty-day siege, a minimum of 750 carts would have been required to make 30,000 trips to load and offload earth into the defensive ditch. Excavating, loading, and unloading these carts would have required a minimum of 110,000 man-hours. With an average of just eight hours of daylight, 1,000 men would have needed about two weeks, including work on Sundays, to carry out this excavation and unloading operation. As this brief discussion makes clear, the difficulties involved simply to fill in part of the ditch at Gana provide some insight into the lengthy period required by Henry I to capture this fortress by storm.

Using the same calculations as at Brandenburg, Henry I would have required a minimum of 3,000–3,500 men to carry out a successful assault on the walls of Gana. Also as had been true at Brandenburg, it is almost certainly the case that Henry's troops suffered very heavy casualties in the attack, perhaps amounting to 1,000 men killed or wounded. It is likely for this reason, as Widukind explains, that the king permitted his men to slaughter all of the male inhabitants at Gana and to take the women and children as slaves.

Objective Prague

Following his capture of Gana, Henry immediately set off southward with his army toward Prague. From Gana, it was a march of some 180 kilometres south along the Elbe River valley to its confluence with the Ultava River. From here, it was 50 kilometres farther along the Ultava to Prague. In the course of this march, Henry's army had to traverse the region now known as Saxon Switzerland (Sächsische Schweiz). As the Elbe River descends northward through the mountain range known as the Erzgebirge, it has carved deep and winding valleys through limestone cliffs that provide numerous opportunities for defenders to set ambushes. Consequently, moving through this region required enormous vigilance, and particularly the effective deployment of scouts.

During the early tenth century, the Elbe likely was navigable all the way to its confluence with the Ultava. In the mid-eighteenth century, King Frederick the Great of Prussia (1740–1786) led tens of thousands of troops along this same route, and carried supplies for his men up the Elbe River. Widukind does not provide any indication that Henry's army faced significant difficulties along his march to Prague, either in terms of enemy resistance or a lack of supplies. Rather, he states with significant brevity that Henry 'came to Prague, the fortress of the Bohemians, and accepted the surrender (*ditio*) of its king'.

It is not surprising that Widukind elides so much information here, and particularly the presence at Prague of the Bavarian Duke Arnulf (died 937). In this context, Widukind was well aware of the resistance that Arnulf had offered to Henry I's claim to rule in East Francia in 919, and also the rebellion by Arnulf's sons against King Otto I in both 938 and 954. However, Arnulf's presence at Prague with an army from Bavaria is recorded in the two Bavarian annals, discussed earlier. Moreover, from a military perspective, the participation of the Bavarians in the campaign is yet another illustration of the use of the pincer movement by two different columns operating against the same objective.

The most likely line of march for Duke Arnulf's troops from Bavaria into Bohemia followed the route Regensburg-Cham-Furth im Walde-Domazlice-Pilsen-Prague. From Regensburg to Furth im Walde, the army had the benefit of travelling along the Regen river valley, with its broad banks and ability to carry supplies by boat or barge. The Bavarian column then entered the valley of the Radbuza River until its confluence with the Berounka River at Pilsen. The Bavarians could then follow this river valley all the way to Prague and meet the army under Henry I's command.

Widukind's emphasis on the large size of the army, and particularly his reference to the 'entire army' available to Henry at Prague, is appropriate, given the enormous challenge posed by the defences there. Prague itself was a large fortress with walls that measured some 1,200 metres, located at the top of a steep hill and further protected by substantial defensive ditches. Prague was further defended by two additional strongholds at Levy Hradec and Vyserad. The first of these was constructed on the Ultava River, 9 kilometres north of Prague. Its walls similarly measured approximately 1,200 metres. Vyserad was built just to the south of Prague, and was also located on a steep hill, with walls measuring 1,300 metres.

According to the formulae set out in the Burghal Hidage, discussed previously, these three fortifications required garrisons in the range of 3,000 men, at a minimum, to defend the collective 3,700 metres of defensive walls. Moreover, given the considerable and growing population density in the Prague region, as seen through excavations, it is likely that the Bohemian leader Duke Wenceslaus had far more men than this available to defend these three powerful strongholds. It is notable, however, that despite his impressive fortifications, Duke Wenceslaus declined to resist the large army that Henry and Arnulf had brought to Prague. Instead, he surrendered to Henry and accepted his authority. It seems likely that Wenceslaus made this decision with knowledge of the events at Brandenburg and Gana, and particularly that Henry had captured both by storm.

In order to make clear to Wenceslaus the futility of armed resistance, Henry required an army that was large enough to pose a credible threat of carrying the walls of the fortifications held by Wenceslaus' men by direct assault. At a ratio of 5 to 1, Henry would have required an army of 5,000 men to storm any one of the three fortresses of Prague, Vyserad, or Levy Hradec, if they were protected only by the minimum effective number of troops. However, the assault on any one of these strongholds would not have been possible without leaving very substantial detachments to guard the other two, and to prevent their garrisons from attacking Henry's army in the rear. Taking into account the likely defensive preparations made by Wenceslaus, and that each of his three strongholds was held by a very large number of defenders, Henry would have required in the neighbourhood of 15,000 effectives to pose a sufficiently credible threat to convince the Bohemian duke to surrender.

From a logistical perspective, supplying an army of this size would not have posed significant difficulties for Henry in light of the highly organized and efficient system of supply in the East Frankish realm. As discussed in detail in Chapter 4, supplying 15,000 men would have required approximately 15 metric tonnes of food per day. If this army were accompanied by 3,000 pack animals and war horses, an additional 30 metric tonnes of hard fodder and grass or hay would have been required each day. If these supplies were carried by cart, the troops at Prague would have required approximately ninety cart loads of supply each day. However, as discussed previously, both the army under Henry I's command and the column under the command of Duke Arnulf marched along rivers that were navigable all the way to Prague. Given the carrying capacity of river barges in this period of approximately 15 metric tonnes, the army would have required three barge loads of food and fodder per day.

These supplies were easily available to the army from the vast network of royal estates, which were maintained by Henry I's government in a manner consistent with his Carolingian predecessors. The royal complex at Magdeburg alone comprised thirty-one estate complexes (*villae*) that produced sufficient surpluses to support 15,000 men and their mounts for a month. In a similar vein, Duke Arnulf of Bavaria had access to both royal and ducal fiscal resources, including the large number of *villae* attached to the complexes at Regensburg and Forchheim. As had been true under the Carolingians, these royal estates were equipped with ample transportation resources to carry food supplies to the royal army. In addition, the numerous royal monasteries also were obligated to provide transportation resources to supply the army, as well.

As our discussion of this campaign makes clear, Henry I drew extensively on the military traditions of the Carolingian Empire, and more broadly to those of the inherited from the later Roman period. The campaign focused on the capture of fortifications in order to control territory. As a result, Henry fielded large armies, which were deployed in pincer movements, like those of the Carolingians. In addition, these large armies required very significant supply, which could only be provided by a proficient and advanced administrative system.

Conclusion

The very successful U.S. Army Gen. William Tecumseh Sherman (died 1891) proclaimed that 'war is Hell', and we affirm that anyone who thinks differently either is abysmally ignorant or delusional. However, some wars are just. Bishop Augustine of Hippo (died 430), a saint of the Catholic Church whose ideas regarding war remain an important guide to thinking about the subject to this day, made clear that there is no such phenomenon as a 'good war'. Rather, he emphasized that sometimes wars are necessary. He believed that when one's adversaries are so evil that their efforts can be stopped only through war, then such a war not only is necessary but it is just. He continued along this line of thinking and concluded that peace only results from victory. This observation makes a great deal of sense to us as the unconditional victory of the Allies over the Axis Powers in 1945 has led to more than two generations of peace among the previous combatants and their posterity.

Throughout the history of Western civilization, war – which we understand as the deployment of armed forces by a government for either offensive or defensive military operations against an adversary – has been commonplace, and the medieval millennium was no exception. It is widely recognized that from the ancient Mesopotamians until very recent times, war, preparation for war, and the aftermath of war has consumed the greater part of the surplus human and material resources in every society in the Western tradition. The European Middle Ages were not an exception to this pattern. It seems self-evident that a society in which not only the leaders but also the great mass of their countrymen invested such a vast proportion of human and material wealth towards military efforts was a society that was organized for war.

Warfare at one point or another affected the lives of almost every man, woman, and child in medieval Europe, either directly as participants in or as victims of military operations or indirectly through the imposition of military-related obligations, taxes, and labour services. As numerous saints' lives written during the medieval millennium emphasize, even hermits in the wilderness often could not avoid the realities of war. Most cities were walled fortresses, often dating back to the later Roman Empire. Smaller towns, and even villages, were provided with defences at great initial construction cost and then had substantial maintenance expenses. Churches and monasteries often were protected by fortifications or constructed within already existing strongholds. Throughout medieval Europe, fortified refuges, especially in frontier regions, dotted the countryside so that the population could find security when the area in which they lived came under attack. The maintenance of these fortresses, as well as the militarily necessary infrastructure of roads, bridges, and ports, imposed additional economic and labour obligations on medieval populations.

The second of our theses, after the idea that society during the Middle Ages was organized for war, is the importance of the Roman inheritance in regard to the nature and

DOI: 10.4324/9781003032878-10

conduct of warfare throughout medieval Europe. We, like historians of medieval Christianity, start from the proposition that early medieval European kingdoms inherited and intentionally maintained a wide range of practices, institutions, physical topography, and ways of thinking about a broad spectrum of matters from the later imperial government in the West. As with medieval Christianity, the relatively few German speakers from beyond the Rhine, who were settled within the erstwhile Roman Empire and rapidly assimilated into a Latin culture, contributed little to the medieval military institutions, just as their rapidly abandoned paganism had little effect on the teachings of the Church. In fact, change over time of the Roman inheritance in the Latin West was very gradual and, in large part, was conditioned by the existing military topography, institutions, and military ideas, and not by some putative influx of Germanic cultural ideas and practices.

Our third thesis is that warfare in medieval Europe was marked both by its complexity and its considerable scale. A main reason why warfare affected such a large part of the population and so many institutions was the very large numbers of combatants and their systems of support, which required vast quantities of arms and supplies. The large scale of military operations required, in turn, the maintenance and further development of advanced techniques in military administration, logistics, transportation (vehicles, roads, and bridges), and architecture. The thousands of fortifications constructed throughout medieval Europe not only were very expensive, but also saw important developments in engineering, as they were built on information left to them from the Romans.

The task of the historian is to convey and explain how the people being studied lived in the context of their own times. To do so requires an understanding by the historian of the topographical, material, intellectual, and cultural realities of that time and place. War, preparations for war, and the aftermath of war were primary realities of medieval life. For medievalists to fail to give proper attention to these phenomena, which medieval chroniclers, historians, and story tellers took as the focus of their work, is to provide a thoroughly skewed view of the Middle Ages to their students and their readers.

Index

Page numbers in *italics* indicate figures; page numbers in **bold** indicate tables.

Abbo of Paris 244, 250, 252
Abd al-Rahman ibn Mu'awiya ibn Hisham 376–377, 379, 382
Abd el-Rahman al Ghafiqi 47
Abels, Richard 85, 88
Abraham ben Jacob 69, 126
Abu al-Qasim (emir of Sicily) 294
Adalbero 365
Adalbold of Utrecht (Bishop) 344
Adalhard of Corbie (Abbot) 181, 332–334, 336, 364
Adhemar of Le Puy (Bishop) 352–353
administrative documents 21–22
Adolf I of Cologne (Archbishop) 213
Aethelbald (King) 69
Aethelberht (King) 69
Aethelred (King) 69
Aethelwulf (King) 69
Afiarta, Paul 348, 349
Alberti, Leon Battista 58
Albigensian Crusade 298
Alcuin 41–42, 58, 367, 368
Alexander III (Pope) 141
Alexander the Great 166
Alexios IV Angelos 251
Alexios Komnenos (Emperor) 202, 239, 249, 296, 352
Alfonso VI of León-Castile (King) 134, 359
Alfonso X of Castile (King) 216
Alfred the Great (King) 69, 70, 117, 264, 265, 283, 304
Allmand, Christopher 339
Alp Arslan (Seljuk leader) 148
Alpert of Metz 14, 251
Alpine passes, map of *200*
American Civil War 275, 324
American Revolutionary War (War of Independence) 84, 275
Ammianus Marcellinus 43, 343
Anastasius I (Emperor) 32, 36, 38, 108
Angevin Empire 130, 139; in late 12ᵗʰ century map *73*

Anglo-Saxon Chronicle 69, 70
animal rations: food for horses 167–169; food for other animals 169; military logistics 167–169; *see also* horses
annales (histories) 15–17; *Annales regni Francorum* 338; *Annals of Cologne* 213; *Annals of Fulda* 14, 283; *Earlier Metz Annals* 333; *Frankish Royal Annals* 292; *Royal Frankish Annals* 290
Anselm of Liège 182
Anselm of Ribemont 317
antiquae consuetudines 60
antiquarianism 57
Apollinaris, Sidonius 364
archaeology, military history and 29
Ardo Smaragdus 368
Aribo, Margrave 339
arithmetic 58–59
armed pilgrimages 132
Arnulf of Bavaria (Duke) 359, 393–394
Arnulf of Carinthia (King) 339
Arnulf of East Francia (King) 282–283
Arrianus, Lucius Flavius 363
Arthurian Cycle poetry 18
artillery: developments in technology 244–245; gunpowder 245–247; impact of, in sieges 298–299; tension 243, 244; torsion 243, 244; traction engine 244
Asbridge, Thomas 331
Asser 264–265
Assize of Arms policies 139, 311
Attila the Hun 56
Augustine of Hippo (Bishop) 57, 395
Augustus (Emperor) 42
Aurelian (Emperor) 56
Avirus (Emperor) 364
Aymer de Valence 281

Bacon, Roger 246
Balderich of Drenthe 251
Baldwin II (King) of Jerusalem 145, 331–332
Barbarian kingdoms, map *45*

Barbarian: forces in pacts outside Roman government 100–101; law codes 60; in Roman standing army 99–100

Barons' Crusade 145

Bartolomeo Colleoni 156

Bates, David 371

battlefield *see* combat

Battle of Hastings, Norman armour *224*

Bavarian March 48

Bayeux Tapestry *224, 232, 267*

Bede of Jarrow 250

Béla III of Hungary (King) 206

Belisarius (general) 109

Benedict (monk) 249

Benedict the Moor 242

Beowulf (poetry) 18, 84, 95, 181, 324, 354

Bernhard (Count) 284

Berthold of Reichenau (author) 310, 334

Black Death 159, 215, 330

Blanche Garde, fortress of 64

Boethius 57, 58

Bohemond of Taranto 202, 296, 346

Boleslav (Duke) 68, 340

Boleslav Chrobry 125

Book of Deeds, The (James I of Aragon) 346

Book of Deeds of Arms and Chivalry (Pizan) 368

Bouvet, Honoré 368

Brown, Elizabeth 119

Brunner, Heinrich 283

Brunner, Karl 23

Brun of Cologne (Archbishop) 366

Bruno of Merseburg 62, 64, 232, 357–358, 369

Bulksu, Khan 53

Burchard of Worms (Bishop) 14

Burghal Hidage 70, 117

Burgundy, map of growth *155*

Al-Bursuqi, Aksungur 331

Byzantine Empire 108, 130, 143, 147–148, 202, 204, 206, 237, 266, 290, 303

Byzantium, map *51*

Cade, Jack 153

Caesar, Julius 11, 14, 42, 248, 249, 297, 363

Caesarius of Arles 43

campaigns: Charlemagne's Spanish (778) 375–383; grand strategy and 330–331; King Henry I of Germany winter (928–929) 384–394; negotiations and planning Charlemagne's 377, 379–380; strategy for Charlemagne's 380–382; *see also* Charlemagne's Spanish campaign of 778; Henry I of Germany (winter campaign 928–929)

Campbell, James 117

Capet, Hugh 51

Capetian dynasty, France 134

Capetians in late 12th century, map of *73*

Capitulare de villis, Charlemagne in 23, 195

Caracalla (Emperor) 100

Carloman (King) 109, 111, 255, 316, 346, 347

Carloman II (King) 51, 181

Carolingian and Ottonian eastern frontiers 65–67; arms and equipment 194; fortifications 269

Carolingian Empire 99; map of division *120*; personal arms and armour 230

Carolingian world: expeditionary levies 112, 114–115; field armies 110–112; impact of organization 117–118; institutions for local defence 116–117; map of Empire of Charlemagne *113*; mercenaries 115–116; military organization of 108–118; residential villas *183*

Cassiodorus 57, 58

Catapult, The (Rihll) 222

Catholic Church 395

cavalry *see* combat; horses

Charlemagne (King) 47–49, 115, 165, 198–199, 330, 370; Alcuin advising 41–42; *Capitulare de villis* of 23; Carolingian court 39; cavalry and 290; diplomacy 346–350; Einhard as biographer 58; fighting weapons in reign of 227; government of 110; grandson Nithard 14; invasion of Muslim-ruled Spain 5; map of empire of *113*; son of Pippin 109; strategic intelligence 335, 336, 338; supplies for army *22*; water route from North Sea to Black Sea 59–60

Charlemagne's Spanish campaign of 778 375–383; diplomatic state of play (771–778) 376–377; failure at Saragossa 382–383; map of Muslim Spain *378*; negotiations and planning 377, 379–380; new plan for 383; strategy and armies in action 380–382; *see also* campaigns

Charles III (King) 51, 115–116, 129

Charles Martel 47, 48, 53, 109, 111, 115, 199, 277, 346, 347, 376, 377, 383

Charles the Bald (King) 14, 24, 60–61, 112, 115–116, 119, 136, 156, 235, 278, 291, 309, 313, 344, 367

Charles the Bold (or Rash) of Burgundy (Duke) 154–156, 247, 322

Charles the German 367

Charles V of France (King) 355

Charles VII of France (King) 154, 211

Charles VIII of France (King) 84

charters 20–21

Childebert II (King) 61

Childeric 102, 105–106, 106, 108

Chilperic I (King) 61, 321

Christianity 2; Constantine the Great and 14, 34; conversion to 46, 53, 68, 143, 315, 360–361; Hungarians 53; medieval 2, 396; military operation and 4; persecution of 352; in Roman state 100, 102
Chronicle (Pere) 345
chronicles: histories and 13–17; *see also* historiographical genres
Chronicon (Thietmar) 42
Cicero 10
Clausewitz 6; Clausewitzian doctrine 82
Clothar I (King) 105
Clovis (King) 44, 46, 102, 105–106, 108–109, 186, 321, 360–361, 370
Cola de Montforte 156
collateral damage 4, 361–362
Colomon of Hungary (King) 202
combat: battle at sea 303–308; battles in the field 274–275; cavalry battles among western armies 291–292; cavalry battles against non-western armies 292–294; cavalry battles on crusade 294–296; cavalry on the battlefield 289–298; commanders in battle 296–298; foot soldiers in 275–285; illustration of Battle of Formigny *287*; illustration of Battle of Roosebeke *279*; illustration of Battle of Stirling Bridge *282*; military codes and discipline 320–322; missile troops on battlefield 285–289; morale 314–324; role of chivalry 322–324; sieges 298–303; tactics, training and morale 4; training 308–314; training for attack 312–313; treatment of enemy combatants 322–324; unit cohesion 319–320; *see also* horses; siege(s); soldiers; warships
Conan of Rennes (Count) 280–281
Concerning the Majesty, Wisdom and Prudence of Kings (Milemete) 246
Conrad I 65
Conrad II (King) of Germany 201, 302
Conrad III (King) of Germany 206
Conrad IV (King) 141, 213
Conrad of Mainz (Archbishop) 206
Conrad the Red of Lotharingia (Duke) 300
Constantine the Great (Emperor) 14, 34, 105, 110, 315, 325, 363
Constantius I (Emperor) 105
consuetudines (regulations) 60, 62
corpus agrimensorum 59
Cossacks 237
Coulson, Charles 63
Crac des Chevaliers, Syria *78, 79*
crusading age logistics 202–211; after First Crusade 204, 206, 208, 211; campaign supplies 211–215; crusades of Emperor Frederick II and St. Louis *210*; Empire of the Comnenoi (1081–1185) *205*; English

exception 214–215; feeding armies 202, 204; Fifth Crusade 208, 211; Fourth Crusade 208, *209*; France 211; German Empire 212–214; Iberian kingdoms 212; routes of First Crusade *203*; Second Crusade 206, *207*; Seventh Crusade 208; Sixth Crusade 208; Third Crusade *207*; warfare and institutionalized taxation 215–217; within Europe and later Middle Ages 211–215
crusading states: cavalry battles on crusade 294–296; crusading armies and 143–150; illustration of King of France leaving for *144*; knighthood in 148–150; map of *76*; map of source of crusaders *133*; map of Templar network *146*; military orders 145, *147*; military organization in 130, 132; Muslim armies of crusading age 147–148; People's Crusade 143; protective equipment developments 231–233; topographies of defence 75, 77–79
Curry, Anne 322
Curthose, Robert 62, 257
Custer, George 290, 324
Customs (Curthose) 257

Danevirke in Schleswig 86–87
Danish Army, East Anglia in 866 *104*
Danishmend Gazi 343
dark age model 57
David (King) of Bible 309
David (King) of Scotland 288
De architectura (Vitruvius) 58, 255
De bello Gallico (Caesar) 249
dediticii 100, 103
Deeds of Charles the Great (Notker) 365
Deeds of Duke William II of the Normans (William of Poitiers) 11
Deeds of Tancred (Ralph of Caen) 18
Deeds of the Archbishops of Trier (Abbo of Paris) 244
Deeds of the Bishops of Cambrai 248
Deeds of the Bishops of Utrecht 213, 214, 369
Deeds of the Saxons (Widukind of Corvey) 123, 256, 369
defence: landscape archaeology and 84–87; medieval starburst fortress in Netherlands *86*; *see also* medieval topographies of defence
Delbrück, Hans 12, 165
De re aedificatoria (*On Construction*) (Alberti) 58
Description of the Fortresses and Regions along the Northern Banks of the Danube 67, 338
Desiderius (King) 347–350, 370
deterrence 357–360
devastation: choosing 355, 357; as strategic tool 354

DeVries, Kelly 83, 238, 286n2, 299, 357
Diocletian (Emperor) 97, 363
diplomacy: choosing devastation 355, 357; devastation as strategic tool 354; strategic role of 346–355, 357; *see also* strategy
Domesday Book, 187, 217, 336, 358
Donatus 57
Dopsch, Alfons 96
Dudo of St. Quentin, *History of the Customs and Deeds of the First Dukes of Normandy* 18

East European states: map of *127*; military organization 126, 128
Ebo of Rheims (Archbishop) 339
Ecclesiastial History (Eusebius) 14
Edessa: crusader state 77; map of *76*
Edgar the Aetheling 56
Edict of Pîtres 61, 116
education *see* military education
Edward I (King) 6, 21, 79, 88, 132, 139, 140, 145, 152, 153, 159, 165, 191, 197, 214, 218, 241, 242, 268, 289, 297, 299, 314–315, 330, 345, 353–354, 365, 370; Conwy Castle *81*; Wales under 79, 81–82, 261
Edward II (King) 191, 201, 215, 235
Edward III (King) 152, 153, 159, 215, 247, 286, 307, 334, 355, 357
Edward the Confessor (King) 333
Edward the Elder (King) 69, 70, 72
Egbert (King) 69
Einhard's *Life of Charlemagne* 17
Ekkehard of St. Gall (monk) 190, 310
El Cid (Rodrigo Díaz de Vivar) 134
Elias of Maine (Count) 285
Elton, Hugh 35, 43n1
Empire of the Comnenoi (1081–1185) map of *205*
Engelard de Cigogné 242
Engels, Donald 166
Engilbert of St. Gall (Abbot) 310, 367
England: campaign supplies 214–215; map of c. 1000 *71*; map under William I *138*; military resources of kings and princes 137, 139–140
Epitoma rei militaris (Vegetius) 34, 84, 164, 195, 229, 237, 310, 312, 354, 366–367, 371, 387
Epitome (Lucius Annaeus Florus) 336
Ermoldus (courtier) 297
Ethelred of Wessex (King) 283
ethnogenesis question, military service and 107–108
Ettel, Peter 256
Etymologies (Isidore) 10, 368
Europe: logistics in pre-crusade 180; map of larger towns of *131*

Eustace the Monk 307
excavation, fortifications 25, *26*, 27, *27*

feorm, standard tax 187
Ferdinand I (King) 134
feudalism 119, 121, 148
Fiefs and Vassals (Reynolds) 119
Fifth Crusade 211, 251; *see also* crusading age logistics; crusading states
al-Fihri, Yusuf ibn 'Abd al-Rahman 376, 379
finger calculus 58
First Crusade 13–14, 164, 184, 366; armed soldiers 230; arms and equipment 193; feeding crusader armies 202, 204; logistics after 204, 206, 208, 211; map of routes of *203*; orations 318; *see also* crusading age logistics; crusading states
Fitz-Osbern, William 333–334
Flügellanzen (winged lance) 229, *229*
FM 7–8: Infantry Rifle Platoon and Squad (military manual) 362
foederati 103, 105; Theodosian Code 101, 102
Folkmar of Corvey (Abbot) 64
Fort Bourtange (The Netherlands), medieval starburst fortress in *86*
fortifications 25, *26*, 27, *27*; barbarian invasions 254; Château Gaillard fortress by Richard the Lionheart *261*; combinations of building materials 256–257; concentric castles and fortresses 260–261; construction of 254–255; earth, timber and stone 257–259; Fort Bourtange *86*; Frankish 255–256; Gallic provinces 35–36; Henry I in 929 campaign *390*; later medieval 261–262; measuring costs of construction 87–88, 90; Roman, within England 55–56; Roman government 34–35; towers and curtain walls 259–260; Trelleborg system of 86–87; *see also* siege technologies
Fourth Crusade 251; logistics of 208; map of *209*; *see also* crusading age logistics; crusading states
France: campaign supplies 211; map of, and principalities (c. 1000) *50*; map of expansion of royal control *135*; medieval bridge Pont Vieux over River Tarn *208*; military resources 134, 136–137; post-Carolingian 72
Frankish spatha *26*
Franklin, Benjamin 237
Franks Casket 23
Frederick Barbarossa (Emperor) 54, 78, 132, 140–141, 145, 149, 206, 213, 215, 322, 342; Lombard league and *55*
Frederick I (Emperor) 253

Frederick II (Emperor) 132, 140, 141, 213; crusades of *210*
Frederick the Great (King) of Prussia 355, 393
French Revolution 217
Fried, Johannes 8–9
Froissart, Jean, 156, 251, 307, 370
From the Foundation of the City (Livy) 14
Frontinus, Sextus Julius 296, 363, 366, 367
Fulk Nerra (Count) 49, 64, 72, 129, 259, 280–281
Fulk of Anjou (Count) 332
Fulk of Jerusalem (King) 64

Gallic Wars (Caesar) 11, 14
Geoffrey Greymantle (Count) 64, 72, 129
Geoffrey Plantagenet (Count) 72, 139, 251, 366, 371
Gerald of Wales 233, 336
German Empire: campaign supplies 212–214; map of Hohenstaufen Empire *142*; military resources of kings and princes 140–142
German Hanse, map of *157*
Germania (Tacitus) 84, 103, 189
Germany: German Hanse *157*; Ottonian organization 121–126
Germar March 48
Gervase of Canterbury 341
gestae, histories 15–17
Ghaznavid Empire 147
Gillingham, John 19, 322–323, 345
Gillmor, Carroll 312
Glaber, Raoul 196
Godfrey of Lotharingia (Duke) 202, 204, 318
Godwinson, Harold 55, 117, 277, 289, 333, 357
Goffart, Walter 9, 103n2
Gospel Book of Emperor Otto III (Richer of Rheims) 239
Gothic architecture 59
Gothic War 46
grand strategy 4, 329; campaign and 330–331; strategy *tout court* 330
Grand Strategy of the Roman Empire from the First Century A.D. to the Third, The (Luttwak) 84, 329
graves 25
Great Charter (Magna Carta) 217
Great Ship of Bayonne (French flagship) 307
Gregory of Tours (Bishop) 9, 14, 41, 42, 44, 102–103, 105–106, 254, 321
Gregory VII (Pope) 62, 350–352
Grierson, Phillip 24
Guiscard, Robert 132, 267, 352
Gundelandus of Lorsch (Abbot) 336
Gundobad ('king') 108
Gundovald (Prince) 341, 345

Guntram (King) 105, 321, 344, 345
Gutenberg Bible, illustrated page from *13*

Hadrian (Pope) 201, 347–350
Haldon, John 87, 360
Halsall, Guy 43n1, 343, 365
Happenings at St. Gall (Ekkehard) 310
Harald Bluetooth (King) 87
Harald Hardrada (King) 304
Hardy, Robert 238
Harper, Kyle 96
Haskins, Charles Homer 60
Hawkwood, John 156
Henry I (King) 62, 65–67, 68, 88, 90, 121, 126, 137, 139, 284–285, 293–294, 297, 340, 365; campaign course 41; Germany's conquest of lands of Hevelli and Sorbs 5
Henry I of Germany 257; background of 384–385; map of 929 objectives *386*; map of Brandenburg defence *388*; map of fortifications for *390*; objective Brandenburg 387, 389; objective Gana 389, 391–393; objective Prague 393–394; winter campaign (928–929) 384–394; *see also* campaigns
Henry I (King) of East Francia/Germany 384–385, 387, 389, *390*, 391–394
Henry II of Germany (King) 54, 62, 72, 124–125, 139, 149, 196, 213, 214, 217, 241, 244, 253, 297, 340, 365, 369
Henry III of Germany (King) 79, 88, 139, 140, 149, 190–191, 242, 245, 268, 288, 297, 299, 314
Henry IV of Germany (King) 54, 62, 139–141, 143, 145, 184, 202, 213, 310, 334, 350, 351, 352
Henry of Huntingdon 333–334
Henry the Lion of Saxony (Duke) 213
Henry V (Shakespeare) 318–319
Henry V of Germany (King) 56, 322, 325, 339, 370
Henry VI of Germany (King) 153, 341
Heribert of Milan (Archbishop) 201
Hermanfrid (King) 9, 344
Hermann of Reichenau 14–15, 191
Herodotos 12
historia, definition of 10
Historiae (Gregory) 14
historians *see* historiographical genres; sources
Histories (Gregory) 9
Histories (Nithard) 313
histories and chronicles 13–17; annales and gestae 15–17; interdisciplinary investigation 27–29; misremembering and writing 8–9; vitae 17; *see also* annales; historiographical genres
historiographical genres: administrative documents 21–22; annales and gestae 15–17;

charters 20–21; histories and chronicles 13–17; images 23–24; letters 19–20; literary works 18–19; material sources 24–27; prescriptive texts 22–23; prosimetric and poetic histories 18; vitae 17; *see also* sources

historiographical sources, interrogating 10–13

History of Geoffrey, Duke of the Normans and Count of the Angevins 366

History of the English (Paris) 237

Hoffmann, Hans Hubert 59

Hohenstaufen Empire, map of *142*

Holy Land 145, 147

Holy Roman Empire 156, 158

Honorius (Emperor) 101

horses: animal rations for 167–169; cavalry on battlefield 289–298; cavalry battles against non-western armies 292–294; cavalry battles among western armies 291–292; cavalry battles on crusade 294–296; commanders in battle 296–298; training cavalry to attack 313–314; training mounted troops 311–312; transport 266–268; *see also* combat

Hospitallers 145, 147, 295

Hugh de Payens 145

human food consumption: carrying food supplies 169–175; logistics for 165–167

human labour 28–29

human physiology 28

Humbert of Silva Candida (Cardinal) 351

Hundred Years' War 95, 215, 238, 241, 247, 251, 285–286, 299, 320, 330, 339, 362, 368, 370; England and France 150–156; illustration of Battle of Crécy *152*; map of *151*; naval battle 307

al-Husayn ibn Yahya ibn Sa'd ibn Ubada 379, 381–382

Iberia 75; campaign supplies for kingdom 212; Spanish and Portuguese reconquest *74*

Iberian Peninsula: arms and equipment 193; military resources of kings and princes 134; military taxes 188

ibn Malik al-Khawlani, Al-Samh 47, 376

ibn Nusayr, Musa 47, 376

ibn Sadaqa, Dubais (Bedouin leader) 331

ibn Tashfin, Yusuf 134

ibn Ziyad, Tariq 46, 47, 376

Imad ad-Din Zengi 298

images 23–24

Ine of Wessex (King) 187

infrastructure *see* military infrastructure; transportation infrastructure

Innocent II (Pope) 145

Institutiones (Cassiodorus) 58

intelligence: captured information 345–346; Francia on Peutinger map *337*; locating the enemy 343; military 335–346; scouts 344–345; secrecy 340–341; strategic 335–336, 338–339; strategic, by enemies of Latin West 341–343; tactical 343

interdisciplinary scholarly investigation 27–29

Iron Gates 36

Isaac II Angelos (Emperor) 206, 251

Isidore of Seville (Bishop) 10, 57

James I (King) of Aragon 212, 216, 242, 346

James of St. George 81, 299

Jefferson, Thomas 170

Jerusalem, crusader states 75, *76*, 77–79

Joan of Arc 56

John (King) of England 136, 152, 242

John de Maidstone 334, 335

John II (King) of France 216, 355, 357

John of Lancaster 56

John of Oxford 336

John of Salisbury 369

Joinville, Jean de 254

Journey of the Pilgrims, 305

Journey of the Pilgrims and Deeds of King Richard 345

Justin I (Emperor) 32, 38

Justinian I (Emperor) 32, 36, 38, 46, 60, 108, 109, 377; map of empire *37*

Justinianic plague 96

Kaeuper, Richard 323

Kalonymous (Rabbi) 143

Keegan, John 275

Keen, Maurice 323

Kilij Arslan (Turkish sultan of Rum) 143, 204, 295–296, 343, 352

Knighthood, crusading states 148–150

Knights of Saint John 147

Köhler, Gustav 243

Komnena, Anna 239

labour obligations, military infrastructure and 63–64

Lampert of Hersfeld (author) 184

landscape archaeology, defence as aspect of 84–87

Landsknechte, German mercenary troops 234

Lanfranc of Canterbury (Archbishop) 336

Lee, Charles (General) 237

Leo III (Pope) 109

Leo IV (Pope) 52, 56

Leo the Deacon 268

letters 19–20

Lex Baiuvariorum 63, 108, 320

lex Julia de vi publica (Julian law on public violence) 101; repeal of 101–102

Lex Ribuaria 103
Lex Salica (law of Salian Franks) 108
Leyser, Karl 323
Liber Pontificalis 249
Life of Charlemagne (Einhard) 17
Life of Henry II (Adalbold of Utrecht) 344
Life of Robert the Pious (Helgaud) 369
Life of Saint Louis (Louis IX) 208
literary works 18–19
Little Key to the World (*Mappae clavicula*)
    252, 254
Liudprand of Cremona 293–294, 300, 340
Lives of the Caesars (Suetonius) 17
Livingston, Michael 357
Livy's *From the Foundation of the City* 14
Llywelyn ap Gruffudd of Gwynedd (prince),
    brother Dafydd and 79, 81
logistics 4, 164–165; animal rations 167–169;
    art and science of 165; campaigning in
    enemy territory 201; carrying food supplies
    169–175; in crusading age 202–211; food
    and fodder in peacetime 180–182; food
    and fodder on campaign 182–186; human
    food consumption 165–167; markets
    185–186; material reality of 165–175;
    mobile field units 178; in pre-crusade
    Europe 180; transportation, in late empire
    179–180; vehicles for transporting supplies
    170–171; *see also* crusading age logistics;
    military logistics
Lombard League, Frederick I Barbarossa and
    55
Lothair I (King) 52, 119, 313, 368
Lothair II (King) 367
Lothair IV (King) 61, 196, 251
Louis (Prince) 245
Louis II (King) 128, 185, 321, 380
Louis III (King) 51, 128, 181
Louis IV (King) 208, 212
Louis IX (King) of France 254
Louis of France (Prince) 306
Louis the Child (King) 65, 384
Louis the German (King) 118, 119, 313, 338
Louis the Pious (Emperor), 48, 67, 111, 115,
    119, 186–187, 297, 321, 338, 364
Louis the Younger (King) 278
Louis VI (King) of France 136
Louis VII (King) of France 206
Louis VIII (King) of France 299
Lucius Annaeus Florus, *Epitome* 336
Luttwak, Edward 84–85, 329, 332

Machiavelli, Niccolò 156
McKitterick, Rosamond 15
Magyars, map *52*
mail armour, Roman government 224–225
Maitland, Frederic 70

Malik Shah (Seljuk leader) 148
Mamluk sultan 79
al-Ma'mun 148
Manuel I Komnenos (Emperor) 206
map(s): Alpine passes *200*; Angevins and
    Capetians in late twelfth century *73*;
    Barbarian kingdoms *45*; Brandenburg
    defence *388*; Burgundian state growth
    155; Byzantium and expansion of Islam *51*;
    campaign of 929 objectives *386*; Carolingian
    Empire division *120*; Carolingian residential
    villas *183*; Crusader states *76*; crusades of
    Emperor Frederick II and St. Louis *210*;
    East European states (c. 1000) *127*; empire
    of Charlemagne *113*; Empire of Comneni
    (1081–1185) *205*; Empire of Justinian
    37; England (c. 1000) *71*; England under
    William I *138*; Europe's larger towns *131*;
    expansion of French royal control *135*;
    fortifications by Henry I in 929 campaign
    390; fortresses of Henry I on eastern frontier
    66; Fourth Crusade *209*; France and its
    principalities (c. 1000) *50*; Francia on
    Peutinger map *337*; Frederick I Barbarossa
    and Lombard league *55*; German Hanse
    157; Hohenstaufen Empire *142*; Hundred
    Years' War *151*; Magyars *52*; Mercian
    supremacy *89*; Muslim Spain *378*; Ottonian
    Empire *122*; Roman Empire in AD 395
    33; routes of First Crusade *203*; Scottish
    wars of independence *192*; Second Crusade
    207; source of Crusaders *133*; Spanish
    and Portuguese reconquest to c. 1140 *74*;
    Templar network *146*; Third Crusade *207*;
    Wales principality and marches *80*
Mappae clavicula (*Little Key to the World*)
    252, 254
Marcus of Eckwersheimn 287
Margueritte of Aixe-sur-Vienne (Viscountess)
    313
Marshall, William 345
Martel, Geoffrey 49
Martianus Capella 57
Mary Rose (ship) 239
material sources 24–27
mathematical calculations 58–59
Mathilda (daughter of Henry I) 62, 139
Maurontius (Count) 376–377, 379
Mézières, Philippe de 339, 340
medieval Europe: Holy Roman Empire
    156, 158; Hundred Years' War 150–156;
    intellectual and legal continuity of Rome's
    military infrastructure 57–60; military
    organization in late 150–158; military
    organization of 3–4; military topography
    of 3; physical continuity of Roman military
    infrastructure 42–43

medieval military history: historiographical
texts 7–9; sources 3, 6–7; *see also* sources
medieval topographies of defence 64–82;
Carolingian and Ottonian eastern frontiers
65–67; Crusader states 75, *76*, 77–79;
Iberia 75; kingdom of Wessex 69–70,
72; map of Angevins and Capetians in
late twelfth century *73*; map of England
(c. 1000) *71*; map of fortresses of Henry
I on eastern frontier *66*; map of Spanish
and Portuguese reconquest to c. 1140 *74*;
post-Carolingian France 72; re-reading 84;
Slavic response 67–69; Wales under Edward
I 79, *80*, 81–82
memory, history writing and 8–9
mercenaries, Carolingian government
115–116
Mercian supremacy, map of *89*
Metalogicon (John of Salisbury) 369
Miesco I (Duke) of Poland 68, 125, 128
Milemete, William de 246
milia passuum, term 38
military campaigns 5; *see also* campaigns
military combat *see* combat
military education: court as military academy
364–365; learning from books 365–368;
military manual 362; reading history
368–370; in Rome 363–364; strategy
362–370
military equipment 4, 25; *see also* military
technology
military history: archaeology and 29; *see also*
medieval military history
military infrastructure: intellectual and
legal continuity of Rome's 57–60;
labour obligations and 63–64; medieval
developments in Roman 56–57; physical
continuity of Roman 42–43; Roman, in
medieval contexts 41–42; Roman law and
medieval practice regarding 60–61
military logistics 4, 164–165; advanced
supply bases and magazines 198–199,
201; arms and equipment 191, 193–197;
campaigning in enemy territory 201;
equipment for professional soldiers
194–196; food and fodder on campaign
182–186; food on the hoof 170; foraging
and plunder 189–191; large-scale weapon
systems 196–197; markets for 185–186;
pack animals 171, 173, 197–198; Roman
military taxes in medieval contexts
186–189; ships 197–198; soldier's pack
169–170; sources of supply for late imperial
175–179; supplied carried by militia troops
182, 184; transportation, in late empire
179–180; transportation and supply
infrastructure 197–199, 201; vehicles

170–171, 197–198; water transport 173,
175; *see also* logistics
military orders, crusading states 145, 147
military organization: barbarian recruits
in standing army 99–100; barbarians in
pacts outside of government 100–101;
Carolingian world 108–118; crusading
age 130, 132; Danish Army in East Anglia
in 866 *104*; food and fodder in peacetime
180–182; German kingdom 121–126;
influences on the East 126, 128; inherited
from Rome 2; late Antique, in West 102–
103, 105–106; late Antique developments
106–108; in late medieval Europe
150–158; late Roman 96–101; medieval
Europe 3–4; Polish account of 126, 128;
post-Carolingian West 119, 121; in post-
Carolingian West 128–130; recruitment of
Rome 97–99; Roman standing army 97
military planning 331–335; groups 332–335;
see also strategy
military religion, soldiers and 315–316; *see
also* Christianity; morale; religion
military resources: England 137, 139–140;
France 134, 136–137; German Empire
140–142; Iberian Peninsula 134; kings and
princes 132, 134–142
military taxes: feorm 187; fodrum 188;
gistum 188; Roman, in medieval contexts
186–189
military technology: artillery 243–247; earlier
medieval personal arms and armour 226–
229; hand-held missile weapons 235–242;
personal arms and armour in late empire
223–226; siege technologies 247–254;
warships 262–268; *see also* personal arms
and armour; siege technologies; warships;
weapons
military topography 3, 32; Carolingian world
47–49; defence and landscape archaeology
84–87; Europe in high and late Middle
Ages 49, 51–56; importance for
government 60–61; labour obligations and
military infrastructure 63–64; late medieval
82–84; licensing and rendition 61–63;
measuring costs of fortress construction
87–88, 90; medieval developments in
Roman military infrastructure 56–57;
medieval topographies of defence 64–82;
physical continuity of Roman military
infrastructure 42–43; re-reading, as
landscapes of defence 84; Roman Empire in
AD 395 *33*; Roman inheritance of medieval
Europe 32, 34–36, 38; Roman military
infrastructure (medieval contexts) 41–42;
Rome's successor states in Late Antiquity
43–44, 46–47; transportation infrastructure

38–41; *see also* medieval topographies of defence

morale: defeating fear and promoting courage 315; military campaigns 314–324; military codes and discipline 320–322; military religion 315–316; orations 317–319; role of chivalry 322–324; treatment of enemy combatants 322–324; unit cohesion 319–320; *see also* combat

Morris, John E. 7

Mummolus (Merovingian General) 344

Muslim armies, of crusading age 147–148

al-Mu'tasim, Abu Ishaq 148

Napoleon Bonaparte (Emperor) 6; death of 95; doctrine 82

Narses (general) 109, 276, 288–289

Nelson, Janet 323

Netherlands, medieval starburst fortress in *86*

Neville, Ralph 318

Nicene Church 96

Nikephoros Phokas (Emperor) 340

Ninth Crusade 145; *see also* crusading age logistics; crusading states

Nithard 14 309, 344

Notitia dignitatum 43, 97, 227

Odo (Count) 49, 51

Odo (Duke) 47

Odo (King) of West Francia 367

Odo of Bayeux (Bishop) 232

Odovacer (Roman general) 46

Offa (King of Mercia) 88

Offa's Dyke 24, 25, 86; defensive work of 331; estimating costs of 88; photograph of *90*; Shropshire, UK *90*

Oman, Sir Charles 6

Omne Datum Optimum, papal encyclical 145

On Rhetoric (Cicero) 10

On the Battles for the City of Paris (Abbo) 250

On the Organization of the Palace (*De ordine palatii*) (Adalhard) 181, 332, 364

On the Variety of our Times (Alpert of Metz) 251

oral society, medieval Europe 8

orations 317–319

Orderic Vitalis 345

Order of Brothers of the German House of Saint Mary 147

Otto I (Emperor) 121, 123–125, 126, 199, 201, 317, 342

Otto I (King) 40, 49, 53–54, 64, 68–69, 123–124, 143, 165, 190, 201, 248–249, 294, 295, 359, 365, 366, 369, 384

Otto II (King) 64, 66, 87, 359

Otto II of Utrecht (Bishop) 213

Otto III (Emperor) of Germany 54, 124, 196, 237, 251

Otto IV (King) of Germany 136, 213

Ottonian Empire: campaign forces 123–125; local defence 125–126; map of *122*; military organization 121, 123–126

Otto of Brunswick 213

Otto of Freising (Bishop) 253

Otto the Illustrious (Count) 385

Paris, Matthew 237

Patton, George S. 340

Pelagius 46

People's Crusade 143, 202, 204, 343

Pere III (King) of Catalonia 344

personal arms and armour: Carolingian developments in 229–231; earlier medieval 226–229; Flügellanz (winged lance) *229*, *229*; helmets and shields 225–226; in late empire 223–226; late medieval developments 233–235; mail armour 224–225, *225*, 232; Normal armour *224*; protective equipment developments through crusading age 231–233; Spangenhelme (helmets) 228; spatha (long sword) 230–231; swords 223–224, 227–228; *see also* military technology; weapons

Peter of Portugal 242

Peter the Saracen 242

Peutinger Table 39

Philip II Augustus (King) 14, 78, 136, 206, 211, 233

Philip IV (King) 136–137, 216, 317, 339, 353–354, 370

Philippidé (William the Breton) 18

Philip the Bold of Burgundy (Duke) 299

Philip the Good 156

Philip VI (King) of France 154, 211, 307, 355

Pippin I (King) 47, 110, 111, 198, 248, 255, 340, 346

Pippin II (King) 109

Pippin III (King) 47, 109, 115, 255, 316, 346, 376–377

Pirenne, Henri 96

Pizan, Christine de 368

poetic histories 19

Policraticus (John of Salisbury) 369

Polybius 363

polyptychs 60, 63

Poor Fellow Soldiers of Christ 145

post-Carolingian France 72

post-Carolingian West, military organization in 128–130

prescriptive texts 22–23

Prestwich, J.O. 335, 365

Prestwich, Michael 166, 191

Prince, The (Machiavelli) 156

Problems for Sharpening the Youth (Alcuin) 58

Procopius 250
procurator tironum 99
prosimetric history 19
protective equipment *see* personal arms and armour
punishment 357–360; waste zones 359–360

Rabanus Maurus of Mainz (Archbishop) 195, 237, 309–310, 312, 313, 367
Ragenardus (count) 309
Ralph of Caen 250, 301, 302, 316; *Deeds of Tancred* 18
Raymond II of Tripoli (Count) 79
Raymond of Toulouse (Count) 353
recruitment, Roman army 97–99
Regarding the Fortification of Encampments 248
Regino of Prüm 235, 291, 310, 313
Regnum Francorum 47, 109, 112, 117–118, 171, 182, 185, 194, 229–230, 255, 300, 344, 348–349
religion: army-wide rites and public 316–317; military 315–316; orations 317–319
Remigius of Rheims (Archbishop) 361
Renaissance Italy, rediscovering Roman technology 58
Report on my Legation to Constantinople (Liudprand) 340
Res Gestae Saxonicae (Widukind of Corvey) 16
Reuter, Timothy 103n2, 165, 365
Reynolds, Susan 119
Richard I Lionheart (King) 78, 140, 206, 217, 241, 253, 260, 268, 278–280, 295, 297, 305, 306, 341–342, 345; Château Gaillard fortress by *261*
Richard II (King) of England 322
Richard II of Normandy (Duke) 369
Richard of Cornwall 288
Richer of Rheims 196, 239, 250, 251
Rihll, Tracey 222
Robert Bruce (Scottish king) 191, 281, 285
Robert II (King) of France 369
Robert II of Flanders (Count) 137
Robert III (Count) of Flanders 353
Robert of Flanders (Count) 202
Robert of Normandy (Duke) 202, 204, 284–285, 295–296
Rodrigo Díaz de Vivar (El Cid) 134
Roger-Bernard III of Foix (Count) 136
Roger I (King) of Sicily 141
Roger II (King) of Sicily 141, 239
Rogers, Clifford 286, 286n2, 343, 344, 355
Rollo 115–116, 129
Roman army: barbarians in 99–100; *magister militum per orientem* 2, *98*; pacts of barbarians outside 100–101; recruitment 97–99; soldiers from Arch of Constantine *99*; standing 97; tax system 98–99
Roman de Rou (Wace) 18
Roman Empire: late Antique military organization in West 102–103, 105–106; map of, in AD 395 *33*; transportation infrastructure 38–41
Romanos IV (Emperor) 148
Roman technology, Renaissance Italy rediscovering 58
Rome: late Antique developments 106–108; military education in 363–364; military organization of late 96–101; military service and ethnogenesis question 107–108; military taxes in medieval contexts 186–189; new military institutions 101–102; organization of 2; technology 58
Royal Frankish Annals 290
Rudolf (anti-King) of Rheinfelden 350, 351
Rudolf I of Habsburg (King) of Germany 142, 212
Rudolf of Coeverden 213
Rule of the Templars, The (Templars) 147
Ruricius of Limoges (Bishop) 364

Sachkritik 13; principles of 12; techniques of 12
St. Jerome 43, 57
St. Louis, crusades of *see* Louis IX
St. Martin of Tours 17
Saladin (Sultan) 242, 279–280, 305, 342, 345
Saladin Tithe 217
Samanids 147
Sancho II (King) 134
Sarantis, Alexander 36
satellites, term 14
Saxon Wars (Bruno of Merseburg) 369
Schneider, Rudolf 243
Scipio Africanus 296–298, 366
Scottish wars of independence, map *192*
Searle, John 27–28
Second Crusade 145; logistics 206; map of *207*; *see also* crusading age logistics; crusading states
Second World War 6–7
Seventh Crusade 208; *see also* crusading age logistics; crusading states
Severus, Sulpicius 17
Shakespeare, *Henry V* 318–319
Sherman, William Tecumseh 395
ships: transportation of cargo 173, 175; *see also* warships
siege(s): fighting with the walls 301–303; impact of artillery 298–299; storming the walls 299–301; *see also* combat
siege technologies: construction of walls 247–249; incendiary devices 254;

motte-and-bailey castle *249*; over the walls 250–252; starving a city into submission 247–249; through the walls 252–253; under the walls 253–254; *see also* fortifications; military technology

Sigibert I (King) 321

Simon (King) 141

Simon de Montfort 298–299, 314

Sir Gawain and the Green Knight 19

Sixth Crusade 208; *see also* crusading age logistics; crusading states

Slavic peoples 67–69

Snorri Sturluson 304–305

soldiers: Anglo-Saxon manuscript depiction *168*; carrying food supplies 169–175; defeating fear and promoting courage 315; equipment for professional 194–196; food consumption for 165–167; food for horses 167–169; food for other animals 169; food on hoof 170; foot soldiers in combat 275–285; foraging and plunder 189–191; hand-held missile weapons 235–242; military codes and discipline 320–322; missile troops deployed on offensive 288–289; missile troops on battlefield 285–289; morale in combat 314–324; orations 317–319; pack animals 171, 173; pack for carrying food supplies 169–170; phalanx deployed in offence 282–285; phalanx in battle 276; phalanx on defence 276–280; preparing battlefield for defensive phalanx 280–281; supplies carried by militia troops 182, 184; training for attack 312–313; training in arms 308–310; training militia troops 310–311; unit cohesion 319–320; vehicles 170–171; *see also* combat; personal arms and armour; weapons

Song of Lewes (Nithard) 314

Song of Roland poetry 18, 19

Sorbian March 49

sources: histories and chronicles 13–17; historiographical genres 13–27; historiographical texts 7–9; interrogating historiographical 10–13; literary works 18–19; medieval military history 3, 6–7; prosimetric and poetic histories 18; *see also* historiographical genres

Spain: map of Muslim *378*; *see also* Charlemagne's Spanish campaign of 778

Star Spangled Banner 84

Statutes of Winchester policies 139

Stephen (King) 139, 149; England 62

Stephen II (Pope) 347

Stephen III (Pope) 348

Stephen of Blois (Count) 202

Strategemata (Stratagems) (Frontinus) 84, 363, 366, 367, 368

strategy 4, 329–331; collateral damage 361–362; devastation as strategic tool 354; Francia on Peutinger map *337*; illustration of great tooth burning of Abby of Maillieres *356*; intelligence 335–336, 338–339; military education as 362–370; military intelligence 335–346; military planning 331–335; punishment and deterrence 357–360; restraint 360–362; role of diplomacy 346–355, 357; secrecy 340–341; tactical intelligence 343; *see also* military education

Strickland, Matthew 19, 238, 323

Suetonius's *Lives of the Caesars* 17

Sulayman ibn Yaqzan al-A'rabi 377, 379, 381–382

Sunni Seljuks 147–148

Supplying War (van Creveld) 164

supply sources: glassware and pottery *177*; late imperial logistics 175–179; production facilities 178–179; Roman system of taxation 178; *see also* logistics

Sweyn II (King) of Denmark 304, 358

Sword Brothers 360

Syria: Crac des Chevaliers *78, 79*; crusader state 75, 77; map of *76*

Tacitus 95, 189; *Germania* 84, 103

Tancred 316, 346

Tassilo of Bavaria (Duke) 347–348

tax system: Roman army 98–99; warfare and institutionalized 215–217

technology: hand-held missile weapons 235–242; military equipment 222–223; *see also* military technology; personal arms and armour; weapons

Templars 145, 147; map of network *146*

Temple of Solomon 145

Teutonic Knights 145, 306, 360

Teutonic Order 147

Thangmar of Hildesheim 196

Theodoric the Great (King) 58

Theodoric the Ostrogoth 46

Theodosian Code 60, 101, 112, 180, 187

Theudebert I (King) 364

Theuderic (King) 280, 344

Thietmar (Count) 284

Thietmar of Merseburg (Bishop and author) 42, 67, 340, 385

Third Crusade 145; defensive phalanx in 278; map of *207*; *see also* crusading age logistics; crusading states

Third Work (Bacon) 246

Thomas Becket (Archbishop) 369

Thurstan of York (Archbishop) 316–317

Topography and Conquest of Ireland, The (Gerald of Wales) 233

tout court, strategy 330
trace italienne, development of 58
transportation: advanced supply bases and magazines 198–199, 201; Anglo-Saxon view of Viking dragon ship *174*; frontier (*limitanei*) 175–176, 179; infrastructure 38–41; infrastructure of supply and 197–199, 201; logistics in late empire 179–180; medieval ship from excavation *174*; mobile field units (*comatitenses*) 175, 178, 179; pack animals 197–198; photographs of road surfaces *172*; ships 197–198; vehicles 197–198; water 173, 175
transportation infrastructure: mile stones 38–39, *39*; ports and rivers 40–41; way stations (*mansiones*) 40
Treaty of Verdun 116, 119
Tree of Battles (Honoré Bouvet) 368
Tristan and Isolde 19
Tughril 147
Turberville, Thomas 339

Ulrich (Bishop) 53
Ulrich of Augsburg (Bishop) 365
Urban II (Pope) 130, 132, 143, 351–352

Valens (Emperor) 97, 343
Valentinian (Emperor) 364
van Creveld, Martin 164
Varro, M. Terentius 364
Vegetius Renatus, Publius Flavius 34, 84, 164, 223, 229, 237, 250, 252, 254, 308, 310, 312, 313, 354, 366–368, 371, 387
Vercingetorix 249
Victorinus of Aquitaine 57
Vikings 17, 49, 51, 72; foraging and plunder 189–190; naval response to 264–265; offence and 283; raids/raiders 35, 36, 59, 116; tribute Danegeld 217
vitae 17
Vitruvius 58, 255
von Geroldseck, Walter 286

Wales: Conwy Castle *81*; Edward I in 79; 81–82
al-Walid, Umayyad caliph 109
Wallace, William 289
Walter of Coutances (Bishop) 341
war and society 6
warfare: complexity of 2–3; foraging and plunder 189–191; geopolitical relations and 4; institutionalized taxation and 215–217; in medieval society 2; *see also* crusading age logistics
War of 1812 275
warrior aristocracy 4

warships: battle at sea 303–308; horse transports 266–268; Hundred Years' War 304–305; later medieval developments 265–266; naval combat in crusading age 304–305; naval response to Vikings 264–265; sailing ships and galley tactics 306–308; shipping in the north 263–264; *see also* combat
water transports: Anglo-Saxon view of Viking dragon ship *174*; medieval ship from excavation *174*; supplies 173, 175
weapons: artillery 243–247; axe (*francisca*) 235; bow and arrow 237–239; crossbows 239–242, *240*; gunpowder artillery 245–247; hand-held missile 235–242; large-scale systems 196–197; mechanically cast projectiles 236–237; personal arms and armour in late empire 223–226; Roman swords 223–224; sling *236*, 236–237; thrown projectiles 235–236
Welf of Bavaria (Duke) 202
Wenceslaus I (Duke) 65
Wenceslaus of Bohemia (Duke) 228
Wenskus, Reinhard 107
Werner, Karl Ferdinand 12
Werner of Merseburg (Bishop) 369
Wessex, kingdom of 69–70, 72
White, Lynn, Jr. 230
Wichmann Billung the Younger 125
Widukind of Corvey *16*, 123, 126, 256, 293, 309, 325, 369, 385, 387, 389, 391–393
Wilbrand of Utrecht (Bishop) 369–370
William I (King), map of England under *138*; William II of Normandy (Duke) 11, 61, 260
William of Malmesbury 366
William of Mortain (Count) 284
William of Poitiers 11, 18, 316, 340
William of Tyre (Bishop) 64, 298
William Rufus (King) 137
William the Breton 14, 18, 233
William the Conqueror (King) 11, 56, 79, 137, 187, 217, 232, 248, 257, 267, 277, 284, 290, 297, 316, 336, 345, 350, 357, 365, 371; *see also* William I (King); William II of Normandy (Duke)
Wipo 301–302
Wolfgang of Regensburg (Bishop) 359

Xenophon 312

Zachary (Pope) 347
Zengi 78
Zeno (Emperor) 46
Zorn, Nicholas 286